Criminal Justice
The System in Perspective

Ronald G. Burns

Carefully scratch off the silver coating to see your personal redemption code.

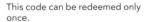

This code can be redeemed only once.

Once the code has been revealed, this access card cannot be returned to the publisher.

Access can also be purchased online during the registration process.

The code on this card is valid for two years from the date of first purchase. Complete terms and conditions are available at learninglink.oup.com

Access Length: 6 months from redemption of the code.

OXFORD
UNIVERSITY PRESS

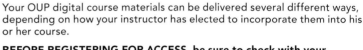

Directions for accessing
Oxford University Press Digital Course Materials

Your OUP digital course materials can be delivered several different ways, depending on how your instructor has elected to incorporate them into his or her course.

BEFORE REGISTERING FOR ACCESS, be sure to check with your instructor to ensure that you register using the proper method.

VIA YOUR SCHOOL'S LEARNING MANAGEMENT SYSTEM

Use this method if your instructor has integrated these resources into your school's Learning Management System (LMS)—Blackboard, Canvas, Brightspace, Moodle, or other.

Log in to your instructor's course within your school's LMS.

When you click a link to a resource that is access-protected, you will be prompted to register for access.

Follow the on-screen instructions.

Enter your personal redemption code (or purchase access) when prompted.

VIA OXFORD learning link

Use this method if you are using the resources for self-study only. **NOTE:** *Scores for any quizzes you take on the OUP site will not report to your instructor's gradebook.*

Visit oup.com/he/burns1e

Select the edition you are using, then select student resources for that edition.

Click the link to upgrade your access to the student resources.

Follow the on-screen instructions.

Enter your personal redemption code (or purchase access) when prompted.

VIA OXFORD learning cloud

Use this method only if your instructor has specifically instructed you to enroll in an Oxford Learning Cloud course. **NOTE:** *If your instructor is using these resources within your school's LMS, use the Learning Management System instructions.*

Visit the course invitation URL provided by your instructor.

If you already have an oup.instructure.com account you will be added to the course automatically; if not, create an account by providing your name and email.

When you click a link to a resource in the course that is access-protected, you will be prompted to register.

Follow the on-screen instructions, entering your personal redemption code where prompted.

For assistance with code redemption, Oxford Learning Cloud registration, or if you redeemed your code using the wrong method for your course, please contact our customer support team at **learninglinkdirect.support@oup.com** or 855-281-8749.

Criminal Justice

The System in Perspective

Ronald G. Burns

Texas Christian University

New York   Oxford

Oxford University Press

Oxford University Press is a department of the University of Oxford.
It furthers the University's objective of excellence in research, scholarship,
and education by publishing worldwide. Oxford is a registered trade mark of
Oxford University Press in the UK and certain other countries.

Published in the United States of America by Oxford University Press
198 Madison Avenue, New York, NY 10016, United States of America.

For titles covered by Section 112 of the US Higher Education Opportunity
Act, please visit www.oup.com/us/he for the latest information about
pricing and alternate formats.

Library of Congress Cataloging-in-Publication Data
Names: Burns, Ronald G., 1968- author.
Title: Criminal justice : the system in perspective / Ronald G. Burns, Texas
    Christian University.
Description: New York : Oxford University Press, [2022] | Includes
    bibliographical references and index. | Summary: "Provides a
    comprehensive overview of the Criminal Justice system, including
    coverage of Law Enforcement, Courts, and the Corrections system"—
    Provided by publisher.
Identifiers: LCCN 2021005443 (print) | LCCN 2021005444 (ebook) | ISBN
    9780190296445 (paperback) | ISBN 9780190296537 (epub)
Subjects: LCSH: Criminal justice, Administration of—United States.
Classification: LCC HV9950 .B873 2022 (print) | LCC HV9950 (ebook) | DDC
    364.973—dc23
LC record available at https://lccn.loc.gov/2021005443
LC ebook record available at https://lccn.loc.gov/2021005444

9 8 7 6 5 4 3 2 1
Printed by Quad/Graphics, Mexico

Contents

MODULE 6 Victims of Crime 79

MODULE 7 Understanding Justice 93

UNIT II LAW ENFORCEMENT

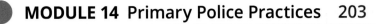

UNIT III COURTS

MODULE 25 Sentencing and Appeals 365

MODULE 26 Juvenile Courts 385

MODULE 27 Future of Courts 402

 CORRECTIONS

 MODULE 28 History of Corrections 416

MODULE 29 Current Organization of Corrections   432

MODULE 30 Corrections Personnel   447

MODULE 35 Future of Corrections **529**

Criminal Justice
The System in Perspective

Welcome to *Criminal Justice: The System in Perspective*. This book provides a refreshing look at the criminal justice system, highlighting the complexities and interconnectedness of crime and justice. *Criminal Justice* focuses on recent research, real-world events, and the criminal case process. After reading this book you will have a firm understanding of how the system works, the many groups that comprise our justice systems, and various important issues surrounding crime and justice.

Through regularly teaching the "Introduction to Criminal Justice" course, it has become clear to me that many students enter the course with just a rudimentary knowledge of the components of the criminal justice system. While students often understand many concepts and issues regarding crime and justice (e.g., arrest and trials), they often lack awareness of how the system functions. This book addresses that concern through adopting a systems-based approach that emphasizes the functioning of the system, while covering all of the primary topics and issues found in other introductory criminal justice texts.

To help students thoroughly understand the criminal case process, *Criminal Justice: The System in Perspective* provides comprehensive content on processing in Unit I of the book, which lays the foundation and framework for understanding the more traditional content of law enforcement, courts, and corrections that comes later. In addition to the robust content in Unit I, the book also includes icons within each module to remind students where they are within the process.

Many students believe they understand how the criminal justice system operates. However, public perceptions of criminal justice are often based on what they see in the media or what they have learned from personal experience with the system, rather than from directed focus or study. The term *criminal justice* itself is often misunderstood. In fact, there is no single "criminal justice system," and such shorthand disguises the variety among practices. Such shorthand also results in misperceptions about how the *systems* of justice at all levels truly work. *Criminal Justice: The System in Perspective* is designed to combat these misperceptions through an approach that highlights the interconnectedness and complexities of crime, justice, and the criminal justice system. While it is acceptable to use the term *criminal justice system* in general reference to the collective actions of our justice systems, there are some differences in how justice is served among jurisdictions. These differences pertain to practices (e.g., the use of discretion) and legal procedure (e.g., sentencing structures). In its thorough coverage of justice-based practices, this book shares both general practices and differences where they exist.

Uncertainties regarding the criminal justice system also stem from various interpretations of the terms *crime*, *criminal*, and *justice*. While crimes are violations against laws, there are numerous social harms that occur within the boundaries of the law. There are also numerous explanations for why crimes occur, which leads to uncertainties regarding guilt or responsibility for harmful acts. The many types of crimes that exist and the circumstances and contexts in which they occur generate varied opinions of their harm(s). Similarly, there are many interpretations of what constitutes "justice." Justice is often defined in terms of "fairness" and "equity," but those terms are subjective in nature. What may seem "just" or "fair" to some may seem unjust or unfair to others. Scholars have long debated whether the term justice can be aptly defined, and if so, what it means. This book does not propose to clearly define what constitutes justice, but instead provides coverage of the types of justice, the difficulties associated with defining the term, and much evidence of how it is considered and applied in the United States.

There is also debate concerning whether the primary components of the justice system—law enforcement, courts, and corrections—truly operate as a system. The term *system* conjures images of a smoothly operating apparatus working harmoniously toward common objectives or goals and adapting and reacting efficiently to changes and emergent events or uncertainties. People expect criminal justice systems to protect society and ensure justice in the face of technological developments and other sorts of challenges over time. Nevertheless, some argue that the components that comprise our justice systems do not necessarily work together harmoniously in certain circumstances or keep pace with our changing world.

Criminal Justice: The System in Perspective provides extensive coverage of the interconnectedness of police, courts, and corrections in the United States and highlights areas where concerns or issues may exist. For instance, Unit II covers the challenges currently faced by police officers in the United States in light of questionable police practices, and Unit IV includes coverage of overcrowded prisons, which are attributable in large part to laws, policies, and courtroom practices that may fail to consider a general lack of prison space and the repercussions of overcrowded facilities.

The decentralized nature of criminal justice within the United States means that there is no single criminal justice authority. Instead, there are many systems at various levels of government guided by constitutional and other legal requirements. In general, criminal justice systems work toward similar goals, although each is notably influenced by factors such as budgeting, politics, laws, societal wants and needs, and technology, among other factors. Given the expansive nature of criminal justice and the many systems in operation, it is not surprising that some systems and components within those systems operate more efficiently than others.

Criminal Justice: The System in Perspective uses the term criminal justice system to refer to the collective body of criminal justice systems within the United States. Criminal justice systems exist at the federal, state, and local levels, and while the overall goal of finding justice within the confines of the U.S. Constitution remains consistent, there are some inconsistencies in structure and practices among each level, particularly at the local levels. The focus in this book is on general practices within these systems, with some attention paid to variations in practices among jurisdictions.

Organization

Criminal Justice: The System in Perspective adopts an approach that covers the core topics (law enforcement, courts, and corrections) you expect to see in an introductory criminal justice textbook, but does so in a flexible organizational framework that helps students truly understand criminal case processing and the workings of criminal justice systems. Rather than setting off important topics such as juvenile justice, drugs, homeland security, and terrorism in their own unit, *Criminal Justice: The System in Perspective* incorporates relevant and recent research and information about these topics in modules throughout the book.

Criminal Justice is composed of four units: Crime and Justice, Law Enforcement, Courts, and Corrections. Each unit is further divided into approximately 8 to 11 modules on discrete topics that instructors can present in any order or combination, depending on the needs of the instructor and the course. Unit I, "Crime and Justice," introduces readers to both crime and criminal justice, providing a foundation for the information that follows. This unit examines the types of crimes and their categorization, considers the ways by which we measure crime, and includes coverage of the extent of crime in the United States both historically and more recently. Also included in Unit I is a discussion of the primary theoretical explanations of crime, victimology, criminal law, and robust coverage of justice, differentiating *Criminal Justice: The System in Perspective* from other introductory textbooks. The justice module in particular provides an overview for students of entry into the system, prosecution and pretrial procedures, criminal case processing, and corrections and reentry into society.

Units II–IV focus specifically on key aspects of the three primary components of the criminal justice system. Each unit includes extensive coverage of the history, organization, personnel, special issues, and future issues related to law enforcement, courts, and corrections. Coverage of history helps contextualize modern-day criminal justice practices, while the accounts of organizational issues address the organization and hierarchy of the agencies within the major components of the criminal justice system. The modules focused on personnel primarily address the recruitment, selection, training, nature, and numbers of individuals working in the respective areas of the system, and coverage of special issues exposes readers to the most significant topics related to each component. The final module of the latter three units addresses the future as it is expected to impact police, courts, and corrections.

Units II–IV also include coverage focused on issues pertaining to juveniles, while Unit II includes a module primarily focused on police practices. The reason for the module focused on police practices is the wide array of controversial and critical issues impacting police officers, their role as gatekeepers to the criminal justice system, and the legal restrictions under which they operate.

The flexible organization of *Criminal Justice: The System in Perspective* provides a refreshing alternative to existing books, one that exposes students to the underpinnings of criminal justice, including criminal case processing, in an easy-to-read format that facilitates comprehension and analysis of the material. Understanding and analysis of the material are also enhanced through the interactive, highly functional pedagogical features and digital materials accompanying the book.

Features and Pedagogy

Criminal Justice: The System in Perspective includes several features and pedagogy that engage students while emphasizing comprehension and promoting critical thinking and analysis.

Icons placed near relevant discussions in the main text refer back to the steps of criminal case processing to remind students where they are within the process. Module 9 includes all icons in its coverage of case processing in general, with each step of the process being brought to life through coverage of a fictitious case following an offender from crime commission through release from prison. A flowchart on the inside front cover uses icons to identify the criminal case-processing steps, and enables readers to best recognize how the content they are reading fits within the broader justice-based actions. Interactive icons in the e-book enable students to access the larger infographic and the Criminal Case Process videos.

Learning objectives tied to the main headings of each module identify the main points that students should know and understand after completing the content. Each learning objective is introduced at the beginning of each module and discussed at the conclusion.

"In the News" features at the start of each module highlight a recent event covered by the media and include questions to get students critically thinking about relevant issues. Links to videos covering the topics addressed are provided in the digital resources.

"Mythbusting" features dispel commonly held inaccurate beliefs, primarily by providing evidence that refutes commonly held perceptions of crime and justice.

"Careers" sidebars provide overviews of the many employment opportunities within criminal justice. This information is strategically placed to correlate with the material under discussion and assist students in becoming aware of and understanding the various career opportunities in the area.

"The System in Perspective" concludes each module and looks back at the opening "In the News" feature and explains how the topic just covered fits in/relates to the overall criminal justice system.

Summaries at the end of each module are organized around the learning objectives and recap the most important points students should remember from each module.

Questions for critical thinking appear at the end of each module and encourage students to think more deeply about and analyze the content.

Key terms are bolded in the main text and listed at the end of each module to identify the most important concepts for students.

A running glossary defines bolded key terms in the margins of the pages on which the terms are first introduced and defined (these definitions appear in popovers about the bolded terms in the enhanced e-book).

Self-Check Assessment questions appear in the enhanced e-book at the end of each section and provide students with the opportunity to reflect upon the material in smaller, more digestible sections. These interactive links enable students to easily access the questions to further challenge their knowledge of the previous section.

"For Further Thought" writing features at the end of each unit encourage students to consider how they would respond to particular situations. These fictitious accounts may ask readers to assume that they are employees within the criminal justice system and must address particular dilemmas. The content helps students better understand the nature of the issues regularly faced within the criminal justice system, and encourages them to think more deeply about the material.

Combined, these helpful features are designed to facilitate student comprehension of the material, introduce readers to critical issues, assist with career preparation, personalize the material, and help make the content come alive.

Welcome to Criminal Justice

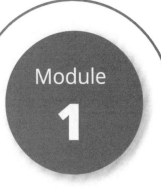

Module

1

Criminal justice fascinates us. We read about it, learn about it from movies and television, and perhaps even experience it firsthand. The effects of our criminal justice system impact us daily.

Where do you get most of your information about crime and justice?

Why are you studying criminal justice? Asking this question may seem like a strange way to begin a book, but it should prompt you to consider your motives or inspiration. Is it because you are interested in criminal justice in general? Are you interested in working in the field? Is it because crime, law enforcement, the courts, and corrections affect many aspects of our daily lives? Or is it because you are interested in studying the field of criminal justice specifically? Likely it is some combination of these reasons. This introductory module addresses the reasons why someone would read a book about criminal justice and considers the various means by which we learn about crime and justice. It also provides a general overview of working in the three primary components of the criminal justice system (law enforcement, the courts, and corrections) and concludes with a brief account of the recent history of criminal justice. These topics will help provide you with a solid foundation on which the remaining modules of this book will build.

The Influences of Criminal Justice

3 Arrest

On May 25, 2020, police officers in Minneapolis, Minnesota, responded to a call that a man had purchased cigarettes with a counterfeit $20 bill. The responding officers saw the man sitting on a car as they arrived at the scene. The suspect, George Floyd, was asked to step away from the car, at which point he physically resisted the officers. The officers noted that Mr. Floyd appeared to be under the influence of drugs or alcohol and in medical distress. They called for an ambulance and attempted to gain control of the suspect.

a hospital, where he was later pronounced dead. Derek Chauvin, the officer who held Mr. Floyd to the ground, was charged with second-degree murder, while the other three officers on the scene were charged with aiding and abetting second-degree murder (*New York Times*, 2020).

The incident was videotaped by a bystander and shared on social media. The footage led to the firing of the involved officers, a Federal Bureau of Investigation civil rights investigation, and rioting and protests in Minneapolis and around the United States. The riots in Minneapolis caused more damage and destruction than any riot since the 1992 unrest in Los Angeles (*New York Times*, 2020).

The officers were able to subdue Mr. Floyd, placing him in handcuffs and pinning him to the ground. The officer who pinned him to the ground did so by lodging his knee in the area of Floyd's head and neck and held it there despite claims from the suspect that he could not breathe. Bystanders surrounded the scene, begging the officer to stop the harmful restraint. Paramedics shortly arrived on the scene and Floyd was taken to

The incident in Minneapolis is by no means unique in the sense that questionable police practices, and justice-based actions in general, have contributed to social unrest. Numerous riots throughout history have been encouraged by questionable justice-related practices and an overall sense of hopelessness and injustice among various groups in society. This case highlights how criminal justice–based actions can have significant consequences.

The criminal justice system, which is one of the most—if not *the* most—visible aspects of justice in society, is often the primary target of criticism when feelings of hopelessness, injustice, and frustration occur. The ongoing impacts of the system are felt to varying degrees in society. In what ways do justice-based actions influence our daily lives? Further, given that many of us are not directly involved in justice-based actions on a regular basis, how do we feel the impacts of or understand such actions? Where do we hear about them?

Why Study Criminal Justice?

Answering the question of why we should study criminal justice requires us to understand what constitutes criminal justice. Put simply, **criminal justice** refers to the practices and procedures by which individuals who violate the law are identified and held accountable. This general definition will be expanded on and discussed thoroughly throughout this book and will include detailed coverage of how we have created and used systems by which we identify and bring offenders to justice.

There is no single **criminal justice system**. Instead, we refer to the collective practices of law enforcement, the courts, and corrections agencies—the topics of Units II–IV of this book—as the criminal justice system. Each state has a criminal justice system, as does the federal government. Within each state there are various levels of government (e.g., counties and municipalities) and numerous law enforcement agencies, courts, and correctional agencies that engage in criminal justice practices. The interworkings and interconnectedness of the primary components are what make their practices system-like.

Despite such a decentralized approach to criminal justice, we often generalize and discuss all criminal justice–based actions as part of one system, which has become an acceptable means to discuss formal criminal justice practices. Much of what is discussed in this book pertains to criminal justice systems in general, with specific examples highlighted throughout. Regardless of the focus, we should study criminal justice because:

- understanding how we address crime in our society will help us ultimately create a safer society,
- studying the field enables us to learn from and address our mistakes and move forward in a positive direction,
- issues relating to crime and justice affect us all in our everyday lives,
- there are millions of employment positions available in the field, and
- studying criminal justice is just plain interesting!

To Create a Safe Society

Consider our world without law enforcement agencies, courts, or correctional agencies. Who would ensure that offenders are identified and brought to justice? Our justice systems exist to help us maintain an orderly society. Without them, we would each be responsible for taking justice into our own hands, or there would be no justice, and we would live in fear for our safety. Studying criminal justice helps us identify best practices and create a fair and safe society for everyone.

Society continues to evolve and change, for instance as new technologies become commonplace. We study criminal justice, in part, to determine how we can adapt to changes and anticipate new developments to protect us from those who violate our laws. Most of us wish to live safe, trouble-free lives, and therefore understanding and improving the agencies charged with ensuring that we can do so is particularly important.

To Learn From Our Mistakes So We Can Make a Better Future

Everyone makes mistakes, including those who set policies for and work within our justice systems. We need to understand where mistakes occur to ensure that they do not

● **Learning Objective 1.1:** Explain why we should study criminal justice.

criminal justice
The practices and procedures by which individuals who violate the law are identified and held accountable

criminal justice system The practices of groups within law enforcement, the courts, and corrections designed to bring offenders to justice

Studying criminal justice helps us create and maintain a safe society. It is important that the field keep pace with changes, including technological developments.

Do you think safety is the most compelling reason to study criminal justice?

happen again. Consider police training, where the focus is often on revisiting problematic situations involving officers who made mistakes and teaching new recruits better options. Some police training academies use technology-based scenarios in which officers are placed in simulators that enable them to better prepare for all the types of situations they will encounter in the field. Doing so helps officers understand best practices ranging from deadly force situations to interacting with the public (Murphy, 2011). The training also enables officers to learn from the mistakes of other officers.

Criminal justice reform has emerged from studying criminal justice practices. We have created and altered laws, courtroom procedures, correctional practices, and law enforcement operations based on examination of mistakes and will continue to do so. More generally, criminal justice policies have shifted throughout history, with the shifts resulting from the study of existing policies highlighting perceived shortcomings.

Reform can also come about with shifts in societal values. Correctional practices, for instance, have changed with the times. In the early 1920s and 1960s, practices were largely based on a more rehabilitative, therapeutic approach; however, they shifted toward a more punitive approach beginning in the late 1970s when it was believed that rehabilitation was ineffective (see Module 28).

To Help Us Address Crime and Justice Issues We Encounter Everywhere

The importance of studying criminal justice is largely evident in the fact that concerns for crime and justice are everywhere. Visit a news website, pick up a newspaper, or watch the news on television. It is very likely that you will encounter one and probably several accounts of someone breaking the law or authorities responding to someone who did. Consider your everyday actions. You likely carry around keys that secure things you do not wish to be stolen, perhaps have a passcode on your phone to restrict access, pass by police officers, remain aware of your surroundings, avoid troublesome areas of the city in which you live, and engage in many other actions that you may not realize in efforts to protect yourself from being victimized.

1 Criminal Act

Regardless of whether we have been the victim of crime, we worry about crime on a regular basis. A report from Gallup (J. McCarthy, 2019) noted that over half (52%) of us believe crime is a very or extremely serious problem.

To Get a Job

The criminal justice system is filled with many career opportunities. These are highlighted in a "Careers" feature that appears throughout this book. Studying criminal justice helps people understand why and how those who work in our justice systems perform their jobs and assists with identifying best practices in the field.

The Bureau of Justice Statistics noted that there are roughly 2.4 million government employees working in policing, courts, and corrections, the three primary components of the criminal justice system (Bronson, 2018). This number does not include the many other employees who also contribute to our justice systems, including those who work in private security, private defense attorneys, and nonprofit groups, such as those that assist inmates as they leave prison. Studying criminal justice enables one to better identify and understand the various positions that exist within the field and assists with job performance once in the field.

To Learn About a Fascinating Field

Perhaps the best reason to study criminal justice is because it is interesting. There is a reason why many television shows, books, movies, and news stories center around crime. It is because many of us are interested in accounts of crime and justice. We want to know why and how people commit crime. We want to know what it is like to live on the other side of the law and what happens to those who do. We are interested in how authorities identify, locate, and catch the "bad guys." Stories of crime and justice fascinate us, which makes studying criminal justice that much more enjoyable.

● **Learning Objective 1.2:** Explain how we learn about criminal justice.

How Do We Learn About Criminal Justice?

Various images come to mind when we hear the term *criminal justice*. Some of us envision a prison or a courtroom, while others may see police officers. Still others may think of criminals. What each of us pictures is based on the information we have encountered through education and experiences over time.

Each module of this book opens with an account of crime "In the News" and each includes a "Mythbusting" section. The former is designed to share a crime- and or justice-related incident in the news and place the content into perspective. The latter is provided to dispel commonly held beliefs regarding different aspects related to criminal justice. These important additions will help you learn about criminal justice from an academic perspective based on research and empirical findings.

We all have perceptions of crime that have formed through various means throughout our lives. Some of these beliefs are closer to reality than others. Among the primary factors that create and shape our perceptions of crime and justice are media accounts, popular culture, personal experiences, and our study of the topics.

Media Accounts

Media accounts of crime and justice largely impact our perceptions of how and why people break the law and what happens to them after they do. The media, discussed more deeply in Module 2, alert us to crimes that may be impacting our communities. However, they have also been accused of disproportionately focusing on the more serious crimes (e.g., rapes, robberies, and murders) and creating an unsubstantiated fear of crime and misperceptions related to crime (Kappeler et al., 2018). Throughout this book, the goal is to dispel some of these misperceptions and provide more accurate information about crime and justice.

Popular Culture

Popular culture largely shapes our beliefs regarding crime and justice. Consider the last five movies you watched. There is a very good chance that one and perhaps several addressed issues pertaining to crime and justice. Television shows also often include crime and justice either as the central focus or tangentially. Perceptions regarding crime and justice are also influenced by music lyrics, including those that discuss police practices and justice in general.

Rap music, in particular, has been criticized for promoting violence, drugs, alcohol, and gang life. The argument centers on the belief that consumers of rap will be influenced by the messages associated with the lyrics (Herd, 2014). Rap music is not the only form of music to be criticized, however; country music has also been targeted for too often emphasizing alcohol use and sexism (A. McCarthy, 2014). Regardless of whether music and other forms of popular culture shape our behaviors, they largely shape our perceptions of crime and justice.

Personal Experiences

If you have ever visited a prison or a jail, ridden along with a police officer on their shift, visited a courtroom while in session, or been stopped by the police, the experience(s) likely shaped your perceptions of crime and criminal justice. Our personal encounters with all aspects of crime and justice influence the manner in which

---

CAREERS

Police officers serve the primary purpose of maintaining order, enforcing the law, and providing services to the public. Among other responsibilities, they respond to calls, patrol their jurisdiction, make arrests, assist citizens, control traffic, write reports, and may be required to testify in courts.

---

we consider both topics. For instance, the police officer who pulled you over for speeding yet did not give you a speeding ticket likely created a positive impression on you. Conversely, the officer who did give you a ticket created a negative one (despite the fact that you likely deserved a ticket if you were speeding).

We all gain a better understanding of crime and justice each time we encounter some real-life aspect of it. Among the ways we can more personally experience the field (aside from working in the criminal justice system or being caught up in it as an offender) are to:

- listen to and converse with those who work in the field or are engaged in crime,
- attend a court hearing,
- ride along with a police officer, or
- visit a jail or prison.

Studying Crime and Justice

Consider the situation of an individual who is deciding whether to attend college and then become a police officer or to join the ranks right out of high school. One could make strong arguments for taking either approach. Practical experience teaches criminal justice personnel the "nuts and bolts" of the field, while higher education generally helps students understand why things are the way they are. Both aspects are vitally important.

One of the joys of studying criminal justice is the diversity of the topics covered. Law enforcement, the courts, and corrections are three different, interesting, and interrelated areas. You may find that one area in particular interests you over the others as you dive deeper into your studies. Or, you may take a more general view of criminal justice and be attracted to the interconnectedness of the field. Regardless, the more you study and focus on criminal justice, the more you will become informed about what truly happens and why it matters. Many outstanding works exist that focus both on why people commit crime and what happens to them when they do. Many of these works are referenced throughout this book.

Working in Criminal Justice

Given that there are roughly 2.4 million people employed in our justice systems (Bronson, 2018), and many more employed in areas related to criminal justice (e.g., private security), there are many employment opportunities in the field. As mentioned previously, throughout this book you will find references to "Careers," designed to highlight some of the many career options in the field. In addition, within each unit of this book is a module that directly addresses personnel issues (see Modules 12, 22, and 30).

- **Learning Objective 1.3:** Describe what it is like to work in the criminal justice system.

Students interested in the field often ask the question: What can I do with a degree in criminal justice? It is often believed that career options in criminal justice are restricted to being a police officer, a lawyer, or a corrections officer. *But . . .* there are so many other options. Table 1.1 provides a broad list of positions within the criminal justice field. Those interested in learning more about specific positions are encouraged to speak with professionals who work in the field or research the positions online or in books.

TABLE 1.1. Some Careers in Criminal Justice

Alcohol, Tobacco, Firearms, and Explosives Special Agent	Customs inspector	Municipal police
Advisor caseworker	Deputy sheriff	Park Ranger
Attorney	Drug Enforcement Administration agent	Parole officer
Border Patrol Agent	Federal Bureau of Investigation	Personnel security specialist
Child advocate	Federal Protective Services Officer	Physical security specialist
Consumer protection specialist	Fingerprint examiner	Postal Inspector
Correctional counselor	Fish and game agent	Private investigator
Correctional officer	Forensic interviewer	Probation officer
Crime scene technician	Highway patrol officer	Secret Service Agent
Criminal investigator	Immigration inspector	State Trooper
Criminal justice policy analyst	Industrial security officer	Substance abuse counselor
Criminal justice researcher	Internal Revenue Service agent	U.S. Marshal
Customs agent	Juvenile hall counselor	Victim assistance coordinator
		Victim's advocate

The positions noted in Table 1.1 require varied levels of education, experience, and skills. Results from a survey of criminal justice practitioners found the following characteristics to be the most valued for working in the field (M. Jones & Bonner, 2016):

- strong verbal communication skills
- good work ethic
- good work habits
- strong initiative
- ethical

The Nature of Police Work

Police officers are considered the "gatekeepers to the criminal justice system," given that they are the ones who initially make the decision to take legal action. Police work is largely reactive in the sense that most police actions occur after a harm has been committed. However, the police also proactively provide many services designed to prevent crime. For instance, many police departments will provide homeowners with a free home security survey that makes suggestions to enhance their safety at home, which may include suggesting that homeowners improve their lighting, trim shrubbery, or purchase better locks to prevent burglaries.

Police officers must be emotionally strong to cope with the troubles they face. Consider that they are summoned to the situations from which we seek to escape. And they respond most quickly to the worst situations. They see people at their worst and deal with victims who are suffering. They are expected to "wear many hats," because we expect our officers to be psychologists, counselors, legal experts, mediators, and medical experts. Too often, we hear about the mishaps that occur in policing when those in law enforcement abuse power or engage in corruption, rather than the many helpful and wonderful things most do on a regular basis without notice or recognition. Unit II addresses these and other aspects of law enforcement.

Working in the Courts

Those who work in our court systems contribute significantly to the search for justice. While there are differences among the courts—for instance, there are courts that hear less serious offenses (e.g., traffic court) and those that hear cases involving more

10
Corrections

Working in criminal justice provides many opportunities to help people and have an impact on society. It also poses many dangers and challenges. There are many areas of employment within law enforcement, the courts, corrections, and related fields that address crime and justice.

What do you think would be the best and worst aspects of working in a prison?

serious crimes (e.g., courts of general jurisdiction)—the ultimate goal of the courts is to find justice through interpreting laws and considering them in relation to the actions in question. This involves many people performing specialized tasks.

Attorneys and judges are the most recognizable workers within the courts, but there are many other positions that contribute to courtroom proceedings (as noted in Module 22). For example, court reporters document courtroom proceedings, bailiffs provide security in the courtroom, and clerks assist with hearings and ensure that all paperwork is prepared.

Courtroom proceedings are much more controlled than what occurs in law enforcement and corrections. In particular, there is a carefully choreographed order to what takes place and when it takes place. Defense attorneys represent the accused, prosecutors represent the state (government), and judges oversee the proceedings to ensure that everything is done in a fair, legal, and judicious manner. In general, careers in the courts are less dangerous and less volatile than careers in law enforcement or corrections. Unit III provides extensive coverage of the courts, including a discussion of those who work in the courts and the actions that take place in courtrooms.

Working in Corrections

Consider waking up in the morning, turning off your alarm clock, and realizing that you soon have to be at a facility that houses individuals deemed unfit to live freely. Or, maybe you look at your planner and see that you have to visit four or five clients who have recently been released from incarceration and are struggling with their adjustment to life outside prison. Working in corrections is complicated, but it can be challenging and rewarding.

Working in corrections differs from working in law enforcement or the courts in the sense that guilt has already been determined, and the goal of corrections workers is to ensure that the penalty is fairly and adequately imposed. Doing so may occur in the community (e.g., when supervising individuals on probation) or in an institution (e.g., a prison or jail).

Unit IV provides coverage of many topics pertaining to corrections, including coverage of the various career opportunities in corrections (as noted in Module 30). Many of the positions include periods of danger and uncertainty, yet they also provide opportunities to help some of the most troubled individuals in our society.

● **Learning Objective 1.4:** Identify the events and developments that notably shaped criminal justice development beginning in the 1960s.

The Recent History of Criminal Justice

The goals and responsibilities of those who work in criminal justice have changed over time, yet in many ways they have remained the same. To best understand crime and justice, it is important to consider how our efforts to identify crime and impose justice have evolved over time. Each unit in this book opens with historical accounts of developments within the respective fields (i.e., law enforcement, the courts, and corrections) with the goal of providing context for the coverage that follows. What follows in this module is a more general view of the most recent history of criminal justice, beginning with a look at how events and occurrences in the 1960s impacted current justice-based practices.

MYTHBUSTING

Justice-Based Practices Emerged Across the United States Consistently

Discussions of the history of crime and justice in the United States typically address the developments as if they emerged consistently across the country. However, there is no easily identifiable history of crime and justice in the United States, given that the country is very large and developed at different stages and faced various challenges. For instance, former justice-based practices in the western portion of the United States developed at a much later time than they did in the eastern portion, simply because initially settlers largely landed in the East. Law enforcement in the West was largely the responsibility of the U.S. Marshals Service (a federal law enforcement agency) as late as the early 20th century, while many cities in the East (e.g., New York, Boston) had established city police departments (Bumgarner et al., 2018). We must look to the past to understand why there are differences in the early 21st century in criminal justice practices, laws, and policies.

The Turbulent 1960s and 1970s

In 1954, the U.S. Supreme Court ruled that segregated public schools for Blacks and Whites were unconstitutional (*Brown v. Board of Education*, 1954). This decision paved the way for a series of Supreme Court decisions that brought about greater civil rights, criminal justice reform, and social disorder. Several Supreme Court decisions offered during this period under Chief Justice Earl Warren notably impacted criminal justice practices and provided greater rights to citizens, including the right for arrestees to be informed of their rights prior to questioning and their rights to legal representation (see Modules 20 and 23 for coverage of these cases).

Social unrest, for instance in the form of protesting, heavily impacted the development of justice-based practices in the 1960s and 1970s. The draft of soldiers to fight in the Vietnam War and the war in general were among the many reasons for the unrest.

What current social issues generate social unrest?

In addition, a series of significant social issues emerged and generated the need for more effective social control during this time. Among the issues troubling the country were:

- a counterculture that promoted drug use and detested authority;
- political instability, particularly as it pertained to the resignation of President Richard Nixon;
- economic and energy crises;
- protests in response to the war in Vietnam; and
- the civil rights movement, which involved efforts to address the social, economic, and political inequality of African Americans in the United States.

1 Criminal Act

criminologists

Scientists who study crime, criminal behavior, and justice-based practices

These and related events led criminal justice historian Samuel Walker to identify the period from 1960 to 1975 as "the most turbulent in all of American criminal justice history" (Walker, 1998, p. 180).

Rioting, protests, and rising crime rates challenged the criminal justice system beginning in the early 1960s. Starting around 1962, there was a large increase in serious crime. The lack of industrial jobs typically held by migrants in large cities and the high unemployment rate among African Americans contributed to serious crime rates continuously rising during this period (Walker, 1998). Figure 1.1 depicts the violent crime rate in the United States from 1960 to 2016 (Kaplan, 2017).

The troubles experienced during the 1960s generated more punitive responses to crime beginning in the 1970s. **Criminologists**—scientists who study crime, criminal behavior, and justice-based practices—cite societal turbulence during the 1970s and violent drug crime in the 1980s as reasons for the shift toward cracking down on crime (Hindelang et al., 1981). Americans grew increasingly fearful of crime, and by 1978 most Americans (85%) believed the criminal justice system should become increasingly punitive (Hindelang et al., 1981). A more conservative, "get tough on crime" approach began late in the 1970s and led to a massive expansion of our justice systems beginning around 1980 (Oliver & Hilgenberg, 2018). The combination of getting tough

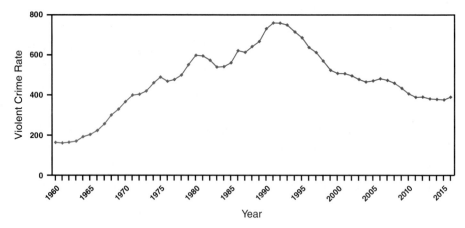

FIGURE 1.1. Violent Crime Rates in the United States, 1960–2016. Violent crime rates increased steadily beginning in the 1970s and continued increasing until the mid-1990s, when they decreased to more moderate levels.

What factors might have had the greatest impact in the fluctuating violent crime rate?

on crime and expanding the criminal justice system had notable impacts that remain evident in the early 21st century.

Responding to the Problems in the 1980s and 1990s

Many of the social problems experienced during the tumultuous 1960s and 1970s dissipated during the 1980s, as the economy recovered and a new approach to policing was introduced in efforts to address earlier problems. As police departments during this period continued to grow in size, many departments changed their philosophical approach from one of strict crime-fighting to **community policing**, which sought to:

- promote partnerships with various groups,
- emphasize problem-solving techniques to address the underlying causes of crime, and
- encourage officers and other personnel to better use and interact with the public.

In addition, tougher laws were passed and enforced to address all forms of crime, including drug offenses, and the prison boom experienced during this time was unprecedented in the history of the United States (see Modules 28 and 32).

The crime rate steadily declined beginning in the early 1990s and continued to do so through the next three decades. A stable and prosperous economy and an enhanced criminal justice system contributed to the reduction in crime (Conklin, 2003).

Homeland Security and the Emergence of New Crimes (2001–Present)

Criminal justice was again brought to the forefront of national attention with the beginning of the 21st century, primarily in response to the September 11, 2001, terrorist attacks. The attacks involved members of the Islamic extremist group al-Qaeda hijacking four airplanes and carrying out suicide missions by crashing the planes into targets in the United States. Two of the planes crashed into the World Trade Center in New York, one was flown into the Pentagon in Washington, DC, and the fourth plane crashed in a field in Pennsylvania after passengers interfered with the terrorists commandeering the plane. Its intended destination upon being hijacked remains uncertain. The attacks resulted in the deaths of nearly 3,000 people and injuries to roughly 6,000.

The terrorist acts generated substantial changes in law enforcement, including at the federal level with the creation of the U.S. Department of Homeland Security (DHS) and at local, county, and state levels. In addition to their traditional law enforcement responsibilities, law enforcement personnel were now expected to play a greater role in combatting terrorism. This increased focus on terrorism as well as the advent of new types of crime reflected what is known as **globalization**, which involves the interaction and integration of ideas and practices among different countries, and created additional concerns for our justice systems.

TERRORISM

As a result of the terrorist attacks, the criminal justice system changed at a quicker pace than at any time in history (Roth, 2011). The creation of the DHS, which relocated all or portions of 22 federal agencies to the department, was the largest reorganization in the federal government in 50 years and resulted in the DHS having more full-time officers with arrest and firearm authority than the Department of Justice. The core missions of the DHS are to:

- prevent terrorism and enhance security,
- secure and manage the United States' borders,
- enforce and administer the United States' immigration laws,

community policing A philosophical approach to policing that promotes partnerships with various groups, emphasizes problem-solving techniques to address the underlying causes of crime, and encourages officers and other personnel to better use and interact with the public

1 Criminal Act

globalization The interaction and integration of ideas and practices among different countries

1 Criminal Act

The September 11, 2001, terrorist attacks had a profound effect on the criminal justice systems in the United States. Added to the existing justice-based practices was a more directed focus on terrorism prevention and homeland security in general.

Have these changes adequately protected U.S. citizens from terrorism? Why or why not?

1 Criminal Act

- safeguard and secure cyberspace, and
- ensure resilience to disasters (U.S. Department of Homeland Security, 2016).

Although the biggest impact of the terrorist attacks was seen for law enforcement, the courts also increasingly faced difficulties associated with prosecuting known terrorists and dealing with terrorism-prompted hate crime cases as they pertained to Arab Americans and others. In addition, correctional agencies confronted the challenges associated with having to compete for resources that were targeted toward fighting a war against terrorism at a time when their domestic prison populations were increasing.

 The emphasis on homeland security generated greater cooperative efforts among criminal justice and related agencies and enhanced information- and intelligence-gathering practices. The costs for the war on terror that followed the attack are estimated to be $1–$5 trillion (Thompson, 2011). Module 10 provides further coverage of the United States' responses to terrorism, particularly as it relates to law enforcement.

TRANSNATIONAL CRIMES AND CYBERCRIMES

Increased globalization has affected justice-based practices in the 21st century, as **transnational crimes**, which are offenses that impact more than one country, have drawn increased attention. Transnational crimes are categorized into three broad categories, including :

- the provision of illicit goods to foreign countries (e.g., drug and weapons trafficking),
- the provision of illicit services in foreign countries (e.g., **human trafficking**, a modern-day form of slavery that involves the use of force, coercion, or fraud to obtain labor or sex), and
- the infiltration of foreign business and government (e.g., fraud, money laundering, political corruption) (Albanese, 2011).

transnational crimes Offenses that impact more than one country.

human trafficking Moving people across and within borders without their consent; it is often done through the use of violence, coercion, and/or deception and is a modern-day form of slavery often used to obtain labor or sex

Developing prevention strategies and effectively enforcing laws pertaining to crimes that cross international borders will continue to challenge justice-based agencies worldwide. Concerns for transnational crimes have highlighted the need for collaborative law enforcement efforts, as well as efforts to further clarify jurisdictional issues and laws (see Module 11) (Reichel, 2013).

Aside from concerns about terrorism and transnational crimes, including both domestic and foreign terrorism, are concerns about crime being committed in new forms. **Cybercrimes** are crimes committed through the use of a computer or other forms of high technology (e.g., a cell phone), in which the device may be used for the commission of or as the target of the offense. These and other technology-based crimes have introduced many new challenges for law enforcement, the courts, and society in general. For example, the Federal Bureau of Investigation's Internet Crime Complaint Center received over 791,000 complaints in 2020, with losses to victims estimated to exceed $4.1 billion (Federal Bureau of Investigation, 2020). These numbers reflect only the incidents in which a complaint was made. Many other cybercrimes went unreported.

Cybercrime, transnational crime, and terrorism are at times interrelated. And they are also not the only challenges facing our justice systems. Responding to crimes such as illegal immigration and drug offenses, as well as competing for government-provided resources (e.g., funding for budgets, personnel), continue to impact law enforcement, the courts, and correctional agencies. Ultimately, justice-based practices in the 21st century face many new challenges. The task for all of us, especially those who are preparing to enter or are already working in the field, is to address those challenges in the most effective manner possible. Studying criminal justice from an academic perspective is a necessary first step.

cybercrimes Crimes committed through the use of a computer (or other related technological device) and a network, in which the computer may be used for the commission of or as the target of the offense

The System in Perspective

The "In the News" feature at the start of this module discussing George Floyd's death and the responses to his death highlights the importance of studying criminal justice. The actions of the officers regenerated anger and anxiousness among those who believe the police too often misuse their powers. The civil unrest that followed this incident highlights the widespread effects of crime and justice in the United States and elsewhere. Images of protestors calling for justice, with police officers attempting to control the protests, went viral. Watching the protests and riots unfold, one could not help but wonder what the police officers were feeling. Civil unrest following questionable justice-based actions has occurred throughout the history of the United States and shows no signs of abating in the near future. The goal for all of us should be to ensure that we better understand crime and justice-based practices to prevent situations like this from happening in the future.

Summary

1. Learning Objectives 1.1: *Explain why we should study criminal justice.*

- There are many reasons why we should study criminal justice. Studying the field helps create a safe society, because we can learn from our mistakes and identify areas of needed improvement.

Further, crime and justice impact our lives regularly. In addition, those who wish to or do work in criminal justice will benefit from studying the field. Finally, it is interesting! Why not study something that many of us find fascinating and captivating?

2. Learning Objectives 1.2: *Explain how we learn about criminal justice.*

• There are many ways to learn about criminal justice. Primarily, we learn about crime and justice through media accounts, such as the news; popular culture, including television shows and motion pictures; our personal experiences with criminal justice, for instance through being caught up in the system or working in it; and studying the field.

3. Learning Objectives 1.3: *Describe what it is like to work in the criminal justice system.*

• There are many positions in criminal justice, including those in policing, the courts, and corrections. Police work involves helping people in many ways, including by addressing dangerous situations and providing various forms of services. Those who work in the courts seek to find justice primarily through examination of the evidence gathered by the police. Attorneys and judges are the most

recognizable courtroom workers, but there are many more positions where individuals work in a much more controlled and structured environment than police officers. Corrections officials carry out the sentences imposed by those who work in the courts. They may work in institutions (e.g., corrections officers) or in the community (e.g., probation officers). Working in corrections can be both dangerous and rewarding.

4. Learning Objectives 1.4: *Identify the events and developments that notably shaped criminal justice beginning in the 1960s.*

• Among the more significant events and developments that shaped criminal justice beginning in the 1960s were various groups fighting for their rights, social unrest, Supreme Court decisions, a "get tough" approach to crime and justice, the increased use of prisons, the war on drugs, the 2001 terrorist attacks, technological advancements, and globalism.

Questions for Critical Thinking

1. What do you believe is the most important reason for studying criminal justice? What makes this reason most important?

2. Aside from the ways discussed in this module, in what other ways do we learn about crime and justice?

3. In which area of criminal justice would you most like to work? What would be the pros and cons of working in that area?

4. Do you believe our efforts directed toward homeland security have been effective? Why or why not?

Key Terms

community policing
criminal justice
criminal justice system
criminologists

cybercrimes
globalization
human trafficking
transnational crimes

For digital learning resources, please go to
https://www.oup.com/he/burns1e

Crime in Context

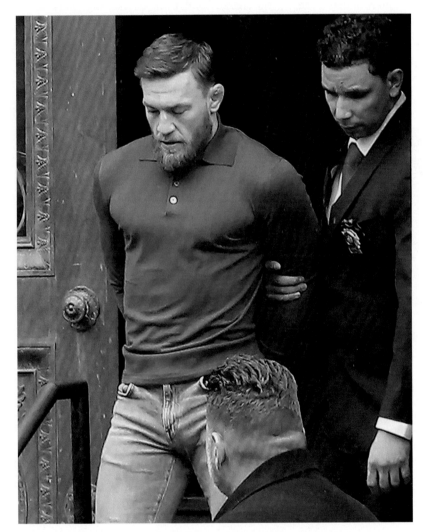

Mixed Martial Arts superstar Conor McGregor is seen here being led out of the New York Police Department's 78th Precinct after spending the night in jail in April 2018. McGregor and members of his team allegedly attacked a bus containing other Mixed Martial Arts fighters and their team. Although he potentially faced 11 years in prison, when he pled guilty he was required to pay for the damage done to the bus, complete 5 days of community service, and attend an anger-management program.

How often do you hear about crime, and how do you hear about it?

MODULE OUTLINE

• **What Constitutes a Crime?**

Learning Objective 2.1: Explain how crime is legislated and identify the elements of a crime.

• **The Costs of Crime**

Learning Objective 2.2: Characterize the various costs that crime imposes on American society.

• **Media and Crime**

Learning Objective 2.3: Explain the media's relationship to crime and criminal justice.

• **Policy Responses to Crime**

Learning Objective 2.4: Illustrate recent shifts in criminal justice policy.

Concern about crime has become part of everyday life. Each day, most of us hear about crime and engage in crime-prevention activities. Crime scares us, intrigues us, and amuses us. It is the topic of legislation, policies, televisions shows, major motion

IN THE NEWS

When Is Intent to Commit a Crime an Actual Crime?

3 Arrest

1 Criminal Act

Jack Sawyer, an 18-year-old living in Vermont, was arrested in 2018 for attempted first-degree murder, two counts of attempted aggravated murder (which refers to a murder that meets certain circumstances; e.g., it was knowingly and intentionally committed), and attempted assault with a deadly weapon after he plotted a mass shooting at his former high school. He was also charged with two misdemeanor

SCHOOL SHOOTING PLOT

POTENTIAL VERMONT SCHOOL SHOOTER TO BE SET FREE
CBS EVENING NEWS — JEFF GLOR

11 Appeal

charges of criminal threatening and carrying a weapon with intent of harming another person. The charges carried a potential life sentence without the possibility of parole.

Sawyer was arrested one day after he stated on social media that he approved of the 2018

mass shooting at Marjory Stoneman Douglas High School in Parkland, Florida, that left 17 people dead and 17 others wounded. Sawyer shared similar school shooting plans of his own and had earlier purchased weapons (Keck, 2018).

Sawyer's attorney appealed the case to the Vermont Supreme Court, arguing that there was no evidence that Sawyer made an attempt to commit a crime. Vermont law required that in order to demonstrate intent, it must be proven that someone has taken an overt action toward committing a crime (Keck, 2018). The court agreed with the attorney, arguing that Sawyer only prepared, but did not attempt, to commit a crime. The four felony charges filed against Sawyer were dropped shortly after the court's ruling (Murray, 2018). A decision resulting from a later hearing that was not open to the public (given Sawyer's status as a juvenile at the time) resulted in Sawyer being adjudicated a "youthful offender" and placed in a residential treatment facility in another state.

This case identifies a challenge regularly faced by criminal justice officials, including law enforcement and those who work in the courts. Authorities do not wish to wait until someone commits a harmful act prior to making an arrest; however, they must recognize individual rights and freedoms. Does posting threatening material on a social media site and buying guns constitute an overt act?

pictures, international relations, everyday conversation, and jokes. Despite our regular exposure to accounts of crime, many of us do not clearly understand the multifaceted nature of crime. This module examines various aspects of crime, beginning with a discussion of the legal elements of a crime, followed by consideration of the costs of crime. Given that our images and perceptions of crime are largely shaped by the media, this module also includes an examination of crime in the media. It concludes with consideration of policymaking in relation to crime.

What Constitutes a Crime?

How would you describe what constitutes a crime to a friend? Is a crime a violation of the law? Is a crime harmful activity? Does a crime require **intent**, or an offender meaning to commit the crime? For our purposes, the definition of a **crime** is a violation of criminal law that is subject to punishment by the government.

Federalism and Legislating Crime

Federalism is the guiding principle on which the United States is organized. **Federalism** means that government power is divided between a central government (the federal or national government) and its constituents (states). This approach differs from a **unitary system of government**, in which all control is allocated to a national government, and from a **confederation**, in which states are sovereign and have supreme authority (Wilson & Dilulio, 2006).

Ultimately, the U.S. Constitution provides the basis for all legislation in the United States. It permits states to govern themselves (e.g., determine what constitutes a crime), except when issues of national welfare are involved.

The **U.S. Congress**, which consists of the U.S. Senate and the U.S. House of Representatives, is the legislative branch of the federal government. Among other responsibilities, Congress determines what constitutes a **federal crime**, or violation of federal laws (e.g., those pertaining to bank robbery, kidnapping, mail fraud).

Each state also has a legislature that determines what constitutes a **state crime**, or violation of state laws (e.g., burglary, theft, robbery). When we use the word "crimes," we are generally referring to state crimes, as opposed to federal crimes, because most crimes are state crimes.

Elements of a Crime

The elements necessary for the commission of a crime have been the subject of much scholarly attention. At the most basic level, the elements include an act, intent, and the occurrence of these two elements simultaneously, or what is known as concurrence. Some scholars provide additional elements and suggest that a crime requires:

- an act (actus reus),
- legality,
- attendant circumstances,
- harm,
- causation,
- intent (mens rea),
- concurrence, and
- punishment (e.g., Hall, 1960).

These elements of a crime may be visible in some incidents, yet difficult to identify or prove in others. Determining whether a crime has occurred sometimes requires interpretation of human behavior.

AN ACT (ACTUS REUS)

Actus reus refers to actions and, in some cases, inactions on behalf of individuals. **Acts of commission**, the most common type of actus reus, involve actions that occurred. **Acts of omission** involve incidents in which a harm occurred by the failure of an individual to meet a designated responsibility. For instance, shooting an individual with a gun would be an act of commission, while failing to pay one's taxes

---

● **Learning Objective 2.1:** Explain how crime is legislated and identify the elements of a crime.

1 Criminal Act

intent (mens rea) An offender meaning or intending to commit a crime

crime A violation of criminal law that is subject to punishment by the state

federalism The division of government power between a central government and its constituents

unitary system of government A system of government in which all control is allocated to a national government

confederation A system of government in which states are sovereign

U.S. Congress The legislative branch of the federal government; it consists of the U.S. Senate and the U.S. House of Representatives

federal crime A violation of federal laws

state crimes Violations of laws created by states

actus reus Actions, and in some cases inactions, on behalf of individuals

acts of commission
Actions that occurred or were committed

acts of omission
Incidents in which a harm occurred by the failure of an individual to meet a designated responsibility

inchoate crimes Offenses that were not completed, but for which there was evidence that the individuals involved were preparing, conspiring, or attempting to commit a crime

attendant circumstances Situations, actions, or characteristics that render particular behaviors criminal

homicide Killing another person

causation The relationship between the act and the harms incurred within crimes

would be considered an act of omission. Individuals cannot be punished for their thoughts; to commit a crime, they must engage in some activity or fail to engage in an activity for which they were accountable or responsible.

There are instances when individuals are held responsible for crimes that they fail to complete, for instance due to incompetence or when law enforcement takes preventive action. Recall the story of Jack Sawyer from the "In the News" feature at the start of this module, in which Sawyer was arrested for making comments about committing a crime, yet did not follow through on his words. **Inchoate crimes** are offenses that were not completed, but there was evidence that the individuals involved were preparing, conspiring, or attempting to commit a crime. In these and related cases, individuals may be charged with "conspiracy" or "attempted" charges.

LEGALITY

Behaviors—regardless of how harmful or immoral—that are not defined as illegal are indeed legal. For example, legislation protecting the environment did not appear in any substantive manner until the 1960s and the creation of the Environmental Protection Agency in 1970 (e.g., Lynch et al., 2014). Accordingly, corporations and others were generally free to pollute rivers and the air. Today, such practices are legislated and regulated by agencies at various levels of government.

ATTENDANT CIRCUMSTANCES

Attendant circumstances involve situations, actions, or characteristics that render particular behaviors criminal. They are particularly important with regard to legality. For instance, **homicide**, which refers to killing another person, is not necessarily illegal. In fact, police officers and military personnel are sometimes expected to commit homicide. Unlawfully killing another person, however, is illegal.

HARM

Crimes require that harm be involved. The extent to which harm is involved in an offense often determines the severity of the penalty involved, as well as the criminal justice efforts put forth in response to the incident. The significance of harm is evidenced in the manner by which we categorize crimes as either serious or nonserious and violent or nonviolent. For example, the difference between assault and aggravated assault (e.g., assault using a deadly weapon) is often the extent of the damages resulting from the violent encounter.

CAUSATION

With respect to crime, **causation** refers to the relationship between the act and the harms incurred. Crimes generally require a demonstration of the relationship between the act, intent, and harms (except in cases of attempted or inchoate crimes). In most cases, this is not difficult to identify. However, there are instances when demonstrating causation can be challenging, including in some white-collar crimes. For example, in cases in which it is necessary to demonstrate the hazards associated with smoking or of exposure of workers to harmful products such as asbestos, the harmful effects of the acts are not immediately apparent.

Harmful acts against the environment, including the pollution of waterways and the air, were largely permitted until the 1960s when laws were passed to prevent these and related environmental harms. Such acts, although harmful, were permitted because they were legal.

Can you think of any other harmful acts that are legal?

INTENT (MENS REA)

Mens rea refers to culpability and one's intent to commit a crime. This requirement helps ensure that those who commit harms but do not intend to do so (for example, a person swinging a golf club who inadvertently strikes another person with the club and injures them) are not fully punished for their actions. Most crimes require a wrongful mind or an intention to commit a harm. **Strict liability offenses**, such as unintentionally speeding or running a red light, do not require criminal intent. These and related actions may be accidental, but the offender would be deemed negligent and/or responsible to some extent.

Related to strict liability and mens rea are the terms *reckless* and *negligence*. For example, individuals who commit harm while acting in a reckless or negligent manner can be held accountable for their actions, even if the result of their actions was not what they intended. The terms are often used synonymously, although they are somewhat different. **Negligence** means that someone neglected to do something, such as save a life when responsible to do so, or to know the laws in a particular jurisdiction. For instance, the use of radar detectors is prohibited in Virginia, and motorists are expected to know the law. It is considered negligence if they use a radar detector. **Recklessness** generally means that an individual was acting in a carefree, atypical manner. An example of reckless behavior would be a gun owner who does not safely secure weapons out of the reach of children.

CONCURRENCE

Concurrence refers to the requirement that the act and intent occur simultaneously to be considered a crime. The absence of one or the other would likely result in the absence of a criminal charge. However, there are some exceptions to the need for concurrence, including:

- strict liability crimes,
- crimes committed while behaving in a reckless or negligent manner, and
- **felony murders** (wrongful deaths that result during the commission of a felony, even if there was no intent by the offender to commit murder); any accomplices can also be found guilty of felony murder.

PUNISHMENT

The final element of a crime is punishment. Laws identify the punishments associated with crimes. Accordingly, there is no crime if there is no associated legal punishment for a behavior. Some behaviors may be considered offensive, harmful, or rude, but they may not be criminal because there is no penalty associated with their commission. For instance, **hate speech**, which includes verbal attacks against a person or group based on a dislike of their attributes, such as race, sexual orientation, and other factors, is protected in part by the First Amendment's granting of freedom of expression. Existing laws only protect against hate speech that is direct, personal, and notably threatening or violently provocative.

The Costs of Crime

When we consider the costs of crime, we often look at the direct impacts, including monetary losses and/or physical harms. However, we often fail to look beyond these impacts to realize how expensive crime is in other ways.

---

mens rea (intent) An offender meaning or intending to commit a crime

strict liability offenses Offenses that do not require criminal intent

negligence Someone neglecting to do something when they are responsible to do so; or failing to know the laws in a particular jurisdiction

recklessness Individuals acting in a carefree, atypical manner

concurrence The requirement that actus reus and mens rea occur simultaneously for the commission of a crime

felony murders Deaths that result during the commission of a felony; punishment for murder applies even if there was no intent by the offender to commit murder

hate speech Verbal attacks against a person or group based on a dislike of their attributes such as race, sexual orientation, and other factors

● **Learning Objective 2.2:** Characterize the various costs that crime imposes on American society.

1 Criminal
Act

Categorizing the Costs of Crime

The costs of crime are often considered in financial terms, specifically in relation to the monetary value of items lost. However, there are many costs aside from the direct loss of property or cash that can be categorized in several ways, including:

● victim costs, including direct financial losses, medical costs, lost wages and earnings, emotional and psychological harms, and property loss and damage;

● criminal justice system costs, including those associated with financing police-, courts-, and corrections-based practices;

● crime career costs, including the money lost by an offender's decision to commit crime rather than engaging in legal and productive behaviors. For instance, those who become career criminals forego working a legitimate job through which they would pay income taxes.

● psychological costs, including the indirect harms and losses incurred by victims, such as pain and suffering and decreased quality of life; and

● loss of tax revenue costs, including the money not collected for criminal endeavors such as gambling, drugs, and prostitution (McCollister et al., 2010).

Calculating the Costs of Crime

Placing a monetary value on emotional or psychological harms is notably difficult. In addition, much of the crime that occurs is not reported or observed. Also lost in many analyses of the costs of crimes are "hidden" crimes, in which the victim is unaware that a crime occurred—for example, when a corporation illegally discharges harmful emissions that cause various health-related problems.

Despite the difficulties in measuring the costs of crime, researchers have offered estimates. One researcher suggested that the annual cost of both reported and unreported Part I offenses in the Federal Bureau of Investigation's Uniform Crime Reports (i.e., criminal homicide, rape, robbery, aggravated assault, larceny-theft, arson, burglary, and motor vehicle theft; as discussed in Module 4) was about $310 billion. The bulk of the costs ($250 billion, or 80.6%) were attributed to violent crimes (Chalfin, 2016). Other estimates of all crimes range from $690 billion to $3.41 trillion (U.S. Government Accounting Office, 2017).

Justice System Costs

Estimating the costs of crime warrants consideration of the costs associated with our justice systems. The crime-related expenses associated with law enforcement, the courts, and corrections are typically included in overall calculations of the costs of crime.

The costs of law enforcement, the courts, and corrections were estimated at $295 billion annually. Almost half (roughly $142 billion, or 48.2%) of the expenditures were on law enforcement, followed by corrections (roughly $88 billion, or 29.9%) and the courts (roughly $64 billion, or 21.8%) (Bronson, 2019). The costs of corrections and law enforcement combined were the fifth largest source of state and local spending in 2017 (Urban Institute, n.d.).

The 2001 terrorist attacks against the United States generated many additional costs to all levels of government. Researchers estimated that public and private sector expenditures on homeland security increased by $44 billion between 2001 and 2005—reflecting security concerns following the attacks. Federal government expenditures constituted the bulk of the spending (Hobijn & Sager, 2007).

Aside from the direct costs of the attacks are the many indirect costs associated with homeland security, including:

- disruptions and security issues at airports,
- business and commerce issues resulting from restrictions on travel into the United States, and
- screening of imports coming into the United States (Gaines & Kappeler, 2012).

Private Security Costs

The **private security industry** also factors into evaluations of the costs of crime and justice. Private security includes individuals, agencies, organizations, and services other than public law enforcement agencies that primarily engage in preventing loss or harm to others. It includes:

- private security officers,
- private detectives and investigators,
- alarm companies,
- armed couriers,
- consultants, and
- personal bodyguards.

Similar to calculating the costs of crime, it is very difficult to determine the costs of private security, although the widespread scope of the private security industry translates into billions of dollars annually spent on private protection from crime and harms (e.g., Dempsey, 2011) (see Module 11 for further discussion of the private security industry).

> **CAREERS**
>
> **Private security officers** protect individuals and businesses. They may personally monitor people/places, or they may use technology to do so. They may be employed by department stores, hospitals, private communities, and banks, and may work directly for these and other groups or for privately owned security companies that contract with them.

private security industry Individuals, agencies, organizations, and services other than public law enforcement agencies that primarily engage in preventing loss or harm to others

Media and Crime

We are typically not exposed to the many long-term costs associated with crime, in large part because much of what we know about crime and justice comes from media accounts. And the media often focus on what is sensational and in the moment. When we refer to the media, we typically mean the following four types of media:

- broadcast media (e.g., film, radio, recorded music, television)
- digital media (e.g., apps, social media sites, websites)
- print media (e.g., books, magazines, newspapers)
- outdoor media (e.g., billboards, signs)

The media continue to expand in terms of size, scope, and impact. While all types of media have connections to both crime and justice, it is information conveyed in the form of "news" via broadcast, print, and digital media that has had notable impacts on perceptions of crime and justice.

● **Learning Objective 2.3:** Explain the media's relationship to crime and criminal justice.

1 Criminal Act

Media Effects on Perceptions of Crime and Justice

Media portrayals of crime and justice significantly affect public perceptions of criminal behavior and criminal justice. In 1956, sociologist C. Wright Mills argued that little of what society perceives as reality is generated by personal encounters. Instead, he noted that many people in society rely on media accounts to shape their reality. Mills's comments still hold true in the early 21st century.

The crime- and justice-related information that comes from media sources has a substantial impact on public perceptions of crime and justice, which subsequently impacts public policy. Media consumers may select and encourage policymakers and other government leaders to react to perceived issues related to crime and justice (Burns & Crawford, 1999). One negative aspect of this relationship is the fact that the media primarily base their practices on generating profits, which means they may disproportionately cover certain types of crime.

Misrepresentations of Crime in the Media

The media may provide skewed coverage of crime by covering certain types of crime at the expense of others. Scholars who study media news coverage of crime suggest that violent, celebrity, and sensationalized crimes are overrepresented in the media (e.g., Kappeler et al., 2018), while crimes that occur most often, such as property thefts, are underrepresented (Jerin & Fields, 2009). Media misrepresentation of crime has created what has been termed the **"carnival mirror" of crime** (Reiman & Leighton, 2013). This expression references the mirrors often found at carnivals and fairs that present distorted images.

Cases involving celebrities and notably horrific crimes receive disproportionate media attention compared with other, far more common, types of crime. The amount of publicity that sensational cases receive distorts public perceptions of crime and criminal justice. These sensational crimes occur infrequently compared to other types of crime and do not truly reflect crime in society. However, by disproportionately covering certain types of crime, the public may believe that crime in their area is more problematic or abundant than it truly is.

Criminal cases have often been compared to a four-tiered wedding cake, with the top layer consisting of celebrated cases, followed by serious and less serious felonies. The bottom layer of the cake, which is the largest, consists of misdemeanors or less serious offenses (Figure 2.1) (e.g., Walker, 2006). The criminal justice wedding cake highlights the fact that most crime consists of misdemeanors, as opposed to the more serious crimes and celebrated cases that are regularly depicted in the media.

Benefits of Media Coverage

While media coverage of crime and justice has been the target of much criticism, because of the aforementioned tendency to cover only the most sensationalized crime, the media often assist in efforts to combat crime and secure justice. For example, media coverage:

- attracts attention to the criminal justice system, which has encouraged reform and development within the field, and prompted individuals to work or study crime and justice;

carnival mirror of crime A reference to media misrepresentation of crime

The news media contribute much to our perceptions of crime and justice. Much of what we understand about criminal justice in general comes from media accounts.

Do you think shedding light on certain types of crime is a good or bad thing for society? Why?

- provides a sense of accountability for criminal justice personnel and agencies through investigative journalism;

- impacts the size of justice-based agencies. For instance, more coverage of crime news resulted in larger departments in some cases (Feinberg, 2002).

- leads to people who come forward with information about crimes, for example through the **Crime Stoppers program**, in exchange for cash rewards;

- assists in recovering abducted children, for instance through the **AMBER Alert system**, or AMBER Plan, which uses media outlets to interrupt radio and television broadcasts with information regarding child abductions; and

- promotes less crime through various public service campaigns (e.g., those pertaining to drug and alcohol abuse).

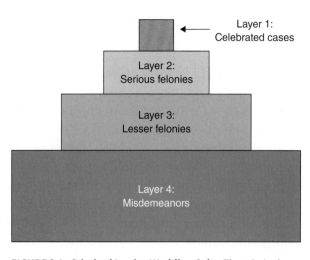

FIGURE 2.1. Criminal Justice Wedding Cake. The criminal justice wedding cake is used to discuss how crime occurs in society. The wedding cake analogy also addresses the influence of high-profile cases, which occur relatively infrequently compared to other types of crime (e.g., misdemeanors), yet command much public attention.

What celebrated cases have you recently heard about?

The Media and Crime Reporting

The media rely on criminal justice agencies as part of their day-to-day operations and vice versa. For instance, reporters and journalists rely on police agencies for accurate and timely crime news, while police agencies can use media outlets to secure the public's assistance in capturing dangerous criminals.

Historically, the relationships between employees within our criminal justice systems and the media has largely been troubled by a sense of distrust and a lack of recognition of the need for both groups to do their job. Criminal justice agencies may feel that the media seek to expose agency wrongdoing or may inaccurately report crime. The media may see criminal justice agencies as being too protective of crime news, or they may believe that the police and other justice-based agencies may misrepresent crime-related information.

Media personnel are assisted by two particularly important pieces of legislation that enable them to obtain and share news: the First Amendment to the U.S.

Crime Stoppers program A media-based program that offers cash rewards to people who come forward with information about a crime

AMBER Alert system A program that uses media outlets to assist in recovering abducted children

MYTHBUSTING

The Media Can Obtain and Publish Whatever Crime-Related Information They Want

It is often believed that the First Amendment, which provides for the freedom of the press, enables the media to publish whatever information it chooses. It is also largely believed that the Freedom of Information Act allows journalists and others to obtain whatever information they want from government sources. While the First Amendment and the Freedom of Information Act do provide assistance for the media and others, there are restrictions. For example, the freedom of the press does not entitle media outlets to publish false information. Further, there are some situations in which the Freedom of Information Act does not apply, including those involving national security and privacy concerns and when the release of certain information may compromise an ongoing investigation.

Freedom of Information Act Legislation that requires government agencies to share their records with the public

● **Learning Objective 2.4:** Illustrate recent shifts in criminal justice policy.

10
Corrections

police public information officers Police personnel who are the spokespersons for police agencies and provide information to media and other sources

policymaking A planned course of action designed to affect persons or issues

deterrence A goal of sentencing that seeks to discourage or dissuade individuals or everyone from committing various behaviors

Constitution and the Freedom of Information Act. The First Amendment established freedom of the press. And the government, with a few exceptions, is prohibited from interfering with the production and distribution of opinions or information. In addition, the **Freedom of Information Act** generally requires government agencies to share their records with the public.

Some justice-based agencies maintain video libraries that provide the media with material that may be needed at critical times. Libraries containing videos and/or photographs of agency-specific duties and responsibilities are sometimes made available to the media when they cannot obtain actual footage of a critical incident. Such footage may involve training practices, behind-the-scenes investigative work, or other nonemergency types of activities. **Police public information officers** are spokespersons for police agencies that provide information to media and other sources. They are often best situated to maintain and administer the media libraries (Boetig & Parrish, 2008).

Policy Responses to Crime

The media are influential in shaping public policy. Increased consumption of news is related to increased levels of fear about crime and stronger support for more punitive criminal justice policies (Dolliver et al., 2018). **Policymaking**, or a planned course of action designed to affect persons or issues, has regularly affected crime and criminal justice throughout much of history. Congress and government leaders throughout the United States regularly grapple with the need to make policies pertaining to gun control, illegal immigration, drugs, and a host of other crime-related concerns. While policies can focus on specific topics (e.g., drunk driving), they can also have broader implications and affect a wider array of issues (e.g., the policies associated with the war on drugs). Criminal justice policy is primarily set by government leaders at the federal, state, and local levels. Each level addresses issues pertaining to its jurisdiction. Policy is proposed to be reflective of the public's interests.

Objectives of Criminal Justice Policymaking

In general terms, the goals of criminal justice policy have fluctuated in the United States throughout history. However, efforts have stressed one or more of the following:

● **deterrence**, which seeks to discourage individuals from committing crime;

● **incapacitation**, which physically prevents people from committing harms and is primarily practiced through the use of **incarceration** (placement in jail or prison);

● **retribution**, which involves imposing some type of punishment that is relatively equal to the harms committed; and

● **rehabilitation**, which attempts to correct or restore a troubled individual to a crime-free life.

Beginning in the late 1970s, a "get tough" approach to crime replaced an emphasis on rehabilitation. This shift signaled the beginning of a notably expanded criminal justice system, extensive resources devoted to punishing criminals, and a reliance on incarceration to deliver that punishment. With regard to the latter, the number of adults under correctional supervision (e.g., in prison or jail or on probation or parole) increased from just under 2 million in 1980 to roughly 6.4 million in 2018. The policy shift has had notable effects, as roughly 1 in every 40 adults in the United States was under some form of correctional supervision as of 2018 (Kaeble & Cowhig, 2018).

Influences on Policymaking

While criminal justice policy is primarily set by government leaders, those leaders must consider the wants of their constituents and others. Influences on policymaking include:

- public opinion: politicians are accountable to constituents to generate or maintain high approval ratings;
- lobbying by corporations, interest groups, and other organizations to generate legislation. For example, in 2015 individuals concerned about harms to the environment created the Texas Grassroots Network, which monitors the energy industry and seeks to influence public policy, at the local and state levels, on oil and gas drilling.
- the media, which identify issues that generate concern for politicians (Burns & Crawford, 1999).

Policies regarding crime and justice must balance the public's need for protection with concerns for imposing on citizens' individual rights. **Due process protections**, which involve efforts to ensure that individual rights and freedoms are not violated, are of particular importance with regard to criminal justice policies.

Policy Changes: Examples

The emphasis on addressing crime, adopted by the United States in the late 1970s, consisted of a compilation of stringent policies directed toward reducing crime and ensuring justice. Among the more notable policies that are reflective of this approach are those directed toward drunk driving and drugs. The policy changes regarding drunk driving are reflective of how criminal justice policy can change in response to the collaborative efforts of various groups. The policy changes regarding drugs exemplify how policies can be heavily enforced and ultimately altered in response to questionable results.

DRUNK DRIVING

Beginning in the 1980s, state and federal legislatures enacted much stiffer penalties for drunk driving. The legislation was largely spurred by public concern over alcohol-related fatal car accidents and by the encouragement and persuasion of an organization known as Mothers Against Drunk Driving. The crackdown included notably tougher punishments for offenders and enhanced efforts to detect and deter driving under the influence of alcohol. The crackdown also featured a collaborative effort between the National Highway Traffic Safety Administration, Mothers Against Drunk Driving, local law enforcement officers, and the Governors Highway Safety Association. Their campaign was supported by national television and radio advertising of the National Highway Traffic Safety Administration's "Drive Sober or Get Pulled Over" campaign.

DRUGS

State and federal legislatures have, for a long time, sought to control the use of drugs. Opium and cocaine initially became illegal in the United States with passage of the **Harrison Narcotics Tax Act** (1914), which is often recognized as the first drug

incapacitation A goal of criminal sentencing that seeks to physically prevent offenders from committing additional crimes; incarceration is an example

incarceration Being physically confined or detained in a jail or prison

retribution A goal of criminal sentencing that seeks to punish offenders; it is based on retaliation, or the "eye for an eye" or "just deserts" approach

rehabilitation A goal of criminal sentencing that begins with understanding why an offender broke the law and proceeds to help them refrain from doing so in the future through education, counseling, and other forms of treatment

due process protections Efforts to ensure that individual rights and freedoms are not violated

1 Criminal Act

9 Sentencing

Harrison Narcotics Tax Act Legislation that outlaws opium and cocaine; it is often recognized as the first drug control policy control policy. Since that time, numerous policies have been established to control all aspects of drugs, including their production, transportation, distribution, and use.

Among the more controversial drug policies enacted were those associated with crack cocaine, which were imposed during the 1980s and into the 1990s. The introduction of crack cocaine during that time was viewed as particularly threatening to society, and notably strict penalties were imposed for crimes involving crack. For instance, the **Anti–Drug Abuse Act of 1986** mandated a minimum sentence of 5 years in prison without parole for possession of 5 grams of crack cocaine. The results, however, generated controversy because the penalties disproportionately impacted African Americans, who were more likely than members of other groups to be associated with crack-related offenses (Kappeler et al., 2018).

Evidence of the government's continued involvement in drug enforcement is found in many areas, including the amount of resources requested and allocated to address drug problems. For instance, there were over 155 million arrests for drug abuse violations in 2019 (Federal Bureau of Investigation, 2020a), most of which were made by local law enforcement agencies. In addition, the federal government has been particularly active in drug enforcement. Almost half of all federal inmates (46.4%) were in prison for a drug offense in 2021 (Federal Bureau of Prisons, 2021). As noted in Figure 2.2, the Drug Enforcement Administration annually makes a substantial number of arrests for offenses involving various types of drugs (Motivans, 2019).

The war on drugs has been criticized for many reasons, including its reliance on flawed policies. The emphasis on getting tough on drug offenders has largely contributed to the expansion of the correctional population and increased spending (as noted above, governments spend roughly $88 billion on corrections annually). The extensive costs of the war on drugs, coupled with public opinion polls increasingly supporting the legalization of marijuana and some other drugs, have contributed to what appears to be a shift in drug control policy.

Anti–Drug Abuse Act of 1986 Legislation that mandated a minimum sentence of 5 years in prison without parole for possession of 5 grams of crack cocaine

3 Arrest

10 Corrections

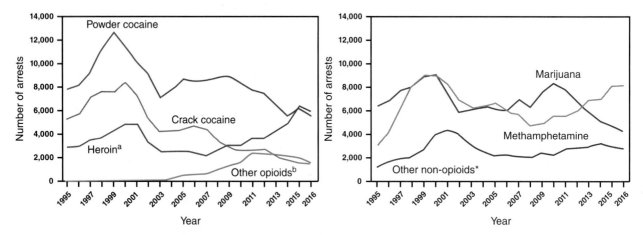

FIGURE 2.2. Drug Enforcement Administration (DEA) Arrests. The DEA annually makes tens of thousands of arrests for various types of drugs. The trend data presented here indicate that the number of arrests for powder cocaine, crack cocaine, and marijuana dropped quite a bit from the late 1990s, while arrests for heroin and other opioids increased. ***Source***: *Bureau of Justice Statistics, based on data from the Drug Enforcement Administration, Defendant Statistical System, fiscal years 1995–2016.*

Note. The unit of count is an arrest by the DEA. Each arrest for an individual is counted separately. Includes state and federal arrests made by the DEA. (Left) [a]Includes heroin, morphine, and opium base. [b]Opioids refer to synthetic compounds that emulate the effects of natural compounds found in the opium poppy. Synthetic opioids are commonly available by prescription but can also be manufactured in labs. (Right) *Includes nonopioid pharmaceutical controlled substances, other depressants, sedatives, ephedrine, pseudoephedrine, hallucinogens, synthetic cannabinoids, other steroids, equipment to manufacture controlled substances, and drug-use paraphernalia.

Do you feel that the shifts in these trends have more to do with the extent to which people use certain drugs, public concern for particular drugs, or agency focus?

The war on drugs has been fought on many fronts, including in other countries, on the seas, at our borders, and on our streets. It does appear, however, that the war may be slowing in its intensity.

Do you believe we should continue fighting the war on drugs, or should we move toward making certain drugs legal?

The aggressive drug control efforts in the United States over the past 4 decades have been tempered in part, and there is evidence of a shift in policy. Two-thirds (66%) of Americans support the legalization of marijuana (J. M. Jones, 2019), and as of 2020, 33 states permitted the use of marijuana for medical purposes and 11 states permitted its use for recreational purposes. Other states are considering whether to follow the states that have legalized it. The apparent shift in policy with regard to drug laws demonstrates the flexibility and fluidness of policies, meaning that they can be altered based on evidence that reform is wanted and needed.

The System in Perspective

The "In the News" story at the start of this module involving Jack Sawyer's alleged intention to cause harm at his school touches on many important topics addressed in this module. The controversy surrounding this case has to do in large part with actus reus and whether Sawyer's actions of posting information about what he intended to do should be considered a crime. Further, those in law enforcement and the courts had to read into whether he had mens rea (intent) to follow through. The case also relates to our perceptions of crime, as school violence has been the focal point of many media accounts in recent years, and authorities wished to prevent the many costs and harms associated with another mass shooting. Authorities had to wrestle with law enforcement policies regarding whether Sawyer committed a crime and an arrest was warranted. Attorneys and the judge involved in the case were required to interpret and respond to Sawyer's actions and the law.

Summary

1. Learning Objective 2.1: *Explain how crime is legislated and identify the elements of a crime.*

- Federal crimes are legislated by the U.S. Congress, which consists of the U.S. Senate and the U.S. House of Representatives and is the legislative branch of the federal government. State crimes are legislated by state legislatures. The elements of a crime include an act (actus reus), legality, harm, causation, intent (mens rea), concurrence, and punishment.

2. Learning Objective 2.2: *Characterize the various costs that crime imposes on American society.*

- The costs of crime include direct monetary losses, pain and suffering, legal costs, costs of the criminal justice system, psychological costs, and public efforts to address crime. All levels of government allocate substantial portions of their budgets to criminal justice.

3. Learning Objective 2.3: *Explain the media's relationship to crime and criminal justice.*

- The media affect crime and justice in many ways, including through their portrayal of crime,

impact on public perceptions, and assistance with crime-fighting and crime-prevention efforts. The media and criminal justice agencies must work cooperatively. Public information officers help criminal justice agencies interact with the media.

4. Learning Objective 2.4: *Illustrate recent shifts in criminal justice policy.*

- Policies can focus on specific topics or be broader in nature. For instance, they may address specific issues, such as driving under the influence of alcohol, or larger issues, such as drug control and sentencing issues. The creation and enforcement of criminal justice policy involves various groups, including criminal justice agencies, government leaders, citizens, corporations, interest groups, and the media. Among the more commonly recognized and more influential policies are those pertaining to the get-tough approach that began in the late 1970s. Influential policies have shaped crime-fighting efforts with regard to drug offenses and drunk driving.

Questions for Critical Thinking

1. Should the police be permitted to arrest individuals who have simply planned a crime? If so, how long should they wait before acting? If not, why?

2. What steps could be taken to reduce the criminal justice system costs of crime?

3. Do you believe the news media should more accurately portray crime? Why or why not? How might they do so?

4. Do you believe all states will legalize marijuana? What about other drugs, such as cocaine or opium? Why or why not?

Key Terms

acts of commission
acts of omission
actus reus
AMBER Alert system
Anti–Drug Abuse Act of 1986
attendant circumstances
carnival mirror of crime
causation
concurrence
confederation

crime
Crime Stoppers program
deterrence
due process protections
federal crime
federalism
felony murders
Freedom of Information Act
Harrison Narcotics Tax Act
hate speech

homicide
incapacitation
incarceration
inchoate crimes
intent (mens rea)
mens rea
negligence
police public information officers
policymaking

private security industry
recklessness
rehabilitation
retribution
state crimes
strict liability offenses
unitary system of government
U.S. Congress

For digital learning resources, please go to
https://www.oup.com/he/burns1e

Types and Categorization of Crime

There are many types of crime and various ways to categorize them. Many crimes have existed throughout much of history (e.g., theft, assault); however, new types of crimes continue to emerge (e.g., cybercrime). This sometimes creates the need for new categories of crime.

What do you believe would be the best way to categorize crimes?

The term *crime* refers to a wide array of illegal actions that can be notably different in nature and degree of harm. For instance, consider that stealing a backpack and murdering someone are both considered crimes. Both acts are harmful and illegal; however, one is violent, and the other involves theft. One is also far more serious than the other and warrants much tougher treatment from the criminal justice system if it is prosecuted. This module addresses the different types of crimes and considers the various ways in which crimes are categorized, beginning with a general classification of crimes. This is followed by classifications of crimes according to the seriousness of the offense and then by the type of action involved.

Social Media and Crime

In April 2018, a 30-year-old man from North Carolina was arrested for soliciting sexual acts from a minor using social media. He was arrested as he arrived at the location at which he and the minor agreed to meet. He was charged with attempted statutory rape, attempted statutory sex offense, attempted first-degree kidnapping, attempted indecent liberties with a minor, felony solicitation of a child under age 16 by computer for the purpose to commit a sex act and appear, and felony fleeing to elude arrest with motor vehicle (Roman, 2018).

Various social media outlets provide opportunities for new forms of crime. Cyberbullying has become increasingly problematic, as have online harassment and internet fraud. These types of cybercrime increasingly occur via social media outlets such as Facebook, Twitter, and Instagram. Social media outlets recognize the opportunities they provide in this respect and have helped fight back.

As one example, Facebook moderators use software that identifies images of children and nudity, which allows the company to enforce restrictions regarding the sharing of images of children in a sexualized context. The company also uses a similar system to catch users attempting to befriend children for sexual exploitation (Paresh, 2018). Do you believe social media outlets have an obligation to identify criminals or potential criminals? Further, how much social media user information should be made available to law enforcement authorities?

3 Arrest

1 Criminal Act

CHILD SEX CRIMES SUSPECT
CRAVEN COUNTY

Morgan Shepard

WITN
witn.com
86°   5:31

Categorizing Crime

It is possible to categorize crimes in different ways. One way of categorizing crimes is by organizing them according to the following groups:

- conventional crime
- white-collar crime
- cybercrime
- organized crime
- hate crimes
- consensual crimes

There is some overlap among these categories; for instance, some acts that are considered organized crime could also be considered white-collar crime. This classification is offered for discussion and conceptual purposes only. Most government agencies,

● **Learning Objective 3.1:** Describe the general categories of crime.

1 Criminal Act

conventional crimes The most common types of crime committed; refers to acts that come to mind when most people think of crime

criminal homicide The willful and illegal killing of one person by another

robbery Taking or attempting to take anything of value from another person or persons through the use of force or threat of use of violence and/or by putting the victim in fear

forcible rape The penetration of the vagina or anus with any body part or object, or oral penetration by a sex organ of another person, without the victim's consent

assault Unlawfully attacking someone for the purpose of inflicting harm

burglary Unlawfully entering a structure to commit a felony or a theft

larceny-theft Unlawfully taking property from the possession of another

motor vehicle theft The theft or attempted theft of a motor vehicle, including boats, cars, motorcycles, and related vehicles

white-collar crime Illegal acts that violate an individual or group's legal responsibility or trust, which often occur during the course of occupational activity; it is typically committed by individuals of high social status for organizational or personal gain

including those that compile crime statistics, typically view crimes as violent or property or as felonies or misdemeanors, as will be discussed later in this module.

Conventional Crime

The most common types of crime committed, and covered by the media, are **conventional crimes**—also known as "street" or "visible" crimes because of the openness and frequency with which they occur. These terms and others (e.g., traditional crime) are often used interchangeably to refer to acts that come to mind when most people think of crime. Conventional crimes often occur in large cities and in public spaces, and they consume many law enforcement resources. The following are some examples of conventional crimes (Federal Bureau of Investigation [FBI], 2020b):

- **criminal homicide:** the willful and illegal killing of one person by another
- **robbery:** taking or attempting to take anything of value from another person or persons through the use of force or threat of use of violence and/or by putting the victim in fear
- **forcible rape:** the penetration of the vagina or anus with any body part or object, or oral penetration by a sex organ of another person, without the victim's consent
- **assault:** unlawfully attacking someone for the purpose of inflicting harm
- **burglary:** unlawfully entering a structure to commit a felony or a theft
- **larceny-theft:** unlawfully taking property from the possession of another
- **motor vehicle theft:** the theft or attempted theft of a motor vehicle, including boats, cars, motorcycles, and related vehicles

White-Collar Crime

White-collar crime is an umbrella term for many illegal activities. Generally, it refers to illegal acts that violate an individual or group's legal responsibility or trust. These acts often occur during the course of employment and are typically committed by individuals of high social status for organizational or personal gain. The term was originally coined by Edwin Sutherland in 1939, although white-collar crimes were committed long before his work. In 1940, Sutherland noted that white-collar crime involved crimes committed by the "upper or white-collar class, composed of respectable or at least respected business and professional men" (Sutherland, 1940, p. 1); he added that a principal aspect of white-collar crime was a violation of delegated or implied trust (p. 3).

Various scholars have enhanced Sutherland's definition of white-collar crime. For instance, in 1996, the National White-Collar Crime Center assembled 15 white-collar crime researchers to assist in clarifying the term. The group identified white-collar crime as:

illegal or unethical acts that violate . . . responsibility of public trust committed by an individual or organization, usually during the course of legitimate occupational activity, by persons of high or respectable social status for personal or organizational gain. (Helmkamp et al., 1996, p. 351)

In his book *Trusted Criminals: White Collar Crime in Contemporary Society*, criminologist David Friedrichs (2010) described various types of white-collar crime:

- **corporate crime:** illegal and harmful acts committed by individuals to promote corporate and/or personal interests. Such acts include illegally dumping toxic chemicals into rivers, knowingly producing faulty and unsafe products, and price gouging.

- **occupational crime:** illegal and harmful acts within the context of one's employment. Examples include medical doctors engaging in unnecessary services, cashiers illegally taking money from a cash drawer, and **"bait and switch" scams** in which consumers are lured into a store by low prices, only to find out that the store does not have the product. Consumers are then offered a more expensive product.

- **government crime:** illegal activities on behalf of government itself, government agencies, government leaders, or individuals who wish to be in government. Such acts include police officers illegally misusing their powers and politicians accepting bribes while in office.

- **state–corporate crimes:** hybrid forms of white-collar crime that involve some combination of governmental and corporate criminals. For instance, some government leaders have been accused of providing favors in the form of large contracts to private corporations.

- **crimes of globalization:** illegal acts that occur or involve different countries. For instance, **money laundering** involves the transfer of illegally obtained funds among financial institutions in different countries.

- **finance crimes:** large-scale illegal or harmful acts that occur in the world of finance and financial institutions. For instance, financial brokers sometimes engage in broker fraud by offering inaccurate, incomplete, or biased information that is designed to benefit the broker and not the investor.

- **contreprenurial crime:** scams, swindles, and frauds that appear as legitimate businesses. For example, in 2009, Bernie Madoff pleaded guilty to 11 criminal counts in relation to a **Ponzi scheme** (a scam in which investors are promised large financial returns as more investors join) that was claimed to involve $65 billion. He received 150 years in prison for his involvement.

- **avocational crimes:** illegal but nonconventional offenses committed by white-collar personnel outside an organization or their occupation. Such acts include income tax evasion and the purchase of stolen goods.

White-collar crime differs from most other types of crimes in these ways (Friedrichs, 2010):

- Those who participate are typically wealthier and more powerful.
- The effects are typically delayed.
- Intent is often more difficult to prove, because the actions are often masked under the guise of conducting business.
- It is more likely to go unnoticed or considered the cost one pays for engaging in certain activities (e.g., investing money).

Cybercrime

One of the most perplexing types of crime is **cybercrime**, which involves the commission of conventional forms of crime (e.g., theft, extortion, fraud) via the use of computers and related technology. Law enforcement officials and the legal system have struggled to keep pace with the constantly changing technology used in this type of crime, which requires updated technology

corporate crime
A type of white-collar crime in which illegal and harmful acts are committed by individuals to promote corporate and/or personal interests

occupational crime Crimes committed within the context of one's employment or occupation

"bait and switch" scams Scams in which consumers are lured into a store by low prices, only to find out that the store does not have the product; consumers are then offered a more expensive product

government crime Illegal activities on behalf of government itself, government agencies, or government leaders

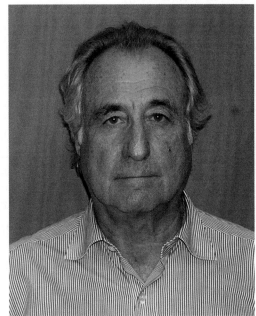

Bernie Madoff was responsible for one of the most impactful white-collar crimes in history. His involvement in the world's largest Ponzi scheme ever resulted in harms that far surpassed many conventional, or street, crimes.

Should nonviolent crimes, including those involving significant losses, be considered as important or significant as violent crimes?

MYTHBUSTING

White-Collar Crime Does No Physical Damage

It is commonly believed that white-collar crime is nonviolent in nature or that it does no physical damage. Many people think that such crimes are simply financially motivated and involve some type of fraud. While many white-collar crimes are financially motivated, the means used to obtain money can have violent consequences. For example, corporations that illegally dump hazardous waste to save money may cause physical harms to the environment and illnesses to individuals who are exposed to the waste. As another example, consider the actions of Volkswagen, which from 2008 to 2015 altered the emissions controls in roughly 11 million of its cars so that the controls would only work to prevent emissions during regulatory testing. The air pollution resulting from the cars that beat those regulatory emissions tests had real physical consequences.

---

state-corporate crimes Hybrid forms of white-collar crime that involve some combination of governmental and corporate criminals

crimes of globalization Illegal acts that occur or involve different countries

money laundering The transfer of illegally obtained funds among financial institutions in different countries

finance crimes Large-scale crimes that occur in the world of finance and financial institutions

contreprenurial crime A type of white-collar crime that involves scams, swindles, and frauds that appear to be legitimate business

Ponzi scheme A scam in which investors are promised large financial returns as more investors join

avocational crimes A type of white-collar crime that involves illegal but nonconventional offenses committed outside an organization or occupation

and training on the part of law enforcement, additional resources, and flexible and encompassing legislation.

Estimates suggest that 90% of adults in the United States use the internet (Pew Research Center, 2019), and evidence points to a substantial worldwide increase in computer crimes and other types of electronic crimes (e.g., INTERPOL, 2019). In estimating the costs of cybercrime, the Center for Strategic and International Studies (2018), a nonprofit organization that seeks policy solutions to challenging problems, noted that the costs of cybercrime to the world economy were between $445 and $600 billion in 2016.

In his book *Understanding and Managing Cybercrime*, Professor Samuel McQuade (2006) outlined the various types of cybercrimes as:

- **writing and distributing malicious code:** the creation and spread of viruses and other harmful information that destroys or alters the information contained in the computers of those who are victimized;
- **credit card theft:** illegally obtaining and/or using credit card information through the use of computers;
- **identity-theft fraud:** illegally obtaining and/or using the identity of another person via the use of computers;
- **cyberterrorism:** the use of technology to engage in terrorism. It involves the use of the internet to promote terrorist causes, communicate with current and potential group members, gather information while planning attacks, and target groups or sites for attack (Damphousse, 2009);
- **interfering with and disrupting computer services:** illegally altering the computer services of another to prevent them from operating properly;
- **unauthorized and illegal file sharing:** illegally distributing information such as music, software, and movie files through the use of a computer; and
- **online harassment:** using a computer to harass others, for instance through sending disturbing images or emails.

Cybercrime differs from conventional crimes in these ways:

- It is often hidden from law enforcement's view.
- It is more likely to be anonymous.

- It is predominantly nonviolent.
- There is often little interaction between the offender and victim.
- It can facilitate victimization on a global scale.

Cybercrimes continue to evolve as offenders find new means to use computers for illegal purposes. It is estimated that there are at least 190 types of **ransomware**, which is software that harms computer files when it is downloaded. Victims may unknowingly download ransomware when they access decoy ads, emails, fake news stories, and related material. Offenders are increasingly taking this type of illegal activity a bit farther by following up the attack and demanding that victims pay money to regain control of their computer or device. The FBI estimated that about 4,000 computers around the world are infected with ransomware every hour (Robbins, 2017).

Organized Crime

Generally, **organized crime**, or **enterprise crime**, refers to criminal enterprises that profit from illegal activities that are typically in great public demand. While it is challenging to define, most definitions include elements of an organized hierarchy, profit through crime, the use of force or threat, and the corruption of public officials.

Organized crime groups often focus their activities around providing goods and services that are otherwise difficult to obtain because they are illegal (e.g., gambling, prostitution, drugs, unregistered guns). Their practices differ because they involve groups of people instead of one individual, and they are more likely to own legitimate businesses, for instance to hide illegally generated revenue, and rely on the involvement of corrupt public officials. For example, organized crime groups may illegally pay corrupt police officers to turn a blind eye to the group's drug trafficking (Lyman & Potter, 2011).

Among the particular types of crimes often associated with organized crime are:

- **human trafficking:** obtaining a person or persons through recruitment, harboring, transportation, or provision and subjecting them by force, fraud, or coercion into involuntary servitude;
- **gambling:** unlawfully betting or wagering money or something else of value. It also includes offering opportunities to gamble and tampering with the outcome of a contest to gain a gambling advantage;
- **prostitution and commercialized vice:** unlawfully promoting or participating in sexual activities for profit;
- **weapons offenses:** violating laws prohibiting the manufacture, sale, purchase, transportation, possession, concealment, or use of firearms or other weapons (e.g., explosives);
- **forgery and counterfeiting:** altering, copying, or imitating something without legal permission to do so, with the intent to present the altered item as the original; and
- **dealing in stolen property:** buying, receiving, possessing, selling, concealing, or transporting any property while being aware that it was illegally taken.

Organized crime in the United States dates back to the early 1800s, when organized street gangs, which largely consisted of new immigrants, worked collaboratively to earn money through violent and illegal means. In the early 21st century, many groups of diverse individuals engage in organized crime. The FBI has identified several groups that operate in the United States or that threaten the country from

cybercrimes Crimes committed through the use of a computer (or other related technological device) and a network, in which the computer may be used for the commission of or as the target of the offense

writing and distributing malicious code The creation and spread of viruses and other harmful information that destroys or alters the information contained in the computers of those who are victimized

credit card theft Illegally obtaining and/or using credit card information through the use of computers

identity-theft fraud Illegally obtaining and/or using the identity of another person via the use of computers

cyberterrorism The use of technology to engage in terrorism

interfering with and disrupting computer services Illegally altering the computer services of another to prevent them from operating properly

unauthorized and illegal file sharing Illegally distributing information such as music, software, and movie files through the use of a computer

online harassment Using a computer to harass others, for instance through sending disturbing images or emails

ransomware
Software that harms computer files when it is downloaded

organized crime Criminal enterprises that profit from illegal activities that are typically in great public demand

enterprise crime Criminal enterprises that profit from illegal activities that are typically in great public demand; also known as organized crime

human trafficking
Moving people across and within borders without their consent; it is often done through the use of violence, coercion, and/or deception and is a modern-day form of slavery often used to obtain labor or sex

gambling Unlawfully betting or wagering money or something else of value; it also includes offering opportunities to gamble and tampering with the outcome of a contest to gain a gambling advantage

prostitution and commercialized vice Unlawfully promoting or participating in sexual activities for profit

weapons offenses
Violations of laws prohibiting the manufacture, sale, purchase, transportation, possession, concealment, or use of firearms or other weapons

afar. These groups include the Italian mafia, Russian mafia, and eastern Europe organized crime groups; Latin American drug cartels; Chinese tongs; Japanese yakuza; and Nigerian groups.

Some international terrorist groups could also be considered organized crime groups because they engage in similar activities to generate money to support their terrorist activities. Global organized crime is estimated to generate about $870 billion in economic profits annually (Dent, 2016).

In recent decades, technological and political advances have made organized crime more global. One researcher found that 70% of the organized crime groups he studied engaged in activities in three or more countries (Van Dijk, 2008). Drug trafficking is the most common illegal activity committed by transnational organized crime groups. But they are also involved in trafficking other things (e.g., people, technology, weapons, and precious gems), counterfeiting, finance fraud, and environmental crimes (Gaines & Kappeler, 2012). Some international organized crime groups also engage in poaching and trafficking in the skin and bones of wildlife from Africa and Southeast Asia (e.g., elephants, tigers, and rhinos).

Hate Crime

Although the term *hate crime* was introduced in the 1980s, the acts that constitute hate crimes have occurred throughout history. **Hate crimes** are offenses motivated by an offender's bias against or hate of the victim's race, religion, disability, sexual orientation, or ethnicity. Native Americans were arguably the first hate crime victims in the United States, and various other groups have been targeted throughout the country's history (Miller & Kim, 2009).

Among the legislative acts that address hate crime is the **Hate Crime Statistics Act** of 1990, which requires the U.S. attorney general to collect data on these types of crime. Data from the FBI (FBI, n.d.b) indicated that in 2018, there were 8,496 hate

Poaching animals is just one of many crimes committed by organized crime groups.

What types of crime come to your mind when you hear the term organized crime?

crime offenses in the United States, most of which (52.4%) involved crimes against persons (e.g., intimidation, assault). Roughly 58% of the offenses were motivated by bias directed toward the victim's race, ethnicity, or ancestry.

Other legislation in the area includes the **Matthew Shepard and James Byrd, Jr. Hate Crimes Prevention Act**, which was passed by Congress in 2009 and is the first federal law to provide protections to transgendered people. The act:

- extended federal hate crime legislation to cover offenses motivated by a victim's actual or perceived gender, sexual orientation, gender identity, or disability;
- provided more money to investigate and prosecute hate crimes; and
- required the FBI to track statistics on hate crimes committed against transgender people.

Among the specific types of crimes often associated with hate crimes are:

- **assaults**,
- **vandalism:** willfully destroying or defacing property without the consent of the owner,
- **criminal homicide**, and
- **harassment:** repeated actions or words that serve no legitimate purpose and are directed at a specific person with the intent to annoy or alarm them.

Consensual Crime

Some crimes, such as rape and murder, are considered wrong in and of themselves, or what is known as ***mala en se***. Other crimes are considered wrong because they are viewed as threats against the moral order, or what is known as ***mala prohibita***. Some types of *mala prohibita* crimes are also referred to as **consensual crimes** because they involve individuals who willingly engage in acts that they may not view as harmful or arguably have no direct victims, like gambling or using drugs.

Consensual crimes may involve acts that not all individuals in society believe are necessarily wrong and, in some contexts, acts that may be legal. Gambling, for instance, is permitted in casinos, and in 2018 the U.S. Supreme Court struck down a law that prohibited commercial sports betting in most states, which opened the door for states to legalize gambling on sports. Certain drugs (e.g., prescription drugs) are legal; others are not.

Consensual crimes can be divisive. Individuals may be frowned on by society or termed *criminals* for engaging in acts that they, and many others, find acceptable. For example, prostitutes are stigmatized in society for their willingness to ply their trade (the term *willingness* is applied lightly, because some prostitutes are exploited or victims of human trafficking). Many are regularly involved with the criminal justice system, and they may have extensive criminal backgrounds. In 2019, there were 26,713 arrests for prostitution and commercialized vice (FBI, 2020a). This figure is much lower than the number of active prostitutes. Some examples of consensual crimes are:

- voluntary prostitution and commercialized vice,
- drug abuse violations,
- gambling,
- liquor law violations, and
- **drunkenness:** drinking alcoholic beverages to the extent that a person's mental faculties and physical coordination are substantially impaired.

forgery and counterfeiting Altering, copying, or imitating something without legal permission to do so, with the intent to present the altered item as the original

dealing in stolen property Buying, receiving, possessing, selling, concealing, or transporting any property while being aware that it was illegally taken

hate crimes Offenses that are motivated, in whole or in part, by an offender's bias against a race, religion, sexual orientation, ethnicity/national origin, or disability

Hate Crime Statistics Act Legislation that requires the U.S. attorney general to collect data on hate crimes

3 Arrest

Matthew Shepard and James Byrd Hates Crime Prevention Act Legislation that extended the 1960 federal hate crime law to cover offenses motivated by a victim's actual or perceived gender, sexual orientation, gender identity, or disability; it provided more money to investigate and prosecute hate crimes and required the Federal Bureau of Investigation to track statistics on hate crimes committed against transgender people

● **Learning Objective 3.2:** Classify crimes by their seriousness.

1 Criminal Act

3 Arrest

10 Corrections

assault Unlawfully attacking someone for the purpose of inflicting harm

vandalism Willfully destroying or defacing property without the consent of the owner

10 Corrections

criminal homicide The willful and illegal killing of one person by another

harassment Repeated actions or words that serve no legitimate purpose and are directed at a specific person with the intent to annoy or alarm them

Classifying Crimes by the Seriousness of the Offense

Crimes are often discussed in terms of being either a felony or a misdemeanor. There are, however, other violations of the law that are categorized with regard to their seriousness, including infractions and treason.

Infractions

Infractions are the lowest level of criminal behavior and are usually punishable by relatively light penalties; offenders are often given a citation or traffic ticket. Some states use the term *petty misdemeanor* instead of infraction. Many traffic offenses, as well as violations of open alcohol container laws, are examples of petty misdemeanors.

Related to infractions are municipal **ordinance violations**, which are infractions against rules created by a municipality. Vagrancy, for which there were 21,896 arrests in 2019 (FBI, 2020a), is an example of an ordinance violation found in many cities. Infractions are the most common violation of the law.

Misdemeanors

Misdemeanors are crimes that are more serious than infractions, yet less serious than felonies (discussed below). They are subject to a variety of punishments, including fines, probation, or up to 1 year of incarceration in jail. The maximum penalties that can be imposed for misdemeanors is defined by law.

Examples of misdemeanors include shoplifting, prostitution, and vandalism. Misdemeanors are committed far more often than more serious crimes, and they warrant less severe penalties, although those penalties may differ by state.

Misdemeanors in Utah, for example, are categorized as follows (Utah State Courts, 2018):

- Class A: possible penalties are up to a year in jail and a fine up to $2,500;
- Class B: possible penalties are up to 6 months in jail and a fine of up to $1,000 or community service; and
- Class C: possible penalties are up to 90 days in jail and a fine of up to $750 or community service.

Felonies

Felonies are crimes that are more serious in nature than misdemeanors. Examples of felonies include murder, rape, and robbery. Felonies are handled more formally by the courts compared to misdemeanors, because more attention is devoted to these cases and the associated penalties are more severe.

Felonies are often subdivided into classes to recognize the various levels of seriousness associated with the crimes. For example, there are four categories of felonies in Utah (listed in order of seriousness), with each having different possible penalties for their commission (Utah State Courts, 2018):

- capital offense: Possible penalties include life in prison, life in prison without parole, or death. Fines are not imposed in capital cases.
- first-degree felony: Possible penalties include 5 years to life in prison and a fine of up to $10,000.
- second-degree felony: Possible penalties include 1 to 15 years in prison and a fine of up to $10,000.
- third-degree felony: Possible penalties include fines up to $5,000 and zero to 5 years in prison.

Treason

Treason, which involves betraying one's country, is considered one of the most serious offenses. Section 3 of Article III of the U.S. Constitution addresses the seriousness of treason in suggesting that treason is limited to levying war against the United States or adhering to their enemies, giving them aid and comfort. Conviction, according to the Constitution, requires two witnesses or a confession in court. The penalty for treason at the federal level is death, or no less than 5 years imprisonment and a fine no less than $10,000.

Charges of treason are not common in the United States. In one more recent example, the federal government filed treason charges against Adam Gadahn, who was raised in the United States and later assisted al-Qaeda in committing terrorist attacks against the country. Gadahn evaded being taken into custody; however, it is believed he died in 2015 (CNN, 2016).

Classifying Crimes by Type of Action

Crimes can also be classified according to the type of action involved. For instance, they may be deemed public order, property, or violent offenses. Public-order crimes are generally less serious offenses that threaten social norms and include acts such as gambling and disorderly conduct. Property crimes, including burglary, involve wrongfully taking something from someone else without the use or threat of force, or damage to the property of others in some instances (e.g., arson). Violent crimes, such as rape or assault, involve the use or threat of force.

Public-Order Crimes

Public-order crimes are crimes that threaten or challenge the moral order, norms, or customs of society. Public-order crimes, including gambling, public intoxication, drug use, and prostitution, occur relatively frequently compared to violent and property crime. Many in society consider these offenses "harmless," although they are prohibited and are indeed violations of the law.

Public-order crimes include a wide array of acts that often do not involve an identifiable, direct victim. The associated punishments are typically much less severe than they are for violent and property crimes. Some of these acts have been legalized in certain jurisdictions. For example, gambling, prostitution, and drug use are permitted in some states.

Public-order crimes are sometimes referred to as **"victimless" crimes**, because there is arguably no direct victim associated with these acts. The term *victimless crime* gained prominence following Schur's (1965) use of the term to describe illegal acts for which no victims complained. The term was later critiqued in the sense that all criminal acts have victims, although the acts may not all have immediate, or direct, victims. Consider drug use. Some people might argue that there are no immediate victims associated with using drugs, but illegal drugs are untaxed, contribute to healthcare costs, and sometimes lead individuals to neglect their civic or parental responsibilities or to act erratically and illegally.

mala en se Acts that are considered to be wrong in themselves

mala prohibita Acts that are considered wrong because they are prohibited

consensual crimes Crimes involving individuals who willingly engage in acts that they may not view as harmful or arguably have no direct victims

● **Learning Objective 3.3:** Classify types of crime by the type of action involved.

1 Criminal Act

Prostitution is among the public-order offenses that regularly challenge our justice systems. These crimes are considered violations against the public order and are typically viewed as more serious in smaller communities compared to larger ones.

What public-order offenses, if any, do you believe should be legalized?

drunkenness Drinking alcoholic beverages to the extent that a person's mental faculties and physical coordination are substantially impaired

infractions The lowest level of criminal behavior that is usually not punishable by confinement; instead, offenders are often given a citation or traffic ticket

ordinance violations Rules, laws, or regulations that apply to a specific village, city, or town

misdemeanors Crimes that are less serious than felonies and are punishable by various means, including fines, probation, or less than 1 year of incarceration in jail

felonies Crimes that are more serious in nature than misdemeanors and are punished in a variety of ways, including a penalty of a year or more of incarceration or the death penalty

treason A crime that involves betraying one's country

public-order crimes Crimes that threaten or challenge the moral order, norms, or customs of society

"victimless" crimes Crimes in which no victim is directly involved

property crime Crimes that involve wrongfully taking something from someone else without the use or threat of force

pyromania A pathological disorder that results in the affected individual feeling the impulsive need to set fires

Property Crimes

Property crime involves either the destruction or the theft of property. Destruction of property occurs in the forms of vandalism and arson. Thefts of property include larceny, shoplifting, fraud, and burglary. In 2019, there were about 12.8 million property crimes in U.S. households, or roughly 101 per 1,000 households (R. E. Morgan & Truman, 2020).

Property crimes do not involve physical harm to individuals. They may be committed for a variety of reasons, such as to obtain money or items that can be sold for money (e.g., theft), as a mean-spirited act (vandalism), or because of a mental illness. Arsonists, for example, may suffer from a pathological disorder known as **pyromania**, which results in the affected individual feeling the impulsive need to start fires.

Violent Crimes

Violent crimes, or **interpersonal crimes**, involve acts in which one person uses, or threatens to use, force against another person. In some instances, the mere threat of violence makes an act violent. For example, robberies involve the use or threat of force to take something from another person while placing the victim in fear. Accordingly, an individual who merely threatens to use force, for example by robbing a bank with a plastic gun that the tellers believe is real, may be charged with robbery if the victims were fearful of violence.

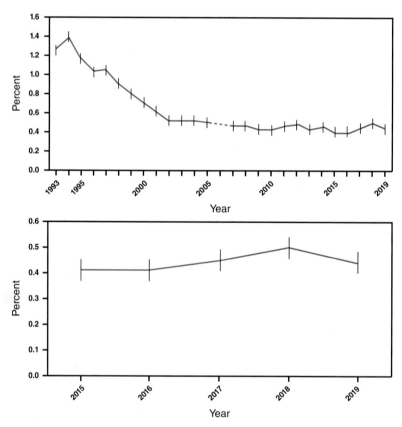

FIGURE 3.1 Violent Crime Offenses, 1993–2019 (bottom graph shows 2015–2019) The rate of violent crime in the United States has dropped significantly since the 1990s. Particularly, the violent crime rate dropped 75% from 1993 to 2019. *Source: From Bureau of Justice Statistics, National Crime Victimization Survey, 1993–2019.*

Do you feel the public is too concerned with violent crime given the relatively low levels compared to earlier decades?

Among the more frequently occurring violent crimes is assault, with simple assaults occurring far more often than aggravated assaults. An assault is considered aggravated when the attack results in serious harm to the victim or involves the use of a weapon to commit the crime. Assaults may also be categorized as aggravated if they involve violence against certain groups, such as the elderly. The most serious forms of violent crime (e.g., rape and criminal homicide) occur relatively infrequently compared to assaults.

Domestic violence is a specific type of violent crime that involves behaviors that cause physical harm, create fear, prevent a partner from doing as they wish, or force a partner to behave in manners they do not wish to. It can involve physical or sexual violence, intimidation, threats, emotional or psychological abuse, and economic deprivation.

The penalties for violent crimes are more severe than they are for property crimes and infractions and could include the death penalty in 34 states. However, not all violent crimes are considered felonies.

Compared to all other types of crime, violent crime is more feared by the public. This is because we are all at various levels of risk with regard to violent victimization (as discussed in Module 6), and we hear about violent crimes regularly in the media (see Module 2). In actuality, the rate of violent crime victimization in 2019 was 21 per 1,000 persons age 12 or older (in other words, about 21 out of every 1,000 people were victimized) (R. E. Morgan & Truman, 2020). Figure 3.1 notes trends in the estimated number of violent crimes, which includes a substantial decrease from 1993 to 2019 (R. E. Morgan & Truman, 2020).

violent crimes, or interpersonal crimes Crimes in which one person uses, or threatens to use, force against another person

domestic violence A specific type of violent crime that involves behaviors that cause physical harm, create fear, prevent a partner from doing as they wish, or force them to behave in manners they do not wish to

The System in Perspective

The "In the News" feature at the start of this module addressed social media and crime. The account demonstrates how crime continues to evolve, as do efforts to secure justice. Computers and social media sites are regularly replacing weapons and urban streets as tools and locations for committing crime. Along these lines, justice-based practices must keep pace, as social media sites and law enforcement agencies determine how they intend to monitor new forms of crime. These concerns with regard to crime and justice must be considered with regard to privacy issues and constitutional rights in general. In other words, we must grant law enforcement officials a certain degree of latitude as they seek to protect us from harm. However, the powers we grant them must not overly infringe on our individual rights. What clouds the situation is that we all have different interpretations of how much power we should grant to law enforcement and others who work in the criminal justice system.

Summary

1. Learning Objective 3.1: *Describe the general categories of crime.*

- Conventional, street, or visible crimes include the offenses we most often associate with the term *crime*, such as robbery, burglary, and assault. Types of white-collar crime include corporate crime, occupational crime, government crime, state–corporate crime, crimes of globalization, finance crimes, contrepreneurial crime, and avocational crime. Cybercrime involves the use of technology to commit crimes. Organized crime is committed by groups who work outside the law, primarily by meeting a public demand for something that is illegal (e.g., drugs). Hate crimes are offenses in which the offender is motivated by bias or hatred based, in whole or in part, on race, color, nationality, religion, gender, ethnicity, sexual orientation, or disability. Consensual crimes involve individuals who willingly engage in acts that are often seen as less harmful than more traditional criminal acts (e.g., gambling).

2. **Learning Objective 3.2:** *Classify types of crime by their seriousness.*

• Infractions are the lowest level of criminal behavior and are usually not punishable by confinement. Instead, offenders are often given a citation or traffic ticket. Related to infractions are municipal ordinance violations, which are infractions against rules created by a municipality. Misdemeanors are crimes that are considered less serious than felonies and are punishable in many ways, including by a sentence of less than a year of incarceration. They are handled more informally by the courts and are committed far

more often than felonies. Felonies are crimes that are more serious in nature than misdemeanors. They can involve a penalty of 1 year or more of incarceration or the death penalty. Treason involves betraying one's country and is considered one of the most serious offenses, because it poses notable threats to the safety of the country.

3. **Learning Objective 3.3:** *Classify types of crime by the type of action involved.*

• Crimes are defined as public-order crimes, property crimes, or violent crimes based on the type of action taken. Public-order crimes, such as going outside without clothing, threaten social norms. Property crimes, such as shoplifting, involve using, destroying, or taking property without the use of force. Violent crimes, such as assault, involve the use or threat of use of force.

Questions for Critical Thinking

1. Which of the following do you believe will have the greatest impact on the United States in the next 20 years: organized crime, crimes of globalization, or cybercrime? Why?

2. Do you believe all individuals who commit infractions should receive a citation, or ticket to appear in court, as opposed to being arrested?

3. Gambling is considered a public-order crime; however, it is permitted in various forms throughout the United States. In what forms is gambling permitted? Do you believe gambling will become increasingly legalized? Why or why not?

Key Terms

assault
avocational crimes
"bait and switch" scams
burglary
consensual crimes
contreprenurial crime
conventional crimes
corporate crime
credit card theft
crimes of globalization
criminal homicide
cybercrime
cyberterrorism
dealing in stolen property
domestic violence
drunkenness

enterprise crime
felonies
finance crimes
forcible rape
forgery and counterfeiting
gambling
government crime
harassment
hate crimes
hate crime statistics act
human trafficking
identity-theft fraud
infractions
interfering with and disrupting computer services
interpersonal crimes
larceny-theft

mala en se
mala prohibita
Matthew Shepard and James Byrd, Jr. Hate Crimes
    Prevention Act
misdemeanors
money laundering
motor vehicle theft
occupational crime
online harassment
ordinance violations
organized crime
Ponzi scheme
property crime
prostitution and commercialized vice

public-order crimes
pyromania
ransomware
robbery
state–corporate crimes
treason
unauthorized and illegal file sharing
vandalism
victimless crimes
violent (or interpersonal) crimes
weapons offenses
white-collar crime
writing and distributing malicious code

For digital learning resources, please go to
https://www.oup.com/he/burns1e

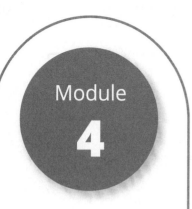

Module

4

Measurement and Extent of Crime

How do we know if crime is increasing or decreasing? There are various ways to measure crime in society. While we will never know exactly how much crime exists, we make estimates that tell us something.

Which sorts of resources do you think could be used to measure crime in the United States?

Measuring crime is challenging. While several methods can be used, each has its limitations. This is why it is best to consider multiple measures to better understand how much crime actually occurs. What we know about the nature and extent of crime primarily comes from government accounts, but other data sources are used as well. This module addresses the measurement and extent of crime, beginning with a look at the Uniform Crime Report and the National Incident-Based Reporting System, both of which are provided by the Federal Bureau of Investigation (FBI). This is followed by coverage of other measurements of crime, including the National Crime Victimization Survey and self-reports, and consideration of crime trends in the United States.

Recording Arrest-Related Deaths

In May 2018, four undercover detectives approached Keeven Robinson as part of a drug investigation. Robinson crashed into two sheriff's vehicles as he fled from the detectives in his car and then tried to run away. He was subdued after climbing over several backyard fences and caught with drugs on him. He died while being taken into custody by the agents. A medical investigation into the death found "significant traumatic injuries" to Robinson's neck, which is consistent with compressional asphyxia (a compression of the lungs that prevents breathing). The case was classified as a homicide and the agents involved in the case were reassigned to desk duty while the case was investigated (Connor, 2018). In 2019, the victim's family filed a civil suit against the officers (WDSUNews.com, 2019).

Cases such as this have regenerated questions regarding how many civilians die while being arrested. Despite the extent to which we measure crime and justice-related actions in the United States, the number of individuals who die during an arrest, or what is considered an arrest-related death, is relatively unknown.

The Bureau of Justice Statistics (BJS) initially started counting what are technically considered arrest-related deaths in 2003, but discontinued doing so in 2014 because the data were believed to be of little value. The BJS noted that during their evaluation of such deaths from 2003 through 2009 and 2011, the program captured an estimated 50% of all incidents. They concluded that the limited data do not permit a census of all such deaths in the United States (Planty et al., 2015).

Among the primary obstacles restricting the collection of accurate data was underreporting, or failing to report by some states. There were also some concerns with understanding what constitutes an arrest-related

death. The BJS notes that "an arrest-related death is defined as any death (e.g., gunshot wound, cardiac arrest, or drowning) that occurs during an interaction with state or local law enforcement personnel" and includes deaths that occur during an attempted arrest or in the process of an arrest, while the person is in law enforcement custody (prior to transfer to jail), and shortly after the arrestee's freedom to leave is restricted. An arrest-related death does not include the deaths of bystanders, hostages, and law enforcement personnel;

2 Investigation

The death of 22-year-old Keeven Robinson was ruled a homicide, authorities said on May 14.

deaths occurring during interaction with federal agents; or deaths by vehicular pursuits absent any police contact.

Not having accurate data regarding the most serious harms associated with police practices results in misunderstanding of the nature of arrest-related deaths. It also limits opportunities for accurate solutions. Why would police departments be apprehensive about reporting arrest-related deaths? How could better reporting practices improve police–community relations?

1 Criminal Act

3 Arrest

Uniform Crime Report

Headlines about crime rates abound in the news:

- "Florida's crime rate hits 47-year low, but violent crime still high"
- "Violent crime in US rises for second consecutive year"
- "Data shows crime rates spike in summer months"
- "Burglaries, vehicle thefts drive New Mexico crime rate"
- "Why is violent crime on the rise—and who is most at risk?"

● **Learning Objective 4.1:** Explain the history, sources, and classifications of the Uniform Crime Reporting Program.

1 Criminal Act

Uniform Crime Reporting Program A program that includes crime-related data based on reports submitted to the Federal Bureau of Investigation by law enforcement agencies

We often encounter media reports such as these, which comment on crime, crime rates, and responses to crimes. However, how can we determine if the claims we read and hear about are justified? In 1930, the **Uniform Crime Reporting (UCR) Program** was introduced. The UCR includes crime data based on reports submitted to the FBI by law enforcement agencies. The data included in the UCR pertain to known offenses and persons arrested by law enforcement. The data are used by:

- police for budgeting, planning, resource allocation, and assessment of police operations;
- chambers of commerce for promoting tourism or relocation;
- social science researchers for use in studying crime;
- legislators for consideration of crime-fighting measures; and
- news media for contextual information in crime reporting.

The History of the UCR

The UCR is the oldest source of crime data in the United States, other than prison statistics. In 1850, the U.S. Census first sought to count the number of persons residing in correctional institutions, and prior to that, a few states compiled crime statistics mainly based on data from courts and prisons. With the exception of the contributions from a few states, much of the data were of little value because not all crimes result in the offender appearing in court or ending up in prison (Rosen, 1995).

International Association of the Chiefs of Police A professional association for law enforcement worldwide

The **International Association of the Chiefs of Police**, which is a professional association for law enforcement worldwide, is largely credited with establishing the UCR. Their interest was primarily to help address media accounts of crime waves that painted an unfavorable view of policing. The first report was published in 1930, with the data collection and analysis provided by the **Bureau of Social Hygiene**, which received grants and donations and was created to address issues pertaining to sex, crime, and delinquency. Later in the same year (1930), the FBI assumed responsibility for collecting, analyzing, and sharing crime data (Rosen, 1995). Essentially, the creation of the UCR was a collaborative effort of these and other groups. Participating local, county, state, tribal, and federal law enforcement agencies have voluntarily provided data for the UCR since it began.

Bureau of Social Hygiene An organization that received grants and donations and was created to address issues pertaining to sex, crime, and delinquency

UCR Data

Annually, the FBI produces several statistical publications based on the data collected by over 18,000 law enforcement agencies that represent 97.7% of U.S. inhabitants. The most prominent publications include the following:

- *Crime in the United States*: a compilation of the volume and rate of crimes in the United States; it includes arrest and law enforcement employee data
- *Hate Crime Statistics*: a publication that includes information about the number of and persons involved (offenders and victims) in hate crimes
- *Law Enforcement Officers Killed and Assaulted*: data on the number of officers feloniously or accidentally killed or assaulted while performing their duties

Law enforcement agencies are not required to participate in the UCR, but most (over 18,000) do so voluntarily. The FBI provides participating law enforcement agencies with a handbook that explains how to classify and score offenses. The handbook provides uniform crime offense definitions, while recognizing that the legal definitions of crimes may vary from state to state. Agencies are expected to make a good-faith effort to comply with the FBI guidelines. The summary of the crime data provided by law enforcement agencies, which is used to describe crime in the United States, is compiled as part of the FBI's Summary Reporting System (SRS).

Part I and Part II Offenses

In sharing data regarding crime in the United States, the FBI categorizes crimes according to Part I and Part II offenses (see Table 4.1 and Module 3 for FBI definitions of some of these offenses). The UCR Program collects arrest data for both Part I and Part II offenses.

Part I offenses consist of 8 crimes that were chosen because they were believed to be most likely to be reported and most likely to occur with enough frequency to provide an adequate comparison across years. For Part I offenses, the FBI also collects data on crimes known to the police, crimes cleared by arrest or exceptional means (discussed in the subsection on "Clearance Rates"), and the age, sex, and race of persons arrested. **Part II offenses** consist of 21 other crimes. These offenses occur more often than Part I crimes, but only arrest data are provided.

Crime Index

Until 2004, seven of the eight Part I offenses (all but arson) were also used to create a **Crime Index**, a single statistic representing the crime rate based on the population in each jurisdiction in the United States. The Crime Index allowed comparison across locations and years. The decision to discontinue the use of the Crime Index came because the index was generally dominated by reports of larceny-theft. The large number of larcenies and thefts overshadowed more serious but less frequently occurring crimes (e.g., murder and rape). This distorted the Crime Index's overall picture of the level of crime in different districts.

Part I offenses
A category of crimes in the Uniform Crime Report that consists of criminal homicide, rape, robbery, aggravated assault, burglary, larceny-theft, arson, and motor vehicle theft

Part II offenses
A category of crimes in the Uniform Crime Report that consists of 21 crimes other than those designated in Part I

Crime Index
A single statistic found in the Uniform Crime Report believed to be representative of the crime rate based on the population in each jurisdiction in the United States

TABLE 4.1. Uniform Crime Report Part I and II Crimes

Part I offenses
- Criminal homicide
- Forcible rape
- Robbery
- Aggravated assault
- Burglary (breaking or entering)
- Larceny-theft (except motor vehicle theft)
- Motor vehicle theft
- Arson

Part II offenses
- Other assaults (simple)
- Forgery and counterfeiting
- Fraud
- Embezzlement
- Stolen property (buying, receiving, possessing)
- Vandalism
- Weapons (e.g., carrying, possessing)
- Prostitution and commercialized vice
- Sex offenses (except forcible rape, prostitution, and commercialized vice)
- Offenses against chastity, common decency, morals, and the like
- Drug abuse violations
- Gambling
- Offenses against the family and children
- Driving under the influence
- Liquor laws
- Drunkenness
- Disorderly conduct
- Vagrancy

Source: From U.S. Department of Justice

Criminal homicide is a Part I offense according to the Uniform Crime Report (UCR) and is the most serious of all crimes.

Do you think the categorization used by UCR makes sense? Do you believe there is a better way to categorize crimes? Why?

3 Arrest

2
Investigation

clearance rates
Data found in the Uniform Crime Report that notes the rate of crimes in which an arrest was made and charges were filed

Clearance Rates

The UCR also provides **clearance rates**, which are based on crimes in which an arrest was made and charges were filed. Crimes can also be cleared by exceptional means, which is when the police have identified a suspect and have enough evidence to support an arrest but the individual cannot be taken into custody immediately or at all. For example, the police may have enough evidence to arrest a suspect who dies or flees to a country with no extradition treaty with the United States before the police can make an arrest.

Clearance rates are calculated by dividing the number of crimes that are cleared by the total number of crimes recorded. For example, if a city experienced 2,500 Part I offenses and cleared 1,250 of the offenses, the clearance rate would be 50% (2,500/1,250 = 0.50). The rates are used to determine, in part, the effectiveness of departments in making arrests following a crime.

Figure 4.1 depicts the percentage of offenses cleared by arrest or exceptional means in 2018 (FBI, 2019). These data show that arrests are not made for most crimes. This reflects the difficult task facing law enforcement when it comes to arrests. Very few crimes are committed within their view. Accordingly, the police largely rely on information from the public to solve crimes, and such information is not always available.

These clearance rate figures also demonstrate that violent crimes are more likely to be cleared by arrest than are property crimes. One reason for this is the interpersonal nature of violent crimes, in which a victim is more likely to provide a description of the offender. Another reason is that the more serious nature of violent crimes warrants a

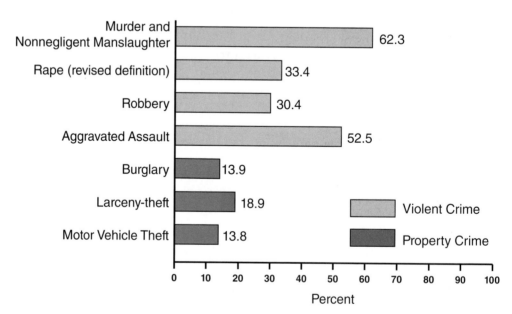

FIGURE 4.1. Clearance Rates, 2018. The clearance rates for violent crimes are typically higher than the rates for property offenses. The interpersonal nature of violent crimes contributes to identifying suspects and offenders. Further, more resources are typically devoted to violent crimes, because they are considered more serious than property crimes.

Do you believe the relatively low rate of property crimes cleared by arrest is a result of violent crimes receiving more law enforcement attention or because property offenders are more difficult to apprehend?

greater amount of investigative attention. Police departments are more likely to have specific task forces designed to solve serious crimes (e.g., homicide task forces) than they would for less serious crimes. Finally, one must also consider that violent crimes are more likely than property crimes to be reported to the police (R. E. Morgan & Kena, 2017).

Limitations of the UCR

The UCR, like other crime data sources, has several limitations. Prominent among them is the **hierarchy rule**, which applies when multiple offenses occur in the same event. According to the rule, reporting agencies only identify the offense highest on the priority list they receive and do not score the other, less serious offense(s). For example, the FBI would only count the murder in a case in which a man kills another man and takes his cell phone. The theft in this case would not be counted.

Another limitation of the UCR concerns the potential for police departments to falsify police reports for political or other reasons. With regard to falsifying reports, police departments may undercount or downgrade some crimes with the intent to make the department look more effective (Van Brocklin, 2012). A final limitation of UCR data is that they do not include crimes that are not reported to police, and most crimes are not reported to the police.

National Incident-Based Reporting System

The data provided in the UCR provide an overview of crime in the United States, but greater detail is needed to more effectively use the data. In response to calls by law enforcement, researchers, and others to enhance the data, the UCR Program formulated the **National Incident-Based Reporting System (NIBRS)** to improve the quality of crime data collected by law enforcement agencies. On January 1, 2021, the NIBRS replaced the FBI SRS and became the only source through which the FBI collects crime data.

About the NIBRS Data

The NIBRS is a reporting system that provides detailed accounts of each crime that is brought to the attention of the police. Among other enhancements to the UCR, it gathers data concerning:

- the circumstances of an offense,
- which offenses are attempted or completed,
- the offender–victim relationship, and
- the age, gender, and race of offenders and victims.

The data collected from the NIBRS provide a more robust account of crime in the United States. For instance, it enables users to determine if a murder resulted from a robbery or argument, whether the victim and offender were related, and the demographics of both the victim and the offender. The NIBRS does not subscribe to the hierarchy rule, which means that all offenses within a single event are recorded.

The data collected as part of the NIBRS cover each single incident brought to the attention of law enforcement and arrest data for the 52 Group A offenses. There are 10 Group B offense categories, although only arrest data are reported for these offenses. Table 4.2 depicts the organization of the NIBRS data (FBI, n.d.a).

TABLE 4.2.   Group A and B Offenses: National Incident-Based Reporting System

GROUP A OFFENSES

Animal cruelty
Arson
Assault offenses:
   Aggravated assault
   Simple assault
   Intimidation
Bribery
Burglary/breaking and entering
Counterfeiting/forgery
Destruction/damage/vandalism of property
Drug/narcotic offenses:
   Drug/narcotic violations
   Drug equipment violations
Embezzlement
Extortion/blackmail
Fraud offenses:
   False pretenses/swindle/confidence game credit card/automated teller
      machine fraud
   Impersonation
   Welfare fraud
   Wire fraud
   Identity theft
   Hacking/computer invasion
Gambling offenses:
   Betting/wagering
   Operating/promoting/assisting gambling/gambling equipment violations
   Sports tampering
Homicide offenses:
   Murder and nonnegligent manslaughter
   Negligent manslaughter
   Justifiable homicide (not a crime)
Human trafficking offenses:
   Commercial sex acts
   Involuntary servitude
Kidnapping/abduction
Larceny/theft offenses:
   Pocket-picking/purse snatching/shoplifting
   Theft from building
   Theft from coin-operated machine or device
   Theft from motor vehicle
   Theft of motor vehicle parts or accessories
   All other larceny
Motor vehicle theft
Pornography/obscene material
Prostitution offenses:
   Prostitution
   Assisting or promoting prostitution
   Purchasing prostitution
Robbery

Sex offenses:
    Rape/sodomy
    Sexual assault with an object
    Fondling
Sex offenses, nonforcible:
    Incest
    Statutory rape
Stolen property offenses
Weapon law violations

GROUP B OFFENSES

Bad checks
Curfew/loitering/vagrancy violations
Disorderly conduct
Driving under the influence
Drunkenness
Family offenses, nonviolent
Liquor law violations
Peeping Tom
Trespass of real property
All other offenses

Source: *Federal Bureau of Investigation Uniform Crime Reporting: https://www.fbi.gov/file-repository/ucr/nibrs-quick-facts.pdf/view*

Participation in the NIBRS

The South Carolina Law Enforcement Division conducted a pilot demonstration of the NIBRS in 1987, and the program has grown steadily since. By 2016, 37% of law enforcement agencies that participated in the UCR reported crime to the FBI using NIBRS data specifications (Waitt, 2017). Beginning in 2021, all agencies that report will use the NIBRS.

Currently, NIBRS data provide enough information to assist the jurisdictions that participate, but it is not comprehensive enough to provide broad generalizations about crime in the United States. In other words, we should not use NIBRS to comment on national crime trends until more agencies participate.

Limitations of the NIBRS

The NIBRS provides more helpful information than most other sources of crime data, but it also requires greater resources on behalf of police officers and departments because they must compile additional, more detailed information about criminal incidents. In addition, the NIBRS crime data consist of only those crimes known to police. This means that unreported crimes are not reflected in the data.

National Crime Victimization Survey

The **National Crime Victimization Survey** (NCVS) provides an estimate of crime in the United States by asking a representative sample of residents living throughout the country about their role as victims in a crime. A **representative sample** is a segment of a larger group that shares or reflects the characteristics of the larger group. For the purposes of the NCVS, researchers gather information from a smaller

● **Learning Objective 4.3:** Describe the history and sources of data used in the National Crime Victimization Survey.

National crime victimization survey A national survey that provides an estimate of crime in the United States by asking a representative sample of residents living throughout the country about their roles as a victim in a crime

representative sample A segment of a larger group that shares or reflects the characteristics of the larger group

dark figure of crime Crimes not reported to the police or found in the Uniform Crime Report; they are included in the National Crime Victimization Survey

segment of the United States, although that segment is believed to be reflective of the U.S. population as a whole. The NCVS is conducted by the BJS within the U.S. Department of Justice.

The History of the NCVS

The NCVS originated in the mid-1960s after President Lyndon Johnson's Commission on Law Enforcement and Administration of Justice, also known as the President's Crime Commission, conducted pilot studies. A primary motivation behind the creation of the survey was to get at the "**dark figure of crime**," or crimes not reported to the police or found in the UCR. It was also created to help provide a benchmark for UCR crime statistics. The survey, first implemented in 1972, was originally called the National Crime Survey.

The NCVS underwent substantial revisions in the 1990s, including:

- a name change to the National Crime Victimization Survey,
- the addition of more direct questions on domestic violence and rape,
- efforts to encourage respondents to recall a wider range of incidents,
- the increased use of phone calls to replace in-person visits, and
- greater efforts to measure victimizations by offenders known to victims.

How It Works

Twice a year, U.S. Census Bureau personnel interview a representative number of households across the United States on behalf of the NCVS. Roughly 95,000 households composed of about 160,000 persons are surveyed each year. Participants are surveyed regularly for 3 years, with seven interviews occurring at 6-month intervals. The first interview is always in person; subsequent interviews may be done by phone.

Study participants are asked about their role as victims of crime. The rationale behind this methodological approach is to provide a more accurate picture of crime in the country. The UCR gathers data only on crimes known to police, but the NCVS proposes to measure all crime, including the crimes that are not reported. It operates under the assumption that victims will share information about all of their experiences as a victim, even if they did not report the incident to the police.

NCVS data are generally more detailed than UCR SRS data (Table 4.3 summarizes some differences between NCVS and UCR), because the NCVS asks questions about the circumstances surrounding each offense:

- time of crime
- place of crime
- use of weapon
- injuries
- financial loss

Further, NCVS data include personal information about victims and offenders:

- age
- gender
- race
- income
- education level

TABLE 4.3. **Differences Between the National Crime Victimization Survey and the Uniform Crime Report**

	NATIONAL CRIME VICTIMIZATION SURVEY	UNIFORM CRIME REPORT—SRS
Data collection	Survey of a representative number of households	Crimes reported to the police, who report them to the Federal Bureau of Investigation
Measure	Rates property crimes per 1,000 households	Rates property crimes per 100,000 inhabitants
Data collection	Derives its data from a survey of a sample of households	Derives its data from actual crime counts reported by law enforcement
Age restriction	Sample includes persons 12 or older	Does not have age restrictions with regard to crimes
Hierarchy rule?	Does not use the hierarchy rule	Uses the hierarchy rule
Definitions	Defines certain crimes differently; for example, burglary is defined as the entry or attempted entry of a residence by a person who had no right to be there	Defines certain crimes differently; for example, burglary is defined as the unlawful entry or attempted entry of a structure to commit a felony or theft
Extent of coverage	Does not measure criminal homicide or arson; does not include consensual crimes	Measures criminal homicide and arson; includes consensual crimes
Sponsor	U.S. Bureau of Justice Statistics	Federal Bureau of Investigation

Arson and criminal homicide are the two Part I offenses not measured by the National Crime Victimization Survey (NCVS). This and other differences make it difficult to compare the Uniform Crime Report and the NCVS. Combined, however, the data provided from both sources provide a more comprehensive account of crime in the United States. Analyzing trends over time provides an even better account.

Which of the two measures do you believe provides a more accurate account of crime?

Excluded from consideration in the sample are:

- crew members of merchant vessels or members of the armed forces living in military barracks,
- institutionalized persons (including prison and jail inmates),
- U.S. citizens living abroad,
- foreign visitors, and
- individuals under the age of 12.

Limitations of the NCVS

Although the NCVS data help provide an account of crime that is in some ways more encompassing than the UCR, the NCVS has some limitations:

- It does not include consensual, or "victimless," crimes such as gambling and prostitution.
- Murder is excluded because victims cannot report.
- It does not include crimes against commercial establishments such as bars and retail stores.
- It lacks concrete evidence to suggest that an event was actually an offense.
- Respondents are expected to determine whether an act was truly a crime and, if so, what kind.
- Memory lapses, misinterpretation of human behavior, embellishment, and lying may hamper the accuracy of the data.
- Respondents may tell an official interviewer what they think the interviewer wants to hear.

1 Criminal Act

● **Learning Objective 4.4:** Explain the contributions and limitations of self-report studies.

Self-Report Studies

Crime data collected by the federal government provide national estimates of crime in the United States. However, there are other means by which crime data are collected, including **self-report studies**, which involve research participants responding to queries or prompts without interference from the researcher. The studies may measure:

- feelings,
- opinions,

- behaviors, or
- beliefs.

This type of research is not necessarily sponsored by a particular agency; self-report studies can be conducted by any researcher. The reason this type of information is valuable is that oftentimes official reports provide only general accounts that mask the details needed for the study of particular groups. For instance, a researcher could study the criminal behaviors of young adults in a particular neighborhood using self-report studies. Such information would be unavailable with official data.

Examples of Self-Report Studies

Self-report studies can be conducted with various groups, such as high school students, drug users, or inmates. In fact, this methodology has been used in numerous studies, including two large-scale surveys: the **National Survey on Drug Use and Health** and **Monitoring the Future**. The National Survey on Drug Use and Health measures the prevalence of alcohol and drug use among household members over age 11. Monitoring the Future asks youths about their viewpoints, attitudes, and experiences with regard to various issues including drug use, views about drugs, delinquency, and victimization.

Self-report surveys have been used with various groups to measure a wide array of issues, including misbehavior among criminal justice personnel. For instance, researchers administered self-report questionnaires to 501 correctional officers and found, among other things, that officers who noted that their supervisors were unsupportive tended to admit to more serious violations of institutional regulations (e.g., having inappropriate relations with an offender) than their peers. The researchers also found that officers who perceived their jobs as less dangerous were more likely to violate the institutional regulations (Worley & Worley, 2013). Findings such as these would be unavailable using any other source of data.

The Benefits of Self-Report Studies

The data generated from self-report studies help address the potential for biases, errors, or restrictive policies associated with official data, simply because the researcher controls the design of the research questions and identifies the target groups. As such, self-report studies have been deemed "one of the most important methodological developments over the past hundred years" (Krohn et al., 2010, p. 510).

Self-report studies provide insight regarding crime and criminal behavior. These studies generally:

- provide more detail regarding less serious crimes (e.g., drug use, minor thefts) that are often not reported to police,
- cover some aspects of the dark figure of crime,
- do not subscribe to the hierarchy rule, and
- provide more fruitful data for theory construction or testing.

The Limitations of Self-Report Studies

Despite their many benefits, self-report studies contain some important limitations. They face the difficulty of soliciting truthful information. Despite efforts to ensure confidentiality, which have improved the accuracy of this type of research, many people may not be willing to openly discuss their criminal behavior.

Self-report studies also sometimes suffer from the use of **convenience samples**, or participants in research studies who are easy to reach (e.g., high school students). Such samples may not be reflective of society as a whole or may lack characteristics

self-report studies An approach to research in which subjects share their feelings, opinions, behaviors, and beliefs in response to queries or prompts without interference from the researcher

National Survey on Drug Use and Health A survey that measures the prevalence of alcohol and drug use among household members over age 11

Monitoring the Future A survey that asks youths about their viewpoints, attitudes, and experiences with regard to various issues including drug use, views about drugs, delinquency, and victimization

convenience samples Subjects in research studies who are easy to reach and include

interviewer effects The influences or biases that those who administer assessments may have on the respondents and responses

● **Learning Objective 4.5:** Discuss recent trends in crime in the United States.

1 Criminal Act

3 Arrest

warranted for the research. For example, they may come from groups that do not generally engage in crime (e.g., the elderly).

Online surveys have addressed some of the interviewer effects inherent in self-report studies. **Interviewer effects** involve the influences or biases that those who administer assessments may have on the respondents and responses. However, there is still the concern that the individuals soliciting the data, or the wording of the questions posed, may bias responses.

Trends in Crime

In light of the different means to measure crime and the limitations associated with each one, it is difficult to discuss the true amount of crime in society. Instead, researchers and policymakers consider possible trends and base their best estimates on multiple sources of data. Recent UCR and NCVS reports suggest that crime rates have dropped significantly since the early 1990s.

Crime Rates: UCR and NCVS

The crime rate increased somewhat steadily from the 1960s until the early 1990s, after which it dropped. Criminologists consider trends or patterns in efforts to provide more confident assessments of crime in society. For example, according to the UCR data, the crime rate dropped almost consistently every year between 1993 and 2016 (as depicted, in part, in Figure 4.2). Looking at trends in data provides some perspective regarding crime in society. Both the property crime rate and the violent crime rate have dropped since the early 1990s.

Many reasons are offered for the notable decreases in the crime rate since the early 1990s. Among the reasons for the drop are:

● the increased number of police officers,

● the rising prison population,

● growth in personal income,

● decreased unemployment,

● decreased alcohol consumption, and

● an aging criminal population (Roeder et al., 2015).

Estimated Number of Arrests

Aside from trends regarding crimes known to the police (the UCR) and victimization rates (the NCVS), the number of arrests also contributes to our overall understanding of crime in the United States. Arrest data do not portray the true amount of crime because arrests are not made following every offense. However, these data do provide an account of the extent to which the police make arrests and offer some glimpse of the crimes that occur most often. Table 4.4 shows that there were more than 10 million arrests in 2019. Roughly 40% of those arrests were for driving under the influence, drug abuse violations, assaults, or larceny-theft. The number of arrests for drug abuse violations was higher than the number of arrests for each of the other offenses.

FIGURE 4.2. Crime (by Volume and Rate per 100,000 Inhabitants) in the United States According to the UCR: 1998–2016. Both property crime rates and violent crime rates have dropped since the 1990s. The property crime rate has dropped significantly, while the violent crime rate decreased moderately. Examining crime rate trends or patterns provides a more robust picture of crime in general. *Source: Adapted from FBI (2018).*

What could explain the more significant reductions in the property crime rate compared to the violent crime rate?

These data suggest that a substantial portion of arrests were for larceny-theft, drug abuse violations, and driving under the influence. While all crimes are noteworthy, these are certainly not the most serious crimes that occur in society. Of note with regard to these data is the fact that most arrests in society involve property-related offenses, particularly larceny-theft.

The global pandemic involving COVID-19 largely impacted crime and crime rates beginning in 2020. Many people were forced to quarantine, remain at home, and generally distance themselves from one another. Businesses shut down for varying lengths of time, and some police officers became less likely to make arrests for minor crimes (Montgomery, 2020). The lack of social interaction and the use of police discretion to overlook some minor offenses will likely have notable impacts on crime rates, particularly those that rely on police reports.

The System in Perspective

The "In the News" feature at the start of this module discussed the death of Keeven Robinson in police custody. His was not the first death of a suspect in police custody, and it will not be the last. Tracking such deaths provides a sense of transparency for the police because the data shed light on what sometimes happens following an arrest. Sharing such data makes police work less "secretive." To be sure, not all deaths that occur in police custody are caused by the police, and this point should also be shared in the data. Government officials should continue to identify means to better collect data on crime and justice-related practices, much like they have with the NIBRS.

The introduction of the NIBRS to provide much more extensive crime data than the UCR highlights the country's recognition of the problem of a lack of accurate information when it comes to crime. Having accurate crime data is important for many reasons.

Many arrests are made for drug abuse violations. Some states have legalized marijuana and others are considering it, particularly in light of the large number of drug-related arrests.

Do you think the recent declines in the crime rate are attributable to the legalization of marijuana in some states? What other factors may be at work?

Primarily, crime counts help us create policy and assist with gauging our crime-prevention and criminal justice practices. They also help us determine which efforts are effective and which may not be and whether we are taking proper care of those who are arrested. Data on crime and justice help law enforcement agencies with budgeting, planning, resource allocation, and evaluations. The data can also be used by other public agencies, such as chambers of commerce and tourism-based agencies. Researchers use the data to study the nature of, causes of, and changes in crime over time. Further, the news media use crime data as part of their reporting practices. The challenge is determining the most effective means to measure crime and justice and how to best share the information.

TABLE 4.4. **Estimated Number of Arrests, 2019**

ESTIMATED NUMBER OF ARRESTS

United States, 2019	
Total[a]	10,085,207
Murder and nonnegligent manslaughter	11,060
Rape[b]	24,986
Robbery	74,547
Aggravated assault	385,278
Burglary	171,590
Larceny-theft	813,073
Motor vehicle theft	80,636
Arson	9,068
Violent crime[c]	495,871
Property crime[c]	1,074,367
Other assaults	1,025,711
Forgery and counterfeiting	45,183
Fraud	112,707
Embezzlement	13,497
Stolen property; buying, receiving, possessing	88,272
Vandalism	180,501
Weapons; carrying, possessing, etc.	153,161
Prostitution and commercialized vice	26,713
Sex offenses (except rape and prostitution)	40,796
Drug abuse violations	1,558,862
Gambling	2,458
Offenses against the family and children	85,687
Driving under the influence	1,024,508
Liquor laws	175,548
Drunkenness	316,032
Disorderly conduct	310,331
Vagrancy	21,896
All other offenses	3,318,453
Suspicion	579
Curfew and loitering law violations	14,653

Source: 2019 Crime in the United States—Estimated Number of Arrests—Table 29, *by the Federal Bureau of Investigation, 2020a (https://ucr.fbi.gov/crime-in-the-u.s/2019/crime-in-the-u.s.-2019/tables/table-29).*
[a]*Does not include suspicion.*
[b]*The rape figure is an aggregate total of the data submitted based on both the legacy and the revised Uniform Crime Reporting definitions.*
[c]*Violent crimes are offenses of murder and nonnegligent manslaughter, rape, robbery, and aggravated assault. Property crimes are offenses of burglary, larceny-theft, motor vehicle theft, and arson.*

Summary

1. Learning Objective 4.1: *Explain the history, sources, and classifications of the Uniform Crime Reporting Program.*

- The creation of the UCR was spurred by police wishing to protect their image, social scientists interested in better understanding crime, and other groups such as the International Association of the Chiefs of Police, which is largely credited with establishing the UCR. The FBI eventually assumed responsibility for overseeing the UCR, which has existed since 1930. The UCR consists of data provided by law enforcement agencies regarding crimes known to the police and persons arrested. Law enforcement agencies at all levels participate. The UCR Program collects arrest data for both Part I and Part II offenses. For Part I offenses, the FBI also collects crimes known to the police, crimes cleared by arrest or exceptional means, and the age, sex, and race of persons arrested.

2. Learning Objective 4.2: *Describe the National Incident-Based Reporting System.*

- The NIBRS uses information gathered from law enforcement agencies to measure crime. It measures many types of crime and offers suggestions regarding the nature and extent of crime in the United States. The NIBRS gathers data concerning the circumstances of offenses, offender–victim relationship, and the age, gender, and race of offenders and victims. It also provides information regarding whether offenses were attempted or completed and does not subscribe to the hierarchy rule. Generally, the NIBRS gathers more detail regarding each criminal incident than does the UCR SRS and addresses some of the limitations associated with the UCR SRS. The relatively limited participation in the NIBRS on behalf of law enforcement stems from departments lacking the resources to collect the data as well as administrators not viewing the data collection efforts as beneficial.

3. Learning Objective 4.3: *Describe the history and sources of the data used in the National Crime Victimization Survey.*

- The NCVS originated in the mid-1960s when President Lyndon Johnson's Commission on Law Enforcement and Administration of Justice conducted pilot studies. A primary motivation behind the creation of the survey was to get at the dark figure of crime. It was also created to help provide a benchmark for UCR crime statistics. The survey was first implemented in 1972. It has undergone revisions through the years.

    Twice a year, U.S. Census Bureau personnel interview a representative number of households across the United States. The primary focus of the questions concerns subjects' involvement as a victim of crime. The BJS identifies a sample of households that will be interviewed for 3 years, with seven interviews occurring at 6-month intervals. The first interview is always in person; subsequent interviews may be done by telephone. Subjects within the study are asked about their role as a victim of crime.

4. Learning Objective 4.4: *Explain the contributions and limitations of self-report studies.*

- The data generated from self-report studies help address the potential for biases, errors, or restrictive policies associated with official data. This type of data collection better facilitates theory construction and testing because researchers design the questions and identify the target group. It generally provides more detail regarding less serious crimes that are often not reported to police and can overcome some of the limitations inherent in official data.

    There are some limitations of self-report studies. For instance, they face the difficulty of soliciting truthful information, and greater efforts to ensure confidentiality are warranted. In addition, they often use convenience samples, which can be problematic in the sense that the subject responses may not be reflective of the larger population, and special consideration is needed with regard to the wording of the questions posed and the administration of the survey.

5. Learning Objective 4.5: *Discuss recent trends in crime in the United States.*

- Prior to the 1990s, crime rates had risen steadily. Beginning in the early 1990s, data from both the UCR and the NCVS have generally suggested that the crime rate is decreasing. More property than violent crime occurs, and most crime is generally nonserious in nature.

Questions for Critical Thinking

1. How much confidence do you have in the accuracy of UCR data? Why?

2. What do you believe are the most significant limitations of NIBRS?

3. Can the NCVS truly measure the dark figure of crime?

4. Have you ever participated in a self-report study? If so, did you answer honestly? Were there any incentives to encourage your participation? If you have never participated in a self-report study, how honest do you think you would be should the opportunity arise?

5. Do you believe the crime rate will increase or decrease in the next 25 years? Explain your answer.

Key Terms

Bureau of Social Hygiene
clearance rates
convenience samples
Crime Index
dark figure of crime
hierarchy rule
International Association of the Chiefs of Police
interviewer effects
Monitoring the Future

National Crime Victimization Survey
National Incident-Based Reporting System
National Survey on Drug Use and Health
Part I offenses
Part II offenses
representative sample
self-report studies
Uniform Crime Reporting Program

For digital learning resources, please go to
https://www.oup.com/he/burns1e

Theories of Crime

Many explanations are offered for why people commit crime. Criminological theory deeply explores various academic disciplines in efforts to describe what prompts people to break the law.

What do you believe most often prompts a person to commit a crime?

Theories are explanations of how things are related, and they are measured using scientific research methods such as observing and documenting behaviors or using surveys to gather information. They are used to explain all sorts of phenomena, including why some people are victimized more than others and involvement in criminal behavior—the topic of this module. Researchers have developed various theories that attempt to explain why people break the law. No single theory explains all crime. This module provides an overview of criminological thought (see Figure 5.1 for a summary of the major areas discussed in this module), beginning with the classical school of criminology. This is followed by coverage of the positivist school of criminology, which primarily consists of biological, psychological, and sociological explanations of crime. This module ends with a look at developmental theories, which consider the effects of changes over one's life span, from youth to maturity.

MODULE OUTLINE

- **Classical School of Criminology**

  Learning Objective 5.1: Describe the major beliefs of the classical school of criminology.

- **Positivist School of Criminology**

  Learning Objective 5.2: Describe the major beliefs of the positivist school of criminology.

- **Biological Explanations of Crime**

  Learning Objective 5.3: Explain how biological factors could influence criminal behavior.

- **Psychological Explanations of Crime**

  Learning Objective 5.4: Explain the major reasons given by psychologists for why crime occurs.

- **Sociological Explanations of Crime**

  Learning Objective 5.5: Describe the major categories offered by sociologists to explain crime.

- **Developmental Theories of Crime**

  Learning Objective 5.6: Identify and describe developmental theories of crime.

IN THE NEWS

Why Do People Commit Crime?

1 Criminal Act

In September 2018, over 100 cases were reported of sewing needles being found in strawberries for sale in Australian supermarkets. No deaths were associated with the acts, but there were injuries. In addition, the associated fear caused national concern that impacted fruit sales in the country. The Australian government responded by raising the maximum prison sentence for tampering

Facebook/Stephanie Chheang

The Guardian

... after several customers found needles hidden inside punnets of strawberries.

with fruit from 10 to 15 years, and there was a $100,000 reward offered for information on who had placed the needles in the berries.

The acts and resulting scare were estimated to cost the fruit industry roughly $130 million (Mao, 2018).

What would prompt someone to commit such acts? Criminologists offered reasons for the acts, and they varied greatly. Perhaps it was revenge against a producer or the public. Or, maybe it was an act of terrorism. Perhaps the individual(s) wished to attract attention, and/or the acts could be a prank. It was also suggested that the individual(s) could be mentally ill. Following much speculation as to the motives in this case, a 50-year-old woman was arrested and told authorities that she did it out of revenge against colleagues whom she felt mistreated her when she was a supervisor on the farm that supplied the fruit to supermarkets (Marsh, 2018).

Much time and effort has gone into trying to understand human behavior, particularly with regard to criminal behavior. There are no simple answers to the question of why people commit crimes. Trying to explain why someone takes drugs or kills another person may seem straightforward (e.g., for pleasure or for revenge). However, not every person who breaks a given law has the same motive. What other factors might explain why someone would place sewing needles in strawberries?

1 Criminal Act

Classical School of Criminology

Criminology is the study of the extent, causes, control, and nature of criminal behavior. Criminologists use theories to explain why people commit crime. **Theories** are not simply suggestions or beliefs; instead, they are rational explanations based on facts about and/or the measurement of relationships of phenomena. For instance, theory construction may involve measuring the effects of poverty on crime and finding that individuals with the lowest family income are at the greatest risk of being involved in the criminal justice system. Good theory is logically constructed, based on the evidence at hand, and supported by subsequent research (Williams & McShane, 2014).

Criminology as a field began in Europe with the **classical school**, which holds that individuals freely decide on their own actions, and do so by rationally weighing the consequences of their actions, in order to avoid pain and seek pleasure. Those who subscribe to **classical theory** believe that people make rational decisions with regard to committing or not committing crime and fear of painful repercussions will discourage criminal behavior. Classical theorists strongly believe that crime can be deterred, primarily through punishment being swift, certain, and sufficiently painful.

● **Learning Objective 5.1:** Describe the major beliefs of the classical school of criminology.

Classical—The decision to commit crime is based on a rational calculation of the risk and reward involved.
Example: An offender steals a car after considering that it is unlikely that they will get caught and that any possible penalty would likely be lenient because this would be their first arrest.

Biological—Characteristics or traits inherent within an individual predispose or prompt them to commit crime.
Example: An offender steals a car because a brain impairment hampered their ability to understand the consequences of their actions.

Psychological—Personality traits, learned behavior, and a damaged mind prompt or predispose individuals to commit crime.
Example: An offender grew up with a mental illness that prohibited them from thinking in a rational manner. They later stole a car believing that it was the best way for them to obtain money.

Sociological—Crime is influenced by social factors, including social relationships and institutions, and focuses on issues such as religion, family, social classes, cultures, and related topics.
Example: An impoverished offender stole a car after being unable to find a job that would allow them to legitimately pay for the car.

Developmental—Crime is influenced by events that occur throughout one's life. These explanations focus on why offending began, why it may continue, why it may become more serious, and why it stops.
Example: An offender stole a car after they lost their job, their wife left them, and the bank foreclosed on their home over the course of 3 months. They had recently begun associating with a group of individuals involved in a car theft ring.

criminology The study of the extent, causes, control, and nature of criminal behavior

theories Means by which we explain natural occurrences by observing and measuring relationships regarding observable phenomena

classical school A school of criminological thought holding that individuals freely decide on their own actions and do so by rationally weighing the consequences of their actions, in order to avoid pain and seek pleasure

classical theory A school of criminological thought proposing that people make rational decisions with regard to committing or not committing crime and that fear of painful repercussions will discourage criminal behavior

FIGURE 5.1. Major Areas of Criminological Thought—Summary. Several schools of thought and many theories propose to explain why crime occurs. Ultimately, explaining crime is difficult, because human behavior is complex and it is challenging to describe why people act as they do.

What do you believe is the most common reason why people commit crime? In which area of thought would that reason fall?

Two early contributors to classical thinking were Cesare Beccaria and Jeremy Bentham. Their influence is evident in the U.S. Constitution, current criminal justice practices, and more recent classical school theories.

Cesare Beccaria

Cesare Beccaria (1738–1794) is one of the major contributors to the classical school of criminology. In his controversial work *An Essay on Crimes and Punishments* (1764/1963), Beccaria addressed the abusive and arbitrary justice-based practices in Europe during the 18th century. Essentially, there was no due process of law, and public officials could deprive individuals of their freedoms without cause. Beccaria believed that punishment for criminal behavior should outweigh the potential gains of committing the crime. He supported a system of justice that served the citizens as opposed to leaders.

Beccaria (1764/1963) believed that crime was a problem of bad laws, not necessarily bad people. He suggested that:

- all people should be treated equally,
- those accused of crimes should be judged by their peers,

- only the laws can identify punishments for crime and determine the instances in which someone suffers punishment,
- punishment should be prompt and effective,
- punishment should be worse than the advantage derived from the crime,
- punishment should prevent criminals from inflicting new harms and deter others from similar acts, and
- punishments that exceed what is necessary for public security are unjust.

Beccaria's work had a substantial impact on crime and justice around the time it was written, and it continues to do so. Beccaria, however, was not the only legal scholar and reformer to influence the classical school's ideas about crime and justice.

Jeremy Bentham

utilitarianism
The assumption that human behaviors are associated with pain and pleasure

Jeremy Bentham (1748–1832) proposed the idea of **utilitarianism**, which assumes that human behaviors are associated with pain and pleasure. Bentham argued that individuals decide what to do by weighing the likelihood and extent of pleasure with the likelihood and extent of pain. He expanded on Beccaria's work with regard to calculations regarding involvement in crime. Figure 5.2 outlines the key principles of the classical school of criminology.

The classical school and its emphasis on free will, rational choice, and utilitarianism were eventually challenged in the 19th century (see the next subsection on the "Positivist School of Criminology") and did not reemerge, to a large extent, until the 1970s. Recent research reflective of the classical school has centered on rational choice and situational crime prevention.

Jeremy Bentham's idea of utilitarianism suggested that people seek pleasure over pain and engage in crime if they believe the pleasure outweighs the pain. He proposed that laws and punishments should reflect this calculus.

Do you believe that punishments should be equal to or greater to the harms associated with the crime? Why or why not?

Rational Choice Theory

Rational choice theory holds that individuals decide whether to commit a crime by considering the potential payoffs (e.g., excitement, money, revenge) in relation to the likelihood of getting caught and the associated punishments. The theory does not assume that we are all equally at risk to commit crime; instead, people's intelligence, social class, and family structure affect their decisions. For instance, according to rational choice theory, individuals with low intelligence would arguably be more likely to engage in crime because they would not have adequate mental ability to weigh the costs and benefits of their actions.

Situational Crime Prevention

Situational crime prevention, an approach based on rational choice theory, involves identifying ways to deter crime by reducing opportunities to commit crimes. To facilitate the understanding of the approach, researchers used four primary categories of techniques that could be useful in deterrence (Clarke & Homel, 1997):

- increasing the perceived effort to commit crime
- increasing the perceived risks of committing crime
- reducing the anticipated rewards associated with committing crime
- producing shame or guilt regarding criminal behavior

- People are rational, and most of their behaviors are based on free will and rational choice
- Pain and pleasure influence human behavior
- It is sometimes necessary to inflict punishment to deter the offender and others who may consider acting in a similar manner
- Justice should be swift and certain
- The punishment for crime should outweigh the benefits derived from crime.

FIGURE 5.2. Key Principles of the Classical School of Criminology. The classical school of criminology is primarily grounded in the belief that people make rational decisions and should be held accountable for them. It holds that punishments should be individualized and deter the offenders and others.

What do you see as some limitations with the classical school of thought?

CAREERS

Crime prevention specialists promote community crime prevention programs, primarily through educating and alerting the public to the various means of protection. They perform public relations, administrative and operational duties, and related tasks.

rational choice theory A theory proposing that individuals decide whether to commit a crime by considering the potential payoffs in relation to the likelihood of getting caught and the associated punishments

The four categories illustrate the emphasis that rational choice theorists place on convincing individuals to abide by the law. **General deterrence** involves efforts to discourage society in general, or large groups of people, from committing crime. This is done, for instance, by imposing harsh penalties to make examples of individuals. **Specific deterrence** involves punishments or restrictions that pertain to a specific individual in an attempt to dissuade that individual from further criminal behavior (e.g., threatening jail time for a substance abuser who visits a bar).

situational crime prevention An approach based on rational choice theory that involves reducing opportunities to commit crimes and the likelihood of victimization

general deterrence A goal of sentencing that seeks to discourage or dissuade everyone from committing harmful behaviors

Positivist School of Criminology

The latter part of the 19th century brought about many social changes, as scholars became more scientific in nature. Criminology redirected its focus from the act to the actor. Criminologists increasingly proposed that individuals did not necessarily act on their own free will (as suggested by classical school theorists) and argued that factors (such as biological, psychological, and social ones) beyond the individual's control influenced their behavior. Figure 5.3 highlights the key principles of the

1 Criminal Act

- Human behavior is influenced by various factors (e.g., physical, social, and mental influences) and is not simply a matter of free will
- Research using scientific methods can explain criminal behavior
- Various biological, sociological, and psychological influences largely contribute to criminal behavior
- Criminals differ from those who don't commit crime

FIGURE 5.3. Key Principles of the Positivist School of Thought. The shift in thinking about crime causation from the classical school to the positivist school was largely grounded in scientific evaluation. Biological, psychological, and sociological factors were more heavily considered, and the theories more directly focused on the individual.

Do you think crime can best be explained by people making rational calculations, or do you believe other forces (e.g., societal or biological) better explain criminal behavior?

● **Learning Objective 5.2:** Describe the major beliefs of the positivist school of criminology.

specific deterrence
A goal of sentencing that seeks to discourage or dissuade specific individuals from committing various behaviors

positivist school of criminology A school of criminological thought that emphasizes the scientific study of crime and the belief that criminal behavior is influenced by factors beyond the control of the individual

positivist school of criminology and demonstrates how explanations of crime shifted from rational choice to more scientific reasons for misbehavior. The positivist school remains the most influential strain of criminology in the United States in the early 21st century.

Early Positivist School Criminologists

French philosopher Auguste Comte (1798–1857) is among the early scholars who heavily influenced the positivist school of criminology. Comte argued that knowledge should be based on a positivist, or scientific, approach that emphasizes observation-based scientific research. Charles Darwin's popular 1859 book *Origin of Species*, which challenged the belief that God created society and suggested that species had evolved through mutation and adaptation, provided further impetus for more scientific evaluation of social phenomena.

Italian scientists Cesare Lombroso (1835–1909) and Enrico Ferri (1856–1929) were among the earliest scholars to move beyond the classical school of thought in favor of more scientific evaluations of criminal behavior. In these early days of science, they proposed relatively crude biological explanations of crime, with the general belief that criminal behavior was predetermined and not the result of rational, individual decision-making.

Bodies of Thought in the Positivist School

The positivist school primarily consists of three bodies of explanation discussed in the subsections that follow: biological, psychological, and sociological. There are other positivist works that seek to explain crime, and there is certainly overlap among the bodies, but these three bodies of thought largely form the backbone of the positivist school of criminology.

● **Learning Objective 5.3:** Explain how biological factors could influence criminal behavior.

Biological Explanations of Crime

Biological explanations of criminal behavior consider various factors within the human body. Early biological theories held that criminals were born, not shaped by society, and could be identified by physical abnormalities. While the early biological explanations of crime have been discarded, advances in the scientific study of the human brain have led to their resurgence in the criminological research literature.

MYTHBUSTING

Criminals Are Bad or Evil People

Many in society believe that all criminals are bad people who regularly violate and have little or no regard for the law. We often label criminals and treat them as if they were a distinct group of people. While there are repeat offenders, career criminals, and those who commit heinous crimes, most crime is minor in nature, most criminals are not repeat offenders or career criminals, and not all criminals are bad people. In fact, many of them are good people who made bad decisions for various reasons. It has been estimated that about 70% of Americans have committed an offense for which they could be incarcerated (Husak, 2008). Does this mean that most of us are bad or evil people? Of course not. Most of us just make bad decisions at one point or another, and some of us get caught, while others do not.

Cesare Lombroso's 1876 publication of *The Criminal Man* largely transformed criminology at the time it was written. Lombroso, influenced by Darwin's earlier work, proposed that criminals were a lower form of life that had not evolved as much as law-abiding citizens. Enrico Ferri, a student of Lombroso's, introduced the term *born criminal* and proposed that crime was caused by various physical, anthropological, and social factors.

1 Criminal Act

Other early positivist scholars focused on biological explanations and proposed that the following were related to crime and criminal behavior:

- low intelligence (which was believed to be inherited) (e.g., Goddard, 1914)
- genetics (Lange, 1919/1930)
- body types and the influence of physiology (e.g., Sheldon, 1949; Glueck & Glueck, 1950); for example, Sheldon argued that mesomorphs (who were muscular and strong) were the most likely to commit violent crime
- differences in the criminal behavior of twins (e.g., Christiansen, 1970)

Other studies conducted at the time found similar results, although in the early 21st century the relationship between physical characteristics and crime is largely unsupported in the research literature (e.g., Vold & Bernard, 1986). While most biological explanations of crime were discarded by the mid-1940s, biosocial explanations have become increasingly prevalent. Biosocial theories recognize the interaction between biological traits and social factors and fall into three categories: biochemical, neurophysiological, and genetic.

Biochemical Theories

Biochemical theories propose that crime is influenced by imbalances in the chemicals in one's body, particularly as they relate to diet, vitamin levels, hormones, or food allergies. Researchers found that hormones such as testosterone and cortisol could play a significant role in an individual committing unethical behavior, such as lying, cheating, and stealing. In one experiment, participants were asked to take a math test and grade their own answers; participants would receive money for each correct answer. The researchers found that participants with higher levels of cortisol and testosterone were more likely to cheat in grading their own papers (Lee et al., 2015).

Environmental contaminants can also influence human behavior, according to some biosocial theories. For example, researchers found that higher levels of lead in the air led to increases in property and violent crime rates, and the association between air-lead levels and crime rates was strongest in poorer areas and weakest in wealthier areas (Stretesky & Lynch, 2004).

Neurophysiological Theories

Neurophysiology is the study of brain activity and the central nervous system in general (e.g., the brain and spinal cord). It has strongly influenced the debate over causes of criminal and **antisocial behavior**—or behaviors that contrast with the customs or expectations of a society. Largely beginning in the 1990s, advanced brain scanning techniques have furthered our understanding of the human brain. Some neurophysiologists believe that brain and physical abnormalities acquired as early as birth or in the womb impact human behavior throughout life (Moffit et al., 1994). Neurophysiology has helped identify slight brain dysfunction and attention-deficit hyperactivity disorder as contributors to antisocial and sometimes criminal behavior. Brain injury is another important, related area, and research suggests that rates of traumatic brain injuries are higher among prisoners and juvenile offenders compared to the general population (Vaughn et al., 2014).

neurophysiology
The study of brain activity

antisocial behavior
Behaviors that contrast with the customs or expectations of a society

1 Criminal Act

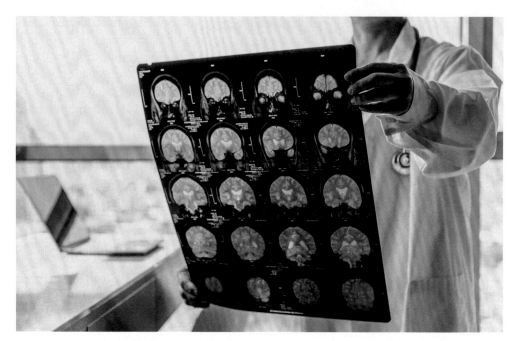

Recent advancements in the study of the brain have helped us better understand how our brains work and influence our behaviors. Damage to particular parts of the brain can result in changes in our behaviors, some of which may contribute to criminal behavior.

Do you believe we should hold individuals accountable for their behavior and punish them if they can prove that damage to their brain influenced their behavior?

10
Corrections

Brain studies gained national attention after several incidents involving the erratic and sometimes criminal behaviors of former National Football League players, whose behaviors were linked to damage to their brains. Among them was former New England Patriots player Aaron Hernandez, who suffered from the most severe case of chronic traumatic encephalopathy ever identified in a person under age 46. Hernandez was 27 years old when he hanged himself in prison while serving a life sentence for murdering a man in 2013. Chronic traumatic encephalopathy results from continued brain trauma and can have significant impacts on victims' decision-making, cognition, and judgment (Kilgore, 2017).

Genetic Theories

Some biological theorists have proposed that criminal traits and predispositions are genetically passed on from parents to their children. According to this view, the criminal behavior of parents can help predict the criminal behavior of children.

Studies have focused on identical twins who were separated since birth, as well as on comparing the behaviors of children and their parents. For example, researchers analyzed twins and found that a large proportion of gambling behavior was explained by genetics, or the heritable traits passed down through generations (Beaver et al., 2010). Despite these and related findings, there is no "crime gene" that is possessed by some and not others. Instead, there are traits that may be passed along genetically that predispose some individuals to act in a manner that would contribute to their involvement in crime.

Psychological Explanations of Crime

While most of the psychologists studying criminal behavior during the 19th century focused more on the body than on the mind, for those who did look to other explanations, the concept of legal insanity came to the forefront. Distinguished physician and author Isaac Ray (1807–1881) questioned whether individuals with brain deficiencies could be held legally responsible for their actions, given that they may not have intended to commit their crimes.

Around the turn of the 20th century, psychologists began to use new measurement techniques to study criminals and others. For instance, Henry Goddard examined intelligence tests provided to inmates and noted that one quarter to one half of prisoners had intellectual defects that prevented them from functioning well in society (Goddard, 1915). Goddard's idea remained dominant until the same survey was administered to World War I draftees (1914–1918), who scored lower than the inmates had (Adler et al., 2007).

Psychological explanations of crime often center around childhood experiences and unconscious thoughts, social learning, mental processes, and personality traits, which are acquired genetically and through interaction with others. Researchers have grouped these explanations into four categories: psychiatric, behavioral, cognitive, and personality.

Psychiatric Explanations of Crime

Austrian neurologist Sigmund Freud (1856–1939) is the father of **psychoanalysis**, which is both a set of theories regarding the impact of the mind on human behavior and a treatment technique. Freud compartmentalized the mind into three regions: the id, ego, and superego. The id is the section of the mind that is interested in immediate gratification and pleasure. The ego rationally evaluates the external world and interacts with the id and the superego, which represents internalized social and moral values.

Although he never offered a theory of crime, Freud noted that many of his patients had felt a sense of guilt before they committed a crime and committed the crime in order to be caught and punished. Their guilty feelings were relieved by the punishment. According to Freud, criminal behavior resulted from an overdeveloped superego generating a strong sense of guilt in the offender's mind (Freud, 1927). Others argued that criminal behavior resulted from an underdeveloped superego and an unregulated id (Aichorn, 1963).

Aside from Freud's psychoanalytical work, other scholars have offered psychiatric explanations of criminal and antisocial behavior. Much of this work centers on mental disorders and crime. For instance, researchers noted that juveniles with psychiatric disorders were significantly more likely than those without disorders to report being involved in violent and property crimes that resulted in arrest. They also found that those with disorders were more likely to report involvement in crimes for which they were not arrested (Coker et al., 2014).

The relationship between mental illness and involvement in the criminal justice system is highlighted in a report from the Bureau of Justice Statistics which noted that roughly 14% of state and federal prisoners and 26% of jail inmates reported experiences that met the threshold for serious psychological distress. The report also noted that 37% of prisoners and 44% of jail inmates were told in the past by a mental health professional that they had a mental disorder (see Module 33 for discussion of mental illness and the incarcerated) (Bronson & Berzofsky, 2017).

● **Learning Objective 5.4:** Explain the major reasons given by psychologists for why crime occurs.

1 Criminal Act

psychoanalysis A set of theories regarding the impact of the mind on human behavior; also a treatment technique

3 Arrest

Behavioral Explanations of Crime

Behavioral theories differ from psychoanalytic and psychiatric explanations of crime in that they assume that human behavior is learned, primarily through interactions with others. The theories generally suggest that behaviors are shaped by reinforcements and punishments to one's actions. Behavioral theories of crime may focus on the influences of role models, both positive and negative (Adler et al., 2018). For example, behavioral theorists would argue that a young child who regularly witnesses disputes being settled via violence is likely to adopt the same approach.

Cognitive Explanations of Crime

Cognitive explanations of crime primarily focus on individuals' mental processes, including:

- how individuals think, learn, and remember;
- how individuals resolve problems; and
- the intelligence of individuals.

Some research studies support a relationship between intelligence and criminal behavior, while others do not. In 1931, Edwin Sutherland (1931) evaluated studies of IQ, criminals, and delinquents and concluded that crime was not caused by a lack of intelligence. This belief was largely held within the field until 1977, when researchers reviewed the existing research and noted that IQ was more important in predicting criminal behavior than was either race or social class. They argued that children who did poorly in school were more likely to engage in delinquency and later criminal behavior than those who did well (Hirschi & Hindelang, 1977).

Scholars James Q. Wilson and Richard Herrnstein later published *Crime and Human Nature* (1985), which also proposed an indirect link between crime and IQ. Further, Herrnstein and Murray, in their controversial book *The Bell Curve: Intelligence and Class Structure in American Life* (1994), noted that low intelligence might contribute to criminal behavior because it could be related to:

3 Arrest

- a lack of success in school and employment,
- desire for immediate gain based on lack of foresight,
- insensitivity to pain or social rejection, and
- the inability to recognize the reasons for obeying the law.

In a nontraditional examination of the possible relationship between IQ and crime, researchers examined self-reported violent offending among individuals with genius-level IQ scores compared to those with average IQ scores. The researchers found that high-IQ individuals reported higher rates of crime and arrest yet lower levels of conviction than control group members (Oleson & Chappell, 2012). The researchers did not offer an explanation for the differences in arrests and convictions. However, it could be that individuals with higher IQ scores are more adept in efforts to avoid conviction. Further research is needed in the area.

The debate regarding whether low intelligence is related to crime is clouded by measurement problems. IQ tests have been criticized for maintaining cultural biases not truly reflective of one's intelligence (Martschenko, 2017).

Personality Explanations of Crime

Personality theories of crime focus on the effects on criminal behavior of various personality traits. Some personality traits, or manners by which we interact and view ourselves and others, arguably predispose individuals to engage in antisocial or criminal behavior. The combination of certain traits forms a criminal personality. Individuals with **antisocial personality disorder** often are short-sighted, are motivated by pleasure, and lack empathy for others. They show a lack of concern for their actions and the consequences their actions have on others. Individuals with varying levels of antisocial personality disorder and other mental illnesses can be found throughout the criminal justice system.

Research regarding the relationship between personality and criminality has focused on:

- differences between the personalities of criminals and noncriminals,
- predicting the criminal behaviors of individuals with particular personalities, and
- quantifying and comparing different types of offenders with regard to personality traits (Adler et al., 2018).

For example, having an aggressive personality can increase the likelihood of violence. Further, the inability to maintain control in frustrating situations can result in individuals committing crimes (Conklin, 2013).

Sociological Explanations of Crime

The field of criminology is a branch of **sociology**, which is the study of social relationships and institutions and focuses on issues such as religion, family, social classes, cultures, and related topics. Sociological explanations of crime argue that crime is a product of social factors, including:

- interpersonal relations,
- differences in the levels of power maintained by different individuals,
- frustration, and
- differences among cultures.

Such explanations of crime often focus on groups, as opposed to the focus on individuals found in the biological and psychological theories of crime.

The beginning of the 20th century saw rapid growth from immigration and industrialization in many U.S. cities. These and related changes contributed to problems, including rising crime rates, which lacked solutions. By the 1920s, sociologists, in particular those at the University of Chicago, had begun to scientifically study the impact of social factors (e.g., living in poverty) on criminal behavior.

Sociological explanations have remained the most prominent body of criminological theories since that time. Sociological theories are often categorized according to whether they address social structure, social processes, or social conflict.

Social Structure Theories

Social structure theories argue that a lack of power in society and living in poverty and deprivation encourage involvement in crime. The theories largely focus on the fact that crime rates are highest in poor, minority neighborhoods with few opportunities. Social structure theories fall into three areas: social disorganization theory, strain theory, and subcultural deviance theory.

SOCIAL DISORGANIZATION THEORIES

Social disorganization theory considers the crime-related effects of the disintegration of conventional values and beliefs often caused by increased levels of industrialization, urbanization, and immigration. It focuses on the impacts of reduced group or

antisocial personality disorder A disorder in which the afflicted often are short-sighted, are hedonistic, and lack empathy for others; they show a lack of concern for their actions and the consequences their actions have on others

sociology The study of social relationships and institutions; it focuses on issues such as religion, family, social classes, cultures, and related topics

social structure theories Theories of criminal behavior proposing that a lack of power in society and living in poverty and deprivation encourage involvement in crime

social disorganization theory A theory that considers the crime-related effects of the disintegration of conventional values and beliefs

1 Criminal Act

● **Learning Objective 5.5:** Describe the major categories offered by sociologists to explain crime.

social unity, or when conventional social values or beliefs are distorted. For instance, one conventional social value is that legal employment is the primary means to obtain money, but some individuals may view crime as a more attractive option.

Researchers Clifford Shaw and Henry McKay, pioneers in social disorganization theory, popularized social structure theory in the 1920s. Their work focused on social and ecological issues as they examined crime rates in relation to identified zones in Chicago. Shaw and McKay found significant differences in crime in particular areas of Chicago. The highest concentration of crime occurred in transitional zones, or areas heavily populated by foreign-born residents. This finding held true regardless of which foreign-born group resided in the area. They further noted that crime rates were highest in the central city and decreased as one moved outward (Shaw & McKay, 1942). More recent work in this area supports these early findings in suggesting that crime rates are highest in heavily populated, poor areas (R. E. Morgan & Kena, 2017).

STRAIN THEORIES

strain theory A theoretical explanation of crime which proposes that crime results from individuals' frustration at their apparent lack of legitimate opportunities for economic and social advancement

Strain theory proposes that crime results from individuals' frustration at their apparent lack of legitimate opportunities for economic and social advancement. Sociologist Robert Merton (1910–2003) argued that crime results from social and economic inequality, and he considered cultural goals (or objectives for which many individuals strive, for instance financial success) and institutionalized means (or legal or proper manner) to achieve them as being strongly related to involvement in crime. Merton's work built on sociologist Emile Durkheim's (1897/1951) earlier work on **anomie**, or a sense of normlessness, in which a breakdown in society's norms results in a feeling of strain.

anomie A sense of normlessness, in which a breakdown in society's norms results in a feeling of strain

Merton (1968) noted that discrepancies between an individual's goals and their means to achieve them result in various adaptations. As an example, assume a young couple wishes to buy their first house. They do not have much money and thus feel strain from being financially unable to purchase a home. As they consider their options, they realize that they can continue to work and earn money to buy a home, not buy a home, or commit crime in order to obtain money to purchase a home immediately. In this case, the couple has a goal (owning a home) and may choose different options to achieve their goal. Whichever option they choose (legal or illegal) will be their adaptation.

general strain theory An expansion of strain theory, which proposes that obtaining material goods is not the only motivation for committing crime; instead, strain perpetuates anger, depression, or frustration, which encourage some criminal behavior

Criminologist Robert Agnew (1992) later introduced **general strain theory**, which builds on Merton's work. Agnew's theory was broader in nature than Merton's work, primarily in the sense that he argued that obtaining material goods is not the only motivation for committing crime. He argued that strain perpetuates anger, depression, or frustration, which encourages some criminal behavior.

SUBCULTURAL DEVIANCE THEORIES

subcultural deviance theories Criminological theories that focus on the effects of subcultures having values and norms that conflict with those of the larger society; the theories propose that individuals who grow up in or are influenced by the values of those subcultures act in accordance with those influences

Society consists of numerous subcultures based on various characteristics, including race, ethnicity, religion, occupation, and others. **Subcultural deviance theories** focus on the effects of subcultures having values and norms that conflict with those of the larger society. These theories propose that individuals who grow up in or are influenced by the values of those subcultures, in particular those subcultures that embrace criminal behavior, act in accordance with those influences.

Several of the more prominent theories based on subcultural influences include criminologist Albert Cohen's (1955) work on gangs. Cohen noted that delinquent subcultures arise from the frustration of working-class youths who desire but cannot achieve middle-class status and success. They may be evaluated by middle-class personnel (e.g., teachers and employers) according to middle-class values and standards that they are ill-equipped to meet. As a result, they may become frustrated and resort to involvement in gangs, which provide a subculture in which they can achieve new forms of status.

Other researchers have also commented on subcultural impacts on crime and delinquency. For instance, researchers Richard Cloward and Lloyd Ohlin (1960) noted that three types of gangs emerge in relation to the subcultures that exist in various areas:

- *Criminal gangs* emerge in communities where many adults engage in crime and influence younger generations.
- *Conflict gangs* emerge in communities where there is little adult crime, and young adults attempt to gain respect through gang violence.
- *Retreatist gangs* emerge in communities with gang activity and consist of youths who were unfit for other types of gangs; members often resort to drug and alcohol use.

Social Process Theories

Social process theories of criminal behavior stress the importance of **socialization**, or the process by which adults and children learn from one another, and interactions between individuals in society. These theories consider the relationships with and influences of other persons and institutions, including schools and churches. Social process theories include social learning theories, control theories, and labeling theory.

SOCIAL LEARNING THEORIES

Social learning theories propose that crime is learned, often from criminal peers. It begins with the belief that people are born good, but over time learn to be bad. Among the more accepted social learning theories is sociologist Edwin Sutherland's (1939) **differential association theory**, which proposes that people's exposure to negative influences encourages them to engage in negative behaviors, including crime. Accordingly, Sutherland argued that individuals who frequently interact with criminals are more likely to become criminals. Sutherland (1939) proposed that family and peer influences are the most powerful but that the following matter with respect to interactions:

- *frequency*: how often the interactions occur (e.g., daily, weekly)
- *duration*: how long the interactions last when they do occur (e.g., a few minutes, hours)
- *priority*: how important the interactions are (e.g., interacting with a new friend or a friend they have had for many years)
- *intensity*: the context of the interaction (e.g., simple greetings or in-depth discussions)

CONTROL THEORIES

Control theories propose that people will misbehave if no controls on their behaviors are in place. Families, social groups, peers, and school are the primary controls that keep people from engaging in antisocial behavior and crime. Sociologist Travis Hirschi (1969) is among the more prominent control theorists. He noted that control theory helps us understand why individuals conform and behave properly, not why they engage in deviance. He identified a series of bonds that help restrict individuals from behaving badly:

- *attachment*: closeness with schools and parents (e.g., close, strong relations with parents or teachers)
- *commitment*: —investment in positive or conventional activities (e.g., educational and career aspirations and opportunities)
- *involvement*: engagement in positive activities (e.g., in athletics or church groups)
- *belief*: ideas held about conventional behavior, regulations, and society's value systems (e.g., maintaining the belief that committing a crime or other antisocial behaviors is wrong)

social process theories Theories of criminal behavior that stress the importance of socialization and interactions between individuals in society

socialization The process by which people learn from one another; people acquiring knowledge, attitudes, values, and habits that are deemed acceptable or normal by a group or the larger society

social learning theories Theories proposing that crime is learned, often from criminal peers; it begins with the belief that people are born good, but over time learn to be bad

differential association theory A criminological theory proposing that people's exposure to negative influences encourages them to engage in negative behaviors, including crime

control theories Theories that propose people will misbehave if no controls on their behaviors are in place

1 Criminal Act

labeling theory
A theoretical explanation of crime that focuses on individuals' reactions to the social judgments or labels placed on them

conflict theory
Theory that is grounded in the belief that power differences in society influence who is viewed as delinquent or criminal and how those individuals are treated

LABELING THEORY

Labeling theory focuses on an individual's reactions to the social judgments, or labels, placed on them. It is based on the works of sociologists Charles Cooley and George Mead. These researchers focused on the impacts and nature of human interactions.

Another sociologist, Edwin Lemert, expanded on the works of these and other early theorists and suggested that people regularly engage in activities that could be considered delinquent or criminal. However, only certain individuals are labeled as such (Lemert, 1967). Lemert distinguished between primary and secondary deviant acts. A primary deviant act is an individual's initial action that causes society to label that person delinquent. Secondary deviant acts occur when such a person accepts the label of delinquency and lives up to it through subsequent actions.

Labeling theory is thus largely grounded in how individuals view themselves. Sociologist Howard Becker (1963) is among the labeling theorists who noted that individuals who are labeled delinquent, criminal, or whatever else will respond according to the status placed on them. Labeling theory proposes that acts are recognized as deviant when individuals or groups deem them as such. The label imposed on individuals separates them from others, and negative labels promote negative behaviors as a matter of self-fulfillment.

Social Conflict

Conflict theory is grounded in the belief that power differences in society influence who is viewed as delinquent or criminal and how those individuals are treated. Proponents of the theory argue that powerful groups in society create and enforce

Conflict theory has been used to explain many crimes committed by powerful groups in society, including those that illegally dispose of waste into waterways. Conflict theorists might argue that the limited enforcement efforts to address environmental crime and the weak punishments imposed when offenders are caught are the result of the power maintained by certain groups in society.

Should environmental crimes be treated as seriously as conventional crimes?

the laws, primarily to their benefit, which subsequently results in targeted, punitive efforts directed toward less powerful groups. Power can be viewed in terms of political power, finances, and related issues.

George Vold (1958) was among the first scholars to apply conflict theory to criminal behavior. He suggested that conflicts between social groups (as a result of their mutual desire for power) are addressed through lawmaking and crime control efforts. Vold noted that groups in society band together out of the belief that collective action best serves their interests.

Conflict theory has spurred several theoretical approaches to crime and justice that are based on power and conflict.

- *Marxist theory*, based on the work of Karl Marx and Friedrich Engels, generally views crime as the result of a capitalist system that exploits the working underclass.
- *Radical criminology (or critical criminology)* expands Marx's work to incorporate the criminal or otherwise harmful acts of government officials and corporate entities.
- *Feminist criminology* considers the power imbalance between males and females in society.

Developmental Theories of Crime

1 Criminal Act

While sociological theories are most often used to explain criminal behavior, some recent explanations of crime incorporate biological, psychological, and/or sociological factors in explaining how changes in human lives impact human behavior. Developmental theories consider the effects of change on human lives that influence human behavior. Such theories can incorporate and intermix social and personal factors into explanations of criminal behavior.

Criminologists Michael Gottfredson and Travis Hirschi's (1990) **general theory of crime** is considered a developmental theory because it modifies social control theory to incorporate biosocial, psychological, routine activities and rational choice theories. This multidisciplinary approach to criminology proposes that poor child-rearing practices and inadequate socialization contribute to poor self-control, which leads to involvement in crime or other harmful acts, such as smoking or drinking underage. The theory recognizes the interconnectedness of various factors and stages of human development, with particular concern for social control. Developmental theories are typically categorized into latent trait theories and life course concepts.

Latent Trait Theories

Latent trait theories generally propose that a master trait that is present at birth or attained shortly thereafter predisposes individuals to engage in crime (e.g., Rowe et al., 1990). While the trait within the individual remains constant, antisocial or criminal behavior occurs when opportunities appear. Such traits could include:

- genetic abnormalities,
- brain impairments,
- defective intelligence, and
- impulsive personalities (Ellis, 1988).

general theory of crime A developmental theory of crime that modifies social control theory to incorporate biosocial, psychological, routine activities, and rational choice theories

latent trait theories Theories proposing that a master trait that is present at birth or is attained shortly thereafter predisposes individuals to engage in crime

● **Learning Objective 5.6:** Identify and describe developmental theories of crime.

We each have specific traits that may be triggered by opportunities. Some people are more aggressive than others and act on that trait when it seems appropriate to them. On a related note, variations in the level of intelligence among people could lead to miscommunication, conflict, or an unawareness of the consequences of one's actions. Latent trait theories focus more on the traits within an individual as opposed to events in one's life that shape their decisions and behaviors.

Life Course Theories

Life course theories consider involvement in or abstinence from crime with relation to the many events and developments that occur throughout one's life. They recognize changes, such as puberty, that can affect whether and how individuals ultimately engage in crime or antisocial behavior. Life course theories also consider the impacts of social factors, environmental influences, and personal behaviors in assessing why and how individuals become involved with crime:

life course theories Theories that consider how criminal careers occur throughout one's life; they recognize that changes in one's life can affect whether individuals may ultimately engage in crime or antisocial behavior

- *Social factors* could include dysfunctional families, unemployment, relationship problems, educational failures, and related issues.
- *Environmental impacts* could involve racism, residing in a high-crime community, being employed in a position with opportunities to commit crime, or living in poverty.
- *Personal behaviors* could include use of illegal substances, actions taken as a result of mental illnesses, or actions taken because of the desire for excitement.

Sociologists Robert Sampson and John Laub (1993) discussed the importance of trajectory and transition with regard to life course theory. **Trajectory** refers to the path of behavior that individuals assume throughout life. **Transition** refers to influential instances, or turning points within the trajectory, that encourage or discourage individuals from engaging in crime. Sampson and Laub argue that both are important in explaining criminal behavior.

trajectory An aspect of life course theory that refers to the path of behavior that individuals assume throughout life

Of particular concern for life course theorists are time periods and contexts. Crime is most often committed by younger persons who eventually age out of criminal behavior. Life course theorists seek to better understand this and other relationships, such as the effects of significant life events, like getting married, moving, and losing a job, on crime (e.g., Piquero & Mazerolle, 2001).

transition An aspect of life course theory that refers to influential instances, or turning points that encourage or discourage individuals from engaging in crime

The System in Perspective

Reflecting on the "In the News" feature at the start of this module, the question remains: Why would someone tamper with fruit? Consider the areas of criminological thought discussed in this module in attempts to explain this behavior. From a biological perspective, one could argue that the offender(s) inherited traits that predisposed them to engage in antisocial behavior. A psychologist might suggest that the offender(s) suffered from a damaged mind as a result of childhood trauma. A sociologist might argue that the individual(s) acted out of frustration from living in poverty while the strawberry manufacturers reaped the rewards of successful businesses. Ultimately, we found out that the act was based on revenge.

The challenge in understanding why people commit crimes is enhanced by the uniqueness of individuals. Each of us is biologically different. We come from various backgrounds, and we lead distinct lives. Our psychological makeups differ, and we have different levels of understanding and interpretations of the world around us. Our differences affect our decisions to engage in crime as well as the means by which we view justice and its imposition.

Summary

1. Learning Objective 5.1: *Describe the major beliefs of the classical school of criminology.*

- The classical school of criminology proposes that individuals commit crime based on rational choice in making decisions regarding pain versus pleasure. Punishments should outweigh the benefits derived from crime, and justice should be swift and certain. Rational choice theory holds that individuals decide whether to commit a crime by considering the potential payoffs in relation to the likelihood of being caught and the associated punishments. Situational crime prevention involves reducing the individuals' opportunities to commit crimes and reducing the likelihood of victimization.

2. Learning Objective 5.2: *Describe the major beliefs of the positivist school of criminology.*

- The positivist school of criminology is more scientific than the classical school. Positivists rely on empirically based, scientifically sound research in explaining crime. The three primary areas of criminological thought within positivism are biological, psychological, and sociological. Biological theories consider various factors within the human body. Psychological theories often center around childhood experiences and unconscious thoughts, social learning, mental processes, and personality traits. Sociological theories argue that crime is a product of social factors, including interpersonal relations, differences in the levels of power maintained by different individuals, frustration, differences among cultures, and related issues.

3. Learning Objective 5.3: *Explain how biological factors could influence criminal behavior.*

- The major biosocial theories fall into three categories: biochemical theories, neurophysiological theories, and genetic theories. Biochemical theories propose that crime is influenced by imbalances in the chemicals in one's body, particularly as they relate to diet, vitamin levels, hormones, or food allergies. Neurophysiological theories involve the study of brain activity and the central nervous system in general. Genetic theories propose that criminal traits and predispositions are genetically passed on from parents to their children.

4. Learning Objective 5.4: *Explain the major reasons given by psychologists for why crime occurs.*

- Psychological theories of crime can be categorized according to psychiatric, behavioral, cognitive, and personality explanations. Psychiatric explanations focus on unconsciousness and the influence of the mind as an explanation of human behavior. Behavioral theorists propose that human behavior is learned through interactions with others and is based on reinforcements and punishments. Cognitive psychologists largely explain criminal and antisocial behavior based on individuals' mental processes, including how those individuals think, learn, and remember. Personality theories focus on the effects of various personality traits on criminal behavior.

5. Learning Objective 5.5: *Describe the major categories offered by sociologists to explain crime.*

- Sociological explanations of crime describe crime as a product of social factors. They are often categorized as social structure, social processes, and social conflict theories. Social structure theories propose that various social and economic forces lead some individuals to commit crime. Theories within this category fall into three well-known areas, including social disorganization theories, strain theories, and subcultural deviance theories. Social process theories of criminal behavior stress the importance of socialization and interactions between individuals in society. Theories within this category include social learning theories, control theories, and labeling theory. Conflict theory is grounded in the belief that power differences in society influence who is viewed as delinquent or criminal and how those individuals are treated.

6. Learning Objective 5.6: *Identify and describe developmental theories of crime.*

- Developmental theories consider the effects of change on human lives that impact human behavior. These theories incorporate and intermix social and personal factors into explanations of criminal behavior. They are typically categorized into latent trait theories and life course concepts. Latent trait theories generally propose that a master trait that is present at birth or attained shortly thereafter predisposes individuals to engage in crime. Life course theories consider how criminal careers occur throughout one's life.

Questions for Critical Thinking

1. How could situational crime prevention be used to address high crime rates in a public housing facility?

2. Which area of criminological thought do you believe explains the largest amount of crime: biological, psychological, or sociological?

3. Do you believe that one's diet could contribute to their involvement in crime? If not, why? If so, do you believe we should restrict at-risk individuals from eating certain foods? Why or why not?

4. Do you believe one's intelligence is related to their involvement in crime? What is the basis for your opinion?

5. Which of the following categories of sociological explanations of crime do you believe best explains shoplifting: social process, social structure, or social conflict? Why?

6. How would you diagram the major events that have shaped your life? Have you experienced more pushes away from or pulls toward crime?

Key Terms

anomie
antisocial behavior
antisocial personality disorder
classical school
classical theory
conflict theory
control theories
criminology
differential association theory
general deterrence
general strain theory
general theory of crime
labeling theory
latent trait theories
life course theories
neurophysiology
positivist school of criminology

psychoanalysis
rational choice theory
situational crime prevention
social disorganization theory
socialization
social learning theories
social process theories
social structure theories
sociology
specific deterrence
strain theory
subcultural deviance theories
theories
trajectory
transition
utilitarianism

For digital learning resources, please go to
https://www.oup.com/he/burns1e

Victims of Crime

Module

6

Crime victims have largely been overlooked by the criminal justice system throughout history. While they receive attention from first responders to crimes and are generally asked for information about their victimization, until recently, their role in the remaining steps of criminal case processing was limited.

Have you been a victim of crime or known someone who has been? If so, how were you or they treated by authorities?

Victims are those who suffer some adverse effect from national disasters, accidents, diseases, or the harms associated with crimes and criminal behavior. Understanding the harms, costs, theoretical explanations, and legal protections associated with victimization is important to the study of crime and justice. This module focuses on these often overlooked, yet essential participants in the criminal justice system, starting with a look at historical events that contributed to the current status of victims in the criminal justice system. This module then discusses the rights and protections of victims in the United States in the early 21st century, followed by an examination of the various harms associated with victimization. Finally, this module ends with a look at theories of victimization followed by a discussion of current trends in victimization and reporting.

MODULE OUTLINE

• The Early History of Victimization

Learning Objective 6.1: Summarize historical changes to the victim's role in the criminal justice system.

• The Rights and Protections of Victims in the Early 21st Century

Learning Objective 6.2: Explain the rights and protections of victims in the United States in the early 21st century.

• The Negative Effects Associated With Victimization

Learning Objective 6.3: Describe the negative effects associated with victimization.

• Theories of Victimization

Learning Objective 6.4: Identify and describe various theories of victimization.

• Recent Trends in Victimization and Reporting

Learning Objective 6.5: Summarize current trends in victimization and reporting.

Asset Forfeiture Program

9 Sentencing

In April 2018, the U.S. Department of Justice awarded the Crime Victims' Financial Restoration Award to the Criminal Division's Program Management and Training Unit. The unit uses funds seized and forfeited by criminals to, among other things, help crime victims.

The U.S. Department of Justice announced that the section had played a key role in

Crime Victims Financial Restoration Award
Money Laundering and Asset Recovery Section
Criminal Division, U.S. Department of Justice
Washington, D.C.
OVC

locating and restoring forfeited funds to crime victims, including over $1.3 billion in the previous 3 years. The bulk of those funds

($772 million) were distributed to roughly 24,000 victims of Bernard Madoff, who is believed to have defrauded victims of roughly $65 billion as part of a Ponzi scheme he oversaw. Madoff was convicted in 2009 and received a 150-year prison sentence. The distribution was the first in a series that will compensate victims with about $4 billion (U.S. Department of Justice, 2018).

Asset forfeiture programs administer assets (e.g., money, cars) that have been seized or forfeited by criminals who obtained the assets as part of their criminal behaviors. The proceeds are often distributed to victims and to support law enforcement efforts.

The programs have been criticized for their potential to encourage law enforcement to be overly aggressive; for instance, some of the assets seized are used to support law enforcement operations. However, these programs seek to help victims and arguably discourage criminal behavior. Do you believe all of the funds secured via asset forfeiture programs should go to victims, or should some portion be allocated to law enforcement? What might be some of the potential challenges or difficulties for the government when allocating resources to crime victims?

The Early History of Victimization

10
Corrections

• **Learning Objective 6.1:** Summarize historical changes to the victim's role in the criminal justice system.

Until the 1820s, when prosecutors in the United States became increasingly involved in initiating criminal cases, victims of crime were responsible for bringing offenders to justice. Courts largely focused on repairing the harms done to the victim by requiring restitution against those who harmed others (A. M. Morgan, 1987). Property offenders were required to replace the stolen goods and provide a bit more (e.g., perhaps repay a stolen horse with two horses). For violent crimes, each injury was worth a prescribed amount of money to be paid to victims (Kelly, 1984). In cases of wrongful death, victims' families were monetarily compensated by the offender (McDonald, 2009).

Over time, government-sponsored prosecutors, and later police forces, assumed responsibility for bringing offenders to justice, as crimes became viewed as offenses against the state as opposed to private disputes. Government-sponsored prosecution became the norm in the late 1800s (Neubauer & Fradella, 2019), and formal policing emerged at different times as the United States continued to expand. With these and related changes, victims became largely an afterthought in the criminal justice system. In addition, victims were sometimes blamed for crimes. They were made to feel that something they did warranted their victimization, leading to the suggestion that victims suffer costs from the criminal incident and their involvement in the criminal justice system (Doerner & Lab, 2002).

The Victims' Rights Movement

The **victims' rights movement** of the 1970s and 1980s tried to put an end to blaming individuals for being victimized and to give victims more of a role in criminal case processing. This movement was generated by the simultaneous occurrence of various social movements and issues during the 1960s and 1970s. Among the contributors to the victims' rights movement were:

- the women's movement, which involved efforts to ensure that women were treated as equals to males;
- increasing crime rates and concerns about increasing crime rates;
- legal reforms, for example through several Supreme Court decisions that provided more rights and protections and restricted government powers;
- promotion of compensation for victims by proponents fighting for additional and enhanced victims' rights;
- mass media, by providing crime stories and focusing on the impacts on victims; and
- increased academic focus on victimology by scholars and researchers (Doerner & Lab, 2002).

The movement received a boost in 1967, when President Lyndon B. Johnson's Commission on Crime suggested that victims should have systematic means to address the harmful effects of criminal victimization and should be more involved in the criminal justice system. The victims' right movement set the stage for greater consideration and involvement of victims in our justice systems.

Government Efforts to Assist Victims

Aside from the suggestion from President Johnson's Commission on Crime, government efforts to address victimization and better involve victims in the criminal justice system are found in various legislative acts and government task forces.

1982 PRESIDENT'S TASK FORCE ON VICTIMS OF CRIME

The President's Task Force on Victims of Crime in 1982 helped victims primarily through improving the services provided to them. The report started a series of changes that resulted in the following (Sgarzi & McDevitt, 2003):

- Victims were able to offer **victim impact statements**—written or oral information about how a crime has affected them—at sentencing.
- Victims were updated regarding the progress of their cases.
- Victims were provided with financial compensation for particular crimes.

victims' rights movement A movement during the 1970s and 1980s that helped put an end to blaming individuals for being victimized and gave victims a larger role in criminal case processing

victim impact statements Written or oral information offered by crime victims that address how the crime has impacted them; they assist sentencing bodies with their decision-making

The victims' rights movement was influential in generating public and official interest in the needs of victims. Protests were among the means by which advocates encouraged actions designed to better help and protect victims.

Aside from providing money, how should the government assist crime victims?

Victim Witness Protection Act Legislation that required the use of victim impact statements in federal trials and encouraged states to adopt a similar approach

Victims of Crime Act Legislation that allocated funds for research on victim needs, for victim compensation, and for victim assistance programs in eligible states that had programs designed to assist victims of sexual assault, spousal abuse, or child abuse

Victim Rights and Restitution Act Legislation through which Congress gave crime victims rights, including the right to be present at court proceedings, notification of the proceedings involving the crime of which they were a victim, and consultation with prosecutors

9 Sentencing

10 Corrections

● **Learning Objective 6.2:** Explain the rights and protections of victims in the United States in the early 21st century.

1982 VICTIM WITNESS PROTECTION ACT

The **Victim Witness Protection Act** of 1982 was legislation designed to strengthen the legal protections for witnesses and victims of federal offenses. The act symbolized the government's renewed interest in helping victims and encouraged states to adopt a similar approach. Among other provisions, the act required the use of victim impact statements in federal trials and provided protections for victims of crime who may have been the target of intimidation or retaliation for reporting the crime (A. M. Morgan, 1987).

1984 VICTIMS OF CRIME ACT

The **Victims of Crime Act** of 1984 allocated funds for various programs designed to help victims, including:

- research on victim needs,
- victim compensation, and
- victim assistance programs in eligible states designed to assist victims of sexual assault, spousal abuse, or child abuse.

The act was amended in 1988 and resulted in the creation of the Office of Victims of Crime, which is in the U.S. Department of Justice and provides guidance and support for crime victims.

1990 VICTIMS' RIGHTS AND RESTITUTION ACT

The **Victims' Rights and Restitution Act** of 1990 gave crime victims the right to be:

- present at court proceedings,
- notified of the proceedings involving the crime of which they were a victim, and
- consulted with by prosecutors.

1994 VIOLENT CRIME CONTROL AND LAW ENFORCEMENT ACT

The **Violent Crime Control and Law Enforcement Act of 1994** provided victims in federal courts permission to speak at sentencing hearings and expanded victim services. It also made restitution mandatory in sexual assault cases. Restitution could be related to repayment for medical services, physical therapy, child-care expenses, lost income, attorney's fees, and any other victim costs resulting from the offense.

By 2003, every state had a crime compensation program and had passed some form of victims' rights legislation. Roughly two thirds of the states passed constitutional amendments that ensure victims' rights (Newmark, 2004; Trulson, 2005).

The Rights and Protections of Victims in the Early 21st Century

Victims' rights vary among the states, although they, and the rights provided by the federal government, generally address two primary areas: (a) the involvement of crime victims in criminal case proceedings and (b) services and compensation to address the harms associated with victimization.

To better ensure the protection and interests of crime victims, states have created bills of rights that have, in some cases, been incorporated into state constitutions. They have also created rape shield laws designed to better address the hardships suffered by victims of rape, in particular. These are by no means the only remedies used.

Victims' Bills of Rights

Victims' bills of rights as found in some state constitutions are a series of legislative acts designed to protect and assist victims of crime. Generally, they share several common elements.

- They identify a legal definition of victim, because there may be uncertainty regarding who is a victim of crime and which victims are eligible for services and compensation (Trulson, 2005). For example, some states limit victim rights to victims of violent felonies or other select types of crime (Davis & Mulford, 2008). Only about 40% of states provide rights to all classes of victims (Howley & Dorris, 2007).

- They often comment on the need for victims to be treated with dignity and include references to the rights of victims to be present and heard during court proceedings involving the defendant (Weed, 1995).

- They typically include the right of victims to be protected from harassment or abuse on behalf of the defendant or someone associated with the defendant (Weed, 1995).

- They often reference victim compensation (Weed, 1995).

An example of a state's bill of rights is provided in Figure 6.1.

Violent Crime Control and Law Enforcement Act of 1994 The largest crime bill in the history of the United States; the act addressed many issues pertaining to crime and justice, including the allocation of over $50 million for the expansion of drug courts, providing victims in federal courts with permission to speak at sentencing hearings, and expanding victim services; it also made restitution mandatory in sexual assault cases

victims' bills of rights A series of legislative acts designed to protect and assist victims of crime

---

The Georgia Crime Victims Bill of Rights, O.C.G.A. 17-17-1, et seq., provides individuals who are victims of certain crimes specific rights. These rights include:

- The right to reasonable, accurate, and timely notice of any scheduled court proceedings or any changes to such proceedings;
- The right to reasonable, accurate, and timely notice of the arrest, release, or escape of the accused;
- The right not to be excluded from any scheduled court proceedings, except as provided by law;
- The right to be heard at any scheduled court proceedings involving the release, plea, or sentencing of the accused;
- The right to file a written objection in any parole proceedings involving the accused;
- The right to confer with the prosecuting attorney in any criminal prosecution related to the victim;
- The right to restitution as provided by law;
- The right to proceedings free from unreasonable delay; and
- The right to be treated fairly and with dignity by all criminal justice agencies involved in the case.

FIGURE 6.1. Georgia's Crime Victims Bill of Rights. The federal government and all states have legislation regarding rights for victims. As noted in Georgia's legislation, the laws generally pertain to victims having certain information, protections, and some role in criminal case processing. *Source:* Crime Victims Bill of Rights, *by Prosecuting Attorneys' Council of Georgia (n.d.). https://pacga.org/ resources/victim-assistance/georgia-crime-victims-bill-of-rights*

What other protections could be provided to assist crime victims in Georgia?

8 Trial

10
Corrections

Effects of Victim Impact Statements

Victim impact statements are permitted in federal sentencing and in virtually all states. Such statements:

- provide information regarding the true harms associated with the crime,
- facilitate the recovery process for victims, and
- enlighten offenders regarding the consequences of their actions (Cassell, 2009).

Some research suggests that victim impact statements have had limited effects on offender sentences and whether an offender receives prison or probation (e.g., Davis & Smith, 1994). Victim impact statements have also been criticized for creating heated emotions that may increase the severity of the punishment (e.g., Wevodau et al., 2014).

Rape Shield Laws

rape shield laws Laws that are designed to limit the ability of a defendant's counsel to introduce evidence regarding the accuser's sexual history during a rape trial; they also protect a victim's identity

Among the protections for crime victims are **rape shield laws**, which are designed to protect a victim's identity and limit the ability of a defendant's counsel to introduce evidence regarding the victim's sexual history during a rape trial. The laws reflect the fact that the sexual history of a victim has no bearing on whether an accused individual has committed a crime, and the victim is not on trial. In the United States, rape shield laws initially appeared in Michigan in 1974. The influences of the victims' rights movement and the enhanced concern for victims in general throughout the United States resulted in almost all states having them within two decades.

In some circumstances, these protective laws do not apply, including cases in which there is evidence that the rape in question was not committed by the defendant or when there is an existing sexual relationship between the accuser and the accused. Critics of rape shield laws contend that they violate a defendant's Sixth Amendment right to confront their accuser.

Victim Services

Various remedies are provided for victims of crimes, with the intent to address any harm associated with their victimization. These services generally include financial compensation, counseling, and notification to victims of their rights and available services (Kilpatrick et al., 1998). Crime victims may be able to recover:

- medical costs (e.g., those associated with physical and emotional harms),
- costs associated with property theft or damage, and
- lost income resulting from an inability to work.

Such compensation may come from offenders through restitution or through public victim compensation programs (see "In the News" for discussion of how some funding is generated to assist victims).

MYTHBUSTING

Sexual Assaults Most Often Involve Strangers

It is commonly believed that most rapes and other types of sexual assaults are committed by strangers. Such incidents are regularly depicted by the media and popular culture as involving someone unknown to the victim (Schwark, 2017). In actuality, most victims of sexual assault know their offenders. Reports of rape and sexual assault committed by strangers regularly hover around 25%, meaning that roughly 75% of these offenses are committed by someone known to the victim (Harrell, 2012).

Despite the progress in addressing victims' rights, most victims do not take advantage of compensation or restitution. This may occur for several reasons, including:

- judges failing to order restitution;
- victims not being made aware of services, compensation, or restitution;
- victims feeling that services will not help address the situation;
- victims not believing they have been victimized; for example, if a company illegally pollutes the environment and negatively impacts the air you breathe, you may not be aware of the harms to your body or that you are being victimized; and
- victims believing that the necessary support can be provided by family or friends (Stohr, 2005).

The criminal justice agencies responsible for providing victims' services often argue that state legislatures do not provide enough funding (Davis & Mulford, 2008). Several steps have been taken to ensure that victims receive the services they should, including creating state constitutional amendments to ensure that victims receive services. Most states created constitutional amendments regarding victim rights (Howley & Dorris, 2007). States have also created compliance programs to:

- educate criminal justice agencies about victim rights,
- assist with training individuals and agencies that provide services, and
- assist victims who feel their needs are not being met (Davis & Mulford, 2008).

An estimated 12,200 victim service providers operated in the United States in 2017. These organizations serve victims of crime or abuse as their primary function or have dedicated staff or programs to assist victims. The large majority (88.5%) of these groups were nonprofit/faith-based (45.1%) or governmental (43.4%) organizations. The government-based providers were most often located in a prosecutor's office or a law enforcement agency (Oudekerk et al., 2019).

Research suggests that the individuals most likely to use victim services are generally those who were the victims of violent crime, as well as individuals who are older, poorer, and less likely to be employed. The same study found that those who did not take advantage of the services chose not to because they had little or no knowledge of the services available to them, they received assistance from friends or family members, or they did not believe the services were worth their effort. Better efforts to educate the public regarding the availability and usefulness of these programs would likely lead more victims to take advantage of them (e.g., Sims et al., 2005).

CAREERS

Crime victim advocates provide various forms of assistance to individuals who have been victimized. They provide information regarding support services and court hearings, may attend court with victims, provide emotional support, may provide counseling, and assist with general victim needs as warranted.

The Negative Effects Associated With Victimization

Crime victims suffer many kinds of costs, including physical, financial, emotional, and psychological ones. As noted in Module 2, victim costs are but one of the categories of the costs of crime. We often only consider the financial losses and physical harms associated with crimes, but there are also many intangible and secondary effects underlying losses.

Learning Objective 6.3: Describe the negative effects associated with victimization.

1 Criminal Act

Intangible Effects

Many of the costs and effects associated with crime can be considered costs and effects associated with victims. For instance, we all pay taxes that support justice systems to protect us from being victimized. We may purchase locks and home security systems to secure us from crime, and the keys we carry are to protect us from victimization. Having to carry keys, remember passwords to protect our bank accounts and the like, and paying more to live in areas with lower crime rates are among the many intangible effects associated with crime and victimization. In addition, victims of crime may have medical costs, for example for counseling or lost wages from being unable to work.

Aside from these more basic intangibles, victims of crime are also at a higher risk of experiencing the following:

- anger
- shame
- depression
- substance use/abuse
- vulnerability
- rage
- concern for their security and the security of others
- distrust of others, including authorities and the police
- post–traumatic stress disorder (Hanson & Self-Brown, 2010; Lurigio, 1987)

Fear of Crime

The costs of victimization are not restricted to individual victims. For example, knowledge of victimization in close proximity to one's residence increases fear of crime among those who were not directly victimized. Researchers found that

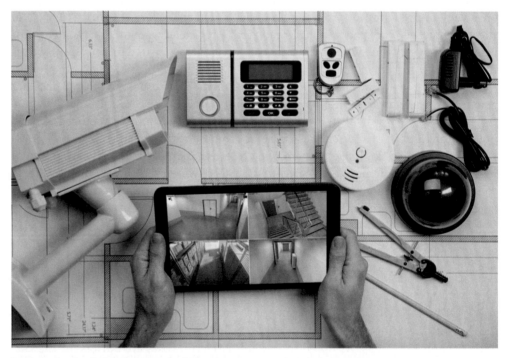

Fear of crime has led to the creation of a large private security industry. We take various actions to protect ourselves, including locking doors, owning weapons, and purchasing home and car alarm systems.

What actions do you take each day to protect yourself from crime?

individuals who live within roughly one block of crime were more fearful of crime than those who did not (Zhao et al., 2015).

Fear of crime has regularly been a concern for many people throughout the United States. A 2017 Gallup poll noted that 30% of Americans lived within a mile of an area in which they would feel unsafe walking alone at night. This percentage has ranged from 30% to 48% of respondents since Gallup first used this measure in 1965 (Newport, 2017). Although 30% is the lowest percentage since the poll began, it remains that 3 of every 10 people fear walking alone at night near their home.

Theories of Victimization

The term **victimology** refers to the study of victims. Historically, the scientific study of crime and justice focused on offenders and the acts they committed (see Module 5). Largely beginning with the victims' rights movement, increased research focused on the roles of victims in crimes. Theoretical explanations of victimization fall into two groups: theories that consider opportunities and focus on elements such as time and space and theories that focus on the interactions of offenders and victims.

Opportunity-Based Theories

Opportunity-based theories consider the activities and practices of victims. For example, the **lifestyle-exposure theory** considers an individual's lifestyle in attempts to explain why some groups or individuals are victimized more than others.

Researchers sought to better understand why males, young adults, and racial minorities were more often victimized than their counterparts. They examined the relationship between social and demographic characteristics in relation to victimization and found that peoples' lifestyle, including the places in which they engage in leisure and vocational activities, influenced their likelihood of being victimized (Hindelang et al., 1978). For instance, individuals who live in safe communities yet work or attend school in high-crime areas are more likely to be victimized than their neighbors who work in areas with low crime rates. The groups most often victimized often engage in lifestyles that pose enhanced risks of victimization. For example, people who buy or sell illegal drugs are at a higher risk of victimization.

Another opportunity-based theory that helps explain victimization was proposed by researchers Lawrence Cohen and Marcus Felson in 1979. They offered the **routine activities theory** to help explain victimization in relation to the activities of individuals within their everyday lives (e.g., where they shop and live and the efforts they take to prevent victimization). In particular, they suggested that people commit crimes when three factors are present in time and space (L. Cohen & Felson, 1979):

- *motivated offenders* (e.g., an individual who is willing and interested in committing a crime);
- *suitable targets* (e.g., an individual walking alone at night while wearing expensive jewelry); and
- *a lack of guardianship* (e.g., a family is away on vacation while their house is burglarized and cannot quickly contact the police).

Cohen and Felson argued that communities where there are large numbers of offenders would experience higher levels of crime, because these three factors were most likely to converge in these areas.

Interaction-Based Theories

Aside from consideration of the opportunities for victimization, the context and nature of interactions between victims and offenders is also important to recognize with regard to understanding victimization. Years ago, a researcher noted that in roughly one-quarter of the incidents he studied, the victim of murder initially acted more aggressively than the eventual offender (Wolfgang, 1958).

More recently, researchers have studied the combined interactions between the victim and offender. Research in this area has focused, in part, on **victim precipitation**, which involves victims provoking or instigating criminal behavior. One study found that 30% of victims of nonlethal personal violence incidents were the first to use violence during the incidents (Muftić et al., 2007). Consider, for example, a bar fight in which one man beats up another man (the victim). The victim had insulted the other man's wife and then started shouting at the husband of the wife whom he had insulted. This incident would be considered victim-precipitated because the victim encouraged the assault.

victim precipitation Acts in which victims provoke or instigate criminal behavior

Recent Trends in Victimization and Reporting

● **Learning Objective 6.5:** Summarize current trends in victimization and reporting.

Data from the U.S. Bureau of Justice Statistics shed light on recent victimizations. Figure 6.2 notes that the percentage of households who were victims of burglary has decreased substantially in recent years (R. E. Morgan & Truman, 2020). The overall rate of property crime victimization is roughly one-third of what it was in 1993 (R. E. Morgan & Kena, 2017). As noted in Module 3, a similar pattern has emerged with regard to violent crime victimization.

Victimization by Demographics

As depicted in Table 6.1, the individuals who were most likely to be the victims of violent crime in 2019 include:

● males, although the differences are slight;

- ● Hispanics and Whites;
- ● individuals ages 18–24;
- ● those who are separated; and
- ● those with the lowest household income (R. E. Morgan & Truman, 2020).

Reporting Practices

Criminal victimizations come to the attention of the police in a variety of ways. For instance, victims, witnesses, or third parties such as school officials or workplace personnel report victimizations to the police. Police on patrol may also personally encounter crime in progress; however, they do so in only about 4%–5% of all crimes (Reiss, 1971). Of particular importance in solving crimes and bringing offenders to justice is crime reporting. Unfortunately, a relatively low percentage of victimizations are reported to the police. In 2019, only about 41% of all violent victimizations were reported to police, and only about 32.5% of property crime victimizations were reported (R. E. Morgan & Truman, 2020).

FIGURE 6.2. Burglary Victimization Rates. The percentage of households who were victims of burglary has steadily declined in the United States, beginning in the early 1990s. There have been years in which the rate increased (e.g., 2011–2012), but the overall trend has been downward. **Source:** Criminal Victimization, 2019 (NCJ 255113), by R. E. Morgan and J. L. Truman, 2020, U.S. Department of Justice, Bureau of Justice Statistics.

What steps do you take to prevent against property crime victimization?

Many reasons exist for the relatively low rate at which victims report crime to the police. These reasons include:

- the fear of retaliation,
- the belief that the police could not or would not do anything about the offense,
- the belief that the victimization was not a crime or was trivial in nature,
- victims handling the incident personally or in some other manner, and
- victims being engaged in an illegal activity at the time of their victimization (Langton et al., 2012).

Crime reporting is important for many reasons; however, most crimes go unreported. Certain groups are more likely than others to report crime, and people have various reasons for not reporting illegal behaviors.

Have you ever witnessed a crime? Did you report it? Why or why not?

Annually, about 3.3 million violent victimizations are not reported to the police (Langton et al., 2012). The most commonly cited reason for not reporting a crime to the police was that the victim dealt with the matter in another way. This could include reporting the crime to a work or school official or handling the situation privately or personally, for instance by warning the offender that they will report the crime if it happens again or threatening them with retaliation.

Victims' failure to report their victimizations has several repercussions, including the inability of victims to receive services, offenders going unpunished, and a lack of a true picture of crime in the community. Understanding why individuals do not report victimizations sheds light on what efforts are needed to persuade victims to report.

TABLE 6.1. Rates of Violent Victimization, by Type of Crime and Demographic Characteristics of Victims, 2018 and 2019

VICTIM DEMOGRAPHIC CHARACTERISTIC		TOTAL VIOLENT VICTIMIZATION[a]		VIOLENT VICTIMIZATION EXCLUDING SIMPLE ASSAULT[b]	
		2018	2019*	2018	2019*
	Total[c]	23.2	21.0	8.6†	7.3
Sex					
	Male	22.1	21.2	7.5	7.5
	Female	24.3	20.8	9.6†	7.0
Race/ethnicity					
	White[d]	24.7‡	21.0	8.2	6.5
	Black[d]	20.4	18.7	10.0	7.0
	Hispanic	18.6	21.3	8.5	10.2
	Asian[d]	16.2†	7.5	5.6†	1.9!
	Other[d,e]	49.2	66.3	20.5	20.9
Age					
	12–17	34.2	35.2	10.1	11.0
	18–24	35.9	37.2	16.3	16.0
	25–34	31.8‡	25.0	11.3	8.9
	35–49	25.2‡	19.5	9.8‡	6.7
	50–64	18.3	18.9	6.4	5.6
	65 or older	6.5	6.0	2.3	1.9

(Continued)

TABLE 6.1. *(Continued)*

VICTIM DEMOGRAPHIC CHARACTERISTIC		TOTAL VIOLENT VICTIMIZATION[a]		VIOLENT VICTIMIZATION EXCLUDING SIMPLE ASSAULT[b]	
		2018	**2019***	**2018**	**2019***
Marital status					
	Never married	33.5	31.2	12.9	11.9
	Married	12.1	11.5	4.1	3.0
	Widow/widower	12.5	10.7	4.3	4.9
	Divorced	39.1†	28.5	14.8	10.7
	Separated	58.2	64.1	20.8	19.5
Household income					
	Less than $25,000	40.8	37.8	19.0‡	14.2
	$25,000–$49,999	23.5	19.7	9.3	7.5
	$50,000–$99,999	16.5	16.6	4.7	5.5
	$100,000–$199,999	19.2	16.2	5.8	3.9
	$200,000 or more	16.3	18.0	3.0†	7.0

Note. Victimization is influenced by various factors, and victimization rates vary by demographics. Some groups (e.g., those who are separated from their spouse or those with the lowest household incomes) have much higher rates of victimization than other groups, such as the elderly. Rates are per 1,000 persons age 12 or older. Includes threatened, attempted, and completed occurrences of those crimes.
***Source:** Bureau of Justice Statistics, National Crime Victimization Survey, 2018 and 2019; and Criminal Victimization, 2019 (NCJ 255113), Table 9, by R. E. Morgan and J. L. Truman, 2020, U.S. Department of Justice, Bureau of Justice Statistics, (https://www.bjs.gov/content/pub/pdf/cv19.pdf). © U.S. Department of Justice, Office of Justice Programs, Bureau of Justice Statistics, September 2020, NCJ 255113*
*Comparison year.
†Difference with comparison year is significant at the 95% confidence level.
‡Difference with comparison year is significant at the 90% confidence level.
!Interpret estimate with caution. Estimate is based on 10 or fewer sample cases or coefficient of variation is greater than 50%.
[a]Includes rape or sexual assault, robbery, aggravated assault, and simple assault. Excludes homicide because the National Crime Victimization Survey is based on interviews with victims.
[b]Includes rape or sexual assault, robbery, and aggravated assault; this category was called serious violent crime prior to Criminal Victimization, 2018.
[c]Statistically significant differences for the total victimization rates are presented using the balanced repeated replication method. Generalized variance function parameters were used to calculate statistically significant differences for the rest of the table.
[d]Excludes persons of Hispanic origin (e.g., "White" refers to non-Hispanic Whites and "Black" refers to non-Hispanic Blacks).
[e]Includes Native Hawaiians and Other Pacific Islanders, American Indians and Alaska Natives, and persons of two or more races.

The System in Perspective

The "In the News" feature at the start of this module discussed an award that the U.S. Department of Justice gave to the division that handles asset forfeiture. The large amount of money that the Department of Justice has collected through these programs and granted to crime victims reflects how much has changed with regard to the treatment and involvement of victims of crime since the victims' rights movement began in the 1970s. Greater protections for victims, more involvement in court proceedings, and enhanced services for victims are primary among the developments that have assisted victims. These and related changes have impacted our justice system in many ways: for instance, police officers are trained to be more sympathetic to victims, prosecutors are more likely to involve victims in the adjudication process, and victim support and compensation groups have emerged throughout the United States. Victims play an integral role throughout our justice systems. The continued funding by the Department of Justice and other groups is necessary to ensure that victims' needs continue to be met.

Summary

1. **Learning Objective 6.1:** *Summarize historical changes to the victim's role in the criminal justice system.*

  - Historically, victims played a central role in criminal justice. Their role diminished over time, as formal policing emerged and prosecutors brought offenders to justice. Beginning in the 1970s and 1980s, victims again became more important in the courts. The victims' rights movement was spurred by the simultaneous occurrence of various social movements and social issues during the 1960s and 1970s. Various legislative efforts generated by the victims' rights movement and other efforts helped victims receive more input in the criminal justice system and some of the services they may require.

2. **Learning Objective 6.2:** *Explain the rights and protections of victims in the United States in the early 21st century.*

  - Compared to years past, victims in the early 21st century have more access to the courts, have more rights and protections, and are treated in a more humane manner. Victims' bills of rights help ensure the proper treatment of victims. Such bills generally identify a legal definition of victim, comment on the need for victims to be treated with dignity, include references to the rights of victims to be present and heard during case processing, protect victims from harassment or abuse, and often provide for victim compensation. These and related services provided to victims demonstrate society's recognition of the need to ensure victims are treated fairly.

3. **Learning Objective 6.3:** *Describe the negative effects associated with victimization.*

  - Crime victims suffer various physical, financial, emotional, and psychological costs. In particular, the costs include physical injuries and associated monetary losses, and victims may suffer from feelings of anger, shame, vulnerability, rage, concern for their security and the security of others, distrust of others, and post–traumatic stress. They may also develop negative feelings for the police. Secondary effects of victimization include increased fear of crime for nonvictims located in proximity to the crime.

4. **Learning Objective 6.4:** *Identify and describe various theories of victimization.*

  - Theoretical explanations of victimization fall into two groups: theories that consider opportunities (e.g., lifestyle-exposure theory, routine activities theory) and those that closely consider the interactions of offenders and victims. The latter theories focus primarily on the dealings between an offender and a victim, as well as the context.

5. **Learning Objective 6.5:** *Summarize current trends in victimization and reporting.*

  - The property and violent crime victimization rates have decreased substantially in recent years. With regard to demographics, males, individuals ages 18–24, those with the lowest household income, and Whites and Hispanics were most likely to be the victim of violent crime. With regard to marital status, individuals who are separated from their spouses were far more likely than others to be the victim of a violent crime.

  With regard to reporting practices, only 41% of violent victimizations were reported to police in 2019, and roughly 32% of property crime victimizations were reported.

Questions for Critical Thinking

1. Why, in your opinion, were victims historically overlooked by the criminal justice system?

2. Do you believe we currently provide too little, too much, or the appropriate level of rights and protections to crime victims? Explain your answer.

3. Have you or someone you know been a victim of crime? If so, what was the most harmful effect?

4. What precautions do you take, if any, in your everyday routines to protect yourself from crime?

5. What could be done to improve crime reporting practices?

Key Terms

lifestyle-exposure theory
rape shield laws
routine activities theory
victim impact statements
victimology
victim precipitation

Victim Rights and Restitution Act
victims' bills of rights
Victims of Crime Act
victims' rights movement
Victim Witness Protection Act
Violent Crime Control and Law Enforcement Act

For digital learning resources, please go to
https://www.oup.com/he/burns1e

Understanding Justice

Module

7

Lady Justice signifies equity and fairness. In her right hand she is often seen holding a set of scales, which symbolizes concern for the strength of and opposition to a case. She holds a double-edged sword in her left hand, which symbolizes the reasoning and justice to be used against any party. She is blindfolded to demonstrate that justice should be as objective and impartial as possible.

What does justice mean to you?

There are many criminology, criminal justice, and justice studies programs in universities and colleges that focus on how offenders are treated for their wrongdoings. Disciplines including sociology, political science, philosophy, and others are also concerned with justice. We regularly hear citizens cry for justice when someone is wronged, and we claim that justice must be swift and certain. We even have scales of justice that symbolize our concern for fairness, individual rights, and due process. Ultimately, while people often use the term *justice*, they generally have trouble describing what it means. This module provides an overview of justice, beginning with coverage of why we need justice, followed by a look at the various types and models of justice.

Finding Justice

1 Criminal
Act

In 2012, 28-year-old George Zimmerman shot and killed an unarmed 17-year-old African American male in Florida. The victim, Trayvon Martin, had been temporarily residing in the gated community in which the incident occurred. Zimmerman, the Neighborhood Watch coordinator for the community, called the Sanford Police Department and reported Martin's behavior as suspicious. A violent encounter ensued between the men following the phone call, resulting in Zim-

Police found Zimmerman with a bloody nose and lacerations on the back of his head. After 5 hours of questioning, the police released Zimmerman without charges. They found no evidence to contradict his version of events. Later, a special prosecutor filed a second-degree murder charge against Zimmerman. Zimmerman pleaded not guilty and was later acquitted.

Although this case occurred in 2012, its justice-related implications remain. Aside from helping to spur the "Black Lives Matter" movement, this case generated international attention in relation to the circumstances regarding Martin's death, the initial decision by police not to arrest or file charges against Zimmerman, and Florida's controversial "Stand Your Ground" law.

merman fatally shooting Martin in the chest. A police report noted that there was no indication that Martin was involved in any criminal behavior when the encounter occurred.

Zimmerman claimed that he shot Martin in self-defense after Martin attacked him.

About 23 states across the United States have stand-your-ground or related laws that generally state that a person may justifiably use force in self-defense, without retreating, when they reasonably perceive an unlawful threat in their home, business, or any place they have a legal right to be (Clark, 2013). Florida's law has been particularly controversial because it resulted in a notable increase in the number of self-defense claims and was not clearly written. Do you believe it is appropriate for citizens to have the right to use force, including deadly force, in self-defense, without retreating, when they reasonably perceive an unlawful threat in their home, business, or any place they have a legal right to be?

Defining Justice

The image of Lady Justice has significance in both the United States and other countries, yet there is uncertainty regarding what truly constitutes justice. Consider the following questions that are often posed about justice-based practices:

● **Learning Objective 7.1:** Define justice and illustrate the consequences of failing to administer justice.

- Do the police regularly violate individual rights, for instance by using too much force when trying to make an arrest?
- Is our criminal justice system biased against the poor and racial and ethnic minorities?
- Do victims receive justice when the offenders who harmed them are incarcerated?
- Is a prison sentence an appropriate punishment for using drugs?

How these questions are answered depends on how justice is defined.

Scholars, philosophers, judges, juries, policymakers, and many others have long struggled with how to define justice and how to determine what constitutes justice. Their difficulty stems from the many perspectives of life in general and views of right and wrong, morality, and fairness. **Justice** can be generally defined as actions that are considered fair, equitable, and morally appropriate. However, these terms are subjective and open to interpretation because of the complexity of human behaviors and beliefs, including our different perceptions of social issues.

justice Actions that are considered fair, equitable, and morally appropriate

Perceptions of Justice

Perceptions change as society changes, which essentially means that justice-based actions and our interpretations of them may change over time. For example, consider the early history of the United States when slavery was legal and widely considered acceptable. In the early 21st century, slavery is viewed as immoral, illegal, and inhumane.

Our perceptions of justice also have changed as society has changed. These perceptions are shaped by powerful influences, including:

- popular culture (e.g., television shows and movies may impact our perceptions of crime and justice),
- the media (e.g., what we read, hear, and watch in the news can shape how we view crime and justice),
- families (e.g., the views of parents and siblings may impact our views of crime and justice),
- friends (e.g., discussions about crime and justice with friends may impact our views), and
- personal experiences (e.g., being arrested, charged, and/or convicted of a crime may impact our perceptions of justice).

The Consequences of Failing to Find Justice

While our criminal justice systems have undergone centuries of reform, history is filled with examples of miscarriages of justice and efforts to fight back. For example, frustration that some racial and ethnic groups have not been treated fairly by the criminal justice system spurred the 2013 **Black Lives Matter** activist movement in the United States. This movement, which campaigns against violence and racism directed toward African Americans, originated after the 2013 acquittal of a Florida man in the shooting of an African American teenager (see the "In the News" feature at the start of this module). The movement gained additional attention following the 2014 deaths of two unarmed African Americans (Michael Brown in Ferguson, Missouri, and Eric Garner in New York City, New York) and the failure of grand juries to indict the officers involved in those shootings. The movement became even more prominent in 2020 following the death of George Floyd in Minneapolis, Minnesota (see Module 1).

Whether or not the miscarriages of justice we have witnessed throughout history have been intentional, failure to appropriately administer justice has several consequences, including:

- innocent people being punished,
- guilty people escaping punishment,
- guilty people being more severely punished than would seem necessary,

1 Criminal Act

Black Lives Matter An activist movement that campaigns against violence and racism directed toward African Americans

6 Grand Jury/ Preliminary Hearing

The Black Lives Matter activist movement emerged in response to what appeared to be misuse of power by police officers against African Americans. The group raises awareness, often through demonstrations and protests, of the injustices committed against African Americans.

What other groups fight to protect against perceived injustices?

appellate courts Courts that hear cases that originated and were decided in trial courts; their primary purposes are to provide accountability for the trial courts and ensure that proper procedures were followed and the law was correctly applied and interpreted

exonerated Being released from prison as a result of the discovery of new evidence suggesting that the individual did not commit the crime for which they were sentenced

11 Appeal

8 Trial

9 Sentencing

- guilty people being punished less severely than would seem appropriate, and
- a lack of confidence in our justice systems.

Failing to ensure justice results in a lack of confidence in our criminal justice systems, as evidenced by Gallup poll results from 2020, which noted that 56% of Whites in the United States had a great deal or a lot of confidence in the police, compared with 19% of Blacks (J. M. Jones, 2020). Further, African Americans are far more likely than Whites to believe that the criminal justice system is biased against Blacks and more likely than Whites to point to racism in the criminal justice system as the reason for the large numbers of incarcerated young Black men (Unnever et al., 2011). Among other things, these findings highlight a significant difference between the groups with regard to belief in the police ensuring justice (Modules 12 and 33 address diversity within our justice systems).

Checks and Balances: Appellate Courts

There are mechanisms in place to provide balance and redress when individuals believe that justice has not been served by our system. For instance, our court systems include **appellate courts**, which may overturn decisions made at trial, for instance if it is believed that the trial court mishandled or otherwise made mistakes in adjudicating a case (see Module 21). Further, there are mechanisms in place to overturn the convictions of those who have been wrongfully convicted. The National Registry of Exonerations (2020) noted that 150 inmates were **exonerated** in 2019, meaning that their sentences were overturned and they were released from prison as a result of the discovery of new evidence suggesting that they did not commit the crime for which they were sentenced.

Types of Justice

Various types of justice address different issues or topics. Of particular importance to this unit (and book) is criminal justice. Other types of justice include procedural justice, retributive justice, restorative justice, social justice, and environmental justice.

Criminal Justice

Criminal justice simply refers to ensuring that lawbreakers are identified and processed appropriately. Criminal justice scholars discuss justice and what it means in relation to crime, social control, deviance, punishments, and law (Arrigo, 1999). Law enforcement, the courts, and correctional agencies are primarily responsible for ensuring justice for criminals. The United States also has distinct systems of justice for juveniles, who have their own court system and correctional agencies (see Modules 26 and 34, respectively).

Procedural Justice

Closely related to criminal justice is **procedural justice**, which refers to ensuring that justice-based processes are fair and just, regardless of individual differences or circumstances. As it relates to criminal justice, procedural justice is evident in the requirement that criminal justice practitioners follow procedural law in ensuring justice. For instance, police officers must follow proper procedure when making an arrest, judges must follow procedure when conducting trials, and probation officers must ensure that their clients are processed appropriately when they violate the terms of their probation. Procedural justice depends on rules being properly followed and consistently applied (Robinson, 2009).

Retributive Justice

Retributive justice is based on the belief that individuals should be treated as they treat others and that if an individual gained an unfair advantage through some illegitimate or illegal means, they must receive some form of punishment that accounts for and equalizes the injustice (Owen et al., 2015). This type of justice is based on the concepts of "just deserts" and **lex talionis**, which means "an eye for an eye." It is evident in current sentencing practices, perhaps most notably in states that use capital punishment, or the death penalty. A primary justification for the use of the death penalty is based on the belief that those who wrongfully kill others should receive the same fate (see Module 25 for a discussion of capital punishment).

Restorative Justice

Restorative justice is the idea that victims and the community should be more involved in repairing the harms resulting from criminal behavior. In addition, efforts should be made to ensure that the offender no longer chooses to break the law. Part of the restoration includes "repairing" offenders, for instance through making them aware of the harms associated with their actions (Van Ness & Strong, 1997). Key components of restorative justice include:

procedural justice A type of justice that ensures justice-based processes are fair and just, regardless of individual differences or circumstances

9 Sentencing

retributive justice A type of justice that is based on the belief that individuals should be treated as they treat others

lex talionis A Latin term that means "an eye for an eye"; it is the law of retaliation, or punishment that corresponds with the harms caused

Capital punishment is perhaps the most obvious form of retributive justice in the United States. Retributive justice is based on the belief that punishments should be equal to the harms imposed.

Should the government be permitted to impose this controversial form of punishment (i.e., capital punishment) for the sake of justice?

restorative justice A type of justice that proposes victims and the community should be more involved in repairing the harms resulting from criminal behavior and efforts should be made to ensure that offenders no longer choose to break the law

9 Sentencing

- victim–offender mediation, in which the two parties meet to discuss the incident in the presence of a mediator;
- family and community involvement;
- forgiveness in the sense that victims, their families, and community members actively attempt to reduce the harms associated with crime; and
- restitution, in efforts to address the harms suffered by the victim.

An example of restorative justice would be a judge imposing a sentence of restitution and a court-ordered mediation session in which the offender and victim meet with a mediator to discuss the crime. The offender could explain why they committed the crime (e.g., to obtain money to buy drugs), while the victim could explain to the offender how the incident changed their life (e.g., they are unable to work and now have many unpaid bills). The meeting would be designed to help better contextualize the incident and move toward repairing the harms associated with it. Modules 25 and 32 discuss restorative justice as a purpose of criminal sentencing and in practice.

Social Justice

social justice A type of justice that considers how societies provide for the needs of their members

Social justice considers how societies provide for the needs of their members. Of particular importance is the extent to which members of subgroups are treated equally (Arrigo, 1999). Social justice refers to ensuring that all members of society receive an equal share of the available benefits and resources. Such goods could include opportunities for advancement, healthcare, housing, personal wealth, and related goods (Clear & Cadora, 2003). One challenge with this and other types of justice is determining what constitutes fairness. For instance, there may be debate regarding whether a fair share should be based on one's contributions or input to society.

Environmental Justice

environmental justice A type of justice that is concerned with the fact that the poor and other less powerful groups are most likely to be affected by environmental harms

environmental equity The fair distribution of environmental risks across all demographic groups

environmental racism Policies, practices, or directives pertaining to environmental harms that disproportionately affect individuals, groups, or communities because of race

A subset of social justice, **environmental justice** is concerned with the fact that the poor and other less powerful groups are most likely to be affected by pollution, contaminated water, hazardous waste, and other forms of environmental damage. It attempts to give these groups a say in the enactment of policies to reduce environmental damage and health hazards. Of importance with regard to environmental justice is **environmental equity**, which involves the fair distribution of environmental risks across all demographic groups, and **environmental racism**, which refers to policies, practices, or directives that disproportionately affect individuals, groups, or communities because of race (Bullard, 1996). One more recent example of environmental racism was the tragedy of a contaminated water supply and the government's slow response in Flint, Michigan, where a majority of residents are Black. The crisis, which began in 2014, resulted from a decision by the government to change the city's source for drinking water in an effort to save money. The result was over 100,000 residents having lead in their drinking water (Eligon, 2016; Pulido, 2016).

Although environmental injustices have occurred throughout history, the study of environmental justice did not appear until the early 1980s. The shift in focus was influenced in large part by a study by the United Church of Christ's Commission for Racial Justice (United Church of Christ, 1987) and Robert Bullard's (1990) book *Dumping in Dixie*. Both works demonstrated that environmental harms were disproportionately located in areas with predominantly non-White residents living in poverty.

More recent evaluations of environmental justice suggest that the problem has improved. Researchers analyzed the penalties imposed by the federal government against corporations that violated environmental laws. They found that the monetary penalties imposed were not related to the demographics of the residents in the areas where the crimes were committed. In other words, companies that committed crimes in mostly minority and poor areas received comparable penalties to companies in other communities (Greife et al., 2015).

Models of Criminal Justice

In 1968, Herbert Packer (1968) wrote *The Limits of the Criminal Sanction*, in which he identified two competing models of criminal justice: the crime control model and the due process model. The models provide a means of thinking about justice-based practices and are not officially recognized in the sense that specific agencies formally declare themselves as subscribing to one or the other. Instead, they are used for analytical purposes. In discussing the need to balance the two approaches, Packer noted that "a person who subscribed to all of the values underlying one model to the exclusion of all of the values underlying the other would be rightly viewed as a fanatic" (p. 154).

The Crime Control Model

The **crime control model** assumes that suppressing crime is the most important aspect of justice-based actions. It proposes that aggressive and efficient enforcement of the law is the primary concern, and failure to do so results in a breakdown of public order. Packer (1968) noted that the crime control model resembles an assembly line, because individuals are swiftly processed through the system. While the crime control model does not completely disregard defendants' legal protections, it places less of an emphasis on them in light of concerns to suppress crime. The crime control model emphasizes:

- social control,
- making many arrests,
- processing cases in a diligent and efficient manner, and
- using the powers of the government to confront crime swiftly.

The adoption of this model often becomes necessary because of a lack of law enforcement and prosecutorial resources, with police departments and prosecutors being asked to "do more with less." Accordingly, the crime control model relies on police officers aggressively enforcing laws, courts swiftly processing the large numbers of individuals who are arrested, and the use of plea bargaining to settle cases (see Module 23) to address the large number of criminal cases.

    The basis of decision-making in the crime control model occurs at the pretrial stages, and discretion plays a significant role. Legally, individuals are considered innocent until proven guilty; however, the crime control model unofficially holds that individuals are generally viewed as guilty upon being arrested, which ultimately means that the use of discretion by police officers (e.g., to arrest or not arrest) is particularly powerful. Prosecutorial discretion during the screening of cases, plea bargaining, and other pretrial procedures also becomes increasingly important (see Module 23). As noted by Packer (1968), "The supposition is that the screening processes operated by police and prosecutors are reliable indicators of probable guilt" (p. 160).

● **Learning Objective 7.3:** Compare and contrast the crime control model and the due process model.

crime control model A model of criminal justice, which assumes that suppressing crime is the most important aspect of justice-based actions

3 Arrest

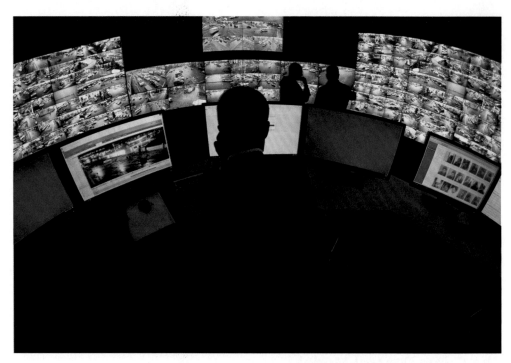

The crime control model emphasizes social control in efforts to ensure a safe society. It includes close monitoring of society, for instance in the form of cameras placed in public spaces. Some people argue that such efforts infringe on our individual rights.

Do you believe our actions are too closely monitored by government officials?

9 Sentencing

MYTHBUSTING

Most Criminal Cases Are Resolved at Trial

It is often believed that criminal cases are resolved at a trial, in which attorneys state and defend their cases, while a judge oversees the proceedings and a jury decides if the accused is guilty or not guilty. However, only about 5%–15% of criminal cases are resolved at trial. Most cases are resolved via informal negotiations between the prosecution and defense in what is known as plea bargaining. Plea bargaining typically involves defendants admitting guilt in exchange for a more favorable outcome of their case (e.g., a reduced sentence). The misperception that most cases are resolved at trial is largely a result of media and popular accounts disproportionately depicting cases going to trial.

The Due Process Model

due process model A model of criminal justice that emphasizes certainty and diligence; it is primarily concerned with recognizing due process rights and freedoms

The **due process model** is primarily concerned with recognizing due process rights and freedoms, even if doing so comes at the expense of controlling crime. Fact-finding and reliability are key components of the due process model, and the primary setting for decision-making is the courtroom. The due process model largely recognizes that individuals are innocent until proven guilty and relies on formal adjudication to determine guilt. Packer (1968) noted that the due process model resembles an obstacle course, with each stage of criminal case processing providing a different set of challenges for the state and protections for the accused. Evidence of the due process model is found, for instance, in the requirement that police officers must follow various procedural laws when conducting stops, searches, and arrests.

The due process model emphasizes:

- certainty and diligence—all cases should be handled with care to ensure that no innocent people are caught up in the system;
- equality—all individuals should be treated in a fair and just manner regardless of race, ethnicity, age, gender, or socioeconomic status;
- legal protections—all individuals should have a right to a trial, legal representation, and appeal; and
- legal guilt—all individuals should have the right to a trial and formal court procedures to assess whether they will be held accountable for a crime.

8 Trial

Comparing the Due Process and Crime Control Models

Perhaps the best way to understand the due process and crime control models is to compare them. Ultimately, justice-based practices that emphasize the due process model will result in fewer arrests and convictions and a lower error rate than those that adopt a crime control approach. However, under the due process model, there is a greater level of confidence that the individuals punished for their behavior are deserving. Figure 7.1 depicts this relationship using fictitious data.

Acts on behalf of criminal justice officials that generate claims of misbehavior often lead to questions regarding concerns for public safety in relation to individual rights. Are we willing to subject ourselves to a greater likelihood of wrongful involvement in the criminal justice system for the sake of reducing the number of criminals on the streets (i.e., the crime control model)? Or, would we prefer to let more guilty offenders go free but feel more confident that the individuals in the system truly deserve to be there (i.e., the due process model)? Table 7.1 compares the two models of criminal justice.

3 Arrest

Balancing Due Process and Crime Control: An Example

An example of the need to balance concerns for due process with crime control involves law enforcement's use of cell phone information. Cell phones provide location-based and related information that can facilitate the investigation of crime. Concerns abound, however, when it is believed that law enforcement has become too invasive in our lives. The American Civil Liberties Union obtained records from 205 police departments across the United States and found that cell phone tracking on behalf of all sizes of law enforcement agencies is more common than officials previously acknowledged. The tracking is often conducted with little or no court oversight (American Civil Liberties Union, 2013).

Cell phone tracking, which was mainly used by federal law enforcement agencies, is becoming increasingly popular among

Due process model

x x x
✓ ✓ ✓ ✓
✓ ✓ ✓ ✓
✓ ✓

Error rate (example) = 23%

Crime control model

x x x x x x x
x x x
✓ ✓ ✓ ✓ ✓ ✓
✓ ✓ ✓ ✓ ✓ ✓
✓

Error rate (example) = 44%

x = Wrongful arrests/convictions
✓ = Justified arrests/convictions

FIGURE 7.1. Arrests and Convictions Examples: The Due Process and Crime Control Models. There are fewer justified arrests and convictions and a lower error rate under the due process model than in the crime control model. There are also fewer wrongful arrests and convictions in the due process model. The data in this depiction were made up to demonstrate the differences between the two models.

Which of the two models would you prefer to live under? Which do you believe you live under?

TABLE 7.1. **Due Process and Crime Control Models Compared**

CRIME CONTROL MODEL	DUE PROCESS MODEL
Perceived guilt	Legal guilt
Plea bargaining/prosecutorial screening	Formal adjudication
Discretion pretrial	Discretion at trial
Assembly line	Obstacle course
Suppress crime	Protect individual rights
Higher error rate	Lower error rate
Higher number of arrests/convictions	Lower number of arrests/convictions
Efficiency	Reliability

local law enforcement agencies for both emergencies and nonemergency investigations. Cell phone companies are benefitting as well, because they charge police departments fees to trace a suspect's location, calls, or text messages. Companies have special law enforcement liaison teams that work with departments, although some departments have acquired their own tracking equipment to bypass the time and expense of having phone companies provide information for them. Many departments require warrants to use phone tracking in nonemergencies, although others use broad discretion to obtain the records on their own, and many departments struggle to understand and abide by the legal requirements associated with cell phone tracking. Despite this, the records obtained by the American Civil Liberties Union showed no indication of departments engaging in wiretapping, or listening to phone calls without court warrants.

Congress, the courts, and some states have passed legislation to tighten restrictions on cell phone tracking. For instance, in June 2018 the U.S. Supreme Court ruled that police generally need a search warrant if they wish to track criminal suspects' movements via their cell phones. It is likely that the struggle between concerns for due process (in this case as they pertain to protecting privacy) and crime control (using cell phone information to track offenders) will persist, and the courts will continue to make decisions as technology continues to develop (see Module 27 for discussion of the courts and technology).

The use of cell phone information in nonemergency situations and without a warrant to track individuals exemplifies Packer's (1968) crime control model. Law enforcement would argue that it is done to provide safety to everyone, even though critics argue that such tracking violates our rights. Ultimately, the goal is to identify and incorporate practices and policies that balance concerns for both crime control and due process. Doing so would help ensure both a decrease in crime and that rights are respected.

The System in Perspective

The "In the News" feature at the start of this module discusses the controversial case involving George Zimmerman and Trayvon Martin and the associated Stand Your Ground laws. Both the incident and the law highlight the complexities associated with finding justice. Some people believe Zimmerman acted properly, while others do not. Relatedly, some people believe the Stand Your Ground laws are necessary for our safety, while others believe they promote violence. There are times when controversial laws are passed and judges and juries make questionable decisions. However, the majority of justice-based practices are relatively fair and noncontroversial.

Summary

1. Learning Objective 7.1: *Define justice and illustrate the consequences of failing to administer justice.*

• Justice is generally defined as actions that are considered fair, equitable, and morally appropriate. The consequences of failing to administer justice include certain groups being treated differently than others, innocent people being punished, guilty people escaping justice, guilty people being punished more or less severely than would seem appropriate, and a loss of confidence in the criminal justice system.

2. Learning Objective 7.2: *Differentiate among the types of justice.*

• Criminal justice involves ensuring that offenders are identified and processed in a fair manner. Procedural justice refers to ensuring that the proper methods are used in identifying and processing the accused. Retributive justice holds that individuals should be treated as they treat others. Restorative justice seeks to repair the harms caused by offenders and restore offenders as law-abiding citizens. Social justice is concerned with providing for the needs of all members of society. Environmental justice addresses the proximity of environmental harms to less powerful groups.

3. Learning Objective 7.3: *Compare and contrast the crime control model and the due process model.*

• The crime control model is concerned with the suppression of crime and the efficient administration of justice. It has a higher error rate than the due process model, encourages plea bargaining, and results in a higher number of arrests and convictions. The due process model is concerned with respecting individual rights and has a lower error rate than the crime control model. It also results in fewer arrests and convictions than the crime control model.

Questions for Critical Thinking

1. How would you define the term *justice*? Can any of the terms you use in your definition be interpreted in multiple ways?

2. How are the types of justice discussed in this module related to one another? Which ones overlap to a greater extent than others?

3. Why do you believe some criminal justice officials or agencies might fluctuate between the due process model and the crime control model under different circumstances?

Key Terms

appellate courts
Black Lives Matter
crime control model
due process model
environmental equity
environmental justice
environmental racism

exonerated
justice
lex talionis
procedural justice
restorative justice
retributive justice
social justice

For digital learning resources, please go to
https://www.oup.com/he/burns1e

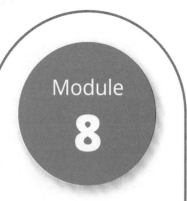

Module

8

Understanding Criminal Law

Laws provide the "boundaries" within which we must behave. They provide guidance and help create an orderly society. Ensuring justice requires that we have sound, enforceable laws and officials who are designated to make sure we all abide by them.

Do you believe our laws ensure equal justice under the law?

Laws provide the rules by which we all must abide. With regard to crime, criminal law notes general behaviors that are deemed illegal and prescribes punishments for the commission of those acts. Such laws largely guide the actions of the criminal justice system, control human behavior, and are symbolic in the sense that they signify that a legitimate system of justice exists to control human behavior. This module covers criminal law, beginning with a discussion of the origins and sources of criminal law. This discussion is followed by a comparison of criminal and civil law. This module ends with an examination of the various defenses that are used in criminal law.

9 Sentencing

1 Criminal Act

Was Justice Served?

In 2018, a Texas man, James Miller, was found guilty of criminally negligent homicide in the 2015 death of Daniel Spencer. Miller was sentenced to 10 years of probation, 6 months in jail, 100 hours of community service, and $11,000 in restitution to the victim's family. He must also wear an alcohol monitoring device for at least a year (Wong, 2018).

The case began when Spencer invited Miller to his home to drink and play music. According to Miller's testimony, Spencer made sexual advances and began moving toward Miller. Miller then stabbed Spencer twice, resulting in his death. At trial, Miller's attorney cited a defense sometimes called "gay panic," in which a defendant can claim that a victim's sexual preferences in conjunction with sexual advances can be used as justification for a violent crime. This defense is permitted in 48 states, although it is controversial. Miller received the criminally *negligent* homicide conviction instead of the criminal homicide (murder) conviction some people thought he deserved (Wong, 2018).

This case leads to several questions regarding justice in our courts. Primary among the questions is whether or not gay panic and related defenses (e.g., "trans panic," which is similar to gay panic although it pertains to gender identity) should be considered as defenses. Further, to some observers the reduced charge and sentence received in this case suggest that reacting violently to a person's sexual orientation is acceptable to some extent. Do you believe gay panic and related defenses are acceptable? Should the charges have been reduced and the sentence be less severe in this case? Why or why not?

8 Trial

Origins of Criminal Law

Criminal law can be traced back to roughly 1754 B.C. In the United States it is largely based on what existed in England when settlers left the country and established the colonies in America along the eastern coast.

The Earliest Laws

One of the earliest known criminal codes was the **Code of Hammurabi** (offered circa 1760 B.C.), which was a set of laws that addressed family law, property rights, and other civil matters. The Babylonian code also provided protections for victims of crimes. King Hammurabi introduced lex talionis, which means "punishment by retaliation." It is the basis of the eye for an eye approach, which means that the

● **Learning Objective 8.1:** Summarize the origins of criminal law in the United States.

Code of Hammurabi The first known legal code; it identified crimes, noted punishments for criminal behavior, and provided settlements for common conflicts

punishment should fit the crime (Wallace & Roberson, 2006). The code was categorized into five sections, including:

- a penal or code of laws;
- a manual of instruction for justice officials and witnesses;
- a handbook of rights and duties of husbands, wives, and children;
- a set of regulations establishing wages and prices; and
- a code of ethics for merchants, doctors, and officials (Roberson et al., 2013).

Twelve Tables Early Roman law created around 450 B.C. that consolidated earlier rules, customs, and traditions into codified law; each table addressed particular aspects of justice

Other early important sources of law include Roman law, particularly the **Twelve Tables**. This codified law, named as such because it was written on 12 ivory tables, was placed in a location for all Romans to see. The Twelve Tables, created around 450 B.C., were punitive in nature (Worrall & Moore, 2014) and consolidated earlier rules, customs, and traditions into codified law. Each table addressed particular aspects of justice. For example, Table I addressed pretrial procedures, and Table II addressed trials.

English Influences

common law Laws adopted by colonists; the laws originated from the early and unwritten laws of England and are derived from ancient practices and customs that have been adopted throughout history

criminal codes Definitions of crimes and their associated penalties as passed by elected legislatures

Criminal law in the United States is grounded in English heritage and is largely based on customs, traditions, and written codes. English colonists who landed in America were tasked with the difficult burden of creating a legitimate system of justice. Their early system of justice recognized **common law**—laws originating from early and unwritten laws in England and derived from ancient practices and customs of various civilizations throughout history. Common law crimes were publicly recognized long before the creation of legislatures, evolved over time, and eventually were replaced by **criminal codes**, which are definitions of crimes and their associated penalties as passed by elected legislatures.

democracy A system of government in which power is delegated to the people

Of particular importance to the colonists was allowing the people to maintain power. The United States is a **democracy**—a term that is derived from two Greek words, *demos* and *kratos*, which combined refer to "power to the people." The democratic approach to government differs from that of some other countries in which there may be:

monarchies Governments headed by royalty in the form of a king or queen

- **monarchies**, which are headed by royalty in the form of a king or queen;
- **oligarchies**, which are headed by a small group of powerful individuals; or
- **dictatorships**, in which one individual maintains power.

oligarchies Systems of government in which power is maintained by a small group of powerful individuals

In democratic countries, such as the United States, power is granted to the people in their ability to hold open elections and generally voice their support or concern for legislation.

dictatorship A system of government in which one individual maintains power

Sources of Criminal Law

The United States is organized around the concept of federalism, which means that power is divided between a central government (in the case of the United States, the national or federal government) and its constituents (in the United States, the states). **Legislatures**, which are legislative bodies that have the power to enact laws, exist within the federal government (Congress) and each of the 50 state governments. Congress serves as the lawmaking branch of the federal government and state legislatures enact laws in their respective states. Aside from legislatures, governmental authority exists in two other branches. The **executive branch** largely enforces the law, and the **judicial branch** primarily interprets the law (Worrall & Moore, 2014).

Criminal law in the United States is primarily found in several sources, including:

- the U.S. Constitution,
- state constitutions,
- the United States Code and state criminal codes,
- municipal ordinances,
- case law, and
- administrative law.

The U.S. Constitution

The **U.S. Constitution** is the supreme law of the land. It identifies the:

- powers of government,
- limitations associated with those powers, and
- protections granted to individuals.

The Constitution, along with the Bill of Rights and other amendments, is the basis on which all laws exist. Legislation in all areas ultimately must conform to constitutional rights and protections.

The **Bill of Rights** consists of the first 10 amendments added to the U.S. Constitution. The amendments were adopted in 1789 and ratified by the states in 1791. Several of the 10 amendments within the Bill of Rights are particularly important with regard to criminal law and criminal justice in general.

- The **First Amendment** protects several basic liberties, including the freedoms of religion, of speech, of the press, to petition the government (e.g., complain to or seek its assistance), and to assemble in groups. The right to freedom of speech is particularly important with regard to hate crime legislation (see Module 3).

- The **Second Amendment** provides the right for people to keep and bear arms and has been and is the focus of much analysis with regard to gun control.

- The **Fourth Amendment** protects individuals from unreasonable searches and seizures and notes that no warrants will be issued without probable cause, supported by oath or affirmation and describing the place to be searched and the persons or items to be seized.

- The **Fifth Amendment** protects individuals from double jeopardy (being tried for the same crime twice) and self-incrimination. It also provides for the right to a grand jury in serious crimes and ensures that the accused is provided due process.

- The **Sixth Amendment** provides various rights to individuals, especially at trial. For instance, it provides for the right to counsel, the right to a trial by a jury, the right to an impartial jury, the right to confront and summon witnesses, the right to a speedy and public trial, and the right to be informed of the nature and cause of the accusation.

- The **Eighth Amendment** prohibits cruel and unusual punishment, excessive bail, and excessive fines.

Although not part of the Bill of Rights, the **14th Amendment** also addresses criminal law in noting, "nor shall any State deprive any person of life, liberty, or property, without due process of the law." **Due process** refers to the legal safeguards that ensure that individuals are treated in a fair and just manner during legal proceedings.

● **Learning Objective 8.2:** Identify and describe the primary sources of criminal law.

legislatures
Legislative bodies that have the power to enact laws

executive branch
The branch of government that primarily enforces the law

judicial branch The branch of government that primarily interprets the law

U.S. Constitution
The supreme law in the United States; it identifies the powers of government, the limitations associated with those powers, and the protections granted to individuals

Bill of Rights The first 10 amendments added to the U.S. Constitution

6 Grand Jury/ Preliminary Hearing

8 Trial

First Amendment
Protects several basic liberties, including the freedom of religion, of speech, of the press, to petition the government, and to assemble in groups

The U.S. Constitution, including the Bill of Rights, addresses several important issues related to criminal law. Various amendments provide protections for our individual rights.

Do you believe the Constitution is the most significant influence on criminal justice-related practices? Why or why not?

Second Amendment

Provides the right for people to keep and bear arms; it has been and is the focus of much analysis with regard to gun control

Fourth Amendment

An amendment to the U.S. Constitution that protects individuals from unreasonable searches and seizures and notes that no warrants will be issued without probable cause, supported by oath or affirmation and describing the place to be searched and the persons or items to be seized

Fifth Amendment

An amendment to the U.S. Constitution that protects individuals from double jeopardy and self-incrimination; it also provides for the right to a grand jury in serious crimes and ensures that the accused is provided due process

Sixth Amendment

Provides various rights to defendants at trial

Two particularly important due process protections in criminal court cases are the presumption of innocence and the need for the prosecution to establish "proof beyond a reasonable doubt" to secure convictions. These due process protections help ensure that individuals enter the judicial system innocent until proven guilty via the presentation of substantial evidence.

Initially, the Bill of Rights applied strictly to the federal government, which meant that states and municipalities were not required to recognize the rights. However, the Supreme Court incorporated most of the provisions of the Bill of Rights into the 14th Amendment's due process clause and applied them to the states beginning in the late 1930s.

State Constitutions

Each state has a constitution that often reflects the U.S. Constitution, although state constitutions are usually more detailed and often a bit longer (Worrall & Moore, 2014). They typically include a bill of rights, which addresses issues related to crime and justice, similar to the U.S. Constitution.

The protections provided in the Bill of Rights that accompanies the U.S. Constitution are the minimum protections that must be extended to individuals facing prosecution. Federal and state law and state constitutions can expand these rights to provide additional protections for the accused.

The United States Code and State Criminal Codes

Federal laws are codified in Title 18 of the **United States Code**, which is the official compilation of federal laws in the United States, and are passed by Congress. Title 18 of the code consists of five parts that address:

- crimes,
- criminal procedure,
- prisons and prisoners,
- corrections of youthful offenders, and
- immunity of witnesses.

Each state has its own criminal codes that are passed by the state legislative bodies, as do other units of governments, such as counties and cities.

Municipal Ordinances

Municipalities may create ordinances (rules created by a municipality) by which they expect individuals to abide. All of these legal codes spell out the criminal laws in each of these areas, allowing cities, towns, and villages to address needs or wants specific to their jurisdiction. Municipal ordinances can be more restrictive than the U.S. and state constitutions. They cannot be more permissive. For instance, a municipal ordinance could not permit the use of carrying a concealed weapon if the state constitution prohibits doing so.

Case Law

Case law is based on the concept of **stare decisis**, which is a Latin term for "stand by the decision." Such judicial precedent means that decisions rendered in earlier court cases set precedent for future cases that are similar in nature. Accordingly, case law is a contributor to criminal law, as the decisions made in earlier cases, based on interpretations of constitutions and statutes, provide standards for subsequent cases. Such judge-made laws demonstrate the quasilegislative function of the courts, because they have some powers to set laws. The use of case law expedites the judicial process since courts can decide cases with much less energy and time as a result of the work exerted in earlier cases.

Administrative Law

In *United States v. Grimaud* (1911), the U.S. Supreme Court ruled that Congress could permit an administrative agency to pass regulations that could be enforced via criminal penalties. As such, **administrative law** contributes to criminal law. It consists of laws, rules, and regulations that address issues such as environmental, consumer, workplace, and public health protections. Federal, state, and local regulatory agencies that have jurisdiction over particular areas often enforce administrative laws. They generally prefer compliance instead of enforcement (e.g., through the use of recalls or warnings) because they have the difficult challenge of balancing consumer and corporate interests. Criminal penalties, however, exist for more egregious violations. For instance, in 2017 the automaker Volkswagen paid a $2.8 billion fine for altering its vehicles so that emissions controls would only work to prevent emissions during emissions tests.

Criminal Versus Civil Law

Civil law addresses disputes between individuals, businesses, and government agencies. It is concerned with laws pertaining to:

- family issues (e.g., marriage, divorce);
- business practices (e.g., contracts, false advertising, the production of faulty products); and
- probate law (e.g., wills, trusts).

Generally, civil law involves **tort law** (which addresses wrongs between individuals and the associated damages), property law, and contract law. In many ways, it is both similar to and different from criminal law.

Civil law and criminal law are similar in the sense that they both:

- control human behavior,
- identify behaviors that are unacceptable,
- include sanctions for wrongful behavior, and
- share some common areas of legal jurisdiction (for example, when a federal regulatory agency has the power to file either criminal or civil charges against automobile companies that fail to produce safe vehicles).

Civil and criminal law differ in the following respects:

- *Scope:* Civil law addresses wrongs between individuals, and criminal law involves offenses against the state. As such, the state calls the accused to court under criminal law, while individuals who believe they have been wronged bring the accused to court in civil law.
- *Sanctions:* The sanction associated with violation of the criminal law can be incarceration or death, while monetary payments are primarily used in civil cases.

Eighth Amendment An amendment to the U.S. Constitution that prohibits cruel and unusual punishment, excessive bail, and excessive fines

14th Amendment An amendment to the U.S. Constitution that provides due process of law

due process The legal safeguard that ensures individuals are treated in a fair and just manner during legal proceedings

United States Code The official compilation of federal laws in the United States

● **Learning Objective 8.3:** Compare and contrast criminal and civil and law.

case law Law that stipulates decisions rendered in earlier cases set precedent for future cases that are similar in nature

stare decisis A Latin term for "stand by the decision"; it is the concept on which case law is based

administrative law Laws, rules, and regulations that address issues such as environmental, consumer, workplace, and public health protections

civil law A body of law that addresses disputes between individuals, businesses, and government agencies

tort law Laws that address wrongs between individuals and the associated damages

11 Appeal

preponderance of evidence The standard typically used to win in civil courts; it requires greater than 50% of the evidence supporting one side or the other

---

● **Learning Objective 8.4:** Explain the types of affirmative defenses in criminal law.

---

proof beyond a reasonable doubt The highest standard of proof used in criminal courts; it requires much certainty that the accused is responsible for the act(s) in question

defenses Responses offered by defendants who seek to demonstrate that they are not legally liable for the crime in question

alibi A defense through which defendants claim that they were physically somewhere other than the crime scene at the time of the crime and therefore could not have committed the offense

affirmative defense A defense offered by defendants who claim responsibility for the actions that caused the harm in a crime, although they provide reasons (defenses) for why they are not criminally responsible

- *Monetary penalties:* Individuals in civil court keep any compensation for damages in civil court, while fines paid in criminal court go to the state.
- *Appeals:* The government typically does not appeal in criminal court, although both parties can appeal in civil court.
- *Standard of proof:* In civil court the standard of proof is generally a **preponderance of evidence**, which means that greater than 50% of the evidence points to something. In criminal court, prosecutors must demonstrate **proof beyond a reasonable doubt** for a conviction, which is the highest standard of proof used in courts and requires much certainty that the accused is responsible for the act(s) in question.

Defenses in Criminal Law

Defenses are responses offered by defendants who seek to demonstrate that they are not liable for the crime in question. Defendants do not have to offer a defense, because it is the prosecutor's responsibility to provide proof beyond a reasonable doubt that a defendant is indeed guilty. If they choose to offer a defense, defendants must introduce evidence to support their claims.

Alibis and Affirmative Defenses

In Latin, the term **alibi** means "somewhere else." Defendants use alibis when they claim that they were physically somewhere else other than the crime scene at the time of the crime and therefore could not have committed the offense. Defendants may use witnesses and enter tangible evidence to support the claim.

Defendants may also enter an **affirmative defense** in which they claim responsibility for the actions that caused the harm in a crime, although they provide reasons (defenses) for why they are not criminally responsible. The various types of affirmative defenses include:

- justifications,
- excuses, and
- procedural defenses.

Justifications

Justification defenses are used when defendants claim that they are responsible for the act in question, but claim their act was acceptable or permitted based on the situation and circumstances. For instance, someone may have killed another person and be charged with murder; however, they may offer the defense that they killed the other person in self-defense or to protect others from being killed. The following are among the more common justification defenses:

- self-defense
- defense of home and property
- defense of others
- necessity
- consent
- resisting unlawful arrest

SELF-DEFENSE

Defendants may claim that they acted in **self-defense** if their actions were taken to protect themselves and they used only as much force as reasonably necessary to thwart the attack, or what is known as proportionality. This defense is generally valid only in unprovoked attacks where there is imminent danger and a lack of suitable alternatives. For instance, defendants cannot claim they acted in self-defense if they were the target of mild aggression (e.g., an insult) and responded with an aggressive response (e.g., the attempt to kill). The "reasonable person" standard is used to determine the extent to which this defense is valid. In other words, the courts consider how a reasonable person would have reacted in the situation, and deadly force is not a reasonable response to nondeadly force. The principle of reasonableness applies to self-defense, protection of others, and protection of property.

DEFENSE OF PROPERTY

Defendants may claim that they were defending their property when they committed the harm in question, although there are some limitations. Generally, one cannot use deadly force to protect property. The defense is restricted to one's premises or property that is in one's possession, such as a cell phone or purse. The defense is not permitted when an individual seeks to retain possession of their property. In addition, the use of mechanical devices, such as electronic fences that shock those who touch them, are not permitted.

The **Model Penal Code and Commentaries** (which was created by the American Law Institute in 1985 to address the existing piecemeal laws that were based on public perception and lacked thorough examination) and others suggest that the loss of life is more important than the loss of property, and thus deadly force generally is not justifiable to protect property. However, there are instances when an armed individual seeks to commit property crime. In these cases, deadly force could potentially be acceptable. Some states, such as Texas, permit deadly force to protect land, natural gas, and other particular types of property (Lawserver, 2018).

DEFENSE OF OTHERS

Defense of others is used when defendants claim their harmful activity was warranted to prevent the additional harm of others. Historically, one could only use this defense if the victim was related. The requirement has been expanded to include all victims, and the third party in this case must act within the same guidelines that apply for the claim of self-defense (e.g., reasonableness). The third party must ensure that they are assisting an innocent victim and cannot simply join a fight to assist a friend who started the fight and may be losing the battle.

NECESSITY

Defendants sometimes claim that their harmful behavior should not be considered criminal because they were acting out of need, or **necessity**. The necessity defense pertains to instances in which an individual had to make a choice between two evils and the apparent crime was the lesser of the two options. The use of necessity as a defense requires a threat of imminent injury for which there are no acceptable alternatives other than their actions, which typically would be considered a crime. For instance, consider the case of lost hikers who are suffering from hypothermia and encounter an abandoned car in a secluded area. They realize the owner is nowhere to be found, so they take the car to save themselves. In other words, the apparent motor vehicle theft was committed out of

justification defenses A series of defenses that are used when defendants claim that they are responsible for the act in question, but their actions were acceptable or permitted based on the situation and circumstances

self-defense
A defense in which defendants claim that their actions were necessary to repel an imminent harm

Model Penal Code and Commentaries
A guideline for states to follow with regard to rational, effective criminal law

Self-defense is a justification defense in which the accused claims that they committed the act in question, but did so to protect themselves.

What problems do you see with the reasonableness standard used to determine the appropriateness of the amount of force one can use to protect themselves?

necessity A defense in which defendants claim that their harmful behavior should not be considered criminal because they were acting out of need

consent A defense in which the defendant claims that a harmful act should not be considered a crime because the victim consented

3 Arrest

Excuses Defenses in which the accused admits to the act in question but states that they are not criminally responsible for doing so because extraordinary circumstances caused them to commit the crime

necessity. This defense can be clouded by the fact that courts consider the extent to which individuals placed themselves in the predicament. In other words, this defense cannot be used if the defendant contributed to the threatened harm.

CONSENT

Some defendants claim that their harmful act should not be considered a crime because the victim consented. In other words, the victim agreed to suffer the harm. **Consent** as a defense provides several challenges for the courts, primarily because a crime is considered a harm against society, not a harm against an individual. The use of consent as a defense is permitted in some cases, however, and the defendant must demonstrate that the consent was voluntary, the victim clearly understood the situation, and no trickery, duress, or coercion was involved. Consent cannot be granted after the harm has occurred. Consent is sometimes brought up in rape and sexual assault cases, in which the accused claims that sexual intercourse occurred, but it was agreed on prior to the act.

RESISTING UNLAWFUL ARREST

Defendants accused of resisting arrest or obstruction of justice may claim that their actions were lawful, if they can demonstrate that they were the subject of excessive force. Some states have laws that enable defendants to use force against officers who are using too much force, but the laws generally do not apply in cases in which the suspect initially used force. The amount of force used against the police must not be excessive.

Excuses

Excuses are similar to justifications in the sense that the individuals admit to the act in question; however, they state that they are not criminally responsible as a result of extraordinary circumstances. Excuse defenses are used when an action was argued to be:

- involuntary (e.g., when someone becomes intoxicated and commits a crime after another person puts drugs in their nonalcoholic drink),
- the product of a cognitive deficiency, or
- the result of outside forces.

Other factors such as age may also be offered to excuse the accused from being criminally responsible for what appears to be a crime. The following are among the more commonly used excuses:

- mistake
- duress
- infancy
- involuntary intoxication
- insanity
- various syndromes

In court, the burden is on defendants to prove that their actions should be excused.

MISTAKE

The requirement that a crime requires mens rea (intent) poses particular challenges for the courts. Establishing intent can be tricky, and requiring it to be present in criminal cases creates additional challenges. Defendants sometimes claim that they committed an apparent crime by mistake. For instance, they may claim that they believed there was no law restricting such action(s), or they simply unknowingly engaged in a wrongful activity (e.g., honestly taking the wrong coat from a coatroom). In such cases there would be no intent, even though the defendant broke the law. Mistake of fact is sometimes permissible as a defense and largely depends on the circumstances of the case. Ultimately, courts consider the honesty and legitimacy in mistake defenses.

DURESS

Duress, which is sometimes referred to as coercion, involves an individual committing a harm based on a threat of harm from another person or persons. It is an individual being coerced, or forced into doing something they otherwise would not have done. Duress is similar to necessity, because they both involve individuals doing something beyond their own volition. However, they differ in the sense that duress essentially does not include as much decision-making, because the threat involved leaves little option.

> **duress** Sometimes referred to as coercion; it involves an individual committing a harm based on a threat of harm from another person or persons

Consider the case in which an individual robs a bank to protect family members who have been kidnapped (the kidnappers have threatened to harm the family members if the individual does not commit the crime). The "bank robber" could claim that they were under duress. There must be a reasonable cause to believe that one's physical well-being is being threatened or that a related serious threat exists for duress to be successfully used as a defense.

INFANCY

Age can also be used as a defense in criminal court. Historically, it has been believed that children under the age of seven are unable to adequately form mens rea and thus have not been held criminally accountable for their misbehavior. Most states require that offenders be at least seven years old before they can be charged with **delinquency**, which is the term used for crimes committed by juveniles.

> **delinquency** Behavior that violates the criminal code and is committed by youth who have not reached a statutorily prescribed age

INVOLUNTARY INTOXICATION

Intoxication can be used as a defense only if the intoxication was involuntary. Intoxication is not restricted to alcohol; individuals who involuntarily become intoxicated as a result of drug use may also offer this defense. Involuntary intoxication occurs in several ways, including:

- the accidental ingestion of alcohol or drugs,
- someone forcing or deceiving another person into drinking alcohol or taking drugs,
- the unexpected side effects from prescribed medications, and
- individuals unknowingly consuming items that have been laced with drugs.

INSANITY

One of the more controversial defenses in criminal law is insanity, which is a legal, not a medical, concept. Of particular concern for the insanity defense is whether a defendant is criminally liable given their mental state at the time. Mental illnesses may or may not be considered insanity, and there are several tests used to determine whether the insanity defense can be used.

Four states (Kansas, Montana, Idaho, and Utah) do not permit the insanity defense, although these states do note that mental disorder can be introduced as evidence to disprove intent, but not necessarily acquit the defendant. These four states dropped the insanity defense in the early 1980s after the attempted assassination of President Ronald Reagan by John Hinckley, who was found not guilty by reason of insanity. In November 2012, the U.S. Supreme Court declined to hear a case from Idaho, which claimed that the insanity defense should be a constitutional right. The Supreme Court has not ruled on whether the Eighth Amendment's protection from cruel and unusual punishment and/or the 14th Amendment's due process clause dictates that all states have the insanity defense (Richey, 2012).

Other states use varying standards for proving the insanity defense. Generally, most states use the definitions found in either the M'Naghten or the American Law Institute Model Penal Code, or what is sometimes referred to as the substantial capacity test. Tests for insanity include the following:

M'Naghten test
The oldest test for insanity; it considers a defendant's intellectual capacity at the time of the offense to understand what they were doing was right or wrong

substantial capacity test A test for insanity that focuses on whether the defendant had substantial capacity, as opposed to total capacity, to understand the rightfulness of their actions

irresistible impulse test An insanity defense that is used when defendants suffer from a mental illness that prevented them from controlling their actions

Durham test A test for insanity holding that a defendant is not criminally responsible if their actions were part of a mental disease or defect

- The **M'Naghten test** is the oldest test, and it considers a defendant's intellectual capacity at the time of the offense to understand that what they were doing was right or wrong. Defendants using this defense must demonstrate that they did not know what they were doing or did not know their actions were wrong.

- The **substantial capacity test** focuses on whether the defendant had substantial capacity, as opposed to total capacity, to understand the rightfulness of their actions. Defendants must demonstrate that they lacked the substantial capacity to appreciate the wrongfulness of their conduct or their ability to control it.

- The **irresistible impulse test** is used when a defendant suffers from a mental illness that prevented control of one's actions.

- The **Durham test** simply holds that a defendant is not criminally responsible if the actions were part of a mental disease or defect.

To be sure, there is some overlap between these defenses, and states sometimes use variations of them. Defendants found not guilty by reason of insanity are not legally guilty and thus are not subject to criminal punishments. They are, however, likely to be civilly committed to psychiatric institutions (Borum & Fulero, 1999).

VARIOUS SYNDROMES
Beginning in the 1970s, the courts permitted claims of various syndromes or disorders that were alleged to affect one's mental state to be used as defenses. These defenses have generated much controversy. Among them are the battered spouse syndrome, post–traumatic stress disorder, and premenstrual syndrome defenses.

- Defendants using the **battered spouse syndrome defense** claim that they were justified in killing or seriously injuring their spouse in light of the abuses they regularly sustained at the hands of their partner and the belief that their life was in danger. Those who use this defense must demonstrate that they feared for their lives.

MYTHBUSTING
The Insanity Defense Is Commonly Used

Many people in society believe the insanity defense is used quite often. However, this defense is only used in about 1% of all cases in the United States and is successful in only about 25% of those cases (Schouten, 2012). Cases involving the insanity defense are generally more likely than other cases to draw the attention of the media, making them appear much more common. Earlier research supported the findings that relatively few cases involve the insanity defense and the defense has a relatively low success rate in the United States (e.g., Steadman, 1985).

- **Post–traumatic stress disorder** has been used as a defense in cases involving individuals who are feeling the mental effects (e.g., stress) of having suffered from some traumatic incident. Symptoms of post–traumatic stress disorder include intense fear or feelings of helplessness, a numbing of the arousal system, anxiety, and anger. The disorder was largely brought to the public's attention following the Vietnam War, when many returning veterans displayed the symptoms, and has largely returned to the public's attention following the wars in Iraq and Afghanistan. The defense requires defendants to demonstrate that the impairment restricted them from forming the necessary intent to commit the crime. Returning war veterans are not the only groups susceptible to the disorder; police officers are at an increased risk as well (see Module 13).

- The American Psychiatric Association recognized **premenstrual dysphoric disorder** as a severe form of premenstrual syndrome. This ailment has been introduced as a defense because some women have claimed that the effects of menstruation (e.g., cramps, nausea, irritability, anxiety, and depression) contributed to their violent behavior. Premenstrual syndrome as a criminal defense was first used in a 1982 case in which a mother was charged with assaulting her child and argued that she suffered from the disorder at the time of the assault (Bird, 1982). The case concluded in a plea bargain, and thus the merits of the defense were not tested. The defense has been used in a handful of other cases, to varying degrees of success.

Procedural Defenses

Laws can be categorized as substantive criminal law and procedural law. **Substantive law** refers to what most people think of when they consider the law: the rules that define criminal behaviors and identify the punishments associated with them. **Procedural law**, in contrast, addresses the legal methods by which the substantive law must be enforced or applied. Primarily, it largely dictates the official behavior of individuals who work in our justice systems. For instance, police officers follow procedural law when they respect a suspect's Fourth Amendment rights against unreasonable seizures, and correctional officers abide by procedural law when they follow the legal requirements for handling a disruptive inmate. The failure of a government official to follow procedural law could result in a defendant being acquitted in court, because a defendant could use a **procedural defense**.

Procedural defenses protect defendants from discriminatory justice-based actions and help ensure that official procedure is followed. They are not related to the actions associated with the crime or the defendant's culpability. These defenses pertain to legal procedure and/or constitutional law. Among the more common procedural defenses are:

- entrapment,
- double jeopardy,
- prosecutorial misconduct,
- expiration of the statute of limitations, and
- police misconduct.

ENTRAPMENT

Defendants use the **entrapment** defense when they claim that government agents induced them into committing a crime. It requires a representative of the government encouraging an individual to commit a crime that they otherwise would have not committed. For instance, defendants who are strongly persuaded to purchase drugs from undercover agents may use this defense, particularly if they initially had no interest in buying drugs.

---

battered spouse syndrome defense
A defense in which defendants claim that they were justified in killing or seriously injuring their spouse in light of the abuses they regularly sustained at the hands of their partner and the belief that their life was in danger

post–traumatic stress disorder
A mental illness in individuals exposed to a traumatic event that causes them to relive the event and experience extended periods of nervousness and being "on edge"; it is sometimes used as a defense in which defendants claim that their behavior was attributed to the mental effects of having suffered from some traumatic incident

substantive law
Laws that dictate our everyday behavior; they define criminal behaviors and identify the punishments associated with them

premenstrual dysphoric disorder
A defense used by some women who claim that the effects of menstruation contributed to their violent behavior

procedural law Laws that address the legal methods by which substantive law must be enforced or applied

procedural defense
A defense in which a defendant claims that a government official failed to follow procedural law

entrapment A defense in which defendants claim that government agents induced them into committing a crime

The entrapment defense is grounded in the belief that the government should not encourage people to commit crime and is designed to protect innocent people and deter police misconduct. Entrapment is primarily used in victimless or consensual crimes such as prostitution, gambling, and drug offenses. It can only be used as a defense in cases involving government agents, including individuals working with the police (e.g., informants) who are considered part of the government.

DOUBLE JEOPARDY

double jeopardy Being tried for the same crime twice; it is prohibited by the Fifth Amendment

Double jeopardy refers to an individual being tried for the same crime on multiple occasions. The Fifth Amendment protects against this in noting, "nor shall any person be subject for the same offence to be twice put in jeopardy of life or limb." It is possible, however, that an individual can be tried twice for the same crime if additional evidence is uncovered and the prosecution has a stronger case.

PROSECUTORIAL MISCONDUCT

Prosecutorial misconduct can exist in various forms, for instance when prosecutors knowingly allow false testimony or evidence or fail to disclose evidence that favors a defendant. Prosecutorial misconduct occurs infrequently, but when it does, the accused may use it as a defense.

EXPIRATION OF THE STATUTE OF LIMITATIONS

statute of limitations A maximum time frame during which criminal charges can be filed

Most crimes have a **statute of limitations**, or a maximum time frame during which criminal charges can be filed. Some crimes, such as murder, have no time limitations. Individuals who commit crimes for which there are limitations and are charged after the expiration date cannot be prosecuted for their behavior.

Procedural defenses are used by defendants who claim that government officials failed to follow the law and proper procedure in the course of their responsibilities. Police misconduct, including lying on the witness stand, may result in defendants being excused for the crimes they committed.

Should defendants be excused for their crime if government officials break the law? Why or why not?

POLICE MISCONDUCT

Police misconduct can also be grounds for a criminal defense. For instance, defendants may be excused for their behavior when officers lie on the witness stand or plant incriminating evidence on suspects (see Module 16 for a discussion of police misconduct).

The System in Perspective

The "In the News" feature at the start of this module describes how James Miller used the gay panic defense in court after killing a man. Miller claimed that he killed the victim, Daniel Spencer, after Spencer made sexual advances and began moving toward him. As a result of using this controversial defense, Miller received a less severe sentence. Legally, Miller was permitted to use this defense, and several other nontraditional defenses have been used in court. It is ultimately up to legislators and the courts to determine the appropriateness of these defenses.

While laws serve many important purposes, they can be the subject of controversy. What one group of individuals might find to be a helpful, necessary law for a safer and more orderly society, another group might find to be a severe violation of their individual rights. It can be difficult to create legislation that is going to appease everyone, and thus legislators must consider multiple factors when constructing, supporting, or arguing against legislative acts.

Summary

1. Learning Objective 8.1: *Summarize the origins of criminal law in the United States.*

- Criminal law in the United States has been impacted by various early legal developments, including the Code of Hammurabi, a set of laws that addressed family law, property rights, and other civil matters. It also provided protections for victims of crimes. Other early important sources of law include Roman law, particularly the Twelve Tables, which was codified law written on 12 ivory tables for all Romans to see. Criminal law in the United States is also heavily grounded in English heritage and is largely based on customs, traditions, and written codes.

2. Learning Objective 8.2: *Identify and describe the primary sources of criminal law.*

- Criminal law in the United States is primarily found in several sources, including the U.S. Constitution, state constitutions, the United States Code, state criminal codes, municipal ordinances, case law, and administrative law. The U.S. Constitution identifies the powers of

government, the limitations associated with those powers, and the protections granted to individuals. Each state has a constitution that often reflects the U.S. Constitution, although state constitutions are usually more detailed. Federal laws are codified in the United States Code, which is passed by Congress. Municipalities may institute ordinances by which they expect individuals to abide. Case law contributes to criminal law because decisions rendered in earlier criminal cases set precedent for future cases that are similar in nature. Administrative agencies have the power to pass regulations in specific areas that could be enforced via criminal penalties and thus also contribute to criminal law.

3. Learning Objective 8.3: *Compare and contrast criminal and civil law.*

- Criminal and civil law are similar because they both guide human behavior, identify the boundaries of our actions, and include sanctions for wrongful behavior. Further, they have some common areas of legal jurisdiction. The two types of law differ in several ways. Criminal law addresses wrongs against the state, and civil law addresses wrongs between individuals. The state calls the accused to court in criminal court, while individuals do so in civil court. There are many more sanctions in criminal court than there are in civil court. In criminal law, monetary penalties go to the state, while in civil law they go to individuals. The state typically does not file appeals in criminal court, but both sides can appeal in civil law. Finally, the standard of proof in criminal law is proof beyond a reasonable doubt, whereas in civil law it is a preponderance of the evidence.

4. Learning Objective 8.4: *Explain the types of affirmative defenses in criminal law.*

• Defendants may use an affirmative defense to accept responsibility for the harms in question, however they must provide reasons why they are not legally responsible. Justification defenses are used when defendants claim that they are responsible for the act in question, but their actions were acceptable or permitted based on the situation and circumstances. Among the more common justification defenses are self-defense; defense of home, property, or others; necessity; consent; and resisting unlawful arrest. An excuse involves the defendant admitting to having committed the act in question but stating that they are not criminally responsible for doing so because extraordinary circumstances caused them to commit the crime. Mistake, duress, age, involuntary intoxication, insanity, and various syndromes are considered excuses. A procedural defense is used when a defendant claims that a government official failed to follow procedural law. Examples include entrapment, double jeopardy, prosecutorial misconduct, expiration of the statute of limitations, and police misconduct.

Questions for Critical Thinking

1. What are the pros and cons of having government power in the control of a dictator as opposed to the democratic structure that exists in the United States?

2. Which source of criminal law do you believe has the greatest influence on our justice systems?

3. What do you believe is the most significant difference between civil and criminal law? Why?

4. Should we be allowed to resist arrest when we believe that the police are making an unlawful arrest? Why or why not?

Key Terms

administrative law
affirmative defense
alibi
battered spouse syndrome defense
Bill of Rights
case law
civil law
Code of Hammurabi
common law
consent
criminal codes
defenses
delinquency
democracy
dictatorships

double jeopardy
due process
duress
Durham test
Eighth Amendment
entrapment
excuses
executive branch
Fifth Amendment
First Amendment
14th Amendment
Fourth Amendment
irresistible impulse test
judicial branch
justification defenses

legislatures
M'Naghten test
Model Penal Code and Commentaries
monarchies
necessity
oligarchies
post–traumatic stress disorder
premenstrual dysphoric disorder
preponderance of evidence
procedural defense
procedural law
proof beyond a reasonable doubt

Second Amendment
self-defense
Sixth Amendment
stare decisis
statute of limitations
substantial capacity test
substantive law
tort law
Twelve Tables
United States Code
U.S. Constitution

For digital learning resources, please go to
https://www.oup.com/he/burns1e

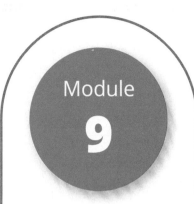

Overview of Criminal Case Processing

Perceptions of justice abound in society and often focus directly on the actions of those involved in our justice systems. Each step of criminal case processing involves events that require consideration of justice.

Do you believe incarceration should be used for nonviolent offenders, or should prison and jail space be reserved for violent criminals?

Entry into the criminal justice system can be life changing for anyone, because it can generate a series of troubling events that may include loss of employment, costly bills, loss of freedom, and a label that will stick with a person forever. Being arrested for committing a crime signifies the beginning of a journey that has several predictable and unpredictable events affected by the decisions of many, including police officers and judges. This module provides an overview of criminal case processing and is organized according to the primary components of the criminal justice system. It begins with consideration of the steps that primarily involve law enforcement, followed by coverage of the actions that occur in the courts. The final section addresses the roles played by correctional agencies. The topics covered in this module are more closely examined in Units II–IV. This module is unique from all others in this book, in that it also includes a fictitious case study (titled "Criminal Justice in Action") that follows an individual through the primary steps of the criminal justice system.

Violating the Fourth Amendment?

A Massachusetts man was arrested in May 2018 for kidnapping, and a search of his home revealed the dead bodies of three victims. The search was facilitated by a ground-penetrating radar device that enabled investigators to search for bodies in an expeditious and thorough manner (Sacks & Zambrano, 2018). Such powerful technology certainly helps investigators; however, it also generates controversy about Fourth Amendment rights protecting citizens from unreasonable searches and seizures.

Law enforcement agencies are beginning to use radar devices that permit them to see through walls and into houses and other dwellings. Reports suggest that over 50 U.S. law enforcement agencies, including the Federal Bureau of Investigation and the U.S. Marshals, had secretly purchased and used the devices as early as 2012 (Heath, 2015). The devices cost roughly $6,000 each and can detect the slightest movements, including breathing, through walls from over 50 feet away.

The use of these devices, which were introduced during the wars in Iraq and Afghanistan, is not controversial when a warrant has been issued. However, there have been occasions in which law enforcement authorities used them without a warrant, and this is what makes them controversial.

A court case in 2014, in which law enforcement officials used a radar device to arrest a man in Denver who was wanted for parole violations, highlighted the potential misuse of radars. In this case and several others, officials peered into homes using the device without a search warrant.

Law enforcement officials and the manufacturer of the devices argue that the radars help protect against criminal behavior and save the lives of law enforcement officials, particularly when they storm buildings or during hostage situations. The devices can also be used to assist other public servants, including firefighters and search and rescue teams. The concern regarding violations of the Fourth Amendment, therefore, is primarily restricted to law enforcement's use of the radars. The U.S. Supreme Court has ruled that officers generally cannot use

3 Arrest

1 Criminal Act

high-tech sensors to obtain information about the inside of someone's home without first obtaining a warrant. Should the police be permitted to use radar devices to see into homes without first obtaining a warrant? Why or why not?

2 Investigation

Law Enforcement: Entry Into the System

The initial steps into the criminal justice system, controlled by law enforcement, have significant implications regarding how well one will fare throughout criminal case processing. Entry into the system typically begins with the police personally seeing or responding to a call regarding a crime. From there, they may investigate the incident, make an arrest, and generally begin the formal processing of the accused.

● **Learning Objective 9.1:** Identify and describe the steps of criminal case processing that primarily involve the police.

CRIMINAL JUSTICE IN ACTION
The Crime

A 22-year-old woman, Alicia Barker, was attacked by a young man while she was walking to her car as she was leaving a restaurant. The man, Freddy Thompson, grabbed her from behind and threated to stab her if she did not cooperate. He demanded her purse, phone, and keys. After she complied, he told her not to contact the po-

lice or he would find her later and things would be worse for her. Freddy then ran off without allowing Alicia to get a good view of him. She did not know the man and only got a quick view of him as he took off. Alicia was not sure what to do next, but ultimately returned to the restaurant and called the police, who arrived shortly thereafter.

2
Investigation

investigations
Studying evidence and facts to identify, find, and ultimately prove the guilt of individuals believed to have committed a crime

Investigations

Law enforcement officials regularly conduct **investigations**, which involve studying evidence and facts to identify, find, and ultimately prove the guilt of individuals they believe committed a crime. Investigations occur when law enforcement officials personally witness a crime or respond to a call regarding one. The primary purposes of the investigation are to determine whether a crime is occurring or has occurred and to gather as much information as possible regarding the incident.

Module 18 discusses different approaches used to conduct investigations. Investigations may be as simple as questioning victims of or witnesses to a crime, or they may involve more advanced techniques such as analyzing hair fibers to see if those found at a crime scene match those taken from a suspect. The duration of each investigation varies depending on several factors, including the seriousness of the crime. Some cases may undergo investigations for years, while others may receive only scant attention.

CAREERS

Investigators collect and analyze evidence in efforts to identify, locate, and demonstrate the guilt of an offender. Searching for evidence, interviewing, interrogating, and collecting and preserving evidence are important aspects of the position. Investigators typically enjoy higher prestige, more flexible work hours, and reduced levels of supervision. Most also have several years of experience as patrol officers prior to assuming their position and are not required to wear a badge or uniform. They may be expected to work irregular hours, because they must respond to crimes as they occur.

Arrest

Arrests involve the seizure and restriction of the freedoms of individuals believed to have committed a crime (see Module 18). They are permitted when there is probable cause to believe that a crime was committed by an individual. Arrests do not signify that an individual is guilty of the crime, because everyone is presumed innocent until proven guilty. Instead, individuals are arrested because the police have probable cause to believe that they may indeed be guilty. Arrestees must be informed of their constitutional rights to remain silent and to have an attorney upon being taken into custody and questioned regarding their involvement in a crime.

Booking

Booking, which is sometimes referred to as processing, involves making or updating an administrative record of an arrestee. It is designed to provide an account of the accused that is necessary for proper record keeping and further case processing. Booking primarily involves collecting the arrestee's immediate possessions (which are

CRIMINAL JUSTICE IN ACTION

The Investigation

The police responded quickly to Alicia's call and offered her assistance. As part of their initial investigation, they asked if Alicia had any injuries (she did not) and for details of the incident, including a description of the man. Alicia could only describe him as being a White male, perhaps around age 24, and wearing jeans and a sweatshirt. The responding officers told her that patrol cars in the area would actively search for a man who fit the description and that they would do their best to find him. They then took her contact information and told her that they would soon be in touch. This was the third time in a month that such an attack had occurred within a mile of this restaurant.

Officers searching the area of the attack found a set of keys that they carefully secured to later examine for fin-

gerprints. The officers also asked workers inside the restaurant and some patrons if they saw or heard anything related to the incident. One worker, Francis Abernathy, mentioned that he earlier saw someone dressed in dark clothes who fit the description of the suspect behind the restaurant as he was taking out the garbage. Abernathy said he did not think much of seeing the man at that time. The police took his information as part of their investigation.

For the next week the police placed several undercover officers in unmarked cars in the area. On the third night of the operation, they saw a White male dressed in dark clothing accost a woman, Susan Brinkman, as she was leaving a bar. Two police officers converged on the scene as Freddy Thompson demanded Susan's purse and jewelry.

Among the many important functions the police perform is making arrests and ensuring public safety. Proper procedure must be followed with each arrest to ensure officer safety and protect the arrestee's rights.

Should the police be required to inform all arrestees of their rights, or should it remain the case that they only need to read the rights to arrestees they wish to question? Why?

3 Arrest

1 Criminal Act

arrest Seizing and restricting the freedoms of individuals believed to have committed a crime

4 Booking

booking Also known as processing; it involves making or updating an administrative record of an arrestee

returned upon release) and gathering information about them, such as date of birth, physical characteristics, and name. It also includes documenting information about the current offense and perhaps placing the arrestee in a local jail or some type of holding cell while awaiting further case processing.

CRIMINAL JUSTICE IN ACTION

Arrests

Freddy ran from the police as he saw them approach. He evaded their foot pursuit, and the officers lost sight of him. He put his sweatshirt in a storm drain to change his appearance, and he tried to quickly make it back to his apartment. However, unbeknown to Freddy, other officers were still in pursuit, and a patrol car met him as he turned a street corner. Freddy did not try to run this time, *because he thought the officer in the car would be looking for a man in a sweatshirt. The officer asked Freddy a few simple questions and then detained him in handcuffs. The undercover officers soon arrived and identified Freddy as the assailant. Freddy was then read his rights and placed under arrest. When asked, he denied involvement in any of the other incidents in the area.*

bail An agreement requiring the accused to post a predetermined amount of money and/or meeting other conditions to be released from custody; it is used to ensure that they will return for later court proceedings

booking officers Officials who work in jails and process arrestees

detention officers Officials who work in jails and are responsible for keeping arrestees safe in custody as they wait to appear before a judge

● **Learning Objective 9.2:** Identify and describe the steps of criminal case processing that primarily involve the courts.

Not all arrestees are booked and detained. Individuals who are arrested for less serious offenses may be released with a notice to appear in court at a later point or allowed to post a specified amount of money (what is known as **bail**) and/or meet other conditions in efforts to ensure that they will return for later court proceedings (Module 23 further addresses pretrial release).

Booking officers, also known as intake and processing clerks, work in jails and process arrestees. **Detention officers** also work in jails and are responsible for keeping arrestees safe in custody until they appear before a judge. Module 18 provides additional discussion of booking.

The Courts: Assessing Responsibility

The courts are the setting for several important steps in criminal case processing. As a case moves forward, defendants are subject to the following:

- charging
- the initial appearance
- preliminary and grand jury hearings
- arraignment
- trial
- sentencing
- appeals

CAREERS

Booking officers are responsible for processing arrestees and may serve the dual role of detention officer by monitoring arrestees awaiting case processing.

Charging

Prosecutors are lawyers for the government who evaluate the cases brought to their attention and determine whether a crime was committed and if the arrestee is the one who appears responsible. They collect information about the arrest and determine what charges, if any, will be brought against the accused. They may decide that not enough evidence exists to move forward with the case, at which point the arrestee must be released. Or, they may support the arrest and then have to decide what charges to file.

CRIMINAL JUSTICE IN ACTION
Booking

Freddy was booked and detained at police headquarters. He was fingerprinted and photographed, and the booking officer placed his possessions (including his wallet and phone) in storage. The booking officer updated his criminal file, which included two burglaries and a drug

offense. A computer-based search was conducted to see if Freddy was wanted for committing other crimes, which he was not. Freddy had no outstanding warrants. He was provided with jail clothing and escorted to a stationhouse holding cell.

Upon deciding to proceed with a case, prosecutors must then determine what crime was committed. In doing so, they consider the facts of the case presented to them. This is an important step in criminal case processing because it has many implications for the arrestee. For instance, being charged with a violent crime would likely result in more serious sanctions than being charged with a property crime (see Module 25 for a discussion of sentencing practices).

CAREERS

Detention officers oversee inmates in custody following an arrest and during the processing of their case. They may also serve the dual role of booking officer.

The Initial Appearance

Criminal case processing for felonies is a bit more formal than it is for misdemeanors and infractions. Cases involving misdemeanors and infractions may be resolved during the defendant's first appearance before a judge, referred to as an **initial appearance** (see Module 23).

5 Initial Appearance

The initial appearance is not a fact-finding stage, and defendants do not offer a defense or enter a plea. Instead, it is designed to inform defendants of the charges against them, their rights, and upcoming court appointments. It is also at this stage when the defendant may be released from custody (pretrial release) and the conditions of that release are determined. Defendants who pose substantial risks to harm others or not return to court upon being released receive stricter conditions of release

CRIMINAL JUSTICE IN ACTION
Charging

The prosecutor assigned to Freddy's case met with the arresting officers and the detectives who later interrogated Freddy. The detectives had questioned Freddy in an attempt to get him to confess to the crime and link him to the previous attacks in the area. Freddy did not confess, and the investigators were unsuccessful in linking Freddy to the earlier incidents. The investigators noted that they would continue investigating,

primarily by asking Francis Abernathy (the restaurant worker) to try to identify Freddy and analyzing fingerprints found on the keys recovered at the crime scene. In response, the prosecutor considered the available facts and was only able to charge Freddy with one count of robbery, because Freddy had used physical force to take Susan Brinkman's cell phone and purse, which he had also discarded in the storm drain.

CRIMINAL JUSTICE IN ACTION
The Initial Appearance

Freddy was brought before a judge on the day after his arrest. He spent the night in a detention cell. At his initial hearing, the judge informed him that he was being charged with robbery in connection with the attack on Susan Brinkman. Freddy was then advised of his rights and given the opportunity to retain his lawyer or to have a different one represent him. Freddy did not have

the resources to hire an attorney, so he requested state-funded representation. He was granted pretrial release after he paid a $7,500 bail bond (which is an agreement between the court and the defendant ensuring that the defendant will return to court if released after being arrested) at his initial appearance and was expected to return to court for further processing in two weeks.

6 Grand Jury/
Preliminary
Hearing

prosecutors
As representatives of the state primarily responsible for ensuring justice, their responsibilities include being actively involved in courtroom proceedings and providing a key link between law enforcement and the courts

initial appearance
A defendant's first appearance before a judge; it is used to resolve less serious cases and address a series of issues pertaining to case processing in more serious cases

or may not be released at all. The courts have ruled that defendants who are taken into custody have a right to appear before a judge within 48 hours of their arrest.

Preliminary and Grand Jury Hearings

Another means by which felony processing generally differs from the processing of less serious offenses concerns the use of preliminary hearings and grand jury hearings. Both of these hearings are designed to provide greater levels of confidence that a crime occurred and the accused is responsible. In so doing, they provide defendants additional protection from unjust prosecution. Some jurisdictions use grand juries, while others use preliminary hearings.

Prosecutors in **preliminary hearings** appear before a judge to explain why the case should continue to be pursued or prosecuted. The prosecutor must demonstrate that there is probable cause to believe that the accused is guilty. If the prosecutor fails to demonstrate probable cause, then the charges filed against the defendant are dropped and they are released from the courts (see Module 23).

Grand jury hearings share the same goals as preliminary hearings: they provide accountability to the prosecution and help protect individuals from wrongful conviction. The primary difference between the two types of hearings involves the use of private citizens in grand juries to replace judges in determining whether probable cause exists to proceed with the case. Grand juries often consist of 6–23 members who are selected in the same manner as jurors in a trial. Grand juries also have the power to conduct their own investigations (see Module 23).

An **indictment** is a charging document issued by grand juries when they believe that the prosecution has provided probable cause that a crime was committed and the accused was responsible. The charging document in a preliminary hearing is known as an **information**.

CRIMINAL JUSTICE IN ACTION
Preliminary and Grand Jury Hearings

Freddy committed his crime in a jurisdiction that uses grand juries to evaluate cases. Following the testimony of witnesses presented by the prosecution (the officers involved and Susan, the victim), the grand

jury met in closed hearings. Less than an hour later, the grand jury noted their probable cause belief that Freddy was responsible for the crime, and an indictment was issued.

CRIMINAL JUSTICE IN ACTION

Arraignments

Freddy was formally arraigned 4 days after the grand jury indictment. At the arraignment, he was again informed of the charges against him (robbery) and asked to enter a plea. Freddy entered a "not guilty" plea, which prompted the court to initiate plans for a trial. At the arraignment, Freddy's attorney entered a pretrial motion to dismiss charges, arguing that Freddy was not responsible for the crime. The judge denied the motion, and Freddy's attorney began preparing for the upcoming trial.

Although grand jury and preliminary hearings are presented as occurring following the initial appearance, they do not necessarily have to. They can occur at other times, for instance prior to an arrest, if the prosecutor wants to ensure that there is enough evidence to make an arrest.

Arraignment

Another important part of criminal case processing is the **arraignment**, which is typically a court hearing in which the accused again hears the charges against them and enters a plea of guilty or not guilty. Attorneys may also begin entering **pretrial motions** at this stage. Motions are requests made to the court regarding particular issues pertaining to the trial (for example, to allow or disallow a piece of evidence). The motions are designed to ensure fairness and equity at the forthcoming trial, or they may be offered in efforts to have the case dismissed. Judges rule on the various motions brought to their attention, and their decisions can have significant impacts on the outcomes of a case (see Module 23).

Most often, defendants enter a guilty plea, which signifies their admission of guilt. They do so as part of **plea bargaining**, which involves the prosecution and defense informally negotiating a settlement and coming to a resolution in a case (often involving a reduced sentence for the defendant). Plea bargain agreements between attorneys must be approved by judges. Only a relatively small percentage of cases (5%–10%) actually go to trial (see Module 24). Defendants do not have the legal right to engage in plea bargaining. They occur only following agreement by the prosecution and defense, and are subject to judicial approval.

Trials

Trials are symbolic of our quest to find justice and proceed through a series of formal steps designed to ensure fairness and resolve disputes. The Sixth Amendment provides the right to a trial by jury for offenders who face a punishment of more than 6 months of incarceration.

Two types of trials are offered to defendants: bench trials and jury trials. **Bench trials** are an expedited form of jury trials in which judges replace the use of jurors. Bench trials are often used for less serious offenses and cases in which the defendant waives their right to a jury trial.

7
Arraignment

preliminary hearings Hearings in which prosecutors appear before a judge to explain why a case should continue to be pursued or prosecuted; the standard of proof is probable cause

grand jury hearings Court hearings in which prosecutors appear before grand jurors to explain why the case should continue to be prosecuted; the standard of proof is probable cause

Many important functions occur in our courts, including bench trials. Judges perform the role of juries in these types of trial, which saves the courts resources and expedites criminal case processing.

What benefit would a defendant receive from a bench trial?

CRIMINAL JUSTICE IN ACTION
The Trial

Freddy's case went to trial roughly 4 months after he was arraigned. Detectives could not link him to the other attacks in the area, so Freddy faced the one charge of robbery. He weighed his options and chose a jury trial in hopes that a jury would be more likely than a judge to find him not guilty. A jury was selected, and they heard both sides present their case. The arresting officers and the victim provided valuable information about what *they witnessed the night of the crime. Freddy and his attorney provided no witnesses other than Freddy, who claimed that he was simply out taking a walk the night he was arrested. The jury deliberated for roughly 2 hours and returned a guilty verdict. Freddy was convicted on one charge of robbery. The judge then set a date for a sentencing hearing.*

8 Trial

Jury trials involve the use of laypersons (jurors) who are carefully evaluated to determine if they can be unbiased in hearing the evidence presented by the prosecution and defense before deciding whether the accused should be found guilty or not guilty. Module 24 discusses the steps of a jury trial in detail. The process begins with finding suitable jurors, after which the attorneys offer introductory remarks regarding the nature of their case. The attorneys then present their evidence to the court. This is followed by closing arguments and the judge providing instructions for juries to deliberate. After deliberating, the jury then offers a verdict.

Sentencing

Upon being found guilty or admitting guilt, offenders are sentenced. Some states permit judges to impose sentences, while others allow offenders to choose whether they want the judge or jury to do so. Some states use guidelines that assist with determining an appropriate sentence, and some sentences are prescribed by the law (for example, some states have specific penalties for individuals who are repeatedly convicted of crimes).

9 Sentencing

indictment A charging document that is issued by grand juries when they believe that the prosecution has provided probable cause to believe a crime was committed and the accused was responsible

Sentences may be imposed immediately following the court's finding of guilt. However, for more serious crimes a sentencing hearing generally happens later to provide the sentencing body some time to better reflect on the case and review reports that are prepared regarding the individual to be sentenced (see Module 25).

Among the primary factors that influence sentences are the criminal history of the offender and the seriousness of the current offense. Offenders who commit less serious offenses and have a limited or no criminal history may receive less punitive sanctions, such as a fine (financial payment to the government) or restitution (repayment in money or services to the offender's victims). Offenders who commit more serious offenses may warrant some type of supervision in the community, such as probation. Offenders with notable criminal histories and/or who committed a serious crime may receive some type of incarceration in prison or jail.

Appeals

11 Appeal

Trial courts host pretrial hearings and trials in which attorneys present their materials and make their arguments. Appellate courts, by contrast, review decisions made in trial courts. In particular, they hear **appeals**, which are requests that they review trial court proceedings and transcripts to ensure that proper procedures were

Sentencing can be controversial because there are various perceptions of what constitutes justice. Some sentences may appear too severe, while others may seem too lenient.

What could be done to improve the consistency of sentencing practices?

information
A charging document that is issued when judges rule in preliminary hearings that probable cause exists to believe a crime was committed and the accused was responsible

plea bargaining
Informal negotiations between the prosecution and defense in efforts to expedite criminal cases; as part of the process, defendants may admit guilt in exchange for a more favorable outcome of their case

bench trials Trials in which judges assess the facts of the case, apply the law, and offer verdicts and sentences; judges replace jurors in determining guilt

---

CRIMINAL JUSTICE IN ACTION
Sentencing

Freddy was sentenced to 6 years in state prison for his conviction of robbery. The judge mentioned that this particular sentence was given in light of the seriousness of *the current offense and with consideration of Freddy's previous criminal record.*

CRIMINAL JUSTICE IN ACTION
Appeals

Freddy appealed his case to an appellate court following his conviction. His argument centered around the severity of the sentence imposed by the trial judge. Freddy claimed that a 6-year sentence violated his Eighth Amendment protection from cruel and unusual punishment.

The appellate judges reviewed the transcript of the trial proceedings, listened to oral arguments from *both the prosecution and the defense, and upheld the lower court ruling. They argued that the judge's decision was appropriate based on the seriousness of the current offense and Freddy's problematic criminal history, which justified such an extended period of incarceration.*

pretrial motions
Requests offered by the prosecution and/or defense prior to trial; they seek to ensure that proper procedures are being followed and defendants' rights are respected

10
Corrections

9 Sentencing

● **Learning Objective 9.3:** Identify and describe the steps of criminal case processing that involve correctional agencies.

jury trials Formal hearings in which laypersons (jurors) hear the evidence presented by the prosecution and defense and make a determination of whether the accused should be found guilty or not guilty

trial courts Courts that decide matters of fact and determine whether a defendant is found guilty; they host various types of court-related hearings in addition to conducting trials

appeals Requests for higher courts to review trial court proceedings to ensure that proper procedures were followed and the punishment was just

followed and the imposed punishment was just. The judges then render a verdict, which often is to uphold the lower court's decision, but they can also overturn the conviction or alter it to some extent (for example, reduce the length of a prison sentence if deemed too harsh). Defendants are not required to appeal their case, and if they choose to do so they have a guaranteed right to one appeal. The appeal must be based on a perceived violation of their constitutional rights. Any further appeals are at the discretion of the higher level appellate court (see Module 21).

Corrections: Imposing Penalties and Rehabilitating

Corrections signify the final stage of criminal case processing. Various sentences can be imposed on convicted offenders, and each must be implemented in a fair and just manner. The sanctions can range from fines and restitution to community corrections (e.g., probation, home confinement, electronic monitoring) to incarceration (e.g., prison) and even capital punishment (i.e., the death penalty).

Fines and Restitution

In certain cases, a sentencing body may believe that incarceration is too harsh for the offender and instead may order one or more of the less restrictive punishments, such as fines or restitution (see Module 25). **Fines** are the most common form of punishment used for individuals who violate the law and involve payment of money to the government. Fines may be issued, for instance, for traffic violations or for criminal trespassing.

 Restitution involves offenders repaying the victims of their crimes for any hardships incurred. Repayment may involve money or services to the victim. For instance, an offender who steals someone's credit card and makes charges to it may be sentenced to repay all of the charges. Similarly, an offender who vandalizes a business or home may be required, as part of their sentence, to fix all damages to the structure.

Community Corrections

The term **community corrections** refers to the series of sanctions that are imposed in the community. These sanctions are considered less punitive than institutional corrections, and they permit monitoring of offenders while they go about their lives. Determining which offenders are suitable to be monitored in the community and which require incarceration is sometimes difficult. Among the more commonly used forms of community corrections are:

● community service,
● probation,
● day reporting centers,
● home confinement and electronic monitoring, and
● parole.

These types of community corrections are discussed in more detail in Module 31.

COMMUNITY SERVICE

Offenders are sometimes sentenced to a specified period of **community service**, which involves offenders being required to perform some type of labor that benefits the community. For example, they may be required to pick up trash along the roadways or wash public service vehicles.

PROBATION

Probation involves offenders being placed under a set of restrictions and supervised in the community. Probationers are assigned to a probation officer, who ensures that the offender remains trouble free and uses community services to address any problems they may have (e.g., substance abuse, anger issues). The greatest percentage of individuals under correctional supervision are on probation. Probationers are heavily restricted in what they can and cannot do while being supervised in the community.

DAY REPORTING CENTERS

Day reporting centers are facilities that are visited by offenders who live at home and are being monitored in the community. They offer various services for offenders, such as counseling, drug testing, treatment, and education. Offenders are required to attend the facilities according to a schedule. For example, they may have to visit before and after they go their job, or they may simply have to stop by daily to be drug tested.

HOME CONFINEMENT AND ELECTRONIC MONITORING

Home confinement, also known as house arrest, is a sanction in which offenders are required to remain within the confines of their home for prescribed periods. They may be permitted to leave their home for particular reasons at specific times, for instance to attend work, school, or counseling.

Home confinement is often used in conjunction with **electronic monitoring**, which involves electronic tracking devices that allow officials to pinpoint the location of an offender. An alert is sent to the official tasked with monitoring the offender in the community (e.g., a probation officer) if the device is removed.

Incarceration or Institutional Corrections

Incarceration, or institutional corrections, refers to being physically confined or detained in a jail or prison. It is used for the most serious offenders and less frequently than the various forms of community corrections.

JAILS

Jails are correctional facilities that serve multiple functions, including the incarceration of offenders serving a sentence of less than 12 months. As noted in Module 32, jails also house individuals who:

- cannot make bail or are denied pretrial release,
- are awaiting sentencing,
- are awaiting evaluation (e.g., mentally ill individuals), or
- are awaiting a hearing for violation of their probation or parole conditions.

Jails are also used to incarcerate those with longer than a year sentence when state prisons are too crowded to house them. Jails are typically operated by local officials, often by sheriff's departments.

PRISONS

Prisons are correctional facilities that house offenders sentenced to incarceration for a year or longer. They are primarily operated by the federal government and state governments and typically have different security levels. The levels separate the most

fines Payment of money to the government for violating the law

restitution A sanction whereby offenders repay the victims of their crimes for any hardships incurred

community corrections Sanctions that are imposed in the community

community service A sanction in which offenders are required to perform some type of labor that benefits the community

probation Conditional freedom granted to an offender, allowing the offender to be supervised in the community under the conditions specified in the probation agreement

day reporting centers A sanction that provides services such as treatment and surveillance to offenders living at home; offenders sentenced to these centers must report regularly to a designated center to help ensure that they are meeting the requirements of their sentence

home confinement Also known as house arrest; it is a sanction that requires offenders to remain within the confines of their home during designated hours of each day

electronic monitoring Electronic tracking devices that allow officials to locate offenders; it is often used in conjunction with home confinement

jails Correctional facilities that house inmates serving less than a year incarceration, those who cannot make bail or are denied release, and those who are awaiting sentencing, evaluation, or a parole or probation violation hearing

prisons Correctional facilities that house offenders sentenced to incarceration for a year or longer

capital punishment Also known as the death penalty; it involves taking the life of an offender in response to their actions

violent or dangerous offenders from those who pose the lowest threat of harming others or escaping.

Given that prison inmates serve longer periods than those in jail, prisons offer more services and treatment options than jails. Prison inmates are more likely to receive employment and educational opportunities and overall assessments of well-being while incarcerated. Prisons also house the most dangerous individuals in society, and thus special attention is devoted to ensure that prisons are safe and secure. Prisons have been challenged by many issues over the years, including overcrowding, a lack of resources, and gang-related conflict (see Module 32).

Capital Punishment

Capital punishment, also known as the death penalty, is the most punitive and controversial sanction that is imposed on convicted offenders. It involves taking the life of an offender in response to their actions (see Module 25) and is used relatively infrequently compared to other sanctions.

Not all states impose the death penalty, and some states that use it do so far less than others. The trend in recent years among states has been toward moving away from the use of capital punishment, primarily because of the high costs involved with imposition of the sentence and the release of individuals from death row after further investigation of their cases determined they were not guilty (Chammah, 2017; Garrett, 2017).

Prisons are imposing facilities that are designed to maintain order and ensure the safety of the prisoners and the people who work there.

Do you believe the heavily controlled nature of prisons helps or hurts the large majority of inmates who return to society?

Release and Parole

Inmates are released from incarceration in one of several ways. A relatively small percentage "max out," meaning that they serve their entire sentence. These ex-inmates will not be monitored in the community upon their release. Most inmates, however, are released early, on average after serving about half of their imposed sentence. These individuals will be monitored after being released, often placed on **parole**.

Parolees, like probationers, face many restrictions while residing in the community. The primary difference between probation and parole is that probation is imposed as a sentence, while parole is granted after one has served a period of incarceration. Some states use mandatory parole, and others use discretionary parole to determine who is to be released early.

CRIMINAL JUSTICE IN ACTION

Incarceration

Freddy served roughly 3 years of the 6-year prison sentence he received. He served his time in a medium-security state prison, where he worked as a cook. He earned a high school equivalency degree while incarcerated and took several life skills courses designed *to help him upon his release. Shortly after entering prison, Freddy found several inmates with whom he shared much in common (e.g., they were from the same neighborhood and of the same race) and generally stayed out of trouble.*

CRIMINAL JUSTICE IN ACTION

Release and Parole

After 3 years in prison, Freddy appeared before a parole board. He described his accomplishments in prison and the fact that he had stayed out of trouble while incarcerated. Freddy was released and assigned to a parole officer whose job it was to monitor Freddy in the community. Freddy was put on parole for 3 years, which is when his prison sentence would have expired. Freddy had worked with counselors in prison to find a job as a line cook at a diner and a small apartment in a new neighborhood upon his release. *While on parole, Freddy was expected to maintain employment at the diner, attend counseling sessions in the community, and generally remain trouble free. He was also expected to regularly meet with his parole officer and abide by several other restrictions. He knew being supervised in the community would be difficult, but it was much better than being in prison.*

Mandatory parole involves inmates being released early after a period of serving time with good behavior. These offenders are rewarded with time off of their sentence for each day they serve and behave while incarcerated. **Discretionary parole** involves the use of **parole boards**, which are composed of officials who evaluate inmates after they have served a period of time. The boards determine whether the inmate appears ready to be released at a parole hearing. Regardless of the type of parole used, most ex-inmates are supervised in the community for a specified time after their release to ensure that they remain free from crime and are using the available community services to stay out of trouble (see Module 31).

parole The supervision of ex-inmates in the community after they are released early from jail or prison

mandatory parole Generally used in states with determinate sentencing structures, it involves the early, conditional release of inmates whose sentence was reduced as a result of time served and earned good time

discretionary parole A means by which inmates are released from prison; it involves the use of parole boards making a determination of whether the inmate appears ready to be released

The System in Perspective

The "In the News" feature at the beginning of this module referenced law enforcement's use of high technology to solve crimes. Such technology, however, poses a risk to our personal freedoms because cameras with the capacity to see through walls could be used in non–law enforcement matters. The controversy regarding freedoms versus protection is found throughout all stages of criminal case processing. The controversy includes debate regarding whether certain actors within the system maintain too much power. For instance, prosecutors are heavily involved in most steps of criminal case processing and make many important decisions along the way.

parole boards
Officials who evaluate inmates after they have served a period of incarceration; they make determinations of whether inmates appear ready to be released

Securing justice is done in many ways and involves various groups of people. The individuals who work in the justice systems may not interact directly with each other, but each plays a role that contributes to the whole. How they perform their jobs and the responsibilities they have vary. We each have different perspectives on how well the agencies and individuals that comprise our justice systems work as a system and whether we have granted those in the system too little or too much power. Regardless, we expect much from the many individuals who work in criminal justice.

Summary

1. Learning Objective 9.1: *Identify and describe the steps of criminal case processing that primarily involve the police.*

- With regard to criminal case processing, the police are primarily involved with investigations, arrests, and booking. Investigations involve studying evidence and facts to identify, find, and ultimately prove the guilt of individuals they believe committed a crime. Arrests entail seizing and restricting the freedoms of individuals believed to have committed a crime. Booking involves making an administrative record of arrestees.

2. Learning Objective 9.2: *Identify and describe the steps of criminal case processing that primarily involve the courts.*

- The courts are home to several important steps of criminal case processing. Court officials review cases and charge the accused or drop charges. Initial appearances occur in courts and serve the purpose of resolving less serious cases. In more serious cases, the courts provide defendants with formal notice of the charges against them, advise them of their rights, inform them of their right to retain a lawyer or to have one appointed to represent them, consider the possibility of pretrial release, and inform suspects of upcoming courtroom activities. Preliminary and grand jury hearings are used to evaluate evidence and determine whether a case should proceed. Arraignments are hearings in which the accused again hears the charges against them and enters a plea, and pretrial motions

may be made. Trials are formal hearings in which evidence is shared to determine whether the accused is found to be guilty or not guilty. Defendants who admit guilt or are found guilty are sentenced in courts, which involves finding a sanction that seems suitable for the offender and their actions. Appellate courts hear appeals regarding decisions made in trial courts and provide a sense of accountability in our justice systems.

3. Learning Objective 9.3: *Identify and describe the steps of criminal case processing that involve correctional agencies.*

- Various sanctions are imposed on offenders, including fines and restitution. Fines are requirements that offenders pay a specified sum of money to the government, while restitution involves the repayment of money or services to victims. In addition, various forms of community and institutional corrections exist. Community corrections includes parole services and sanctions that are imposed while the offender remains in the community, including community service, probation, day reporting centers, and home confinement with electronic monitoring. Institutional corrections includes jails and prisons. Jails are used for various purposes, including to incarcerate offenders serving sentences of less than a year. Prisons are used to incarcerate offenders sentenced to a year or more. Capital punishment, or the death penalty, is the most severe and controversial sanction.

Questions for Critical Thinking

1. Aside from investigations, arrests, and booking, what other important activities do the police perform to ensure justice?

2. What images come to mind when you hear the term *courts*? Do you envision a judge, an attorney, or a defendant? Are they engaged in a trial? Why do you think this image came to mind?

3. How could a probation sentence be more punitive than incarceration? Do you believe that all offenders who commit a violent or otherwise serious crime should be incarcerated? Why or why not?

Key Terms

appeals
arraignment
arrest
bail
bench trials
booking
booking officers
capital punishment
community corrections
community service
day reporting centers
detention officers
discretionary parole
electronic monitoring
fines
grand jury hearings
home confinement

indictment
information
initial appearance
investigations
jails
jury trials
mandatory parole
parole
parole boards
plea bargaining
preliminary hearing
pretrial motions
prisons
probation
prosecutor
restitution
trial courts

For digital learning resources, please go to
https://www.oup.com/he/burns1e

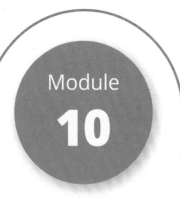

Module

10

MODULE OUTLINE

- **English Influences and the Development of Policing in the United States**

  Learning Objective 10.1: Explain how early English methods of informal social control influenced the development of formal policing both in England and in the United States.

- **The Political Era (1840–1930)**

  Learning Objective 10.2: Describe the characteristics of the political era.

- **Reforming the Police: The Reform Era (1930–1980)**

  Learning Objective 10.3: Describe the characteristics of the reform era.

- **Bringing Back the Community: The Community Era (1980–Present)**

  Learning Objective 10.4: Describe the characteristics of the community era.

- **Terrorism and Homeland Security**

  Learning Objective 10.5: Explain how the threat of terrorism has influenced local policing.

136

History of Law Enforcement

Much has changed from the days when police technology was limited and officers focused mainly on providing services.

How do you think advances in technology, such as the increased use of automobiles versus a reliance solely on horseback and foot patrol, played a role in the changing nature of the job?

What do the police do, and how has their role changed over time? How and why did the police shift from providing a variety of services to citizens toward becoming primarily concerned with fighting crime? To answer these questions and others and to understand current police practices, we must first examine the historical developments that preceded them. Module 10 addresses the history of policing as it originated in England and developed in the United States.

Community Policing, Bridging Relationships, and Getting Back to the Roots of Policing

1 Criminal Act

In January 2017, the U.S. Department of Justice (DOJ) announced that it had found reasonable cause to believe that the Chicago Police Department engaged in a pattern of using force, including deadly force, which violated the Fourth Amendment's protection against the use of excessive force by law enforcement (*Graham v. Connor*, 1989). The report noted that officers behaved in a manner that resulted in the unnecessary use of force against suspects. The problems allegedly stemmed from the failure to properly train officers regarding how to deescalate potentially violent situations and the failure to conduct effective investigations into the uses of force by officers. The city of Chicago and the DOJ agreed to work together, with consideration of community input, to address the deficiencies (DOJ, 2017).

Chicago is not alone in dealing with these issues related to use of force. For instance, in 2015 the DOJ issued a scathing report accusing Cleveland, Ohio, police officers of routinely violating suspects' rights and using excessive force, being too quick to use their weapons, firing guns at people who were not immediate threats, and abusing suspects in custody. The report also noted that the department failed to adequately investigate the incidents and discipline the officers involved (DOJ, 2014). In response, the city of Cleveland and the DOJ signed an agreement

that required the city to create an organization that was more responsive to and engaged with the citizens it serves.

The proposed resolutions in both of these cases (and others of a similar nature) included establishing stronger police–community relations. Relations between the police and some of the communities they serve have suf-

fered in recent years, primarily in response to controversial police practices. The police and the public have had a volatile relationship throughout history, as the levels of support for and confidence in the police have fluctuated.

English Influences and the Development of Policing in the United States

While the police practices of 19th-century England remain visible in 21st-century U.S. policing, formal policing in England did not always exist. Citizens largely relied on one another to bring offenders to justice and protect themselves and assumed personal responsibility for what is currently recognized as police work. The military sometimes addressed the most serious crimes, such as offenses against public officials or the king (Oliver & Hilgenberg, 2006).

● **Learning Objective 10.1:** Explain how early English methods of informal social control influenced the development of formal policing both in England and in the United States.

Informal Social Control

Kin policing involved a victim's family members bringing an offender to justice (Germann et al., 1970). Citizens provided safety and security for community members by responding to any calls to arms when a crime occurred and generally helping each other by providing strength in numbers. The communal living arrangement in which

kin policing An early form of informal social control that involved a victim's family members bringing an offender to justice

tythings Early England living arrangements that consisted of 10 families living communally

hundreds Early England living arrangements that consisted of roughly 10 tythings (or roughly 100 families), an appointed leader, and perhaps assistants to organize any law enforcement and justice efforts

shire A group of several hundreds; Early English families living communally

Bow Street Runners A group of men who proactively searched for lawbreakers in the Bow Street region of London and were paid a sum of money for each individual they brought to court

London Metropolitan Police Act The act that essentially created the London Metropolitan Police, which was the first urban police department in the Western world

Bobbies The name given to officers in the London Metropolitan Police Force in recognition of Sir Robert Peel

citizens protected one another through responses to crime and with crime-prevention efforts was necessary in the absence of formal policing. All adult males in the community were expected to respond when someone was harmed or felt threatened.

Some communities were assembled into **tythings**, groups of roughly 10 families from which a tythingman was selected and responsible for organizing any necessary law- and justice-based efforts. Larger communities, known as **hundreds**, consisted of roughly 10 tythings, an appointed leader, and perhaps assistants to organize any law enforcement and justice efforts. Tythings and hundreds expanded as the populations in these areas increased. A group of several hundreds was known as a **shire**, in which a shire reeve and assistants were designated to organize and lead any law enforcement and justice-based actions. The shire reeve was the precursor to the modern-day sheriff. The designated law enforcement leaders in the tythings, hundreds, and shires also served as judges (Oliver & Hilgenberg, 2006) and typically performed their duties on an as-needed basis, because victimization and crime levels varied among communities, much as they do in the early 21st century.

The practice of having multiple families live in close proximity to one another and protect fellow citizens was known as the **frankpledge system**. As part of the approach, citizens agreed to respect the law, help maintain order, and bring offenders to court, for instance through raising the hue and cry upon being victimized (Uchida, 1993). The hue and cry was a call for able-bodied males to pursue and capture an offender. Further, the frankpledge system entailed night watch and day ward systems, in which designated watchers would alert residents of impending dangers such as fires, crime, and dangerous weather.

Informal social control was well suited for small societies where most neighbors knew each other. In early England, the reliance on citizens to protect one another would eventually become less effective as small towns and villages grew into large cities. Many residents left small towns in hopes of prosperity in big cities, and England became less agrarian and more industrial. As cities grew, citizens faced increased levels of frustration and poverty. Ultimately, informal social control became less effective and the need for more formal law enforcement services emerged.

Emergence of Formal Law Enforcement Services

London magistrate Henry Fielding responded to the increasing levels of disorder brought about by bigger cities in the Bow Street region of London by hiring a group of men who proactively searched for lawbreakers. He paid the **Bow Street Runners**, as they were called, a sum of money for each individual they brought to court. These efforts somewhat reflect current police patrol practices, but they generated controversy. Londoners were not accustomed to having government officials monitor their behavior. Further, citizens were apprehensive about the potential for runners to misbehave and intentionally make wrongful apprehensions for pay. Nevertheless, the Bow Street Runners were effective in cleaning up the crime problems in the area.

Fielding's approach of paying individuals to proactively address crime inspired the **London Metropolitan Police Act** of 1829. The act essentially created the London Metropolitan Police, which was the first urban police department in the Western world. England's home secretary, Sir Robert Peel, was an avid supporter of formal policing and immediately provided direction for the department. Peel adopted a community-oriented approach that emphasized professionalism, effective police–community relations, and crime prevention. He believed that it was better to prevent crime than to aggressively respond to it. The officers were called "**Bobbies**" after Peel's nickname, Bob, and they wore uniforms designed to look like civilian clothes. They patrolled regular beats and were required to be at least 5 feet 7 inches tall and under the age of 35. Many were former officers in the army (Roth, 2005).

Initially, public opinion of the police was low, because citizens believed the police were too often monitoring their behaviors and intruding into their lives, much as the military had done. Citizens, particularly those of the lower classes, were apprehensive about having another group of government officials monitoring them (Oliver & Hilgenberg, 2006). However, public opinion began to change in response to Peel's efforts to reform and refine police practices and improve community relations, and the general approach of assisting rather than controlling residents.

The Development of Policing in the United States

While policing in the United States can be traced back to U.S. slave patrols—which existed in every Southern colony by 1750 and have been recognized as the first American police departments (Dulaney, 1996)—the emergence of formal law enforcement in the United States largely reflects the development of policing in England. As settlers arrived in the new country, they relied primarily on informal social control. The need for more formal law enforcement emerged as villages and towns expanded, diversified, and experienced greater levels of crime, unabated drunkenness, and economic troubles.

Given the country's commitment to liberties and freedoms, early Americans were apprehensive about formal law enforcement and of government having too much control over their lives (Wadman & Allison, 2004). Nevertheless, the first police departments in the United States appeared in cities along the East Coast, as settlers largely arrived and resided in these areas. Following three major riots and increasing violence in the early 1830s, Boston created the first permanent police force in the United States in 1838 (Bopp & Shultz, 1972). New York faced similar problems and also responded by creating a police department in 1844. Policing emerged in other areas at different times as settlement and expansion occurred.

The Political Era (1840–1930)

During the **political era of policing**, government leaders heavily influenced officers, departments, and police practices. Members of law enforcement also had close personal relationships with the communities they served and often provided non-crime-fighting services for the general public, such as helping the elderly obtain medicines, assisting the homeless with lodging, and looking after wayward youth. Patrol officers during this time primarily used foot patrol, or walking their beats, which encourages greater police–community interactions and promotes stronger relations among groups. They most often communicated with others in their department using call boxes, whistles, and telegraphs and responded to reports of crime and incidents they personally witnessed.

The Spoils System

The **spoils system**, in which politicians rewarded individuals who supported their candidacy with employment, was quite evident during the political era of policing. Professor James Chriss noted that "there was no pretense of choosing officers on the basis of objective criteria of competence or ability. Rather, officers during the Political Era were chosen on the basis of political loyalty and ascribed characteristics such as family connections, race or ethnicity, or friendship" (Chriss, 2011, p. 29). In addition to their influence on personnel issues, politicians set the goals and activities for the police; this was problematic because it often led to corruption and a general lack of professionalism.

● **Learning Objective 10.2:** Describe the characteristics of the political era.

political era of policing The period of time during which politicians heavily influenced officers, departments, and police practices (1840–1930); members of law enforcement also had close personal relationships with the communities they served and often provided non-crime-fighting services for the general public

Spoils system
The practice of politicians rewarding individuals who support their candidacy with employment; it was quite evident during the political era of policing

Police officers during the political era established close ties with the communities they served. The reliance on foot patrol meant that the officers were often in contact with the citizens they served.

How might foot patrols help in early 21st-century efforts to improve police–community relations?

1 Criminal Act

prohibition The time when the selling, transporting, and manufacturing of alcohol was illegal (1919–1933); police corruption became particularly widespread during this period as organized crime grew

The Civil War, Prohibition, and Civil Unrest

Several events during the political era significantly affected policing. One of the most significant was the Civil War (1861–1865), which resulted from tensions and contradictory views between Northern and Southern states over slavery, the rights of states to govern their own affairs, and the political and legal status of Blacks (Roth, 2005). Passage of the 13th and 14th Amendments (in 1865 and 1868), which abolished slavery and provided Blacks with citizenship and equal protection under the law, respectively, signified major progress with regard to equality in the United States. The new legislation, however, provided new challenges for policing. Because police were the front-line defenders of protecting these newly granted rights, officers had to deal with high levels of racial tensions.

Another event that had a great impact on policing during the political era was **Prohibition** (1919–1933). During Prohibition, the selling, transporting, and manufacturing of alcohol were illegal. Police corruption became particularly widespread during this period as organized crime grew to supply the demand for alcohol and would often bribe police officers and politicians to overlook the illegal behavior. Public perceptions of the police suffered because many citizens disapproved of Prohibition, and the police had to enforce these unpopular alcohol laws.

Rioting and civil unrest also occurred with increasing frequency during the political era. Riots in cities such as Tulsa, Oklahoma, in 1921 and Rosewood, Florida, in 1923 originated in response to racial tensions. The police were called on to quell the riots and unrest, but they were generally untrained in how to do so.

Historical Accounts

Several historical accounts of policing during the political era provide some insights about early police departments in the United States. For instance, historian P. J. Ethington examined the creation of a progressive police bureaucracy in San Francisco from 1847 to 1900, which was perhaps the most professional police department in the United States. Among other proactive accomplishments, Ethington (1987) noted that the department was:

- administered by career officers,
- staffed by dedicated, highly paid patrol officers who were qualified for their positions, and
- relatively free of partisan control

Data collected from the journal of a late 19th-century Boston patrol officer also shed light on early policing. In particular, an analysis of the 1895 journal entries found that police officers in Boston at the time provided an equal balance of service and law enforcement. Generally, the officers:

- protected private property,
- let citizen complaints guide much of their actions, and
- served as mediators and low-level magistrates when handling conflicts among citizens (von Hoffman, 1992).

The continued growth of towns and villages into large cities resulted in many significant challenges for police departments. Historian Joseph Laythe documented policing in Eugene, Oregon, from 1862 to 1932, when the city underwent significant growth and change. Laythe notes several issues that were common to policing in most U.S. cities at the time (Laythe, 2002):

- problematic police practices, such as targeting what were deemed "dangerous classes," including transient farm workers, immigrants, the unemployed, and loggers
- scandals, including accusations that the police chief and an officer had become intimate with two young, intoxicated girls
- various forms of police misconduct, including circumventing due process rights of arrestees

Reforming the Police: The Reform Era (1930–1980)

- **Learning Objective 10.3:** Describe the characteristics of the reform era.

Police corruption was problematic during the political era, and the need for reform and improved educational standards for police officers was evident. Attempts to address these and related concerns emerged through the efforts of several key police reformers and led to the **reform era of policing**, also known as the "progressive era" or the "professional era." The reform era sought to reform, advance, and generally professionalize policing. This period was characterized by an emphasis on crime-fighting—more so than providing services or maintaining order—particularly through innovations such as patrol cars, two-way radios for patrol cars, and motorcycles, which became particularly popular by the mid-1930s (Wadman & Allison, 2004).

reform era of policing Also known as the "progressive era" or the "professional era"; it was the period during which the goal was to reform, advance, and generally professionalize policing (1930–1980); it was characterized by an emphasis on crime-fighting

Key Reformers and Reforms

Reform-era efforts were spurred in large part by August Vollmer, who is considered by some the "Father of American Policing" (Oliver, 2008, p. 84). Vollmer's contributions include largely reforming police management techniques; improving recruitment, retention, and training practices; and emphasizing the need for crime prevention. He promoted formal education among officers and was among the early police chiefs to use fingerprinting technology and motorcycle and bicycle patrols (Oliver, 2008).

Vollmer's efforts, along with those of other reformers, including his protégé O. W. Wilson, and a series of reports spurred reform. In 1931, President Hoover's National Commission on Law Observance and Enforcement, also known as the Wickersham Commission, issued a series of reports that highlighted the need for reforms and police professionalism. The reports documented gross abuses of power, including the beating of suspects and regular violations of constitutional rights. In addition, Wilson authored two influential books on police administration and introduced a personnel management system that remains in use in the early 21st century. Wilson was among the first proponents of automobile patrol and one-person patrols (instead of two-person) to conserve department resources.

The increased focus on crime-fighting during the reform era, at the expense of other functions, however, had repercussions. Because fewer officers walked their beats and automobiles were more commonly used, police had less personal interaction with the public. This in turn led to poorer police–community relations.

1 Criminal Act

The Civil Rights Movement and More Civil Unrest

As has been the case throughout all periods of policing in the United States, several events affected police practices during the reform era. After World War II, a period of peace and prosperity ensued, and the suburbs grew as the inner cities, composed of higher concentrations of minorities and the poor, declined. Rising crime rates in inner cities prompted the police to largely adopt a crime control approach.

The civil rights movement, which began in the late 1950s, involved protests against the social, economic, and political inequality of African Americans in the United States. Demonstrators at these nonviolent protests were often confronted by White police officers with limited training (Miller & Hess, 2005). The police often arrested large numbers of protestors and quickly resorted to using force instead of controlling the situation in a less violent manner, such as through effective communication.

3 Arrest

Rioting in many U.S. cities between 1964 and 1968 was largely perpetuated by tensions between the police and African American communities. Often, the unrest followed a situation involving questionable police practices. For instance, the Watts, California, riots occurred during a 6-day period in 1965. A 21-year-old Black motorist, Marquette Frye, was arrested for drunk driving. The arrest involved an argument and then a fight between Frye and the officers, which in turn resulted in many members of the community protesting and rioting. The damages included 35 deaths, 864 injuries, and over $200 million in property damage (Folkart, 1986). Although the arrest altercation sparked the riots, underlying problems such as high unemployment rates and police racism were identified as large underlying causes.

Poor police–community relations, a lack of officer training in response to civil disturbances, and general racial tensions aggravated many of the riots occurring during this time (A. D. Perez et al., 2003). In 1966 alone, there were at least 38 major riots across the United States. The effects of the rioting were disturbing in terms of lives and costs. A week-long riot in Detroit in 1967 resulted in 43 deaths and an estimated $40 million in property damage, for example (M. D. White, 2007). Compounding the financial and victim-related costs were the harms done to police–community relations, because the police were tasked with controlling populations that were generally unsupportive of the police prior to the riots.

Concerns from the public and the government regarding the general social disorder of the times and questionable police practices encouraged the creation of several national commissions to assess the issues and identify solutions. These commissions included the 1965 President's Commission on Law Enforcement and Administration of Justice (also referred to as the President's Crime Commission) and the National Advisory Commission on Civil Disorders (also known as the Kerner Commission). The President's Crime Commission called for greater professionalization of policing and police officers, for instance through encouraging departments to become more community oriented. The Kerner Commission identified institutional racism, discrimination, and unemployment as primary causes of the social unrest. It also cited poor police–community relations and a lack of African American police officers, police professionalism, and effective training and supervision as contributing factors (National Advisory Commission on Civil Disorders, 1967).

Landmark U.S. Supreme Court Decisions

Policing during the reform era was also influenced by a series of landmark U.S. Supreme Court decisions under the guidance of Chief Justice Earl Warren. Some of the court's decisions rendered in several cases during the 1960s continue to influence policing. Among the more influential cases were:

- *Mapp v. Ohio* (1961), in which the court ruled that the **exclusionary rule**, which prohibits the introduction of illegally seized evidence into courtroom proceedings, applied in all courts within the United States;
- *Miranda v. Arizona* (1966), in which the court noted that suspects must be informed of their rights prior to being questioned in police custody. Otherwise, the information obtained during the interrogation is inadmissible in court; and
- *Terry v. Ohio* (1968), in which the court specified the conditions under which police officers can stop and question individuals.

The distancing of the police from the public, reliance on technology, emphasis on crime-fighting, and rising crime rates resulted in calls for innovation in policing. Police recruiting practices contributed to the tension between inner-city residents and the police, in part because recruits tended to come from police families or have military backgrounds, and police departments were primarily staffed with White males (Wadman & Allison, 2004). The reform era truly highlighted the difficulties associated with police work and the need for the police to be more than strictly crime-fighters. By the end of the 1970s, it had become evident that a philosophical shift in policing was needed, one that would enable the police to better cooperate and associate with the public.

Bringing Back the Community: The Community Era (1980–Present)

Social unrest during the 1960s and 1970s highlighted many of the limitations of police putting too much emphasis on crime control and neglecting to build and foster relationships with the communities they served. The police were increasingly the target of public concern primarily as a result of:

- increasing crime rates;
- research highlighting the limitations of law enforcement practices too focused on crime-fighting;
- increased fear of crime;

exclusionary rule Prohibits the introduction of illegally seized evidence into courtroom proceedings

● **Learning Objective 10.4:** Describe the characteristics of the community era.

- many minority citizens believing they were being treated unfairly;
- the anti–war and civil rights movements that challenged police practices;
- reduced financial support for the police, which forced police agencies to do more with fewer resources; and
- the community crime control movement and private security beginning to provide competition to the police (Peak & Glensor, 2004, pp. 13–14).

One of the most significant changes in policing began around the early 1980s, when many departments made a philosophical shift toward becoming more community oriented. The shift of many departments toward a community-oriented approach reflected a return to the roots of policing, when early police departments formed close relationships with citizens and often relied on them to help address crime. This shift back to those early core principles has ushered in what experts refer to as the **community era of policing**. This era has been characterized by proactive police efforts to better involve the community and address crime and crime-related problems.

This philosophical approach to policing commonly known as community policing or "community-oriented policing" promotes partnerships with various groups, emphasizes problem-solving techniques to address the underlying causes of crime, and encourages officers and other personnel to better use and interact with the public. As a result of community policing, the organizational structure of police departments shifted: Officers were now expected to provide a wide array of services and not focus strictly on crime-fighting.

As noted in Figure 10.1, the primary elements of community policing include community partnerships, organizational adjustments, and problem-solving. Community partnerships encourage a more holistic approach to addressing crime and may include collaborative efforts with groups such as other government agencies (e.g., zoning boards), the media, private businesses, service providers, and community members and groups. Organizational transformation includes adjustments within the police agency with regard to community policing, for instance in relation to how officers are managed, the organization of the personnel, the training of personnel, and technology-related issues. The final primary element of community policing is a problem-solving approach that proceeds through a series of steps designed to address the underlying causes of crime and related problems.

A Focus on Problem-Solving

Herman Goldstein (1990) is credited with introducing **problem-oriented policing**. He believed a primary limitation of police practices was that the police were incident driven and too reactive. The steps involved in the problem-solving process include scanning, analysis, response, and assessment (which form the acronym SARA):

- *Scanning* involves identifying issues that require attention.
- Following the identification of a problem, departments *analyze* the nature and extent of the problem, which guides the response they take.
- Analysis of the problem is followed by a *response*, or several responses, which may include assistance from other agencies.
- The final step in the problem-solving process is *assessment*, which involves evaluating the effectiveness and outcomes of their efforts and determining whether the problem remains. If the problem remains, the evaluators will seek to determine if they misidentified the problem, misanalyzed the nature and extent of the problem, and/or perhaps implemented an incorrect response.

community era of policing The era of policing beginning in the 1980s that has been characterized by proactive police efforts to better involve the community and address crime and crime-related problems

problem-oriented policing A style of policing that seeks to address the causes of crime and disorder, as opposed to reacting to crime; the problem-solving process involves scanning, analysis, response, and assessment

The Primary Elements of Community Policing

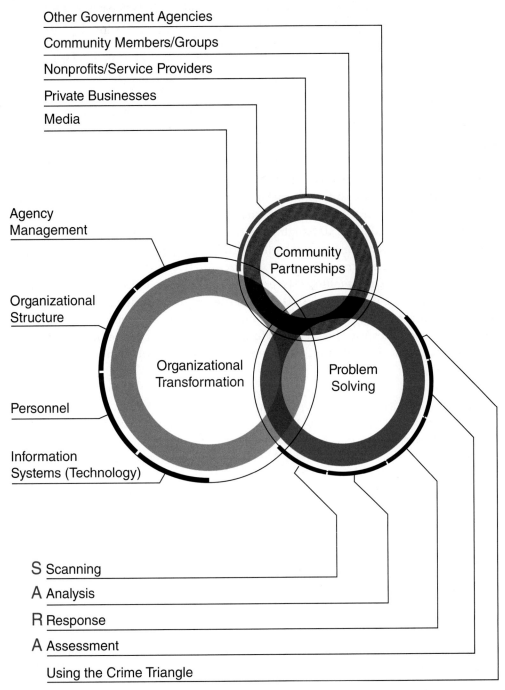

Other Government Agencies

Community Members/Groups

Nonprofits/Service Providers

Private Businesses

Media

Agency Management

Organizational Structure

Personnel

Information Systems (Technology)

Community Partnerships

Organizational Transformation

Problem Solving

S Scanning

A Analysis

R Response

A Assessment

Using the Crime Triangle

FIGURE 10.1. Community policing. This figure depicts the primary elements of community policing, including the interconnectedness of community partnerships, problem-solving, and organizational transformation. *Source:* Community Policing Defined, *by Community Oriented Policing Services, 2014, U.S. Department of Justice (http://www.cops.usdoj.gov/pdf/vets-to-cops/e030917193-CP-Defined.pdf).*

Do you believe police departments should be required to adopt certain aspects of community policing in efforts to improve police–community relations? Why or why not?

Evaluating the Effectiveness of Community Policing

Community policing promotes a more accurate view of police functions and acknowledges the importance of alliances between the police and other groups and the inability of the police to address crime single-handedly. The proactive approach facilitates officers using information gathered in communities with discretion, makes more effective use of patrol resources, and helps highlight community problems and target appropriate police responses (Goldstein, 1997). Other benefits of community policing include greater police accountability to the public and a commitment to crime prevention.

The effectiveness of community policing efforts is largely evaluated in terms of citizen satisfaction and public cooperation rather than response times and crime rates. However, effectiveness is difficult to measure, primarily because it is difficult to assess the effects of a philosophical shift in policing. The crime rate has dropped significantly since the early 1990s, while the number of community-oriented departments has increased. Figure 10.2 highlights the number of departments that have included a written community policing plan. However, many factors aside from police practices influence crime rates.

The death of George Floyd (see Module 1) while being apprehended by Minneapolis police officers in 2020 reignited many of the earlier concerns about police mistreatment of African Americans. Protests and riots resulted from this and related incidents, which left fewer resources for police departments to engage in community policing, yet a greater need to do so. Contributing to the

Populations Served	Maintained a Plan
1,000,000 or more*	80.0%
500,000–999,999	72.4 ‡
250,000–499,999	78.0
100,000–249,999	61.7 †
50,000–99,999	62.3 †
25,000–49,999	56.6 †
10,000–24,999	51.1 †
2,500–9,999	37.9 †
2,499 or less	35.8 †
All departments	42.1
All officers[a]	65.8

FIGURE 10.2. Departments with a written community policing plan. Although only 42% of police departments had a written community policing plan, larger departments were more likely than smaller ones to do so. Larger departments, of course, are more likely than smaller ones to encounter crime and related problems. *Source: Brooks (2020).*

†Difference with comparison group is significant at the 95% confidence level.

‡Difference with comparison group is significant at the 90% confidence level.

[a]Reflects the percentage of officers whose departments maintained a written community-policing plan. This is calculated by multiplying the result for each department by its size. The size of the department is the sum of the number of full-time sworn officers and part-time sworn officers (who are counted as the equivalent of 0.5 full-time sworn officers) employed by that department.

Why would larger departments be more likely than smaller ones to mention community policing in their mission statement?

difficulties of implementing community policing practices was the global concern for COVID-19. Police departments were restricted in the extent to which they could closely interact in positive situations with the general public (Montgomery, 2020), a key component of community policing.

The civil unrest led to many calls for defunding the police, which refers to redirecting some of the funding typically allocated to police departments to other services such as counseling, assistance with homelessness and mental health concerns, job training, and violence-prevention programs (Fernandez, 2020; Ray, 2020). Calls for defunding the police do not suggest the abolition of the police. Instead, they focus on redirecting police resources and responsibilities.

The Los Angeles Riots and the War on Drugs

Regardless of the actual or alleged contributions of community-oriented policing, police departments in the community era have faced some of the same issues as in the preceding periods of policing, such as civil unrest and riots. For instance, in 1992, riots that broke out in Los Angeles led to 43 deaths. The event that preceded the riots was the acquittal of police officers who had been seen on video beating a Black motorist, Rodney King. The acquittal may have been the immediate impetus for the riots, but there were also underlying tensions resulting from minority group perceptions that they were the targets of social injustice.

The Christopher Commission, which was assembled following the Rodney King incident in part to examine claims of Los Angeles Police Department officer misbehavior, stated in its report that "there is a significant number of officers in the LAPD who repetitively use excessive force against the public and persistently ignore the written guidelines of the Department regarding force" (*Report of the Independent*, 1991, p. 3). The commission further noted that "the problem of excessive force is aggravated by racism and bias," and "failure to control (problem) officers is a management issue that is at the heart of the problem" (p. 4).

Policing during the community era has also been shaped by the "war on drugs," which was a government campaign begun by President Richard Nixon in 1971. The campaign involved targeting the manufacturing, transport, and use of illicit drugs. Since that time, the government has spent over $1 trillion fighting the war, and drug arrests have contributed in large part to the increased rates of incarceration seen beginning in the 1980s (Branson, 2012; Pearl, 2018). Despite these efforts, drug use remains relatively popular among a sizeable percentage of youth and adults. For instance, in 2018, nearly 1 in 5 people in the United States aged 12 or older (19.4%) admitted to having used an illicit drug during the previous year (Substance Abuse and Mental Health Services Administration, 2019). Street-level law enforcement efforts have been prominent in the war on drugs because the criminal justice system, and especially policing, is expected to address drugs and drug-related crimes, such as gang crimes, turf wars over the right to distribute drugs, and the commission of crimes to purchase drugs (Levitt, 2004).

Neighborhood Crime Watch programs are often part of a police department's approach to community policing. These programs encourage residents in a community to assist the police through reporting suspicious behaviors and are symbolic of a community's concern for crime.

Should the police mandate that residents who live in high-crime areas create a Neighborhood Crime Watch group?

1 Criminal Act

10 Corrections

● **Learning Objective 10.5:** Explain how the threat of terrorism has influenced local policing.

terrorism Unlawfully using force and violence to intimidate or coerce others in furtherance of political or social objectives

1 Criminal Act

Community Oriented Policing Services A component within the U.S. Department of Justice that promotes community policing

Terrorism and Homeland Security

Terrorism is defined and categorized in many ways, largely because of different interpretations of terrorist acts. What may be viewed as terrorism by one group may be viewed as a form of freedom-fighting by others. However, the term terrorism has been broadly defined as "the unlawful use of force and violence against persons or property to intimidate or coerce a government, the civilian population, or any segment thereof in furtherance of political or social objectives" (Purpura, 2007, p. 469). Some commonalities among definitions of terrorism include:

● acts often committed by an organized group of individuals,

● acts motivated by politics,

● acts featuring violent behaviors, and

● acts designed to inflict harm beyond the immediate attack (Burns, 2013).

Terrorism can be domestic or international. It crosses international boundaries and may include acts or threats from foreign sponsors of terrorism, formalized terrorist groups such as al-Qaeda and the so-called Islamic State, and loosely organized groups. The Islamic State, in particular, has engaged in various terrorist attacks in different countries to intimidate government leaders and citizens and promote their political and religious beliefs. Domestic terrorists have also been responsible for several high-profile attacks (e.g., the Oklahoma City federal building bombing in 1995) and many low-profile ones, such as those that have occurred at abortion clinics around the country. Terrorists exploit opportunities and deficiencies in law enforcement practices (Finn, 2010).

Ramifications of the September 11, 2001, Terrorist Attacks

The 2001 terrorist attacks against the United States in some ways ushered in a new era of policing (Oliver, 2006). The attacks came at a time when police departments were increasingly engaged in community policing and the crime rate was dropping. The resources directed toward community policing were, in large part, redirected toward protecting the homeland (Wallace-Wells, 2003). Shortly after the attacks, President Bush proposed zero funding for the **Community Oriented Policing Services**, a component within the DOJ that promotes community policing. Among other contributions, Community Oriented Policing Services provided funding for local agencies to hire roughly 70,000 new community-oriented officers between 1994 and 2000 (Wallace-Wells, 2003). While Congress ultimately restored some, but not all, of the funding for the program, economic strains in many local departments led community policing to become more of "an add-on" to homeland security efforts than a primary focus (Wallace-Wells, 2003, p. 34).

Homeland security efforts largely pertain to protecting the United States from terrorist attacks, but more broadly, homeland security entails protecting citizens from any type of harm that threatens the nation. In highlighting the significance of policing in relation to homeland security, one researcher noted that "the world of policing has been rapidly and radically transformed. Our military and intelligence communities cannot succeed in defending us without the active cooperation of well-informed and well-prepared local police agencies" (O'Connell, 2008, p. 456).

Following the terrorist attacks, police departments faced several new issues, including:

● a decrease in budgets,

● the need to train officers in how to deal with terrorist threats and other threats to the homeland,

MYTHBUSTING

Militarized Policing Is an Effective Form of Crime Control

Police departments have increasingly resembled the military in terms of the weapons they possess and the uniforms they wear. The use of military-type weapons and tactics was originally restricted to the most serious situations (e.g., incidents involving hostages and shooters); however, SWAT teams, which use military gear and were created primarily to deal with emergency situations, have also commonly been used to search suspects' homes for drugs (American Civil Liberties Union, 2014).

Evidence suggests that militarizing the police can increase violence. The reason for this is that military equipment is used against enemies, and individuals may perceive themselves to be enemies when they see the police in military gear. Citizens often feel threatened by the police in military gear, and angry crowds respond violently when they feel they are being treated unfairly (Eichenwald, 2014). Why do you think the police have become more militarized in recent years?

- an increased number of hate crime attacks against Middle Easterners and Muslims,
- the need to replace reserve military personnel who had previously worked in policing and were summoned for overseas military activity, and
- the recruitment of new individuals, because many who would have become police officers chose to enlist or remain in the military for the wars in Afghanistan and Iraq (Chapman et al., 2002).

Local police departments assumed greater responsibilities following the attacks, because in addition to their traditional law enforcement practices, they had to better prepare for terrorist threats, cooperate to a greater extent with other agencies, and conduct greater surveillance and intelligence efforts. Such responsibilities create a challenge, for instance as researchers noted that the attacks "resulted in many, and sometimes conflicting, claims as to what local law enforcement should do in terms of terrorism prevention and response" (Stewart & Morris, 2009, p. 297).

Cooperation Among Law Enforcement and Concerns About Privacy

The decentralized nature of law enforcement has traditionally hampered cooperative law enforcement efforts. However, the 2001 terrorist attacks prompted a significant restructuring of federal law enforcement (e.g., Ward et al., 2006), including the creation of the Department of Homeland Security. As a result of the restructuring, all or part of 22 existing federal agencies became part of the department. In addition, many new task forces and fusion centers were established. Fusion centers are run by state and local law enforcement agencies. They collect information from regional jurisdictions and may contain either only terrorist-related information or all types of criminal behavior.

In the aftermath of the 2001 terrorist attacks and others, **intelligence-led policing** is increasingly being used by police departments across the United States (Crank et al., 2010). This type of policing uses

CAREERS

Intelligence support analysts collate and analyze statistical data for law enforcement agencies. The information they prepare is shared with various groups, both internally (e.g., administrators and line personnel) and externally (e.g., the media, the general public).

intelligence-led policing A type of policing that uses real-time crime and data analyses to direct regular patrol and specialized units; it is supported by surveillance and intelligence-gathering practices

USA PATRIOT Act Passed in 2001, it provided funding for local law enforcement to protect the homeland; it enabled law enforcement agents to use greater levels of surveillance, enhanced the punishments associated with terrorist acts, and facilitated better relationships and communication among levels of law enforcement

real-time crime and data analyses to direct regular patrol and specialized units (Carter, 2004), and is supported by surveillance and intelligence-gathering practices. Real-time policing also involves the sharing of information among law enforcement agencies.

Local police departments have increasingly established intelligence units and engaged in greater levels of cooperation with federal agencies (see Module 11). With increased intelligence-gathering capabilities come concerns about privacy and respect for individual rights. Surveillance and intelligence-gathering efforts in particular have generated concerns that law enforcement is becoming too invasive. For example, the **USA PATRIOT Act** of 2001 provided funding for local law enforcement to protect the homeland. The act enabled law enforcement agents to use greater levels of surveillance, enhanced the punishments associated with terrorist acts, and facilitated better relationships and communication among levels of law enforcement (Oliver, 2007). However, the act was viewed as controversial by some because it was believed to grant law enforcement greater powers to infringe on the rights and freedoms of citizens (e.g., Bloss, 2007). President Barack Obama signed the PATRIOT Sunsets Extension Act of 2011, which extended three key provisions of the act that provided continued powers for law enforcement regarding roving wiretaps, searches of business records, and conducting surveillance of individuals suspected to be involved in terrorist attacks yet not linked with a terrorist group. The extended parts were renewed in 2015, to extend until 2019, with the provision that the National Security Agency cease its mass phone data collection program. This means the National Security Agency will need a federal court order to obtain information about targeted individuals.

The System in Perspective

The "In the News" feature at the beginning of this module highlighted accounts of police officers in Chicago and Cleveland using excessive force, which resulted in calls for revised departmental policies and efforts to promote stronger police–community relations. Controversial police practices have historically hampered the relationship between the police and the public. There have been times when public trust in the police erodes and public support for the police diminishes. These tumultuous periods are typically addressed by efforts from both groups to repair any damages done.

George Orwell once noted that "the most effective way to destroy people is to deny and obliterate their own understanding of their history." This quote highlights the importance of understanding history in order to shape the future. The hope is that by examining the history of policing, we can learn from mistakes and move forward in a more positive manner.

Examining the history of policing also highlights the independence, yet interconnectedness of the criminal justice system. Prior to the development of formal policing, citizens were expected to bring offenders to justice. Those with the financial means to do so often hired others for the job. It was, in large part, the efforts of a magistrate (Henry Fielding) that helped create modern policing. Police departments represented the final piece of the criminal justice system, as courts had existed and correctional practices occurred prior to policing. The relationship between the police and the courts continuously evolved, as did the functions and responsibilities of police officers.

Summary

1. Learning Objective 10.1: *Explain how early English methods of informal social control influenced the development of formal policing both in England and in the United States.*

- Early English methods of social control were informal in nature and contributed to the development of formal policing. Citizens protected one another and eventually designated specific individuals (shire reeves) to be the primary law enforcement agents. As cities and towns grew larger, informal social control became increasingly limited, which led to the Bow Street Runners becoming the model for proactive police practices. The group was responsible for bringing offenders to justice. The approach was effective and contributed to the creation of the London Metropolitan Police Department.

- Policing in the United States emerged in a similar manner to policing in England. Residents initially relied on informal social control (including the frankpledge system) and created police departments when informal social control became less effective in fighting crime. The appearance and responsibilities of the officers were similar, and they shared the need to establish and maintain positive relations with the public.

2. Learning Objective 10.2: *Describe the characteristics of the political era.*

- Policing during the political era was heavily influenced by politicians, who maintained much control over police departments through the spoils system and other political influences. Police corruption became particularly problematic during this time, and several significant events including the Civil War, Prohibition, passage of the 13th and 14th Amendments, and rioting influenced police work.

3. Learning Objective 10.3: *Describe the characteristics of the reform era.*

- The reform era was characterized by an emphasis on crime-fighting, poor police–community relations, and the isolation of the police from the public. The civil rights movement, rioting, and several important Supreme Court decisions influenced policing during this time.

4. Learning Objective 10.4: *Describe the characteristics of the community era.*

- The community era began in response to policing in the reform era becoming too focused on crime control at the expense of community relations. There was a clear need for police departments to establish better relationships with the communities they served. This era involved many police departments adopting a new philosophical approach to policing that focused on problem-solving and better integrating the public with regard to police practices. The era was also characterized by increased efforts to fight the war on drugs.

5. Learning Objective 10.5: *Explain how the threat of terrorism has influenced local policing.*

- The terrorist attacks against the United States in 2001 notably changed local law enforcement. Reserve military personnel who worked in policing were summoned for military activity. In addition, many individuals who might have become police officers enlisted or remained in the military instead. Police during this time have had to deal with increased numbers of hate crime attacks and terrorist threats, all while dealing with privacy issues associated with increased surveillance. While cooperation with other agencies and enhanced intelligence efforts have helped police to do their jobs, community policing has arguably taken a backseat.

Questions for Critical Thinking

1. Do you see any elements of the frankpledge system in 21st-century efforts to address crime? Explain your answer.

2. What were the primary limitations of policing during the political era? Do any of these challenges remain?

3. What do you believe were the most significant events that occurred during the reform era that impacted policing?

4. Do you consider community policing to be a hybrid of the political and reform eras? Why or why not?

5. How has local policing changed in an age where the threat of terrorism looms large?

Key Terms

bobbies
Bow Street Runners
community era of policing
Community Oriented Policing Services
exclusionary rule
frankpledge system
hundreds
intelligence-led policing
kin policing
London Metropolitan Police Act

political era of policing
problem-oriented policing
prohibition
reform era of policing
shire
spoils system
terrorism
tythings
USA PATRIOT Act

For digital learning resources, please go to
https://www.oup.com/he/burns1e

Current Organization of Law Enforcement

Module
11

Law enforcement in the United States is largely decentralized, with law enforcement agencies existing at all levels of government.

Do you believe that the future of law enforcement will involve greater levels of centralization? Why or why not?

Law enforcement in the United States is decentralized, resulting in many different agencies at the federal, state, and local levels. Most law enforcement agencies, particularly police departments, are found at the local level. At the international level, two organizations (INTERPOL and the United Nations) assist with international law enforcement issues. This module starts with a discussion of the decentralization of law enforcement before providing an overview of the organization of local, state, federal, and international law enforcement. The module ends with a discussion of the growth of private security.

MODULE OUTLINE

- **Decentralization**

  Learning Objective 11.1: Illustrate the characteristics of the decentralized approach to law enforcement in the United States.

- **Local Law Enforcement**

  Learning Objective 11.2: Summarize the law enforcement agencies that are considered local law enforcement.

- **State Law Enforcement**

  Learning Objective 11.3: Identify the primary responsibilities of state law enforcement agencies.

- **Federal Law Enforcement**

  Learning Objective 11.4: Summarize the key features of the most prominent federal law enforcement agencies.

- **International Law Enforcement**

  Learning Objective 11.5: Describe the primary functions of INTERPOL and the United Nations regarding international law enforcement.

- **Private Security**

  Learning Objective 11.6: Compare and contrast public policing and private security.

INTERPOL and Collaborative International Efforts to Address Crime

In 2018, INTERPOL, an international police agency that promotes cooperation among countries to address international crimes, coordinated efforts among 116 countries that seized 500 tons of illicit pharmaceuticals and resulted in 859 arrests. The operation, titled Pangea XI, also resulted in the seizure of over 110,000 illicit medical devices (e.g., hearing aids, surgical instruments) and the closure of over 3,600 web links, including websites, social media pages, and online marketplaces that sold the fake and unlicensed goods (Interpol, 2018). INTERPOL worked with police, customs, and health regulatory agencies from all of the involved countries.

Selling illicit pharmaceuticals and medical devices online has become an attractive practice for some criminals, given the high costs of these items and the historical lack of regulation and enforcement. Addressing cybercrimes can be challenging without the assistance of a central agency to coordinate efforts among countries. INTERPOL's efforts in Pangea XI demonstrate the need for an international law enforcement agency and the importance of cooperative and coordinated crime-fighting efforts among countries. What other international crimes would likely warrant attention from INTERPOL? Do you believe the role of INTERPOL will expand in the near future? Why or why not?

Liam Gimon
INTERPOL Illicit Goods and Global Health unit

Decentralization

The United States has a **federalist** system of political organization, which means that powers are distributed to national, state, county, and local levels. As a result, the powers and authority to enforce the law in the United States are **decentralized**—with no central unified law enforcement agency. This is in contrast to some countries that have highly centralized police forces, such as Sweden, France, Italy, and Spain. The decentralized organizational design of law enforcement in the United States emerged as colonists and later groups feared the federal government having too much control over their daily lives and because Americans have long believed that local problems are best addressed by local authorities (Barkan & Bryjak, 2014).

A decentralized organizational approach to law enforcement allows local departments to more directly understand the wants and needs of their communities. It also permits members of local communities to more easily direct their concerns or complaints to the police department than if they had to contact a national office.

● **Learning Objective 11.1:** Illustrate the characteristics of the decentralized approach to law enforcement in the United States.

Decentralization has limitations, however, because it may result in lack of coopera-tion, an uneven or unequal quality of service depending on community resources, a disjointed response to crime, and overlapping jurisdictions (Bumgarner, 2006).

With decentralization comes the need for cooperation among law enforce-ment agencies within and across levels, for example through the roughly 200 **joint terrorism task forces** found in cities across the United States. The joint terrorism task forces are small groups of highly trained investigators, analysts, linguists, SWAT experts, and other specialists from dozens of U.S. law enforcement and intelligence agencies that are designed to combine the resources of federal, state, and local law enforcement. The groups primarily address terrorism and related threats, with most of the task forces created following the 2001 terrorist attacks (Federal Bureau of Investigation [FBI], n.d.). Collaboration among departments at all levels has increased in recent years, primarily in response to technological advancements facilitating such cooperation, as well as concerns for homeland security.

Despite the decentralized approach, law enforcement agents generally share the same goals of responding to and preventing crime, although their specific duties, responsibilities, and practices differ. The differences among law enforcement agen-cies are attributable to many factors, including the level of government at which an agency exists, public needs, jurisdictional issues, and departmental needs.

Of particular importance with regard to the organization of law enforcement agencies is **jurisdiction**, which refers to the authority or responsibility that law en-forcement has over a particular area. Jurisdiction may be geographical (Roberg et al., 2015) or based on subject matter. In general, law enforcement agencies are bound by the geographical, or territorial, areas in which they operate. For instance, a county law enforcement agency has territorial jurisdiction over the county it serves, but not over other counties. With regard to subject matter jurisdiction, some specialized agencies maintain subject matter jurisdiction over particular types of crimes. For ex-ample, the Bureau of Alcohol, Tobacco, Firearms and Explosives (ATF) has primary federal jurisdiction over the manufacture, import, and transport of firearms, ammu-nition, and explosives. Most local law enforcement agencies have broad subject mat-ter jurisdiction and relatively small geographical jurisdiction compared to federal law enforcement agencies.

federalist A system of government in which the powers are distributed to national, state, county, and local levels

decentralized With regard to law enforcement, it refers to the absence of a central unified law enforce-ment agency

joint terrorism task forces Small groups of highly trained investigators, analysts, and law enforce-ment specialists that are designed to combine the resources of federal, state, and local law enforcement to address terrorism and related issues

jurisdiction The power or right to exert one's legal power over an-other; it can be considered in terms of geography, sub-ject matter, and the func-tions and responsibilities of a court

Local Law Enforcement

Local law enforcement agencies include rural, suburban, county, and municipal police departments; sheriff's departments; and various special jurisdiction law enforcement agencies, including university/college campus police and law enforcement groups that protect transportation systems. Local law enforcement groups work cooperatively in many ways, largely in response to limited budgets that require a sharing of resources (e.g., jails and crime labs), the close geographical proximity of some cities and towns, and the need for departments to collaborate on crimes that cross jurisdictional boundaries.

● **Learning Objective 11.2:** Summarize the law enforcement agencies that are considered local law enforcement.

Responsibilities of Local Law Enforcement

Local law enforcement agencies primarily have three general responsibilities: main-taining order, providing services, and fighting crime. Through these functions, the police come into contact with the public on a relatively frequent basis. For instance, in 2018 an estimated 61.5 million U.S. residents over age 15, or 24% of the popula-tion, had face-to-face contact with a police officer in the prior 12 months, most com-monly during a traffic stop (Harrell & Davis, 2020).

Traffic stops constitute a notable portion of a patrol officer's responsibilities. It could be argued that they embody all of the primary responsibilities of policing: for instance, they address violations of the law, ensure our safety on the streets, and help maintain order.

Do you believe that the police are overzealous with regard to traffic citations, or should they become more active in controlling driver behavior?

Organization of Local Law Enforcement

Local departments are typically administered by a police chief or sheriff, under which there are a host of supervisory and administrative positions (e.g., captains, sergeants). Further, larger local departments may include various types of investigators, public information officers, marshals, constables, canine (K-9) handlers, polygraph operators, training personnel, and human resource specialists. There were 12,261 local police agencies and 3,012 sheriff's offices as of 2016, with the majority of personnel in these departments being sworn officers (C. Brooks, 2020), meaning that they have the power to make arrests. Nonsworn personnel perform many important services, including many administrative support functions such as providing research and statistics, accounting services, police dispatch, information technology, and forensics. Figure 11.1 notes the organizational design of the Fort Worth Police Department, including the wide array of services provided by the department.

Urban Versus Rural Law Enforcement Agencies

There is much variation among large and small local law enforcement agencies. Officers who work in big-city police departments engage in much more crime-fighting and order maintenance than their counterparts who work in rural areas, where the need to provide non–law enforcement services (e.g., engaging in searches and rescues) is more common. Officers who work in medium-size cities generally perform more of an equal combination of service and crime-fighting duties. Larger departments are generally more specialized than other departments with regard to particular services. For instance, traffic response teams are more likely to exist and respond to motor vehicle accidents in larger cities (where more accidents occur) than

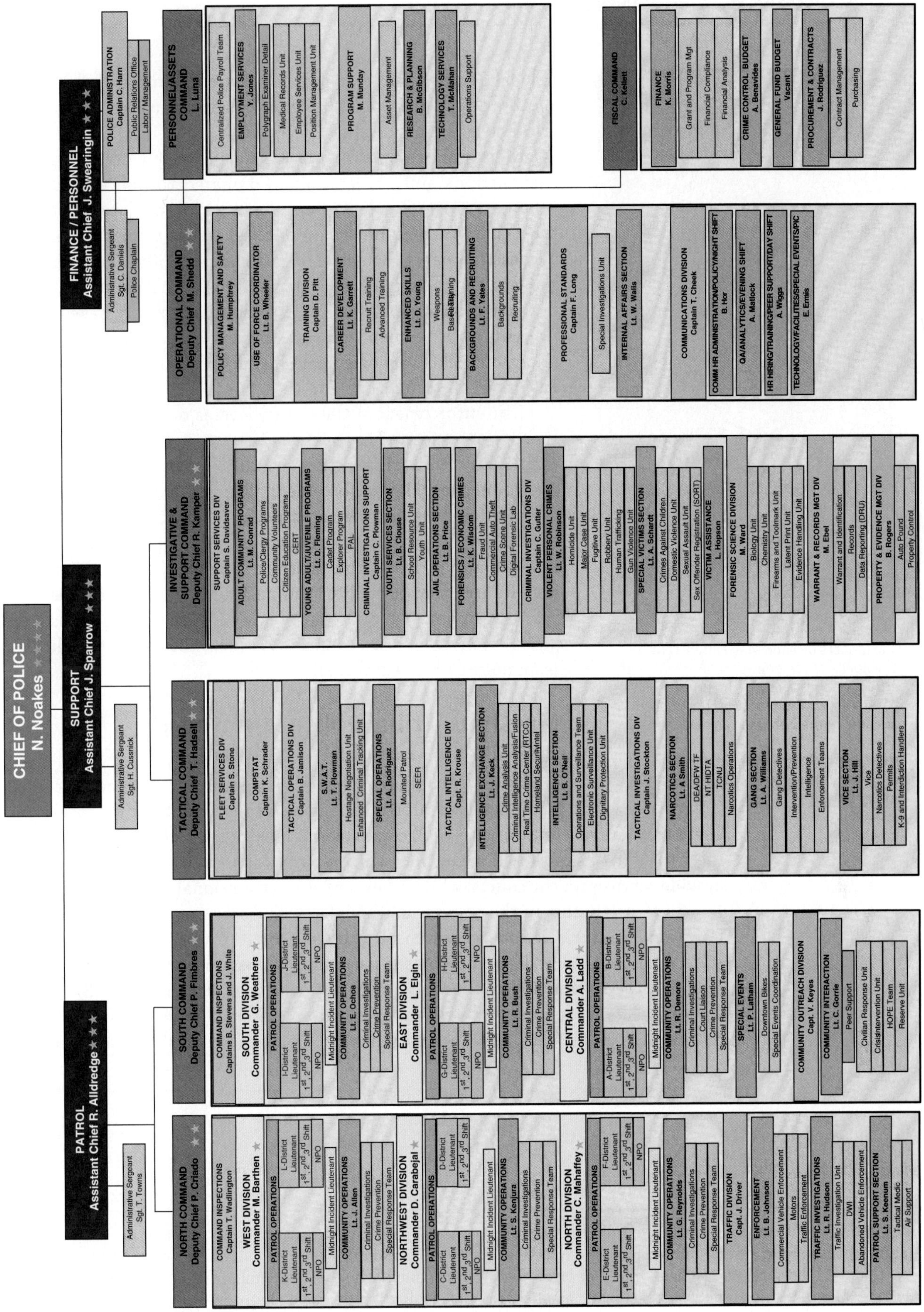

FIGURE 11.1. Organizational Design for Fort Worth, Texas, Police Department. The Fort Worth Police Department is organized into three primary areas: patrol, support, and finance/personnel. The department is further divided within these areas. *Source: Fort Worth Police Department (2021).*

What are the pros and cons of having such a detailed organizational design?

Police canine officers provide many important services. The ability of the dogs to search for drugs, explosives, and missing persons and protect police officers by subduing or intimidating noncooperative suspects are among the benefits canines provide.

In what other ways do you believe dogs, or perhaps other animals, can assist police officers?

in smaller cities. Larger departments are also more likely to have specific divisions or units designed to address particular types of crimes (e.g., homicide units).

Most police departments are small, which notably affects their actions and expectations. Compared to police officers in urban areas, rural police officers have a closer relationship with their constituents and are more likely to use informal means to address low-level incidents (e.g., Cebulak, 2004). For instance, they may be more likely to help resolve personal disputes instead of making an arrest. Smaller departments typically have a lower percentage of women officers compared to larger departments (Langton, 2010) and often have higher crime clearance rates (e.g., Falcone et al., 2002).

Law enforcement at the county level is primarily provided by sheriff's deputies and in some cases county police officers. Despite their many similarities, there are differences among municipal and county-level law enforcement agencies. Among the more notable differences are the tasks performed by these groups, the effects of politics in selecting leaders, their practices, funding sources, and jurisdictional matters (Burns, 2013). For instance, sheriffs are often elected to their positions, while police chiefs are typically appointed, and county law enforcement agencies have jurisdiction over entire counties. As such, they are more likely to respond to calls in rural areas.

Marshals, Tribal Police, and Special Jurisdiction Law Enforcement

Constables/marshals, tribal police agencies, and some special jurisdiction law enforcement agencies also operate at the local level. There are relatively few (roughly 638) constable/marshal agencies (Reaves, 2011), and their roles vary across and sometimes within states. For example, some primarily provide services for the courts, while others engage in traditional police practices.

There is variation in the manner in which law enforcement exists on tribal lands, for example as jurisdiction over offenses in Indian country may lie with the federal, state, or tribal agency, depending on the particular offense, the characteristics of the offender, the victim, and the location of the offense (e.g., Hickman, 2003). For instance, an offense committed by a Native American on Indian lands falls under the jurisdiction of tribal police, while other crimes may be addressed by the county sheriff.

MYTHBUSTING

Most Police Departments Employ a Large Number of Officers

When you think of the typical police officer, it is easy to imagine them as one among many in a big-city police department. To be sure, most officers work for large departments. However, most police departments employ a relatively *small number of officers*. For instance, in 2013 there were 49 local police departments (0.4% of all local departments) that employed 1,000 or more sworn personnel. These agencies employed 33.9% of all full-time sworn personnel. In contrast, there were 5,895 local departments (47.8%) that employed 9 or fewer officers. The United States has a relatively large number of small towns compared to a small number of big cities, which is why most police departments, in fact, employ a small number of officers.

As a result of the **Major Crimes Act** of 1885, most serious crimes such as murder, arson, and manslaughter that occur on tribal lands fall under the jurisdiction of federal authorities, while tribal authorities have jurisdiction over less serious crimes, such as burglary and theft. Tribal police departments face many limitations and challenges, including:

- increasing crime on reservations,
- poor equipment,
- limited budgets,
- inadequate management practices,
- a lack of political support, and
- high personnel turnover (Wakeling et al., 2001).

There are roughly 1,700 special jurisdiction law enforcement agencies in the United States, with some of these agencies operating at the state level, although many would be considered local law enforcement. Special jurisdiction law enforcement agencies are categorized into five areas:

1. Public buildings and facilities
2. Natural resources
3. Transportation systems and facilities
4. Criminal investigations
5. Special enforcement

The bulk of special jurisdiction agencies (65%) provide services for public buildings and facilities, including schools, hospitals, public housing, and government buildings (Reaves, 2011).

> **CAREERS**
>
> **Canine (K-9) officers**, or canine (K-9) handlers, are sworn officers who oversee the proper use and care of police canines. They take care of the canine, remain updated with regard to training, and respond to a variety of calls for service in which canine services are required.

> **CAREERS**
>
> **Fire marshals, or arson specialists,** help determine the origins and causes of fires through investigations and the collection of evidence. They are employed by law enforcement agencies, fire departments, and insurance companies.

Major Crimes Act Passed in 1885, it attempted to clarify law enforcement jurisdiction in Native American lands by noting that most serious crimes fall under the jurisdiction of federal authorities, while tribal authorities have jurisdiction over less serious crimes

State Law Enforcement

In 2016, 47 shootings in a 14-month period in the Chicago area prompted the Illinois State Police to more closely patrol the expressways and work with the Chicago Police and the Cook County Sheriff's Department. In 2018, three young adults were shot in an 8-day span, and six others were injured within a month, in Syracuse, New York. The incidents led New York Governor Andrew Cuomo to send 10 New York State Police officers to assist the local authorities. Patrolling highways and assisting and cooperating with other law enforcement agencies are among the primary functions of state law enforcement groups.

Creation of State Law Enforcement

Texas and Massachusetts were the only two states to have a state police force prior to 1900, but by 1925 nearly all states had one. State law enforcement agencies emerged out of the need to:

- assist local law enforcement agencies that lacked resources or training,
- investigate crimes that crossed jurisdictional boundaries,

1 Criminal Act

● **Learning Objective 11.3:** Identify the primary responsibilities of state law enforcement agencies.

- provide law enforcement services in areas without municipal or county police protection, and
- address labor disputes such as strikes (Lyman, 2010).

Functions of State Law Enforcement

Each of the 50 states in the United States has a primary state law enforcement agency. Most of the primary state law enforcement agencies are state police agencies, followed by highway patrol agencies and departments of public safety (Reaves, 2011). State police agencies have broad law enforcement responsibilities, similar to those found in local police departments. They often include a combination of state-level regulatory and enforcement agencies that:

- provide traffic regulation on the state's roads and highways;
- regulate drivers' license renewals and motor vehicle inspections;
- collect, analyze, and distribute crime data;
- investigate crimes;
- operate crime labs;
- provide emergency management services;
- engage in intelligence gathering and counterterrorism;
- protect natural resources;
- train and cooperate with local law enforcement agencies; and
- collaborate with federal law enforcement groups.

Organization of State Law Enforcement

State law enforcement agencies vary with regard to their organization (centralized or decentralized) and emphasis on functions. Centralized agencies combine state highway patrol with the investigative components and are typically called state police. Decentralized agencies, which are found most often in the Midwest, West, and South, create distinct agencies such as the highway patrol and a division of law enforcement. For instance, South Carolina has several state law enforcement agencies, including the two primary ones: the South Carolina Department of Public Safety (which houses the South Carolina Highway Patrol) and the South Carolina Law Enforcement Division (which is a statewide investigative law enforcement agency). The geographic or other qualities specific to the state may also influence functions and responsibilities. For instance, states with many miles of coastland to protect face different responsibilities than do states without coastal regions, while states with an abundance of highways face another set of issues.

Some states also have specialized units to regulate particular industries or areas. For instance, the Florida Fish and Wildlife Conservation Commission enforces the laws designed to protect fish and wildlife and protects Florida's waterways. The Nevada Gaming Commission and the Nevada Gaming Control Board are state agencies tasked with regulating casinos throughout Nevada. Other states have similar law enforcement and regulatory agencies to address special needs.

Federal Law Enforcement

Federal law enforcement agencies are perhaps the most prestigious in law enforcement. They are often depicted in major motion pictures and television shows using advanced investigative skills to solve crimes. An estimated 132,000 federal law enforcement officers are found throughout roughly 100 federal agencies in the United States, providing a wide array of services (C. Brooks, 2019). While the FBI, ATF, Drug Enforcement Administration (DEA), Secret Service, and U.S. Marshals Service (USMS) are perhaps the most widely known, the Internal Revenue Service, U.S. Postal Inspection Service, Food and Drug Administration, and Environmental Protection Agency are among the many other agencies that also employ federal law enforcement agents who specialize in various areas.

Functions of Federal Law Enforcement

The nature of federal law enforcement work varies by agency (see Table 11.1) and position, but in general, federal law enforcement officers engage in the following functions (C. Brooks, 2019; Reaves, 2012a; see Figure 11.2).

Table 11.1 depicts the primary responsibilities of the more commonly known federal law enforcement agencies.

- *criminal investigations*, including the collection of evidence, the execution of warrants, the identification and seizure of illegal goods, surveillance, and the analysis of information pertaining to criminal cases
- *corrections and detention*, including the duties involved with the custody, control, and transport of inmates, pretrial detainees, and detained illegal aliens
- *police response and patrol*, including the response to complaints and reports of illegal behavior, the arrest of offenders, traffic and crowd control, and the provision of emergency services
- *inspections*, including the regulation of industries to ensure compliance with regulations and laws
- *court operations*, including the supervision of offenders on federal probation or parole and the monitoring of individuals who received pretrial release
- *security and protection*, including services related to ensuring the security and safety of buildings, records, assets, or persons (such as judges, foreign officials, and government officials)

Organization of Federal Law Enforcement

In some ways, the organization of federal law enforcement is simpler than that of state and local law enforcement because there is only one federal

2
Investigation

10
Corrections

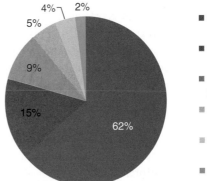

- Criminal investigations
- Corrections and detention
- Police response and patrol
- Inspections
- Court operations
- Security and protection

FIGURE 11.2. Percentage of federal law enforcement officers, by primary function. The primary function of the majority of federal law enforcement in 2016 was related to criminal investigations.

Based on your familiarity with the police, how would this pie chart look if it depicted the primary functions of local law enforcement?

TABLE 11.1. Primary Responsibilities of Common Federal Law Enforcement Agencies

AGENCY	RESPONSIBILITIES
U.S. Customs and Border Protection	Customs and Border Protection officers protect U.S. borders at official ports of entry. Border Patrol agents prevent the illegal entry of people and contraband.
U.S. Immigration and Customs Enforcement	Immigration and Customs Enforcement promotes homeland security and public safety by enforcing criminal and civil laws pertaining to customs, border control, trade, and immigration.
U.S. Secret Service	Secret Service Special Agents investigate financial crimes, counterfeiting, computer crime, and related offenses and provide protection for the White House, other presidential offices, and the main Treasury building. The agency also provides protective services for the president, the vice president, their families, and select other individuals.
Bureau of Alcohol, Tobacco, Firearms and Explosives	Special agents enforce federal laws pertaining to the illegal use and distribution of firearms; the illegal use and storage of explosives; acts of arson, bombings, and terrorism; and the illegal diversion of alcohol and tobacco products.
Drug Enforcement Administration	Special agents investigate major narcotics violations, enforce the laws concerning illegal drugs, and seek to prevent and respond to drug trafficking.
Federal Bureau of Investigation	Special agents are responsible for the criminal investigation and enforcement of over 200 categories of federal laws. Their priorities include public corruption, civil rights violations, organized crime, white-collar crime, violent crime, and major theft.
U.S. Marshals Service	The agency receives all individuals arrested by federal agencies and is responsible for their custody and transportation until they are sentenced. Deputy marshals provide security for federal judicial buildings and personnel.
Federal Bureau of Prisons	The bureau oversees inmates who have been incarcerated for violating a federal law. It also holds inmates who have committed felonies in Washington, DC.

Controlled Substances Act

The statute prescribing federal U.S. drug policy regarding the manufacturing, importation, possession, use, and distribution of drugs in the United States

government. However, federal law enforcement has its own type of complexity. The many federal agencies have highly specialized jurisdictions and together cover a great variety of responsibilities. Federal law enforcement agencies have territorial jurisdiction over the entire United States and its territories, but the subject jurisdiction of most federal agencies is narrowly defined. For example, the DEA is the lead agency for enforcement of the **Controlled Substances Act**, which is the statute prescribing federal U.S. drug policy regarding the manufacturing, importation, possession, use, and distribution of drugs in the United States. The DEA has territorial jurisdiction not only in the United States, but also in pursuing drug investigations abroad; however, its subject matter jurisdiction is primarily related to drug enforcement.

Following the 2001 terrorist attacks against the United States, the Homeland Security Act of 2002 created the cabinet-level **Department of Homeland Security (DHS)** and transferred all or parts of 22 existing federal agencies under its purview (Figure 11.3), including U.S. Customs and Border Protection, the U.S. Immigration and Customs Enforcement, and the Secret Service. The overall mission of the DHS is to "safeguard the American people, our homeland, and our values" (DHS, 2016).

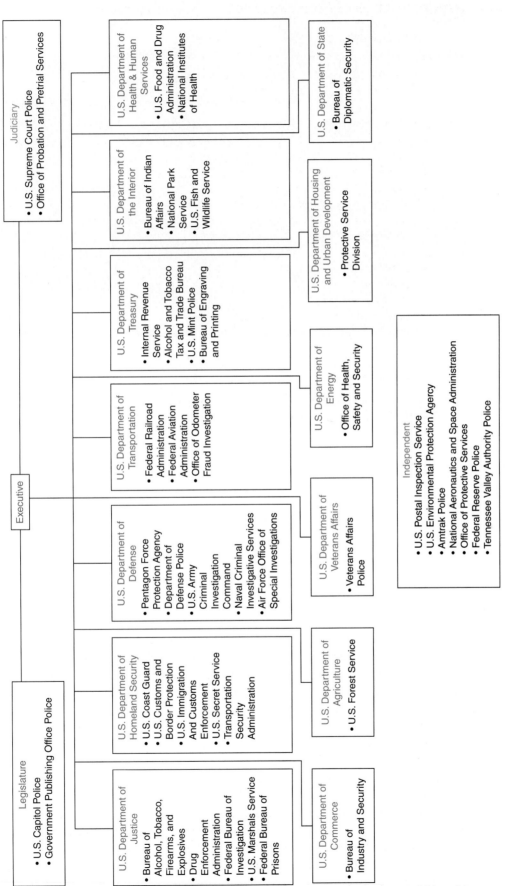

Sampling of Federal Agencies That Have Law Enforcement Power

Legislature
- U.S. Capitol Police
- Government Publishing Office Police

Executive

Judiciary
- U.S. Supreme Court Police
- Office of Probation and Pretrial Services

U.S. Department of Justice
- Bureau of Alcohol, Tobacco, Firearms, and Explosives
- Drug Enforcement Administration
- Federal Bureau of Investigation
- U.S. Marshals Service
- Federal Bureau of Prisons

U.S. Department of Homeland Security
- U.S. Coast Guard
- U.S. Customs and Border Protection
- U.S. Immigration And Customs Enforcement
- U.S. Secret Service
- Transportation Security Administration

U.S. Department of Defense
- Pentagon Force Protection Agency
- Department of Defense Police
- U.S. Army Criminal Investigation Command
- Naval Criminal Investigative Services
- Air Force Office of Special Investigations

U.S. Department of Transportation
- Federal Railroad Administration
- Federal Aviation Administration
- Office of Odometer Fraud Investigation

U.S. Department of Treasury
- Internal Revenue Service
- Alcohol and Tobacco Tax and Trade Bureau
- U.S. Mint Police
- Bureau of Engraving and Printing

U.S. Department of the Interior
- Bureau of Indian Affairs
- National Park Service
- U.S. Fish and Wildlife Service

U.S. Department of Health & Human Services
- U.S. Food and Drug Administration
- National Institutes of Health

U.S. Department of Commerce
- Bureau of Industry and Security

U.S. Department of Agriculture
- U.S. Forest Service

U.S. Department of Veterans Affairs
- Veterans Affairs Police

U.S. Department of Energy
- Office of Health, Safety and Security

U.S. Department of Housing and Urban Development
- Protective Service Division

U.S. Department of State
- Bureau of Diplomatic Security

Independent
- U.S. Postal Inspection Service
- U.S. Environmental Protection Agency
- Amtrak Police
- National Aeronautics and Space Administration
- Office of Protective Services
- Federal Reserve Police
- Tennessee Valley Authority Police

FIGURE 11.3. Organization of the Larger Federal Law Enforcement Agencies. Federal law enforcement agencies are spread throughout different branches of the federal government. The bulk of agencies are located within the executive branch, including those within the U.S. Department of Justice (e.g., the Federal Bureau of Investigation) and the Department of Homeland Security (e.g., the Secret Service).

Do you believe all federal law enforcement agencies should be housed in one department, instead of such a decentralized approach? Why or why not?

Department of Homeland Security A cabinet-level department created with the Homeland Security Act of 2002 whose mission is to protect the American people, its homeland, and its values

The Department of Homeland Security was created to provide a more centralized approach to federal law enforcement. The department is responsible for many law enforcement functions, including preventing terrorism, securing U.S. borders, and thwarting cybercrime.

Should such important functions be the responsibility of one department, or should they be dispersed among different departments?

The primary areas of focus for the DHS are:

- preventing terrorism and enhancing security,
- securing and managing U.S. borders,
- enforcing and administering U.S. immigration laws,
- safeguarding and securing cyberspace, and
- ensuring resilience to disasters.

U.S. Department of Justice A department in the federal government that includes the Federal Bureau of Prisons, the USMS, the FBI, the DEA, and the ATF

The DHS quickly surpassed the **U.S. Department of Justice (DOJ)**, which includes the Federal Bureau of Prisons, the USMS, the FBI, the DEA, and the ATF, as the federal department employing the greatest number of federal officers that are authorized to make arrests and carry a firearm. Table 11.2 highlights the larger federal agencies employing individuals with arrest and firearm authority.

As of 2016, most federal law enforcement personnel were employed by agencies within the DHS (47%) or DOJ (33%; C. Brooks, 2019). An additional 11.7% of federal law enforcement personnel were employed by agencies in some other executive branch of the federal government, and others were placed in the judicial branch (3.1%), legislative branch (1.4%), or independent agencies (3.7%).

Offices of Inspector General Offices charged with preventing and detecting fraud, abuse, waste, and other criminal violations pertaining to federal programs, employees, and operations

Of note in Table 11.2 is the large percentage of federal law enforcement officers working for Customs and Border Protection (33% of all federal law enforcement officers) and the many federal law enforcement officers working in the offices of inspector general. **Offices of inspector general** are charged with preventing and detecting fraud, abuse, waste, and other criminal violations pertaining to federal programs, employees, and operations.

TABLE 11.2. Full-Time Federal Law Enforcement Officers in Federal Agencies, 2016

	NUMBER OF FULL-TIME OFFICERS	PERCENTAGE OF ALL FEDERAL OFFICERS
Total	132,110	100.0
Offices of Inspectors General	3,869	2.9
Total executive/judicial/legislative/ independent federal law enforcement agencies, other than Offices of Inspectors General	128,241	97.1
Executive departments:		
Department of Agriculture		
Forest Service	514	0.4
Department of Commerce		
Bureau of Industry and Security	108	0.1
National Oceanic and Atmospheric Administration, Office of Law Enforcement	126	0.1
Office of Security	38	<0.1
Secretary's Protective Detail	11	<0.1
Department of Defense		
Pentagon Force Protection Agency	777	0.6
Department of Energy		
National Nuclear Security Administration	302	0.2
Department of Health and Human Services		
Food and Drug Administration, Office of Criminal Investigation	231	0.2
National Institutes of Health, Division of Police	77	0.1
Department of Homeland Security		
Customs and Border Protection	43,724	33.1
Immigration and Customs Enforcement	12,400	9.4
Federal Emergency Management Agency, Mount Weather Police	78	0.1
Federal Protective Service	1,007	0.8
Office of the Chief Security Officer	26	<0.1
Secret Service	4,697	3.6
Department of the Interior		
Bureau of Indian Affairs, Office of Justice Services	352	0.3
Bureau of Land Management	253	0.2
Bureau of Reclamation	24	<0.1
Fish and Wildlife Service	619	0.5
National Park Service Rangers	1,822	1.4
Park Police	560	0.4
Department of Justice		
Bureau of Alcohol, Tobacco, Firearms and Explosives	2,675	2.0
Drug Enforcement Administration	4,181	3.2
Federal Bureau of Investigation	13,799	10.4
Federal Bureau of Prisons	19,093	14.5
U.S. Marshals Service	3,788	2.9
Department of Labor		
Division of Protective Operations	15	<0.1

(Continued)

TABLE 11.2. *(Continued)*

	NUMBER OF FULL-TIME OFFICERS	PERCENTAGE OF ALL FEDERAL OFFICERS
Department of State		
Bureau of Diplomatic Security	1,215	0.9
Department of the Treasury		
Bureau of Engraving and Printing Police	182	0.1
Internal Revenue Service, Criminal Investigation Division	2,198	1.7
U.S. Mint Police	292	0.2
Department of Veterans Affairs		
Police Department	3,839	2.9
Other federal law enforcement agencies:		
Administrative Office of the U.S. Courts		
U.S. Probation and Pretrial Services	3,985	3.0
Amtrak		
Amtrak Police Department	427	0.3
Environmental Protection Agency		
Criminal Investigation Division	214	0.2
Government Publishing Office		
Uniform Police Branch	48	<0.1
National Aeronautics and Space Administration		
Office of Protective Services	51	<0.1
Smithsonian Institution		
Office of Protective Services	620	0.5
Supreme Court of the United States		
Supreme Court of the United States Police	156	0.1
Tennessee Valley Authority		
Tennessee Valley Authority Police	53	<0.1
U.S. Capitol Police	1,773	1.3
U.S. Postal Service		
U.S. Postal Inspection Service	1,891	1.4

Source: Adapted from C. Brooks, *Federal Law Enforcement Officers, 2016—Statistical Tables* (NCJ 251922), 2019, U.S. Department of Justice, Bureau of Justice Statistics.

● **Learning Objective 11.5:** Describe the primary functions of INTERPOL and the United Nations regarding international law enforcement.

International Law Enforcement

In our increasingly global society, criminal activity from identity theft to terrorism does not stop at national borders. **Globalization** refers to the international integration of cultural, social, and economic issues among countries that have historically been distinct from one another. The international nature of crime and justice requires greater interaction among countries, particularly with regard to law enforcement efforts. Currently, INTERPOL and the United Nations are best suited to provide international law enforcement. These groups are well-situated and are prepared to address the changing and complex nature of international crime and terrorism.

INTERPOL

INTERPOL is the world's largest international police organization, with 194 member countries as of May 2021. The organization facilitates international police cooperation and supports and assists all organizations, authorities, and services that seek to prevent or confront international crime. According to its constitution, INTERPOL cannot intervene or act in a manner that is motivated by a political, military, religious, or racial character. A particularly important service provided by INTERPOL is the facilitation of international police cooperation among countries, especially those that have poor relations. The four core functions of INTERPOL are:

- securing global police communication services,
- providing operational data services and databases for police,
- providing operational police support services (e.g., through the agency's incident response teams, which are sent to requesting members in times of natural disaster or in the wake of a major or very serious crime), and
- offering police training and development; the agency does not typically provide direct, traditional police services on an international level.

INTERPOL has a National Central Bureau in every member country, which is usually a division of a national police or investigative agency. The National Central Bureau provides a contact point for all INTERPOL operations. The U.S. National Central Bureau is co-managed by the U.S. DOJ and the U.S. DHS. It is staffed with law enforcement personnel from federal, state, and local law enforcement agencies who work closely with DOJ personnel.

The United Nations

The **United Nations** (UN) is an international organization that consists of 193 countries in the early 21st century. It was founded in 1945 and addresses issues including human rights, sustainable development, terrorism, disarmament, health emergencies, and gender equality. The UN Security Council is a group within the UN, composed of 15 member states, that assesses the existence of threats to the peace or acts of aggression and may recommend the UN to take action to keep or restore international peace and security, for instance through economic sanctions or international military action.

The UN has been instrumental in facilitating treaties and agreements, including the Convention Against Transnational Organized Crime (2000) and the Convention Against Corruption (2003). In addition, the UN has led or participated in over 65 international peacekeeping missions or operations since 1948. These missions have involved efforts from law enforcement agencies from 89 countries, although military personnel have played a larger role in the UN peacekeeping efforts than have police agencies (Haberfeld et al., 2008).

Regional Organizations and Nongovernmental Organizations

Perhaps the best example of international crime-fighting on a regional scale is the European Police Office, better known as **Europol**. This organization was created in 1998 to confront international crime, address the removal of border controls in the European Union, and serve as a clearinghouse of information (Bruggeman, 2002; Gerspacher, 2008). Europol largely resembles a smaller version of INTERPOL; it is composed of member states working collaboratively to provide various forms of law enforcement assistance to countries that comprise the European Union.

globalization
The interaction and integration of ideas and practices among different countries

INTERPOL The world's largest international police organization; it facilitates international police cooperation and supports and assists all organizations, authorities, and services that seek to prevent or confront international crime

United Nations
An international organization that was founded in 1945 and addresses issues including human rights, sustainable development, terrorism, disarmament, health emergencies, and gender equality

Europol Also known as the European Police Office, this organization was created in 1998 to confront international crime, address the removal of border controls in the European Union, and serve as a clearinghouse of information

nongovernmental organizations
Typically not for profit, they are organizations set up by groups that are run independent of governments, although they may receive funding from governments, businesses, foundations, or individuals; they provide a wide range of services, including efforts to address various types of human rights violations and crimes

● **Learning Objective 11.6:** Compare and contrast public policing and private security.

The difficulties inherent in policing the globe have inspired regional-based and **nongovernmental organizations** (NGOs) to help address international crime. NGOs are typically not for profit and are set up by groups that are run independent of governments, although they may receive funding from governments, businesses, foundations, or individuals. They provide a wide range of services, including efforts to address various types of human rights violations and crimes. For instance, Human Rights Watch is an NGO that protects human rights internationally by exposing and investigating abuses. Amnesty International is another NGO that seeks to protect the rights of individuals worldwide. NGOs have the benefit of working across borders and organizations more easily than can government organizations. These groups, however, often suffer from a lack of funding (Aguilar-Millan et al., 2008).

Private Security

Businesses, homeowners, and others have become increasingly concerned about crime prevention and the limitations of public policing. In response, the security field has expanded in terms of personnel and the services it provides. While not a formal level of law enforcement, the private security industry provides significant law enforcement–related services. In addition to security services, private security may include alarm companies, private detectives and investigators, courier services, consultants, and personal protection services. The types of positions in the industry are varied and include positions such as bodyguards, home or business alarm technicians, and security contractors, such as those individuals who are contracted by the government to provide security and protection services in dangerous facilities and locations worldwide.

Private Security Services

Roughly 2 million people work in private security domestically (Roberson & Birzer, 2010), which is far more than the estimated 1 million persons working in state and local law enforcement (Hyland & Davis, 2019). The general objectives of private security positions include:

● enforcing policies and procedures concerning security in general, including access control and employee safety;
● maintaining a safe and productive workplace environment;
● assisting with on-site incidents as needed, for instance if a customer needs immediate medical attention; and
● identifying and reporting conditions and incidents considered breaches of security or potential security hazards, for instance if a customer enters a restricted area of a building (Hess & Wrobleski, 1996).

More specific goals and functions of private security include:

● perimeter and internal security,
● fire protection,
● personnel and information security,
● risk management,
● asset protection,
● disaster and emergency preparedness,
● locating drugs in the workplace, and
● control of workplace violence (Nalla, 2001).

Private Security and Public Law Enforcement Similarities and Differences

Private security and public law enforcement generally seek the same outcomes. Both entities are responsible for protecting businesses and citizens. Some individuals enter the private security field as a stepping-stone to a career in policing, while for many others, private security is the next step after having worked in policing or served in the military. Among the common attributes of those who work in private security or public law enforcement are the ability to follow the chain of command, and being accustomed to wearing a uniform.

The contributions of private security groups to providing safety and security in the public and private sectors have increased in the past several decades and are expected to continue growing in the years ahead.

Why do you think businesses and industry rely so heavily on private security instead of the police?

Despite these and other similarities, private security and public policing differ in important ways. While police officers act as agents of the government and have extensive authoritative powers, private security personnel have limited authority that is dictated by the laws of the state in which they operate. Police officers must undergo much more extensive training than private security personnel, and accrediting agencies more strongly influence the actions of police officers. Generally, private security officers have the same legal powers as citizens. Many states define and regulate the authority of private security personnel, sometimes permitting security personnel to carry a weapon or search, detain, and arrest individuals.

A final notable difference between public law enforcement and private security is the overall approach to their job. Private security is largely proactive, because those in the field attempt to prevent crime or harm before it happens. By contrast, public law enforcement is largely reactive in the sense that officers often respond to calls regarding incidents that have already occurred.

The interconnectedness of public and private policing is evident in the existence of public security positions, such as special deputies who perform many of the same functions as private security personnel but are employed by the government. Special deputies may work part-time (or volunteer) in providing security during civic events such as parades and fairs. The USMS assigns special deputy marshals to provide security at courthouses (U.S. Marshals, 2020). More generally, the federal government employs over 10,000 contract security officers to protect federal offices and buildings (Fischer et al., 2008).

The System in Perspective

The "In the News" feature at the start of this module highlighted the role of INTERPOL in coordinating law enforcement efforts from various countries to address the distribution of illicit pharmaceuticals. This account provides a glimpse of how law enforcement may be organized in the future. Globalism has encouraged international crime and put pressure on countries across the globe to work more collaboratively. On a national scale, similar trends are emerging. For instance, the law enforcement agencies found at various levels of government in the United States are increasingly working together to address crimes that cross jurisdictions and to better address crimes through information sharing and collaborative efforts. Greater levels of cooperation among the agencies and various non–law enforcement groups (e.g., the private security industry) have emerged in recent years. These efforts involve greater use of task forces and may perhaps lead to regional law enforcement agencies that could oversee the law enforcement operations in designated regions of the country.

Summary

1. Learning Objective 11.1: *Illustrate the characteristics of the decentralized approach to law enforcement in the United States.*

- A decentralized approach to law enforcement helps disperse power and provides greater accountability. It permits departments to better understand what is needed, provides greater local control over police operations, and requires greater levels of cooperation among departments. Decentralization is sometimes criticized for the unequal quality of services provided by different departments, the lack of a national policy regarding police practices, and the overlap in jurisdictions among agencies at different levels of government.

2. Learning Objective 11.2: *Summarize the law enforcement agencies that are considered local law enforcement.*

- Local law enforcement consists of rural, suburban, municipal, and county police departments; sheriff's departments; and various special jurisdiction law enforcement agencies. Rural departments are small in size and generally have more free time compared to their counterparts in suburban and urban departments. Big-city police departments engage in more crime-fighting activities and provide more order maintenance than other departments. Suburban departments typically fall between the rural and municipal departments with regard to crime-fighting activities, order maintenance, and the provision of service. County police departments and sheriff's departments provide law enforcement services for their respective county. Sheriff's departments often assist the courts, and both types of agencies provide law enforcement services in unincorporated areas that lack a police department. Special jurisdiction law enforcement agencies provide law enforcement services in particular settings (e.g., schools) or in relation to specific types of crimes (e.g., gaming or gambling laws).

3. Learning Objective 11.3: *Identify the primary responsibilities of state law enforcement agencies.*

- State law enforcement agencies provide many services. Primarily, they patrol highways, conduct investigations, protect natural resources, and collect, analyze, and distribute crime data. They also provide training for other law enforcement agencies and assist and cooperate with other agencies, for instance with regard to crimes that are difficult for local authorities to solve.

4. Learning Objective 11.4: *Summarize the key features of the most prominent federal law enforcement agencies.*

- Many agencies provide law enforcement services at the federal level. Among the more prominent are the U.S. Customs and Border Protection, which protects U.S. borders and prevents the illegal entry of people and contraband; Immigration and Customs Enforcement, which enforces laws involving customs, border control, trade, and immigration; the Secret Service, which investigates financial crimes and provides protective services; the ATF, which oversees laws regarding the diversion of alcohol and tobacco products and enforces laws pertaining to firearms, explosives, arson, bombings, and terrorism; the DEA, which enforces laws pertaining to illegal drugs; the FBI, which investigates and enforces laws pertaining to over 200 categories of federal laws; and the USMS, which is responsible for overseeing the processing of all arrestees at the federal level and provides security for federal courts and personnel.

6. Learning Objective 11.5: *Describe the primary functions of INTERPOL and the United Nations regarding international law enforcement.*

- Although there is no international police force, INTERPOL and the UN are the organizations that appear to be best suited to provide international law enforcement. Neither group is a police force, per se; however, each provides assistance for law enforcement agencies. INTERPOL facilitates cooperation among police agencies worldwide and supports and assists all organizations, authorities, and services that help prevent or confront international crime. The UN facilitates treaties and agreements and participates and leads international peacekeeping missions or operations.

7. Learning Objective 11.6: *Compare and contrast public policing and private security.*

• Private security and public law enforcement generally seek the same outcome, as they are responsible for protecting businesses and citizens. Individuals within both fields share many attributes, such as the ability to follow orders, and being accustomed to wearing a uniform. However, private security agencies are not government entities. The groups also differ with regard to their legal power. Private security companies focus more on preventing crime and harm, whereas public law enforcement agencies are more concerned with recognizing and responding to crimes.

Questions for Critical Thinking

1. Law enforcement in the United States is largely decentralized. Do you think we could better address crime if we centralized our law enforcement agencies to some extent, for instance by organizing all law enforcement services into five regional departments responsible for addressing crime in designated states?

2. What advantages and disadvantages do you see in working for a small versus a large local police department? Explain your answer.

3. Do you consider law enforcement at the state level a hybrid of local policing and federal law enforcement? Why or why not?

4. Currently, most federal law enforcement agencies are in the U.S. DOJ and the U.S. DHS. What would be the pros and cons of placing all federal law enforcement agencies under one department?

5. Do you believe there will someday be continental law enforcement agencies that have jurisdiction to enforce the laws in all countries on the seven continents? For instance, do you anticipate there will someday be the "North American Police Department" or something akin to that? Why or why not?

6. How can private security firms work most productively with local police? What potential issues might arise from such cooperation?

Key Terms

Controlled Substances Act
decentralized
Department of Homeland Security
Europol
federalist
globalization
INTERPOL

Joint Terrorism Task Forces
jurisdiction
Major Crimes Act
nongovernmental organizations
Offices of inspector general
United Nations
U.S. Department of Justice

For digital learning resources, please go to
https://www.oup.com/he/burns1e

Module

12

Police: Personnel and Community Relations

Protestors around the country marched in response to controversial police practices following the shooting of Michael Brown by a Ferguson, Missouri, police officer in 2014. The incident led to an investigation and several changes within the Ferguson Police Department, including enhanced training practices.

Do you believe that more training could have prevented the death of Michael Brown and others who have been harmed by the police? Why or why not?

Police officers regularly make life-or-death decisions and choices that affect the liberties of individuals. Accordingly, many steps are taken to attract qualified individuals and to properly prepare them through regular training. This thorough vetting and training process is essential because poor hiring decisions may have disastrous consequences.

This module begins with an examination of personnel issues in policing, including the size and demographics of police forces in the United States. This is followed by a discussion of police subculture and a consideration of the recruitment, selection, and training of police officers. The end of the module addresses police–community relations.

Does Having More Officers on the Streets Reduce Crime?

IN THE NEWS

In May 2019, the New York City Police Department began its fifth year employing "Summer All-Out," which is an effort to reduce crime in troubled New York City neighborhoods. The program involves taking some officers from their desk jobs and administrative positions and deploying them and others to historically high-crime neighborhoods.

Prior to particpating in the program, the assigned officers are required to attend a day-long refresher training course that focuses on neighborhood policing and deescalation techniques (Cohen & Prendergast, 2015; New York City Police Department, 2019). The program has demonstrated success in reducing crime. The department noted that Summer All-Out 2018 was responsible for 8 fewer murders (a 36% drop) and 11 fewer shootings (a 16% reduction).

Does simply adding officers to the streets reduce crime, as the 2018 results suggest? Or was the refresher training course the key to the reductions? Ultimately, various factors affect crime rates, and additional research in the area is needed to determine what, specifically, contributes to the success of this program and others like it. If you were the New York police chief, would you make Summer All-Out efforts part of your standard operating procedure? Why or why not?

1 Criminal Act

NYPD LAUNCHES 'SUMMER ALL-OUT' PROGRAM WITH ADDITIONAL OFFICERS TO REDUCE CRIME AND VIOLENCE

Size and Diversity of Police Departments

Policing has become institutionalized in the United States, as evidenced by the roughly 18,000 state and local law enforcement agencies that employ over 1 million people full-time. Most of the individuals in these agencies are sworn personnel, meaning that they have the power to make arrests, and most agencies operate at the local level of government (Hyland & Davis, 2019). Police departments have been steadily increasing in size over the years. With that increase in size has come more diversity. Diversifying police departments brings with it officers with different perspectives on life, the job, and citizens, which is a primary reason why departments have sought to diversify.

Size of Police Departments

Most state and local law enforcement agencies are small; 71% of departments served fewer than 10,000 residents in 2016. However, the comparatively few large police departments employ the majority of police officers. For instance, in 2016, less than

● **Learning Objective 12.1:** Describe the typical police department in terms of size and demographics.

3% of local police departments served a resident population of 100,000 or more, but those departments employed 52% of all officers (Hyland & Davis, 2019).

The number of individuals working in law enforcement agencies has increased steadily over the years. Between 1997 and 2016, the number of officers working in local agencies increased by 11%, and a similar increase was noted with regard to state law enforcement (10%). As of 2016, there were over 1 million people working in local and state law enforcement agencies as both civilians and officers (Hyland & Davis, 2019).

Police agencies continue to expand, and the number of police officers and detectives is expected to grow by 5% from 2019 to 2029 (U.S. Bureau of Labor Statistics, 2021). Many people believe that having more police officers reduces crime. However, researchers in one study noted that increases in police manpower did not lead to greater deterrent effects in high-crime areas (Kleck & Barnes, 2014).

Racial and Ethnic Minorities in Police Departments

Racial and ethnic minorities have long been underrepresented in policing because of a lack of aggressive efforts to recruit minority candidates, as well as fears by such candidates that they would not be accepted by fellow police officers (Carter & Radelet, 1999). However, local police departments, and law enforcement agencies in general, have increasingly sought to diversify their workforces because of the many benefits, which include:

- helping to gain the public's trust and confidence, which leads to better police–community relations;

- enabling officers from various cultural backgrounds opportunities to offer insight to their fellow officers, supervisors, and the general public; and

- contributing to the resolution of situations in which cultural or language barriers are problematic.

affirmative action programs Programs designed to promote the hiring of disadvantaged groups who have suffered from discrimination

Title VII of the Civil Rights Act of 1964 Legislation passed in 1964 that prevents governments, unions, employment agencies, and private employers with 15 or more employees from discriminating based on color, race, sex, religion, or national origin

Equal Employment Opportunity Act of 1972 Legislation that extended the Civil Rights Act of 1964 to state and local governments

Efforts to diversify police departments have been aided by legislation and **affirmative action programs** designed to promote the hiring of disadvantaged groups who have suffered from discrimination. For example, **Title VII of the Civil Rights Act of 1964** prevents governments, unions, employment agencies, and private employers with 15 or more employees from discriminating based on color, race, sex, religion, or national origin. The **Equal Employment Opportunity Act of 1972** extends the 1964 act to state and local governments.

Efforts to diversify policing have generally been successful. In 2016, about 71% of full-time sworn local police personnel were White, 12.5% were Hispanic/Latino, and 11.4% were African American (Hyland & Davis, 2019). The percentage of Hispanic/Latino officers has increased by 61% from 1997 to 2016, while the percentage of African American officers has remained somewhat constant. Overall, the percentage of racial and ethnic minorities has increased by 150% since 1987, when minorities made up about 14.6% of local police officers, compared to 27% in 2016 (Hyland & Davis, 2019; Reaves, 2015a). Figure 12.1 notes the increasing percentages of minority representation among local police officers from 1997 to 2016.

These numbers, however, while important, mask problems in cities where minority officers may be underrepresented. For example, in 2015 the Ferguson Police Department drew much national attention following the shooting death of Michael Brown. Highlighting the problematic situation in Ferguson was the fact that the majority of Ferguson's population (66%) was Black, and yet the department had a total of only 4 Black officers on a force of 53 (Alcindor & Penzenstadler, 2015).

Akin to other minority groups, Hispanics have faced many limitations in becoming police officers, and their historical underrepresentation in policing has been

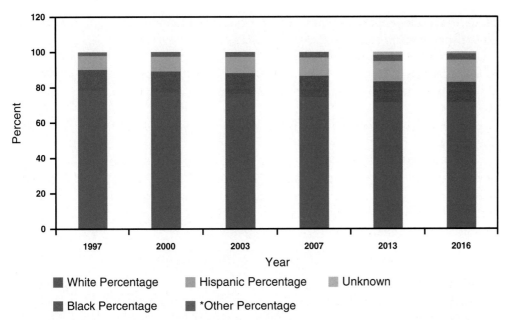

FIGURE 12.1. Minority Representation Among Full-Time Local Law Enforcement From 1997 to 2016. The percentage of minority group representation in local law enforcement has increased and will likely continue to increase in the future. Efforts to diversify police departments, for instance through recruitment efforts directed toward racial and ethnic minorities, have largely altered the demographics of many police departments. *Source:* Local Police Departments, 2013: Personnel, Policies, and Practices *(NCJ 248677), p. 5, by B. A. Reaves (2015a), U.S. Department of Justice, Bureau of Justice Statistics.*

What do you believe are the primary benefits of diversifying police departments?

attributed to language barriers and the fact that Hispanics were not aggressively recruited by police departments (Alcindor & Penzenstadler, 2015). Asian Americans have also been poorly represented in police departments across the United States (Dempsey & Forst, 2014).

Women in Police Departments

Women have served in law enforcement since 1845, although their role has changed over the years. Initially, they were considered "police matrons" and were expected to be social workers instead of police officers. Accordingly, they dressed in street clothes and patrolled areas where children were likely to misbehave (Barkan & Bryjak, 2014).

MYTHBUSTING

Men Are Better-Suited to Police Work Than Women

Many people believe that women are not physically strong or "tough" enough to handle the more violent, demanding aspects of the job. In reality, female officers perform the job as well as male officers. And, with regard to some aspects of the job (e.g., communicating and acting in a less authoritarian manner), they outperform men. For instance, a study of differences in male and female officer practices found that females were less likely than males to use extreme controlling behaviors and were better equipped to deescalate potentially violent situations more effectively than males (Rabe-Hemp, 2008). The belief that women are not well suited for police work is largely based on the myth that much police work only involves violent confrontations (Lersch, 2013).

The number of females in policing has increased over time, but women still constitute a small percentage (roughly 13%) of police officers. Women police officers were historically restricted in their responsibilities, but have proven to be well qualified to perform the responsibilities associated with police work.

What efforts do you believe would be most effective in recruiting more female officers?

culture Values, behaviors, beliefs, and material objects that collectively identify a people's way of life; it shapes behaviors, personalities, and outlooks

subculture Cultural patterns, including values, meanings, and behavioral patterns, that identify some segments in the population as distinct from other groups

● **Learning Objective 12.2:** Explain what police subculture is and what factors influence and what factors shape it.

In 1970, women comprised roughly 2% of law enforcement officers; however, the 1972 passage of an amendment to Title VII of the Civil Rights Act of 1964 led to an increase in the number of women in policing. The percentage of women in law enforcement has increased steadily in recent years, from 8% in 1987 to 12.8% in 2019 (Statista, 2020).

The increased number of women in policing has encouraged police departments to reconsider several personnel policies. Scheduling officers in an accommodating manner to assist with family and other responsibilities and moving officers to lighter work (e.g., desk jobs) during pregnancy are among the changes that have been made to attract more female officers. As the historical barriers that discouraged many women from engaging in police work have diminished, more departments have begun proactively recruiting women. Evidence suggests that females can do the job as well as males, and they tend to work well with female victims of sexual assault, who may not wish to speak to male officers. Further, females may be better at deescalating potentially violent encounters through less aggressive means (e.g., Rabe-Hemp, 2008). They generally have better communication skills and generate more cooperation and trust during interactions with the public when compared with male officers (Lonsway et al., 2003).

Police Subculture

There is a strong sense of solidarity in policing—often referred to as the police subculture—that contributes to officers' outlooks on life, their job, and the people with whom they interact. **Culture** refers to values, behaviors, beliefs, and material objects that collectively identify a people's way of life; it shapes behaviors, personalities, and outlooks (McNamara & Burns, 2020). **Subculture** refers to cultural patterns, including values, meanings, and behavioral patterns, which identify some segments in the population as distinct from other groups (e.g., McNamara & Burns, 2020). Some researchers have identified a police subculture that is characterized by officers sharing very similar beliefs and attitudes and exhibiting similar behaviors within their job. They say this subculture is shaped by a number of factors (Burns, 2013):

- formal and practical education
- shared occupational tasks
- use of force, authority, and weapons
- general shared norms and expectations

The decision to become a police officer in some ways signifies the beginning of the socialization process of police officers into the police subculture. Socialization refers to people acquiring knowledge, attitudes, values, and habits that are deemed acceptable or normal by a group or the larger society, and it is shaped by various factors and stages of police officer development. Among the factors are the relationships formed with fellow cadets at the police academy and the training that occurs at the academy.

An important byproduct of the socialization of police officers is the development of a particular police personality. For instance, noted police scholar Jerome Skolnick (1966), in a classic work, commented on the personality of police officers, particularly as it is formed by two aspects of police work: the constant exposure to danger and the need to use force and authority to confront dangerous situations. In response to these and related aspects of police work, officers may become suspicious of the general public and defensive about the actions of their fellow officers.

Not all researchers agree, however, on the existence of a police subculture, or that if one does exist, that culture is influential (e.g., Cochran & Bromley, 2003; Paoline et al., 2000). For example, a study on sheriffs' deputies in Florida found that the deputies were not overly concerned with crime control and were more strongly oriented to service, which contrasts with what would be expected of law enforcement officers who subscribed to a police culture that often leads to excessive use of force, suspicion of the public, and a focus on crime-fighting (Cochran & Bromley, 2003).

Police Recruitment and Selection

During the political era, very little attention was devoted to police personnel issues, and officers were typically hired based more on their support for politicians than on their qualifications. However, in the early 21st century, police officers are hired, promoted, rewarded, and dismissed based on their competency. **Civil service commissions** throughout the United States provide oversight by ensuring that bias, political influence, and favoritism do not impact personnel decisions (M. D. White & Escobar, 2008).

Effective recruitment efforts are essential for police agencies. Failure to properly recruit qualified candidates results in wasted resources and ineffective police services. Recruitment efforts differ from selection. Recruiting personnel primarily involves identifying and attracting individuals who might be suitable and interested in a career in policing. Selecting officers involves evaluating the personnel who have been recruited or otherwise applied for a position.

The Recruitment Process

Police **recruitment** involves generating a pool of interested candidates from which individuals will be selected for further evaluation and consideration. Despite the importance of recruiting the best candidates, many departments face a scarcity of resources,

civil service commissions
Commissions throughout the United States that provide oversight by ensuring that bias, political influence, and favoritism do not impact personnel decisions

recruitment
The practice of generating a pool of interested job candidates from which individuals will be selected for further evaluation and consideration

● **Learning Objective 12.3:** List the typical minimum eligibility requirements to become a police officer and the examinations used as part of the screening process.

FIGURE 12.2. Recruitment Advertisement. Recruitment efforts may include job advertisements, such as this one, which includes the minimum requirements and benefits associated with the position. **Source:** *Mount Lebanon Police Department (2019).*

What important information do you believe is missing from this ad?

and only a small percentage of departments with a small number of officers have a permanent recruiting office (Taylor et al., 2006). The recruitment process generally consists of three components, including the establishment of minimum requirements, the actual recruitment effort, and the applicant's decision to apply for a position. Many resources can be saved through initially informing people of the minimum requirements of the job.

Minimum Requirements for Becoming an Officer

The minimum requirements for becoming a police officer vary across departments and are influenced by factors such as laws, court decisions, and each department's determination regarding what qualities and characteristics make an effective police officer. Further, departments sometimes alter their minimum requirements in response to their actual or expected applicant pool. For instance, departments facing tough competition for few candidates in a rural area may lower their minimum requirements to ensure that they fill their vacancies. The minimum eligibility requirements for a police officer position may include:

- residency requirements;
- physical requirements (height, weight, and age);
- educational requirements;
- medical disqualifiers; and
- criminal history restrictions.

RESIDENCY REQUIREMENTS

residency requirements
Regulations which mandate that police officers live within a prescribed distance from the department for which they are employed

Residency requirements mandate that police officers live within a prescribed distance from the department for which they are employed. Roughly 40% of local police agencies have residency requirements (Reaves, 2012b). The rationale for having residency requirements is that they:

- permit officers to understand the issues within their community and allow them to become better connected with the area,
- improve police–community relations,
- deter crime, and
- enable officers to respond quickly to emergency situations.

Despite their benefits, residency requirements do have some drawbacks, and some states prohibit them, while police agencies seem to be moving away from them. The trend is toward letting officers live outside the department's boundaries with the goal of attracting the most qualified candidates (Alpert et al., 2015). Residency requirements may:

- limit the size of the applicant pool;
- oblige officers to live in areas that they cannot afford, that are crime-ridden, or that have poor schools;
- prevent officers from reducing their stress level by getting away from police work; and

- contribute to officers becoming too familiar with their neighbors and correspondingly more lenient (or punitive) with regard to enforcement practices (e.g., K. Johnson, 2006).

PHYSICAL REQUIREMENTS

Physical requirements such as those pertaining to height, weight, and age have changed over the years. Police departments historically required candidates to be within a specific height and weight range. These requirements were challenged in courts, and the result has been that many departments require that an applicant's weight and height be proportional (Roberg et al., 2015).

Departments have generally required applicants to be between the ages of 21 and 35. There is debate regarding the minimum age at which one should be allowed to become an officer. For instance, some argue that 19- to 21-year-olds are too young to handle the challenges of police work, although raising the minimum age limit restricts the applicant pool (e.g., Decker & Huckabee, 2002). The maximum limit emerged out of consideration for the sometimes strenuous nature of police work. Congress passed the **Age Discrimination in Employment Act of 1967**, which was designed to prevent maximum age limits for employment and address discrimination against older Americans. The act initially applied to law enforcement agencies, but Congress has since exempted them. Departments can choose their own maximum age requirement; however, the requirement cannot be more restrictive than the standards they used prior to the act (Gaines & Worrall, 2012).

Age Discrimination in Employment Act of 1967 Legislation passed in 1967 that was designed to prevent maximum age limits for employment and address discrimination against older Americans; the act initially applied to law enforcement agencies, but Congress has since exempted them

EDUCATIONAL REQUIREMENTS

Most police departments (84%) require a high school degree, and about 15% of departments have some type of college requirement. Only 1% of local police departments have a 4-year degree requirement (Reaves, 2015a). Some police reformers argue that officers should be required to have a 4-year degree, and police officers in the early 21st century are generally more highly educated than at any point in the history of policing. The increased levels of education among police officers are attributable, in part, to increased education-based hiring standards and incentives for educational attainment in some departments. The changing nature of policing, with its emphasis on community policing, increased use of technology, and concerns for homeland security and civil liberty issues, arguably warrants more highly educated officers (Roberg & Bonn, 2004). In 2013, officers were twice as likely to work in a department with a college requirement for new officers (32%) than in 1993 (Reaves, 2015a).

HEALTH REQUIREMENTS

Police departments typically have general requirements regarding applicants' mental and physical health, including eyesight and hearing specifications. Physical and psychological wellness are typically evaluated during the selection process. The exam is provided by a doctor selected by the candidate or the department and typically includes consideration of whether the candidate has any preexisting back, knee, or heart problems that may be aggravated during the course of police work. The costs of losing an officer to illness or injury can be substantial to police departments, and thus special efforts are taken to assess the long-term health of potential officers. Drug testing is also part of the medical examination.

CRIMINAL HISTORY RESTRICTIONS

All departments consider applicants' criminal histories. Having a criminal record does not necessarily preclude someone from becoming a police officer, because police departments recognize that people sometimes make mistakes. Of particular concern are the types and frequency of any criminal behavior and the time elapsed since one's last involvement in crime. For instance, being convicted of a less serious (e.g., petty theft) offense that was committed 10 years prior to applying for a police position is much more tolerable than having been convicted for a violent crime in the past year. There is also a distinction made between arrests and convictions, with conviction of a crime being considered more serious. Most departments will reject candidates with a felony conviction.

While drug use is a concern among police departments, a zero-tolerance policy will hamper recruitment efforts. Accordingly, departments have had to develop an acceptable level of tolerance for past drug use, which varies widely by department. Issues considered include the type of drug used, how often the candidate used drugs, and the time elapsed since last use. Regular, recent use of more serious drugs, such as heroin, is considered more alarming than having experimented with less serious drugs, for example marijuana, 10 years prior. Figure 12.3 depicts the Fort Lauderdale, Florida, Police Department's policy regarding drug use.

The Recruitment Effort

Police recruitment efforts typically involve the internet and visits to high schools, colleges, military bases, local gatherings (e.g., fairs or parades), and related areas and events. A department's website is also particularly important for hiring purposes. Police recruiters target particular groups of individuals by visiting areas typically frequented by the target group. For example, recruiters might visit a women-only workout facility to recruit women. Researchers have found that departments most commonly target individuals with prior police experience, college graduates, racial and ethnic minorities, and women (Taylor et al., 2006).

APPEALING TO MOTIVATIONS

One of the most effective ways to hire qualified individuals may be to appeal to their motivations for becoming a police officer. Researchers found that job security, the benefits associated with the job, and the opportunity for early retirement were the most influential motivators for individuals who entered police work (M. D. White et al., 2010). Some individuals are attracted to police work because of the salaries. The average base salary for police officers was $54,561 in 2020 (Indeed, 2020). Police officers in large departments generally have higher salaries than their counterparts who work in smaller departments (Reaves, 2015a).

FINANCIAL INCENTIVES

Police departments sometimes offer financial incentives or perks for employees in the attempt to attract qualified candidates. For instance, in 2020 the Orono, Maine, Police Department offered $10,000 signing bonuses to eligible officers, payable over 5 years, and other departments have offered similar bonuses. Some departments offer "finder fees" to officers who recommend applicants who eventually become officers. For instance, the San Diego Police Department offered officers $3,000 if they recruited a rookie officer who successfully completed the academy and training and $4,000 if they recruited veteran officers (Garrick, 2018). Further, departments may pay for relocation expenses, and some offer helpful interest rates (or no interest) on home-buying loans or provide a vehicle-take-home program for officers (Martinez, 2006).

Police Officer Selection

The selection process follows recruitment efforts and is by no means an exact science. Identifying both the qualities that contribute to success in a police career and which candidates will be most successful has long challenged police officials. Research in

The Fort Lauderdale Police Department is responsible for conducting a thorough background investigation in an attempt to determine the moral character of an applicant pursuant to § 943.13(7), Florida Statutes. The Police Department standards for evaluating a candidate's moral character shall include, but shall not be limited to, the candidate's use of controlled substances.

1. Drug Policy

The unlawful use of any controlled substances, as designated by Florida State Statutes, by an applicant shall be reviewed by police management to determine if the applicant is considered to be of good moral character. This determination shall be made based on all relevant facts, including the type of controlled substance used, the date of the last use, the frequency of use, and the age of the applicant at the time of use.

A. After a management review of all relevant facts, an applicant shall either continue in the hiring process or if they fail to meet the police department's standards for past drug use, they will be classified as either
Permanently Disqualified (DQ), which does not allow applicant to reapply for the position of police officer or Failed Background (FB) which allows an applicant to reapply as a police officer in one (1) year.

B. If any of the following are indicated it shall result in an automatic permanent disqualification:
(1). Other than marijuana, Adderall XR or Mydayis, any past use of a Schedule I or Schedule II drug as defined by the U.S. Drug Enforcement Administration, used in an illegal or recreational manner will result in an automatic permanent disqualification.
(2). Use of marijuana and Adderall XR or Mydayis (non-prescribed) twenty (20) times or more over the applicant's lifetime and within three years of application will result in an automatic permanent disqualification. No exception to existing standards shall be provided for marijuana, or its derivatives, as a drug or substance that is prescribed, recommended or dispensed for medical purposes, when such is prohibited under federal law.
(3). Any use of illegal drugs after having been employed by a police or corrections agency, in a police or corrections capacity will result in an automatic permanent disqualification.
(4). Past sale of any illegal drug as defined by Florida State Statutes will result in an automatic permanent disqualification.
(5). The Assistant Chief of the Support Services Bureau may grant an exemption to illegal drug use by an applicant prior to becoming 21 years of age, based on a totality of the circumstances.

C. If any of the following are indicated, it will result in an automatic Failed Background;
(1). Abuse of any prescription drug within five (5) years of application
(2). Any more than experimental use of steroids not prescribed by a doctor for a medical condition and not within five (5) years of application.
(3). Use of any illegal drugs within three (3) years of an application for employment as a police officer.
(4). Marijuana, whether it is used medically or recreationally used within 3 years of application, as long as it remains a violation of the Federal Controlled Substances Act.
(5). Any use of Cannabidiol (CBD) and other products containing Tetrahydrocannabinol (THC) within three (3) years of application may be grounds for a failed background.

FIGURE 12.3. The Fort Lauderdale, Florida, Police Department's policy regarding drug use. The department is responsible for conducting a thorough background investigation in an attempt to determine the moral character of an applicant pursuant to § 943.13(7), Florida Statutes. Each police department will have a similar policy, with the primary considerations often involving the frequency and recency of drug use and the type of drug used. *Source:* Hiring Police Officers, *by Fort Lauderdale Police Department, 2020 (https://www.flpd.org/home/showdocument?id=4168).*

What would your drug policy for officers entail if you were a police chief?

the area has suggested that law enforcement officials consider five factors in determining a candidate's likelihood of success in policing (Guffey et al., 2007):

- moral character
- physical fitness
- an even temper under stressful conditions
- excellent judgment
- dependability

The selection process primarily involves two types of assessments: screening practices and evaluations. Screening practices offer information regarding each candidate's history and involve consideration of whether candidates meet the basic requirements for the position, including an assessment of each candidate's driving record, credit history, and criminal history. Candidates undergo a series of thorough background checks as part of the screening process, which may require candidates to submit a wide array of data, often including information such as their work history, their previous and current places of residence, names and contact information of friends and family members, and contact information of personal references. In addition to initial screening requirements, candidates must undergo a series of evaluations. Particularly, candidates may be required to undergo:

- a written aptitude test,
- a polygraph examination or voice stress analyzer,
- a psychological evaluation and personality inventory,
- a personal interview,
- a physical agility test,
- a medical exam, and
- a drug test.

Not all departments subject each candidate to all of these evaluations and screening practices. Each department has a specified set of requirements that are used throughout the selection process. The extent to which departments weigh each assessment and the individuals who evaluate the results vary among departments.

WRITTEN APTITUDE TESTS

Written examinations used in the selection of police officers may be developed by the department internally or purchased from an outside source. About half of all local police departments require candidates to complete a written aptitude test as part of the selection process (Reaves, 2010). Historically, the written exams taken by candidates primarily measured cognitive ability and were completed via paper and pencil. The use of computers has improved the administration and evaluation of the exams. Computer-assisted testing permits the use of more contextual and situational-based policing material, and video-based selection tests are replacing standardized written tests in some departments.

POLYGRAPH EXAMINATIONS AND VOICE STRESS ANALYZERS

Polygraph examinations measure one's heart rate, blood pressure, breathing rate, and perspiration in response to a series of questions and statements, including information candidates provided on their background questionnaire. The goals of the examination are to ensure accuracy of the information and note any psychological irregularities (DeCicco, 2000).

polygraph examinations
Tests that measure one's heart rate, blood pressure, breathing rate, and perspiration in response to a series of questions and statements; the goals of the examination are to ensure accuracy of the background information and note any psychological irregularities

Polygraph examinations are prohibited from use in the private sector per the **Employee Protection Act of 1988**, but they are permitted for use by government agencies. This type of assessment is used by about one quarter of all local police departments (Reaves, 2010).

The use of polygraphs has generated some controversy because the test may lack credibility. Taking a polygraph exam is stressful for some applicants, which can result in false positives—for example, candidates being accused of lying when they are telling the truth (Roberg et al., 2015). Some departments have replaced polygraph examinations with **voice stress analyzers**, which measure small frequency modulations heard in human voices that are believed to happen when someone is lying. The analyzers appear to be less intrusive to candidates and easier to administer than polygraph tests, although they too are questionable with regard to their ability to detect deception. They are used by relatively few departments (roughly 5%; Reaves, 2010).

PSYCHOLOGICAL EVALUATIONS AND PERSONALITY INVENTORY

Psychological evaluations of police officer candidates are designed to assess whether the individuals are emotionally stable, mature, sociable, independent, and able to function in stressful situations (DeCicco, 2000). Their use in the police officer selection process has increased over the past several decades (Roberg et al., 2015). Certified psychologists conduct this aspect of the screening process, which can be conducted in writing, orally, or both, and offer recommendations regarding whether candidates appear suitable for police work. Historically, police departments used general psychologists and psychiatrists to conduct the evaluations. However, departments are increasingly using examiners who specialize in law enforcement hiring. Despite their relative popularity, the accuracy of personality tests and psychological evaluations with regard to determining officer suitability has been questioned.

The Minnesota Multiphasic Personality Inventory-2, the Inwald Personality Inventory, and the California Personality Inventory are among the more commonly administered exams. Regardless of the exam that is administered, the results are analyzed by trained professionals (typically psychologists) who seek to identify candidates who exhibit emotional issues (e.g., anger management problems) and those who would be psychologically strong as a police officer (e.g., they can effectively control their emotions). Among the areas of evaluation are impulse control, judgment, honesty, integrity, biases, and the ability to handle stress and work well with others. Among the concerns associated with these exams are the lack of consensus regarding which personality characteristics are most appropriate for policing, whether personality characteristics predict an individual's effectiveness in the job, and how accurately personality tests measure personality traits.

PERSONAL INTERVIEWS

Oral interviews are often used to determine the final ranking of the candidates. The interviewers may consist of ranking officers, the police chief, psychologists, and investigators, and there may be more than one oral interview. Thus, the interviews require many resources. Generally, the raters assess each interview with particular concern for confidence, motivation, dedication, appearance, poise, judgment, and spoken communication skills. There is much subjectivity inherent in evaluating candidates based on an oral interview, and, accordingly, there is some concern regarding the reliability of oral interviews (Doerner, 1997).

PHYSICAL AGILITY TESTS, MEDICAL EXAMS, AND DRUG TESTS

Most departments use physical agility tests, medical exams, and drug tests. Physical agility tests evaluate a candidate's ability to effectively perform the duties of a police

Employee Protection Act of 1988 Legislation passed in 1988 that prohibited the use of polygraph examinations in the private sector, but not for government agencies

voice stress analyzers Devices that measure small frequency modulations heard in human voices that are believed to happen when someone is lying

officer. The tests include scaling walls, hurdling obstacles, running long distances, push-ups, sit-ups, a host of agility tests (e.g., side lunges, squat thrusts), and related evaluations. Departments often have distinct requirements for both men and women with regard to physical strength tests and may have different standards for candidates based on age.

Most candidates will be required to undergo a medical examination to assess whether they are physically healthy enough to perform the job. Among other assessments, the examining physician will check for proper reflexes and blood pressure and determine if each candidate has proper eyesight, height-to-weight ratio, and hearing. Medical examinations for new officer candidates are required by 89% of local police departments (Reaves, 2010).

The medical examination may also include a drug test, or the test may be administered at another point. The tests are outsourced to medical facilities in most departments; large departments often have the ability to test in house (Swanson et al., 2012). A urine sample is typically collected from candidates as part of the test, although a small number of departments test hair samples, which provide evidence for longer periods of time (Mieczkowski, 2004). Candidates are typically tested for the presence of marijuana, cocaine, phencyclidine, opiates, and amphetamines. Many departments do not test police officers after the initial preemployment screening. Those that do test again often do so about every 2 years (Test Country, n.d.).

Police departments vary in terms of the standards that specify the drug-related behaviors they find acceptable. Some departments are more tolerant of previous drug use than others (Gaines & Kappeler, 2011). Of particular consideration are the recentness of drug use, the frequency of drug use, the types of drugs used, and involvement in the sale and transport of drugs. Applicants are often given the opportunity to discuss their drug usage, and many departments have more liberal policies than in the past, especially when it comes to marijuana use, given social changes and greater levels of acceptance of use in certain states (Roberg et al., 2015).

ASSESSMENT CENTERS AND OTHER CONSIDERATIONS

Some departments use assessment centers to supplement and expand on the traditional testing methods used to select police officers (and to help determine promotions). The centers typically use written evaluations, role-play exercises, videotaped situational assessments, problem-solving exercises, and oral presentations. The assessment center approach involves a series of tests that are believed to be more reflective of police work than are traditional police candidate evaluations (DeCicco, 2000).

The order in which the tests/evaluations used to evaluate candidates are administered is based largely on the cost of the evaluation and the number of individuals taking the tests. Some evaluations are more costly than others, so departments often choose to include the more costly examinations when the pool of candidates has dwindled. For instance, written tests are generally less expensive than most other evaluations and are thus commonly administered early in the selection process. Most of the evaluations included in the selection process are graded on a pass–fail scale, with the written exam and the oral interview generally being the exceptions, and are often used to rank applicants.

Peace Officer Standards and Training Commission State agencies that regulate the minimum police training standards set by each state and help ensure that training curricula are in accord with training standards

● **Learning Objective 12.4:** Differentiate between basic, field, and in-service training.

Police Training

Various state agencies typically regulate the minimum police training standards set by each state and help ensure that training curricula are in accord with training standards. Most states use a **Peace Officer Standards and Training (POST) commission** to regulate officer training. For instance, the New Jersey Division of Criminal Justice Police Training Commission is responsible for developing and certifying basic training courses for various types of police officers in New Jersey.

At a minimum, police officer training should be designed to teach officers the fundamentals of police work, promote alternative solutions to troubling situations, and instill the values and ideals of the department within the officers (Flynn, 2002). Applicants selected to become police officers soon begin months of formal training. Police officer training can be categorized according to basic, or preservice training; field training; and in-service training.

Basic Training

Basic training takes place at the police academy and is designed to instill in new officers the skills and knowledge relevant to police work. The training occurs at the beginning of officers' careers and largely shapes their overall practices and effectiveness. Each new officer recruit in local police departments in 2016 was required to complete 816 academy training hours, on average (C. Brooks, 2020). Table 12.1 notes that the largest number of hours was devoted to firearms skills (71 hours), defensive tactics (60 hours), and criminal/constitutional law (53 hours; Reaves, 2016).

Research suggests that several factors appear to affect success at the police academy include a recruit's:

- reading level (higher recruit reading level was positively related to better performance),
- age (older candidates performed less well), and
- gender (males outperformed females).

The same research found no association between academy performance and military experience, college credits, and city residency (M. D. White, 2008).

Police academies operate in various ways. The differences include the qualifications of instructors, the number of hours required, and the emphasis placed on different topics. Further, some academies are residential and allow trainees to return home only on weekends, while others permit cadets to return home each day. Other differences among academies involve the administration of the facilities. For instance, most big-city police departments in the United States have their own police academies, while smaller localities send their officers to regional or state training facilities. Some colleges and universities also provide training for police cadets.

Upon being sworn in and assigned to regular duty after completing basic training, officers are typically placed on probation for anywhere from 6 months to 2 years, as designated by departments. The probationary period enables departments to better assess new officers and easily dismiss those who seem unsuited for police work. While an officer may perform admirably at the academy, their performance in the real world may not be up to the necessary standards in the field. Officers may be released for a variety of reasons during this probationary time, for instance if they neglect to enforce the law, believe the laws do not apply to them, or do not apply what was learned at the academy during their police shifts. The dismissal of an officer who

CAREERS

Police training officers develop, implement, and provide training programs in law enforcement academies. They teach, update, and revise courses with concern for currency of content and instruction and relevance to policing.

CAREERS

Police officer training coordinators perform administrative tasks pertaining to the scheduling and coordination of various types of training classes for sworn and civilian employees. They analyze, research, and develop training courses independently or jointly with other law enforcement agencies or government groups.

basic training
Training that takes place at the police academy and is designed to instill in new officers the skills and knowledge relevant to police work; it occurs at the beginning of officers' careers and largely shapes their overall practices and effectiveness

TABLE 12.1. Major Areas of Basic Training in State and Local Law Enforcement

TRAINING AREA	PERCENTAGE OF ACADEMIES WITH TRAINING	AVERAGE NUMBER OF HOURS OF INSTRUCTION REQUIRED PER RECRUIT[a]
Operations		
Report writing	99	25
Patrol procedures	98	52
Investigations	98	42
Traffic accident investigations	98	23
Emergency vehicle operations	97	38
Basic first aid/CPR	97	24
Computers/ information systems	61	9
Weapons/defensive tactics/use of force		
Defensive tactics	99	60
Firearms skills	98	71
Use of force	98	21
Nonlethal weapons	88	16
Self-improvement		
Ethics and integrity	98	8
Health and fitness	96	49
Communications	91	15
Professionalism	85	11
Stress prevention/ management	81	6
Legal education		
Criminal/ constitutional law	98	53
Traffic law	97	23
Juvenile justice law/ procedures	97	10

[a]*Excludes academies that did not provide this type of instruction. From Bureau of Justice Statistics, Census of Law Enforcement Training Academies, 2013, Table 6; and a State and Local Law Enforcement Training Academies, 2013 (NCJ 249784), by B. A. Reaves, 2016, U.S. Department of Justice, Bureau of Justice Statistics.* **Source:** *From U.S. Department of Justice, Office of Justice Programs, Bureau of Justice Statistics, July 2016, NCJ 249784*

field training Training designed to reinforce what officers learned during basic training, provide additional information about specific aspects of the job, and ensure that officers can apply what they learned at the academy; it involves new officers working closely with field training officers

field training officers Skilled and experienced officers who, in providing field training, assist rookie officers as they move from the academy to the streets and evaluate new officers' performances

completes the probationary period is more difficult and must be based on cause and abide by the requirements designated by contracts with police unions and/or civil service regulations.

Field Training

Field training is designed to reinforce what officers learned during basic training, provide additional information about specific aspects of the job, and ensure that officers can apply what they learned at the academy. Field training involves new officers working closely with skilled and experienced officers—**field training officers (FTOs)**. FTOs serve two primary purposes: assisting rookie officers as they move from the academy to the streets and evaluating a new officer's performance. FTO programs require extensive documentation of each trainee's performance (Doerner & Hunter, 2006). Among other benefits, field training provides an opportunity for continued training beyond the academy. New officer recruits in local police departments in 2016 were required to complete 628 field training hours, on average (C. Brooks, 2020).

Academy training is crucial, but it does not fully prepare officers for all that they will encounter on the job. For instance, while the police academy may train cadets on how to best interact with the public, actually interacting with the public, particularly in culturally diverse communities, is quite different. New officers may be unprepared for their own reactions and those of the public. Among the many things that rookie officers learn from experienced officers is how to temper their anxiety, enthusiasm, nervousness, and other emotions while on the

Police training helps prepare officers for encounters on the streets; however, officers cannot fully prepare for police work solely through training at the police academy.

Do you believe officers should be required to spend additional hours training at the police academy, or are they better served by gaining experience on the streets?

job. The influence and guidance a rookie officer receives from their FTO may have long-lasting effects, and thus it is important that officers with strong policing skills are selected as FTOs.

In-Service Training

Experienced officers at all stages of their careers must periodically undergo **in-service training** to keep abreast of changes in the field, developments regarding laws and ordinances, changes in technology, and new department policies. Some officers must also undergo such training if they are promoted or if they change or plan to change job assignments. For instance, officers preparing to go undercover may receive specialized training, while those being promoted to sergeant may go through supervisory or managerial training. Officers in local police departments were required to undergo an average of 35 in-service training hours in 2016 (C. Brooks, 2020).

In-service training may occur internally in departments, for example through brief discussions or sessions at roll call or broadcasting over vehicle radios. Or, trainees may be sent to other locations such as a state training facility. The external training provided to officers may be brief (a day or a few days) or could last several weeks or months. The use of online professional training for in-service and other types of training has also grown over the past several years.

At a minimum, in-service training is designed to enhance overall officer professionalism and enable police officers to keep pace with the constant changes associated with police work.

in-service training
Training provided to officers in efforts to keep them abreast of changes in the field, developments regarding laws and ordinances, changes in technology, and new department policies; some officers must also undergo such training if they are promoted or if they change or plan to change job assignments

Dangers of Improper Training

Training is vital to effective policing, and officers are typically well prepared upon being trained. Training, however, does have its limitations, which include:

- incomplete program content (e.g., some programs may not cover significant aspects of policing);
- subpar training facilities and equipment;
- requirement of full-time cadet attendance (e.g., officers who work and attend the academy encounter scheduling and work-related difficulties);
- lack of follow-up evaluation; and
- need for greater quality control of instructors (Burns, 2013).

The failure to properly train officers has many repercussions, including:

- negative police–community relations,
- wasted resources,
- dangers to the public,
- ineffective crime control and prevention efforts, and
- increased civil litigation.

With respect to the last point, federal statute Title 42, United States Code, Section 1983, allows individuals to hold government employees and, under some circumstances, their employers accountable for violation of rights under the U.S. Constitution. Counties and municipalities can face litigation if individuals believe their rights have been violated by a failure to adequately train officers (M. J. King, 2005). The U.S. Supreme Court ruled in *City of Canton v. Harris* (1989) that "deliberate indifference" is the standard required to demonstrate the presence of a problematic policy when an individual claims that their constitutional rights were violated as a result of a failure to train. Deliberate indifference refers to consciously or recklessly disregarding the consequences of one's actions or failing to act.

Police–Community Relations

As noted in Module 10, strong police–community relations benefit the police in many ways. Community involvement in addressing crime and related problems is at the core of community policing, because citizens provide input, assistance, and guidance for the police. Problematic relations with the communities they serve contribute to the police having a more difficult time performing their duties, as evidenced by recent events in Baltimore, New York City, Minneapolis, and other cities around the United States in which the public openly displayed their concerns with police practices.

One of the more important reasons to diversify police departments is to facilitate police–community relations, for instance by departments demonstrating their willingness to openly accept individuals from all groups. In general, Americans have high levels of support for and confidence in the police. There are, however, notable differences among groups. Generally, Whites are most likely to express satisfaction with various aspects of policing, while African Americans typically report low levels of satisfaction. Surveys conducted in 2019 and 2020 by the Pew Research Center highlight the perceptions different groups have of the police. Among the findings were the following:

- Blacks (84%) were far more likely than Whites (63%) to believe that Blacks are treated less fairly than Whites by the police.
- Far fewer Blacks (52%) than Whites (78%) believed that ethical standards of police officers were high or very high.
- Whites (78%) were more likely than Hispanics (74%) and Blacks (56%) to state that they had a fair amount or great deal of confidence in police (Gilberstadt, 2020; Horowitz, 2019).

African American Relations With Police

Many factors have contributed to problematic relations between the police and African Americans, including a lack of communication between groups, officer abuse of force, stereotyping, racism, and overrepresentation of African Americans in the

Learning Objective 12.5: Summarize the factors that have contributed to problematic relations between the police and members of minority groups.

3 Arrest

Controversial police practices around the United States often generate public protest. The deaths of some African Americans at the hands of police in recent years have hampered police–community relations. It is often argued that diversifying police departments will help address problematic relations.

What else could be done to promote more positive police–community relations in communities with large percentages of minorities?

criminal justice system. African American leaders and others point to the disproportionate number of African Americans stopped, interrogated, searched, and arrested by police as evidence of biased policing. For instance, African Americans constitute roughly 13% of the U.S. population, but they accounted for 27.4% of all arrests in the United States in 2018 (Federal Bureau of Investigation, 2020a). The overrepresentation of African Americans, however, may also be a result of the actions of African Americans. In other words, it may be the case that African Americans are more likely to engage in activities that draw the attention of the police. Arguably, the overrepresentation of African Americans in the criminal justice system results from combination of biased policing and the actions of African Americans, although the extent to which each explains the overrepresentation is difficult to discern.

Racial profiling, which is the practice of targeting or suspecting individuals based not on behavior but on race or ethnicity, is particularly important with regard to any discussion of policing and African Americans. Some evidence indicates that traffic stops disproportionately target African Americans (Smith & Petrocelli, 2001). In 2015, Black drivers (9.8%) were more likely than White and Hispanic drivers (7.6%) to be stopped while driving a motor vehicle (E. Davis et al., 2018). Profiling, however, can be based on ethnicity, age, socioeconomic status, and other factors, and it occurs everywhere, from airports to job interviews.

racial profiling
The practice of targeting or suspecting individuals based not on behavior but on race or ethnicity

Hispanic/Latino Relations with Police

In commenting on the relationship between the police and Hispanic/Latino groups, researchers have noted that "underlying the relationship between Latinos and police is a history of conflict, mistrust, and misunderstandings." They added that the opportunities for police interactions with Hispanic Americans have increased as the Hispanic population continues to grow (C. Perez & McCluskey, 2004, p. 68).

There has historically been a sense of distrust and general tension between Hispanics and the police. In some cases, for those who have moved to the United States from other countries, the distrust stems from the actions and behaviors of law enforcement personnel in their countries of origin (Cafferty & Engstrom, 2000). For instance, law enforcement personnel in Mexico, South America, and Central America are generally less professional than police officers in the United States, and this may reinforce negative perceptions of the police.

In addition, difficulties between Hispanics and the police may arise as a result of cultural and language barriers (McNamara & Burns, 2020). For example, Hispanic Americans who speak in Spanish or fail to make eye contact may appear threatening to officers who do not speak the language and do not understand what is being communicated.

The relationship between Hispanics and the police has also been influenced by national immigration policies. Given that many immigrants, both legal and illegal, who enter the United States are Hispanic, this group, in particular, largely feels the effects of concerns for and reactions to immigration. For instance, nearly half of Latinos surveyed (44%) noted that they would hesitate to report criminal victimization to the police out of fear that they would be asked about their immigration status (Theodore, 2013). Generally, the victimization of immigrants is underreported, primarily in light of the hardships associated with appearing in court (e.g., having to take time off of work), uncertainty about the proceedings in the U.S. justice systems, language barriers, and various cultural differences (C. Davis & Erez, 1998). The 2016 election of Donald Trump as president of the United States reignited concerns regarding immigration, because Trump adopted a tough approach that included mass deportation of illegal immigrants currently in the United States.

Citizen Outreach Programs

The problematic relations between the police and certain groups in society have led to calls for police departments to establish better relations with the communities they serve, and many departments have taken action. Greater levels of communication, openness, and citizen involvement in policing arguably improve police–community relations. Departments have increasingly incorporated citizen outreach programs to promote police–community relations and facilitate community policing efforts.

Among the community outreach programs offered by departments are civilian review boards, citizen police academies, citizen patrols, and police ride-along programs. **Civilian review boards** consist of community members who offer input regarding questionable police practices. **Citizen police academies** offer citizens the opportunity to train in various areas of police work. **Citizen patrols** involve citizens undergoing a period of training prior to being equipped with a radio and sent out to patrol particular areas. These volunteers are expected to contact the police as warranted and provide additional surveillance for departments. Police **ride-along programs** enable citizens to better understand police work by allowing participants to accompany officers on their shifts.

There are many benefits to getting the public more involved in policing, and many of these outreach programs serve to improve police–community relations. Results from a study of citizen police academies in Tennessee found that involvement in these sorts of programs significantly and positively influenced participants' familiarity with local law enforcement, the police chief, crime in the community, and the criminal justice system (Lee, 2016). Other research on citizen police academies notes that graduates of the program have more trust in the police (Becton et al., 2005) and more positive perceptions of the police (Brewster et al., 2005).

civilian review boards Community outreach programs offered by police departments that involve community members offering input regarding questionable police practices

citizen police academies Community outreach programs that offer citizens the opportunity to train in various areas of police work

citizen patrols Community outreach programs in which citizens undergo a period of training prior to being equipped with a radio and set out to patrol particular areas; these volunteers are expected to contact the police as warranted and provide additional surveillance for departments

ride-along programs Community outreach programs that enable citizens to better understand police work by allowing participants to accompany officers on their shifts

The System in Perspective

Conventional wisdom suggests that placing more officers on patrol will reduce crime. And, as noted in the "In the News" feature at the beginning of this module, the New York Police Department believed they could impact crime by having more officers on the streets. However, simply having more police officers on the streets is not enough unless those officers are properly selected and trained and work in departments with positive and supportive cultures. Police departments constantly face many important personnel decisions, including those regarding recruitment, selection, training, and how to best use officers. Of particular importance to police personnel is quantity and quality. In other words, it is important to have enough officers on the streets, but it is also important to have professional officers who perform the job without bias toward any group and in a manner that best benefits the department and community.

Summary

1. Learning Objective 12.1: *Describe the typical police department in terms of size and demographics.*

- The typical police department is relatively small, with the majority of departments serving populations of fewer than 10,000 residents. Most police officers, however, work for large departments. Further, most police officers are White (about 73%) and male (about 87%). The demographics of police officers are changing, however, as more females and members of racial and ethnic minority groups become involved in policing.

2. Learning Objective 12.2: *Explain what the police subculture is and what factors shape it.*

- The police subculture refers to the similarities among police officers with regard to their values, beliefs, attitudes, and practices within their job. It is used to explain why officers often act in a similar manner and is shaped by an officer's education, work experiences, and the nature of police work.

3. Learning Objective 12.3: *List the typical minimum eligibility requirements to become a police officer and the examinations used as part of the screening process.*

- The minimum eligibility requirements for a police officer position typically include residency requirements; height, weight, and age requirements; educational requirements; medical disqualifiers; and criminal history restrictions. In addition to initial screening requirements, candidates may undergo a series of evaluations prior to selection for employment, including a written exam, polygraph examination, psychological evaluation, a personal interview, and a physical agility test.

4. Learning Objective 12.4: *Differentiate between basic, field, and in-service training.*

- Basic training provides officers with the foundation of skills and education required to perform the job. It requires candidates to spend time at the police academy studying police operations, weapons/self-defense/use of force, legal aspects, and self-improvement issues. Field training supplements basic training and is designed to reinforce and help officers apply what is learned during basic training, while providing additional information about specific aspects of the job. In-service training primarily attempts to keep experienced officers abreast of changes in the field and generally applies to officers at all stages of their career. Some officers undergo specialized training if they are promoted or change job assignments.

5. Learning Objective 12.5: *Summarize the factors that have contributed to problematic relations between the police and members of minority groups.*

- Many factors have contributed to problematic relations between the police and minorities, including officer abuse of force, racial profiling, stereotyping, overrepresentation of minorities in the criminal justice system, a lack of effective communication between the groups, and racism. Further, concerns regarding immigration have hampered relations between the police and the Hispanic community.

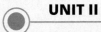

Questions for Critical Thinking

1. What do you believe are the most effective ways for police departments to diversify the ranks?

2. There are both positive and negative aspects of the police subculture. What steps could be taken to enhance the positive aspects and reduce the negative aspects on officers and the public?

3. If you were setting policy for a police department, would you include residency requirements for officers? Why or why not?

4. What factors are related to a recruit's performance in the police academy? What could be done to assist groups that do not perform as well as others?

5. Which type of community outreach program do you believe would best address tensions between the police and racial and ethnic mjnorities?

Key Terms

affirmative action programs
Age Discrimination in Employment Act of 1967
basic training
citizen patrols
citizen police academies
civilian review boards
civil service commissions
culture
Employee Protection Act of 1988
Equal Employment Opportunity Act of 1972
field training

field training officers
in-service training
Peace Officer Standard and Training commission
polygraph examinations
racial profiling
recruitment
residency requirements
ride-along programs
subculture
Title VII of the Civil Rights Act of 1964
voice stress analyzers

For digital learning resources, please go to
https://www.oup.com/he/burns1e

Personal Toll of Police Work

Module

13

Police officers encounter many disturbing and stressful issues that most people will not encounter in their lifetime.

What type of training or preparation do you believe would best prepare officers for the stressful challenges associated with the job?

Stress and health problems are not unique to law enforcement. However, the challenging nature of police work leads to a greater risk of health problems and other related issues than is found in most other civilian occupations. While police departments have made efforts to address the harmful byproducts of policing through wellness and support programs, more work needs to be done.

This module begins with a look at the stressors of law enforcement, followed by a discussion of substance abuse and why officers may misuse drugs or alcohol. This module then describes how police work can contribute to divorce and other family problems. This module ends with a look at health-related problems to which police officers are particularly susceptible, as well as the increased risks of suicide faced by those working in law enforcement.

MODULE OUTLINE

- **Stress**

  Learning Objective 13.1: Identify the categories of police stressors.

- **Substance Abuse**

  Learning Objective 13.2: Discuss why officers may misuse drugs or alcohol.

- **Family Problems**

  Learning Objective 13.3: Describe how police work can contribute to family problems.

- **Health Problems**

  Learning Objective 13.4: Identify the types of health problems to which police officers are particularly susceptible.

- **Suicide**

  Learning Objective 13.5: Explain why police officer suicide rates are higher than average.

3 Arrest

Addressing Police Stress

In 2015, Eric Casebolt, a McKinney, Texas, police corporal, resigned after he was caught on video violently trying to subdue an African American teenage girl in a bikini outside a public pool. The officer had responded to a report of a fight at a pool party. The video showed the officer shoving ithe girl's face in the ground, placing his knee on her back, and cursing and shouting. Casebolt also pulled out his gun when a crowd formed around them. He later apologized for his actions through his attorney, stating that he was under much stress that day because he earlier responded to two calls involving a suicide and an attempted suicide.

A grand jury declined to indict the officer; however, the young girl's family filed a $5 million federal lawsuit, alleging that the officer violated the girl's constitutional rights and held her without probable cause. They also claimed that the department was liable for failing to properly train the officer (Chiquillo, 2017). In 2018, the young girl's legal guardian agreed to a legal settlement with the city of McKinney and received $148,850. Six others on the lawsuit each received $6,000.

Police officers across the United States regularly encounter stressful situations. How they respond to that stress affects their own health, well-being, and professionalism on the job. Should the supervisors of the corporal in McKinney have prevented him from further working after what was a particularly stressful day? Should the number and nature of stressful calls officers take be considered by police supervisors?

Eric Casebolt resigned after responding to several stressful calls that prompted him to use too much force in a later situation. The harmful effects of stress and other byproducts of policing often go unnoticed.

What could police departments do to assist officers with dealing with stress-related problems?

Stress

● **Learning Objective 13.1:** Identify the categories of police stressors

Defined as "an unpleasant state of arousal in which people perceive the demands of an event as taxing or exceeding their ability to satisfy or alter those demands" (Brehm et al., 1999, p. 500), **stress** is perhaps the most significant personal consequence of police work. While sometimes small levels of stress may be beneficial, for instance in encouraging individuals to more closely focus on the task at hand (e.g., Folkman, 2008), high levels are often associated with negative effects. How officers respond to stress and its effects has widespread implications.

stress An uncomfortable state of arousal in which individuals perceive the demands of an incident as difficult or beyond their ability to satisfy or alter those demands

Sources of Stress

The harmful effects of policing include stressful situations that can result in psychological and physical harm. The high level of stress associated with police work stems from many aspects of the job. Researchers have categorized the stressors (sources of stress) as those that are:

- external to policing, including negative media coverage of police work;
- internal to policing, including excessive paperwork and shiftwork;
- related to police practices, including danger and the need to gain control of situations; and
- individual to the officer, such as dealing with unresolved family issues (Ayers & Flanagan, 1992; Terry, 1981).

Researchers found that shiftwork is related to stress in police officers. In particular, they found that officers who worked the afternoon and night shifts reported experiencing more stressful events than their colleagues who worked the day shift (Ma et al., 2015). Not all officers are subject to the same levels of stress on the job because individuals handle situations differently, and different departments, shifts, and beats provide varying levels of stressful situations.

Female officers face several unique stressors compared to male officers. Among them are:

- sexism,
- feeling the need to prove one's self,
- a lack of role models or mentors,
- negative attitudes of male officers, and
- lack of acceptance into the police subculture (McCarty et al., 2007).

Further, female officers appear to be more likely than males to report being treated differently by supervisors because of their gender (Sousa & Gauthier, 2008).

Physical and Emotional Reactions to Stress

Stress leads to both physical and emotional effects. The physical reactions to being regularly exposed to stress include:

- headaches,
- heart disease,
- ulcers,
- sleep disturbances, and
- muscle aches.

The emotional reactions to high levels of stress include:

- fear,
- guilt,
- irritability,
- anger,
- anxiety, and
- sadness.

Officers may also experience nightmares, memory lapses, difficulty in decision-making, and a lack of concentration. Officers exposed to high levels of stress are at a greater risk of certain behavioral issues, for instance in the form of absenteeism, divorce, suicide, limited motivation, substance abuse, and withdrawal from nonpolice friends (Gershon et al., 2009; Kirschman, 2007; Roberg et al., 2015). Prolonged exposure to stress can also result in **burnout**, which involves officers losing their enthusiasm for the job and being incapable of performing up to standards.

Post–Traumatic Stress Disorder

It is estimated that 7%–19% of officers may experience a particular stress, known as **post–traumatic stress disorder (PTSD)**, following their involvement in a traumatic incident such as a shooting or physical fight (Carlier et al., 1997; Kirschman, 2018; Marmar et al., 2006). This estimate does not include officers who suffer many of the same symptoms associated with PTSD, yet are not diagnosed as suffering from the disorder. Some studies suggest that roughly 34% of officers suffer from symptoms associated with PTSD, but fail to meet the standards of a full diagnosis of the disorder (Kirschman, 2018). PTSD may contribute to intense fear or feelings of helplessness. The affected officers may continuously revisit the traumatic experience, which amplifies the effects of the incident. Ultimately, there may be a numbing of the arousal system, and officers may find difficulty in both their work and nonwork lives (Cross & Ashley, 2004). It was noted that alcohol use combined with PTSD results in a 10-fold increase in the likelihood of an officer committing suicide (Violanti, 2004).

There are two main methods of coping with stress: action-oriented approaches or avoidance. Action-oriented approaches address the problem and include lifestyle changes, counseling, and therapy. In Kansas City, Missouri, for example, training at the police academy includes 4-hour sessions during which they learn how to recognize, avoid, and deal with stressful situations as they pertain to secondary trauma—when individuals are traumatized by witnessing trauma experienced by someone else. Participants are taught muscle relaxation exercises, breathing techniques, and other calming methods they can use both on and off the job (Rice, 2015).

The second, and more problematic, way of dealing with stress is through the use of avoidance strategies, which may include withdrawal from families, smoking, drinking alcohol, or misusing other substances (He et al., 2002). Avoidant coping methods are considered the least effective approach to addressing stress (Ben-Zur, 2009).

Substance Abuse

According to research, police officers appear to be at a higher risk than the general public for drug abuse and alcohol use disorders (Cross & Ashley, 2004). One study found that approximately 11% of male officers and 16% of female officers had engaged in at-risk levels of alcohol use in the previous week, and over one-third of all officers had reported binge drinking in the previous month (Ballenger et al., 2011).

burnout Officers losing their enthusiasm for the job, which leaves them incapable of performing up to standards

post–traumatic stress disorder A mental illness in individuals exposed to a traumatic event that causes them to relive the event and experience extended periods of nervousness and being "on edge"; it is sometimes used as a defense in which defendants claim that their behavior was attributed to the mental effects of having suffered from some traumatic incident

● **Learning Objective 13.2:** Discuss why officers may misuse drugs or alcohol.

As mentioned, the use of mind-altering substances as coping mechanisms for the stress associated with the job is one explanation for officers misusing drugs and alcohol. Other factors include social ones, for instance peer pressure, social isolation, and being part of a subculture that approves of and encourages alcohol use (Violanti et al., 2011). In addition, officers may be more likely to show solidarity by gathering in bars after work to debrief or socialize. It was found that the yearning to "fit in" with other officers was one of the primary reasons cited by officers for drinking (Lindsay & Shelley, 2009).

Officers who use alcohol and drugs generally do so for the same reasons as civilians: for recreational purposes and to cope with problems. However, the challenges associated with police work place officers at a higher risk of self-medicating or consuming alcohol as a coping mechanism to deal with stressful encounters, which subsequently puts them at a higher risk of developing alcohol or substance abuse issues when compared to the general population (Richmond et al., 1998, Violanti et al., 2011). Alcohol and substance abuse can have numerous negative consequences, both personally and professionally, for police officers (Swatt et al., 2007).

With respect to drugs in particular, police officers are in a unique position. They are regularly exposed to drugs and drug offenders and are often left generally unaccountable in their patrol cars. These factors have encouraged some officers to engage in illegal drug use or to sell drugs. Little information regarding the extent of officer drug use is available, primarily because such information is not often collected, and the information is often withheld from the public when it is (Mieczkowski, 2002). Results from drug tests conducted by various departments suggest that a very small percentage of officers (0.5%–1.1%) tested positive for drugs in their system (Lersch & Mieczkowski, 2005; Smalley, 2006).

Family Problems

The effects of regularly encountering troubling situations at work can make officers cynical and closed off emotionally. While these characteristics may be necessary for one's physical and emotional survival on the job, they may be detrimental to personal and family relationships. Several job-related aspects of policing that contribute to problematic family issues are:

- rotating shifts,
- the dangers of the job,
- community expectations of the officers, and
- intrusion of the work into the home, either in a real way, for example with respect to storing weapons, or in an emotional way, for example with respect to mood swings (Scrivner, 1991).

● **Learning Objective 13.3:** Describe how police work can contribute to family problems.

Domestic Violence

Domestic violence issues are a concern with policing. One study reported that at least 40% of police families experience domestic violence, compared to 10% of families in general, while another noted that 24% of older, experienced officers had been involved in domestic violence, which was nearly 2.5 times the rate for nonpolice families (cited in Cheema, 2016).

1 Criminal Act

Police officers are at a high risk of engaging in domestic violence given several critical aspects of the job:

- the stressful nature of police work, including the exposure to danger and shiftwork
- the rigid, militaristic management style often found in police departments
- the emphasis on maintaining control of situations and the use of violence if needed to gain control

These sorts of tactics do not translate well to family life. Of particular concern with regard to domestic violence in police families is the treatment of victims. Many victims of officer-involved domestic violence are apprehensive or fearful to report their victimization because they believe their complaints will not be taken seriously or treated in a fair manner. Victims often believe that the officer's position will protect the offender, are often fearful that their report will result in the offender losing their job, and sometimes fear further abuse from the officer/family member (Cohen et al., 2013).

Steps have been taken to address the underreporting of officer-involved domestic violence in the form of legislation. Various states have passed laws that mandate specific protocols in domestic violence cases involving officers, and the International Association of Chiefs of Police has developed a model policy to address these types of incidents. In addition, in 2005, Congress passed the **Crystal Judson Domestic Violence Protocol Program** when it reauthorized the Violence Against Women Act. The program provides funding to police departments that adopt protocols that address domestic violence cases involving officers. Among the protocols that have been adopted are:

- educating police officers regarding domestic violence,
- better screening job applicants,
- counseling officers, and
- properly investigating and responding to complaints of domestic violence involving the police (Cheema, 2016).

Further, the **Domestic Violence Offender Gun Ban**, which is often called the Lautenberg Amendment in recognition of its sponsor, Senator Frank Lautenberg (D-NJ), was an amendment to the Omnibus Consolidated Appropriations Act of 1997. It bans access to firearms by individuals who are convicted of domestic violence. This ban impacts police officers, because carrying a firearm is an essential requirement for the position. The legislation has led to conflict between several groups that protect police interests (including the Fraternal Order of the Police and the National Association of Police Organizations) and victims' rights advocates (Adelman & Morgan, 2006). The amendment has withstood various legal challenges since its passage.

Divorce

Police officers appear to be at a high risk for divorce given the stressful nature of police work. Irregular working hours (including shift work) and regularly dealing with traumatic situations can contribute to marital stress (Roberg et al., 2015). It is a commonly held belief that the divorce rate for police officers is higher than that of the general population (e.g., Aamodt, 2008; Territo & Sewell, 2007) because of the stress and nature of police work in general and the characteristics of the individuals who choose to go into policing. Some researchers, however, have noted that the divorce rate for police officers is lower than the average divorce rate for other occupations (McCoy & Aamodt, 2010).

Crystal Judson Domestic Violence Protocol Program A program passed by Congress in 2005 that provides funding to police departments that adopt protocols to address domestic violence cases involving officers

Domestic Violence Offender Gun Ban Also known as the Lautenberg Amendment; it was an amendment to the Omnibus Consolidated Appropriations Act of 1997 and bans access to firearms by individuals who are convicted of domestic violence

Police Officers Experience the Highest Rates of Divorce

Some reports suggest that police divorce rates are as high as 75% and that police officers have the highest or second highest divorce rate in the United States compared to other occupations (Aamodt, 2008). This perception is in part due to factors that predominantly affect police officers, such as irregular working hours, exposure to dangerous situations, and failure to properly handle the stresses associated with the job. Despite these and other claims that have regularly shaped the public perception that divorce

rates for police officers are notably high, there was little empirical evaluation of police divorce rates until the research of Shawn McCoy and Michael Aamodt (2010).

McCoy and Aamodt (2010) noted that the divorce rate for officers was 14.47%, compared to the national average of 16.96%. Further, they found that even within law enforcement in general, police officers have lower rates of divorce than animal control officers, fish and game wardens, and parking enforcement officers.

Health Problems

Aside from the physical aspects of police work, which can result in officers being physically harmed or killed, police officers are particularly susceptible to other health problems and may experience accelerated rates of:

- heart disease,
- diabetes,
- hypertension,
- cancer of the liver and colon, and
- depression.

> **Learning Objective 13.4:** Identify the types of health problems to which police officers are particularly susceptible.

Each of these health problems could impact an officer's performance and overall well-being. For instance, **diabetes**, which is a life-threatening disease in which one's body does not produce or respond to the hormone insulin properly and results in the abnormal processing of carbohydrates and high levels of glucose, can be brought on by regularly consuming a diet high in fat, calories, and cholesterol and a lack of physical exercise. Officers often eat unhealthy meals while on patrol. In addition, officers riding in patrol cars often do not get the physical exercise they need.

Police officers also have higher rates of depression than the general public (Larned, 2010). **Depression**, which can be hereditary or brought on by other factors, produces feelings of isolation and hopelessness. Officers may be reluctant to share their depression with other officers or openly seek assistance for the disorder out of fear of being seen as weak or losing respect from other officers (Larned, 2010).

Contributing to the health-related concerns for police officers was the global pandemic resulting from the spread of COVID-19. Police officers are not always able to social distance from the individuals with whom they interact, and more so than in most other occupations, they must closely interact with people. More officer lives were lost in 2020 because of the virus compared to all other causes of death combined (Montgomery, 2020; Officer Down Memorial Page, 2020). Many other officers contracted the virus on the job and suffered notable health concerns.

It remains unclear if the reason officers are more likely than those in other occupations to experience health-related problems is because of the high levels of stress in policing or because of the lifestyle of individual police officers. Drinking excessive

diabetes A life-threatening disease in which one's body does not produce or respond to the hormone insulin properly and results in the abnormal processing of carbohydrates and high levels of glucose; it can be brought on by regularly consuming a diet high in fat, calories, and cholesterol and a lack of physical exercise

depression A mental illness involving feelings of dejection, isolation, and hopelessness; it can be hereditary or brought on by other factors

levels of alcohol also puts individuals at risk for particular illnesses, as does regularly being exposed to and in personal contact with a variety of offenders who may have contagious diseases or illnesses and no access to appropriate healthcare.

Suicide

● **Learning Objective 13.5:** Explain why police officer suicide rates are higher than average.

A report from the Centers for Disease Control and Prevention noted that protective services, which includes policing, are among the occupations with the highest levels of suicide (Peterson et al., 2018). A number of factors contribute to the increased likelihood of officers committing suicide:

- high level of stress (pressure to always make correct decisions while on the job)
- disproportionate number of males in policing (males are more likely than females to kill themselves)
- substance abuse (alcohol is a factor in most police suicides)
- involvement in deviance and corruption
- false accusations
- easy access to and familiarity with firearms
- depression
- financial and familial problems
- social isolation and cynicism
- guilt over a fellow officer's death or severe injury
- physical and mental health problems

Gathering data on police suicides is difficult because police departments are sometimes reluctant to share such information with researchers (O'Hara et al., 2013). Nevertheless, Blue H.E.L.P., an organization that seeks to help law enforcement officers with various issues (e.g., mental illness) that could lead to suicide, estimated that there were 454 suicides by active-duty law enforcement personnel between January 1, 2016, and June 31, 2019 (Blue H.E.L.P., 2019). The group noted that there were a record 228 suicides in 2019 alone. Most of the officers who died were male (90%), and about 25% were veterans with over 20 years of service (Barr, 2020). Other research suggested that the average age of law enforcement personnel who committed suicide was 40, firearms were the most prevalent means of suicide (roughly 82%), and intimate partner problems appeared to be the most common reason for the decision of officers to take their lives (K. Roberts, 2019).

The number of police suicides may be underreported, because some cases may be intentionally misclassified as "accidents" to protect the reputation of the officer and/or the department (Violanti, 1996). The strong bond among police officers may encourage a department to misclassify a suicide as another type of death to protect the reputation of the officer. Further, an officer suicide generally reflects negatively on a department because it suggests that the department failed to provide adequate psychological counseling and other types of support for the officers.

Police departments have increasingly begun to offer services to help officers and their families address the stressful aspects of police work, and they have implemented programs to prevent suicides. For instance, departments often make peer support programs and mental health professionals available to officers, and employee assistance programs have been implemented in many departments. In Tennessee, the

Metro Nashville Police Department's Behavioral Health Services offers family support groups and provides a place for family members of officers to process emotions and destress, build supportive networks of other family members, and obtain helpful information (Nashville, 2018).

Officers have increasingly taken advantage of these types of support programs (O'Hara et al., 2013), and departments have encouraged officers to report critical warning signs in other officers, including:

- talk of committing suicide or talk of death,
- isolation from family and friends,
- giving away personal items, and
- neglecting one's hygiene and appearance (Larned, 2010).

The System in Perspective

Police officers see the worst aspects of society on a regular basis. They rush to the most problematic situations and are expected to not let what they encounter personally affect them. Corporal Casebolt, referenced in the "In the News" feature at the start of this module, was seemingly impacted by a stressful shift. His particularly challenging day arguably contributed to him misusing his power.

Physically and mentally sound police officers are vital to effective policing. Officers who are stressed or otherwise suffering the ill effects of police work may be unable to perform their jobs well. They may experience health, psychological, and family-related problems and may resort to substance abuse and even suicide when the hardships of the job get to be too much. The repercussions of not addressing these burdens may negatively impact many people, including an officer's family, their co-workers, and the public they serve.

Summary

1. Learning Objective 13.1: *Identify the categories of police stressors.*

- The sources of police stress have been categorized according to stressors that are external to policing (e.g., negative media coverage of police work); internal to policing (e.g., excessive paperwork and shiftwork); related to police practices (e.g., facing danger and the need to gain control of situations); and associated with individual officers (e.g., dealing with unresolved family issues).

2. Learning Objective 13.2: *Discuss why officers may misuse drugs or alcohol.*

- Police officers appear to be at a higher risk than the general public for drug abuse and alcohol use disorders, primarily as a result of the use of mind-altering substances as coping mechanisms for the difficulties associated with the job; the emphasis on being "macho," which could encourage officers to drink more, as well as more frequently; and the solidarity among officers who may gather in bars after work to debrief or socialize. Officers are regularly exposed to drugs and drug offenders and are often left generally unaccountable in their patrol cars, which could encourage officers to engage in illegal drug use and/or selling drugs.

3. Learning Objective 13.3: *Describe how police work can contribute to family problems.*

- Officers may become cynical and emotionally distant in response to dealing with troubling situations. Rotating shifts, the dangers of the job, community expectations of the officers, and the intrusion of the work into the home (e.g., storing weapons and officer moodiness) have also contributed to family problems such as domestic violence and divorce.

4. Learning Objective 13.4: *Identify the types of health problems to which police officers are particularly susceptible.*

- Police officers are particularly susceptible to various health problems, including accelerated rates of heart disease, diabetes, hypertension, indigestion, and liver and colon cancer. COVID-19 posed additional concerns for officers beginning in 2020.

5. Learning Objective 13.5: *Explain why police officer suicide rates are higher than average.*

- Policing is among the occupations with the highest levels of suicide, primarily because of the higher level of stress in police work, the disproportionate number of males in policing, substance abuse, involvement in deviance and corruption, easy access to and familiarity with firearms, depression, false accusations, financial and familial problems, social isolation and cynicism, guilt over a fellow officer's death or severe injury, and physical and mental health problems.

Questions for Critical Thinking

1. How could police administrators best ensure that officers are not suffering from the ill effects of stress?
2. Is it hypocritical for officers to drink more, as well as more often than individuals in other occupations? Why or why not?
3. Do you believe officers who engage in domestic violence should be punished more severely than civilians, given the fact that officers are responsible for upholding the law? Why or why not?
4. What actions could be taken by officers to ensure they live healthier lives and are not as susceptible to such a large number of health issues?
5. Do you think law enforcement officers are more likely to commit suicide because of the stressful nature of the work or off-duty problems?

Key Terms

burnout
Crystal Judson Domestic Violence Protocol Program
depression
diabetes

Domestic Violence Offender Gun Ban
post-traumatic stress disorder
stress

For digital learning resources, please go to
https://www.oup.com/he/burns1e

Primary Police Practices

Module

14

Solving crimes is an important aspect of crime control. Much police work is reactionary in nature and requires cooperative efforts among many groups.

Do you believe the police spend too much time responding to crime and too little time preventing crime?

Police officers regularly perform a wide array of tasks, from responding to fights and stopping drunk drivers to assisting stranded motorists and moving the homeless away from businesses. The primary functions of policing are preventing crime, serving the population, and keeping order. While these functions are different, they often overlap. For instance, police officers engaged in order maintenance may make arrests—acts that would be considered crime control. Similarly, officers who provide particular services to the community, for example bringing mentally ill individuals to receive treatment after they are found wandering in traffic, may simultaneously be engaged in order maintenance. This module addresses the most important parts of police work: crime control, the provision of service, and order maintenance, as well as patrolling and policing juveniles.

MODULE OUTLINE

- **Crime Control**

  Learning Objective 14.1: Describe the extent to which officers focus on crime control.

- **Service**

  Learning Objective 14.2: Illustrate how providing public service differs by department size and how it promotes positive police–community relations.

- **Order Maintenance**

  Learning Objective 14.3: Explain why zero-tolerance policing is closely related to order maintenance.

- **Patrol**

  Learning Objective 14.4: Differentiate among the patrol strategies.

- **Policing and Juveniles**

  Learning Objective 14.5: Identify the delinquency prevention efforts taken by police.

IN THE NEWS

1 Criminal Act

Order Maintenance and Large-Scale Events

On April 15, 2013, two bombs exploded near the finish line of the Boston Marathon. The bombs killed 3 people and injured 264 others. The suspects were eventually identified from surveillance video, and one was killed and the other arrested as the two sought to evade authorities (Merica, 2013). More recently, in October 2017, 58 people were killed and 850 injured after a man used multiple rifles to shoot from the 32nd floor of a hotel room at a crowd

of roughly 22,000 people who were attending a country music festival on the Las Vegas strip. The shooting ceased when the man took his own life (Corcoran & Baker, 2018).

Marathons are problematic primarily because the competitions are spread out over 26.2-plus miles. Following the Boston Marathon bombing, law enforcement authorities in other cities that host major marathons changed their policies. Among the actions

taken by law enforcement in Chicago and New York, for example, were the requirement that family members who wished to be at the finish line go through special screening, the prohibition of bags of any kind, the requirement that runners use plastic bags to store goods, the expansion of inspection areas, an increase in the number of fences used, and an increase in the number of uniformed and undercover officers.

Festivals present difficulties for law enforcement because of the large numbers of people in relatively small places. The Las Vegas incident was problematic for law enforcement given that large hotels exist on the strip, and it would have been extremely difficult and burdensome to screen all customers who were staying in the hotels.

Marathons and outdoor festivals present particular challenges for law enforcement in maintaining order, because law enforcement must ensure the safety of both participants and spectators, while not hindering athletes, performers, or spectators/audience members from enjoying the experience. Finding an appropriate balance requires cooperation among many parties and planning before and during an event.

Fortunately, police departments and other first responders have used these tragic incidents as learning tools in efforts to provide greater levels of security for all involved. For instance, a 158-page after-action report was prepared following the Las Vegas incident. Should public police agencies be responsible for providing security at sporting events and large festivals, or should the organizers, league, sponsors, participants, or teams be responsible for paying for protection?

Learning Objective 14.1: Describe the extent to which officers focus on crime control.

Crime Control

The police engage in crime control when they enforce traffic laws, investigate criminal cases, collect evidence, interview witnesses, testify in court, make arrests, patrol neighborhoods, and perform related enforcement-oriented actions. The manner through which they engage in each of these tasks is sometimes the subject of controversy; for instance, enforcing the law may interfere with respecting individual rights. Officers are expected to use their powers appropriately, although the definition of appropriate behavior varies. The emphasis that officers and departments place on crime control efforts shapes public perception of police work and influences the overall effectiveness of each department.

Time Spent on Crime Control

Despite the general public's perception of police officers as primarily enforcers of the law, police officers spend relatively little time actually engaged in strict crime-fighting activities. For instance, an estimated 24% of U.S. residents over age 15 had face-to-face contact with a police officer in 2017 (Harrell & Davis, 2020). Police–citizen contacts occur relatively infrequently, and when they do occur, they often do not involve the use of force. Officers who work in large cities are more engaged in crime control efforts than are their counterparts who work in smaller departments, given that much crime occurs in large cities.

Balancing Crime Control and Individual Rights

Finding the correct balance between respecting individual rights and enforcing the law has historically challenged police departments and officers. For example, officers who aggressively enforce the law by writing many speeding tickets are sometimes criticized for being overzealous. There is no consensus among the general public, the police, politicians, police administrators, and other groups regarding what constitutes the perfect balance between crime control and individual rights. As noted in Module 7 with regard to Packer's models of criminal justice, there are distinct differences in the means by which some groups administer justice.

Selective Enforcement and Styles of Policing

In practice, the police engage in **selective enforcement** of the law, whereby they enforce some of the laws some of the time. As such, there is variation among officers regarding their practices. While some officers adopt a "by the book" approach in which almost all offenses are formally addressed, others take a more relaxed approach. For instance, some officers responding to a fight among two young adults might make arrests, while others might let the parties leave the scene with a warning. Such use of discretion contributes to different styles of policing.

selective enforcement The practice of police officers whereby they enforce some of the laws some of the time

Several researchers have categorized police officer types based on their policing styles:

- Professor Susan White (1972) identified "tough cops" and "crime-fighters" who view crime control as their primary functions. Tough cops are outcome oriented, with less of a concern for the means by which they enforce the law. Crime-fighters believe their role is to strictly enforce the law and that any other action (e.g., providing service) is not real police work.
- Broderick (1987) and Muir (1977) identified "enforcers," who are primarily concerned with crime control. These individuals primarily focus on enforcing the law, even if that may involve violating individual rights.
- J. Q. Wilson (1968) depicted a legalistic style of policing that includes officers who make high numbers of arrests and issue high numbers of traffic citations. Such officers generally believe that police work is primarily about enforcing the law for the sake of removing dangerous people from the streets, and they are more likely to use aggressive and coercive means. They are often less concerned about providing service to citizens or respecting individual rights.

This categorization of officer styles includes only those who generally believe that crime control is the primary or sole function of police work. The researchers compared these officers to other types of officers, including those who emphasized the provision of service, avoided confrontation, or sought to solve problems. Ultimately, all officers perform various functions, but some emphasize certain functions over others.

● **Learning Objective 14.2:** Illustrate how providing public service differs by department size and how it promotes positive police–community relations.

Service

One of the most significant aspects of police work is the provision of services to citizens. The service-related aspects of policing involve activities that typically do not involve disruptions of social order, nor are they violations of the law (R. R. Johnson & Rhodes, 2009). Most police activities are service related. Recent departmental shifts toward community-oriented policing have resulted in police officers and departments more openly engaging with the public and a greater level of police services than in preceding decades.

Types of Services

We often look to the police to assist us in times of trouble, regardless of whether an incident involves a crime. Police departments are available to the public 24 hours a day, 7 days a week. The type of services that officers most often provide depends on the characteristics of the community being served. In general, however, the police provide the following sorts of services:

- searching for runaways and missing elderly persons
- assisting motorists in times of trouble
- providing medical attention or assisting emergency medical personnel
- offering various crime-prevention programs
- rescuing lost or troubled animals
- providing directions to lost citizens

Service is important because it helps people. This is exemplified by the officers from the Bedford, Texas, police department's Repeat Victimization Unit. They work closely with the mentally ill by visiting them regularly (accompanied by mental health professionals), listening to their concerns, ensuring that they are taking their necessary medications and attending therapy sessions, and providing various other types of assistance (Mitchell, 2014). Another example of the importance of police services involves drug overdoses. Police officers are often the first to respond to drug overdoses, and, akin to other medical emergencies, immediate assistance is required. To better address a growing number of heroin overdoses, police departments are increasingly carrying antidotes that can instantly reverse opiate overdoses (Leger, 2014).

Service in Small Towns Versus Large Cities

Individuals who reside in more affluent communities expect, and often receive, higher levels of service than those who live in impoverished neighborhoods. There are also differences in the service provided depending on the size of the town or city. Researchers examined the services provided by police by comparing citizen demands for services in urban areas and small towns. They found that smaller departments received proportionately more service-related calls, such as assisting emergency medical technicians, responding to fire alarms and assisting fire departments, general citizen assistance, and animal control. Large, urban police departments typically received calls involving medical problems/assistance with emergency medical personnel, general citizen assistance, and assistance with disabled vehicles or individuals who were locked out of their vehicle (R. R. Johnson & Rhodes, 2009).

Positive Community Relations

Some officers choose policing as a career because of their interest in assisting others. They may view themselves as social service agents who can positively influence the community. Their orientation toward providing service contributes to positive police–community relations. Researchers found that police are more likely to garner the support of the public when they provide greater levels of service. For example, when examining crime victims' satisfaction with police responses to calls in five districts in Louisville, Kentucky, researchers found that an officer's level of concern for the victim also highly related to overall satisfaction with police services (Tewksbury & West, 2001).

Providing service often involves police officers and departments working closely with community groups and agencies, which promotes cooperative efforts in the community and establishes stronger bonds with various groups. Further, officers who provide service to the public can better identify where problems exist. Police officers are regularly in direct contact with a large number of individuals who are in need of various social, psychological, medical, and related services. Efforts by officers to assist these individuals and others arguably contribute to lower crime rates. The global pandemic that largely impacted communities beginning in 2020 heavily impacted opportunities for police departments to interact with citizens. Special precautions such as masks and gloves became mandatory as officers tried to continue providing various types of service.

Order Maintenance

Order maintenance is defined as the role of the police in keeping the peace (Dempsey & Forst, 2014), and it "has become a staple of the touted missions of police agencies nationwide" (Gau & Gaines, 2012, p. 46). Order maintenance–related activities constitute a significant portion of an officer's duties. Examples of such activities include:

- assisting with accidents and emergencies on highways and streets to ensure that traffic proceeds smoothly;

● **Learning Objective 14.3:** Explain why zero-tolerance policing is closely related to order maintenance.

**order mainte-
nance** The role of the
police in keeping the peace

- controlling crowds at large events (such as athletic events, political national conventions, and protests); and
- ensuring that intoxicated individuals do not disrupt the public peace.

These types of duties are distinct from traditional efforts directed toward enforcing the law because they involve more of a focus on ensuring that citizens have a better quality of life.

Types of Order Maintenance

Order maintenance can be both reactive and proactive. Officers engage in reactive order maintenance when restoring a community to normalcy following a natural disaster. For example, police departments in West Virginia provided order maintenance following flooding in the state that left 23 dead and resulted in physical destruction. The police were also tasked with preventing looting and responding to armed citizen patrols that emerged in efforts to address the looting (Beck, 2016) Proactive order maintenance may involve a police presence at a major sporting event; for instance, police help ensure that both vehicular and pedestrian traffic moves swiftly. Protestors recently demonstrated in many cities across the United States following several instances in which it was believed that the police were misusing their powers against Black males. The police were called in to ensure that the protests did not become violent or exacerbate into riots. The police have provided this type of order maintenance throughout history.

**broken windows
hypothesis** The belief
that offenders perceive order maintenance problems
as opportunities to commit
crimes primarily because
it appears citizens in the
area do not care about their
community

Scope of Order Maintenance

Order maintenance can be large or small in scope. The police typically engage in small-scale order maintenance as part of their daily routines, for instance when they respond to noise complaints. On a larger scale, police departments often work cooperatively with city leaders and community groups to assist neighborhoods, for instance in fixing up or demolishing abandoned buildings, discouraging and removing graffiti, or removing abandoned vehicles.

Assisting stranded motorists and responding to traffic accidents are among the services the police provide that can also be considered order maintenance. Some cities have specialized traffic response groups or departments, whose members are not police officers, that respond to traffic problems.

Should cities continue moving in the direction of having such departments, with the goal of freeing police officers to focus more on addressing crime?

Order Maintenance as a Policing Style

In the early 1980s, researchers Wilson and Kelling introduced the **broken windows hypothesis**, which argues that offenders perceive order maintenance problems as opportunities to commit crimes, primarily because it appears citizens in the area do not care about their community. The hypothesis centers around the need to address signs of disorder (e.g., a broken window in an abandoned building) in efforts to reduce citizens' fear of crime and send the message that crime and disorder are taken seriously in the community (J. Q. Wilson & Kelling, 1982). Following the introduction of the broken windows hypothesis, some departments adopted the order maintenance style of policing, which emphasizes the aggressive enforcement of minor crimes. The premise is that the prevention of minor crimes will contribute to the prevention of more serious crimes.

Order maintenance policing addresses the nagging quality-of-life issues (e.g., noise emanating from loud parties) that negatively influence communities. The aggressive policing of minor crimes is designed to send a message to offenders and potential offenders that crime and unruly behavior will not be tolerated. Police discretion plays a significant role, particularly since aggressively enforcing petty crimes or violations may appear as overenforcement of the law on behalf of the police. In particular, the public may view police practices that crack down on minor offenses as disproportionate to the harms being committed (Harcourt, 2001). There is evidence that order maintenance policing disproportionately affects minority groups and the poor (D. E. Roberts, 1999).

Researchers examined the effects of order maintenance policing on New York City homicide and robbery rates between 1988 and 2001 and found statistically significant, although small, crime reduction effects of order maintenance policing. They concluded that the influence of aggressive order enforcement on the reduction in homicide and robbery rates in New York City during the 1990s was modest at best (Rosenfeld et al., 2007). More recently, researchers analyzed the existing research on policing disorder and found that strategies designed to reduce disorder in communities do indeed reduce the levels of crime. They also noted that aggressive order maintenance strategies focused on individual disorderly behaviors resulted in significant crime reductions (Braga et al., 2015).

Zero-Tolerance Policing

A more aggressive version of order maintenance policing is **zero-tolerance policing**, which "has become a familiar feature of the crime control landscape" (Newburn & Jones, 2007, p. 221). Zero-tolerance policing is rooted in the broken windows hypothesis and seeks to aggressively address small infractions (e.g., urinating in public and loitering) that could lead to larger ones. It focuses on particular types of behaviors and is place specific, which makes it suitable for the use of crime mapping and analyzing hot spots to determine where intervention is required.

Zero-tolerance policing could be considered both order maintenance policing and crime control. To be sure, the police are maintaining order through addressing smaller crimes and instances of disorder; however, they are typically doing so by enforcing the law and attempting to control larger crimes. While the approach seemed to have positive results in some cities and has been adopted by police agencies around the country, it does have some limitations. Particularly, the style of policing associated with zero tolerance is seen by some as overly aggressive and has contributed to an increased number of police misconduct charges (Amnesty International, 1996). For instance, the city of Baltimore's zero-tolerance approach, which began in 1999, resulted in a substantial increase in the number of arrests and much opposition from civil rights advocates and prosecutors. In 2006 the American Civil Liberties Union and the National Association for the Advancement of Colored People sued the city regarding its policing practices, claiming that the police engaged in a pattern of citizen abuse in which thousands of people were arrested without probable cause. The city settled the case in 2010 and agreed to move away from zero-tolerance policing. The approach has been deemed a contributor to the rioting that occurred in the city in 2015, and the U.S. Department of Justice noted that the approach to policing resulted in repeated violations of statutory and constitutional rights of citizens and hampered relations between the public and the police (Coburn, 2016).

Patrol

The provision of service, controlling of crime, and maintenance of order by the police are facilitated by police patrol. Regardless of whether the police are making an arrest or assisting a stranded motorist, police patrols serve many necessary functions

zero-tolerance policing A style of policing that is rooted in the broken windows hypothesis and seeks to aggressively address small infractions that could lead to larger ones

3 Arrest

● **Learning Objective 14.4:** Differentiate among the patrol strategies.

and are vital to most police operations. Patrol officers perform much of the unglamorous, day-to-day work in policing, and the results of their efforts largely shape the effectiveness, and the public's perception of, policing. Although patrol officers are located at the lowest level of the police organizational hierarchy, they provide a key link between the department and the community. Patrol work is dangerous and difficult, but it can also be very rewarding, given the greater levels of autonomy and responsibility, the variety of tasks, and the opportunities to directly assist others (Miller, 1995). Given its importance, most departments allocate extensive resources to patrol. The primary functions of patrol include:

- protecting and defending lives and property;
- repressing criminal and delinquent behavior;
- identifying, apprehending, and convicting offenders;
- encouraging the flow of traffic and reducing traffic accidents;
- creating a sense of community and citizen satisfaction; and
- maintaining order and public safety (Adams, 2001).

Patrol Shifts

Eight-hour shifts have been the traditional practice in policing patrols; however, some departments have implemented 10-hour and sometimes 12-hour shifts. Officers with higher levels of seniority in a department often receive the preferential beats and shifts.

Officers who work the day shift (typically 8 a.m. to 4 p.m.) have the most interaction with the general public. Officers working the evening shift (typically 4 p.m. to 12 a.m.) often deal with more problematic issues such as traffic accidents, misbehaving students who are no longer in school, domestic disturbances, bar fights, and drunk driving. Officers working the night shift (typically 12 a.m. to 8 a.m.)—also known as the **graveyard shift** given that many businesses are closed and it is also often eerily quiet—do a lot of observing and may be more suspicious of individuals who are out and about.

Patrol officers experience gaps of inactivity during their shifts between the times they respond to citizens' calls for service, or what is known as **downtime**. Research suggests this downtime constitutes roughly 70%–79% of an officer's shift (Famega, 2005). Officers may use their downtime for police-related activities such as writing reports or conversing with other officers. Some officers spend their downtime preparing for various situations, such as going over scenarios in their minds or memorizing streets and directions. Others pass the downtime by visiting places in the community such as convenience stores, fire stations, and related places. Shift assignments and the overall workload of a department influence the extent to which officers have downtime and the nature of their overall patrol practices.

Types of Patrol

Officers engage in several types of patrol. Decisions to use different types of patrol are based on the need to address particular types of crime, qualm public concerns, or generate positive police–community interactions. The types of patrol can be categorized according to the strategies behind different patrols and the means by which patrol is conducted.

- **Preventive patrol**, also known as **routine patrol**, primarily involves officers driving around their beats, responding to calls, and observing citizen behavior. Officers in patrol cars may deter crime through their presence or the

graveyard shift The overnight shift for police officers; typically the 12 a.m. to 8 a.m. shift when many businesses are closed and it is also often eerily quiet

downtime Gaps of inactivity between the times officers respond to citizens' calls for service

preventive patrol Also known as routine patrol, it primarily involves officers driving around their beats, responding to calls, and observing citizen behavior

routine patrol Also known as preventive patrol, it primarily involves officers driving around their beats, responding to calls, and observing citizen behavior

unpredictability of their presence. However, much of what the police do stems from citizen calls for service.

- **Directed patrol** is a proactive approach to patrolling in which officers use uncommitted time to address particular issues or locations. Computerized crime mapping and, more generally, statistical analyses of crime patterns and trends are used by many departments to identify problematic areas and times of day, thus providing information to guide directed patrol practices.

- **Saturation patrol** involves police departments allocating a larger-than-typical number of police officers to a hot spot. For instance, departments concerned about burglaries in a particular neighborhood can provide additional patrol cars in the area.

- **Aggressive patrol** involves patrol officers proactively addressing specific types of infractions and crimes such as driving under the influence. For instance, departments using aggressive patrol may have officers set up sobriety or seat-belt checkpoints, conduct more frequent speed checks, or aggressively seek outdated vehicle registrations or vehicle inspection stickers.

Patrol has also been categorized according to the means by which police officers engage in patrol. Historically, officers patrolled on foot, and foot patrol remains a common practice among most departments. The Bureau of Justice Statistics noted that local police departments used several types of patrol to supplement routine automobile patrol services, with foot patrol (55%) being the most common. Other types of patrol include bicycle (32%) and motorcycle (16%) (Reaves, 2010).

directed patrol A proactive approach to patrolling in which officers use uncommitted time to address particular issues or locations

saturation patrol A patrol strategy in which police departments allocate a larger-than-typical number of police officers to a hot spot

aggressive patrol A type of patrol in which officers proactively address specific types of crimes and infractions

Foot Patrol

An influential earlier study, known as the Newark Foot Patrol Experiment, examined the efficacy of foot patrol in Newark, New Jersey, and found that additional officers on foot patrol resulted in citizens:

- being more satisfied with police services,
- feeling safer and less likely to be victimized, and
- perceiving crime to be less of a problem than did residents in areas patrolled primarily by motorized patrol (The Police Foundation, 1981).

Several researchers noted the crime-reduction benefits of foot patrol (Piza & O'Hara, 2012; Ratcliffe et al., 2011). In response to these and other studies that highlighted the benefits of foot patrol, officers walking beats have become increasingly common, especially as many departments have assumed a community-oriented approach. Compared to officers using most other forms of patrol, officers on foot patrol have greater opportunities to more directly interact with the public, gain information regarding crimes and various other problems, and generally promote positive police–community relations.

Automobile/Motorcycle Patrol

Automobile patrol is the most popular form of police patrol, given its associated benefits including its mobility, ease of transporting arrestees and weapons, and safety. Motorcycle patrol has also become an effective tool for traffic patrol, because motorcycles are fast, can navigate in places automobiles sometimes cannot, and are not as visible to the public as are police cars. Three- or four-wheeled motorcycles are sometimes used for patrolling beaches or difficult-to-reach wooded areas inaccessible by car. Despite these benefits, motorcycles can be dangerous in inclement weather, and

Police patrol practices serve many useful purposes. Among them is the ability of police officers to detect drivers under the influence of drugs or alcohol. Police in some jurisdictions aggressively address such crimes, for instance through the use of sobriety checkpoints, in which officers stop motorists and ensure that they are not driving under the influence.

Do you believe such practices are justifiable, given that motorists are stopped and evaluated even though the large majority are not driving while intoxicated?

they are limited in what they can transport (e.g., they cannot be used to transport arrestees or carry special weapons and tools).

Bicycle Patrol

Bicycles have become an increasingly popular method of police patrol, particularly as departments have become more community oriented. Officers patrolling on bicycles can better interact with citizens than can patrol officers in motorized vehicles, and bicycle patrol officers are well suited to patrol parks, bicycle and walking trails, and other locations that are inaccessible to cars. Bicycles are limited in many of the same ways as motorcycles in that they cannot be used to transport individuals, are of little value in bad weather, and cannot carry specialized tools and weapons. Research suggested that officers engaged in bicycle patrol had over twice as much contact with the public compared with officers patrolling in an automobile (Menton, 2008).

Mounted Patrol

Mounted (horseback) patrol has many of the same strengths and weaknesses as bicycle patrol, although it is more effective with regard to crowd control. Mounted patrol officers are physically elevated compared to the crowds they may be used to control; thus, they enable officers to see much of what is going on and can be intimidating to potential offenders. Mounted patrol officers can also be beneficial with regard to public relations, because officers can directly interact with the general public, especially young children who may be excited to see a horse.

Marine, Snow, and Air Patrol

Boats, jet skis, and wave runners are used by officers engaged in marine patrol. Marine patrol officers address boating rules and regulations, provide emergency assistance, and may focus on drug trafficking efforts. Snowmobiles are sometimes used for similar purposes in areas with a cold climate. Some departments also use air patrol: Officers in helicopters or planes fly above highways and city streets and provide information to officers on the ground. Helicopters are particularly effective during high-speed chases or locating and rescuing individuals in remote locations. However, the costs of purchasing, using, and maintaining a helicopter or plane prevent many departments from incorporating this type of patrol.

Policing and Juveniles

Police departments have long been involved in the lives of children and young adults. They have sought to establish positive interactions with juveniles (those under age 18), for instance through police involvement in athletic leagues for children and young adults and through a greater police presence in schools. The police also offer numerous crime-prevention programs designed to make positive impressions on juveniles. In the past, arresting a youth and formally processing him or her in the juvenile justice system was used in only the most serious cases. Beginning in the 1980s, however, the police became more punitive in their treatment of juveniles.

Delinquency

Delinquency in most states refers to behavior that violates the criminal code and is committed by youth who have not reached a statutorily prescribed age. There is some variation in the age at which individuals are considered youths. In most states (45), the maximum age of jurisdiction is age 17, while in 5 states (Georgia, Michigan, Missouri, Texas, and Wisconsin) the maximum age is 16. Much of the difficulty for police officers when addressing delinquency and youthful misbehavior stems from the belief that young people are particularly impressionable and can change more easily than adults. However, some believe that all people, including youths, should know not to break the law.

For the past 20 years or so, there has been a steady decline in the number of arrests of children and young adults. As noted in Figure 14.1, the juvenile arrest rate peaked in 1996 and has declined consistently thereafter. Many factors could explain the decreased rates of arrests (Greenwood & Turner, 2011):

- shifts in cultural norms, with fewer juveniles turning to drugs and violence (e.g., B. D. Johnson et al., 2006)
- the use of evidence-based and generally more effective prevention programs designed to discourage juveniles from misbehaving
- a reduction in the enforcement-oriented approaches taken by police in response to juvenile delinquency beginning in the 1980s

In 2019, there were roughly 697,000 arrests for individuals under the age of 18, which was the fewest number of juvenile arrests in nearly 4 decades (Office of Juvenile Justice and Delinquency Prevention, 2020). The number of arrests is

● **Learning Objective 14.5:** Identify the delinquency prevention efforts taken by police.

delinquency
Behavior that violates the criminal code and is committed by youth who have not reached a statutorily prescribed age

3 Arrest

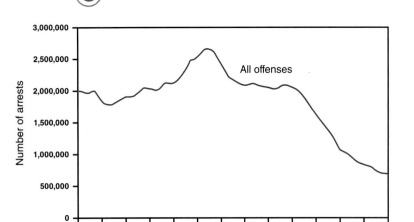

FIGURE 14.1. Juveniles arrested from 1982 to 2019. The juvenile arrest rate is currently in decline and has been for over 20 years. Arrests rates do not directly portray the extent to which the police interact with juveniles, because officers regularly encounter juveniles in nonarrest situations.

In what other ways do the police interact with juveniles?

notably much lower than the number of contacts in which the police could have made an arrest. While images of gang-involved, violent juvenile offenders are popular in the media, the large majority of offenders in the juvenile justice system do not return to the juvenile justice system, and most offenders never enter the system in the first place.

Schools provide a setting for delinquency and related activities and problems, such as underage drinking, using tobacco, vandalizing property, and fighting. The increased presence of law enforcement at schools has resulted in many behaviors that were once handled informally becoming part of a youth's official record and contributes to the "**school-to-prison pipeline**": students having contact with the justice system as a result of more punitive approaches to addressing school-related problems (Crawford & Burns, 2016).

school-to-prison pipeline A term that refers to the increasing patterns of students having contact with the justice system as a result of more punitive approaches to addressing school-related problems

Researchers assessed the impact of various protective measures such as law enforcement, security policies, and school/neighborhood characteristics on school violence with consideration of the racial composition of schools and grade levels. The researchers noted that minority schools often faced higher levels of reported violence and had a heavier law enforcement presence than predominantly White schools. The enhanced law enforcement efforts at predominantly minority schools had mixed or counterproductive results for reducing school violence, leading the researchers to suggest that the environments in which the schools are located and the characteristics or culture of the schools should be considered in efforts to reduce violence on campus (Crawford & Burns, 2016).

Police Discretion and Juveniles

Historically, the police had a wide array of discretion when addressing delinquency. Prior to the 1960s, juveniles had limited legal protections. That began to change, particularly in 1967, when the U.S. Supreme Court ruled that juveniles were entitled to the same procedural protections as adults (*In re Gault*, 1967). In the early 21st century, there are a few slight differences with regard to procedural law for juveniles compared to adults, and most are designed to protect the best interest of the youth. The laws vary among the states; for instance, there are some limitations regarding interrogations, booking, fingerprinting, and photographing as they apply to juveniles. Some states require the presence of a lawyer or parent prior to a juvenile waiving their rights.

1 Criminal Act

status offenses Violations of the law by juveniles that would not be an offense if committed by adults (e.g., truancy, drinking alcohol)

The amount of discretion an officer has is reduced as crime seriousness increases, but most juveniles engage in low-level offending. Of particular interest is the need for officers to contend with **status offenses**, which are violations of the law that would not be an offense if committed by adults. Status offenses include actions such as truancy, drinking alcohol, smoking, running away from home, and curfew violations. Ultimately, police discretion with regard to juveniles is impacted by a series of legal and extralegal variables.

Legal variables:

- the seriousness of the offense
- prior police contacts with the police
- the amount of evidence
- input from the complainant

Extralegal variables:

- appearance
- demeanor
- attitude
- gender
- race/ethnicity
- socioeconomic factors

When officers encounter delinquency and related youthful misbehavior, they have several options, including:

- initiating formal delinquency or criminal proceedings in which individuals are sent to juvenile court;
- advising and releasing the individual to a parent, guardian, or social service agency;
- referring the juvenile to other individuals or agencies that address delinquency;
- warning the juvenile and taking no further action; or
- taking no action.

Officers arresting juveniles must notify parents or guardians when they take the juvenile into custody, contact juvenile intake personnel, and ensure that juveniles who will be detained are out of sight and sound of adult arrestees.

3 Arrest

Delinquency Prevention Efforts

The police interact with juveniles under many conditions, including both positive and negative situations. Much police work involves helping others, and juveniles are often prime targets. Accordingly, police departments provide many programs designed to prevent delinquency and dissuade youths from misbehaving. These programs exist both within and outside schools.

Larger departments more often have the personnel and budgets to allocate resources directly toward programs that address crime and delinquency and that confront and protect juveniles (Reaves, 2015a). Many police departments create specialized units to best address issues such as child abuse, juvenile delinquency, and gangs. For example, in 2013, roughly 90% of local police departments that employed 100 or more officers had designated personnel to address child abuse, 83% had personnel to address gangs, and 82% allocated personnel to confront delinquency. These percentages were all higher than similar counts in 2003 (Reaves, 2015a). While all police officers encounter troubling youthful behavior at some point, specialized units are trained to address these and related areas (e.g., drug abuse prevention, school safety, bullying).

Police departments often use schools in their efforts to address delinquency prevention. There are several techniques and programs currently in use.

Drug Abuse Resistance Education One of the most popular efforts offered by police and targeted toward juveniles; the program involves officers encouraging children to resist drugs through classroom-based instruction

school resource officers Sworn officers who work in schools to prevent disorder and enhance police–community relations

gang intervention units Specialized police units that address delinquency and related behaviors through targeting gangs and gang-related activity

Gang Resistance Education and Training Program (G.R.E.A.T.) Established in 1991 and modeled after the Drug Abuse Resistance Education program, it involves law enforcement officers providing classroom content to children and young adults covering topics such as life skills, problem-solving, and alternatives to delinquency

police athletic leagues Outreach programs by the police in which officers host various types of sports leagues that enable them to more closely and positively interact with youth and generally discourage delinquency

Police Explorer programs Programs that enable juveniles to better understand the law and police work; they are experience- and education-based programs that facilitate police–youth relations

- **Drug Abuse Resistance Education (DARE).** One of the most popular efforts offered by police and targeted toward juveniles, this program involves officers encouraging children to resist drugs through classroom-based instruction. The program seeks to build positive relationships with students, although discouraging results regarding the effectiveness of the program (e.g., Rosenbaum & Hanson, 1998) have caused the program's budget to be reduced.

- **School resource officers (SROs).** The use of SROs has increased since the mid-20th century, as many local police departments increasingly allocate sworn personnel to work in local schools (Theriot, 2009). The increased use of SROs has been attributed to increased concerns for juvenile delinquency and student victimization, as well as increased federal funding (Na & Gottfredson, 2013). The use of officers in schools also enhances police–community relations.

- **Gang intervention units.** Police officers also address delinquency and related behaviors through the use of gang units, which target gangs and gang-related activity. For instance, the Winston–Salem Police Department's Gang Unit in North Carolina partners with community groups and agencies in focusing on the suppression of gang-related crimes in the city. The unit uses intervention strategies and educational programs in efforts to deter youths and others from joining gangs.

- **Gang Resistance Education and Training Program (G.R.E.A.T.).** Among the more popular programs targeted toward discouraging youth from joining gangs is G.R.E.A.T., which was established in 1991 and modeled after the DARE program. G.R.E.A.T. involves law enforcement officers providing classroom content to children and young adults, including a 13-lesson curriculum for middle school students and a 6-week course for elementary school children. The lessons cover topics such as life skills, problem-solving, and alternatives to delinquency. Families are also involved to encourage reinforcement of what is taught in the classroom. Over 13,000 sworn officers from the United States and other countries have been trained and certified to teach the curricula, which has reached more than 6 million youths (G.R.E.A.T., 2017). Research evaluations of G.R.E.A.T. have been generally positive, and the program appears to have some effect on reducing gang involvement and improving police–youth relations (Esbensen et al., 2011).

- **Police athletic leagues.** The police work with youth through police athletic leagues, in which the police host various types of sports leagues that enable the police to more closely and positively interact with youth and generally discourage delinquency.

- **Police Explorer programs.** These programs enable juveniles to better understand the law and police work. They are experience- and education-based programs that facilitate police–youth relations. The programs promote life skills and character development and provide students an insider's view of police work. Participants provide assistance at community functions, attend local meetings, and may ride along with police officers. The programs offer opportunities to attend conferences, compete against other Explorer groups, and generally learn more about law enforcement, and are provided at the state and federal levels as well.

The System in Perspective

Effective police practices are vital to a well functioning criminal justice system and our safety. The "In the News" feature at the start of this module highlighted the important role the police play in ensuring our safety, as well as the challenges police face when large groups of people assemble. Maintaining public order is just one of many duties we expect of police; we also expect them to enforce the law and provide various types of services. The police rely on many other personnel and agencies within our justice systems in meeting these expectations. For instance, they may work with juvenile justice officials when implementing prevention programs or parole officers when enforcing the laws regarding parole violations. They also work with prosecutors when sharing the evidence from a crime and judges when requesting warrants to search homes or make arrests.

Summary

1. Learning Objective 14.1: *Describe the extent to which officers focus on crime control.*

- Officers focused on crime control typically address all violations of the law. However, most officers spend very little time controlling crime. Police interactions with the public occur less frequently than is often perceived by the public, and relatively few of the interactions involve the use of force.

2. Learning Objective 14.2: *Illustrate how providing public service differs by department size and how it promotes positive police–community relations.*

- Research has suggested that smaller departments receive proportionately more service-related calls than urban police departments. Compared to officers in large cities, officers in small towns were more likely to respond to less serious calls. Providing service promotes positive police–community relations. It encourages the public to support the police, promotes cooperation between the police and various groups, builds stronger bonds between groups, and enables the police to better identify where problems exist, all of which arguably contribute to lower crime rates.

3. Learning Objective 14.3: *Explain why zero-tolerance policing is closely related to order maintenance.*

- Zero-tolerance policing is closely related to order maintenance because it is rooted in the broken windows hypothesis and seeks to address minor and serious violations and infractions that could lead to larger ones. It focuses on particular types of behaviors and is place specific, which means it is suitable for the use of crime mapping and analyzing hot spots to determine where intervention is required.

4. Learning Objective 14.4: *Differentiate among the patrol strategies.*

- Preventive, or routine, patrol primarily involves officers driving around their beats, responding to calls, and observing citizen behavior. Directed patrol is a proactive approach to patrolling in which officers use uncommitted time to address particular issues or locations. Saturation patrol involves police departments allocating a larger-than-typical number of police officers to a hot spot. Aggressive patrol involves patrol officers proactively addressing specific types of infractions or crimes such as driving under the influence.

5. Learning Objective 14.5: *Identify the delinquency prevention efforts taken by police.*

- The police engage in various delinquency prevention efforts, both within schools and in the community. Primary among the delinquency efforts are programs such as G.R.E.A.T., DARE, Police Explorers, and police athletic leagues. School resource officers and gang intervention units also seek to prevent delinquency.

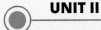

Questions for Critical Thinking

1. How does selective enforcement of the law both benefit and hamper police work?

2. Should the police be obligated to provide services to the community beyond crime-fighting? Why or why not?

3. How is order maintenance related to community policing?

4. How do the different shifts worked by police officers influence the individuals they encounter and the calls they receive? If you were an officer, which shift would you prefer, and why?

5. Should the police treat juveniles differently from adults? Why or why not?

Key Terms

aggressive patrol
broken windows hypothesis
directed patrol
downtime
Drug Abuse Resistance Education
gang intervention units
Gang Resistance Education and Training Program
graveyard shift
order maintenance
police athletic leagues

Police Explorer programs
preventive patrol
routine patrol
saturation patrol
school resource officers
school-to-prison pipeline
selective enforcement
status offenses
zero-tolerance policing

For digital learning resources, please go to
https://www.oup.com/he/burns1e

Police Use of Force

The authority to use deadly force makes policing relatively unique compared to other occupations. It has also generated much controversy, because the consequences associated with the misuse of deadly force are significant. The large majority of police shootings are justified, but there are times when mistakes lead to lives lost.

Do you believe that the police too often use deadly force?

The police are granted special powers to use force when appropriate. However, what constitutes "appropriate" has long been debated in society. Given the relatively dangerous nature of police work, the police are themselves subject to having force used against them, and they must be trained to protect themselves in order to protect us. Recent concerns regarding the police misuse of force, particularly against African Americans, has led to civil unrest and claims that something must be done to control the police. Retaliation against the police in the form of shootings and protests has also occurred in many cities. This module addresses the extent to which the police use force, the types of weapons they are equipped with and trained to use, and the violence they themselves face.

MODULE OUTLINE

- **The Extent and Nature of Police Use of Force**

  Learning Objective 15.1: Differentiate between the political threat and reactive explanations of police use of deadly force.

- **Weapons and Protection**

  Learning Objective 15.2: Identify the types of weapons officers most commonly carry and their primary means of protection.

- **Violence Against the Police**

  Learning Objective 15.3: Explain the extent to which officers are harmed on the job, as well as the most dangerous situations they face.

Controversial Police Practices and Retaliation

On October 3, 2018, Chinedu Okobi died after sheriff's deputies in San Mateo County, California, used a Taser on him. A Taser is a device that shoots prongs into a person's body and then sends electrical jolts throughout the system in order to subdue the person. Okobi had been running in and out of traffic when

the deputies arrived, and he then assaulted a deputy who initially approached him (Ho, 2018). An investigation of the incident

resulted in no criminal charges being filed against the officers involved.

Two months prior to this incident, another man died less than 20 miles away from where Okobi was killed after police Tasered him several times in attempts to subdue him. A third man died earlier in the year after police Tasered him in his home. In fact, the use of Tasers resulted in the deaths of an estimated 50 people in 2015 (Ho, 2018). The particular incidents in San Mateo led county officials there to reconsider the use of these types of shock weapons that are supposed to be alternatives to lethal weapons or guns.

The police are expected to always use force appropriately, although there is sometimes discussion as to what is considered appropriate, as well as different accounts of what happens during police–citizen interactions. The aforementioned Taser deaths and other related incidents in recent times have brought officer use of force to the forefront of public attention. What can be done to better ensure that police use of force is monitored and citizens better understand the conditions under which the police may use force? Should the laws regarding police use of electronic shock devices be similar to those that apply to their use of deadly force?

The Extent and Nature of Police Use of Force

Learning Objective 15.1: Differentiate between the political threat and reactive explanations of police use of deadly force.

Officers are sometimes required to make important, split-second decisions involving numerous variables. For instance, in Cleveland, Ohio, in 2014, 12-year-old Tamir Rice was shot and killed by police officers after they responded to a call of a person pointing a gun at people in a local park. Following the shooting, it was determined that the young boy was pointing an Airsoft gun that lacked the orange tip that signifies that such guns are not true firearms. The case involving the officer was brought before a grand jury, which declined to indict the officer given that it appeared Rice was drawing a weapon. The city of Cleveland, however, ultimately settled a lawsuit filed by Rice's family by awarding $6 million to the family. From 2014 to 2019, approximately 153 others holding toy guns were killed by officers who believed the suspects they shot were brandishing real, not toy, guns (officers must make quick decisions and cannot always discern what type of gun is involved) (Diaz, 2019).

BB guns and Airsoft guns that resemble lethal weapons were most commonly involved (Sullivan et al., 2016).

Much research on policing centers on the use of force by police officers; however, the use of force against police officers is also important. Violent acts committed by and/or against police officers are known as **police violence**. Police violence can be justified or unjustified, legal or illegal, and deadly or nondeadly. Most instances of police use of force are justified, legal, and nondeadly. The U.S. Supreme Court ruled in *Graham v. Connor* (1989) that per the Fourth Amendment, the objective reasonableness standard applies when citizens claim that the police have used excessive force. Excessive force is simply defined as a level of police use of force that exceeds the required limit. The court suggested that questionable cases should be evaluated according to what a reasonable officer would do in the situation, given the totality of the circumstances, including the severity of the crime and whether the suspect poses an immediate threat, is resisting arrest, or is attempting to flee.

police violence
Violence by and against the police; it can be justified or unjustified, legal or illegal, and deadly or nondeadly

We grant police the power to use force and expect that they will always do so properly. Such power is necessary given the nature of police work; however, there have been questions at times regarding what constitutes an acceptable amount of force and what is the proper use of force. Along these lines, it is well understood that some officers and some departments use force at a higher rate than others.

The Extent of Police Use of Force

A significant challenge to police officers when engaging in violence is that they must continue to operate within the boundaries of procedural law, even though suspects who attempt to evade arrest or assault officers do not. Further, suspects will sometimes do whatever it takes to flee from the officer(s), which subsequently means officers must protect themselves and others while preventing the suspect from escaping. Officer use of force has sparked riots, generated millions of dollars in lawsuits, and led to deaths and substantial legislation. It has also helped officers apprehend many dangerous persons and protected both officers and citizens. According to a survey conducted by the U.S. Department of Justice's (DOJ's) Bureau of Justice Statistics on police use of nonfatal force in 2017:

- nearly 1.25 million (roughly 2%) of the 61.5 million U.S. residents over age 15 who had contact with the police experienced threats or the use of force;
- males (3.0%) were more likely than females (1.1%) to experience the threat of force, as were Blacks (3.8%) and Hispanics (3.4%), compared to Whites (1.5%);

MYTHBUSTING

Police Use of Force Is Common

Media accounts can make it appear that the use of force by the police is widespread. While it is true that officers working certain shifts or in certain areas face more violent encounters than other officers, overall police use of force remains relatively rare (W. R. King & Matusiak, 2013). For instance, the U.S. Bureau of Justice Statistics noted that the police had roughly 61.5 million personal contacts with persons age 16 or older in 2017, yet only about 1.25 million (2%) of those contacts involved the threat or actual use of force (Harrell & Davis, 2020). The police are required to respond to the most dangerous and violent situations, which would suggest that they engage in violent encounters regularly. However, the data suggest otherwise.

- approximately 51% of those who experienced the threat or use of force during their most recent contact believed the action was excessive. Blacks (62.9%) were more likely than Whites (44.3%) to believe the action was excessive; and
- the use of handcuffs was the most commonly used type of force (2.2%) (Harrell & Davis, 2020).

These findings must be interpreted with caution, however, because they only involve the subjects' perceptions of officer behavior and not the perceptions of the officers.

Deadly Use of Force

In August 2014, a White police officer, Darren Wilson, responded to a robbery call in Ferguson, Missouri, and encountered two men who fit the description of the robbers. A struggle ensued between Michael Brown, a Black man, and Officer Wilson. There was no video of the altercation. Some witnesses claim that Brown had his arms up and was surrendering, while other accounts (including Officer Wilson's account) suggested that Brown was moving toward the officer in an aggressive manner when Officer Wilson shot and killed him (*Ferguson Unrest*, 2015). A DOJ investigation suggested that Brown was not surrendering, and a St. Louis grand jury failed to indict Officer Wilson. The DOJ stated that Wilson was acting in self-defense and cleared him of any civil rights violations in the incident.

Shortly after the incident, both violent and peaceful protests occurred in cities throughout the United States. The incident attracted national attention and directed much negative attention toward the department and policing in general. Compounding this incident were several other shootings of Black males within a relatively short time by White officers, including those in Minnesota, Florida, and Louisiana. The death of George Floyd in 2020 by a Minneapolis police officer (as addressed in Module 1) perpetuated the concerns for police brutality, primarily as it is directed toward African Americans. The incident sparked social unrest in the form of riots and protests across the United States.

The use of deadly force, the most severe and rarest form of force police use, is particularly controversial and most closely scrutinized. Police officers may use deadly force to protect themselves or others. In *Tennessee v. Garner* (1985), the U.S. Supreme Court set the standard for police use of deadly force. The court ruled that deadly force may only be used to apprehend fleeing felons when "it is necessary to prevent the escape and the officer has probable cause to believe that the suspect poses a significant threat of death or serious physical injury to the officer or others." Prior to the court's decision, officers in some states were permitted to shoot felons who fled from the police, under what was known as the **fleeing felon rule**.

Several high-profile, controversial police killings in recent years drew attention to the lack of tracking in regard to these incidents. In response, Congress passed the **Death in Custody Reporting Act of 2013**, which mandates that states receiving federal criminal justice assistance grants report all deaths in law enforcement custody, including the deaths of individuals who have been arrested or are being detained.

Explaining Police Use of Force

The differences in the frequency of the use of deadly force among officers have been explained from two perspectives. **Political threat explanations** hold that police use of deadly force is most likely to occur in areas where there are notable racial or economic differences, largely in response to the divisions between groups. **Reactive explanations** hold that police killings are more prominent in areas with high violent crime rates or where officers are working under difficult conditions (Jacobs & O'Brien, 1998; Terrill & Reisig, 2003).

fleeing felon rule An earlier standard regarding police use of deadly force which noted that deadly force could be used to subdue an offender who committed a felony and was attempting to escape from the police

Death in Custody Reporting Act of 2013 Legislation passed by Congress that mandates that states receiving federal criminal justice assistance grants report all deaths in law enforcement custody

political threat explanations The argument that police use of deadly force is most likely to occur in areas where there are notable racial or economic differences, largely in response to the divisions between groups

reactive explanations The argument that police killings are more prominent in areas with high violent crime rates or where officers are working under difficult conditions

Understanding the causes of police violence in general is difficult given the varied nature of police work. No particular factor alone influences an officer's decision to use force, although the most influential factors can be categorized according to individual officer characteristics, suspect characteristics, and the nature of the environment in which an incident occurs. For instance, researchers found that male officers were more likely than female officers to use force, although suspect behavior was the most powerful predictor of police use of force. Specifically, suspects who possessed a weapon and those who attempted to flee were more likely than their counterparts to have various types of force used against them (Crawford & Burns, 2008).

Research in the area of police violence suggests that departments with more restrictive use of lethal force policies have lower numbers of shootings and deaths (e.g., M. D. White, 2001), and those with more restrictive policies with regard to less-lethal use of force used force less often than departments with more permissive policies (Ferdik et al., 2014; Terrill & Paoline, 2017). There is concern, however, that more restrictive policies may place police officers and the public at a greater risk of harm (Terrill & Paoline, 2013).

A 2016 Gallup poll asked a sample of Americans what they believed was the single most important action that could be taken to reduce the number of deadly encounters between Black males and the police in the United States. The largest percentage of respondents suggested that general, structural changes were needed (36%), including building relations, communicating, and having a better understanding of groups. This category was followed by a belief that changes among Blacks were necessary (27%), as were changes in the police and police operations (21%; Newport, 2016).

Weapons and Protection

Police officers use various techniques and tools to enforce the law. Primarily they use verbal commands, but as situations escalate, they progress to using various weapons, including lethal weapons such as firearms and less-lethal weapons such as batons, pepper spray, Tasers, and stun guns. In addition, officers are increasingly being encouraged to wear body armor (Reaves, 2015b) and to use body cameras for protection. Officers must be proficient with their weapons and protect themselves for their safety, as well as the safety of others.

Weapons

Police officers using deadly force primarily use their sidearm, or pistol. Some patrol cars also carry shotguns or rifles for incidents that may require mid-range or long-range shooting. Specialized units, such as SWAT teams, use more powerful guns, such as semiautomatic guns, which fire at a higher rate. Shotguns have also been used to fire stun bags and chemical munitions (in an act of less-lethal force).

Aside from firearms, officers regularly carry various less-lethal weapons including **conducted-energy devices (CEDs)**, which deliver an electrical charge that disrupts an individual's central nervous system for a moment so that an officer may gain control of an individual without being injured (Cronin & Ederheimer, 2006). Researchers found that compared to agencies that did not use CEDs, agencies that used the devices experienced lower rates of officer injuries, suspects with severe injuries, and officers or suspects receiving injuries that required medical attention. CEDs have become increasingly popular (Roberg et al., 2015), although there is some debate regarding the situations in which the CEDs should be used and the potential harms they can impose. For instance, it was reported that at least 50 people died in

● **Learning Objective 15.2:** Identify the types of weapons officers most commonly carry and their primary means of protection.

conducted-energy devices Less-lethal weapons that deliver an electrical charge that disrupts an individual's central nervous system for a moment so that an officer may gain control of an individual without suffering injury

Police officers are expected to be proficient with various weapons, including Tasers (one is shown in this image). The failure to properly use the weapon, or using the weapon in an inappropriate situation, can have many repercussions, including the loss of lives, jobs, and freedoms.

Would you be in favor of more or fewer police officers being equipped with Tasers?

the United States between January and December in 2015 during incidents in which the police used Tasers (Ho, 2018).

Among the more commonly authorized less-lethal weapons in 2016 were pepper spray, which was authorized by 97.3% of all local police departments, followed by batons (96.9%) and CEDs, such as Tasers and stun guns (92.4%). All large local police departments permitted the use of three types of weapons (see Table 15.1) (C. Brooks, 2020).

Officers choose which weapons to use based on each situation, primarily as it relates to a suspect's behavior. For instance, a suspect who does not respond to verbal commands may be subject to the officer using pepper spray. Officers are trained to understand to what extent and when they must escalate their use of force, and some departments use guidelines for escalation, or a **continuum of force**, which dictates the levels of force officers should use in relation to a suspect's behavior (Figure 15.1). A basic continuum includes the following (escalating from least harmful to most harmful):

1. Verbal commands
2. Physical restraints
3. Chemical agents
4. Tactical weapons
5. Firearms

continuum of force A guideline for the escalation in police use of force, which dictates the levels of force officers should use in relation to a suspect's behavior

TABLE 15.1. Selected Nonlethal Weapons Authorized by Local Police Departments

PERCENTAGE OF LOCAL POLICE DEPARTMENTS THAT AUTHORIZED LESS-LETHAL WEAPONS, BY SIZE OF POPULATION SERVED, 2016

POPULATION SERVED	BATON	BLUNT-FORCE PROJECTILES[a]	CHEMICAL-AGENT PROJECTILES[b]	CONDUCTED-ENERGY WEAPONS[c]	EXPLOSIVES	PEPPER SPRAY[d]
1,000,000 or more*	100.0	86.7	100.0	100.0	73.3	100.0
500,000–999,999	100.0	96.6†	96.6†	89.7†	79.3	100.0
250,000–499,999	100.0	96.0†	100.0	98.0†	74.0	98.0†
100,000–249,000	98.4†	96.2†	96.2†	96.2†	65.6‡	98.4†
50,000–99,999	98.9†	92.1	84.8†	92.9†	51.6†	97.3‡
25,000–49,999	96.7†	78.2‡	74.9†	89.0†	20.7†	99.9†
10,000–24,999	92.0†	56.3†	52.3†	91.6†	9.9†	94.5†
2,500–9,999	90.5†	36.0†	34.4†	90.3†	6.3†	92.0†
2,499 or less	82.3†	25.1†	31.7†	82.8†	3.2†	85.4†
All departments	88.5	41.6	42.5	87.7	9.9	90.8
All officers[e]	96.9	71.0	80.0	92.4	42.4	97.3

Source: U.S. Department of Justice, Office of Justice Programs, Bureau of Justice Statistics, August 2020, NCJ 254826

*Comparison group.
†Difference with comparison group is significant at the 95% confidence level.
‡Difference with comparison group is significant at the 90% confidence level.
[a]For example, bean bags or rubber bullets.
[b]For example, CS (tear) gas or oleoresin capsicum pellets.
[c]For example, Tasers or stun guns.
[d]Oleoresin capsicum spray or foam.
[e]Reflects the percentage of officers whose departments authorized less-lethal weapons. This is calculated by multiplying the result for each department by its size. The size of the department is the sum of the number of full-time sworn officers and part-time sworn officers (who are counted as the equivalent of 0.5 full-time sworn officers) employed by that department.

Protection

Much training (both preservice and in-service) addresses the means by which police can protect themselves. Officer safety is a high priority for training academies and police departments alike. Officers use several means to protect themselves, including properly confronting each situation with members of the public, regularly wearing body armor, and using in-car and body-worn cameras.

ENCOUNTERS WITH THE PUBLIC

Officer safety begins with an understanding of how to properly confront each encounter with the public. Consider, for instance, how police officers approach a vehicle they have pulled over. They park behind the motorist, gather information about the vehicle they stopped (if they have not already done so), and approach the vehicle with caution. They immediately look into the vehicle, noticing the actions of the driver and anyone else inside, as well as any contents in the vehicle. They then verbally engage

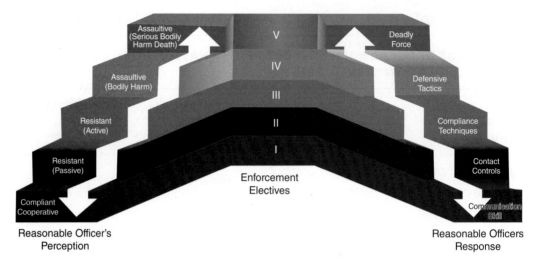

FIGURE 15.1. Enforcement Electives With Regard to the Continuum of Force as Used by the U.S. Border Patrol. The continuum of force is used to help officers and all of us better understand what would be a reasonable response to perceived threats. It is used for guidance, however, because each situation is different, and strictly staying within the enforcement electives may not be the most effective approach. *Source: U.S. Border Patrol (2021).*

What might be problematic about always requiring officers to abide by the continuum?

the motorist. Any breakdown in this general account of how to properly approach a vehicle could result in the officer being harmed. As another example, officers confronting potentially dangerous situations may wait for backup prior to addressing the situation. However, there are times, unfortunately, when officers follow proper procedures, yet are still harmed, because there are limitations to how far following proper procedures can protect an officer.

BODY ARMOR

Changes in the design and use of body armor have assisted in providing protection for the police. The use of body armor by police began in the mid-1970s, and its use has steadily increased since that time (LaTourrette, 2010). Early body armor for officers was much bulkier than it is in the early 21st century, which led to officers storing the armor in the trunks of their patrol cars and putting it on only when encountering what they perceived to be particularly dangerous situations. The armor worn by police officers today is much sleeker and lighter, enabling officers to constantly wear the protection without much discomfort or restriction. As noted in Table 15.2, most police departments (79%) have body armor requirements for police officers, with the majority of departments (71%) requiring officers to wear armor at all times (Reaves, 2015b).

Body armor requirements for patrol officers have steadily increased since the 1990s, when only roughly 30% of departments required officers to wear armor at all times or in some circumstances (Reaves, 2015b). In 2010, the U.S. attorney general noted that local police departments would lose millions of dollars in federal assistance if they did not require officers to wear body armor (K. Johnson, 2012).

One study estimated that equipping all officers with body armor would save at least 8.5 lives each year and would largely outweigh the costs of not doing so. The same study noted that body armor more than triples the likelihood that officers shot in the torso will survive (LaTourrette, 2010). The drawbacks to outfitting officers with body armor include the costs of purchasing the armor and the added weight to officers. Officers in

TABLE 15.2. Body Armor Wear Requirements for Local Police Departments

POPULATION SERVED	TOTAL (%)	AT ALL TIMES (%)	IN SOME CIRCUMSTANCES (%)
All sizes	79	71	8
1,000,000 or more	92	64	29
500,000–999,999	93	80	13
250,000–499,999	93	78	15
100,000–249,999	89	80	9
50,000–99,999	93	89	4
25,000–49,999	95	89	7
10,000–24,999	91	83	8
2,500–9,999	85	78	8
2,499 or fewer	62	54	7

Detail may not sum to total because of rounding.

Source: *Bureau of Justice Statistics, Law Enforcement Management and Administrative Statistics (LEMAS) Survey, 2013, Table 2 (https://www.bjs.gov/index.cfm?ty=pbdetail&iid=5321). © U.S. Department of Justice, Office of Justice Programs, Bureau of Justice Statistics, July 2015, NCJ 248767*

southern states are sometimes hesitant to use the armor in the hot summers, when the armor makes the heat more difficult to contend with (K. Johnson, 2012).

CAMERAS

The use of cameras by police officers also provides protection; for instance, individuals who interact with the police are aware that their actions are being recorded and may be less likely to attempt to assault or otherwise harm the officer. The use of cameras to document police practices began with the use of in-car cameras and has since expanded to body-worn cameras. As noted in Figure 15.2, most law enforcement agencies used some type of recording device (either audio or visual) in 2016.

The International Association of Chiefs of Police (2004) noted that in-car cameras improve officer safety, and many officers agree. The association surveyed officers after they had used them for some time and found that one-third of the officers noted that they felt safer as a result of having the cameras in their cars. Departments of all sizes have increasingly used the technology, with just over two-thirds (69%) having them in 2016 (Hyland, 2018; Reaves, 2015b).

Police departments are also increasingly using body-worn cameras. Akin to the use of in-car cameras, officers and departments in general believe

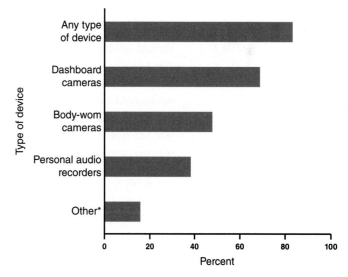

FIGURE 15.2. General-Purpose Law Enforcement Agencies With Recording Devices, by Type of Device, 2016. Most police departments used dashboard cameras as of 2016, and almost half of all departments had acquired body-worn cameras. Some departments use personal audio devices as well. ***Source:*** Body-Worn Cameras in Law Enforcement Agencies, 2016 *(NCJ 251775), by S. S. Hyland, 2018b, U.S. Department of Justice, Bureau of Justice Statistics.*

Do you believe that all departments should be required to use recording devices? Why or why not?

that this technology can improve their safety (Jennings et al., 2014; Hyland, 2018), although less than half of departments (47%) used them in 2016 (Hyland, 2018). The use of body-worn cameras is relatively new to policing, as the technology continues to evolve and departments locate funding for the devices. In a 2014 program implemented by then-president Barack Obama, approximately $20 million in DOJ funding was provided to assist departments in purchasing and maintaining body-worn cameras (Bud, 2016; Sommers, 2016).

Violence against the Police

Learning Objective 15.3: Explain the extent to which officers are harmed on the job, as well as the most dangerous situations they face.

In 2016, a man fired an assault weapon and a shotgun at the Dallas Police headquarters, damaging police cars and shattering windows at the facility. He also planted explosives outside the building. The man was later shot by SWAT officers following a chase to a suburb of Dallas, and no officers were injured or killed. Prior to his death, the man claimed that the police were responsible for having his child taken from him. Aside from attacks on the department, officers face many other dangerous situations.

The tension and frustration resulting from police shootings in 2014–2016 led to several acts of retaliation against the police, including an incident in which two New York City Police Department officers were shot to death in their patrol car by a man seeking retaliation for a police shooting in Ferguson, Missouri. This was followed by a 2016 incident in Dallas, Texas, in which five police officers were killed by a gunman at the conclusion of a peaceful Black Lives Matter march in the city. Ten days later, a gunman killed three law enforcement officers in Louisiana in what was believed to be an act of retaliation against the police for the shootings (Braden-Perry et al., 2016). These and related incidents highlight the volatile and dangerous nature of police work.

While much attention, including scholarly attention, is devoted to officer use of force, officers receive extensive training, both prior to and in service, with regard to protecting themselves from harm. In 2013, recruits at police academies across the United States received an average of 60 hours in defensive tactics, 71 hours in firearms skills, 21 hours regarding the use of force, and 16 hours concerning the use of nonlethal weapons (Reaves, 2016). The types of defensive tactics taught at the academies are noted in Figure 15.3.

1 Criminal Act

The Federal Bureau of Investigation (FBI) annually publishes reports concerning law enforcement officers killed during a felonious act, which provides some insight regarding violence against officers (FBI, 2020b). The report noted the following:

- A total of 48 law enforcement officers were feloniously killed in line-of-duty incidents during 2019.
- Most of the deaths (45) involved male officers, and most were White (40).
- The victims had an average tenure of 13 years of experience in law enforcement.
- The greatest number of officers feloniously killed were shot with firearms (44).

The number of police officers feloniously killed in the line of duty has notably decreased over time, largely as a result of improved training for officers, enhanced requirements for officer protection, and improved body armor worn by officers.

The FBI also tracks the number of law enforcement officers assaulted. An estimated 56,034 officers were assaulted while performing their duties in 2019, with about 30.7% of those assaults resulting in injury. The largest percentage of officer victims (30.4%) resulted from responding to disturbance calls (FBI, 2020b).

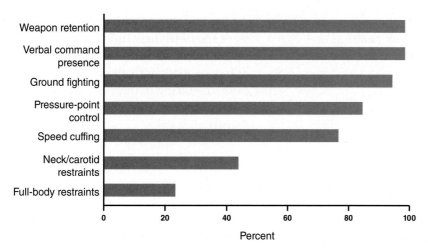

FIGURE 15.3. Techniques Covered in State and Local Law Enforcement Training Academies in the United States, 2013. Law enforcement training academies were most likely to include training on weapon retention and verbal commands in 2013. They were least likely to train future officers on full-body restraints. **Source:** State and Local Law Enforcement Training Academies, 2013 *(NCJ 294784), by B. Reaves, 2016, U.S. Department of Justice, Bureau of Justice Statistics.*

Should all officers be trained in each of these important areas, given the danger associated with police work?

The System in Perspective

The "In the News" feature at the beginning of this module highlights the controversial nature of police violence. Electric-shock weapons are viewed as an alternative to lethal force, because they enable officers to subdue threats from a distance. However, findings that their use has resulted in deaths have prompted critics to argue that they are not necessarily nonlethal. The power and expectation to use force under certain circumstances distinguish police work from many other occupations. The volatile nature of police work requires officers to sometimes make split-second decisions that have life-or-death consequences. The repercussions of using what appears to be too much force include criminal charges and being brought to criminal court.

Summary

1. Learning Objective 15.1: *Differentiate between the political threat and reactive explanations of police use of deadly force.*

- Political threat explanations propose that police use of deadly force is most likely to occur in areas where there are notable racial or economic differences, largely in response to the divisions between groups. Reactive explanations hold that police killings are more prominent in areas with high violent crime rates or where officers work under difficult conditions.

2. Learning Objective 15.2: *Identify the types of weapons officers most commonly carry and their primary means of protection.*

- Police officers carry an assortment of lethal and nonlethal weapons and are expected to be proficient with each one. The most commonly carried weapons by police officers are firearms, pepper spray, batons, and CEDs (such as Tasers and stun guns). Officer protection is largely facilitated by properly confronting each situation, along with the use of body armor and cameras.

3. Learning Objective 15.3: *Explain the extent to which officers are harmed on the job, as well as the most dangerous situations they face.*

- In 2019, a total of 48 law enforcement officers were feloniously killed in line-of-duty incidents. Male officers were far more likely than female officers to be victims, and the greatest number of officers who were feloniously killed were shot with firearms. An estimated 56,034 officers were assaulted while performing their duties in 2019, with about 31% of those assaults resulting in injury. The largest percentage of officer victims resulted from response to disturbance calls.

Questions for Critical Thinking

1. Are the police given too much power to use force? Should we restrict the amount of force police are permitted to use? Explain your answer.

2. Looking into the future, what kinds of weapons, both lethal and nonlethal, do you envision the police will carry and use?

3. What steps could be taken to better protect officers from being assaulted or killed while on the job?

Key Terms

conducted-energy devices
continuum of force
Death in Custody Reporting Act of 2013
fleeing felon rule

police violence
political threat explanations
reactive explanations

For digital learning resources, please go to
https://www.oup.com/he/burns1e

Police Misconduct

A Detroit police officer was arrested in 2017 for domestic violence and was suspended with pay while the department investigated the case. He was charged with assaulting a woman he had dated. He is just one of many officers who have been accused of acting outside the laws they are responsible for enforcing.

Should the officer have been suspended while the case was investigated given that he is legally innocent until proven guilty?

MODULE OUTLINE

- **Defining Police Misconduct**

  Learning Objective 16.1:
  Explain how police misconduct is classified.

- **Controlling Misconduct**

  Learning Objective 16.2:
  Distinguish among means of controlling police misconduct.

- **Sanctioning Misconduct**

  Learning Objective: 16.3
  Describe the sanctions used to address police misconduct.

Police officers are first and foremost human beings and thus are subject to the same shortcomings of human behavior as everyone else. However, the police are granted special powers not found in other jobs and are also held to higher standards of behavior than individuals in most other occupations. As a result, misconduct by police—whether it be excessive use of force, property crimes, lying under oath, neglecting one's legal responsibilities, or other related acts—generates particular concern. The officers who misbehave also make it difficult for the large majority of officers who do not engage in police misconduct. Departments regularly take steps to prevent officer misconduct, both on and off the job. This module defines police misconduct and then discusses the ways that departments prevent such behavior, as well as the sanctions used to address misconduct when it occurs.

IN THE NEWS

3 Arrest

When Police Officers Break the Law

When we think of police misconduct, we often think first of excessive use of force and biased policing. However, those are not the only offenses for which officers have been accused and prosecuted. In fact, much like ordinary citizens, the police commit a wide assortment of offenses.

In 2017, seven Baltimore police officers were arrested on federal racketeering charges for stealing drugs and guns and extorting up to $200,000 from victims (Simpson, 2017). Other incidents during the same period included a rookie police officer with the Miami Police Department being arrested on robbery charges for allegedly robbing some of the motorists he pulled over (Allen, 2017), and two Detroit police officers were convicted of using their status as police officers to rob drug dealers (Ainsworth, 2017).

These and related incidents emerged when many in society were questioning the role of the police, police practices, police training, and police–community relations. Some argue that the incidents brought to our attention are isolated incidents and not reflective of policing in general. Others argue that such actions occur more frequently and highlight the need for improvement with regard to police practices. Arguably, the increased use of cameras, both by police and by the public through their phones, has brought to light practices that have long gone unnoticed. Do you believe the police engage in more or fewer acts of misconduct in the third decade of the 21st century compared to 10 years ago? How about 25 years ago?

● **Learning Objective 16.1:** Explain how police misconduct is classified.

Defining Police Misconduct

In September 2017, a White St. Louis police officer was acquitted in court and thus was not held criminally responsible for fatally shooting a young Black male. The St. Louis Metropolitan Police Department anticipated civil unrest following the announcement of the verdict, and several of the department's officers texted each other about their excitement for the opportunity to physically harm the protestors. Civil unrest followed, and during the protest three St. Louis officers threw a man on the ground and beat him with a baton, even though the protestor was complying with the officers' commands. The protestor/victim in this case was an undercover police officer and 22-year police veteran. Three officers were indicted for assault in this case, and another officer was indicted for her role in lying to investigators (Elfrink, 2018). While these acts of police misconduct are not reflective of general police practices, they do highlight the potential for misconduct and the many forms in which it can occur. Police misconduct is categorized in a variety of ways, including as police crime, deviance, corruption, and abuse of authority (Kappeler et al., 1998).

Police Crime

Police crime involves criminal behavior committed by police officers while on duty. Examples include:

- stealing money from drug dealers,
- stealing property while investigating a burglary, and
- perjury, or lying while under oath.

In 2018, a former Baltimore police officer admitted to the Federal Bureau of Investigation that he had stolen money, lied in police reports, and misused electronic surveillance equipment. He admitted his behaviors when interviewed as part of the bureau's investigation into a public corruption investigation involving police officers (Fenton, 2018).

Police Deviance

Police deviance refers to unethical activities that do not conform to the high standards expected of members of the criminal justice system (Maher, 2003, p. 355). Examples include:

- intentionally failing to alert the department of availability to respond to calls,
- sleeping in one's patrol car, and
- being disrespectful to members of the public.

As a specific example, in 2018, two Chicago police officers faced department sanctions for police deviance. This occurred after a photo of the officers sleeping in their patrol car went viral on Facebook (Francisco, 2018).

Police Corruption

Corruption includes the misuse of authority for an officer's personal gain or that of others. Examples include:

- aggressively requesting free items from a convenience store,
- accepting a bribe from a speeding motorist, and
- using official databases for personal, not professional, reasons.

In October 2017, as an example of police corruption, a Georgia police sergeant was convicted in federal court for taking bribes in exchange for providing access to restricted law enforcement information. He was arrested after accepting a bribe of $5,000 to search a sensitive police database and provide restricted information (CBS 46, 2017).

Police Abuses of Authority

Abuses of authority include intentional actions in the course of police work that are designed to inflict harm on others or violate individual rights. Abuses of authority may:

- be physical in nature (e.g., excessive force);
- be psychological (e.g., verbal abuse or harassment); or
- pertain to enforcing the law (e.g., illegal searches and seizures) (Barker & Carter, 1994).

In 2018, as an example of abuse of authority, a former police officer from Ohio pleaded guilty to a charge of deprivation of rights under color of law. The officer was caught on video kicking a handcuffed suspect in the head (Associated Press, 2018).

1 Criminal Act

police crime Criminal behavior committed by police officers while on duty

police deviance Unethical activities committed by police officers; the acts do not conform to the high standards expected of members of the criminal justice system

corruption A type of police misconduct that includes the misuse of authority for an officer's personal gain or that of others

abuses of authority Acts of police misconduct that include intentional actions in the course of police work that are designed to inflict harm upon others or violate individual rights

noble cause corruption A type of corruption in which officers misuse their powers for the sake of what they believe is "justice"

Noble Cause Corruption

Officers also sometimes misuse their powers and engage in misconduct for the sake of what they believe is "justice," or what is known as **noble cause corruption** (Crank & Caldero, 1999; Delattre, 1996). There are many types of noble cause corruption, which may include officers who use too much force when encountering suspects who have violently harmed helpless victims, including during acts of domestic violence. Or, officers may commit perjury on the witness stand in hopes that offenders will be sanctioned for their crime even if proper procedures were not followed. For instance, an officer in Chicago testified in court that he pulled over a suspect for an illegal lane change and smelled marijuana as he waited for the suspect to hand over his license and proof of insurance. He stated that he then ordered the suspect from the car, searched the car, and found a pound of marijuana and so arrested the suspect. The in-car video suggested otherwise. It showed the officer approaching the car and reaching into the window to unlock the door. The officer was then depicted ordering the driver to step out, at which time he was frisked, handcuffed, and brought to the police patrol car prior to the car being searched (Editorial Board, 2015).

Measuring Police Misconduct

It is difficult to determine the extent of police misconduct, largely because of the challenges associated with measurement. These challenges include:

- a lack of agreement regarding what, specifically, constitutes misconduct;
- departments being protective of releasing information concerning officer misconduct;
- the inability to detect much officer misconduct; and
- a lack of national statistics regarding officer misconduct.

1 Criminal Act

It is assumed that many incidents involving police misconduct are not brought to the attention of authorities or are handled informally within the departments, because departments are sometimes apprehensive about releasing such negative information. In an effort to measure the extent of police crime, researchers analyzed media sources of reports of officers who were arrested. Their work provides some account of the extent to which officers engaged in various types of crime.

Among their findings, the researchers noted that police crimes occur relatively frequently: They identified 6,724 arrest cases involving 5,545 police officers from 2005 to 2011. They noted that simple assault and driving under the influence were among the more common charges, and over half (54%) of the arrested officers lost their job. Violence-related crime appeared more frequently than other types of offenses, such as drug-related, alcohol-related, and profit-motivated crimes (Stinson et al., 2016).

Another study focused on police deviance and misconduct specifically in Arizona from 2000 to 2011 and analyzed charges of misconduct filed with the Arizona Peace Officer Standards and Training Board. The researchers found that most of the cases involved line-level officers (80.3%), and most involved males (88.9%). They found a wide range of acts of misconduct, with failure to perform their responsibilities (32.6%) accounting for the largest percentage of acts, followed by untruthful behavior (e.g., filing false reports, 16.5%). They also found that the more serious forms of misconduct, including the ones that often generate media coverage, such as profit-motivated corruption (6.9%), sexual misconduct (6.8%), and excessive use of force (1.0%), occurred relatively rarely (Huff et al., 2018).

Effects of Police Misconduct

Officers who misbehave typically draw negative attention to all officers, their departments, and policing in general. There are many negative effects associated with police misconduct, including the fact that police criminal behavior undermines the legitimacy of policing and hampers confidence in the police. Police misconduct is also seen as hypocritical because officers are trusted to enforce the law in a fair and just manner. Officers who break the law break that trust with fellow officers and the public. Small-scale police misconduct is more likely to occur than large-scale misconduct, and it could lead to more serious forms of officer misbehavior.

Controlling Misconduct

There are numerous ways through which departments and other groups seek to control police misconduct, both before and after it occurs. Police accountability primarily exists in two forms: internally and externally. Internal forms of police accountability include the presence of an effective internal affairs division; proper recruitment, selection, and training of officers; coworker influences; and department procedures that guide officer behavior. Externally, civilian review boards, appointed commissions, the media, and the general public provide police accountability.

Internal Police Accountability

Positive police leadership and effective and clear departmental policies promote professional behavior. In addition, **internal affairs** units, sometimes referred to as Offices of Professional standards, are internal police units that evaluate and investigate allegations of questionable police conduct. Internal affairs units typically report directly to the chief or deputy chief. They can be reactive and proactive, for instance by responding to complaints and conducting investigations on their own. They protect the public by deterring officers from misconduct and protect the department and officers from frivolous or false claims of officer misconduct.

As noted in Module 12, properly recruiting, selecting, and training officers also helps prevent misconduct, as does regularly tracking cases of misconduct. Teaching police ethics and integrity both prior to and in service helps ensure that officers are aware of the boundaries under which they must operate. In 2013, 98% of all police academies offered an average of 8 hours of training in ethics and integrity, while 85% offered an average of 11 hours in professionalism (Reaves, 2016).

Finally, **early warning systems**, or early intervention systems, have facilitated the identification of problem police officers through the use of computer programs that permit supervisors to closely monitor officers who regularly receive complaints. Police departments have also increasingly incorporated cameras on officers and in police cruisers with the goals of providing more accountability for officers and protecting them against claims of misbehavior.

External Police Accountability

Civilian review boards, also referred to as citizen complaint boards, and external review boards are also used by many departments to provide accountability in policing. They are important primarily because they involve the citizenry in police practices by allowing nonpolice personnel to help monitor department operations with a particular emphasis on complaints against police. The organization and functions

● **Learning Objective 16.2:** Distinguish among means of controlling police misconduct.

internal affairs Sometimes referred to as Offices of Professional Standards, it is an internal police unit that evaluates and investigates allegations of questionable police conduct; internal affairs units typically report directly to the chief or deputy chief

early warning systems Also known as early intervention systems, they are systems that facilitate the identification of problem police officers through the use of computer programs that permit supervisors to closely monitor officers who regularly receive complaints

CAREERS

An **inspector general** oversees an office that provides oversight for agencies by preventing and investigating inefficient or illegal operations. These offices are often charged with addressing fraud, waste, abuse, embezzlement, and mismanagement. They are typically found in the federal government, but they also exist in state agencies and at the local level, including some local-level police departments. The Los Angeles Police Department, for example, has an Office of Inspector General that has oversight over the department's internal disciplinary process.

of review boards vary among departments; for instance, some permit board members (some of whom are paid and some who volunteer) to review complaint investigations conducted by investigators from the police internal affairs unit. Other jurisdictions permit board members to conduct investigations of allegations of misconduct of police officers, and others provide a combination of these approaches (De Angelis et al., 2016).

These boards became popular during the 1960s and 1970s when citizens became increasingly concerned with police practices, although various forms of citizen oversight in policing existed decades earlier. An estimated 11.3% of local police departments, which employed 35.4% of all local officers, used a citizen complaint review board in 2016 (C. Brooks, 2020).

Various external commissions have been assembled to investigate claims of police misconduct. The commissions have been appointed by government leaders, including the president, and have provided insight regarding police misconduct.

Wickersham Commission In 1931, it criticized the police for widespread corruption and misconduct, including accusations of officers engaging in unprofessional conduct with regard to interrogating suspects and the use of force

- The **Wickersham Commission** (1931) criticized the police for widespread corruption and misconduct, including accusations of officers engaging in unprofessional conduct with regard to interrogating suspects and the use of force.

- The **National Advisory Commission on Civil Disorders (1967–1968)**, also known as the **Kerner Commission**, noted that police practices contributed to the civil unrest occurring in the 1960s. It suggested that the officers engaged in unprofessional conduct particularly through aggressive enforcement practices, inadequate training, poor supervision, and overzealous patrol practices.

- The **Knapp Commission** was assembled in 1970 and speculated that half of the New York City Police Department engaged in corruption.

- The **Mollen Commission** (1992) investigated police corruption in New York and found that officers who engaged in the most serious forms of corruption began to engage in misconduct through the beating and abuse of suspects.

MYTHBUSTING

Officers Who Receive Many Complaints Are Problematic

Upon assuming control of a problematic police department, many chiefs promise to "clean up the department." They begin by looking at citizen complaints against officers. This may seem to be an appropriate approach, but not all officers who receive many complaints are problematic officers. In fact, they may be exceptional officers. For example, it may be the case that an officer makes many legitimate arrests, and thus in retaliation, offend-

ers will file false complaints (even though doing so is illegal). Additional considerations include the communities in which the officers work (for instance, residents in the area may not like the police), the nature of the complaints, and the shifts the officers work. To be sure, citizen complaints assist in identifying problematic officers, but the nature and context of those complaints must be considered.

The Department of Justice investigated the Ferguson, Missouri, police department and found that the officers regularly violated the rights of African Americans. The police shooting of Michael Brown ignited a series of protests regarding police practices and the subsequent investigation.

What steps can be taken to better ensure that police officers appropriately use force against suspects?

- The **Christopher Commission**, assembled in 1991, argued that the failure of the Los Angeles Police Department to control police brutality largely contributed to the civil unrest that occurred in Los Angeles.

The U.S. Department of Justice also investigates claims of police violations of civil rights through its Civil Rights Division. For instance, the department conducted an independent investigation into the death of Freddie Gray after he died while in the custody of Baltimore police officers (Rector, 2017).

Other external groups that help control police misconduct are the news media, which provide a sense of accountability for the police through investigative journalism and more traditional news reporting, and citizens, who play an important role through filing complaints and lawsuits. Citizens play a particularly important role, and departments must have proper procedures for citizens to file complaints. Many departments provide complaint forms in multiple languages to provide non–English speaking citizens the opportunity to file a complaint. Figure 16.1 provides an example of a complaint form used by the Albuquerque, New Mexico, Police Department.

Research examining citizen complaints against police officers in eight cities found variation among departments with regard to the types of complaints received and the outcomes of those complaints. Generally, however, they found that improper use of force (22%) and officer discourtesy (20%) constituted many of the complaints, and a small number of officers accounted for a disproportionate number of complaints. Younger and less experienced officers were more likely than their counterparts to generate citizen complaints (Terrill & Ingram, 2016).

National Advisory Commission on Civil Disorders Also known as the **Kerner Commission** (1967–1968), the commission noted that police practices contributed to the civil unrest occurring in the 1960s; it suggested that the officers engaged in unprofessional conduct particularly through aggressive enforcement practices, inadequate training, poor supervision, and overzealous patrol practices

Knapp Commission A commission assembled in 1970 which speculated that half of the New York City Police Department engaged in corruption

Mollen Commission A commission which in 1992 investigated police corruption in New York and found that officers who engaged in the most serious forms of corruption began to engage in misconduct through beating and abuse of suspects

Christopher Commission A commission assembled in 1991 that argued that the Los Angeles Police Department's failure to control police brutality largely contributed to the civil unrest that occurred in Los Angeles

Official Use ONLY: Date/Time Received: Received by: CPC#.   Assigned to:

Civilian Police Oversight Agency (CPOA)
Albuquerque Police Department Complaint or Commendation Form

This form can be hand-delivered to the CPOA office located at the
Plaza Del Sol Building, 600 2nd st. NW Room 813, Albuquerque, NM 87102
Fax: 505-924-3775
Email: cpoa@cabq.gov
Mail: CPOA, P.O. Box 1293
Albuquerque, NM 87103
TTY (800) 659-8331

Please complete as much information as possible below. The CPOA only accepts complaints and commedations for the Albuquerque Police Department. In order to make sure your accessibility needs are being met, such as sign language interpretation or help completing this form, please contact the CPOA at 505-924-3770.

I want to file a: ☐ Complaint ☐ Commendation ☐ Interested in Medlation? ☐ Yes ☐ No ☐ I need more information

Information about you:
First: _____ Last: _____ Middle: _____

Home: ( ) _____ - _____ Cell/Work ( ) _____ - _____ Best time to Call? _____

Email: _____ Preferred Language: _____ Date of Birth: ____/ ____/ _____

Street: _____ Apt:: _____

City: _____ State: _____ Zip Code: _____

Optional: This section is for statistical purposes only.

Gender: Male/Female/Other: ____Race/Ethnicity: White/Hispanic/Native American/African American/Asian/Other____

Sexual Orientation: Heterosexual/Homosexual/Bisexual/Other:

Do you have a Mental lilness?☐ Yes ☐ No

Do you struggle with homelessness? ☐Yes ☐ No

Information about the incident:

Date: ____/ ____/ _____ Time: _____AM/PM

Address/Location: _____
                   Street   Apt   City   State   Zip Code

Information about the Albuquerque Police Department employee(s) Involved:

Name: _____ Man/I.D. #: _____

Name: _____ Man/I.D. #: _____

Are you submitting this form for someone else? ☐ Yes ☐ No   Did you witness this incident? ☐Yes ☐No

Name of the person you are submitting this form for: _____ Phone: ( ) _____ - _____

Additional Witness:

Name: _____ Phone: ( ) _____ - _____

Address/Location: _____
                   Street   Apt   City   State   Zip Code

STATEMENT

Briefly summarize what happened (attach additional pages or documents if needed).
It is important to provide as much information as possible describing the incident in full detail including: location, date, time, officer/employee(s) involved, and witnesses.
If names are not known, please include a detailed description of the officer(s) involved.

_____

_____

_____

_____

_____

_____

_____

_____

_____

_____

_____

_____

_____

_____

_____

_____

_____

_____

What outcome are you seeking?

_____

_____

_____

> The information provided in this statement is true and factual to the best of my knowledge and will become public record once filed.
>
> I understand I may be required to appear in the Civilian Police Oversight Agency office for an interview or to provide other investigative assistance, as necessary.
>
> I understand that if i file a complaint, it is unlawful and against APD Policies for anyone to retaliate against me for the filing of this complaint.
>
> _____   _____
> Signature   Date

OFFICE USE ONLY: APD personnel who receive misconduct complaints must notify a supervisor immediately. Supervisor shall submit complaint to Internal Affairs by the end of the shift following the shift in which the complaint was received.

APD Superviser signature:_____ Date: _____ Time Received: _____ AM/PM

FIGURE 16.1. A Complaint Form Used by the Albuquerque, New Mexico, Police Department. Enabling citizens to file complaints against police officers is an important part of police–community relations. Those who wish to highlight questionable police practices must be able to feel safe from retaliation by the department and should be made aware of the process for doing so. Further, departments need to ensure that proper responses are made to the complaints. **Source:** *Albuquerque Police Department (n.d.).*

Do you believe it is problematic that complaints against the police are filed with the police? Should there be some type of third party involved in the process?

Sanctioning Misconduct

● **Learning Objective 16.3:** Describe the sanctions used to address police misconduct.

There are several sanctions for officers who are found to have engaged in misconduct. More serious cases will likely be addressed formally, in accord with a department's legal procedures. Less serious infractions are typically handled less formally; they may include a warning or no action may be taken. The methods and processes through which misconduct and corruption are addressed are administrative in nature, although civil and criminal charges may result. For instance, in 2019 a former Houston Police Department officer was charged with two counts of murder after he allegedly lied to justify warrants for a drug raid that resulted in two people being killed and five officers wounded (Madani & Li, 2019).

To address misbehavior internally, departments may:

decertification A punishment for police misconduct in which police administrators work with state accreditation and regulatory boards to remove an officer of their state certification to be a police officer

- fire misbehaving officers;
- opt for **decertification**, in which police administrators work with state accreditation and regulatory boards to remove an officer of their state certification to be a police officer;
- place misbehaving officers on administrative leave with or without pay, reassign officers to administrative tasks, or relocate them to less opportunistic positions;

punitive probation A sanction for police misconduct that involves closely monitoring and assessing the actions of problematic officers over a period of time

- place officers on **punitive probation**, which involves closely monitoring and assessing the actions of problematic officers over a period of time;
- reprimand officers: **reprimands** are written citations and accounts of infractions that are kept in officers' personnel files;
- require officers to undergo additional training with regard to specific aspects of police work; and

reprimands Written citations and accounts of infractions that are kept in officers' personnel files

- mandate that officers with psychological, anger, drug, or alcohol problems get counseling.

The System in Perspective

The incidents of police misconduct described in the "In the News" feature at the start of this module shed light on a very small sample of the many types of misbehavior by police that have been documented. Stealing drugs and guns, extorting money from victims, and robbing motorists are very serious offenses, but they are not the only acts of misconduct that have been identified. To be clear, most police do not misbehave while on the job. However, one high-profile incident in which an officer misuses their powers may negatively affect opinions of policing in general. The police are the gatekeepers to the courts and corrections, and we depend on them to act professionally and ethically in order for the criminal justice system to function effectively. They, like everyone else, may end up in our courts and correctional facilities if they break the law.

Summary

1. Learning Objective 16.1: *Explain how police misconduct is classified.*

- Police misconduct includes police crime (e.g., officers breaking into a house and stealing items when responding to a burglary call), occupational deviance (e.g., officers failing to respond to calls in a dangerous part of town out of concern for their safety), corruption (e.g., officers accepting a bribe from a stopped motorist), and abuse of authority (e.g., when an officer uses too much force to subdue a victim).

2. Learning Objective 16.2: *Distinguish among means of controlling police misconduct.*

- Several methods are used to control misconduct, including the law, internal review boards, civilian review boards, recruitment, selection, training, and early warning systems. Departments have also increasingly used cameras, both on officers and in police vehicles, to provide greater accountability for officers. The media and citizens also help address police misconduct.

3. Learning Objective 16.3: *Describe the sanctions used to address police misconduct.*

- Officers caught engaging in misconduct are subject to sanctions including termination, the filing of civil or criminal charges, decertification, placing the officer on administrative leave, relocating them to another unit or division, punitive probation, additional training, counseling, or a reprimand.

Questions for Critical Thinking

1. What form of police misconduct do you consider most damaging, and why?
2. Do you believe that internal affairs divisions, which consist of law enforcement personnel evaluating the questionable behaviors of other law enforcement personnel, can be objective in their evaluations? Why or why not?
3. What sanctions would be most appropriate for an officer engaged in less serious forms of misbehavior, such as accepting free meals when it is against department policy or not ticketing friends who are speeding? What sanctions would be appropriate for officers engaged in more serious forms of misconduct, such as using excessive force?

Key Terms

abuses of authority
Christopher Commission
corruption
decertification
early warning systems
internal affairs
Kerner Commission
Knapp Commission

Mollen Commission
National Advisory Commission on Civil Disorders
noble cause corruption
police crime
police deviance
punitive probation
reprimands
Wickersham Commission

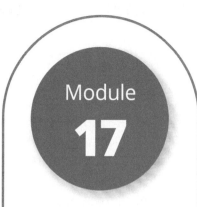

Module

17

MODULE OUTLINE

- **Search and Seizure**

  Learning Objective 17.1:
  Compare probable cause with
  reasonable suspicion.

- **The Exclusionary Rule**

  Learning Objective 17.2:
  Explain the exclusionary
  rule and identify the
  exceptions to it.

- **Legal Requirements for an Arrest**

  Learning Objective 17.3:
  Identify when a warrant is
  required to make an arrest.

- **Interrogations and Confessions**

  Learning Objective 17.4:
  Note when a Miranda
  warning is required.

Police and Constitutional Law

Police practices must conform to the U.S. Constitution, which was written in 1787 and has been interpreted by the courts ever since. Several amendments to the Constitution directly impact police work: The Fourth Amendment pertains to searches and seizures, and the Fifth Amendment provides protections against self-incrimination.

What other amendments impact policing?

Constitutional law guides police practices, and interpretations of the U.S. Constitution dictate how the police perform their duties. Accordingly, the police must abide by procedural law when conducting all aspects of their job, including searching, stopping, frisking, and arresting individuals. The uniqueness of each police–citizen encounter, however, requires interpretation of the Constitution and of human behavior. This module addresses the topics of search and seizure, the exclusionary rule, the legal requirements for an arrest, and interrogations, all in the context of constitutional law as it pertains to policing.

Searches Following Lawful Arrests

In 2013, Danny Birchfield drove his vehicle into a ditch in North Dakota. The police believed he was intoxicated, and Birchfield failed the sobriety and breath tests. He refused to consent to a chemical (blood) test required by state law. As a result, he was charged with a misdemeanor for refusing to consent to the test. Birchfield claimed that the law requiring a chemical blood test violated his Fourth Amendment right against unlawful search and seizure.

In 2016, the Supreme Court agreed with Birchfield when it ruled, in a 7–1 decision in *Birchfield v. North Dakota*, that searches following lawful arrests may include breath tests, but not blood tests on suspected drunk drivers. The Supreme Court noted that breath tests do not violate privacy in a significant way, but blood tests are more intrusive and thus not allowed without consent (Kopan & de Vogue, 2016).

The Supreme Court ruling impacts police departments nationwide. The court continues to interpret the Constitution and its amendments in efforts to ensure that the need to protect society is balanced with individual rights and freedoms. In this case, the decision came down on the side of the protection of freedoms and rights and restricting law enforcement practices. Do you believe the Supreme Court got it right in this case? Should officers be allowed to conduct blood tests on suspected intoxicated drivers?

IN THE NEWS

1 Criminal Act

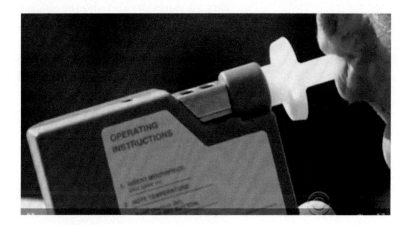

Search and Seizure

Police searches and seizures are guided by the Fourth Amendment, which states:

> The right of the people to be secure in their persons, houses, papers, and effects, against unreasonable searches and seizures, shall not be violated, and no Warrants shall issue, but upon probable cause, supported by Oath or affirmation, and particularly describing the place to be searched, and the persons or things to be seized.

Ultimately, the Fourth Amendment governs police practices as they pertain to arrests with and without warrants, searches with and without warrants, and the seizure of evidence. Evidence seized illegally cannot be used in court.

In *Brinegar v. United States* (1949, p. 338, U.S. 175–176), the Supreme Court noted that probable cause exists when "the facts and circumstances within the officers' knowledge, and of which they have reasonably trustworthy information, are sufficient in themselves to warrant a belief by a man of reasonable caution that a crime is being committed." **Probable cause** is the standard of proof required in four particularly important aspects of police work:

- searches and seizures of property without a warrant
- searches and seizures of property with a warrant

3 Arrest

● **Learning Objective 17.1:** Compare probable cause with reasonable suspicion.

probable cause
The standard of proof required in searches and seizures of property without a warrant, searches and seizures of property with a warrant, arrests with a warrant, and arrests without a warrant

reasonable suspicion The standard of proof required for officers to stop individuals acting in an unusual manner which may suggest that a crime is taking or has taken place and the individual acting suspiciously may be dangerous and/or responsible

stop and frisk Also known as a threshold inquiry or field inquiry; it involves officers briefly detaining and patting down individuals they believe may pose a risk

frisks The practice of police patting down or running their hands along the clothes of suspects to check for weapons

- arrests with a warrant
- arrests without a warrant

The courts have ruled that probable cause may be based on an officer's observation of misconduct, the expertise of officers, circumstantial factors, and information brought to the attention of officers.

Stopping and Frisking

Stops are designed to prevent crime or assess whether a crime has taken place. Stops are permitted when officers observe unusual behavior that leads them to have a **reasonable suspicion** that a crime is taking or has taken place and the individual acting suspiciously may be dangerous and/or responsible. Stops must be temporary in duration and should not last longer than is necessary for law enforcement to accomplish its purposes (del Carmen & Hemmens, 2017). In conducting the stop, officers must self-identify as a police officer and make reasonable inquiries. They may determine that an individual is not problematic, or they may investigate further, and the encounter may lead to a **stop and frisk**, also known as a threshold inquiry or field inquiry (Wrobleski & Hess, 2006).

Frisks involve police patting down or running their hands along the clothes of suspects to check for weapons. The protection of lives is the sole purpose of frisking suspicious individuals (del Carmen & Hemmens, 2017). Frisks are restricted to areas

The police must have probable cause to believe that a crime was committed to make an arrest. What constitutes probable cause may differ among individuals; for instance, the police may believe they are justified in making an arrest, while a suspect does not.

Do police have too much power in making arrests, or do the laws and policies place too many restrictions on officers?

where suspects may be concealing weapons or other devices that could provide harm to the officer or others. Frisks cannot become explorations to determine if suspects have any type of evidence that could be used against them.

The Supreme Court attempted to clarify the law regarding stopping and frisking in *Terry v. Ohio* (1968) when it ruled that seizures occur when an officer restrains an individual's freedom and a search occurs when an officer explores an individual's possessions via a pat-down search. The court ruled that officers may detain a person briefly without probable cause if they believe the person committed a crime. Stopping and frisking an individual is distinct from and does not constitute an arrest, despite the restricted freedoms involved.

Searches With a Warrant

Searches are designed to obtain incriminating evidence. Search warrants are issued by a magistrate or judge with jurisdiction over the area to be searched. Officers seeking a warrant must first prepare an **affidavit**, which is a written statement establishing probable cause to conduct a search. The officer presents the affidavit to a judge and swears under oath that the information included in the document is truthful. The affidavit must clearly note the reasons for the anticipated search, the names of the individuals presenting the affidavit, and the items to be seized. The judge then determines if probable cause exists and, if so, may issue a warrant. Searches are restricted to the items, areas, and persons noted in the affidavit and must occur shortly after being approved.

affidavit A written statement establishing probable cause to conduct a search

When serving a warrant, officers must generally announce their authority and presence upon approaching a residence (*Wilson v. Arkansas*, 1995). If no one responds, they may forcibly enter the dwelling by knocking down the door or breaking a window, or they may contact an apartment manager to provide access to the dwelling. **No-knock searches**—searches that do not require an announcement—are permitted by state statute, and also require judicial approval. Generally, they are permitted in cases in which it is anticipated that the individual whose residence is to be searched will be uncooperative and may potentially destroy or remove the objects of the search.

no-knock searches Police searches that do not require an announcement; they are permitted by state statute and require judicial approval

Searches Without a Warrant

Although all searches should be supported by a warrant, there are situations in which a warrant is not necessary. These situations include the following:

- *if consent is provided*: Individuals may grant the police permission to conduct a search without a warrant, although the permission must be voluntary, meaning that the police did not threaten or coerce the individual.

- *exigent circumstances*: Exigent circumstances are situations in which police have probable cause, but there is no time to secure a warrant (e.g., if the suspect is likely to flee).

- *searches following a lawful arrest*: The Supreme Court ruled that officers may conduct a warrantless search simultaneously with a lawful arrest, although the search must be restricted to the immediate vicinity of the arrest (*Chimel v. California*, 1969). The court also ruled that in addition to searching the immediate vicinity of the arrestee, officers may also conduct a protective sweep of the premises without a warrant (*Maryland v. Buie*, 1990). The sweep, often referred to as a "**Buie sweep**," is permitted to help ensure the safety of the officers.

- *searches of motor vehicles*: The Supreme Court noted that permission to grant a warrantless search of an automobile is dependent on the officer's probable cause in believing that there are illegal contents within the vehicle, and the vehicle would be gone by the time the officer obtained a warrant (*Carroll v. United States*, 1925). Vehicles may also be searched without a warrant when it is believed by officers

Buie sweep Officers conducting a warrantless sweep of an arrestee's premises following a lawful arrest; it is permitted and done to help ensure the safety of the officers

administrative searches Searches conducted by government investigators to assess whether there are violations of government regulations

plain view doctrine An exception to the warrant requirement that permits officers to seize evidence without a warrant if it is in view of the officer, although the police must have justification for being present to view the evidence

hot pursuit exception Permits officers to enter places otherwise protected by the Fourth Amendment without a search warrant if they are in pursuit of a suspect based on probable cause

● **Learning Objective 17.2:** Explain the exclusionary rule and identify the exceptions to it.

that they were used in the commission of a felony, for instance as a getaway car or to store stolen goods (*New York v. Belton*, 1981). In 2009, the Supreme Court ruled that an arrest of the occupants of a vehicle does not justify a warrantless search of the vehicle unless the search is necessary to ensure the safety of officers and others and to preserve evidence supporting the arrest (*Arizona v. Gant*, 2009).

- *situations involving stops and frisks*: Assuming that an officer has conducted a legal stop and frisk, the officer is permitted to conduct a warrantless search if it is believed that the suspect has an item that may pose a danger to the officer or others (*Minnesota v. Dickerson*, 1993).

- *Administrative searches and inspections*: Government investigators conduct **administrative searches** to assess whether there are violations of government regulations. These searches are typically conducted by individuals authorized by local ordinances or administrative agencies (e.g., building inspectors) instead of police officers. There are three types of administrative searches: entrance into private residences for code violations, entrance into commercial buildings for inspection, and searches of regulated businesses (del Carmen & Hemmens, 2017).

- *searches due to special needs beyond law enforcement*: These searches typically do not involve the police, although they may assist. They are often conducted by other public agencies or groups and may include searches at schools, searches of probationers and parolees, and searches at airports by Transportation Security Administration personnel, for example (del Carmen & Hemmens, 2017).

Further, the **plain view doctrine** holds that officers may seize evidence without a warrant if it is in view of the officer, although the police must have justification for being present to view the evidence. In addition, under the **hot pursuit exception**, officers are permitted to enter places otherwise protected by the Fourth Amendment if they are in pursuit of a suspect based on probable cause.

The Exclusionary Rule

The failure to abide by the rulings and laws surrounding search and seizure may result in the application of the **exclusionary rule**, which prohibits the use, in court, of illegally seized evidence (Figure 17.1). The rule was originally introduced in the federal criminal justice system in 1914 (*Weeks v. United States*, 1914) and was formally applied to the states in 1961 (*Mapp v. Ohio*, 1961). The exclusionary rule was designed to deter police misconduct and respect individual rights.

Since its inception, the exclusionary rule has undergone much scrutiny, and several exceptions to the rule have been introduced. The exceptions fall within four categories: good faith, inevitable discovery, purged taint, and independent source.

Good Faith Exception

The **good faith exception** permits the introduction of illegally seized evidence if an officer makes an honest and reasonable error (del Carmen & Hemmens, 2017). The exception was established by the U.S. Supreme Court in two 1984 **companion cases**, which are two or more cases that have been consolidated by an appellate court because they involve a common legal issue. The cases were *United States v. Leon* and *Massachusetts v. Sheppard*, both of which involved the appropriateness of evidence seized by the police.

Inevitable Discovery Exception

The **inevitable discovery exception** permits the introduction of illegally seized evidence, if it can be shown that the evidence would have or might have been obtained even if the officer had not illegally seized it. In *Nix v. Williams* (1984), the U.S. Supreme Court set the standard for this exception when it ruled that officers who were searching for the body of a murdered young girl would have located the girl, even without Williams's input, which led to the body. Williams was asked by a police officer for assistance in locating the body, without having been read his Miranda rights and without having an attorney present. The court ruled that officers who had been searching in the area would have ultimately found the body even without Williams's input, which was wrongfully obtained.

Purged Taint Exception

The **purged taint exception** permits the introduction of illegally obtained evidence, if suspects willfully offer the information. The origin of the exception is traced back to the U.S. Supreme Court case *Wong Sun v. U.S.* (1963), in which police illegally arrested the defendant, who then provided the officers with information regarding his involvement in a crime. Under the **"fruit of the poisonous tree" doctrine**, which holds

exclusionary rule Prohibits the introduction of illegally seized evidence into courtroom proceedings

good faith exception An exception to the exclusionary rule that permits the introduction of illegally seized evidence if an officer makes an honest and reasonable error

companion cases Two or more court cases that have been consolidated by an appellate court because they involve a common legal issue

inevitable discovery exception An exception to the exclusionary rule that permits the introduction of illegally seized evidence if it can be shown that the evidence would have or might have been obtained even if the officer had not illegally seized it

purged taint exceptions An exception to the exclusionary rule that permits the introduction of illegally obtained evidence if suspects willfully offer the information

"fruit of the poisonous tree" doctrine An extension of the exclusionary rule which holds that any secondary information or evidence collected as a result of an illegal search is also inadmissible in court

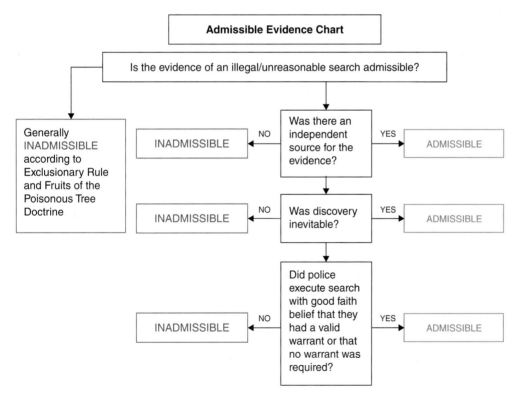

FIGURE 17.1. *Is the Evidence Admissible?* Evidence gathered from an illegal or unreasonable search is generally inadmissible under the exclusionary rule. The U.S. Supreme Court, however, has offered several exceptions to the rule and identified the conditions under which illegally seized evidence is admissible in court.

Do you believe that the exclusionary rule is necessary? Should evidence implicating an individual in criminal behavior be permissible regardless of how it was obtained?

independent source exception
An exception to the exclusionary rule that permits the introduction of illegally seized evidence if the police are able to demonstrate that the information was obtained from a source unrelated to the illegal search or seizure

that any secondary information or evidence collected as a result of an illegal search is also inadmissible in court (*Silverthorne Lumber Co. v. United States*, 1920), the information provided by the defendant would be inadmissible in court. The defendant in this case, however, under his own will, returned to the police department and signed a document stating that his admission was accurate.

Independent Source Exception

The **independent source exception** permits the introduction of illegally seized evidence, if the police are able to demonstrate that the information was obtained from a source unrelated to the illegal search or seizure (*United States v. Crews*, 1980). In reviewing the *Crews* case, the U.S. Supreme Court noted that even though the police illegally detained the defendant, he could be held accountable for his actions, if evidence suggesting his guilt emerged unrelated to the police misconduct.

● **Learning Objective 17.3:** Identify when a warrant is required to make an arrest.

Legal Requirements for an Arrest

An **arrest** occurs when police take a person into custody after the commission of an offense (*State v. Murphy*, 1970). Arrests require either physical force or the submission to the use of authority (*California v. Hodari D*, 1991). Words alone do not constitute an arrest; there must be "governmental termination of freedom of movement through means intentionally applied" (*Brower v. County of Inyo*, 1989). Arrests are considered the most intrusive form of seizures and thus involve greater restrictions on police officers.

Arrest Warrants

The U.S. Constitution requires officers to obtain an arrest warrant prior to making an arrest. Not doing so could lead to officers facing claims of false imprisonment and civil liability, if it is later determined that the arrest was not based on probable cause. Despite the benefits of securing a warrant prior to making an arrest, most arrests are made without an arrest warrant (del Carmen & Hemmens, 2017). This is because officers are permitted to make warrantless arrests if:

3 Arrest

arrest Seizing and restricting the freedoms of individuals believed to have committed a crime

public offenses
Felonies or misdemeanors committed in the presence of law enforcement

- a felony or misdemeanor is committed in their presence, known as a **public offense**;
- there is probable cause and an emergency situation exists;
- there is a danger to the officer; or
- a crime was committed in a public place.

Similar to a search warrant, arrest warrants require an affidavit noting the facts of the case and affirmation by an officer that the information is accurate (Figure 17.2 depicts an arrest warrant). Warrants vary in form among states, but they typically include the following:

- the name of the issuing officer
- the name of the person to be arrested
- the offense charged
- an order for the officer to bring the arrestee before the court issuing the warrant
- the date the warrant was issued
- the signature of the judge or other court official

A judge or some other impartial official signs and issues the warrant if they believe that probable cause to make an arrest exists. Officers request a

---

AO 442 (Rev. 11/11) Arrest Warrant
_____

UNITED STATES DISTRICT COURT
for the

United States of America	)	
v.	)	Case No.
	)	
	)	
	)	
_____	)	
Defendant		

ARREST WARRANT

To: Any authorized law enforcement officer

　　　　YOU ARE COMMANDED to arrest and bring before a United States magistrate judge without unnecessary delay
(name of person to be arrested) _____ ,
who is accused of an offense or violation based on the following document filed with the court:

☐ Indictment　　　☐ Superseding Indictment　　☐ Information　　☐ Superseding Information　　☐ Complaint

☐ Probation Violation Petition　　☐ Supervised Release Violation Petition　　☐ Violation Notice　　☐ Order of the Court

This offense is briefly described as follows:

Date: _____

　　　　　　　　　　　　　　　　　　　　　　_____
　　　　　　　　　　　　　　　　　　　　　　　　　　Issuing officer's signature

City and state: _____

　　　　　　　　　　　　　　　　　　　　　　_____
　　　　　　　　　　　　　　　　　　　　　　　　　　Printed name and title

Return
This warrant was receive on *(date)* _____, and the person was arrested on *(date)* _____ at *(city and state)* _____ . Date: _____ .　　　　　　　　　　_____ 　　　　　　　　　　　　　　　　　　　　　　　　　*Arresting officer's signature* 　　　　　　　　　　　　　　　　　　　　　　_____ 　　　　　　　　　　　　　　　　　　　　　　　　　*Printed name and title*

FIGURE 17.2. *An Arrest Warrant.* Arrest warrants are generally required to make arrests, although there are situations in which one is not needed. The warrant requests information regarding the individual to be arrested and the reason(s) for the arrest. Failure to provide vital information results in officers not receiving a warrant.

Should we eliminate the need for arrest warrants and trust that officers will always use their best judgment? Why or why not?

"John Doe" warrant when they do not know the name of the individual they wish to arrest. Such requests are permitted when there exists probable cause to believe the individual committed a crime and the request includes a description of the accused, which would enable their identification with reasonable certainty.

3 Arrest

"John Doe" warrant
A type of arrest warrant requested by officers when they do not know the name of the individual they wish to arrest

3 Arrest

8 Trial

● **Learning Objective 17.4:** Describe when a Miranda warning is required.

Other Tools for Bringing Suspects Into Custody

Police officers also use tools other than arrest warrants to bring suspects into custody or hold them accountable by the courts. For instance, officers may issue a citation or a summons that directs the accused to appear in court at a specified date and time. The issuance of traffic tickets is one example. Many state statutes also permit officers to issue citations in response to minor crimes. Citations do not require the accused to be taken into custody, although their failure to appear in court at the time and date noted may result in the issuance of an arrest warrant (del Carmen and Hemmens, 2017).

Interrogations and Confessions

Prior to 1964, the admissibility of a defendant's admission of guilt or confession was based on whether it was voluntary and was determined on a case-by-case basis. Involuntary statements, for instance statements forced or coerced by the police, cannot be used in court because they violate the due process clause of the Fifth and 14th Amendments. The voluntariness requirement stems from *Brown v. Mississippi*, in which the Supreme Court ruled that a confession obtained from a suspect through police use of force was inadmissible (*Brown v. Mississippi*, 1936).

The Fifth Amendment states that "No person . . . shall be compelled in any criminal case to be a witness against himself, nor be deprived of life, liberty, or property, without due process of law." In addition to other interpretations of this amendment, the courts have ruled on when confessions and admissions of guilt are admissible as evidence in a criminal trial. The ruling in *Miranda v. Arizona* that "the prosecution may not use statements . . . stemming from custodial interrogation of the defendant unless it demonstrates the use of procedural safeguards effective to secure the privilege against self-incrimination" (*Miranda v. Arizona*, 1966) is perhaps the most influential law enforcement case decided by the U.S. Supreme Court. Figure 17.3 depicts a Miranda card carried by some officers to assist them as they inform suspects of their rights.

Per the *Miranda* decision, suspects:

● must be informed of their right to remain silent and that anything they say can be used against them in court;

● must be informed of the right to the presence of an attorney and that one will be appointed if they cannot afford one, if they choose to have one; and

● have the right to terminate the interrogation at any time.

Miranda warnings are only necessary when a suspect:

● has been taken into custody, and

● is to be interrogated, or questioned by law enforcement.

Officers Must inform You of Your Rights Upon Arrest

Many people believe that the police must inform you of your Miranda rights upon being arrested and that the failure to do so means that the arrest is invalid. In reality, however, the police are required to inform you of your rights only when you are detained and the police wish to question you. They do not need to offer the Miranda warning for arrests without interrogations. The offering of the rights is designed to protect individuals from self-incrimination; thus, the warnings are required only when an individual is in custody and being questioned.

Warnings are not required when the questioning of a suspect does not involve information that could be self-incriminating. The court ruled that volunteered statements offered by suspects are not protected by the Fifth Amendment and are not affected by the *Miranda* decision (*Miranda v. Arizona*, 1966). Officers are not required to interrupt an individual offering a volunteered statement to inform them of their Miranda protections. However, officers must cease questioning a suspect if at any time prior to or during an interrogation the suspect wishes to remain silent. Further, the **public safety exception** permits officers to question individuals in custody if the need for answers is imperative for public safety (*New York v. Quarles*, 1984). In the *Quarles* case, police officers apprehended a man in the area near where they were approached by a woman who said she had just been raped. The man fit the description of the rapist provided by the woman, and upon arresting him the police noticed that he had an empty gun holster. The police asked where the gun was prior to informing him of his Miranda protections, and the man identified the location of the weapon. The U.S. Supreme Court ruled that the gun was admissible in court as evidence under the public safety exception.

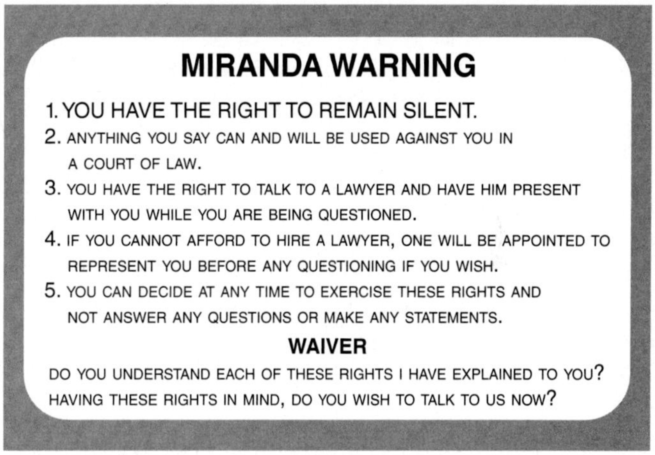

MIRANDA WARNING

1. YOU HAVE THE RIGHT TO REMAIN SILENT.
2. ANYTHING YOU SAY CAN AND WILL BE USED AGAINST YOU IN A COURT OF LAW.
3. YOU HAVE THE RIGHT TO TALK TO A LAWYER AND HAVE HIM PRESENT WITH YOU WHILE YOU ARE BEING QUESTIONED.
4. IF YOU CANNOT AFFORD TO HIRE A LAWYER, ONE WILL BE APPOINTED TO REPRESENT YOU BEFORE ANY QUESTIONING IF YOU WISH.
5. YOU CAN DECIDE AT ANY TIME TO EXERCISE THESE RIGHTS AND NOT ANSWER ANY QUESTIONS OR MAKE ANY STATEMENTS.

WAIVER

DO YOU UNDERSTAND EACH OF THESE RIGHTS I HAVE EXPLAINED TO YOU? HAVING THESE RIGHTS IN MIND, DO YOU WISH TO TALK TO US NOW?

FIGURE 17.3. Miranda Warning Card. Miranda warnings inform suspects of their rights and are required when suspects have been taken into custody and are going to be questioned by law enforcement officers. Some officers carry cards such as the one depicted here, which may include the warnings in multiple languages to assist them in diverse communities.

Why is it necessary for the police to inform individuals of their rights?

public safety exception An exception to the Miranda warning requirement that permits officers to question individuals in custody without reading them their rights if the need for answers is imperative for public safety

The System in Perspective

Various U.S. Supreme Court decisions have impacted police practices, including the decision made in *Birchfield v. North Dakota* (as noted in the "In the News" feature at the start of this module) in which the court noted that blood tests on suspected drunk drivers are not permitted without consent. This decision applies to all law enforcement officers in the United States, because the Supreme Court is the highest court in the country. The police are regularly impacted by court decisions, and they must abide by procedural laws as they apply to many important aspects of police work, including arrests, searches, seizures, and interrogations. The U.S. Constitution provides the "rules" for all justice-based practices. Courts at all levels have interpreted the Constitution and, in doing so, have granted powers to and placed restrictions on all who work in the system.

Summary

1. Learning Objective 17.1: *Compare probable cause with reasonable suspicion.*

- Probable cause exists when "the facts and circumstances within the officers' knowledge and of which they had reasonably trustworthy information are sufficient in themselves to warrant a man of reasonable caution to believe that a crime is being committed." Reasonable suspicion is the standard that requires officers to have a rational belief, or legitimate reason, to believe that an individual is involved in a crime or is dangerous.

2. Learning Objective 17.2: *Explain the exclusionary rule and identify the exceptions to it.*

- The exclusionary rule holds that all illegally obtained evidence will be excluded from government consideration in a criminal trial. It was designed to deter police misconduct and respect individual rights. The exceptions to the

exclusionary rule include good faith, inevitable discovery, purged taint, and independent source.

3. Learning Objective 17.3: *Identify when a warrant is required to make an arrest.*

- The U.S. Constitution requires officers to obtain an arrest warrant prior to making an arrest except if they witness a felony or misdemeanor, if there is probable cause and an emergency situation exists, if there is a danger to the officer, or if a crime was committed in a public place.

4. Learning Objective 17.4: *Describe when a Miranda warning is required.*

- Miranda warnings are only necessary when a suspect has been taken into custody and is to be interrogated, or questioned by law enforcement. They are not required when the questioning of a suspect does not involve information that could be self-incriminating.

Questions for Critical Thinking

1. How would you define probable cause?
2. Does the exclusionary rule hamper police practices? Should we give the police more powers to conduct searches?
3. Can an officer arrest a young man who is acting suspiciously in the officer's presence? Why or why not?
4. It is sometimes argued that the requirement for officers to issue a Miranda warning hampers police work and that it frees guilty people and needs to be eliminated. There are also strong arguments in support of keeping the requirement. Do you believe we should keep or eliminate the need for officers to issue the warning? Why?

Key Terms

administrative searches
affidavit
arrest
buie sweep
companion cases
Exclusionary Rule
frisks
"fruit of the poisonous tree" doctrine
good faith exception
hot pursuit exception
independent source exception

inevitable discovery exception
"John Doe" warrant
no-knock searches
plain view doctrine
probable cause
public offenses
public safety exception
purged taint exceptions
reasonable suspicion
stop and frisk

For digital learning resources, please go to
https://www.oup.com/he/burns1e

Police Investigations and Arrests

Criminal case processing begins with an investigation that may be followed by an arrest. Proper procedures must be followed in both steps. Further, decisions to investigate and make an arrest, as well as the means by which they are conducted, are influenced by a host of factors.

Do you believe that the police have too much power with regard to investigating crimes, or should we grant them additional powers, for instance with regard to searching and arresting suspects?

Police officers control entry into the criminal justice system because they make stops and arrests that set in motion what can be a long series of steps for defendants. Entry into the criminal justice system can be life changing for anyone. It may signify that an individual will never again be free. It may also generate a series of troubling events that can include loss of employment, costly bills, and a label that will stick with the person forever. Entry into the system begins with the police viewing or responding to a crime, which perhaps prompts further investigation, an arrest, and the formal processing of the accused. This module examines the initial steps of criminal case processing: investigations, arrests, and booking procedures.

The Role of Polygraphs in Investigations

IN THE NEWS

In 2006, David Stodden's wife Mary and his daughter Susanna were shot to death along the Pinnacle Lake Trail in Washington. Twelve years later, in 2018, David took a third polygraph examination as investigators sought to determine if he was responsible for the shootings. The first two examinations in years prior had been deemed inconclusive, and after 3 hours of investigation during the third exam, investigators believed that David was not a suspect in the case (Wilkinson, 2018).

Polygraph examinations, often referred to as "lie detector tests," are one of many tools used by investigators to solve crimes. The tests measure physical reactions (e.g., heartbeat rate) to questions in efforts to detect deception. They are used to both identify and eliminate potential suspects. Their accuracy has been questioned, yet departments still use them, among many other methods, to solve crimes. In this case, David Stodden was eliminated as a potential suspect based on

his performance in a third examination. Do you believe polygraph examinations should be used by law enforcement as part of their investigations? What are the potential problems associated with using a deception-based test that is not always 100% accurate?

Investigations

The entertainment media have long depicted heroic, crime-fighting detectives, which has shaped public perceptions of detectives, investigations, and detective work in general. Many large police departments have specialized investigation divisions that focus on specific crimes, such as homicide or sex offenses. Other large departments and most small departments have investigative units staffed by investigators who are considered generalists and investigate all types of offenses. Nationally, 10%–15% of a police department's sworn personnel (or individuals who have taken an oath to uphold the law and have arrest and firearm authority) are located in a detective unit (Gaines & Kappeler, 2011). In addition to investigators and detectives, police officers also conduct investigations, and their work as first responders to crime scenes is vital to the likelihood of making an arrest.

There is no single way to investigate crimes, and the organization and structure of investigative units within police departments vary according to multiple factors. Each investigation provides new challenges that require creativity, diligence, and organizational skills on behalf of police officers and detectives.

2
Investigation

● **Learning Objective 18.1:** Specify the factors that influence decisions to investigate a potential crime.

Who Investigates

2
Investigation

Patrol officers sometimes conduct investigations, although the bulk of their investigative work occurs primarily after initially responding to a reported or observed crime. Responding officers conduct a preliminary investigation, primarily through interviewing witnesses, victims, and suspects. If no arrest is made, the information culled at this stage is used as the basis for more elaborate investigations conducted by detectives or investigators. Patrol officers may also investigate crimes during their downtime, or when they are not responding to calls for service. Less serious crimes, such as traffic offenses, are more likely to be investigated by patrol officers, while more serious crimes, such as rapes or murders, will likely be investigated by detectives.

Investigators are assisted by various groups, including:

- forensic scientists,
- crime scene units,
- lab technicians,
- victims,
- witnesses,
- the general public—citizen input is the most significant factor in solving crimes,
- the media, and
- state-level investigative agencies, in instances of high-profile, serious cases, or if local departments lack resources.

The Decision to Investigate

2
Investigation

Investigations vary in length and in whether they are reactive or proactive. The extent to which a crime is investigated and the nature of the investigation are often largely influenced by the type of crime and the available resources. Departments and investigative units, particularly those in large cities, may lack the resources to thoroughly investigate each crime. Accordingly, they typically prioritize cases and devote investigative resources based on offense seriousness and other factors.

Research on detective decision-making with regard to the attention they devote to cases found that the status of the victim, the status of the accused, and media publicity impacted the extent to which a case received attention. For instance, cases involving a victim with a high socioeconomic status or extensive media coverage received more attention from detectives than did cases in which the victim had a low socioeconomic status or there was not extensive media coverage of the case (Corsianos, 2003). Ultimately, investigators consider whether their efforts will result in enough evidence to build a case and bring charges against a suspect or suspects.

Investigative Tools

Detectives use various tools to help them solve crimes. Among the most important are communications skills, which are crucial to interviewing and interrogations. However, investigators also rely on other methods of information gathering, including surveillance, police lineups, informants, decoy units, sting operations, and polygraph tests.

● **Learning Objective 18.2:** Describe the tools used during investigations.

Communication Skills

Communication skills are very important for detectives, primarily because they rely so heavily on gathering information from others during interviews and interrogations. **Interviewing** is used to gather information from individuals who are familiar with a case, such as first responders and witnesses. **Interrogations** are used with suspects or persons of interest in a case and to test information and hopefully obtain a confession and conviction. A primary difference between interrogations and interviews is the need to inform individuals of their due process rights, including the issuance of Miranda warnings with regard to interrogations. These warnings are not necessary when conducting interviews because the individual being questioned is not under arrest. Aside from the need to effectively communicate, investigators and detectives must have strong research and analytical abilities and skills.

Surveillance

Surveillance entails observing suspects to gain information and can be used in three manners: fixed (e.g., by staying in one location), moving (e.g., through following a suspect), or electronic (e.g., through the use of wiretaps and other audiovisual devices) (Lyman, 2010). Law enforcement agencies use many tools in their surveillance efforts, including:

- radars;
- surveillance vans equipped with video recorders, night-vision devices, periscopes, radios, and scanners;
- unmanned aerial vehicles;
- **vehicle tracking systems**, which enable investigators to track vehicles using devices placed on a suspect's vehicle and global positioning systems; and
- closed-circuit television systems, which were particularly helpful in identifying the perpetrators of the 2013 Boston Marathon bombing. See Module 19 for further discussion of surveillance.

Police Lineups

Police lineups are often used when an eyewitness may be able to identify a suspect. Lineups typically involve the eyewitness being asked to identify the suspect from viewing either photographs (which may be used when a suspect is not yet in custody) or four to six individuals lined up along a wall at the police station. Lineups have been criticized on various grounds, including the potential for administrators to influence eyewitnesses (Clark et al., 2013). In a study of the influences of informed administrators and police lineups, researchers found that the target photo was over twice as likely to be selected when the lineup was administered by an administrator who was aware of who the suspect was compared to administrators who were unaware (Canter et al., 2013).

One approach to combat consciously or subconsciously influencing an eyewitness is to make the lineup double-blind, so that the police personnel conducting the lineup are unaware of the suspect's identity. An alternative to the lineup approach is to show suspects to an eyewitness individually, instead of in a group, to reduce the likelihood of the eyewitness choosing the individual who most closely resembles the suspect.

Informants

Investigators sometimes use informants to help build and solve cases. **Informants** are individuals who provide information in expectation of some benefit or reward

interviewing
The practice of gathering information through questioning individuals who are familiar with a case; those being questioned do not need to be informed of their rights

interrogations
The practice of questioning suspects or persons of interest in a case to test information and hopefully obtain a confession and conviction; those being questioned must be informed of their rights

2
Investigation

surveillance An investigative technique in which suspects are observed to gain information and can be used in three manners: fixed, moving, or electronic

Police lineups assist with investigations because they provide witnesses with the opportunity to identify suspects. Lineups have been criticized because of the potential for administrators to persuade witnesses. Several steps have been taken to address this limitation.

Do you believe witnesses too often select the individual in the lineup who "most closely" resembles the suspect or the individual who undoubtedly looks like the suspect? What could be done to improve the effectiveness of police lineups?

2
Investigation

vehicle tracking systems An investigative technique in which investigators track vehicles using devices placed on a suspect's vehicle and global positioning systems

from police or prosecutors. Informants may be rewarded for their input through money or a reduced sentence or penalty for their cooperation. Ethical and credibility issues are sometimes concerns when using informants, for instance because reducing an informant's penalty on a criminal charge in exchange for information arguably minimizes the likelihood of justice in response to the informant's criminal behavior. Further, informants may provide law enforcement authorities with inaccurate information, and informants may be at risk of retaliation if their identity is exposed.

Decoy Units and Sting Operations

Decoy units are used in criminal investigations to provide opportunities for individuals to engage in criminal acts. Either the undercover officers or officers located nearby respond to the crime if and when it occurs. The units essentially involve officers placing themselves in vulnerable positions in efforts to attract criminals. For instance, undercover officers may pose as prostitutes in efforts to arrest individuals who seek their services. Such tactics are similar to **sting operations**, in which officers pose as criminals with the intent to gain access to offenders. For example, in Minnesota in 2018, three men were arrested for several felonies, including solicitation of a child through electronic communication, following a sex sting operation in which an officer posed as a 15-year-old female. The men were arrested when they arrived to meet a person they believed was a young girl (Ebel, 2018). Both decoy units and sting operations involve officers going undercover with the goal of gathering information and attracting and identifying criminals.

1 Criminal Act

police lineups A method of investigation in which an eyewitness is asked if they can identify a suspect from either photographs or individuals lined up along a wall at the police station

Polygraph Tests

Polygraph tests measure an individual's physiological reactions to questions. They are used to detect deception, clear suspects, locate evidence, and confirm statements. The use of polygraphs in court has been questioned, and not all states permit their use. For instance, the U.S. Supreme Court noted that there was no consensus that polygraph testing is reliable (*United States v. Scheffer*, 1998). Nevertheless, polygraph testing can be useful in some investigations and under some circumstances. In 2014, one of the most notorious murder cases in Oklahoma was solved through the assistance of a polygraph. Prior to taking the polygraph, the offender in the case was not much of a suspect. The man agreed to take the polygraph exam, however, and results from the evaluation led officials to find remains of a body from a murder

2
Investigation

victim and shell cases at the land owned by the offender's father. The man was found guilty of murdering three people between 2008 and 2011 (Lowry, 2014).

CAREERS

Polygraph specialists examine individuals to discern truthful and false responses. They are licensed and trained to administer polygraph exams to witnesses, suspects, and others involved in criminal cases. Polygraph examiners must be certified through the American Polygraph Association after taking courses at an accredited school and passing a state-administered exam.

Choosing to Arrest

Arrest is a suspect's formal entry into the criminal justice system. It is the first of a series of steps that may ultimately result in some penalty. Hence, careful consideration is required before making an arrest. Depriving an individual of their freedom requires that officers act in strict accordance with the law. Arrests do not mean that an individual is guilty, because arrestees are innocent until proven guilty. And not all arrests are justifiable (e.g., there may have been insufficient evidence

> **MYTHBUSTING**
>
> ## Investigators Rely on Science to Solve Most Crimes
>
> Scientific advancements, such as DNA and fingerprint analyses, have greatly assisted investigations, and policing in general. Popular television programs like *CSI* have contributed to the widespread belief that such scientific procedures are used to solve most crimes. However, actual police investigations continue to rely primarily on the accounts of victims and witnesses (Cordner, 2013).

for an arrest). Arrests are warranted only when there is probable cause to believe a crime was committed and the individual accused was responsible. The decision to arrest can be challenging, because the facts of each case are not always clearly evident to police officers.

Legal Requirements for Making an Arrest

The law requires that officers establish probable cause to make an arrest, and from a procedural standpoint, officers should document the circumstances of the crime and the arrest. As discussed in Module 17, probable cause is the standard of proof required in four particularly important aspects of police work: arrests with a warrant, arrests without a warrant, searches and seizures of property with a warrant, and searches and seizures of property without a warrant. The courts have ruled that probable cause may be based on an officer's observation of misconduct, the expertise of officers, circumstantial factors, and information brought to the attention of officers.

The police must also keep in mind the need to gather and secure evidence, with the goal of building a case against the suspect. Failing to abide by the law may result in any evidence seized being inadmissible in court, and wrongful arrests may result in civil litigation filed against the officer or the officer's department.

Arrest statistics do not reflect the level of crime in the United States because most crimes are not reported to the police, and arrests are not made in every case that is reported. The likelihood of an arrest in a case is based on a number of factors, including the seriousness of the crime. For instance, violent crimes are more likely than property crimes to result in an arrest because these cases warrant greater investigative attention, and victims are more likely to report the crime and be able to identify a suspect.

The police also have the option to issue **field citations**, more commonly known as "tickets," which require a person to appear in court on a specific day and time to answer charges. Field citations are most commonly associated with driving violations; however, they are also sometimes used in lieu of custodial arrests for nonviolent offenses when the accused seemingly poses no risk of harm to the community.

Factors That Influence an Officer's Decision to Arrest

While many criminal justice professionals exercise discretion in their work, the police in particular do so when deciding whether to make an arrest. Factors that influence an officer's decision fall into three categories: situational, personal, and environmental (Figure 18.1).

1. *Situational factors*: Situational factors have received the bulk of research attention with regard to police–citizen encounters and include the characteristics of the interactions between suspects and the police. Among the more commonly

● **Learning Objective 18.3:** Categorize the factors that influence decisions to arrest.

3 Arrest

informants
Individuals who provide information in expectation of some benefit or reward from police or prosecutors; they may be rewarded for their input through money or a reduced sentence or penalty for their cooperation

decoy units Police units used in criminal investigations to provide opportunities for individuals to engage in criminal acts; either the undercover officers or officers located nearby respond to the crime if and when it occurs

sting operations An investigative technique in which officers pose as criminals with the intent to gain access to offenders

polygraph examinations Tests that measure one's heart rate, blood pressure, breathing rate, and perspiration in response to a series of questions and statements; the goals of the examination are to ensure accuracy of the information and note any psychological irregularities

3 Arrest

field citations More commonly known as "tickets," they are citations that require a person to appear in court on a specific time and day to answer charges

letter of the law Typically associated with officer responses to more serious offenses, it refers to officers having limited discretion and being more likely to enforce the law

spirit of the law Typically associated with officer responses to less serious offenses, it refers to officers having much more discretion and being more likely to act in a less punitive manner

cited situational factors influencing officers' decisions to arrest is the seriousness of the offense; for instance, violent crimes are more likely to warrant an arrest than property crimes (Burns, 2013; Dempsey & Forst, 2014). Officers responding to more serious offenses (e.g., violent crimes) act under the **letter of the law**, in which they have limited discretion and are more likely to act in a punitive manner. Officers encountering less serious crimes (e.g., property offenses or minor domestic disputes) may act under the **spirit of the law**, in which they have more discretion and may act in a less punitive manner (Burns, 2013). Other situational factors include whether an officer personally viewed the crime, the presence of police backup, and whether a weapon was used in the crime.

2. *Personal factors (characteristics of the arresting officer and the suspect)*: Although they do not appear to be particularly strong predictors of police behavior (e.g., Riksheim & Chermak, 1993), officer characteristics that may influence arrest decisions include demographics (e.g., age, race/ethnicity, gender, socioeconomic status), attitudes, and years of experience. For instance, researchers found that an officer's gender has little impact on the decision to make an arrest (Novak et al., 2011). Suspect characteristics, including race, age, gender, demeanor, socioeconomic status, and other variables, also appear to be related to

Situational Factors
(e.g., backup, seriousness of offense, weapons, crime committed in presence of officer)

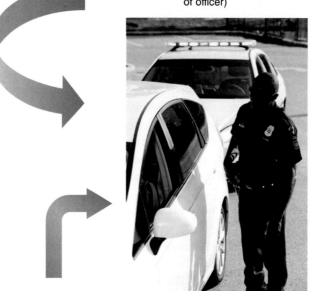

Personal Factors
(e.g., race, class, ethnicity, age, gender, demeanor)

Environmental Factors
(e.g., crime rate, socioeconomic factors, publicity)

FIGURE 18.1. The Decision to Arrest. Situational, personal, and environmental factors all play a role in an officer's decision to arrest. Some factors are more powerful than others, and each arrest situation is unique. Primary among the considerations to make an arrest are the seriousness of the offense and the evidence to suggest an arrest is warranted.

Which of the three categories of factors affecting an officer's decision to arrest is the most powerful? Which one do you believe is least powerful? Why?

officer decisions to arrest. For instance, researchers estimated the effect of race on police decisions to arrest and found with strong consistency that minority suspects were more likely to be arrested than White suspects (Kochel et al., 2011).

3. *Environmental factors*: Environmental factors involve variables that extend beyond the immediate area of an arrest. Among the more prominent environmental factors that influence police decisions to arrest are the neighborhood's crime rate and socioeconomic level, community pressure to make an arrest, and the publicity surrounding a case. Research regularly finds that arrest rates are higher in lower socioeconomic areas than in other areas, and police generally act more punitively toward individuals in the lower socioeconomic strata (L. W. Brooks, 2010).

3 Arrest

The use of force is sometimes required during an arrest, because officers may need to use handcuffs/restraints, weapons, or tactics to control a suspect. Decisions to use force during an arrest situation are influenced by many of the same variables that affect decisions to make an arrest. Officers are generally permitted to use only the amount of force necessary to subdue a suspect during an arrest (police use of force is more fully discussed in Module 15).

Booking

Suspects are booked and charged with a crime after being arrested. Booking is usually completed prior to the arrestee's initial appearance in court; however, it may occur after the initial appearance. **Booking** is the first step in the disposition of an arrestee and consists of creating an administrative record of the accused.

5 Initial Appearance

4 Booking

Processing

Sometimes referred to as "processing," booking primarily involves officers:

- collecting a suspect's personal information, including name, date of birth, and physical characteristics;
- recording information about the suspect's alleged crime;
- conducting a criminal background check;
- collecting DNA samples and fingerprinting, photographing, and searching the suspect;
- confiscating any personal property held by the suspect (the property is returned upon release); and
- placing the suspect in a police station holding cell or local jail.

booking Also known as processing; it involves making or updating an administrative record of an arrestee

One of the more controversial aspects of the booking process involves the collection of DNA samples. The collection of a DNA sample helps law enforcement identify suspects and offenders, in part because it is stored in databases that can be easily accessed. The concern is that doing so is considered by some to be an infringement on privacy to a much greater extent than fingerprinting or other forms of information that are collected (e.g., photos). An individual's DNA can reveal much more about a person, including their proneness to disease or illness. In a controversial 2013 decision, the U.S. Supreme Court ruled that arrestees being detained for a serious offense may have to submit to a cheek swab of their DNA (*Maryland v. King*, 2013) and that doing so is reasonable per the Fourth Amendment, which generally protects against illegal searches and seizures.

● **Learning Objective 18.4:** Summarize the booking process.

4 Booking

10
Corrections

5 Initial
Appearance

holding facilities
Detention facilities similar
to jails, although they
generally do not hold
individuals who have been
sentenced; they temporar-
ily hold arrestees who are
awaiting court hearings

4 Booking

Dealing With Uncooperative Suspects

Officers sometimes face resistance from a suspect during booking. The formal entrance into the criminal justice system can be stressful, and some arrestees act in
an irrational and even violent manner. Thus, officers sometimes use restraints or
seek additional assistance when dealing with uncooperative suspects. For example,
in 2018 a woman arrested in Cleveland, Ohio, for driving while intoxicated became
combative during the booking process. The woman stabbed herself with an ink pen
and tried to bite an officer. She was restrained by officers and taken to a local hospital for evaluation (Cleveland, 2018). Most bookings, however, do not involve suspect
resistance.

Detaining Suspects

Not all arrestees are booked and detained. For instance, the booking process for simple offenses merely includes gathering the name of the arrestee; the name of the arresting officer; the date, time, and location of arrest; and the circumstances of the
arrest. Individuals arrested for minor offenses in some jurisdictions are permitted
to post a predetermined amount of bail, or they are released with a citation requiring them to appear in court at a later date, much like a traffic citation. Juveniles who
are arrested are referred to the juvenile justice system. Further, if additional evidence
emerges that refutes the probable cause belief on which an arrest was made, the arrestee is released.

Arrestees detained following an arrest are held in a holding cell or lockup, which
are typically located in police departments or precinct houses. **Holding facilities** are
similar to jails, although they generally do not hold individuals who have been sentenced. These facilities temporarily hold arrestees who are awaiting court hearings,
including their initial appearance before a judge.

Detention officers are responsible for keeping arrestees safe in custody until they
appear before a judge. Officers use restraints (e.g., handcuffs), holding cells, jails, or
any other means to prevent individuals from escaping. They consider several factors
in assessing the extent to which an arrestee should be restrained, including the arrestee's prior record, the officer's perception of the potential for the arrestee to resist and cause harm to the officer(s) or others, and the current offense. In ensuring
the arrestee's health and safety, booking and detention officers must obtain medical
assistance for arrestees as needed. They must also consider the potential for harm
or violence upon placing certain individuals in the same holding cell (e.g., rival gang
members).

Of particular concern during the booking process is to determine if the arrestee
is in danger of committing suicide while detained. In 2015, Sandra Bland was found
hanged in her cell after being arrested in Texas. Following Bland's death and similar deaths in Texas, the Texas Commission on Jail Standards changed its jail intake
form, which previously relied on inmates to self-report whether they were at risk of
suicide. The revised form includes questions asked by jailers and is designed to elicit
information that could be used to better determine if someone is at risk.

The System in Perspective

The "In the News" feature at the beginning of this module highlighted the role of
polygraphs in criminal investigations. Many people believe that polygraphs, also
known as lie detectors, are very effective tools for catching criminals. Their use, however, is somewhat limited and questionable, given concerns about their reliability in

measuring deception. Fortunately, investigators have multiple tools at their disposal to solve crimes. Effective, successful investigations are vital for effective policing, as well as ensuring that justice will be served. The power to arrest distinguishes policing from other occupations, and reflects the importance of discretion in police work. Upon being arrested, the accused is booked and will soon enter the courts.

Summary

1. **Learning Objective 18.1:** *Specify the factors that influence decisions to investigate a potential crime.*

   - Decisions to investigate crimes are often based on available resources, the level of publicity surrounding a case, the seriousness of the offense, the presence and extent of accessible evidence, the credible identification of a perpetrator, and sometimes the socioeconomic levels of victims.

2. **Learning Objective 18.2:** *Describe the tools used during investigations.*

   - The many tools and tactics used during criminal investigations include communication skills, surveillance, police lineups, photo lineups, informants, decoys, sting operations, and polygraph testing.

3. **Learning Objective 18.3:** *Categorize the factors that influence decisions to arrest.*

   - The factors that influence an officer's decision to make an arrest have been categorized

into situational factors (e.g., the seriousness of the offense, whether an officer personally viewed the crime, the presence of police backup, whether a weapon was used in the crime); personal characteristics of the officer and suspect (e.g., demographic variables, years of service, suspect demeanor); and environmental factors (e.g., a neighborhood's crime rate and socioeconomic level, community pressure to make an arrest, and the publicity surrounding a case).

4. **Learning Objective 18.4:** *Summarize the booking process.*

   - The booking process primarily involves collecting an arrestee's personal information; recording information about their alleged crime; conducting a criminal background check; fingerprinting, photographing, and searching the arrestee; confiscating the arrestee's personal property; and placing the arrestee in a holding cell or local jail.

Questions for Critical Thinking

1. What factors do you believe are most influential regarding the decision to investigate a crime? Which factors do you believe should be most influential? Which should be least influential? Explain your reasoning.

2. Which investigative tools do you believe are most important for solving violent crimes? Would the same tools be as effective in solving crimes involving drug trafficking? Explain your answer.

3. Identify one factor within each of the following categories that you believe is most influential in the decision to arrest. Justify your choices.

- officer characteristics
- suspect characteristics
- situational factors
- environmental factors

4. What would be the pros and cons of using the following groups to provide booking services for all arrestees?

- police or sheriff's departments
- corrections officials
- a specific agency created to provide booking services

Key Terms

decoy units
field citations
holding facilities
informants
interrogations
interviewing

letter of the law
police lineups
spirit of the law
sting operations
surveillance
vehicle tracking systems

For digital learning resources, please go to
https://www.oup.com/he/burns1e

The Future of Policing

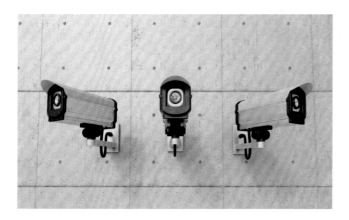

Closed-circuit cameras assist the police in many ways, for example by providing greater levels of monitoring of behaviors in public places. Their use has been criticized as being too intrusive into our lives.

Do you believe the cameras infringe on our privacy?

There is much uncertainty with regard to what the future holds; however, society continues to believe that the police should provide effective protection and services. Police departments are constantly challenged in their attempts to keep pace with social changes, and the most effective departments of the future are likely the ones that are already planning for what is ahead. This module addresses several important issues that are expected to influence the future of law enforcement, including technological innovations, immigration and demographic changes, economic issues, and concerns for drugs and international crime.

MODULE OUTLINE

- **Technology**

  Learning Objective 19.1: Characterize the technological advancements that have assisted law enforcement.

- **Immigration and Demographic Changes**

  Learning Objective 19.2: Illustrate how demographic changes and immigration influence policing.

- **Economics**

  Learning Objective 19.3: Identify the economic factors that affect policing.

- **Drugs and International Crime**

  Learning Objective 19.4: Explain the impact of drugs and international crime on police practices.

IN THE
NEWS

Drones, Underage Drinking, and Policing in the Future

3 Arrest

South Padre Island, Texas, is a major spring break destination for college students. The city has fewer than 3,000 permanent residents, although as many as 75,000 college students visit the barrier-island town each spring. The local police department prepares months in advance for the influx of students, including

arrests for public intoxication during the 11 prior months of the year was 294.

In 2016, to prepare for the spring breakers, the police purchased two drones and have continued to use them and other technology to best prevent and respond to crime. The drones are equipped with high-resolution cameras that enable officials to monitor the behaviors of the crowds from above (Holley, 2016). Other departments around the country are also using drones to monitor behavior. Police officials cite the utility of drones in providing a safe environment; however, others claim the drones violate one's right to privacy and provide an obvious example of the police becoming too intrusive into our lives.

The use of drones by the police is one example of how technology is changing police work. Who would have believed in 1950 that law enforcement agencies in the early 21st century would be capable of patrolling in unmanned aircraft or that police cars would be equipped with computers? Picture police officers in the year 2050. What do they look like? What are their primary functions, and how do they perform those functions? Are they still called police officers? Now, picture police officers in the year 2100 and ask yourself the same questions.

1 Criminal Act

the associated problems. As an example, in March 2015 the police arrested 270 people for public intoxication. The combined number of

Technology

There is little doubt that technology has and will continue to assist and challenge policing. Technology has become increasingly used as a crime-fighting tool, as well as a means to commit innovative crimes. Technology helps law enforcement agencies in many ways. For instance, it is used for:

● **Learning Objective 19.1:** Characterize the technological advancements that have assisted law enforcement.

- records management,
- investigations,
- personnel records management,
- sharing information,
- dispatch,
- booking,
- managing patrol,
- allocating resources,

- scanning license plates and driver's licenses, and
- accessing information from various databases.

Many departments still employ out-of-date technology. But the agencies that have upgraded their systems have been much more effective in terms of ensuring public safety (Daly, 2013). The future of law enforcement will likely be influenced by the various existing forms of technology, including mobile digital terminals, crime mapping, predictive policing, computer-assisted training, management information systems, surveillance, video recording, digital photography, cell phones, and robotics, as well as new technology.

CAREERS

Dispatchers receive and share (dispatch) emergency and routine calls to patrol units. They also perform record checks and maintain computerized and written reports. They often instruct callers on how to respond to situations while awaiting emergency response personnel.

Mobile Digital Terminals

Mobile digital terminals and laptop computers permit officers to communicate with dispatchers and others via electronic transmission. Mobile digital terminals are basically high-powered laptops that are mounted and wired into a police car and allow officers to obtain necessary information in the field. These terminals and laptops enable officers to communicate with dispatchers via a keyboard and computer, instead of a voice system (e.g., radio), and are particularly helpful for officers who wish to check license plates, driving records, criminal records, vehicle registrations, and driver's licenses. About 90% of local police officers were employed by a department that provided in-field computerized access to vehicle and driving records in 2013 (Reaves, 2015a). Figure 19.1 identifies the percentage of local police officers

mobile digital terminals High-powered laptops that are mounted and wired into a police car that allow officers to obtain necessary information in the field

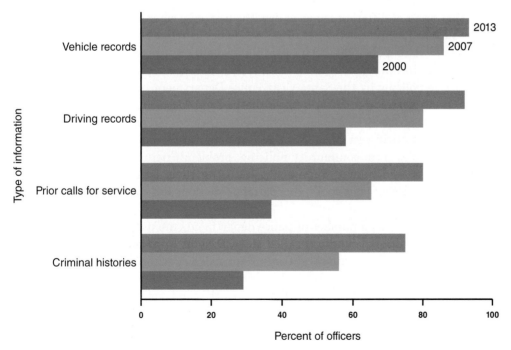

FIGURE 19.1. Percentage of Officers With In-Field Computer Access to Information. There has been a substantial increase in the percentage of officers with computer access to information since 2000. In addition, the quality and extent of the data have improved. **Source:** *Reaves, B. A. (2015b). Local police departments, 2013: Equipment and technology (NCJ 2,48,767). U.S. Department of Justice, Bureau of Justice Statistics July 2015, NCJ 248767*

Are you concerned that law enforcement agencies may have access to too much information, including personal histories?

in 2000, 2007, and 2013 who were employed by a department that provided in-field computer access to information.

Crime Mapping

Crime analysts historically used simplified maps to assess crime in their jurisdictions. The practice of pin-mapping crimes has been replaced in many departments by technology-driven geospatial crime-prevention programs. Computerized crime mapping via Geographic Information Systems applications enables researchers to analyze multiple layers of data to identify relationships between times, trends, officer shifts, locations, and other factors. Crime mapping assists with crime prevention and control because it can be used to:

- map calls for service,
- assess resource allocation,
- assist with community-oriented and problem-oriented policing practices, and
- inform patrol officers with regard to crime patterns.

The technology also facilitates community policing practices. For example, the Clearwater Police Department, in Florida, works with a private company to regularly post a crime map that depicts crime in the city, alerts residents to crimes in their area, and encourages citizens to assist in solving crimes (Lonon, 2016). The use of crime mapping in policing is expected to grow in the future (Reaves, 2010).

Predictive Policing

predictive policing
An approach to policing that incorporates software that uses algorithms to anticipate the time, location, and suspects involved in a crime

Some departments engage in **predictive policing**, which incorporates software that uses algorithms to anticipate the time, location, and suspects involved in a crime. This approach relies on the compilation and analysis of information in identifying hotspots and predicting when a crime will occur. The analyses consider the types of crime that occur at different times of day, the locations where the crimes occur, and factors such as juveniles being out of school (which is related to increases in crime). Based on the data, police can better speculate where their resources will be needed. This approach has provided positive results; for instance, a study involving the use of predictive policing by the Santa Cruz Police Department in California noted decreases in burglaries and motor vehicle thefts. *Time Magazine* identified predictive policing as one of the 50 best inventions for 2011 (Friend, 2013).

Predictive policing enables police departments to be more proactive. It incorporates principles from community policing, problem-oriented policing, evidence-based policing, and related approaches by using tools and techniques such as mapping and analyzing hot spots, geospatial prediction, and social network analysis (Pearsall, 2010).

Data-Driven Approaches to Crime and Traffic Safety Initiatives to merge crime and traffic data to lower crime rates and traffic accident violations with limited or no additional funding

Relatedly, a growing number of police departments are using an initiative (with limited or no additional funding) called **Data-Driven Approaches to Crime and Traffic Safety** to merge crime and traffic data to lower crime rates and traffic accident violations. The data are analyzed by geomapping and help determine hot spots where crime and accidents occur, which guides the deployment of police resources (Kerrigan, 2011).

computer-assisted instruction
Also known as computer-based training, it enables police personnel to undergo training via computers that also provide evaluation

Computer-Assisted Training

Training and evaluation have been and will continue to be influenced by technology. **Computer-assisted instruction**, or computer-based training, enables police personnel to undergo training via computers that also provide evaluation. The use of computers to create simulated, virtual scenarios in which officers engage in seemingly real-life situations has enhanced training practices. Officers may use training programs that assess their decision-making abilities with regard to shoot/no-shoot situations, or they may safely hone their driving skills in police-pursuit driving simulators. The use of computer-assisted instruction also reduces the need for personnel to conduct training sessions and makes training more convenient for officers, who can train at a convenient location and at their own pace.

Management Information Systems

Many police administrative functions are also now performed through computers and related technologies. Management information systems, or record management systems, have reduced the amount of time and resources needed to conduct many administrative functions within police agencies. Such programs enable police officials to effectively and efficiently coordinate and disseminate information pertaining to the following:

- personnel
- case tracking
- evidence and property
- detention
- booking
- officer reports
- finances
- equipment

Storing information in these programs reduces the need for bulky paperwork, enables easy access to the information, and facilitates advanced statistical analyses of the information.

Surveillance

Police surveillance efforts have increasingly relied on technological advancements. Investigators building a case or seeking arrests use advanced listening, recording, and viewing devices, among other tools, to conduct surveillance operations. Surveillance efforts have been enhanced through the increased use of vehicles equipped with video recorders, periscopes, radios, scanners, and other items (see Module 18) (Gray, 2013). Recent developments in the area include radars that permit law enforcement personnel to see through walls via the use of radio waves that detect movement from over 50 feet away.

2
Investigation

THERMAL IMAGING AND NIGHT-VISION DEVICES

Thermal imaging and night-vision devices enable officers or investigators to view the behavior of suspects in the dark. Advanced flashlights and lighting apparatus in general facilitate police work, for instance to heavily illuminate crime scenes in remote locations. In addition, high-technology flashlights better enable officers to detect pieces of evidence (e.g., body fluids and hair) (Schultz, 2008). Aside from the increased levels of brightness advanced technology has brought to policing, some jurisdictions are using passive alcohol sensors attached to flashlights to assist officers in detecting alcohol on motorists' breath.

Some departments have equipped officers with flashlights that also serve as passive alcohol testers. With this device, officers can detect alcohol on a person's breath or in the air from up to 10 inches away, with or without the suspect's cooperation. Upon the detection of alcohol, officers would then conduct more thorough tests for the presence of alcohol, as prescribed by law.

What potential benefits and limitations do you see with regard to police using this type of device?

unmanned aerial vehicles Also known as drones, they are unmanned aircraft increasingly used for various law enforcement purposes

UNMANNED AERIAL VEHICLES AND TETHERED BALLOONS

Unmanned aerial vehicles, or drones, are increasingly being used to map crime scenes, control traffic, and protect the U.S. border (Crank et al., 2010). They may also be used to assist in SWAT team operations, tracking fugitives, and locating missing persons. The drones are controlled by a laptop computer and contain a powerful camera that can be aimed at and zoomed in on particular locations. They may have infrared heat-seeking devices and can be equipped with less-lethal systems such as Tasers, a bean bag gun, or a stun baton.

Similar to drones are surveillance balloons, which are being used by the U.S. Border Patrol along some portions of the U.S.–Mexico border. The tethered balloons fly up to 55 feet in the air and carry cameras that can zoom in on a license plate. The balloons are being used to address human smuggling, drug trafficking, and illegal immigration. Despite their many proposed benefits, the use of drones has been criticized as being too invasive (Sorcher, 2013).

1 Criminal Act

VEHICLE TRACKING SYSTEMS AND CLOSED-CIRCUIT TELEVISION

Surveillance practices may also involve the use of vehicle-tracking systems, which require the placement of a transmitter for tracking purposes on a suspect's vehicle. The transmitter then sends a signal that enables law enforcement to identify the location of the vehicle. Global positioning systems have largely enhanced vehicle tracking practices. Further, closed-circuit television systems and security cameras enhance surveillance practices. Cities across the United States have incorporated cameras at busy traffic intersections to identify individuals who run red lights. Closed-circuit television has also been useful in preventing and solving crimes. It was instrumental in the identification of the individuals deemed responsible for the Boston Marathon bombing in 2013. Closed-circuit television is used to monitor human behavior in public areas, and like many other surveillance technologies, it has been both deemed helpful with regard to crime control and condemned as an infringement on privacy.

Video Recording

Police departments have increasingly used video cameras mounted to the dashboard of police patrol cars and on the bodies of officers. The digital evidence in the form of a video recording addresses claims of wrongful police behavior, provides evidence from talkative prisoners, and provides training footage. Lapel cameras have become increasingly popular because they address some of the limitations of video cameras mounted in cars; for instance, in-car cameras can only record in the direction in which they are set up. Body cameras follow an officer wherever they go. An estimated 89% of local police departments used some type of video camera technology in 2013 (Reaves, 2015b), including the types of technologies depicted in Table 19.1.

Digital Photography

Digital photography provides images of crime scenes, mug shots, photos of wanted persons, photo lineups, and age-progression photographs that help identify missing persons. These photos have greatly assisted searches for wanted suspects, because police personnel can alter photographs to better visualize what a suspect may look like in the years ahead and after alterations to their appearance. Digital photographs of wanted persons or vehicles can also be easily distributed to officers in patrol cars and the general public.

Cell Phones

Cell phones are another form of technology used by the police. The popularity and functionality of cell phones in the early 21st century have contributed to many

TABLE 19.1. Use of Selected Video Technologies by Local Police Departments

TYPES USED BY PATROL OFFICERS

POPULATION SERVED	ANY TYPE (%)	IN-CAR VIDEO CAMERAS (%)	BODY-WORN CAMERAS (%)	WEAPON-ATTACHED CAMERAS (%)	OTHER TYPES OF CAMERAS FOR SURVEILLANCE OF PUBLIC AREAS (%)
All sizes	76	68	32	6	49
1,000,000 or more	71	57	21	14	86
500,000–999,999	80	73	30	7	87
250,000–499,999	70	63	20	9	87
100,000–249,999	75	70	19	10	76
50,000–99,999	70	63	26	11	68
25,000–49,999	79	76	22	9	67
10,000–24,999	75	71	26	9	62
2,500–9,999	80	71	34	8	51
2,499 or fewer	72	64	35	3	35

*Note. Use of selected video technologies by local police departments, by size of population served, 2013. **Source:** Law Enforcement Management and Administrative Statistics (LEMAS) Survey, U.S. Department of Justice, Office of Justice Programs, Bureau of Justice Statistics, July 2015, NCJ 248767*

people owning and using them on a regular basis. The Pew Research Center reported in 2019 that 96% of Americans owned phones, including 81% who owned smart phones (Pew Research Center, 2019). What many people fail or forget to realize is that their phone is a tracking device that provides information about day-to-day activities. Law enforcement has increasingly taken advantage of the popularity of cell phones and the data they contain to investigate crimes. Concerns abound, however, about the invasion of privacy (see Module 7).

Robotics

Robotics involves using robotic devices to perform functions traditionally performed by humans. Such devices are often used in cases involving bombs or situations in which it is believed that explosives may be involved. Robots can search potentially dangerous areas, conduct x-rays, and deliver items to suspects who do not wish to interact with law enforcement officials. For instance, robotics could be used to deliver a cell phone to a hostage taker who does not wish to directly confront the police. Technology in this area has expanded rapidly, and robots have become increasingly agile and functional.

robotics The use of robotic devices to perform functions traditionally performed by humans

New Technological Advancements

Many other technological advancements will influence the future of policing, including:

- lasers that enable officers to detect the chemical composition of substances in a short period of time,
- more effective language translators,
- advanced cameras for K-9 units, and
- more advanced automatic license plate recognition devices (Schultz, 2008).

TABLE 19.2. Use of Gunshot Detection Systems by Local Police Departments

POPULATION SERVED	PERCENTAGE
All sizes	4
1,000,000 or more	50
500,000–999,999	30
250,000–499,999	28
100,000–249,999	11
50,000–99,999	12
25,000–49,999	6
10,000–24,999	5
2,500–9,999	6
2,499 or fewer	1

Source: From Law Enforcement Management and Administrative Statistics (LEMAS) Survey, *by Bureau of Justice Statistics, 2013; and* Local Police Departments, 2013: Equipment and Technology *(NCJ 248767), by B. A. Reaves, 2015, U.S. Department of Justice, Bureau of Justice Statistics.*

Police departments and researchers are also:

- testing the usefulness of devices that emit directional intense sounds that could stun suspects, enabling police to more peacefully subdue noncooperative suspects;
- developing global positioning system bullets that could be shot onto the vehicles of fleeing suspects to enable remote tracking; and
- using gunfire locator systems, which may also incorporate global positioning system technology, to detect and identify the location of gunfire or other weapon fire through the use of acoustic and/optical sensors. As noted in Table 19.2, large local police departments were most likely to use a gunshot detection system in 2013.

Immigration and Demographic Changes

Police officers have historically been involved with addressing concerns related to illegal immigration, and departments are directly impacted by demographic changes. Concerns regarding undocumented immigrants place police officers in difficult situations, primarily because these individuals may be hesitant to use police services, and they may also be the target of victimization. Anticipated demographic changes in society largely involve increases in racial and ethnic diversity and an aging population.

Immigration

Law enforcement plays a particularly important role with regard to immigration issues, especially in light of concerns for illegal immigration and homeland security. Police officers are caught in the middle of a difficult struggle, as policymakers try to find solutions that suit the various interests in an increasingly diverse United States.

● **Learning Objective 19.2:** Illustrate how demographic changes and immigration influence policing.

Illegal immigration poses significant challenges for many groups, including the police. Undocumented immigrants consume a notable portion of police attention in some jurisdictions in relation to outstanding warrants and gang activity (MacDonald, 2004). They are also particularly vulnerable to criminal victimization and other forms of abuse because they are less likely than others to contact the police for assistance for fear of deportation (e.g., Sampson, 2008).

In 2014, then-president Obama responded to the lack of a clear policy and approach to immigration by proposing to protect roughly 5 million undocumented immigrants from deportation; sending additional Border Patrol agents, judges, and U.S attorneys to border areas; and permitting foreign workers trained in high-tech fields to enter and stay in the United States. Regardless of these and other plans, the police remain largely responsible for identifying and detaining illegal immigrants. However, doing so can be particularly challenging and controversial. For example, legislation in Arizona intended to increase public safety permits officers to stop and question, based on reasonable suspicion, individuals believed to be illegally in the country. The legislation generated support from certain corners but criticism from others. A delegation of police chiefs from cities across the United States assembled by the Police Executive Research Forum noted that the legislation makes their job more difficult, because it:

- contributes to more crime,
- hampers relations between police and immigrant communities,
- intimidates illegal immigrants who may be crime victims or witnesses, and
- diverts policing efforts from more serious crimes to identifying, arresting, and processing undocumented immigrants (Hsu, 2010).

The 2016 election of Donald Trump as president of the United States generated additional discussion on immigration, given Trump's stance toward immigration during his presidential campaign. Trump announced that he would curtail illegal immigration by constructing a wall to separate the United States from Mexico and encourage and support the use of advanced technological devices to catch those seeking to illegally cross the border. He also proposed the mass deportation of illegal immigrants currently residing in the United States. In so doing, he proposed to revoke former president Barack Obama's earlier actions to protect undocumented immigrants who came to the United States as children.

President Donald Trump's tough stand on immigration had notable impacts during his years in office. In particular, illegal immigration into the United States slowed by roughly 40% during his first month in office. Further, arrests of illegal aliens increased (Frum, 2017). Joe Biden became president in 2021 and has proposed to soften many of the tough stances taken by the Trump administration with regard to immigration issues.

MYTHBUSTING

Increases in Immigration Lead to Increases in Crime

There is a long-standing belief in the United States that increases in immigration will lead to increases in crime. The belief is based on perceptions that immigrants will bring criminal tendencies from their country, resulting in higher crime rates. Research, however, suggests the opposite. In particular, areas with higher numbers of immigrants have lower rates of crime, and foreign-born individuals are less likely than U.S.-born individuals to commit crimes (Bersani & Piquero, 2017).

11 Appeal

Police officers and administrators are caught in the debate over illegal immigration in several ways. The status of illegal immigrants warrants police attention, and several municipalities have created additional ordinances targeted toward illegal immigration. For instance, the city of Hazleton, Pennsylvania, earlier passed the Illegal Immigration Relief Act that included fines for landlords who rent to illegal immigrants. An ordinance in Farmers Branch, Texas, also sought to ban landlords from renting property to people who are in the United States unlawfully. A lower court ruled that the Farmers Branch ordinance was unconstitutional, noting that immigration laws should be enforced by the federal government. The ordinance in Hazleton was also denied by the courts and appealed to the U.S. Supreme Court. In both cases, the U.S. Supreme Court declined to review the case, and so the lower court rulings stand.

Demographic Changes

Both legal and illegal immigration contribute to demographic changes, which have effects on policing. All signs point to increased diversity in the United States in the years to come (Lanier & Jockin, 2009). The number of Hispanics is expected to continue growing, which means law enforcement must ensure that Hispanic Americans, as well as members from other underrepresented groups, are better represented among the police ranks and that cultural and communication barriers do not pose challenges for police personnel.

Police departments must also be cognizant of an increasingly older population. Individuals are living longer, healthier, more productive lives these days in large part because of better healthcare practices. This means they are more likely to be involved in crime as offenders and victims. Figure 19.2 depicts the increase in the elderly population in the United States from 1990 to 2020.

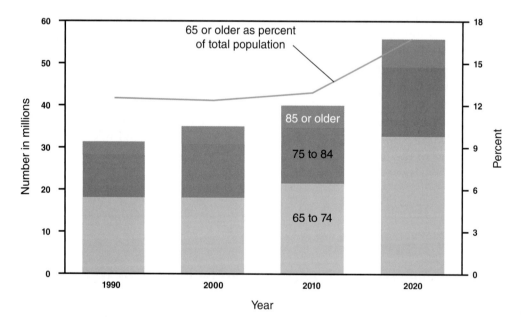

FIGURE 19.2. *Increases in the Elderly Population in the United States.* In light of the increased number of the elderly, cities and police departments will likely encounter higher levels of crimes by and against the elderly. They must also address retirement pensions that are paid to retired officers living longer lives. *Source: Crimes Against the Elderly, 2003–2013 (NCJ 248339), by R. E. Morgan, 2014, U.S. Department of Justice, Bureau of Justice Statistics.*

What particular concerns should police consider with regard to addressing elderly victims and offenders?

Economics

Economics have always impacted policing, because departments rely on funding for resources, and the strength or weakness of the economy can influence crime rates. For instance, in 2013 the city of Detroit declared bankruptcy, becoming the largest municipality in the United States to do so. Among many other effects, Detroit police officers were being asked to do more with less, because resources were notably scarce throughout the department, and officer pensions were placed in jeopardy. Upon shedding $7 billion of debt per the bankruptcy agreement, Detroit was able to hire 200 additional officers.

Economic factors regularly affect police practices, as evidenced in the budgets police departments receive, the amount and nature of crime to which officers must respond, the number of individuals interested in careers in law enforcement, and other areas. Police departments that operate in areas affected by economic stress are likely to feel the effects in many ways.

- Department budget cuts can negatively affect the number of individuals that can be hired, the extent of the searching and hiring efforts, pay raises, training, and equipment.
- Police response times may increase with fewer officers on duty, which may negatively influence public perceptions of the police and hamper enforcement efforts.
- Patrol practices may be restricted by fuel costs.
- Interaction with the public may be hampered because of the need to have all on-duty officers responding to calls.
- Public education programs and general community policing practices may suffer.

Times of economic prosperity, or "economic comfortableness," typically provide greater opportunities for departments to increase their staff, improve their technology and other resources, better reward their employees, and engage in greater training opportunities. However, when the period of prosperity ends, the departments that have given pay raises or hired additional personnel must be prepared to address the costs.

Times of economic stress encourage police departments to rely more heavily on the private sector and volunteers to assist with traditional police practices. For instance, private security companies can provide security services at major events, and volunteers may assist police departments with administrative tasks. Police departments may also consolidate services; for instance, police departments in adjoining municipalities have combined forces with the goals of best using resources and saving money.

Economic factors also influence crime. Periods of economic prosperity generally result in less crime than periods of economic strain (Rosenfeld & Messner, 2010). A stronger economy and lower unemployment rate generally result in less crime, because there are more legitimate means and opportunities for individuals to obtain money. Unfortunately for policing, crime rates typically increase and the police suffer various types of hardships during economic downturns. However, economic downturns also typically prompt more individuals to consider police work as a career, primarily because there are fewer available positions in the private sector.

● **Learning Objective 19.3:** Identify economic factors that affect policing.

Economics impact many aspects of policing, including the training, staffing, equipment, and benefits of the police force. When the city of Detroit filed for bankruptcy, many former police officers saw a reduction in their benefits and pensions. We depend on the police to provide safety and security; however, economic crises may result in threats to our well-being.

Should it be the responsibility of the federal government or state governments to ensure that all police departments are economically sound?

● **Learning Objective 19.4:** Explain the impact of drugs and international crime on police practices.

Drugs and International Crime

Other issues anticipated to effect policing in the future include drug crime and international crime. Drug crimes remain problematic for the police, because officers invest many resources in addressing drug crimes, and crimes related to drugs in general (e.g., turf wars over the right to sell drugs) and the war on drugs persist. In addition, increased globalization has contributed to the internationalization of crime. Law enforcement has had to and will need to continue to respond to crimes that cross international borders. Inconsistencies among laws, lack of cooperative efforts, jurisdictional issues, and problematic international relations have challenged law enforcement agencies in their efforts to address international crime.

Drug Crime

Drug use and drug-related crimes will continue to influence police practices. The psychedelic movement of the 1960s and the crack cocaine epidemic of the 1990s are among the prominent events to significantly alter police practices. Most recently, the increasing use of several synthetic club drugs (e.g., methamphetamine) has created new challenges for police because drugs can now more easily be prepared in one's home.

Drug enforcement efforts occur both internationally and domestically and involve law enforcement agencies at all levels. The war on drugs has been fought in schools, in communities, at our borders, in foreign countries, and elsewhere (see Module 2). Ultimately, the war on drugs consumes a great deal of resources, has contributed to police corruption, and has hampered police–community relations. For instance, the temptation to profit from the illegal drug trade or use illegal drugs has encouraged some officers to break the law.

Drug enforcement efforts have hampered police–community relations in many ways. The war on drugs has notably affected urban, African American males who have often been targeted or profiled by the police as being involved in drug-related (and other types of) crimes. The police in many urban communities have come to be seen as the enemy. Individuals who are arrested by the police for drug offenses often feel that the police should be targeting more serious, violent offenders (Walker et al., 2018).

There is some evidence, however, that the heavy enforcement of drug crimes may be waning, particularly for low-level drug offenses. A handful of states have legalized marijuana, and over half have legalized it for medicinal purposes (Rubin, 2016). The trend appears to be toward the legalization of marijuana, which could free many resources for police officers who would not have to enforce the laws surrounding such offenses. The increased legalization of marijuana could contribute to additional concerns for police; for instance, they would likely have to respond to more motorists driving under the influence of drugs. Research conducted 3 years after marijuana was legalized in Colorado and Washington, however, suggests that there have not been many detrimental effects. For example, teen marijuana use was unchanged, marijuana arrests were

The war on drugs has extended to many areas, including schools. Police officers have made notable efforts to remove drugs from schools and prevent them from ever entering.

What police antidrug efforts have you noticed in the schools you have attended?

down, and traffic fatalities remained consistent with prelegalization rates. Legalization has increased tax revenues in both states (Drug Policy Alliance, 2016).

International Crime

International crime and law enforcement efforts to address these crimes notably influence police practices and will become increasingly important as international travel, commerce, and communication become easier. Module 11 highlighted international law enforcement efforts. Among the primary challenges in fighting international crime are the lack of cooperation and poor relations among some countries, the lack of consistency in laws among countries, and jurisdictional issues. For instance, acts that may be illegal in one country may be legal in other countries (e.g., viewing child pornography). And even when there is consistency among laws, some countries have poor relations that would hamper cooperative efforts to address international crime.

1 Criminal Act

International crimes are essentially traditional forms of crimes that cross the borders of multiple countries. They provide many challenges for law enforcement officials and include offenses such as (Sciarabba & Sullivan, 2010):

- terrorism: acts of violence designed to spread fear for political or ideological reasons;
- organized crime: crimes committed by groups of individuals who work collectively;
- human trafficking: the involuntary movement of individuals within and across borders (often through force or deception);
- high-technology crime: crimes committed using electronic and digitally based technology such as cell phones, computers, and tablets; examples include money laundering, identify theft, and online gambling;
- drug trafficking: the selling, transport, or import of illegal drugs;
- illegal weapons trafficking: the selling, transport, or import of illegal weapons;
- environmental crimes: illegal acts that harm the environment (e.g., water and air pollution, the destruction of forests); and
- international gang-related crime: crimes committed by gangs that cross international boundaries (e.g., the Central American gang MS-13 has committed violent crimes in cities across the United States) (Lynch et al., 2017).

The System in Perspective

As noted in the "In the News" feature at the start of this module, using drones to monitor students on spring break is one of the many ways technology is being used to assist police officers. Drones enable law enforcement personnel to more easily monitor the behaviors of large groups of people while using fewer resources. However, the use of drones and other forms of technology has been criticized on the grounds that they restrict freedoms and infringe on privacy rights. Technology will continue to play a very important role in policing, but many factors beyond technology will influence policing in the future, including changes in demographics, the economy, immigration, and globalism. The effects of these and other factors will also influence the courts; for example, legislation will need to address how the police use technological advancements that may enable law enforcement to potentially become too invasive in our lives.

Summary

1. Learning Objective 19.1: *Characterize the technological advancements that have assisted law enforcement.*

- The future of law enforcement will continue to be influenced by various existing forms of technology, including mobile digital terminals, crime mapping, predictive policing, computer-assisted training, management information systems, surveillance, video recording, digital photography, cell phones, and robotics.

2. Learning Objective 19.2: *Illustrate how demographic changes and immigration influence policing.*

- Changing demographics in the United States stem from increased legal and illegal immigration as well as trends toward living longer. Illegal immigration and harsh measures against it can hamper relations between police and immigrant communities, intimidate undocumented immigrants who may be crime victims or witnesses, and divert police efforts from more serious crimes. Immigration in general has produced a more diverse country and increasingly diverse police forces. An aging population will lead to greater involvement in crime and victimization by the elderly.

3. Learning Objective 19.3: *Identify the economic factors that affect policing.*

- Economic factors affect the budgets police departments receive, the crime rate, the number of individuals interested in careers in law enforcement, police response times, public perceptions of the police, and public education programs. Departments are more likely to consolidate during budget crises, and private security plays a more significant role. In times of economic prosperity, departments may increase and better reward their staff, improve their technology and other resources, and engage in greater training opportunities.

4. Learning Objective 19.4: *Explain the impact of drugs and international crime on police practices.*

- The psychedelic movement of the 1960s and the crack cocaine epidemic of the 1990s significantly altered police practices because they improved coordination among all levels of law enforcement, produced new forms of corruption, and poisoned police–community relations in many places. The introduction and increasing use of several synthetic club drugs have created new challenges for police. International crime, drug related and otherwise, will require more cooperation among different countries' police departments in the future.

Questions for Critical Thinking

1. Which new technological advancement do you think has had the greatest influence on police practices? Which has likely had the least impact on policing? Defend your answers.

2. What level of law enforcement (federal, state, or local) do you believe is best situated to address concerns over illegal immigration? How could that level of law enforcement better address the problems associated with the issue of illegal immigration?

3. Assume you are the police chief of a medium-sized police department. You just found out that your budget was cut in half because of the poor economy. How will you cut your budget? Will you reduce personnel or training opportunities? Will you issue pay cuts? How will these actions impact the department?

4. Which of the following do you believe will pose more significant challenges for police departments in the future: international crime or drug crime? Defend your answer.

Key Terms

computer-assisted instruction
Data-Driven Approaches to Crime and Traffic Safety
mobile digital terminals

predictive policing
robotics
unmanned aerial vehicles

For digital learning resources, please go to
https://www.oup.com/he/burns1e

History of Courts

Judge Roy Bean was appointed as a justice of the peace in Pecos County, Texas, in 1882. Judge Bean had no legal training and used his saloon as a courtroom. He discouraged the use of defense attorneys and rarely used jurors. When he did use them, they were often chosen from among his best saloon customers. However, despite the lack of professionalism and respect for individual rights common in the early West, Judge Bean's judicial actions and practices were generally seen as helpful.

Would you consider Judge Bean's actions "criminal" in the sense that constitutional rights were routinely violated? Why or why not?

Our court systems have evolved over time, as have courtroom practices. Historically, conflicts were addressed primarily by the individuals involved. As societies developed, became more complex, and grew in size, methods of informal social control became less effective and the need for more formal efforts emerged. Legal codes and forums in which disputes and conflicts could be formally addressed arose in the form of criminal law and the courts. This module begins with a look at the development of early English courts, followed by discussions of early U.S. courts after colonization up until the Civil War and then following the Civil War. The end of this module discusses more recent court developments and the impact of U.S. Supreme Court decisions.

Frontier Justice Now and Then

On July 28, 2016, Paul O'Neal, a Black man, was driving a stolen vehicle in Chicago, Illinois, when police attempted to stop him. Reportedly unarmed, O'Neal was shot in the back by an officer who chased him both in a vehicle and on foot. The officer said he saw O'Neal reach into his waistband and believed that the young man was going to shoot him. An investigation following the O'Neal incident initially found that the officers involved in the incident may have violated several procedural requirements; however, no charges were filed against them. Shortly after the incident, Chicago Police Department officials warned officers that gangs had met to plan acts of retaliation against the police (Seelye, 2016). The O'Neal death was one of several recent incidents in which a Black man was killed by police across the United States, and the gang-alleged retaliation was designed to be a response to perceived injustices by the police both in Chicago and nationwide. In May 2017, 8 months after O'Neal was killed, two Chicago officers were shot by a gang member (Ruthhart, 2017). It is not clear if the shootings were an act of retaliation.

In another situation involving possible retaliation, in 2014, Ismaaiyl Brinsley had mentioned to some friends and family that he was angry over police shootings in Staten Island, New York, and Ferguson, Missouri. In December, Brinsley drove from Baltimore, Maryland, to Brooklyn, New York, where he shot and killed two unsuspecting New York City Police Department officers as they sat in

their patrol car. He then killed himself (Mueller & Baker, 2014).

Brinsley's actions, and those planned by the gangs in Chicago, as well as several other less serious acts of retaliation against the police, resemble the vigilante style of justice that existed on the Western frontier in the United States. When individuals do not believe that formal means of justice are effective, sometimes they take the law into their own hands. Can you think of other examples when vigi-

 1 Criminal Act

POLICE TRACE GUNMAN'S DIGITAL ACTIVITIES

lante justice occurred in recent history? What were the circumstances of those incidents and how do they relate to the practices found in the early West?

Early English Courts

English common law heavily influenced the development of laws and the court system in the United States. Colonists brought with them many of the same rules and procedures that existed in England. However, they ultimately established a system that best fit their needs and interests and that sought to limit the power of the government to impose its will in local legal matters.

Learning Objective 20.1: Summarize the developments of the early English courts.

Blood Feuds and the Code of Hammurabi

The earliest means of resolving disputes or seeking justice involved wars, fights, duels, and feuds. **Blood feuds** were used in some primitive cultures whereby the family members of a victim killed by another person had the right and obligation to

blood feuds
One of the earliest means of resolving disputes or seeking justice, they were used in some primitive cultures whereby the family members of a victim killed by another person had the right and obligation to kill the murderer or a member of the offender's family

weregild An early means of settling disputes among Germanic tribes of Europe, it was the practice of offenders paying an amount of money to the deceased victim's family; the amount paid was based on the social status of the victim

8 Trial

compurgation
A method for clearing an individual accused of a crime through a series of oaths and by others attesting to the innocence of the accused; it would occur if the evidence was unconvincing or if an individual refused to confess or lacked witnesses

oath-helper
Individuals who assisted both plaintiffs and the accused in compurgation by swearing under oath that the accused was innocent or guilty

trial by ordeal
Used in early English cases in which the plaintiff could not obtain enough oaths, it involved the accused being required to perform particular dangerous acts, and their survival was viewed as fate determining their innocence

kill the murderer or a member of the offender's family. This type of resolution existed in early Greek civilization until around 621 B.C., when a statesman named Draco was commissioned to write a new law that eliminated blood feuds (Roth, 2005). In some cultures, a payment to the deceased's family could be made in lieu of violence; for instance, Germanic tribes of Europe offered **weregild** (or "man price"), in which the amount paid was based on the social status of the victim.

However, early English courts and Western legal traditions, in general, can be traced to the first known legal code—the Code of Hammurabi—dating back to 1760 B.C. The code identified crimes, punishments for crime, and settlements for common conflicts. Generally, officials worked with the king to settle disputes and assess whether the accused was guilty of a crime against their state (Spohn & Hemmens, 2009). The officials who performed these tasks were akin to modern-day judges.

Court Practices in the Hundreds and Shires: 401–700

Early English adjudicatory practices were notably informal in nature. Between the 5th and 7th centuries A.D., various invasions of England resulted in tribal kinship. The various kingdoms in England were subdivided and ruled by the king, who was considered a military leader and landlord (Roth, 2005). Communities were organized into tythings, hundreds, and shires (see Module 10). Court was held once a month or so in the hundreds, with local freeman resolving cases according to local custom (Marcham, 1937). The shire court, composed of all freemen in the shire, handled all cases involving land ownership and cases that could not be resolved in the hundred courts (Keeton, 1966). Shire reeves were the liaison between the king and the shire and the principle judicial and administrative officers.

Compurgation and Ordeal: 1066–1215

By about 1200, national law replaced local and regional customs of the shires and hundreds. Royal judges now applied the law throughout England (Walsh, 1932). Court cases in England between 1066 and 1215 generally involved the victim bringing forth their case to the court by swearing an oath and pledging property as collateral. If there was enough evidence to convict, the case was decided immediately (Steury & Frank, 1996). If not, cases were decided primarily by two means: compurgation and ordeal.

Compurgation was a method for clearing an individual accused of a crime through a series of oaths and by others attesting to the innocence of the accused (Oliver & Hilgenberg, 2006). Compurgation would occur if the evidence was unconvincing or if an individual refused to confess or lacked witnesses.

In compurgation, generally, the plaintiff (accuser) took a series of oaths and employed an "**oath-helper**" to assist with their case by swearing that the accused was innocent. The number of oaths taken depended on the social status of the plaintiff and the seriousness of the crime (Oliver & Hilgenberg, 2006). The value of each oath was tied to the value of the oath-taker's life as determined by the court. For instance, oaths offered by noblemen were worth more than oaths offered by freemen. Women, slaves, and other less powerful groups had no declared value under the law and had to have other individuals swear on their behalf. Accusers were required to offer more oaths than defendants (the accused). Some consider this requirement for more oaths by the plaintiffs a precursor to our current recognition of the accused being innocent until proven guilty (Fuller, 2014).

Cases in which the plaintiff could not obtain enough oaths were resolved by **trial by ordeal**, in which the accused was required to perform particular dangerous acts and their survival was viewed as fate determining their innocence. Religion was particularly influential, and priests would say mass and preside over the trials (Oliver & Hilgenberg, 2006). Surviving these tasks was thought to be a sign from God that the individuals were innocent. Courts would select the ordeal to be used. The primary types of trial by ordeal included the following (Bartlett, 1986; Holten & Lamar, 1991):

- trial by cold water—the accused was submerged into very cold water

- trial by hot water—the accused was required to grab a stone from boiling water

- trial by hot iron, also known as trial by fire—the accused was required to carry a hot rod for a certain distance

In trials by ordeal, the accused was required to perform dangerous acts (that would be considered particularly inhumane by 21st-century standards) that would determine innocence. Basing one's culpability for an offense on a strong faith in religion and the belief that higher powers should determine one's fate are among the foundations on which our current court practices are based.

What factors, aside from evidence pertaining to a crime, should impact one's culpability?

England inherited **trial by battle** as a means of litigation following the 11th-century Norman Conquest when England was invaded and occupied by an army of Norman, Breton, and French soldiers. Trial by battle involved plaintiffs and defendants agreeing to settle their differences via an agreed-on location and weapon, such as a battle-axe (Kinnane, 1952).

In 1166, the **Assize of Clarendon** established that 12 men from each hundred and 4 others from each township would determine who was responsible for a crime and order the sheriff to bring them to the court (Stuery & Frank, 1996). Significantly, this precursor to a grand jury involved local citizens as opposed to government representatives who filed charges (Oliver & Hilgenberg, 2006). Over time, the grand jury evolved into its current form, and grand jurors were tasked with assessing whether there was enough evidence to file charges against the accused.

6 Hearing

8 Trial

trial by battle
An early means of litigation that emerged in England following the 11th-century Norman Conquest; it involved plaintiffs and defendants agreeing to settle their differences via an agreed-on location and weapon, such as a battle-axe

Development of Grand Jury and Jury Trials: 1215–1642

Compurgation and ordeals were used less frequently as the English criminal justice system developed. In 1215, a council within the Roman Catholic Church determined that priests could no longer say mass and preside over the trials because they already played too many roles in the communities (Oliver & Hilgenberg, 2006). To replace trials by ordeal, the precursor to the modern-day grand juries and jury trials emerged, in which citizens became more involved. Initially, the accused was given the option of being detained indefinitely or participating in a jury trial. If they were detained indefinitely and died in prison, their land would be passed to their heirs. However, if they were found guilty in a trial, their lands would be forfeited to the king (Baker, 1990).

Trial jurors often consisted of the same individuals who served on the grand juries because of their familiarity with the cases. In the 1350s, defendants were given the option of barring grand jurors from serving on trial juries (Kempin, 1973). In many instances, trial jurors were selected from outside the community. As a result, they had to be introduced to the evidence and facts of the case (Green, 1985).

In the 15th century, religious strife increased, and the king began to use the courts as a tool of oppression (Fuller, 2014). He created the **Court of the Star Chamber**—so named because it was composed of his councilors and met in a room with stars painted on a ceiling in the palace of Westminster Abbey—to address

5 Initial Appearance

particular offenses such as rioting, perjury, and conspiracy. The court engaged in serious acts of repression before it was abolished in 1641 (Steury & Frank, 1996):

- Suspects were interrogated in secrecy.
- Torture was used as a fact-finding tool.
- No jury trials were used.
- Accusations were brought without evidence.
- The accused were not informed of the identity of the persons making the accusations.

Early Court Reform: 1650–1750

The court system in England continued to evolve in the 17th century. Legislation guiding courtroom proceedings emerged, and cases were brought before **justices of the peace**, who were also known as magistrates and responsible for hearing cases and preserving the king's peace. With regard to the former, the **Habeas Corpus Act of 1679** permitted imprisoned individuals to request a hearing before a judge to make the charges against them public. Judges determined whether the confinement was justified or the accused should be released or remain imprisoned before trial (Oliver & Hilgenberg, 2006).

Additional components of the judicial process that emerged during this time and remain in the United States in the early 21st century include the following (Friedman, 1993; Fuller 2014; Oliver & Hilgenberg, 2006):

- the opportunity for defendants to challenge jurors who appear to be biased
- the fact that a verdict of the jury is final upon a decision to acquit (free or exonerate someone)
- the hiring of **solicitors** (lawyers) by victims to present their cases
- the use of defense attorneys, particularly around the 1730s

Early U.S. Courts

The United States has two levels of criminal courts: federal and state. Federal courts hear cases that involve violations of federal laws, while state courts hear cases involving violations of state laws (see Module 21). State laws are passed by state legislatures and govern the behavior of all individuals within the respective state. Federal laws, for example, those addressing kidnapping, bank robbery, and mail fraud, are passed by Congress and approved by the president. State courts hear the bulk of criminal cases, because most cases are adjudicated (decided) at the local level. The structure and jurisdiction of U.S. courts, however, has not always been clearly defined. In fact, early U.S. courts operated in a variety of means with very little oversight. The earliest U.S. courts date back to colonial times, when many English settlers arrived on the east coast of the United States and began the difficult process of creating a new country.

Courts in Colonial America: 1607–1763

British colonization of America began in 1607, and the original colonies were viewed as corporations chartered by the king of England. The colonies were limited with regard to making laws, and English common law guided

CAREERS

Attorneys may practice civil law or serve as a prosecutor or defense lawyer in criminal courts. They interpret and apply the law by identifying and presenting the facts of a case. They must hold a juris doctorate and an attorney's license to practice law. Strong analytical, speaking, and argumentation skills are often required for the position.

legislation. However, it was unclear as to which acts were binding on the colonies (Abadinski, 1988; Oliver & Hilgenberg, 2006), and the colonists increasingly viewed the courts as a tool for the English Crown and mistrusted English rule (Chroust, 1965).

Colonial American courts largely reflected English courts, although there were distinct differences. English courts :

- were more advanced from a legal standpoint;
- were more numerous, complex, and highly specialized;
- possessed more formal decor and pomp and circumstance (formality); and
- were more likely to provide due process protections (Surrency, 1967).

Colonial courts originated through royal charters, governors acting on behalf of the king, and legislation by colonial leaders (Holten & Lamar, 1991). They varied quite a bit across colonies because of differing local customs, beliefs, and religious interests (Holten & Lamar, 1991). For instance, the Massachusetts Bay Colony charter of 1629 established one general court that made laws and administered justice (Foote, 1976), while in New York the English created a system of courts that would become the first permanently established court system in the United States (Foote, 1976). Additional courts were created as towns and villages increased in size and crime increased. Biblical codes were often adopted in the northern colonies, while laws governing slavery were enacted in the south.

There were no law schools in colonial America; thus, budding attorneys went to England to study (Abadinski, 1988). Lawyers in America learned their trade through apprenticeships, although they also often maintained employment in other areas (Friedman, 1985). While lawyers were often viewed with hostility by the colonists—particularly by those who were poor and saw lawyers as members of the privileged class (Pound, 1953)—lawyers nevertheless played an important role in U.S. history; of the 56 signers of the Declaration of Independence, 25 were lawyers (Abadinski, 1988).

The Constitutional Convention and the Bill of Rights: 1776–1787

The 1776 American Revolution largely occurred because the colonists believed the English Crown was treating them unfairly. The break with England affected justice-based practices and provided an opportunity for the colonists to create a constitution and criminal codes and further separate themselves from English rules and laws. The U.S. Constitution, including the first 10 amendments—also known as the Bill of Rights—offered much guidance for the courts (see Figure 20.1).

The evolution of U.S. courts was also notably influenced by the **Constitutional Convention** in Philadelphia in 1787, in which disagreement occurred over the structure of state and federal (national) courts. The debate largely centered on whether there should be a federal court system distinct from state courts. States' rights supporters, later known as **Anti-Federalists**, believed that a strong federal court system would restrict individual liberties and viewed the creation of a federal court system as a threat to the power maintained by state courts. They proposed that federal crimes should be decided in state courts and the U.S. Supreme Court should only hear appeals from state courts.

● **Learning Objective 20.2:** Trace the development of early U.S. courts following colonization until the Civil War.

justices of the peace Also known as magistrates, they were responsible for hearing cases and preserving the king's peace; they remain in use to a limited extent in the early 21st century, particularly in rural areas

Habeas Corpus Act of 1679 An act that permitted imprisoned individuals to request a hearing before a judge to make the charges against them public; judges determined whether the confinement was justified or the accused should be released or remain imprisoned before trial

Solicitors A historical term used to refer to lawyers

Courts in colonial times in the United States were modeled after those established in England. The formality, for instance with regard to dress and headwear, is evidenced in this depiction of a 1735 case in which Andrew Hamilton defends John Peter Zenger. Zenger, a printer and journalist in New York, was tried for libel after he printed articles critical of the colony's governor.

How does this depiction of early court practices differ from what we see in our courts in the early 21st century?

6 Hearing

9 Sentencing

6 Hearing

8 Trial

11 Appeal

6 Grand Jury/
Preliminary
Hearing

8 Trial

THE BILL OF RIGHTS

AMENDMENT I

Congress shall make no law respecting an establishment of religion, or prohibiting the free exercise thereof; or abridging the freedom of speech, or of the press; or the right of the people peaceably to assemble, and to petition the government for a redress of grievances.

AMENDMENT II

A well regulated militia, being necessary to the security of a free state, the right of the people to keep and bear arms, shall not be infringed.

AMENDMENT III

No soldier shall, in time of peace be quartered in any house, without the consent of the owner, nor in time of war, but in a manner to be prescribed by law.

AMENDMENT IV

The right of the people to be secure in their persons, houses, papers, and effects, against unreasonable searches and seizures, shall not be violated, and no warrants shall issue, but upon probable cause, supported by oath or affirmation, and particularly describing the place to be searched, and the persons or things to be seized.

AMENDMENT V

No person shall be held to answer for a capital, or otherwise infamous crime, unless on a presentment or indictment of a grand jury, except in cases arising in the land or naval forces, or in the militia, when in actual service in time of war or public danger; nor shall any person be subject for the same offense to be twice put in jeopardy of life or limb; nor shall be compelled in any criminal case to be a witness against himself, nor be deprived of life, liberty, or property, without due process of law; nor shall private property be taken for public use, without just compensation.

AMENDMENT VI

In all criminal prosecutions, the accused shall enjoy the right to a speedy and public trial, by an impartial jury of the state and district wherein the crime shall have been committed, which district shall have been previously ascertained by law, and to be informed of the nature and cause of the accusation; to be confronted with the witnesses against him; to have compulsory process for obtaining witnesses in his favor, and to have the assistance of counsel for his defense.

AMENDMENT VII

In suits at common law, where the value in controversy shall exceed twenty dollars, the right of trial by jury shall be preserved, and no fact tried by a jury, shall be otherwise reexamined in any court of the United States, than according to the rules of the common law.

AMENDMENT VIII

Excessive bail shall not be required, nor excessive fines imposed, nor cruel and unusual punishments inflicted.

AMENDMENT IX

The enumeration in the Constitution, of certain rights, shall not be construed to deny or disparage others retained by the people.

AMENDMENT X

The powers not delegated to the United States by the Constitution, nor prohibited by it to the states, are reserved to the states respectively, or to the people.

Constitutional Convention Held in 1787, it was the convening of officials to frame the U.S. Constitution; among other accomplishments, they established the structure of U.S. courts; the debate largely centered on whether there should be a federal court system distinct from state courts

FIGURE 20.1. The Bill of Rights. Of particular importance in the Bill of Rights in relation to courtroom procedures are the Fourth Amendment through the Eighth Amendment. The Fourth Amendment addresses illegal searches and the need for warrants to be issued by the courts for searches. The Fifth Amendment comments on grand jury requirements, double jeopardy, self-incrimination, and due process protections, among other things. The Sixth and Seventh Amendments address rights regarding trials, and the Eighth Amendment prohibits excessive bail and fines and protects against cruel and unusual punishment. These and other amendments contain vague terms, such as due process, which had to be clarified over time.

Was it appropriate for those who composed the Bill of Rights to be vague with respect to the role of the courts? Why?

Here, George Washington is shown presiding over the Constitutional Convention of 1787. At the convention, a compromise was reached that vested judicial power in one Supreme Court and other courts to be determined by Congress.

Looking back at history from the vantage point of the present, do you believe the compromise that provided for state and federal courts was the best solution at the time, or should the Framers have created only federal or only state courts? Why?

Anti-Federalists
States' rights supporters who believed that a strong federal court system would restrict individual liberties and viewed the creation of a federal court system as a threat to the power maintained by state courts

nationalists Also known as **Federalists**, they distrusted the prejudices of the states and believed a strong national government would support economic and political cohesiveness for the new country; they supported the creation of federal courts

The Anti-Federalists faced opposition from the **Nationalists** (later named the **Federalists**), who distrusted the prejudices of the states and believed a strong national government would support economic and political cohesiveness for the new country. The Federalists believed that the state courts, with their own "provincial prejudices," would be unable to create a uniform body of law that would enable businesses to flourish. Accordingly, they supported the creation of federal courts (Neubauer & Fradella, 2017, p. 63).

A compromise was reached at the convention, in which it was decided (and noted in Article III, Section 1, of the U.S. Constitution) that "the Judicial Power of the United States, shall be vested in one supreme Court, and in such inferior Courts as the Congress may from time to time ordain and establish." This, in turn, left Congress with the task of determining how to structure the judicial system. In the early 21st century, we have a Supreme Court that considers cases from state courts and federal courts (see Module 21).

Post–Revolutionary War Courts in the West

Increased European immigration in the north following the Revolutionary War contributed to religious and cultural tensions, and the west, which was largely unsettled, lagged far behind the east with regard to court development (Neubauer & Fradella, 2017). The discovery of gold in the west prompted many individuals to relocate, but the lack of established laws and other means of formal social control meant that individuals were often required to protect themselves (Abadinski, 1988).

Law was applied in an informal, sometimes violent manner. Judges who were often ignorant of the laws and sometimes illiterate presided over cases in makeshift courtrooms (Abadinski, 1988). The legal systems that existed in the frontier were often a synthesis of systems formed in other states (Friedman, 1985).

Ordinance of 1787 Also known as the Northwest Ordinance, it was an attempt by the national government to address the lawlessness in the West; it prescribed the law for most of the western territories

One notable attempt by the national government to address the lawlessness in the West was the **Ordinance of 1787**, otherwise known as the Northwest Ordinance, which prescribed the law for most of the western territories (Oliver & Hilgenberg, 2006). A similar ordinance, the Ordinance of 1798, was created to govern the southwest territories acquired by the United States. Essentially, these acts were passed based on the need to establish law and in anticipation of forthcoming statehood. They placed lawmaking powers into the hands of a governor and three judges, who were tasked with passing legislation that was in the best interest of, and best suited to, the geographic areas (Oliver & Hilgenberg, 2006). A more formal approach was adopted following statehood.

Judicial Acts Affecting the Courts: 1789–1925

Following ratification of the Constitution, Congress passed several laws to clarify uncertainties regarding the structure of the courts. These laws included the Judiciary Act of 1789, the Judiciary Act of 1801, and the Court of Appeals Act of 1891, among others.

JUDICIARY ACT OF 1789

Judiciary Act of 1789 Legislation that sought to clarify uncertainties regarding the structure of the courts and provided a foundation on which our current court system exists; the act established a federal judicial system

The **Judiciary Act of 1789** provides a foundation on which our current court system exists. The act, which was viewed as a victory for the Federalists, established a federal judicial system that included (Oliver & Hilgenberg, 2006):

- *one Supreme Court*, which was designed to be a six-member court with five associate justices and headed by a chief justice (justices were chosen by President Washington and confirmed by the Senate);
- *thirteen district courts*, which were essentially the trial courts; and
- *three circuit courts*, which consisted of two supreme court judges and a district court judge who would ride on horseback or a carriage to locations under their purview and hear appeals from the district courts (Foote, 1976).

Washington chose John Jay as the first chief justice, and the Supreme Court met for the first time in 1790. Although it was viewed as a victory for the Federalists, the act was considered a compromise, because it addressed some of the Anti-Federalists concerns; for instance, the boundaries of the district courts were drawn along state lines and federal district judges were required to be residents of their district (Richardson & Vines, 1970).

JUDICIARY ACT OF 1801

Judiciary Act of 1801 Legislation that created many new judgeships and expanded the jurisdiction of the lower federal courts; this change, however, lasted only briefly

Following passage of the Judiciary Act of 1789, Federalists argued for greater powers of the federal judiciary, because they long supported the development and expanded use of the federal courts, which resulted in the **Judiciary Act of 1801**. The act created many new judgeships and expanded the jurisdiction of the lower federal courts. This change, however, lasted only briefly. With the election of Thomas Jefferson (who was an Anti-Federalist with regard to court structure) as president and support from Anti-Federalists in Congress, the act was quickly repealed and the court system returned to its previous form (Neubauer & Fradella, 2017).

COURT OF APPEALS ACT OF 1891

Court of Appeals Act of 1891 Legislation that created new courts known as circuit courts of appeals, which released the burden of the Supreme Court from hearing many types of minor offenses so it could instead focus on more substantive cases

It was not until the late 1800s when Congress again expanded the jurisdiction of the federal courts and added new circuit court judges. The **Court of Appeals Act of 1891** represented a victory for the Federalists, because it created new courts known as circuit courts of appeals. The act released the burden of the Supreme Court from hearing many types of minor offenses so it could instead focus on more substantive cases (Spohn & Hemmens, 2009).

ADDITIONAL LAWS REFINING THE FEDERAL JUDICIARY

The basic jurisdiction of the federal court system has largely remained intact since 1925. However, Congress has continued to pass laws that further refined the structure and operations of the federal judiciary:

- The **Judges Bill of 1925** gave the Supreme Court greater control over the cases it heard (Neubauer & Fradella, 2017).
- The **Federal Magistrate Act of 1968** created U.S. magistrate judges who had limited jurisdiction to assist district court judges, for instance through setting bail and overseeing initial appearances (see Module 21).
- The U.S. Sentencing Commission was tasked with creating sentencing guidelines in 1984.

Judges Bill of 1925
Legislation that gave the Supreme Court greater control over the cases it heard

Federal Magistrate Act of 1968 Legislation creating U.S. magistrate judges who have limited jurisdiction to assist district court judges, for instance through setting bail and overseeing initial appearances

Court Developments From the Civil War through the World Wars

The Civil War brought a host of new challenges to the United States. Rising industrialization and increases in the country's population, particularly in the large cities that were emerging, created new challenges. Ultimately, the courts were ill-prepared to meet the needs of the changing society. Among the key developments following the Civil War were the increased use of plea bargaining, the creation of new courts such as city courts and specialized courts like family and juvenile courts; the establishment of probation and parole; efforts to ensure that the accused were afforded their rights to an attorney; and attempts to combat judicial corruption.

● **Learning Objective 20.3:** Summarize the key developments that shaped U.S. courts following the Civil War through World War II.

Plea Bargaining

Following the Civil War, the increase in criminal caseloads and the more frequent use of public prosecutors largely contributed to an increase in the use of plea bargaining (when a defendant admits guilt in exchange for some form of leniency, typically a reduced sentence). The process had existed since colonial times and gave courts greater flexibility in sentencing options (Oliver & Hilgenberg, 2006). Despite the diminished role of juries that accompanied the increase in plea bargaining, there was little public outcry until the 1920s (Walker, 1998).

City Courts and Juvenile Courts

Among the most significant changes following the Civil War was the creation of city courts to deal with the increasing amount of crime in urban areas and the use of specialized courts to address issues such as family relations. The ever-changing nature of the courts resulted in varying court structures, little uniformity, and overlapping jurisdictions that exist to this day in some locales.

In 1899, the first juvenile court in the United States was created. The court was intended to save troubled youths by preventing them from committing more crimes and protecting them from exposure to adult

The progressive era was a time when many changes impacted justice-based practices. Among the more notable developments was the increased development and use of distinct courts for juveniles. These courts promoted a more rehabilitative (or treatment-oriented) approach than adult courts.

Why do you think there is a distinct court system for juveniles?

progressive era
The period when several important justice-related developments emerged (1900–1920), including the proliferation of juvenile courts, the establishment of probation and parole, and efforts to ensure that defendants were afforded their Sixth Amendment right to an attorney

9 Sentencing

criminals. The creation of juvenile courts was just one of the many contributions to the administration of criminal justice found in the **progressive era** (1900–1920) of criminal justice reform. Ultimately, the creation of distinct juvenile courts enabled authorities to focus on the specific needs and issues pertaining to juveniles. The courts' emphasis on crime prevention and rehabilitation remained through much of the 20th century.

Probation, Parole, and Sixth-Amendment Rights to an Attorney

Among other developments within the courts were the establishment of probation (which involves offender supervision in the community in lieu of incarceration) and parole (which involves offender supervision in the community following a period of incarceration) and efforts to ensure that defendants were afforded their Sixth Amendment right to an attorney. In 1914, the first public defender's office opened, and others soon followed across the country (Walker, 1998).

Fighting Judicial Corruption

The U.S. Supreme Court shifted its concern from economic regulation in the 1930s to civil liberties in the 1940s, a focus that continued for the next several decades (Oliver & Hilgenberg, 2006). Judicial corruption had become problematic during Prohibition, because judges were among the public officials who were sometimes bribed by organized crime groups intent on selling alcohol. In response, the American Bar Association proposed to implement a system of judicial selection that involved consideration of judges' performances on the bench (Oliver & Hilgenberg, 2006). Judicial selection had been controversial throughout the 19th century (Walker, 1998), because it was believed that voters in elections did not know who would make an effective judge. Reformers were also concerned that, because of election politics, judges would decide cases in a manner that was politically popular as opposed to based strictly on the law (Neubauer & Fradella, 2017).

Court Developments Since the 1950s

A notable shift occurred in court practices in the 1950s. Beginning in 1954, with Chief Justice Earl Warren at its helm, the U.S. Supreme Court issued several decisions that emphasized individual rights and freedoms. However, during the 1960s and 1970s there was an increase in crime rates, which led to a more punitive approach beginning in the 1980s which involved tougher sentencing practices and restrictions on individual rights and freedoms. This crackdown on crime was accompanied by an expansion in the number of courts, judges, and attorneys to address the rising crime rates. These and other events resulted in unprecedented numbers of individuals under correctional supervision and reflect some of the more relatively recent developments of the courts.

● Learning Objective 20.4: Explain how U.S. Supreme Court decisions impacted the relatively recent development of U.S. courts.

The Warren Court: 1953–1969

The appointment of U.S. Supreme Court Chief Justice Earl Warren in 1953 ushered in a period when the Supreme Court heard and decided a number of cases that continue to regularly affect the criminal justice system. The Supreme Court's intervention during this time was viewed by many scholars, including historian and professor Samuel Walker as being among "the most important developments in the history of American criminal justice" (Walker, 1998, p. 191). The series of court decisions began with *Brown v. Board of Education* (1954), in which the court voted to desegregate Southern schools and continued with several other important cases that recognized concerns for civil rights and liberties. Among them were the following:

- *Mapp v. Ohio* (1961), which mandated that states were bound by the protections granted through the exclusionary rule
- *Gideon v. Wainwright* (1963), which provided all indigent defendants with the right to counsel
- *Escobedo v. Illinois* (1964), which provided the accused with the right to counsel during interrogations
- *Miranda v. Arizona* (1966), which required police officers to inform arrestees of their rights prior to interrogation
- *Duncan v. Louisiana* (1968), which extended the right to a jury trial to the states

A Shift Toward Crime Control

Beginning in the 1980s, the emphasis on protecting individual rights shifted in favor of crime control. This shift was in part because the Supreme Court became increasingly composed of conservative justices. The court, under chief justices Warren Burger (chief justice from 1969 to 1986) and William Rehnquist (1986 to 2005), limited the due process protections earlier granted by the Warren court. Among other acts, the court:

- created a "good faith" exception to the exclusionary rule (in *U.S. v. Leon*, 1984), which holds that evidence illegally obtained may be used in court if the individuals who seized the evidence believed they were acting in good faith;

Chief Justice Earl Warren, the 14th chief justice of the U.S. Supreme Court, oversaw a court that ruled on many important issues, including ones that impacted criminal justice practices as many groups were fighting for equal rights.

Which of the Warren court decisions do you believe had the most significant impact on the criminal justice system?

8 Trial

5 Initial
Appearance

11 Appeal

9 Sentencing

- added a public safety requirement as part of the Miranda warning (*New York v. Quarles*, 1984), which allows information obtained without a Miranda warning to be admissible as evidence at trial, if the information was collected in circumstances when there was great danger to public safety;

- ruled that suspects did not have the right to bail, despite the Eighth Amendment's protection against excessive bail (*U.S. v. Salerno*, 1987); and

- restricted appeals by death row inmates (Walker, 1998).

Mandatory minimum sentences enacted in the late 1970s and early 1980s directed toward habitual offenders were characteristic of legislators' and the courts' concern for greater consistency in sentencing and getting tough on repeat offenders. These are but a few of the many crime control efforts that began in the 1980s and contributed to unprecedented growth in the U.S. correctional population (see Module 32 for a more in-depth discussion of this issue).

An Expansion of Our Legal Systems

More recent developments in the history of the courts have included an expansion in the numbers of courts, lawyers, law schools, and cases since the mid-20th century. For example, the growth in the number of lawyers has been exponential:

- prior to the Civil War: ~20,000 (Friedman, 1993)
- end of the 19th century: ~114,000 (Friedman, 1993)
- as of 2020: over 1.3 million (American Bar Association, 2020)

The numbers of law schools and students attending those schools has also increased. For instance, there were 135 law schools in the United States as of 1963–1964 and slightly less than 50,000 students. By contrast, in 2017 there were 197 law schools approved by the American Bar Association, with a combined enrollment of roughly 114,500 (American Bar Association, 2021).

The numbers of cases heard in both state and federal courts have increased as well since the 1950s. While in 1950 there were 37,720 criminal cases heard in federal courts, there were 90,473 criminal defendant filings in U.S. district courts in 2019 (Administrative Office of the U.S. Courts, 2020; Federal Judicial Center, 2017). The increased number of caseloads in criminal courts has resulted in backlogged courts and the need to dispense of cases in a swift manner. This has largely shifted much of the courtroom decision-making from judges and juries to attorneys engaging in plea bargaining (see Module 23).

To be sure, there have been other changes in the courts since the 1950s, several of which are addressed in other modules within this unit. These include reform efforts by some states to eliminate the distinction between courts of limited jurisdiction and courts of general jurisdiction and instead have one level of courts (see Module 21). Another notable change concerns juvenile courts. While the 1980s ushered in a period of more punitive responses to juvenile delinquency, more recently there has been a shift toward rehabilitation (see Module 26). Most recently, the courts have had to continue functioning with strong consideration of the spread of COVID-19. The National Center for State Courts (2020c) noted that the most common efforts taken by state courts to address concerns for the virus were:

- restricting or ending jury trials;
- restricting entrance into courthouses;
- generally suspending in-person proceedings;
- granting extensions for court deadlines, including deadlines to pay fees or fines; and
- encouraging or requiring teleconferences and videoconferences in lieu of hearings.

The ability of the courts to function effectively in light of these and related changes is vital to our efforts to secure justice.

The System in Perspective

Acts of retaliation and revenge are not new. As noted in the "In the News" section at the start of this module, acts of retaliation against the police in the early 21st century in many ways resemble the frontier justice of the past. However, society has progressed since the early days when taking the law into one's own hands was more common. Today, we rely much more heavily on the courts to ensure that justice is served. The courts play an integral role in the administration of justice. As with other components of the criminal justice system (e.g., law enforcement and corrections), various factors, including wars and public concern for crime, have affected the development of and reform within the courts. Understanding the history of our courts is necessary to better understand current justice-based practices and the integral role the courts play in finding justice.

Summary

1. Learning Objective 20.1: *Summarize the developments of the early English courts.*

- Early English court practices were influenced by religion, the Code of Hammurabi, and the Norman Conquest of 1066. The courts used a variety of tactics to adjudicate cases, including compurgation, trial by battle, and trial by ordeal. Other developments included the Assize of Clarendon, which brought about the use of grand juries; the Court of the Star Chamber, which highlighted the potential for abuse in the courts; and the Habeas Corpus Act of 1679, which permitted the accused to appear before a judge to make the charges against them public.

2. Learning Objective 20.2: *Trace the development of early U.S. courts following colonization until the Civil War.*

- Court development in the United States was largely modeled after the English court system. Colonists originally were heavily controlled by England, although they eventually distanced themselves from English law and established their own court system and laws. Each colony modified its courts according to local customs, beliefs, and religious practices. The American Revolution and the creation of the U.S.

Constitution further facilitated the development of U.S. courts. Debate at the Constitutional Convention concerned whether the United States should have strictly federal courts or state courts. The result was a combination of both, largely as a result of various acts, including the Judiciary Act of 1789, the Judiciary Act of 1801, and the Court of Appeals Act of 1891.

3. Learning Objective 20.3: *Summarize the key developments that shaped U.S. courts following the Civil War through World War II.*

- Court development in the United States following the Civil War was largely affected by the need for the country to recover from the devastation of the war and increased urbanization and rising crime rates. City and specialized courts were created to address the social problems, and the first juvenile court was established in 1899. Judicial corruption became increasingly problematic during this time, which resulted in reform efforts to better professionalize the courts.

4. Learning Objective 20.4: *Explain how U.S. Supreme Court decisions impacted the relatively recent development of U.S. courts.*

• The appointment of Chief Justice Earl Warren in 1953 brought about a series of changes that affected the courts. Among the cases to impact the courts were *Mapp v. Ohio* (1961), which mandated that states were bound by the protections granted through the exclusionary rule; *Gideon v. Wainwright* (1963), which provided all indigent defendants with the right to counsel; *Escobedo v. Illinois* (1964), which provided the right to counsel during interrogations; *Miranda v. Arizona* (1966), which required police officers to inform arrestees of their rights prior to interrogation; and *Duncan v. Louisiana* (1968), which extended the right to a jury trial to the states. Several court cases beginning in the 1980s further affected the courts, including a "good faith" exception to the exclusionary rule (in *U.S. v. Leon*, 1984) and a public safety requirement to the requirement of a Miranda warning (*New York v. Quarles*, 1984). The court also ruled that suspects did not have the right to bail, despite the Eighth Amendment's protection against excessive bail (*U.S. v. Salerno*, 1987), and restricted the number of appeals for death row inmates.

Questions for Critical Thinking

1. What ethical concerns were involved with the practices used in the Court of the Star Chamber? Do you believe some of the same practices are employed in today's U.S. courts? Discuss your answer.

2. How would the organization of our court system differ today if there had not been a compromise at the Constitutional Convention and the proposals offered by the Federalists had been adopted in full?

3. What two court developments during the progressive era of criminal justice reform do you believe most significantly impacted the courts? Why?

4. Which 1960s Supreme Court decision do you believe had the greatest effect on courtroom practices? Why?

Key Terms

Anti-Federalists
Assize of Clarendon
Bill of Rights
blood feuds
Code of Hammurabi
compurgation
Constitutional Convention
Court of Appeals Act of 1891
Court of the Star Chamber
federalists
Federal Magistrate Act of 1968
Habeas Corpus Act of 1679

Judges Bill of 1925
Judiciary Act of 1789
Judiciary Act of 1801
Justices of the Peace
nationalists
oath-helper
Ordinance of 1787
progressive era
solicitors
trial by battle
trial by ordeal
weregild

For digital learning resources, please go to
https://www.oup.com/he/burns1e

Current Organization of Courts

The ultimate goal of any court is to find justice. This image of the New York State Court of Appeals, with multiple judges, is notably different from the image many of us have of courts where only one judge presides.

What image comes to mind when you hear the word **court?**

Much like there is no single "criminal justice system" in the United States, there is no single "court system." There is a federal court system that processes federal crimes, and each of the 50 states has courts that address state laws. The state and federal court systems include both trial courts, which convict or adjudicate defendants, and appellate courts that provide oversight of the trial courts. This module begins with a look at the distinctions between trial and appellate courts and continues with an examination of the organization of both the federal and the state court systems. This module ends with a discussion of the roles and contributions of specialized courts, which were created to better address particular types of criminal cases.

Overlapping Court Jurisdiction

IN THE NEWS

1 Criminal Act

In June 2015, 21-year-old Dylann Roof killed nine people, all of whom were African American, following a bible study in a church in Charleston, South Carolina. Roof admitted that these victims were selected, in part, because they were African American.

State and federal prosecutors had to work collaboratively, primarily because South Carolina was one of three states without a hate crime statute (a law that increases penalties for crimes committed based on hatred or bias toward a victim's gender,

A jury sentenced Roof to death in January for killing nine black churchgoers in June 2015.

9 Sentencing

race, religion, or sexual orientation, etc.). The lack of a state-level hate crime statute

meant that the hate crime charges had to be filed in federal court. While the state prosecutor had jurisdiction (authority) over the murder charges, the federal and state prosecutors had to decide which courts would hear the case.

In January 2017, a federal judiciary sentenced Roof to death, and in June of the same year Roof pleaded guilty to nine murder charges, three attempted murder charges, and a weapons charge in state court. In addition to the death sentence he received in federal court, Roof received nine consecutive life sentences and three consecutive 30-year sentences in state court (Croft & Smith, 2017).

The Dylann Roof case demonstrates, in part, the complexity of the organization of U.S. courts. Roof's case was considered in both state and federal courts, because both levels of government had some jurisdiction. Cooperation was essential to determine where best to prosecute Mr. Roof for the various acts. While not all criminal cases are as complex as this one, most require different degrees of cooperation, understanding, professionalism, and resources. Given that Dylann Roof initially received the death penalty in federal court, was it necessary to expend court resources by having him face charges in state court? Why or why not?

Trial Versus Appellate Courts

Courts can be categorized in several ways, but they are primarily recognized in terms of their jurisdiction. With regard to the courts, **jurisdiction** is the power or right to exert one's legal power over another and can be considered in terms of:

● Learning Objective 21.1: Distinguish trial courts from appellate courts in the United States.

- *geography*: For instance, a crime occurring in Montana will generally be heard in Montana and not a different state.

- *subject matter*: For instance, trial courts of limited jurisdiction primarily hear misdemeanor and civil cases involving small amounts of money.

- *functions and responsibilities of a court*: For instance, trial courts are where both sides share evidence pertaining to the crime in question with the goal of determining whether the accused is guilty, and appellate courts generally review cases that were originally decided in trial courts to ensure that no constitutional rights were violated at trial.

There are some situations in which a state (or states) and the federal courts have **concurrent jurisdiction** over the accused, meaning that both courts have jurisdiction over a case and a decision must be made as to where the accused should stand trial (as discussed in the "In the News Feature" dealing with Dylann Roof). Such cases could involve:

- crimes punishable under both federal and state laws,
- certain civil rights claims,
- class action suits,
- issues involving the U.S. Constitution, or
- environmental regulations.

Trial Courts

Trial courts decide matters of fact, and they determine whether a defendant is found guilty. They exist in both the state and the federal court systems and process a large majority of criminal court proceedings. Trial courts are generally overseen by one judge and may include witnesses testifying, hearings, trials, and/or juries. Trial courts also provide a sense of oversight to lower courts, such as **justice of the peace courts**. These courts are often found in rural areas and are controlled by local government. There is no appellate oversight in justice of the peace courts, and so defendants who appeal cases heard in these courts must have their case retried, or what is known as trial de novo, by a trial court of general jurisdiction (Neubauer & Fradella, 2017).

Civil cases are also resolved in trial courts, although the procedures differ to some extent from criminal cases. As noted in Module 8, civil cases involve disputes between individuals, and thus there is no prosecutor or prosecution. Among the functions of civil trial courts are the following (Neubauer & Meinhold, 2013):

- making each party aware of the complaint that has been filed
- overseeing pretrial procedures
- conducting the trial
- ensuring that any out-of-court agreements are upheld (for example that construction materials or equipment is returned to their rightful owners, per an agreement)

Appellate Courts

Appellate courts hear cases that originated and were decided in trial courts. The primary purposes of appellate courts are to provide accountability for the trial courts and to ensure that proper procedures were followed and the law was correctly applied and interpreted. Defendants convicted and sentenced in a trial court have the right to appeal, one time, to an appellate court. If the appellate court upholds the decision of the trial court, the appellant is not guaranteed another appeal, because decisions to hear a second or third appeal are at the discretion of the higher level appellate courts.

Appellate courts do not hear new testimony nor do they consider new evidence. Instead, they review the trial court proceedings via a transcript of the case and listen to oral arguments from the prosecution and defense regarding the substantive nature of the appeal. Unlike trial courts that generally have just one judge overseeing a trial, multiple judges generally oversee appeals. In addition, appellate court judges typically offer written reports justifying their decisions, whereas trial court judges rarely do so (see Module 25).

jurisdiction The power or right to exert one's legal power over another; it can be considered in terms of geography, subject matter, and the functions and responsibilities of a court

concurrent jurisdiction The power of both state and federal courts to hear a case; officials work together to decide in which level of court the accused should stand trial

8 Trial

trial courts Courts that decide matters of fact and determine whether a defendant is found guilty; they host various types of court-related hearings in addition to conducting trials

justice of the peace courts Lower trial courts that are often found in rural areas and are controlled by local government

11 Appeal

appellate courts Courts that hear cases that originated and were decided in trial courts; their primary purposes are to provide accountability for the trial courts and ensure that proper procedures were followed and the law was correctly applied and interpreted

8 Trial

The Federal Court System

The federal criminal court system consists of three levels: U.S. district courts, U.S. courts of appeals, and the U.S. Supreme Court. Federal courts primarily hear cases in three situations (Spohn & Hemmens, 2009):

- when the United States is a party
- when individuals are from different states
- when there are violations of laws passed by Congress or the U.S. Constitution

There are also other federal courts, such as **Article III courts**, which hear cases that fall under Article III of the Constitution (e.g., the U.S. Court of International Trade and the Foreign Intelligence Surveillance Court) and **Article I tribunals**, which are legislative courts (e.g., U.S. Tax Court, U.S. Court of Appeals for Veterans Claims, U.S. Court of Federal Claims, and military courts). **Legislative courts** are courts that were created by the legislature as opposed to courts that were created by the U.S. Constitution. They are established for some specialized purpose (Figure 21.1).

U.S. District Courts

The 94 **U.S. district courts** spread throughout the United States and its territories are the trial courts of the federal judicial system. Eighty-nine can be found throughout the 50 states, and a district court is also located in Puerto Rico, the Virgin Islands, the District of Columbia, Guam, and the Northern Mariana Islands (Figure 21.2). Each state has at least one district court, and no court's jurisdiction can

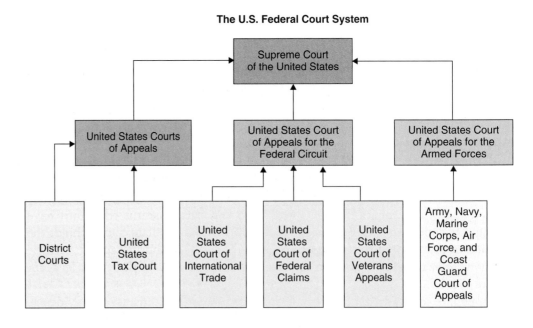

FIGURE 21.1. Federal Criminal Court Structure. Federal offenses are typically heard in U.S. district courts, which are the trial courts in the federal system of justice. Appeals are heard in U.S. courts of appeals and possibly in the U.S. Supreme Court.

Do you believe the federal court system is too complex? If so, how might you simplify it? If not, why not?

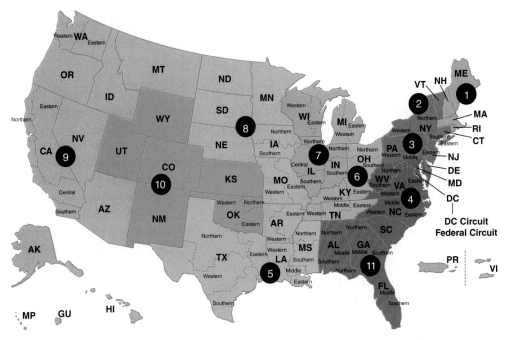

FIGURE 21.2. Geographical Boundaries for U.S. District and Circuit Courts. The U.S. districts are noted in the perforated lines within the states. The numbers reflect 11 of the 132 circuits in which appeals are heard in the federal system. The remaining 2 circuits are for the federal circuit and the District of Columbia. *Source: Administrative Office of the U.S. Courts on behalf of the Federal Judiciary, 2020 (https://www.uscourts.gov/sites/default/files/understanding-federal-courts.pdf).*

How could the organization of the districts be enhanced?

Article III courts Federal courts that hear cases that fall under Article III of the Constitution (e.g., the U.S. Court of International Trade and the Foreign Intelligence Surveillance Court)

Article I tribunals Legislative federal courts that were created by legislature as opposed to courts that were created by the Constitution; they address specialized issues, including taxes and veterans' claims

legislative courts Courts created by legislature as opposed to courts created by the Constitution; they are established for some specialized purpose

U.S. district courts The trial courts of the federal judicial system

extend beyond state lines per the Judiciary Act of 1789 (see Module 20). States with larger caseloads have multiple district courts, while others have only one.

U.S. DISTRICT COURT JUDGES

The number of district court judges in each district is determined by caseload sizes. As of October 2020, there were:

- 677 authorized judgeships in the U.S. district courts,
- 9 Supreme Court justices,
- 179 judges in the courts of appeals,
- 9 judges in the U.S. Court of International Trade, and
- 16 judges in the U.S. Court of Federal Claims (U.S. Courts, 2020a).

U.S. district court judges are nominated by the president and confirmed by the Senate and generally are appointed for life. They may be removed from the bench only through impeachment and conviction, which has occurred just a few times in U.S. history. They serve many of the same functions as state trial court judges. U.S. district court judges:

- preside over trials and pretrial activities,
- approve plea agreements,
- oversee settlements in civil cases,
- apply higher court rulings,

habeas corpus petitions Writs filed by prisoners contesting the constitutionality of their confinement

consent decrees Agreements between parties involved in a case to cease the alleged improper or illegal activity

U.S. magistrate judges Judges who assist federal judges through performing all of the same tasks as district court judges with the exception of trying and sentencing felony defendants

11 Appeal

U.S. courts of appeals Federal appellate courts that hear appeals from cases first tried in the U.S. district courts within their circuit

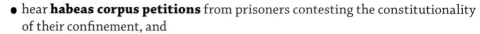

- hear **habeas corpus petitions** from prisoners contesting the constitutionality of their confinement, and

- supervise **consent decrees**, which are agreements between parties involved in a case to cease the alleged improper or illegal activity (e.g., employment discrimination or providing poor jail conditions).

U.S. MAGISTRATE JUDGES

U.S. magistrate judges are a subcomponent of U.S. district courts and were created by Congress in 1968 to ease the burden of the district courts. Magistrates are permitted to perform all of the same tasks as district court judges, with the exception of trying and sentencing felony defendants. They may preside over misdemeanor and petty offense cases and oversee many preliminary hearings, such as those involving the setting of bail and issuing of search warrants. Magistrate judges are selected by the district court judges, and full-time magistrates are appointed for 8-year terms. Part-time magistrates are appointed for 4 years. Magistrate judges have played an increasingly important role as federal caseloads have increased over time (Neubauer & Fradella, 2017).

U.S. DISTRICT ATTORNEYS

There are 93 U.S. district attorneys in the 94 U.S. districts throughout the United States and its territories, with 1 attorney serving in each of the districts, with the exception of Guam and the Northern Mariana Islands, where a single U.S. attorney serves both areas. The number of charges filed for criminal offenses has lately decreased or increased in U.S. district courts, depending on the attorney general in the position. For example, when Eric Holder held the position (2009–2015), he directed federal prosecutors to ensure that the cases they prosecuted served "a substantial federal interest" (Holder, 2013), while Attorney General Jeff Sessions, confirmed to the position in 2017, proposed to increase the number of prosecutions in the years ahead (Gramlich, 2017). Filings for defendants prosecuted for immigration (34% of all defendant filings) and drug (28%) offenses remained most numerous in 2019 (Figure 21.3).

U.S. Courts of Appeals

The 13 **U.S. courts of appeals** are federal appellate courts that hear appeals from cases first tried in the U.S. district courts within their circuit. Eleven of the 13 circuits are noted in Figure 21.2. The other 2 circuits are an appellate court for the federal circuit and one for the District of Columbia. The former hears specialized appeals regarding certain kinds of government contracts, patents, and trademarks. It also hears specified types of claims against the U.S. government, federal personnel, and veterans' benefits (Neubauer & Fradella, 2017). U.S. courts of appeals hear appeals for both civil and criminal cases.

U.S. COURTS OF APPEALS JUDGES

Similar to judges in district court, the judges presiding over the U.S. courts of appeals are nominated by the president and confirmed by the Senate, and the number of judges in each circuit varies according to caseload: The number of judges within each circuit ranges from 6 (the First Circuit) to 29 (the Ninth Circuit). Each circuit has a chief judge who has supervisory responsibilities and is selected based on seniority.

U.S. COURTS OF APPEALS PROCESS

The courts of appeals typically use panels of three judges from the circuit who read the arguments and listen to oral arguments from the prosecution and defense. The panel then discusses the case and decides whether to uphold or reverse the lower court decision. Although a panel of three judges is typically used, on occasion all the

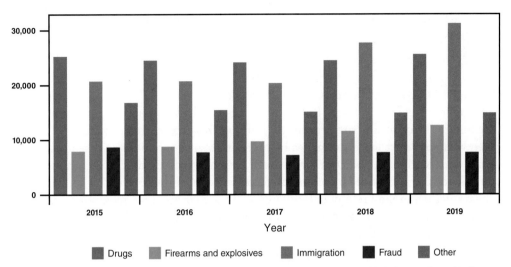

FIGURE 21.3. Criminal Defendants Filed, by Offense. The most commonly filed charges from 2012–2017 were for drug offenses, closely followed by immigration offenses. *Source:* U.S. District Courts—Judicial Business 2019, *by U.S. District Courts, 2020 (https://www.uscourts.gov/us-district-courts-judicial-business-2019).*

Should drug offenses be such a large focus of the federal court system? Why or why not?

judges in the circuit may sit in on a case, or what is known as sitting *en banc*, and decisions are made by a majority vote (Spohn & Hemmens, 2009).

Decisions offered by U.S. courts of appeals exhaust a defendant's right to have their appeal heard. Defendants may, however, appeal their case to the U.S. Supreme Court, although the court is not obligated to hear the case.

U.S. Supreme Court

The **U.S. Supreme Court** is the only court specifically created by the U.S. Constitution. It is the highest court in the land, which means that it has authority over the 51 distinct legal systems in the United States (one in each state and the federal government). The court consists of one chief justice and eight associate justices. Supreme Court judges, akin to other federal judges who are appointed under Article III of the U.S. Constitution, are nominated by the president and confirmed by the Senate, and they serve for life.

HOW THE U.S. SUPREME COURT SELECTS CASES

The U.S. Supreme Court justices choose what cases they will hear from the appeals already adjudicated in the federal U.S. circuit courts and the highest courts at the state level. Annually, the U.S. Supreme Court receives thousands of petitions for a **writ of certiorari**, which is an order from the lower courts to send the case records forward to the Supreme Court for review. The "rule of four" is used to determine if a case will be heard by the court, which means that four of the nine justices must agree to hear a case.

The court typically accepts only 100–150 of the more than 7,000 cases it is asked to review each year (U.S. Courts, 2020b). Decisions to not hear cases do not necessarily mean that the court agrees with the lower courts' rulings. Instead, the court chooses cases that may have national significance or cases in which lower courts may have ruled in conflicting ways (Spohn & Hemmens, 2009). Likewise, decisions made in state courts will generally only be reviewed by the Supreme Court if they pertain to a federal matter. For instance, in 1985, the court set the standard for the use of deadly force for law enforcement in *Tennessee v. Garner* (1985), which originated in

U.S. Supreme Court
The highest court in the land; it has authority over the 51 distinct legal systems in the United States

11 Appeal

writ of certiorari
An order from a superior court to the lower courts to send the case records forward for review

state court (see Module 15). The court will also often listen to questions involving important legal matters in which there is conflict, such as inconsistencies among state laws (Spohn & Hemmens, 2009).

HOW THE U.S. SUPREME COURT HEARS CASES

All nine justices sit for cases. Both the defense and the prosecution present their case before the court and are granted 30 minutes. No jury is used or witnesses heard, given that the court largely engages in appellate review—reviewing cases that have been tried—although the court does have original jurisdiction in certain circumstances, for instance those involving disputes between states. For each appellate case it hears (which is the large majority of cases), the justices have received a record of prior proceedings and printed briefs containing the arguments of each side.

THE U.S. SUPREME COURT'S TERM

The Supreme Court begins its annual term on the first Monday in October and continues until late June or early July. The term is divided between "sittings," which involve the justices hearing cases and offering opinions, and "recesses," when the justices consider the business before the court and write opinions. Sittings and recesses alternate at roughly 2-week intervals. During the summers, the justices regularly analyze new petitions for review, consider motions and applications, and prepare for the cases scheduled for the fall (Supreme Court of the United States, 2021).

Administration of the Federal Court System

The federal and state court systems cannot operate without a host of people and groups in support roles, including members of the courtroom workgroup (see Module 22) and sentencing commissions (see Module 25). Several groups are also involved in the support and administration of the federal court system. These include the following:

- **Judicial Conference of the United States:** Created in 1922, this is the principal policymaking body with regard to the administration of the federal courts. The group considers and proposes improvements with regard to various areas of the federal court system, including civil procedure, criminal procedure, bankruptcy procedure, appellate procedure, and rules of evidence.
- **Administrative Office of the U.S. Courts:** Created in 1939, this group performs administrative support functions for the federal judiciary, including legal, financial, management, and information technology support.
- **Federal Judicial Center:** Created in 1967, this center provides training and research for federal judges. Its responsibilities include recommending improvements in the administration and management of the federal courts.
- **U.S. Sentencing Commission:** Created in 1984, this is an independent agency in the judicial branch of the U.S. government that establishes sentencing policies for the federal government, advises Congress regarding crime policies, and provides information on federal crime and sentencing issues.

State Court Systems

State courts handle the bulk of criminal cases in the United States simply because most crimes committed are violations against state, not federal, laws. The courts heard about 84 million cases in 2018 and have jurisdiction over a wide array of issues, including, but not exclusively, criminal matters. In 2018, the bulk of the

Judicial Conference of the United States The principal policymaking body with regard to the administration of the federal courts; the group considers and proposes improvements with regard to various areas of the federal court system, including civil procedure, criminal procedure, bankruptcy procedure, appellate procedure, and rules of evidence

Administrative Office of the U.S. Courts Created in 1939, this office performs administrative support functions for the federal judiciary, including administrative, legal, financial, management, and information technology support

Federal Judicial Center Provides training and research for federal judges; its responsibilities include recommending improvements in the administration and management of the federal courts

9 Sentencing

U.S. Sentencing Commission An independent agency in the judicial branch of the U.S. government that establishes sentencing policies for the federal government, advises Congress regarding crime policies, and provides information on federal crime and sentencing issues

incoming **caseloads**—which refers to new cases filed, cases reopened, and cases reactivated in state trial courts—pertained to matters involving:

- traffic (53%),
- criminal offenses (20%),
- civil disputes (20%),
- domestic relations (6%), and
- juveniles (1%) (National Center for State Courts, 2020a).

8 Trial

Like the federal court system, state courts are categorized according to whether they are trial or appellate courts. However, court structures vary in many ways. For instance, some states have unified court systems with three levels of courts across the state, while others have four. Further, most states have two levels of appellate courts, and some only have one. Most state trial court systems include two general levels of trial courts (courts of limited and general jurisdiction) and two levels of appellate courts (intermediate appellate and state supreme).

A handful of jurisdictions have only one level of state courts in which all trials are processed. The distinction between trial courts of limited and general jurisdiction is often based on issues such as case complexity, case types, and monetary values (Schauffler et al., 2016). Figure 21.4 depicts the general levels of courts found in most state court systems, as well as alternate names for the courts.

State Trial Courts of Limited and General Jurisdiction

State courts of limited jurisdiction are the most common among the courts. There are 14,000 to 16,000 limited-jurisdiction courts in the United States (Schauffler et al., 2011), and these courts hear the bulk of court cases. In 2018, courts of limited jurisdiction in states that used a two-tiered court structure (including both courts of limited and general jurisdiction) heard 54.8 million (roughly 77%) of the 83.8 million cases (Court Statistics Project, 2020).

Courts of limited jurisdiction primarily hear cases involving:

- traffic infractions;
- petty theft;
- disturbances of the peace;
- alcohol and drug offenses;
- low-level civil offenses, such as those involving domestic relations (e.g., divorce, child custody), estates (also known as probate court), and personal injury issues; and
- preliminary stages of felony hearings, such as conducting initial appearances, making bail decisions, and holding hearings regarding the appointment of counsel for indigent defendants.

Courts of limited jurisdiction are **courts of record**, which means that formal transcripts of the actions in these courts are created for use at the appellate level. Some of the problems associated with the lower courts include:

- inadequate financing,
- inadequate facilities,
- lax court procedures, and
- unbalanced caseloads (Neubauer & Fradella, 2017).

The group of courts responsible for the major trials in the state system are collectively known as **state courts of general jurisdiction**. The geographical

State Supreme Courts
• supreme court • court of appeals • supreme judicial court • court of criminal/civil appeals • supreme court of appeals

Intermediate Courts of Appeal (exist in 41 states)
• appeals courts • appellate courts • appellate divisions • courts of appeals

State Trial Courts of General Jurisdiction
• circuit courts • district courts • superior courts • supreme courts • courts of common pleas

State Trial Courts of Limited Jurisdiction
• county courts • municipal courts • justice of the peace courts • city courts • lower courts • inferior courts

FIGURE 21.4. State Criminal Court Structures. The bullets represent the different names of the courts at each level, because they are referred to by different names in different states. The two lower levels of courts (the courts of limited and general jurisdiction) are primarily trial courts. The next two levels (intermediate courts of appeal and supreme courts) are appellate courts. Eight states have collapsed the two levels of trial courts into a single tier. The single tier of trial courts is referred to differently among states: For instance, the trial courts in California are called superior court, while in Illinois they are known as circuit courts.

How could the organization of the courts be improved, or simplified?

● **Learning Objective 21.3:** Outline the organization of the state court systems.

caseloads The number of new cases filed, cases reopened, and cases reactivated in court

state courts of limited jurisdiction The most common among the courts, they are the lower level trial courts; they hear the bulk of court cases

courts of record Courts in which formal transcripts of the actions are created for use at the appellate level

5 Initial Appearance

8 Trial

state courts of general jurisdiction The group of courts responsible for the major trials in the state systems

jurisdiction of these courts is usually defined at the county level. These courts hear the cases that are considered more serious in nature than those heard in the courts of limited jurisdiction and may hear appeals from the lower courts. Akin to courts of limited jurisdiction, they are courts of record.

In 2018, state courts of general jurisdiction were the location for the roughly 15.3% of court cases heard in the 42 states that used a two-tiered court system. The greatest percentage of these cases were civil cases (35%), followed by domestic relations (21%), criminal (23%), and traffic (16%) cases (Court Statistics Project, 2020).

Moving Toward Court Unification

Across states, some jurisdictions do not have courts of limited jurisdiction, while others have several thousand of them. Court reformers view the inconsistencies, overlap, and general disorganization of trial courts, particularly trial courts of limited jurisdiction, as problematic. Since the 1990s, there has been a shift as states have generally decreased their use of courts of limited jurisdiction and moved toward a single-tiered or **unified court system**, which processes all case types in a single trial court (LaFountain et al., 2014; Malega & Cohen, 2013). As of 2020, 8 states had single-tiered court systems, with the remaining 42 states and territories having two-tiered systems (Court Statistics Project, 2020).

Unified court systems shift judicial administration from local courts to centralized administration and control (Neubauer & Fradella, 2017). This leads to the following (Berkson & Carbon, 1978):

- a simplified court structure
- centralized administration
- centralized rule making
- centralized judicial budgeting
- statewide financing of the judiciary

Administration of the State Trial Court System

State trial courts are technically a component of the state court system. However, they often receive funding from multiple sources, including the federal, county, and local governments. A central office in each state is responsible for the administration of the state's trial court system. These administrative offices of the court:

- assist with research and planning,
- provide technical assistance,
- serve as a liaison to the legislature,
- disperse state court statistics, and
- offer public information.

State Courts of Appeal

States historically only had one level of appellate courts, which was known as the state court of last resort. An increasing number of appeals resulted in the need for some states to create a second level of courts to hear appeals, or what are known as **intermediate appellate courts**. Only 13 states had permanent intermediate appellate courts in 1957. Six states added intermediate appellate courts between 1980 and 1998 (Malega & Cohen, 2013). Today, 41 of the 50 states have two-tier systems consisting of intermediate courts of appeal and courts of last resort (or state supreme courts).

Larger states typically have several intermediate appellate courts and sometimes divide them into criminal and civil sections. In 2018, the total incoming caseload

11 Appeal

Appellate Courts Often Overturn Many Trial Court Decisions

Appellate courts exist to provide correction for the trial courts. Accordingly, defense attorneys who fail to win at trial often provide their clients with a sense of hope that the trial court decision will be overturned by an appellate court. In practice, however, appellate courts relatively rarely reverse a trial court decision. For example, in fiscal year 2017, the California Court of Appeals reversed only about 7% of the cases it considered (Judicial Counsel of California, 2018). Criminal appeals rarely succeed because the rules of appeals apply primarily to serious errors, and courts often find that no serious errors occurred (Neubauer & Fradella, 2017).

of all state appellate courts was 234,000, with most cases (about 70%) heard by the intermediate appellate courts (Court Statistics Project, 2020).

State appellate courts generally hear the following:

- *appeals by right*, which are reviews of the lower courts that appellate courts must hear;
- *appeals by permission*, which are discretionary in nature and subject to an appellate court agreeing to review the case;
- *death penalty cases*, which involve appeals pertaining to cases in which a defendant received capital punishment and the case is undergoing appeal; and
- *original proceedings/other appellate matters*, which involve writs, judiciary proceedings, advisory opinions, and related issues.

State Supreme Courts

State supreme courts, or state courts of last resort, exist in each state. Two states, Texas and Oklahoma, have a court of last resort for civil appeals and one for criminal appeals. All states have an odd number of judges on their supreme court, with a range of five to nine judges. A seven-judge court is typical for most states.

Appeals from the trial courts are heard by state supreme courts in states that do not have intermediate appellate courts. State supreme courts use their discretion to decide if they will hear an appeal in states with intermediate appellate courts. Akin to the U.S. Supreme Court, state supreme courts typically hear relatively few cases (around 100 or so), although most have notable effects on legal issues and government within their jurisdiction (Neubauer & Fradella, 2017).

Specialized Courts

The federal and state court systems include various **specialized courts** that focus directly on particular types of crime or adjudicate certain types of defendants. These courts, which are sometimes referred to as "**problem-solving courts**" or "specialty courts," have become increasingly popular (Strong et al., 2016).

Specialized courts in the state system include the following:

- community courts
- domestic violence courts
- drug courts
- family relations courts

unified court system
Court systems that use a single-tiered organization of trial courts, thus eliminating the distinction between courts of limited jurisdiction and courts of general jurisdiction

intermediate appellate courts
A second level of courts that hear appeals; in the early 21st century, 41 states have intermediate courts of appeal

11 Appeal

state supreme courts Also known as state courts of last resort, they are the highest appellate court in each state

● **Learning Objective 21.4:** Describe the types of specialized courts.

specialized courts
Also known as problem-solving or specialty courts, they include various courts that focus directly on particular types of crime or adjudicate certain types of offenders

problem-solving courts Also known as specialized or specialty courts, they include various courts that focus directly on particular types of crime or adjudicate certain types of offenders

individualized justice Justice-based approaches designed to best meet an offender's need; they are often associated with problem-solving courts

- juvenile courts
- mental health courts
- military tribunals
- veterans courts

Specialized courts in the federal system include the following:

- U.S. Court of Appeals for the Armed Forces, which reviews court martial convictions in the armed forces
- the U.S. Court of Federal Claims, which hears tax cases and other cases involving monetary claims against the United States
- the U.S. Court of International Trade, which hears cases involving customs, unfair import actions, and other issues regarding international trade
- The U.S. Court of Appeals for Veterans Claims, which reviews decisions offered by the Board of Veteran Appeals
- the U.S. Tax Court, which addresses disputes between citizens and the Internal Revenue Service

Specialized courts have the benefit of involving court officials who develop expertise in particular types of social problems (Dorf & Fagan, 2003). While these courts differ to some extent, they all seek to address social problems, change the behavior of defendants through judicial supervision of rehabilitative approaches, and collaborate with social service providers and community agencies (e.g., community groups, victim advocates, employment services personnel, and treatment providers; Berman & Feinblatt, 2001). Compared to traditional courts, problem-solving court personnel are more likely to:

- collaborate with individuals not traditionally associated with the courtroom workgroup;
- focus on **individualized justice**, or justice-based approaches designed to best meet an offender's need;
- involve judges who are more directly involved in the monitoring and accountability of the individuals who come before the court;
- have access to much more information about each case in order to make better decisions;
- be concerned with the outcomes of cases, as opposed to simply processing cases; and
- involve the community and its many resources in addressing social problems (Marble & Worrall, 2009).

Although specialty courts are relatively new, there are over 3,000 problem-solving courts, and they are found in all U.S. states. Drug courts (44%) and mental health courts (11%) were the most common types of problem-solving courts identified in a U.S. Bureau of Justice Statistics census (Strong et al., 2016). Figure 21.5 depicts the number of problem-solving courts in the United States in 2012 (the most recent year for which these data are available). It is expected that the number of specialized courts will grow because focusing on specific problems and special populations seemingly provides positive results.

Drug Courts

Drug courts often address adult felony drug cases involving nonviolent offenders with substance abuse problems. The courts are not designed for drug traffickers and dealers. Early drug courts largely resembled diversionary programs concerned

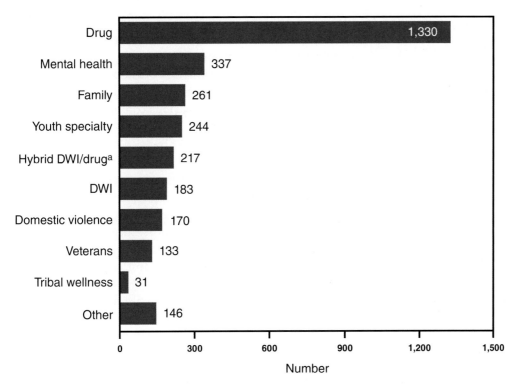

ᵃHandles alcohol- or drug-dependent offenders also charged with a driving offense.

FIGURE 21.5. Number of Problem-Solving Courts. This figure depicts the wide variety of special issues addressed by problem-solving courts. Drug courts (44%) were the most common form of problem-solving courts in the United States, followed by mental health (11%) courts. The "Other" category includes courts that focus on cases involving the homeless, prostitution, elder abuse, gambling, and parole violations. **Source:** Census of Problem-Solving Courts, 2012 *(NCJ 249803), by S. M. Strong, R. R. Rantala, and T. Kyckelhahn, 2016, U.S. Department of Justice, Bureau of Justice Statistics.*

Do you see the use of problem-solving courts increasing or decreasing in the future?

with improving the efficiency and speed with which drug cases were resolved. More recent drug courts are more concerned with the treatment and rehabilitation of offenders. These courts increased in popularity in the 1990s via support from the federal government; for instance, the **Violent Crime Control and Law Enforcement Act of 1994** allocated over $50 million for the expansion of drug courts across the United States (Olson et al., 2001). Research generally suggests that drug courts are effective in reducing recidivism (reoffending) (e.g., Berman et al., 2007). The effectiveness of drug courts at the state level prompted the creation of similar courts in the federal system.

Domestic Violence Courts

The first **domestic violence court** appeared in Florida in 1992, and they have grown in number since. Domestic violence courts differ from other specialty courts because they generally consider the victim's needs to a greater extent than offender rehabilitation. The emphasis is often on protecting victims and offering offender accountability over offender treatment (Berman et al., 2007). Evaluations of domestic violence courts suggest that they can be helpful for victims, although there are mixed results regarding their effectiveness for offenders (Marble & Worrall, 2009).

Homelessness, Gun, Mental Health, and Community Courts

Various other specialty courts exist throughout the United States. For instance, a court for the problems associated with homelessness was created in San Diego in

drug courts
Specialized courts that typically address adult felony drug cases involving nonviolent offenders with substance abuse problems

Violent Crime Control and Law Enforcement Act of 1994 The largest crime bill in the history of the United States; the act addressed many issues pertaining to crime and justice, including the allocation of over $50 million for the expansion of drug courts, providing victims in federal courts with permission to speak at sentencing hearings, and expanding victim services; it also made restitution mandatory in sexual assault cases

domestic violence court Specialized courts that address cases related to domestic violence; the emphasis in these courts is often on protecting victims and offering offender accountability over offender treatment

mental health courts Specialized courts that contain dockets of mentally ill individuals who are assessed and processed by court personnel and clinical specialists

community courts Courts that address many quality-of-life crimes such as prostitution, trespassing, and vandalism; they use various community services to address the root causes of problems in the community

1989 (American Bar Association, n.d.b), and New York City established a gun court to address cases involving felony gun possession. **Mental health courts** originated in Florida in 1997, and contain dockets of mentally ill individuals who are assessed and processed by court personnel and clinical specialists. **Community courts** exist throughout the United States to address many quality-of-life crimes, such as prostitution, trespassing, and vandalism. These courts use various community services to address the root causes of problems in the community.

Veterans Courts

Veterans courts, or veterans treatment courts based on the drug and mental health treatment courts, are designed to assist veterans with substance abuse problems, mental health issues, and other concerns. For example, the Tarrant County Veterans Court Diversion Program in Texas offers veterans facing prosecution for certain offenses, such as driving under the influence, a judicially supervised treatment option if they meet certain criteria. To be eligible for participation in the program, defendants must be veterans or current members of the U.S. Armed Forces (including the reserves), National Guard, or State Guard. They must have a clinical diagnosis of a brain injury, mental illness, or mental disorder, which includes post–traumatic stress disorder that resulted from military service or a similar hazardous duty that affected their criminal conduct (Ciesco, 2018).

Participants in the program receive an individualized treatment plan, including education and counseling provided by outside agencies. Successful completion of the program results in the participant's case being dismissed. Failure to complete the program results in the cases being returned to the court of origin for continued prosecution. The program in Tarrant County has proven successful, for instance as the judge who oversees the cases noted that the recidivism rate was only 7% (Ciesco, 2018).

Veterans courts provide helpful alternatives for veterans who find themselves involved in the criminal justice system. The programs have become increasingly popular, as veterans suffering from substance abuse, mental illness, and related problems can obtain specialized treatment by court systems specifically created to meet their needs.

Does the idea of offering specialized treatment for veterans seem fair to you? Why or why not?

The System in Perspective

Some crimes, such as the ones committed by Dylann Roof at a South Carolina church (as noted in the "In the News Feature" at the start of this module), can be processed in state and/or federal courts. In fact, the dual jurisdiction of the Roof case and the debates over where to prosecute Roof highlight the complexity of the organization of our court systems, which differ, sometimes significantly, across states. Although efforts to reform and streamline the courts continue, there is much work to be done. The vital role played by the courts in criminal case processing means that it is important for those who enter the courts in any capacity (whether as defendants, victims, or employees) to understand the levels of functionality and organization.

Summary

1. Learning Objective 21.1: *Distinguish trial courts from appellate courts in the United States.*

- Trial courts decide matters of fact and determine whether a defendant is found guilty. Appellate courts hear cases that originated and were decided in trial courts. The primary purposes of appellate courts are to provide accountability for the trial courts. Appellate courts do not hear new testimony, nor do they consider new evidence. Instead, they review the trial court proceedings via a transcript of the case and listen to oral arguments from the prosecution and defense regarding the substantive nature of the appeal. Multiple judges oversee appeals, as opposed to just one judge in trial courts. Appellate courts also differ from trial courts because appellate court judges typically offer written reports justifying their decisions, whereas trial court judges rarely do so.

2. Learning Objective 21.2: *Explain how a federal crime could be heard by the U.S. Supreme Court.*

- The federal criminal court system consists of three levels: U.S. district courts, U.S. courts of appeals, and the U.S. Supreme Court. A federal case would make it to the Supreme Court after first being heard in the U.S. district courts and following an appeal heard in the U.S. courts of appeals. Cases reach the Supreme Court through a writ of certiorari after being heard in a U.S. court of appeal. The Supreme Court does not hear all cases; it uses discretion in selecting cases that have the most significant impacts.

3. Learning Objective 21.3: *Outline the organization of the state court systems in the United States.*

- State court systems are generally organized into state trial courts of limited jurisdiction, state trial courts of general jurisdiction, intermediate courts of appeal, and state supreme courts. States use various names to refer to these different courts, and only 41 of the 50 states have intermediate courts of appeal. Some states have combined the trial courts of limited jurisdiction with the trial courts of general jurisdiction, opting to have one level of trial courts instead of two.

4. Learning Objective 21.4: *Describe the types of specialized courts in the United States.*

- Various types of specialized courts exist to address particular types of crime and/or offenders. Specialized courts in the federal system include the U.S. Court of Appeals for the Armed Forces, the U.S. Court of Federal Claims, the U.S. Court of International Trade, the U.S. Court of Appeals for Veterans Claims, and the U.S. Tax Court. Among the specialized state courts are drug courts, which typically address drug cases involving nonviolent offenders with substance abuse problems; domestic violence courts, which seek to best resolve domestic violence cases and protect victims; mental health courts, which are designed to assist mentally ill offenders in the courts; community courts, which seek to address many quality-of-life crimes, such as trespassing and vandalism; and veterans courts, which assist current and former members of the armed forces in the courts.

Questions for Critical Thinking

1. Do you believe appellate courts would be more effective if, instead of reviewing transcripts and hearing oral arguments, they conducted a new trial with the appellate court judges overseeing the case? Why or why not?

2. Given that the U.S. Supreme Court hears only 100–150 cases per year, would you support the creation of an additional Supreme Court that provided the same functions, in efforts to increase the number of cases heard in the highest court? Discuss why or why not.

3. Some states have consolidated the number of trial courts they have, switching from two levels of trial courts to one. What would be the pros and cons of adopting this unified organizational approach?

4. Do you believe we should further specialize our courts? For instance, should we have "property crime courts" and "violent crime courts"? Along these lines, should we, in addition or instead, create courts designed for other categories of individuals (e.g., single-mothers, first-time offenders, etc.)? Why or why not?

Key Terms

Administrative Office of the U.S. Courts
appellate courts
Article I tribunals
Article III courts
caseloads
community courts
concurrent jurisdiction
consent decrees
courts of record
domestic violence court
drug courts
Federal Judicial Center
habeas corpus petitions
individualized justice
intermediate appellate courts
Judicial Conference of the United States
jurisdiction

justice of the peace courts
legislative courts
mental health courts
problem-solving courts
specialized courts
state courts of general jurisdiction
state courts of limited jurisdiction
state supreme courts
trial courts
unified court system
U.S. courts of appeals
U.S. district courts
U.S. magistrate judges
U.S. Sentencing Commission
U.S. Supreme Court
Violent Crime Control and Law Enforcement Act of 1994
writ of certiorari

For digital learning resources, please go to
https://www.oup.com/he/burns1e

Courtroom Personnel

It takes a lot of organization for courts to successfully function. Various individuals perform a wide array of tasks to help find justice. The roles and expectations of the many individuals who work in the courts or briefly participate in court proceedings are well defined, but each court case is unique.

Which individual do you believe has the most significant role in ensuring that justice is served?

Courtrooms across the United States are filled with individuals who are there for various reasons. The uniqueness of courtroom happenings, including the diverse backgrounds and interests of individuals assembled for a common purpose, contributes to our fascination with courtroom proceedings. This module examines the roles of the various individuals found in courtrooms, beginning with a look at the primary actors, including judges, prosecutors, and defense attorneys. This is followed by an examination of others who work in the courts, such as court administrators, court reporters, bailiffs, and clerks of court. Finally, this module ends with a discussion of others in the courtroom who typically play instrumental roles in the adjudication process, including witnesses, defendants, jurors, and audiences.

MODULE OUTLINE

• **Primary Actors in the Courts**

Learning Objective 22.1: Identify the primary actors in the courts and describe their responsibilities.

• **Contributors Who Work in the Courts**

Learning Objective 22.2: Identify the contributors who work in the courts and summarize their primary responsibilities.

• **Contributors Who do Not Work in the Courts**

Learning Objective 22.3: Identify the prominent groups who contribute to but do not work in the courts, and briefly describe their contributions.

Is It Time for Professional Jurors?

In 2019, Joaquin "El Chapo" Guzman was convicted in a Brooklyn, New York, federal court on charges of drug trafficking, weapons violations, and operation of a continuing criminal enterprise. He received a life sentence plus 30 years, and was required to forfeit more than $12.6 billion. Guzman, who for many years headed Mexico's Sinaloa drug cartel, had gained international notoriety for twice breaking out of high-security prisons in Mexico. Despite Guzman's conviction, however, reports surfaced that jurors in his initial

Joaquin "El Chapo" Guzman's defense team said in court filings that jurors repeatedly disregarded instructions...

trial were following media coverage of the case, despite repeated instructions from the judge for them not to do so. As a result, Guzman's attorneys plan to seek a new trial (K. McCoy, 2019).

Serving on a jury can be a long and tedious endeavor, and individuals may face personal and financial hardships from not being able to work and/or being away from home. Individuals asked to serve on a jury typically have

no training in the law, and some states do not permit jurors to take notes. Jurors sometimes let their emotions get in the way of common sense or logic and may suffer psychological effects from viewing grisly crime or autopsy photos. A negative attitude about serving on a jury may also influence case outcomes.

Some have suggested that instead of using laypersons, we should consider the use of professional jurors who would be evaluated and trained to serve full-time on juries (Frank, 2014). These salaried, career individuals could be taken from the ranks of retired judges, lawyers, and law professors, or the individuals could go through other formal training. The use of professional jurors would create new jobs, and the money currently used to pay jurors could offset some of the costs of employing professional jurors. Further, the use of professional jurors would eliminate the hardships on jurors' personal lives, because the professional jurors would be employed by the courts.

There would be some drawbacks to using professional jurors, however (Diamond, 2011). For example, professional jurors might overthink cases or act as attorneys or judges instead of jurors. Further, they would be costly. The cost of paying jurors under the current system is much lower than what it would be to hire full-time professional jurors. In addition, using professional jurors would result in the general public being less involved in the adjudication process. How might the use of professional jurors potentially contradict aspects of the Sixth Amendment, for instance as it pertains to the right to a trial by one's peers? Would you support or oppose the use of professional jurors? Why?

● Learning Objective 22.1: Identify the primary actors in the courts and describe their responsibilities.

Primary Actors in the Courts

The courtroom setting has been loosely compared to a boxing match, particularly with regard to trial proceedings (Burns, 2007). The prosecution and defense serve as the combatants who square off before evaluative bodies in the form of a judge—akin to the boxing referee tasked with ensuring proper procedures are followed. In some cases, a jury offers verdicts of guilty or not guilty, much like the judges in a boxing match offer their opinion regarding who won the match. Finally, more generally, both the courts and the boxing matches generate interest and audiences, and both events involve individuals from all walks of life.

The United States uses an **adversarial legal system** that involves two parties—the prosecution and defense—presenting their cases before a judge and perhaps a jury. The burden of proof is on the prosecution (the state) to demonstrate beyond a reasonable doubt that the defendant is culpable for the crime in question. Both the prosecution and the defense may present evidence to support their arguments, and they may cross-examine (ask questions of) witnesses who are placed on the stand by the opposing party. Judges oversee these and other events that occur in courtrooms, with the goal of ensuring that proper procedure is followed and justice is served. The primary actors in the courtroom include the judge, prosecutors, and defense attorneys. Through working with one another in the courts on a regular basis, the primary actors become familiar with one another and engage in a series of exchange relations. They then develop a culture of shared norms and expectations (Eisenstein & Jacob, 1977).

Judges

Generally, **judges** are responsible for ensuring that courtroom proceedings operate in a fair manner. A judge's powers depend on the type of judge they are and the responsibilities they may be asked to assume:

- In **bench trials**, judges assess the facts of the case, apply the law, and offer verdicts and sentences.

- In jury trials, judges decide only the legal matters and often offer sentences.

- In appellate courts, judges review cases previously decided in the trial courts and determine whether the trial court proceedings were appropriate.

Aside from the more traditional judges found in busy courtrooms across the United States are **lay judges**, who are more commonly found in rural areas. They are sometimes also referred to as a magistrate, a justice of the peace, or an associate judge, and are not lawyers. They are more commonly found in areas where it may be difficult to find lawyers who are interested in being a judge (Spohn & Hemmens, 2009). The requirements for lay judges are much less stringent. For instance, in Colorado the only requirements to be a lay judge are to have a high school degree and to be a registered voter. Lay judges serve on state courts of limited jurisdiction in 22 states, although in 14 of those states a defendant has the right to seek a new trial before a judge if they receive a jail sentence. Seven states permit lay judges to impose jail sentences (Ford, 2017).

A JUDGE'S ROLE

Judges are placed in powerful positions within the criminal justice system. Legally, they retain much control over courtroom proceedings and play a role in:

- arrests (e.g., through issuing warrants),
- initial appearances,
- bail hearings,
- preliminary and grand jury hearings,
- arraignments,
- plea bargaining,
- trials,
- sentencing, and
- appeals.

adversarial legal system The legal system used in the United States, which involves the prosecution and defense presenting their cases before a judge and perhaps a jury; the burden of proof is on the prosecution to demonstrate beyond a reasonable doubt that the defendant is culpable for the crime in question

9 Sentencing

judges Court officials who are responsible for ensuring that courtroom proceedings operate in a fair manner

bench trials Trials in which judges assess the facts of the case, apply the law, and offer verdicts and sentences; judges replace jurors in determining guilt

lay judges Judges who are nonlawyers and are sometimes referred to as magistrates, justices of the peace, or associate judges; they serve on state courts of limited jurisdiction in most states and a small number serve on state courts of general jurisdiction

---

MYTHBUSTING

All Judges Are the Same

Given the role of judges in ensuring that the law is properly applied and procedures are followed, it would be easy to assume that all judges are similar. In practice, however, there are notable differences among judges, with some being more focused on disposing cases, some more sympathetic to defendants' needs, and others who emphasize law and order. In response to the differences among judicial practices, attorneys sometimes "judge shop" by strategically offering motions for continuances, which are postponements of hearings or trials in court, and motions for a change of judge to find one who they believe will be more likely to support their arguments in court and thus provide more favorable decisions (Neubauer & Fradella, 2017).

In practice, however, judges often informally share their powers with the other primary actors in the courtroom. In addition, not all judgeships are alike. For instance, judges in state courts of limited jurisdiction have heavier caseloads and more extensive administrative responsibilities, and they deal with conflict on a more regular basis than other judges.

THE SYMBOLISM OF A JUDGE

Judges are considered symbols of justice. Several aspects distinguish judges from others in the courtroom and suggest a high level of prestige and respect:

- a judge's robe
- a judge's use of a gavel
- the requirement that everyone rise upon a judge's entrance into the courtroom
- the elevation of the judge's bench over the rest of the courtroom
- the fact that federal positions and some state positions are lifetime appointments
- a judge's salary; Table 22.1 notes the relatively high level of pay for various levels of judges.

THE SELECTION OF A JUDGE

The selection of federal judges is straightforward. The U.S. Constitution notes that the president, with the advice of the Senate, nominates judges for the federal judiciary. The nominees must be approved by the Senate (Neubauer & Fradella, 2017).

TABLE 22.1. State-Level Judicial Salaries, 2020

TYPE OF JUDGE	AVERAGE SALARY AS OF 2020
Courts of last resort, chief	$186,164
Courts of last resort, associate judge	$181,224
Intermediate appellate courts	$174,504
General trial courts	$162,590

Source: Survey of Judicial Salaries, National Center for State Courts, 2020b (https://www.ncsc.org/__data/assets/pdf_file/0017/51164/JSS-Handout-July-2020.pdf).

The variation in the court systems among the states, however, results in several means by which judges are selected, and states may use different procedures depending on the level of the position being filled:

- *Appointment*: Most appellate court judges are appointed by judicial nominating committees, governors, or legislators. Federal judges are appointed for life. Judges in state courts of general jurisdiction and intermediate appellate courts generally serve average terms of 7 years, and judges on state courts of last resort serve an average of 15 years (Malega & Cohen, 2013). A limitation of appointing judges involves the potential for selecting judges based on their political support for the appointing entity, as opposed to selecting the most qualified individual for the position (T. E. George & Yoon, 2014).

- *Partisan or nonpartisan elections*: Judicial elections are used in the selection of trial court judges in most states (29). The idea of electing judges emerged during Andrew Jackson's presidency (1829–1837), because it was believed that voters should determine who is qualified and suitable for judgeships. Most states that use elections use nonpartisan elections to avoid any problems associated with perceptions of judges being more accountable to members of one political party than another. Critics of judicial elections argue that many voters have very little knowledge of a judge's qualifications and thus often vote based on political party affiliation or other reasons that may have little relation to a candidate's suitability for being a judge. It is also suggested that well-positioned special interest groups can influence elections and that elections strip judges of their dignity by requiring them to run campaigns that can become increasingly negative in tone (Hull, 2010). State supreme court spending totaled roughly $39.7 million in the 21 states that held elections in 2017–2018, with much of the funding (27%) coming from special interest groups (Keith et al., 2019).

- *Merit selection*: **Merit selection** proposes to limit the effects of politics, elections, and favoritism from the selection of judges. Merit selection is a hybrid approach that incorporates various judicial selection approaches. It is often known as the **Missouri Bar Plan** (or the Missouri Plan), in reference to Missouri being the first state to adopt it in 1940. Merit selection begins with the creation of a judicial nominating commission, consisting of lawyers and laypersons, that provides a list of potential candidates to the governor, who then chooses one from the list. The new judge then undergoes an uncontested vote after a defined period, which varies from 1 to 12 years. Voter approval results in the judge remaining on the bench.

Merit selection or Missouri Bar Plan
A means of selecting judges that is a hybrid approach incorporating various judicial selection approaches, including appointment and election

THE REMOVAL OF A JUDGE

Given the significance of the responsibilities of judges and the high levels of independence, concerns about judicial misconduct arise. Judges are expected to be impartial and objective in performing their duties. The American Bar Association created a **Model Code of Judicial Conduct**, although each state has its own set of ethical guidelines. The goals of the guidelines are to promote ethical judicial behavior and encourage confidence in the courts. **State judicial conduct commissions** evaluate complaints about judges and often work informally to address any concerns. Serious concerns may result in the commission recommending to the state's highest court that problematic judges be removed (Neubauer & Fradella, 2017).

Removing judges from the bench for a case or permanently can be difficult. Prosecutors and defense attorneys in many states can motion that a judge be removed from a case for cause, for instance if a judge has a vested interest in the case (e.g., it involves a close associate). Judges are sometimes removed from the federal

Model Code of Judicial Conduct
A set of ethical guidelines created by the American Bar Association; the goals of the guidelines are to promote ethical judicial behavior and encourage confidence in the courts

state judicial conduct commissions
State commissions that evaluate complaints regarding judges

courts permanently via impeachment, which involves accusation by the House of Representatives and a trial in the Senate. This occurs only rarely. In the history of the courts, only 15 judges have been impeached by the House, and 8 were convicted by the Senate and removed from the bench. Other judges have resigned during the Senate's investigation (Federal Judicial Center, n.d.a).

States note the procedures and causes for removing state judges in state constitutions, which includes impeachment by the state legislature and **recalls**, which involve a special election in which voters note their support or disapproval for the judge in question. These processes are somewhat cumbersome, however, so states have created judicial disciplinary commissions that investigate complaints against judges. For instance, the Colorado Constitution created the Commission on Judicial Discipline to investigate allegations of judicial misconduct or general inappropriate behavior. The commission consists of 10 members: 4 citizens, 2 attorneys, 2 district court judges, and 2 county court judges (Colorado Commission on Judicial Discipline, n.d.).

recalls Special elections in which voters note their support or disapproval for specific judges

Prosecutors

prosecutors
As representatives of the state primarily responsible for ensuring justice, their responsibilities include being actively involved in courtroom proceedings and providing a key link between law enforcement and the courts

As a representative of the state primarily responsible for ensuring justice, **prosecutors** have a great deal of discretion because they perform many functions throughout criminal case processing. For instance, they:

- provide a key link between law enforcement and the courts;
- work with police in response to crimes—officers must be aware of the prosecutor's preferences with regard to the level of evidence required for prosecution. For instance, officers do not wish to go through the process of making an arrest and have the charges dropped by a prosecutor who believes the officer had no legal justification for the arrest or failed to follow legal procedure in some other manner;
- are part of the executive branch and considered law enforcement personnel and gatekeepers to the criminal justice system—they decide if, what, and how many charges should be filed in each criminal case; and
- participate actively in courtroom proceedings, such as:
  - initial appearances,
  - bail hearings,
  - filing charges,
  - preliminary and grand jury hearings,
  - arraignments,
  - trials,
  - sentencing, and
  - appeals.

3 Arrest

Prosecution is notably decentralized in the United States. Prosecutors work in various levels of court, and different prosecutors' offices may handle the same case. For example, a city attorney may handle the preliminary stages of a felony case, while a district attorney prosecutes the case at the trial court of general jurisdiction (Neubauer & Fradella, 2017).

11 Appeal

FEDERAL PROSECUTORS

The U.S. Department of Justice handles prosecutions in federal court. The **U.S. attorney general**, who is a member of the president's cabinet, heads the department, which consists of numerous attorneys working on various types of caseloads. Three groups prosecute crimes at the federal level, including the Office of the Solicitor General, the Criminal Division, and U.S. attorneys.

- The **Office of the Solicitor General** represents the U.S. government before the U.S. Supreme Court in federal appeals.

- The **Criminal Division** prosecutes some nationally significant criminal cases and provides some supervision over U.S. attorneys.

- **U.S. attorneys** are the primary litigators for the federal government. The 93 attorneys in the United States are assisted by over 5,400 assistant U.S. attorneys and are appointed by and serve at the discretion of the president with the advice and consent of the Senate. According to Title 28, Section 547, of the United States Code, U.S. attorneys are responsible for:

  - the prosecution of criminal cases brought by the federal government,

  - the prosecution and defense of civil cases in which the United States is a party, and

  - the collection of debts owed the federal government that are administratively uncollectable.

STATE PROSECUTORS

Prosecution in state courts is decentralized, with the authority to prosecute state crimes found at the state, county, and local levels. Each state has a **state attorney general**, who is the state's chief legal officer. Their responsibilities are often noted in state constitutions, although their most important tasks include providing legal advice to other state agencies and representing the state when state practices are challenged in court (Neubauer & Fradella, 2017). For example, Arkansas attorney Leslie Rutledge filed an appeal in 2017 regarding a federal judge's order that had blocked the state from enforcing new laws that tightened restrictions on abortions (Satter, 2017).

Despite being the state's chief legal officer, state attorneys general rarely engage in local criminal procedures and do so only when local attorneys need assistance or fail to meet their responsibilities (Roberson et al., 2013). Figure 22.1 depicts the duties and responsibilities of the Vermont Office of Attorney General.

U.S. attorney general A member of the president's cabinet who heads the U.S. Department of Justice and oversees prosecutions in the federal government

Office of the Solicitor General The office responsible for representing the U.S. government before the U.S. Supreme Court in federal appeals

Criminal Division Prosecutes some nationally significant criminal cases and provides some supervision over U.S. attorneys

U.S. attorneys The primary litigators for the federal government

state attorney general A state's chief legal officer

VERMONT OFFICE OF ATTORNEY GENERAL

ELECTION AND TERM

The Attorney General is elected every two years at the same time and manner as other Vermont statewide elected officials.

SCOPE OF AUTHORITY

The Attorney General may represent the state in all civil and criminal matters as at common law and as allowed by statute. The Attorney General shall also have the same authority throughout the state as a state's attorney.

GENERAL POWERS

The Attorney General shall have the general supervision of criminal prosecutions, shall consult with and advise the state's attorneys in matters relating to the duties of their office, and shall assist them by attending the grand jury in the examination of any case or in the preparation of indictments and informations when, in his judgment, the interests of the state require it.

FIGURE 22.1. *Duties and Responsibilities—Vermont Office of Attorney General.* The Office of Attorney General has a large scope of authority and is responsible for many important functions in the court system. In Vermont, an election is conducted every 2 years to select the attorney general. ***Source:*** *Vermont Office of the Attorney General (https://ago.vermont.gov/about-the-attorney-generals-office/duties-responsibilities/).*

What are the pros and cons of choosing a new attorney general every 2 years?

Prosecutors are elected officials in most states, and their position is often in high demand in large urban areas because of the high pay, associated level of prestige, and large support staffs. Sparsely populated areas may have part-time prosecutors who have no support staff (Roberson et al., 2013).

PROSECUTORIAL DISCRETION

Perhaps one of the most significant aspects of the prosecutor's role is the decision to file charges in a case. Most prosecutors' offices do not have specific criteria designating when a case should be prosecuted, and so prosecutors must use discretion. Various factors influence prosecutorial decisions in filing charges, including the following:

- seriousness of the offense
- relationship between the victim and offender
- level of evidence to support prosecution
- criminal history of the suspect
- concern and/or media attention devoted to the case (e.g., high-profile cases with extensive media coverage often limit prosecutorial discretion)

Ultimately, a series of legal and extralegal variables influence prosecutorial discretion. Prosecutors may decide *not* to file charges for several reasons, including not having enough resources to prosecute a case or a lack of evidence to successfully go forward with a case. Prosecutors may adhere to public opinion when it does not support charging a particular offender, and prosecutors may drop a case or reduce charges if they feel a potential penalty is too severe for the crime. Diversion (e.g., when a prosecutor does not file charges against a suspect who successfully completes substance abuse treatment) and plea bargaining are also alternatives to filing charges.

Prosecutors' offices generally operate under a series of different policies with regard to their decision to prosecute, including legal sufficiency, trial sufficiency, system efficiency, and defendant rehabilitation (Jacoby, 1980):

- **Legal sufficiency** refers to the prosecution of cases when all legal elements are present, meaning that there is enough evidence to successfully prosecute the case.
- **Trial sufficiency** refers to the prosecution of cases where there is a strong likelihood of winning at trial.
- **System efficiency** refers to the way that offices consider their caseloads in light of the high volume of cases and lack of resources for prosecution; offices with high caseloads are more likely to screen out cases for diversion.
- **Defendant rehabilitation** refers to foregoing prosecution in favor of diversion, particularly with regard to first-time nonviolent offenders, if there is an acceptable perceived likelihood of rehabilitation.

Some important Supreme Court decisions have affected prosecutorial discretion, including *Berger v. United States* (1935), in which the court ruled that prosecutors' primary interest should be in finding justice, not simply winning cases. Other cases focused on the protections granted to prosecutors in the course of their work, including *Imbler v. Pachtman* (1976), in which the court noted that prosecutors have absolute immunity, or are protected from civil liability regarding their decisions to initiate and pursue criminal prosecution.

COMMUNITY PROSECUTION

One increasingly common alternative to traditional prosecutorial practices is **community prosecution**. Similar to community policing, and also based on Wilson

legal sufficiency
The prosecutorial use of discretion that favors only proceeding with cases in which all legal elements are present

8 Trial

trial sufficiency
The manner by which prosecutors' offices consider their caseloads by prosecuting cases primarily when there is a strong likelihood of winning at trial

system efficiency
The manner by which prosecutors' offices consider their caseloads in light of a high volume of cases and lack of resources for prosecution

defendant rehabilitation (prosecutors)
A prosecutorial policy of foregoing prosecution in favor of diversion if there is an acceptable perceived likelihood of rehabilitation

and Kelling's (1982) broken windows theory (see Modules 10 and 14 for elaboration on this topic), community prosecution involves greater efforts to engage the community in crime-fighting, solving problems, and generally enhancing citizens' quality of life. Community prosecution involves cooperation and collaboration between prosecutors and individuals, both within and outside the criminal justice system. It is based on the belief that prosecutors should not only prosecute cases, but also improve public confidence in the justice system, solve public safety problems, and prevent crime. Prosecutors working under this approach better communicate with community residents, local and national groups, and the police to address community problems and measure their success more on citizen quality of life and community attitudes than on the number of convictions (e.g., Wolf, 2010). Community prosecution efforts typically target individuals accused of less serious crimes.

community prosecution As an alternative to traditional prosecutorial practices, it involves greater efforts to engage the community in crime-fighting, solving problems, and generally enhancing citizens' quality of life; it requires cooperation and collaboration between prosecutors and individuals both within and outside the criminal justice system

The Fulton County District Attorney's Office in Georgia opened its first community prosecution office in July 2000, and it has since expanded to nine offices. The offices are strategically placed to provide visibility and accessibility to residents and offer a grassroots approach that promotes cooperation between police, prosecutors, organizations, and the community in general (Office of the Fulton County District Attorney, 2014).

Defense Attorneys

Defense attorneys provide representation for the accused, and all who enter criminal court have the right to an attorney. The attorney may be secured privately, which means that the defendant pays for the attorney's services. Most individuals who enter criminal court, however, are poor, or indigent, and rely on representation provided by the state. **Indigency** is typically determined by:

defense attorneys Lawyers who provide representation for the accused; they may be secured privately or provided by the state

- a defendant's income level,
- whether the defendant receives public assistance,
- a sworn application, and
- a defendant's debt level.

indigency The state of being poor or needy

Public defenders, judges, and court personnel are typically responsible for indigency screening (Langton & Farole, 2010). A small percentage of individuals choose to represent themselves, in what is known as ***pro se*** legal representation.

pro se The practice of individuals representing themselves in court

THE ORIGINS OF INDIGENT DEFENSE

The Sixth Amendment states that "in all criminal prosecutions, the accused shall enjoy the right. . . to have the assistance of counsel for his defence." As written over 200 years ago, this protection seemingly meant that judges could not prevent defendants from having counsel. It was not interpreted to mean that the state would provide representation for them until the twentieth century. Interpretation of the Sixth Amendment with regard to this issue changed beginning in the 1930s in light of a series of court cases:

- *Johnson v. Zerbst* (1938) led to the appointment of lawyers for indigent criminal defendants in the federal courts.
- *Betts v. Brady* (1942) resulted in only defendants accused of a capital offense being permitted state-appointed representation at the state level.
- *Gideon v. Wainwright* (1963) overturned the court's decision in *Betts* and ruled that all indigent defendants have a right to self-representation; the decision applied only to state felony cases.
- *In re Gault* (1967) extended the right to counsel to juvenile courts.

11 Appeal

- *Argersinger v. Hamlin* (1972) extended the right to representation by counsel to all cases that may result in incarceration, including misdemeanors and petty charges.
- *McKaskle v. Wiggins* (1984) ruled that trial judges may appoint standby counsel (for consultation only) when defendants represent themselves.

The right to representation for the indigent generally begins once they are arrested and continues through the time when their first appeal is concluded. Questions about the effectiveness or quality of indigent representation have led various states to reform their indigent defense systems. The somewhat vague "**objective standard of reasonableness**" the Supreme Court established as criteria for assessing the quality of representation (*Strickland v. Washington*, 1984) has contributed to variations in the quality of defense provided to indigent defendants.

Per the 1964 **Criminal Justice Act**, each of the 94 federal judicial districts in the United States has a system designed to appoint representation for indigent defendants in federal court. The Criminal Justice Act requires each district to provide counsel via federal public defenders or panels of private attorneys (often referred to as panel-appointed attorneys). In state courts, indigent representation is provided in three ways: public defender offices, assigned counsel, and contract systems. State-administered indigent systems closed an estimated 2.7 million criminal, appellate, civil, and juvenile cases in 2013 (Strong, 2016).

PUBLIC DEFENDER OFFICES

Public defender programs began in Los Angeles County in 1914. These programs, which use salaried staff attorneys who provide representation strictly for the indigent, are most often found in large cities where most crime occurs. The primary benefits of this approach include the experience and qualifications of the attorneys who are hired based on their qualifications and experience in the courtroom. In addition, public defenders' familiarity with the courtroom personnel helps them better understand how the court operates, as well as the orientations of the courtroom actors. However, there are concerns that their familiarity could lead attorneys to become too cordial with the courtroom actors at the expense of justice for their clients (Metcalfe, 2016). Public defender offices also often suffer from limited funding, which hampers efforts to offer particularly strong defenses (Lee, 2016). For example, they may not have investigators on staff who can find and provide evidence to effectively represent their client. Most indigent cases are assigned to public defenders. Extending the right to counsel in state courts resulted in a substantial increase in the number of public defender offices in the United States (McIntyre, 1987).

ASSIGNED COUNSEL SYSTEMS

Assigned counsel systems involve the courts appointing attorneys as needed to represent the indigent. The attorneys are selected from a list of available attorneys, who are generally paid on an hourly basis or via a flat fee rate. Assigned counsel is often used in small cities and rural areas, where the amount of crime is low and need for a permanent public defender office is not necessarily warranted.

Assigned counsel systems exist in two forms: ad hoc and coordinated. The ad hoc model is most commonly used and involves the assignment of willing attorneys that are in the courtroom at the time. The coordinated model involves a court administrator overseeing the appointment of counsel. The coordinated model is arguably more effective, because the court can better control who takes the cases (Siegel et al., 2011). For instance, the court can set minimum qualifications for being in the assigned counsel program and appoint attorneys based on their areas of expertise.

objective standard of reasonableness The criteria for assessing the quality of representation provided to indigent defendants

Criminal Justice Act Legislation that required the federal judicial districts to establish a system to provide indigent defense

public defender programs A means by which indigent representation is provided; they include salaried staff attorneys who represent the poor and are most often found in large cities

assigned counsel systems A means of providing indigent defense in which the courts appoint attorneys as needed to represent the poor; the attorneys are selected from a list of available attorneys; this approach is often used in small cities and rural areas

Among the limitations of the assigned counsel approach is the possible lack of motivation to strongly represent the accused given the small amount of pay attorneys receive relative to the pay earned in their private practices (Cohen, 2014).

CONTRACT SYSTEMS

Contract systems involve governments and private attorneys, bar associations, or law firms contracting to represent indigent clients in a jurisdiction for a specified period of time and at a designated rate. This system is primarily used in a handful of rural counties, mostly in Western states (Cole et al., 2004). Among the limitations of this approach is contracting agencies underbidding one another to secure the contract and ultimately devoting limited resources to indigent cases out of concern for costs.

EFFECTIVENESS OF INDIGENT DEFENSE

Do individuals fare better when they secure their own counsel versus relying on the counsel provided by the state? The research findings are generally mixed with regard to case processing outcomes in relation to private versus state-provided representation. Some researchers found no or few differences (e.g., Hartley et al., 2010), while others noted that defendants with public defenders were more likely to be detained prior to trial, more likely to be convicted, and less likely to have their cases dismissed (M. R. Williams, 2013). In comparing the types of state-provided counsel, researchers noted that defendants with assigned counsel received less favorable outcomes compared to defendants who were represented by public defenders (Cohen, 2014; Roach, 2014). Table 22.2 shows the types of indigent representation in use by states and the percentage of cases closed by each in 2013. Over two-thirds of cases closed were through public defender offices, followed by assigned counsel and contract counsel.

THE NATURE OF WORK FOR DEFENSE ATTORNEYS

Defense attorneys face many struggles and challenges, particularly with regard to their clientele. Defendants do not always trust that their representation is adequately doing their job. In addition, those requiring state-provided counsel are generally clients who face financial difficulties, and they may believe the criminal justice system works against them (Cole et al., 2004).

contract systems
A means of providing indigent representation in which governments and private attorneys, bar associations, or law firms contract with the state to represent indigent clients in a jurisdiction for a specified time and at a designated rate

TABLE 22.2. Indigent Representation

TYPE OF REPRESENTATION	NUMBER OF STATES USING	PERCENTAGE OF CLOSED CASES
Public defender offices	27 states and the District of Columbia	67
Assigned counsel	16 states	20
Contract counsel	14 states and the District of Columbia	13

Note. Some jurisdictions use a combination of methods. For instance, the court might assign particular types of indigent cases (e.g., drug cases) to attorneys under contract with the court and use a public defender's office for all other cases. ***Source:*** State-Administered Indigent Defense Systems, 2013 (NCJ 250249), by S. M. Strong, 2016, U.S. Department of Justice, Bureau of Justice Statistics.

Defense attorneys have been called "the least powerful members of the courtroom work group" (Neubauer & Fradella, 2017, p. 189), and they depend on the actions of prosecutors and judges throughout all steps of the adjudication process (Cole et al., 2004). Ultimately, however, the job of defense attorneys is to provide representation to individuals who appear in court and defend liberties as duly required by the Constitution. Such representation may include demonstrating that one is not guilty of the charges filed, or it may involve ensuring that their clients receive appropriate penalties if they are found guilty. Defense attorneys work with many individuals who are indeed guilty of the crimes for which they are charged; however, defendants are still entitled to have their case heard in a court of law and to receive fair outcomes.

Defense attorneys engage in a great deal of counseling for their clients. They:

- advise defendants of the formal steps of criminal case processing,
- provide information on possible plea bargains and pleas,
- prepare clients for expected outcomes,
- share information about the courtroom actors (roles and motivations), and
- seek, generally, to best prepare clients for the courtroom.

Confidentiality is an important aspect of the defense attorney's relationship with their client. **Attorney–client privilege** protects defense attorneys from having to disclose information their clients share with them. This standard can provide moral challenges for defense attorneys who must sometimes work around or balance what they have been told by their clients (i.e., defendants) with their interest in securing justice. Ultimately, defense attorneys are bound to a set of professional ethics and legal parameters. They cannot deliberately mislead the court or engage in perjury.

attorney–client privilege A standard that protects attorneys from having to disclose information their clients share with them

Contributors Who Work in the Courts

Aside from the primary actors in the courtroom, many contributors are needed to process criminal cases. The contributors to case processing can be categorized as to whether they are employed by the court or an agency that largely works in the courts. Among the more prominent contributors who work in the courts are bailiffs, court recorders, court administrators, and clerks of the court. These individuals may be actively involved in the courtroom proceedings, or they may provide behind-the-scenes contributions that facilitate the work of the primary actors.

Bailiffs

1 Criminal Act

● **Learning Objective 22.2:** Identify the contributors who work in the courts and summarize their primary responsibilities.

In June 2017, a Washington man who was sentenced to prison assaulted his attorney and fought with four court bailiffs (Komo Staff, 2017). In a separate incident, two court bailiffs were killed and a sheriff's deputy was injured when an inmate grabbed the deputy's gun outside of a holding cell in Michigan (Ellis, 2016). These are but a few of the dangerous events that occur in courtrooms across the United States. These cases highlight the volatility of the courtroom experience and the importance of the various courtroom personnel, including the individuals who subdued the attackers in these cases.

Bailiffs, who may also be called "marshals" or "court officers," provide a law enforcement presence in the courtroom. They are typically armed peace officers who are expected to maintain safety in the courts. The specific duties of the bailiff include:

- transporting incarcerated defendants into and out of the courtroom,
- assisting judges,

- delivering court documents,
- announcing the judge's entrance into the courtroom,
- preventing defendants from escaping,
- supervising the jury when it is sequestered,
- controlling media and public access to jurors, and
- providing overall security for the courthouse.

CAREERS

Bailiffs are uniformed law enforcement officers who provide courtroom security and escort prisoners and jury members into and out of the courtroom. They are the law enforcement authority in the courtroom. U.S. Marshals serve as bailiffs in the federal courts; sheriff's deputies largely provide bailiff services in state courts.

The U.S. Marshals Service provide bailiff services in the federal courts, while bailiffs are typically provided by sheriff's deputies in the state courts. Accordingly, the job requirements for becoming a bailiff typically fall under the responsibilities associated with being a sheriffs' deputy or a U.S. Marshal. Some bailiffs are nonsworn, unarmed personnel, although most bailiff positions are filled by some type of law enforcement agency. There were roughly 18,900 bailiffs in 2018, and their median annual salary was $49,870 (U.S. Bureau of Labor Statistics, 2019).

Court Reporters

Court reporters, who are also known as stenographers (given their use of a stenotype machine), document the courtroom proceedings. They prepare written transcripts that can be used for various purposes, for instance when judges wish to revisit earlier portions of a trial for clarification or, most important, as a primary source of documentation in cases heard in the appellate courts. Many court reporters use computer-aided transcription software that provides more efficient documentation of courtroom proceedings.

bailiffs Sometimes called "marshals" or "court officers," they provide a law enforcement presence in the courtroom; they are typically an armed peace officer who is expected to maintain safety in the courts

11 Appeal

court reporters Also known as stenographers, they document the courtroom proceedings by preparing written transcripts of courtroom proceedings

Bailiffs provide a much needed sense of security in courtrooms. They provide law enforcement services in what can be particularly volatile settings.

What specific challenges do you believe bailiffs face, and what steps could they take to best ensure that courtrooms remain safe?

CAREERS

Court reporters, who are sometimes known as stenographers, document courtroom proceedings as official transcripts. They work both within and outside courtrooms for both legal and private organizations. They transcribe spoken or recorded speech into written form. Many community colleges and technical schools offer certificate programs to become court reporters, and many states require them to become licensed by the state or certified by a professional association.

In addition to a stenotype machine that permits reporters to use a type of shorthand that is decoded and provided on a monitor, reporters may also use audio equipment to record the proceedings, or what is known as **electronic reporting**. The technology used in electronic reporting notes who is speaking and what is said during proceedings. **Voice writing** is another method used by court reporters. It involves reporters speaking directly into a voice silencer, which is a stenomask containing a microphone. Reporters repeat the testimony offered in court into the mask/microphone, and the mask dampens the sound and prevents anyone from hearing what they say.

Some court reporters are considered employees of the court, while others are self-employed or work for private companies. There were roughly 15,700 court reporter employment positions in 2019, and the median annual pay for the position was $60,130 (U.S. Bureau of Labor Statistics, 2020a).

electronic reporting
The use of audio equipment by court reporters to record courtroom proceedings

voice writing
A means by which transcripts are made in court; it involves court reporters speaking directly into a voice silencer; reporters repeat the testimony offered in court into the silencer

Court Administrators and Clerks of Court

Court administrators work behind the scenes to ensure that cases flow in an efficient and timely manner and that the courts run effectively and smoothly (Spohn & Hemmens, 2009). They have assumed many of the tasks earlier performed by judges, clerks of court, and prosecutors. Generally, court administrators:

- oversee the scheduling of hearings and cases,
- maintain court records,
- oversee budgeting,
- plan space utilization, and
- manage courtroom personnel.

Similar to court administrators, **clerks of court** provide administrative services to the courts. The primary difference between the two is that clerks of court are more visible in the courtroom. They largely assist with the immediate needs of the events taking place in courtrooms. In some smaller jurisdictions, the court administrator serves as the clerk of court. Clerks of court are the record keepers and are sometimes referred to as "register of probate," "clerk," or "county clerks of court." Clerks of court:

CAREERS

Court administrators perform administrative and management functions within the court system. For instance, they assist judges with court calendars, case flow, court budgets, and personnel management. The minimum requirements for the position vary; some positions require a bachelor's degree, while others may require a master's degree. Professional certification may also be required.

- schedule court cases,
- collect fees,
- make deposits for the courts,
- administer jury selection,
- swear in witnesses,
- mark physical evidence as directed by a judge,
- maintain custody of the evidence,
- maintain court records,
- provide information about the courts, and
- help recruit, hire, and train staff.

Clerks of courts in some states are granted limited judicial powers, for instance as they pertain to issuing warrants. Court clerks may be required to hold a law degree or have extensive administrative experience, depending on the size of the court in which they work and the extent of their responsibilities. Some courts, particularly smaller state courts, may be willing to employ individuals with lower levels of education. The skills required for the position include accounting, budgeting, human resources, and word processing.

> ### CAREERS
>
> **Clerks of court** provide clerical assistance for a variety of administrative responsibilities in the courts. Among their responsibilities are maintaining case records, preparing statistical reports, and administering the oath to jurors and witnesses. Many positions require a high school degree, although professional certification and advanced degrees may be required, particularly for promotion.

Contributors Who Do Not Work in the Courts

Numerous groups contribute to the operations of a court but do not work within the courts. Among the prominent groups that fall into this category are jurors, witnesses, paralegals, defendants, spectators, and the media.

8 Trial

Jurors

The Sixth Amendment provides defendants the right to a trial by jury, although states have the right to decide the size of criminal jury trials. Historically, juries were composed of 12 individuals, and 12-member juries are required in all capital offense cases (cases in which the sentence may be the death penalty) and are still used in many states, particularly in serious criminal trials. Many states use smaller juries (6 to 8 members) for less serious criminal trials in efforts to reduce costs (Anwar et al., 2012). Juries include alternates who substitute for members who need to be excused during the trial (see Module 24 for additional information on jurors).

JURY QUALIFICATIONS

The process of identifying potential jurors varies to some extent among the states and even among some areas within states. Some larger areas use a jury commissioner who selects persons within their district to potentially serve on a jury. In other areas, the clerk of court is responsible for compiling the list. Specific qualifications to serve on a jury vary among the states, although generally, potential jurors must be (Roberson et al., 2013):

- a citizen of the United States,
- at least 18 years old, and
- a resident of the jurisdiction for a specified time, typically 1 year.

Serving on a jury is a **civic duty**, which means it is a responsibility of citizens to their government. However, juveniles, convicted felons, and individuals who recently served on a jury are excluded in most jurisdictions. Further, individuals in select occupations such as law enforcement, members of the armed services on active duty, and emergency response personnel are excused. Others may be excused if they can provide the court with a convincing reason.

JURY SELECTION

Juries are expected to be reflective of society with regard to values and beliefs, and the Sixth Amendment holds that juries must be impartial. As such, the method(s) by

court administrators Court officials who ensure that cases flow in an efficient and timely manner; among other responsibilities, they oversee the scheduling of hearings and cases, maintain court records, oversee budgeting, plan space utilization, and manage courtroom personnel

clerks of court Employees of the court who provide administrative services to the courts; they largely assist with the immediate needs of the events occurring in courtrooms

● **Learning Objective 22.3:** Identify the prominent groups who contribute to but do not work in the courts, and briefly describe their contributions.

civic duty A responsibility that citizens have to their government; jury duty is an example

which a jury panel is selected becomes important. Potential jurors are identified from several sources, including:

- voter registration lists,
- motor vehicle registration lists,
- unemployment and welfare rolls,
- water service customer lists, and
- tax-related information.

The use of multiple sources in compiling a list of potential jurors assists with ensuring that all eligible individuals are considered. The challenges sometimes associated with assembling juries has led for some to call for the use of professional, full-time jurors (recall the "In the News: Is It Time for Professional Jurors?" at the start of this module).

Witnesses

lay witnesses Eyewitnesses to a crime considered in court

character witnesses Witnesses who provide information regarding the demeanor, nature, character, behavior, and other traits of the defendant to assist the court in determining whether the individual would be likely to commit the crime for which they are accused

Witnesses provide testimony and sometimes expert input at trials. Most witnesses who testify in court are **lay witnesses**, who may be eyewitnesses to the crime in question. **Character witnesses** are also used to provide information regarding the demeanor, nature, character, behavior, and other traits of the defendant. A character witness may assist the court in determining the likelihood of a defendant committing the crime for which they are accused. Victims may also serve as witnesses, although they are not required to do so (see Module 6 for more information on victims).

Witnesses are summoned to court via a **subpoena**, which is a written document that may be served by a law enforcement officer or an officer of the court, or it may be mailed. Depending on the jurisdiction, subpoenas may be issued by a judge, prosecutor, clerk of court, or defense attorney (Roberson et al., 2013). The document notifies the witnesses that their services are required in court. Those who fail to appear may be charged with contempt of court, which can bring about a penalty ranging from a fine to incarceration. Witnesses may only offer accurate information of which they have direct knowledge. They are typically not permitted to offer **hearsay testimony**, which involves evidence offered indirectly from someone who heard information from others.

subpoena A written document that is used to summon witnesses to court

hearsay testimony Evidence offered not from someone with personal knowledge of the situation in question, but from someone who heard information from others

The courts may also issue a **subpoena duces tecum**, which is a court order requiring the person named in the document to produce documents such as records, computer files, books, or other tangible items for the courts. Individuals who receive this type of subpoena are not required to offer oral testimony in court. The document is sometimes referred to as a "subpoena for the production of evidence."

WITNESS CHALLENGES

Being asked to testify as a witness in court can provide various challenges, including:

- lost work days,
- the need to rearrange travel plans,
- difficulty traveling to and from the court,
- finding child care,
- fear of being cross-examined in court,
- fear of having one's credibility challenged in a public forum, and
- fear of offering testimony leading to punishment of an individual present in the courtroom.

subpoena duces tecum A court order requiring the person named in the document to produce documents such as records, computer files, books, or other tangible items for the courts

Many states have recognized the potential hardships associated with testifying in court. Thus, most states may reimburse witnesses for expenses incurred and time lost in relation to their involvement in the case, but they may not be paid for testifying or not testifying, nor can they be paid for the substance of their testimony (McRae & Nortman, 2012). Judges in some jurisdictions must endorse the subpoena if travel expenses are to be incurred. Technology has addressed, to some extent, the logistical problems associated with subpoenaing witnesses who must travel long distances or cannot physically be in court at a specific time, and video deposition testimony is sometimes used.

Video deposition is sometimes used in cases when a witness is unable to physically attend a court hearing. The use of this technology saves court resources and helps ensure that all evidence can be shared in court.

What would be a limitation of using video deposition?

EXPERT WITNESSES

Expert witnesses are called into court to offer their opinions regarding various issues based on the specialized skills and knowledge they may have in particular areas relevant to the courtroom proceedings. For instance, they may be experts in the area of psychology, ballistics, handwriting, or fingerprint analysis. Expert witnesses who testify in court must present their findings and share their information in a manner that can be understood by jurors (e.g., they must avoid specialized language and jargon that would not be understood by jurors and other members of the court).

Expert witnesses are often paid for their input in court. However, past research suggests that those who are highly paid for their services and testify frequently are perceived as "hired guns" by jurors, who generally neither like nor believe them (Cooper & Neuhaus, 2000).

expert witnesses Witnesses who are called into court to offer their expert opinion regarding various issues; they have specialized skills and knowledge in particular areas that may be relevant to the courtroom proceedings

Paralegals

Paralegals are also known as legal assistants. Paralegals:

- perform administrative and clerical tasks for lawyers,
- research and prepare cases,
- research laws,
- investigate the facts of a case,
- obtain and draft legal documents (e.g., affidavits),
- interview defendants and witnesses,
- attend and schedule hearings, and
- generally support attorneys as needed (National Association of Legal Assistants, 2017).

paralegals Also known as legal assistants, they perform administrative and clerical tasks for lawyers, research and prepare cases, research laws, investigate the facts of a case, obtain and draft legal documents, interview defendants and witnesses, attend and schedule hearings, and generally support attorneys as needed

They perform much of the legwork for attorneys, although they do not provide legal advice to clients or set legal fees, and they do not represent clients in court. Their specific responsibilities vary according to the size and orientation of the firm or agency for which they are employed. For example, paralegals in smaller firms tend to be generalists, and those who work in larger firms tend to be specialists and focus on particular phases of a case.

The nature of the work of paralegals is largely dependent on their area of specialization, if any. Among the areas of the law in which paralegals can specialize are the following:

- employee benefits
- criminal

- corporate
- personal injury
- litigation
- bankruptcy
- immigration
- family
- real estate
- intellectual property

corporate paralegals
Paralegals who provide legal assistance for corporations, for example by preparing employee contracts, shareholder agreements, companies' annual financial reports, and stock-option plans

litigation paralegals
Paralegals who conduct research for lawyers, maintain documents received from clients, and retrieve and organize evidence for use at trial

8 Trial

As examples, **corporate paralegals** typically prepare employee contracts, shareholder agreements, companies' annual financial reports, and stock-option plans. **Litigation paralegals** conduct research for lawyers, maintain documents received from clients, and retrieve and organize evidence for use at trial.

Paralegals first appeared in the early 1960s and have played an increasingly important role in the courts since. There are currently about 337,800 paralegal and legal assistant employment positions in the United States, and the 2019 median pay was $51,740 (U.S. Bureau of Labor Statistics, 2020b).

Defendants

Defendants have strong interests in courtroom proceedings. They may offer information that influences the direction of the courtroom actors with respect to:

- decisions about counsel,
- cooperation with counsel,
- accounts of the incident(s) in question,
- decisions about plea bargaining, and
- decisions about whether to appeal.

Media and Spectators

The media and spectators provide a sense of accountability for the courts. They also share information regarding courtroom activities. The Sixth Amendment's requirement to a public trial contributes to the presence of the media and spectators in courtrooms.

In 1936, the American Bar Association examined the issue of pretrial publicity, particularly as it relates to the media. Among their recommendations were prohibiting the following:

- picture taking in the courtroom
- telegraph wires in courthouses
- radio broadcasts and movies of a trial
- vaudeville appearances of jurors or principals after proceedings
- interviews with jurors after a trial ("Criminal Trial Publicity," 1936)

Electronic media coverage of criminal proceedings in federal trial courts is permitted and is at the discretion of the presiding judge. Such coverage includes broadcasting,

CAREERS

Paralegals, also known as **legal assistants**, assist lawyers by conducting much of the background work for cases. They research laws and prior cases, investigate facts and evidence, write legal documents and briefs, coordinate communications, and keep records of all documents. They generally perform clerical and administrative duties for lawyers. Most have an associate's degree or a certificate in paralegal studies.

televising, recording, or taking photographs in federal trial courts. Judges are responsible for ensuring that coverage of the proceedings:

- is respectful of the rights of the involved parties (e.g., defense and prosecution),
- does not unduly distract participants, and
- does not interfere with the overall administration of justice.

Photographs and video coverage of U.S. Supreme Court hearings is prohibited by Federal Rule 53 (created in 1946). The rule was expanded in 1972 to include television cameras and video footage. Following legislation that was proposed (but not passed) in 1999 to allow cameras into Supreme Court hearings, the court began releasing audio of oral arguments upon the conclusion of all arguments (Kessler, 2013).

Spectators also contribute to the courts by providing a sense of accountability. The openness of court hearings is grounded in the roots of court development. Court hearings were public spectacles where citizens would gather to view the proceedings and ensure that the courts were operating in a fair manner. Opening the courts to the public provides a sense of accountability and transparency, but it also generates several concerns, ranging from security issues to personal conduct. Some courts provide information regarding the expectations of spectators in court. The information is also sometimes directed at those who participate in the hearings (e.g., witnesses, defendants).

The System in Perspective

The allegations of juror misconduct in the Joaquin "El Chapo" Guzman case, as discussed in the "In the News" feature at the start of this module, demonstrate some of the limitations of using laypersons in juries. Jurors in that case (and many other criminal cases) sacrificed their time and effort to find justice, but the entire criminal case could be in jeopardy as a result of the alleged misconduct. Jurors are just one of the many crucial players in our justice system. All players in a courtroom serve important functions, and they also largely rely on each other for support and guidance. The subsystems found in courtrooms across the country contribute to the overall functioning of the courts, which subsequently contributes to the overall functioning of our justice system.

Summary

1. Learning Objective 22.1: *Identify the primary actors in the courts and describe their responsibilities.*

- The primary actors in the courts are judges, prosecutors, and defense attorneys. Judges are responsible for ensuring the courtroom proceedings operate in a fair and efficient manner. They are involved in many steps of the adjudication

process: they oversee hearings, act as a jury in bench trials, and often impose sentences. Prosecutors are representatives of the court who are responsible for ensuring justice. They provide a key link between the police and the courts and have much discretion in determining whether to file charges, how many charges to file, and what charges will be filed. Defense attorneys can be both public or private, and they represent the accused in all steps of the adjudication process. Indigent defense is provided by public defenders, assigned counsel systems, and contract systems.

2. **Learning Objective 22.2:** *Identify the contributors who work in the courts and summarize their primary responsibilities.*

 • Contributors who work in the courts include bailiffs, who provide law enforcement services in the courts; court reporters, who document the court proceedings; court administrators, who ensure that cases flow in an efficient and timely manner by overseeing scheduling of cases and hearings, maintaining court records, overseeing budgeting, planning space utilization, and managing courtroom personnel; and clerks of court, who provide administrative services to the courts and may have limited judicial powers.

3. **Learning Objective 22.3:** *Identify the prominent groups who contribute to but do not work in the courts, and briefly describe their contributions.*

 • Contributors who do not work in the courts include jurors, who offer verdicts; witnesses, who provide testimony and sometimes expert input; paralegals, who perform administrative and clerical tasks for attorneys; the media, which provide accounts of what happens in court; and the general public, which has historically provided a sense of accountability to courtroom proceedings.

Questions for Critical Thinking

1. Which of the primary courtroom actors do you believe has the greatest amount of discretion in court proceedings? Provide three examples of how this actor uses discretion in court.

2. Which contributor who works in the courtroom do you believe provides the most important functions? Who do you believe provides the least important functions? Discuss.

3. Should courtroom proceedings be open to the public? Should they be televised? Why or why not?

Key Terms

adversarial legal system
assigned counsel systems
attorney–client privilege
bailiffs
bench trials
character witnesses
civic duty
clerks of court
community prosecution
contract systems
corporate paralegals
court administrators
court reporters
Criminal Division
Criminal Justice Act
defendant rehabilitation

defense attorneys
electronic reporting
expert witnesses
hearsay testimony
indigency
judges
lay judges
lay witnesses
legal sufficiency
litigation paralegals
merit selection
Missouri Bar Plan
Model Code of Judicial Conduct
objective standard of reasonableness
Office of the Solicitor General
paralegals

pro se
prosecutors
public defender programs
recalls
state attorney general
state judicial conduct commissions
subpoena

subpoena duces tecum
system efficiency
trial sufficiency
U.S. attorney general
U.S. attorneys
voice writing

For digital learning resources, please go to
https://www.oup.com/he/burns1e

Courtroom Practices and Pretrial Procedures

Defendants are required to appear in court for a series of pretrial hearings and
potentially a trial. Among the more common pretrial hearings are the initial
appearance, preliminary and grand jury hearings, and the arraignment.

***How might technology be used to reduce the number of appearances
defendants are required to make in court?***

Following an arrest and booking, criminal cases move into the courts,
and several important pretrial procedures begin. Pretrial procedures
play a central role in criminal justice proceedings given that only a
relatively small percentage of cases (5%–10%) go to trial. This module
covers the basics related to pretrial procedures, starting with a discussion of charging and initial appearances in court and then continuing
with a look at preliminary hearings and grand jury hearings, as well as
arraignments. This module concludes with an examination of diversion and plea bargaining. Much occurs in the courts prior to trials, and
many important decisions are made throughout each step.

Bail Recovery Efforts

In May 2017, seven bail recovery agents in Nashville, Tennessee, were indicted on first-degree murder charges in the killing of an unarmed man and the wounding of another man. Two of the men later reached plea deals with prosecutors, and one man was charged with reckless endangerment with a deadly weapon. The trials involved nearly 3 weeks of testimony, nearly 50 witnesses, almost 200 pieces of evidence, and over 5 hours of jury deliberations (Babich, 2019).

Bail recovery agents work with the private bail industry to ensure that defendants who have been bailed out of court by a private bonding agency return for court proceedings. The indictment pertained to an incident in which the bail recovery agents shot at four men and pursued their car for several miles. In this case of mistaken identity, none of the men in the car being chased was wanted on outstanding charges (Associated Press, 2017a). In an earlier incident in May 2015, two armed bail enforcement agents, also in Tennessee, forced their way into the apartment of a woman and her children. The agents were searching for a man who did not live in the dwelling. They eventually left the apartment, but the mother and her children were shaken by the situation (Autler, 2015). These situations help explain why bail enforcement can be so controversial in the United States.

Individuals who are released from custody via a surety bond sign an agreement with a bonding agency that grants bail recovery agents rights that extend beyond those maintained by public law enforcement. The private agreement between the parties (i.e., the defendant and the bonding agency) means that bail recovery agents are not representatives of the state. Thus, they are not bound by as many procedural guidelines and constitutional limits as local law enforcement agents when it comes to searches and seizures and informing suspects of their protections regarding self-incrimination and the right to counsel.

The lack of regulation and oversight of the bail enforcement industry has been problematic. Some states have modified the broad powers of bail enforcement agents through court decisions and statutes, and some have

1 Criminal Act

sought to better regulate bail enforcement agent licensing and occupational requirements. What do you believe can be done to help ensure that bail enforcement agents do not infringe on the rights of innocent individuals? Should bail recovery agents be bound by the same procedural guidelines and constitutional limits as law enforcement officers? Why or why not?

Charging

Prosecutors provide a key link between the police and the courts. Officers need to be aware of the level of evidence needed for a prosecutor to file charges so they do not make an arrest and find the charges are dropped. Prosecutors vary with regard to the quality and quantity of evidence they require to file charges, and they maintain a great deal of discretion and limited accountability for their decision-making.

● **Learning Objective 23.1:** Describe the prosecutor's role in charging suspects.

3 Arrest

4 Booking

information A charging document that is issued when judges rule in preliminary hearings that probable cause exists to believe a crime was committed and the accused was responsible

indictment A charging document that is issued by grand juries when they believe that the prosecution has provided probable cause to believe a crime was committed and the accused was responsible

complaint A charge, which requires support by oath or affirmation of the victim or arresting officer, that an offense was committed by a particular person

ordinance violations Violation of rules, laws, or regulations that apply to a specific village, city, or town

● **Learning Objective 23.2:** Describe the primary purposes of the initial appearance.

5 Initial Appearance

Filing Charges

Officers who make an arrest typically consult with supervisors, investigators, or the district attorney regarding the criminal charge(s) to be filed while the arrestee is processed by a booking officer. Prosecutors have the legal power to determine the charges to be filed, but some choose to share this power with police officers. In some urban areas, assistant prosecutors are available at all times of the day to consult with the police regarding the decision to formally file charges. Prosecutors are not obligated to file charges against a suspect following arrest, and the prosecutor may drop the case if they feel that an arrest is not warranted because of a lack of evidence or legal justification for the arrest.

Charging Documents

Prosecutors prepare a charging document if they believe an offense is chargeable. There are three primary types of charging documents: an information, an indictment, and a complaint.

- An **information** is the charging document that emerges from a preliminary hearing.
- An **indictment** is filed when a grand jury finds probable cause to proceed with a case.
- A **complaint** is a charge that a misdemeanor offense or an **ordinance violation** (a violation of a rule or regulation that applies to a specific community, such as having one's lawn properly mowed or not playing loud music during the night) was committed by a particular person; it requires support by oath or affirmation of the victim or arresting officer.

The Initial Appearance

Sometimes called the *first appearance* or *magistrate's review*, the **initial appearance** is the first time a defendant is brought before a judge or magistrate. At this stage, a defendant is informed of the charges against them and may or may not be granted pretrial release. Throughout criminal case processing, and especially with regard to the initial appearance, felonies are addressed a bit differently from misdemeanors. Misdemeanors typically receive less attention than felonies, simply because the harms involved are less serious and the penalties less severe. Suspects charged with felonies are more likely to be taken into custody and are processed in a more formal manner than those charged with misdemeanors.

Misdemeanors

For petty offenses or infractions—which often involve individuals responding to a citation or ticket—magistrates may conduct a **summary trial** and sentence offenders at the initial appearance. At this point, the case is concluded, and no further action is required. Magistrates may also dismiss the case if they believe there is not enough evidence to warrant further processing. The informality and emphasis on efficiency at the initial appearance for misdemeanor cases is primarily a result of the large number of such cases and a general lack of resources to devote to each one.

Felonies

In felony cases, the initial appearance involves bringing defendants before a judge for the purposes of:

- providing them with formal notice of the charges against them;

- advising them of their rights, including their right to retain a lawyer or to have one appointed to represent them;
- considering the possibility of pretrial release; and
- informing suspects of the upcoming courtroom activities.

Defendants who are taken into custody have a right to appear before a judge within 48 hours of their arrest. In the 1943 Supreme Court case *McNabb v. U.S.*, the court ruled that any confessions made after an unreasonable delay between an arrest and an initial court appearance would be inadmissible. Following this case, 48 hours became the standard maximum time a defendant should have to wait between arrest and an initial appearance.

If the state believes the defendant did not commit the crime, the prosecutor may draft a **nolle prosequi**, which notes that the government is foregoing prosecution of the case. This may occur after the defendant was charged with a crime and perhaps new evidence emerged suggesting that they were not responsible. It could also happen if the prosecutor more closely examines the evidence and does not feel that they have a strong case or the defendant dies after being charged. Upon such a filing, the defendant is released from the system, although prosecutors may later decide to again file charges, for instance upon the discovery of additional evidence. In some cases, the prosecutor's decision to file a nolle prosequi requires approval by a judge.

Notification of Charges and Defendant Rights

As provided by the Sixth Amendment, defendants have the right to be informed of the charges against them, which is done at the initial appearance. The Sixth Amendment also provides defendants with the right to counsel. While the right to counsel exists prior to the initial appearance (for example, during questioning), defendants are reminded of their right at the initial appearance. Defendants who choose to represent themselves must competently and voluntarily waive their right to counsel.

Defendants who are found to be indigent must sign an affidavit affirming their impoverishment. Jurisdictions use public defenders, assigned counsel, and contract systems to represent the indigent (see Module 22). Further, some attorneys provide indigent defense **pro bono**, or on a volunteer basis, and law school students and prepaid legal service programs also provide assistance for the indigent.

Pretrial Release

Jurisdictions often use **pretrial service programs** that gather and share with the court information about defendants, particularly with regard to their level of risk upon being released from custody. The programs also identify release options for defendants and supervise them prior to trial (Mahoney et al., 2001). Suspects charged with serious crimes, those believed to be dangerous, and those deemed a flight risk are most likely to be detained until trial, otherwise known as pretrial detention.

The primary considerations with regard to **pretrial release** are ensuring that:

- innocent individuals are not wrongfully detained,
- defendants will return to court for hearings, and
- defendants will not commit crimes while released.

While defendants are not guaranteed pretrial release and not all can afford it, a Bureau of Justice report on case processing in the 75 largest counties in the United

initial appearance A defendant's first appearance before a judge; it is used to resolve less serious cases and address a series of issues pertaining to case processing in more serious cases

8 Trial

summary trial A trial conducted by magistrates for a petty offense or infraction

3 Arrest

nolle prosequi A notice by the prosecutor stating that the government is foregoing prosecution of a case

pro bono Legal services offered on a volunteer basis

pretrial service programs Programs used in some jurisdictions that gather and share with the court information about defendants, particularly with regard to their level of risk upon being released prior to trial

pretrial release The release of defendants prior to trial with special conditions or requirements

States suggested that roughly 62%–64% of felony defendants were released prior to their cases being resolved (Reaves, 2013).

Decisions regarding pretrial release affect outcomes in criminal case processing. For instance, pretrial detention may encourage defendants to plea bargain, and detained defendants are more likely to be convicted and receive more punitive sentences, perhaps because of their inability to adequately prepare their case (Gottfredson & Gottfredson, 1988).

SETTING BAIL

Setting bail for individuals who are taken into custody and are to be released is one of the most important purposes of the initial appearance. In some jurisdictions, bail is predetermined and release is granted at the booking stage. This typically occurs for less serious offenses, primarily misdemeanors, for which a schedule or chart is used to determine the conditions under which a defendant is released. In other jurisdictions, the decision to release or not, and under what conditions, is typically made by a judge or an appointed hearing officer. Judges and officers primarily consider:

- the seriousness of the current offense,
- whether the defendant is likely to return to court for upcoming hearings (e.g., are they a flight risk?)
- the defendant's prior record, and
- background information of the defendant (e.g., family ties, substance abuse problems).

bail An agreement requiring the accused to post a predetermined amount of money and/or meet other conditions to be released from custody; it is used to ensure that they will return for later court proceedings

Bail is an agreement that the defendant will return to court when expected to do so. It is the most common form of pretrial release and is provided by the Eighth Amendment, which notes that "excessive bail shall not be required." Bail bonds often involve cash deposits, but can come in the form of property or other valuables. Defendants generally post a specific amount of money as part of the requirement. Failure to abide by the terms of the agreement without justification for doing so results in bail forfeiture, and the suspect is deemed a fugitive from justice. **Bench warrants**, which are warrants issued by a judge requesting the arrest of an individual who violated a court order, are issued for fugitives' arrest, and additional charges are filed for the newly committed offense.

bench warrant
Warrants issued by a judge requesting the arrest of an individual who violated a court order

MONETARY BAIL

Judges may impose monetary bail and the percentage of the bail amount that must be paid to secure release. The money paid is returned (minus some court costs) if the defendant returns for all further court proceedings. Among the different types of release are the following:

fully secured bail A type of pretrial release in which defendants post the full amount of the bail that is set; defendants who return to court at all specified times will receive the bail they posted

- **Fully secured bail** requires defendants to post the full amount (100%) of the set bail. For instance, if a judge sets fully secured bail at $10,000, it means the defendant has to pay $10,000 to be released. Defendants who return to court at all specified times will receive the bail they posted.

deposit bail Requires defendants to pay a percentage of the bail that is set; however, they are responsible for the full amount of the bond if they do not return to court as expected

- **Deposit bail** requires defendants to pay a percentage (e.g., 10%) of the set bail; however, they are responsible for the full amount of the bond if they do not return to court as expected. For instance, if a judge sets deposit bail at $10,000, assuming the established percentage is 10%, it means the defendant has to pay $1,000 to be released. Defendants who fail to show up in court as expected would lose their $1,000 and have to pay the $9,000 balance.

- **Unsecured bond** involves the setting of a bail amount (e.g., $10,000), although no monetary payment is required for release. Defendants who fail to return to court as expected would be responsible for the full bail amount.

Defendants without the financial resources to post bail sometimes use a bail bonding agency, which posts the bail and typically charges the defendant an extra 10%–15% fee. This approach is known as **surety bond**. Defendants using this approach sign an agreement with a private bonding agency, which is accountable for the bail amount if the defendant fails to return for future court hearings.

Bonding agencies use bail recovery agents to help ensure that defendants return to court. Private bonding is not used in all jurisdictions. Several states have outlawed it in response to various concerns (see "In the News: Bail Recovery Efforts") and replaced it with state-operated pretrial services. These state agencies assist with bail decision-making and monitor individuals on release to ensure that they appear in court as expected and meet any conditions imposed on them.

NONMONETARY RELEASE

Some defendants are released prior to trial without having a financial bail amount set. These types of release typically involve offenders with strong ties to the community who have been accused of committing less serious offenses. Among the types of nonmonetary release are the following:

- **Release on recognizance** is a promise from defendants that they will return to court. Failure to return to court results in the judge issuing a bench warrant.

- **Conditional release** involves defendants having to meet specific requirements if they wish to be released prior to trial. Failure to meet the requirements results in the issuance of a bench warrant.

- **Third-party custody** involves a third party (e.g., the defendant's attorney, a relative, or a counselor) assuming responsibility for the defendant's future attendance in court. Failure to meet the requirements results in the issuance of a bench warrant for the defendant's arrest.

Bail enforcement agents, or fugitive recovery agents, assist with ensuring that defendants released prior to trial appear in court. These individuals are also sometimes referred to as bounty hunters. They have been the topic of many motion pictures and television shows. Shown here is Duane Chapman, also known as Dog the Bounty Hunter from the television show with the same name.

Do you believe popular culture depictions of bounty hunters are accurate? Should private agencies be permitted to capitalize on the misfortunes of those caught up in the criminal justice system?

unsecured bond A means of pretrial release that involves the setting of a bail amount, although no monetary payment is required for release; defendants are responsible for the full bail amount should they fail to return to court

Preliminary and Grand Jury Hearings

Felonies are serious crimes that warrant substantial penalties. Accordingly, felony case processing includes additional steps—preliminary and/or grand jury hearings—to help protect defendants from unjust prosecution. These steps are used to further examine evidence and help ensure that case processing has been handled appropriately. The two types of hearings differ in the manner in which they occur (see Table 23.1), yet their goals are generally the same. Both hearings seek to:

- **Learning Objective 23.3:** Compare and contrast preliminary and grand jury hearings.

TABLE 23.1. Comparing Preliminary and Grand Jury Hearings

	PRELIMINARY HEARINGS	GRAND JURY HEARINGS
Standard of proof: probable cause	Judge determines whether probable cause exists	Laypersons determine whether probable cause exists
Formal charging document	Formal charging document is an information	Formal charging document is an indictment
Type of proceedings	Proceedings open to the public	Proceedings held in closed sessions
Right to counsel	Defendants have the right to counsel, to be present, and to offer evidence	Defendants in most states have no right to counsel, to be present, or to offer evidence
Efficiency and cost	More efficient; quicker and thus less costly because there is no need to assemble a grand jury	More costly in terms of resources
Interests served	Reflects prosecutor and judge's decision to proceed with a case, not necessarily the public's interest	More representative of public interest

surety bond The means by which defendants without the financial resources to post bail secure their release through the use of a bail bonding agency

release on recognizance Pretrial release on the promise from defendants that they will return to court

conditional release Defendants having to meet specific requirements if they wish to be released prior to trial

third-party custody A means of pretrial release in which a third party assumes responsibility for the defendant's future attendance in court

- protect individuals from unwarranted prosecution,
- instill greater levels of confidence in criminal justice practices,
- help determine if a crime was indeed committed, and
- help determine if the defendant was indeed responsible for the crime in question.

The required level of proof in grand jury and preliminary hearings is *probable cause,* which is much lower than the required *proof beyond a reasonable doubt* required for a criminal conviction at trial. The lower level of proof means that few cases are rejected at preliminary and grand jury hearings.

States vary in their use of preliminary hearings and grand juries. Some states use preliminary hearings as a primary step to trial, while others use them prior to sending the defendant's case over to a grand jury. Further, about half of the states require that all felonies, and in some instances misdemeanors, be presented to a grand jury. The remaining states hold that the accusation may be presented to a judge or magistrate in a preliminary hearing instead of to a grand jury (Roberson et al., 2013).

Preliminary Hearings

Preliminary hearings resemble abbreviated trials and are sometimes called "bind over hearings," "probable cause hearings," or "preliminary examinations." They primarily consist of the prosecution presenting evidence before a judge. The hearing is open to the public. Judges preside over preliminary hearings and offer decisions regarding the need for further case processing. They consider the evidence presented and the legality of the arrest and searches.

Defendants and their representation attend the preliminary hearing, with both sides swearing in and presenting evidence. Defendants have the right to waive the preliminary hearing, and they may do so, for instance if they decide to plead guilty or seek to avoid negative publicity that might emerge from the hearing. However, approval from the judge and prosecution is required to do so. Prosecutors may wish to conduct a preliminary hearing for the purposes of having on record the testimony of witnesses who may not be available at the trial. Further, the preliminary hearing is the only procedure to consider the existence of probable cause in states with no grand jury provisions.

Following the preliminary hearing, judges may:

- bind over the defendant to trial or a grand jury (depending on procedure),

- reduce the charges (an option in most states), or

- dismiss the accused should the judge find no probable cause to believe the accused is guilty.

Few cases are dismissed at the preliminary hearing, simply because establishing probable cause is often not overly difficult at this stage. Judges typically find that probable cause exists and order the suspect held for further case processing (Neubauer & Fradella, 2017). In most cases bound for trial, prosecutors then file an information, which signifies that they wish to take the case to trial.

Grand Jury Hearings

Like preliminary hearings, **grand jury hearings** assess whether enough evidence presented by the prosecution (including witness testimony, photographs, and documents) exists to justify further processing. Also akin to preliminary hearings, the standard of proof is probable cause. However, unlike preliminary hearings, grand juries have investigative powers to subpoena witnesses and documents, and they meet in closed sessions to protect those under investigation from unwarranted publicity (Neubauer & Meinhold, 2017).

Sometimes grand juries may be assembled prior to an arrest. For instance, a prosecutor who has evidence against a high-profile individual (e.g., a mayor) may assemble a grand jury to determine if the jurors believe there is enough evidence to support the arrest. This would be done to prevent the negative publicity that would accompany the wrongful arrest of a high-profile individual.

A FIFTH AMENDMENT RIGHT

The Fifth Amendment states that all citizens are guaranteed the right to indictment by a grand jury, although the 1884 Supreme Court case *Hurtado v. California* declared that states were not bound to this law. As such, states are divided in the use of grand juries; 24 states require grand juries for most or all felonies; 24 states and Washington, DC make them optional for most felonies; and 2 states do not use grand juries (Connecticut and Pennsylvania) (Figure 23.1; Neubauer & Fradella, 2017). Where optional, grand juries are typically selected when:

- the case is of notable political or public significance,

- the investigative powers of the grand jury are preferable, or

- one or more witnesses may be reluctant to speak in an open setting, such as a courtroom (Worrall, 2004).

6 Grand Jury/ Preliminary Hearing

preliminary hearings Hearings in which prosecutors appear before a judge to explain why a case should continue to be pursued or prosecuted; the standard of proof is probable cause

grand jury hearings Court hearings in which prosecutors appear before grand jurors to explain why the case should continue to be prosecuted; the standard of proof is probable cause

3 Arrest

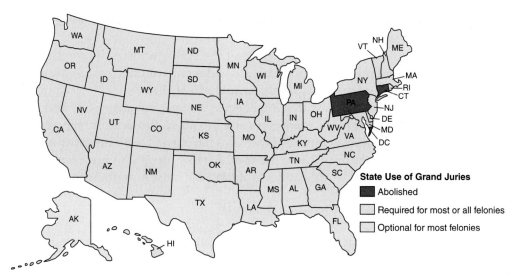

FIGURE 23.1. State Use of Grand Juries. States are divided in the use of grand juries: 24 states require grand juries for most or all felonies, 24 states and the District of Columbia make them optional for most felonies, and 2 states do not use grand juries. The required use of grand juries appears largely in the northeastern, mid-Atlantic, and southeastern states. Western states largely make the use of a grand jury optional. ***Source:*** *Neubauer, D.W., & Fradella, H.F. (2017).* America's Courts and the Criminal Justice. *Cengage Learning Inc. Reproduced by permission.*

Do you support the use of grand juries? Why or why not?

More recently, the use of grand juries in the United States has diminished, primarily because the hearings consume more resources than a preliminary hearing and grand juries so often indict suspects. This has led some critics to question their effectiveness in providing oversight (Scheb & Scheb, 2009).

GRAND JURORS

Grand juries may range in size from 6 to 23 members, but often consist of 19 members who serve terms that may last from one to several months, but generally no more than 3 months (Roberson et al., 2013). They consist of private citizens who are selected via various means. Most states choose them at random (e.g., from voter registration lists), and others permit judges and sheriffs to offer the clerk of court names of potential jurors (Neubauer & Fradella, 2017). Volunteers are also used in some jurisdictions. At minimum, grand jurors are required to be:

- at least 18 years old,
- citizens of the United States,
- residents of the jurisdiction in which they are to serve, and
- able to communicate in English.

GRAND JURY PROCESS AND OUTCOMES

During a grand jury hearing, the prosecution presents its evidence. Defendants do not have the right to challenge the state's case, and defendants in most states do not have the right to counsel during grand jury proceedings.

There are three possible outcomes of a grand jury hearing. Grand juries generally issue one of the following:

true bill Also known as a bill of indictment, it is issued by grand juries when they find probable cause for the continued prosecution of a defendant

- **true bill**, or bill of indictment, if they find probable cause to believe the defendant is guilty based on the state's evidence

- **no bill**, if they fail to find probable cause; the case is then dismissed
- **presentment**, in cases in which probable cause is found through their own investigation

LIKELIHOOD OF INDICTMENTS

Grand juries overwhelmingly find probable cause to indict defendants, leading critics to argue that grand juries are generally tools for prosecutors to indict whomever they want. The high likelihood of indictments most likely stems from the following (Burns, 2007):

- the low level of proof required (probable cause)
- the need in most states for only half to two-thirds of the votes to find probable cause
- the inapplicability in some jurisdictions of the exclusionary rule at grand jury hearings (which forbids the introduction of illegally seized evidence)
- the permission of hearsay testimony about what someone who has not testified in court has said, or what is commonly known as secondhand communication
- effective screening practices on behalf of prosecutors who dismiss cases they find unworthy of grand jury consideration

An exception to the likelihood of indictments being issued pertains to killings by police. In such cases, the grand jury system typically favors the accused police officers because of the wide discretion given to police officers with regard to the use of force (McKinley & Baker, 2014). This has caused some controversy.

Arraignment

After an indictment, presentment, or information is filed, cases proceed to an **arraignment**, typically a brief hearing that is the final step prior to trial. At an arraignment, defendants hear the charges (included in the charging document) against them. After the charges are read, defendants must then enter a plea. Also at an arraignment, the attorneys may begin offering pretrial motions, which are oral or written requests to the court to make decisions regarding particular issues prior to the trial, and pretrial discovery begins. Discovery involves the sharing of information on behalf of the prosecution and defense. Following an arraignment, prosecutors cannot change the charges. If they wish to do so, they must formally file new charges, and the pretrial process begins anew.

Entering a Plea

Defendants typically enter one of three pleas in response to the charges. Specifically, they enter a guilty, nolo contendere, or not guilty plea.

GUILTY

Defendants may plead guilty to the charges originally filed against them, or they may plead guilty to reduced charges following a plea bargain agreement (discussed later in this module). Regardless, defendants who plead guilty sacrifice many constitutional protections, and so judges do not always accept guilty pleas. A judge may rule that a not guilty plea be entered if they feel the defendant offered a guilty plea under duress or because they lacked awareness of the situation. Judges are required

no bill An outcome of grand jury hearings which signifies that the grand jury failed to find probable cause, at which point the case is dismissed

presentment An outcome of a grand jury investigation in which they found probable cause and the need for further case processing

● **Learning Objective 23.4:** Identify the significant events that occur during an arraignment.

7 Arraignment

arraignment Court hearings in which the accused again hears the charges against them and enters a plea

nolo conten-dere "No contest"; a plea that is legally recognized as guilty and is offered by defendants who do not wish to admit guilt; it protects defendants from having an admission of guilt used against them in any subsequent civil trial

Insanity As it pertains to the courts, it is a legal, as opposed to medical, issue that is interpreted differently among the states with regard to whether they use the defense, how to define insanity, and the burden of proof needed to demonstrate insanity

8 Trial

to inform defendants entering a guilty plea of the possible sanctions associated with the charges filed against them. Sentencing follows a guilty plea.

NOLO CONTENDERE

Sometimes a defendant does not wish to contest the charges, and so they may plead **nolo contendere**, which is legally recognized as a guilty plea although the defendant does not admit guilt. A plea of nolo contendere protects defendants from having an admission of guilt used against them in any subsequent civil cases. Nolo contendere pleas also benefit defendants who may not wish to admit guilt even though they wish to cooperate with the court and engage in plea bargaining.

Nolo contendere pleas are permitted in the federal courts and in the courts of about half of the states. Some states that permit nolo contendere pleas require approval from the judge, while defendants in other states must obtain the agreement of the judge and prosecutor. Defendants are sentenced following a plea of nolo contendere.

NOT GUILTY BY *"REASON OF INSANITY"*

Defendants in some states are permitted to enter a "not guilty by reason of insanity" defense, which suggests the defendant is not responsible for the crime because they lacked the mental capacity to understand their actions. Some other states require such defendants to enter a not guilty plea and demonstrate insanity at trial. Some states also permit defendants to enter a "guilty but mentally ill" plea, which requires the offender to receive mental treatment followed by prison time (Borum & Fulero, 1999; Palmer & Hazelrigg, 2000).

Insanity, as it pertains to the courts, is a legal, as opposed to medical, issue that is interpreted differently among the states with regard to whether they use the defense, how to define insanity, and the burden of proof needed to demonstrate insanity. The insanity defense is used relatively rarely in the courts, and when it is used, it does not often result in an acquittal. The federal government permits use of the defense, as do most states, with the exception of Kansas, Montana, Idaho, and Utah (see Module 8).

NOT GUILTY

Defendants who enter not guilty pleas are informed by judges of their rights regarding the forthcoming trial, and the judge assesses the ability of the defendant to stand trial. A formal evaluation of the defendant's competency to stand trial may be requested. Not guilty pleas are more often offered in cases involving serious crimes than in cases involving less serious crimes. Some defendants refuse to respond to the charges and in turn stand mute. Such noncooperation is viewed as a not guilty plea. Standing mute rarely occurs, and is often done as a sign of protest of the court and/or legal system.

A trial date is set when defendants plead not guilty. Trials are usually scheduled to occur within 2 to 3 weeks following the arraignment. The reason for the prompt scheduling is the **Speedy Trial Act**, which originated in 1974 and was amended in 1979 and 1984. It is designed to ensure that federal defendants are promptly brought to

James Holmes was convicted on 24 counts of murder and 140 counts of attempted murder following his actions at a movie theater in Aurora, Colorado, in 2012. Prior to the shooting, he had been receiving treatment for mental health problems. He entered a plea of not guilty by reason of insanity. Following his conviction, he was sentenced to 12 consecutive life sentences, in addition to 3,318 years in prison without parole.

Do you believe that individuals suffering from mental illness should be punished for criminal behavior, or should they receive treatment?

trial per their Sixth Amendment right to a speedy trial. The act requires that suspects must be charged with an offense within 30 days following their arrest (or the receipt of a summons) and brought to trial in no less than 30 and no more than 70 days. Federal courts and many state and local jurisdictions adhere to the federal provisions offered in the act.

Pretrial Motions

In preparing for trial, prosecutors and defense attorneys may ask the court to grant various **pretrial motions**. Motions may be requested at any time following a not guilty plea and the start of trial. Judges consider written motions (or petitions), brief arguments, and oral arguments from the involved attorneys. Separate hearings may be held to consider pretrial motions. There are several standard motions offered in preparation for trial, although attorneys may make unique motions in relation to their case. Most motions are offered by the defense. The granting of pretrial motions can significantly affect the outcome of a case. Charges may be dropped or plea bargaining negotiations may be initiated or influenced depending on a judge's decision to grant or deny specific motions. The more commonly offered motions are noted in Figure 23.2.

Pretrial Discovery

Discovery is a pretrial procedure that begins at the arraignment and continues until the trial. This stage provides an opportunity for both the defense and the prosecution to learn more about each other's case. Generally, **discovery** is the disclosure of information that is primarily used to prevent one side from introducing unexpected

Speedy Trial Act
Legislation designed to ensure that federal defendants are promptly brought to trial per their Sixth Amendment right to a speedy trial

pretrial motions
Requests offered by the prosecution and/or defense prior to trial; they seek to ensure that proper procedures are being followed and defendants' rights are respected

2
Investigation

discovery The disclosure of information between prosecutors and defense attorneys; it is primarily used to prevent one side from introducing unexpected evidence at trial

---

COMMONLY OFFERED PRETRIAL MOTIONS

- **Motion to dismiss.** This motion is typically filed by the defense, who argues that the case should be dismissed and the defendant released, for instance due to insufficient evidence and due process violations. Judges may grant two types of dismissals, including those with prejudice, in which case the defendant cannot be recharged with the same crime; and those without prejudice, which means that the case will not proceed to trial, but the prosecutor may address the problematic issue and re-file charges.

- **Motion to determine the competency of the accused to stand trial.** This motion proposes that the defendant's mental ability should be evaluated to determine if she or he is fit to stand trial. Attorneys offer this motion to protect mentally ill persons from being convicted of criminal acts.

- **Motion to suppress evidence obtained through an unlawful search or seizure.** This motion proposes that certain evidence should not be allowed to be introduced at trial because it was gathered in violation of the Fourth Amendment. It is one of the more commonly filed motions.

- **Motion to suppress confessions, admissions, or other statements made to the police.** This motion seeks to suppress evidence with consideration of the Fifth Amendment protection against self-incrimination and the Sixth Amendment right to counsel. The primary concerns with regard to this motion are whether the confession was coerced, Miranda warnings were properly administered, and the defendant knowingly, intelligently, and voluntarily waived those rights.

- **Motion to require the prosecution to disclose the identity of a confidential informant.** This motion, offered by the defense, requests that the prosecution identify a source of its information, regardless of whether or not an informant was granted confidentiality.

- **Motion for a change of venue.** Criminal cases are often held in the jurisdiction in which the offense in question occurred. Pretrial publicity surrounding a case may encourage attorneys to request that a case be relocated to an area where there is less or no awareness of the case.

- **Motion for a continuance.** The prosecution or defense may request a continuance, or postponement of a case due to a variety of reasons such as illness and the need for more time to prepare.

FIGURE 23.2. Commonly Offered Pretrial Motions. Attorneys may offer motions prior to trial in efforts to ensure that neither side has an unfair advantage and justice can be served in a fair and just manner. The decisions of judges to allow or disregard motions can have notable impacts on case outcomes.

Which of the above motions do you believe to be most significant? Why?

evidence at trial. In 1963, the U.S. Supreme Court ruled that the prosecutors must disclose material obtained during investigations that is favorable to the defense, or what is known as **exculpatory evidence** (*Brady v. Maryland*, 1963).

exculpatory evidence Evidence obtained by the prosecution during investigations that is favorable to the defense; the Supreme Court ruled that such evidence must be shared with the defense

States vary greatly in the type of information that is subject to discovery. Some states require that only a defendant's statements and physical evidence must be shared with the defense; in other states, there is a presumption that the prosecutor will share almost all of the evidence against a defendant (Spohn & Hemmens, 2009).

Pretrial discovery occurs through defense attorneys making oral requests to prosecutors for permission to view the discoverable material and defense attorneys making written requests to the court in the form of a motion seeking permission to view the prosecution's evidence. A recent development in some jurisdictions has been the automatic informal discovery for particular types of evidence, which eliminates the need for filing motions and court orders.

Laws governing discovery are constantly changing, although the trend is toward broadening the right of discovery for both the defense and the prosecution (Ferdico, 2005). In the early 21st century, the prosecution is provided some discovery rights by the federal government and most states, although it has no constitutional right to discovery.

● **Learning Objective 23.5:** Define diversion and describe when it is used.

Diversion

diversion Halting or suspending formal proceedings with the agreement that the defendant will meet some agreed-on obligation

Some defendants are provided with opportunities for **diversion**, which involves halting or suspending formal criminal proceedings prior to conviction, with the agreement that the defendant will meet some agreed-on obligation. Pretrial diversion is an informal feature in criminal case processing, which is voluntary, not guaranteed, and is not offered to all offenders. Jurisdictions have criteria to determine which defendants are eligible to participate in pretrial diversion. For instance, New York permits diversion for first-time offenders who commit nonviolent misdemeanors and have employment problems. The programs, which generally target first-time and/or nonviolent offenders, serve to do the following (Schmalleger & Smykla, 2009):

In 2017, professional golfer Tiger Woods was arrested for driving under the influence (DUI). He agreed to plead guilty to a lesser charge of reckless driving. As part of the plea agreement, Woods agreed to enter a diversion program offered by Palm Beach County, Florida, the location where Woods was arrested, for first-time DUI offenders. The program required Woods to spend a year on probation, pay a $250 fine and court costs, attend DUI school, and provide 50 hours of community service. He also had to attend a workshop in which victims of impaired drivers discuss how their lives have changed since their victimization (Associated Press, 2017b). Woods successfully completed the program and had the offense removed from his criminal record.

Do you believe diversion is an appropriate option for those who drive under the influence? Should its use depend on whether someone dies or is injured as a result?

- reduce crime by providing specific treatment programs
- ease the number of individuals in the criminal justice system
- assist with removing the stigma associated with involvement in the justice system
- address the belief that not all offenses warrant criminal case processing

Failure to meet the terms of the diversion agreement will result in the formal processing of the individual in the criminal justice system. Successful completion of the agreement will result in the dismissal of the charge(s). Diversion may involve the services of agencies within and outside the criminal justice system, and it may occur at any point in criminal case processing. There are many options available for those who undergo pretrial diversion. Among the options are:

- *counseling*, for example in relation to anger management;
- *treatment*, for example in relation to alcohol and drug abuse;
- *life skills*, for example in relation to parenting and managing finances;
- *education*, for example by requiring individuals to obtain a General Educational Development certificate or partake in adult literacy programs; and
- *community service*, for example by requiring individuals to contribute to the community in some way, such as providing service to underprivileged children or the homeless.

10
Corrections

Research generally suggests that pretrial diversion programs offer a helpful alternative to traditional processing in the criminal justice system. They also assist the courts by easing caseload pressures and reducing the jail and prison populations (Camilletti, 2010).

Plea Bargaining

While we often envision criminal cases being heard in a court of law and decided by a judge and jury, the large majority of criminal court cases are disposed of via plea bargaining. **Plea bargaining** involves informal negotiations between the prosecution and defense. Defendants, as part of their plea agreement, admit guilt in exchange for a more favorable outcome of their case, including a reduced sentence, an alternative form of sentence (e.g., probation instead of incarceration), a reduced number of charges, or a softer label (e.g., being charged with assault instead of a sex offense).

The large majority of criminal court cases, ranging from roughly 85% to 95%, are resolved via plea bargaining. Such leniency often comes in the form of a reduced sentence. An assessment of felony defendants in the 75 largest counties in the United States noted that nearly all convictions for both felonies and misdemeanors resulted from guilty pleas rather than criminal trials (Reaves, 2013).

Supreme Court Cases Related to Plea Bargaining

Plea bargaining has been around for much of the history of the U.S. courts, although it became particularly controversial in the 1960s (Neubauer & Fradella, 2017). The Supreme Court upheld the constitutionality of plea bargaining in several Supreme Court cases:

- In *Boykin v. Alabama* (1969), the court ruled that guilty pleas must be intelligent and voluntary, meaning that the defendant should not be forced into plea bargaining and must be aware of the conditions in the agreement.
- In *Brady v. United States* (1970), the court established the constitutionality of plea bargaining, but noted that its use should not encourage innocent people to plead guilty.
- In *Santobello v. New York* (1971), the court encouraged the proper administration of plea bargaining and added that legal remedies exist when plea bargain agreements are broken.
- In *Missouri v. Frye* (2012) and *Lafler v. Cooper* (2012), the court ruled that defendants are entitled to effective assistance of counsel during plea bargaining.

● **Learning Objective 23.6:** Describe the benefits and disadvantages of plea bargaining.

8 Trial

9 Sentencing

plea bargaining
Informal negotiations between the prosecution and defense in efforts to expedite criminal cases; as part of the process, defendants may admit guilt in exchange for a more favorable outcome of their case

9 Sentencing

charge bargaining Defendants pleading guilty to a less serious charge than the one originally filed, which may ultimately reduce the penalty involved

count bargaining Defendants pleading guilty to some, but not all of the charges filed against them; this may reduce the potential penalties defendants face

sentence bargaining Defendants pleading guilty and receiving an agreed-on sentence that is less than the maximum

8 Trial

Procedures Related to Plea Bargaining

A plea bargain agreement between the prosecution and the defense must be approved by a judge, and the defendant must be aware of and approve the agreement. Judges may also actively engage with the attorneys in plea bargaining or attend, but not participate in, the negotiations. However, most judges simply ratify the agreements between the parties.

Defendants do not have the legal right to engage in plea bargaining. And, in some cases, a prosecutor or defense attorney may not wish to engage in plea bargaining based on the strength of the case. The seriousness of the charge and the strength of the prosecution's case are among the most important considerations in plea negotiations. Prosecutors, for instance, would be less likely to engage in plea bargaining if they have a particularly strong case. Other factors that have impacted plea negotiations are the defendant's prior record and various extralegal variables, including age, gender, employment, and race (Bernstein et al., 1977; Harris & Springer, 1984).

Defendants have the right to contest or withdraw their guilty plea under certain conditions (Siegel et al., 2011):

- if the prosecutor coerced the defendant into making the agreement
- if the prosecution fails to uphold their end of the bargain
- if it was determined that a defendant's constitutional rights were violated, for instance by law enforcement officials

Types of Plea Bargains

Plea bargaining agreements come in various forms, although the ultimate goals are often a quick and secure conviction for the prosecution and a favorable, less punitive deal for the defense. Attorneys may engage in charge bargaining, count bargaining, and sentence bargaining.

- **Charge bargaining** involves defendants pleading guilty to a less serious charge than the one originally filed (e.g., agreeing to burglary instead of robbery), which may ultimately reduce the penalty involved.

- **Count bargaining** involves defendants pleading guilty to some, but not all, of the charges filed against them, with the agreement that the other charges will be dropped; this may reduce the potential penalty the defendant faces.
- **Sentence bargaining** involves defendants pleading guilty and receiving an agreed-on sentence.

"The prosecutor says you have to roll over."

Plea bargaining involves a lot of discretion on the part of judges. Prosecutors and defense attorneys can be creative in proposing deals, but judges must approve any deals that are made.

Do you believe plea bargaining distorts justice by encouraging defendants to plead guilty, perhaps even when they are not guilty? Why or why not?

Advantages of Plea Bargaining

Plea bargaining has many benefits, which largely explains its prevalent use. Among the benefits of plea bargaining are:

- *quick disposition of criminal cases*: Our court system could not provide jury or bench trials in a timely manner for all who enter the courts;
- *savings in terms of resources and funds*: The courts simply do not have the resources to provide trials for

all who are accused of committing a crime, nor does the state have adequate funding to provide indigent defense if a large number of defendants wish to go to trial;

- *reduced uncertainties associated with trials*: Plea bargaining reduces the uncertainties associated with trials and the adjudication process in general; and

- *protection of victims from possibly having to testify at trial*: It is sometimes difficult for victims to discuss their victimization publicly. Plea bargaining eliminates the need for victims to testify.

8 Trial

Disadvantages of Plea Bargaining

Despite the advantages of plea bargaining, there are several negative features that make the process controversial. Among the disadvantages of plea bargaining are:

- *the inherent lack of due process*: The informality and emphasis on the efficiency inherent in plea bargaining results in less concern for due process and a greater emphasis on administratively processing defendants;

- *filing of more serious charges*: Plea bargaining often leads prosecutors to file the most serious charges (or overcharge) in anticipation of settling for lesser charges;

- *undermining of the integrity of the justice system*: Plea bargaining removes the administration of justice from judges and gives it to attorneys, which was not part of the original design of the court process;

9 Sentencing

- *reduced punishment associated with the crime*: Plea bargaining may lead to defendants who are guilty of crimes receiving lesser sentences than what may be viewed as an appropriate penalty for their crimes; and

- *encouragement for innocent persons to admit guilt*: Plea bargaining may encourage innocent individuals to admit guilt and accept a reduced penalty out of fear that they may not be able to successfully defend themselves in court and may be convicted and receive a more severe sentence.

In light of these limitations, some jurisdictions have sought to ban or limit plea bargaining. For example, in 1975, Alaska's then–attorney general banned all forms of plea bargaining. While the courts did not become notably overburdened, as some expected, the number of misdemeanor trials increased substantially following the decision. By 1990, however, an Alaska Judicial Council study found that plea bargaining had again become common practice, in part because of changes in personnel in the state's attorney general office and declines in state revenue (Carns & Kruse, 1992). More recently, Alaska again addressed plea bargaining by prohibiting it for defendants accused of the most serious classes of felonies, all cases of sexual assault, cases involving sexual abuse of a minor, and domestic violence cases (Boots, 2013).

The System in Perspective

One could argue that the tragic incident involving the death of an innocent man resulting from the actions of a bail enforcement agent (as discussed in the "In the News" feature at the start of this module) was unfortunate, but that it does not necessarily represent a breakdown in the criminal justice system. Or, one could argue that giving private bonding agencies expanded powers beyond those permitted to law enforcement agents means the government was to blame in this miscarriage of justice. Regardless, each step in criminal case processing serves an important purpose, and each requires cooperation and professionalism from the individuals involved. A breakdown at any stage may result in injustice. The majority of the time, cases progress through the system as intended, without substantial problems. This is a result of the many policies and procedures that have been implemented over time and the many agencies, organizations, and individuals that work collaboratively as part of the criminal justice system.

Summary

1. Learning Objective 23.1: *Describe the prosecutor's role in charging suspects.*

- Prosecutors are empowered to determine the charges to be filed, although some share the decision with the arresting police officer(s). They may decline to file charges for different reasons. They use discretion in charging suspects, and their decisions are influenced by various factors, such as the seriousness of the offense. They provide a key link between the police and the courts.

2. Learning Objective 23.2: *Explain the primary purposes of the initial appearance.*

- The initial appearance in felony cases involves bringing defendants before a judge to provide them formal notice of the charges against them, advise them of their rights, consider pretrial release, and inform them of the upcoming courtroom activities. The initial appearance in less serious cases involves defendants responding to the charges against them and likely a resolution to the case.

3. Learning Objective 23.3: *Compare and contrast preliminary and grand jury hearings.*

- Preliminary and grand jury hearings both require probable cause as the standard of proof, seek to protect individuals from unwarranted prosecution, and help ensure a crime was committed and the defendant was responsible for the crime in question. They differ with regard to who determines whether probable cause exists, the name of the formal charging documents used, the formality and openness of the proceedings, the right to counsel, and the required resources. Further, grand juries can initiate their own investigations and are believed to better reflect the public interest.

4. Learning Objective 23.4: *Identify the significant events that occur during an arraignment.*

- The most significant events that occur during an arraignment are the accused once again being informed of their rights, the accused entering a plea, and attorneys offering pretrial motions. Defendants typically enter a plea of guilty, not guilty, or nolo contendere. Some refuse to cooperate with the courts, in which case they are viewed as being not guilty.

5. Learning Objective 23.5: *Define diversion, and describe when it is used.*

- Diversion involves halting or suspending formal criminal proceedings prior to conviction with the agreement that the defendant will meet some agreed-on obligation (such as attending anger-management therapy). It is primarily used with first-time, nonviolent offenders who would seemingly benefit from the opportunity to get treatment and avoid formal processing in the criminal justice system.

6. Learning Objective 23.6: *Assess the benefits and disadvantages of plea bargaining.*

- Among the benefits of plea bargaining are the quick disposition of criminal cases, the certainty of conviction, the reduced time served by those who plead guilty, and the protection of victims from having to testify at trial. Among the disadvantages of plea bargaining are the inherent lack of due process, the encouragement it provides to prosecutors to file the most serious charges (or overcharge) in anticipation of settling for lesser charges through plea bargaining, the undermining of the integrity of the justice system, the reduced punishment associated with the crime, and the encouragement for innocent persons to admit guilt.

Questions for Critical Thinking

1. Do you believe judges would be better situated than prosecutors to determine what charges to file in criminal cases? Why or why not?

2. What do you believe is the most significant aspect of an initial appearance? Why?

3. Should we continue to use grand juries, which provide opportunities for the general public to become more involved in justice-based practices? Or, should we eliminate them in favor of preliminary hearings, which save the courts' resources?

4. Which pretrial motion do you believe most significantly impacts criminal cases? Why?

5. Imagine you are a judge hearing the case of a first-time offender who was caught with drugs while he was breaking into cars. The defendant claims his actions were prompted by his lack of money, education, and employment. Would you offer this defendant the opportunity for pretrial diversion? If so, what would be the conditions? If not, why not?

6. Do you believe that plea bargaining will continue to be the primary means by which cases are resolved in the courts? Why or why not?

Key Terms

arraignment
bail
bench warrant
charge bargaining
complaint
conditional release

count bargaining
deposit bail
discovery
diversion
exculpatory evidence
fully secured bail

grand jury hearings
indictment
information
initial appearance
insanity
no bill
nolle prosequi
nolo contendere
ordinance violations
plea bargaining
preliminary hearings
presentment

pretrial motion
pretrial release
pretrial service programs
pro bono
release on recognizance
sentence bargaining
Speedy Trial Act
summary trial
surety bond
third-party custody
true bill
unsecured bond

For digital learning resources, please go to
https://www.oup.com/he/burns1e

Trials

Criminal trials consist of a variety of steps and processes designed to find justice. They essentially involve two parties—the defense and prosecution—presenting their cases, with a judge as the "referee" and an arbitrator in bench trials. In jury trials, laypersons serve as the arbitrators.

Do you believe the trial is the step of criminal case processing that most accurately reflects our concern for finding justice? Why or why not?

Although most cases are plea bargained, criminal trials garner much of the public attention devoted to courts, and trials remain an important stage in criminal case processing. Trials can be dramatic, suspenseful, and frustrating. Careful attention is required at each step of a criminal trial to protect defendant rights. This module begins with a brief look at bench trials, before continuing with an examination of the stages of criminal trials, including jury selection, opening statements, the presentation of evidence, closing arguments, and judges' charges to the jury. This module ends with a look at jury deliberations and the verdict.

MODULE OUTLINE

- **Bench Trials**

  Learning Objective 24.1: Discuss the benefits and disadvantages of bench trials.

- **Jury Selection**

  Learning Objective 24.2: Explain how potential jurors are identified and removed from consideration from serving on a jury.

- **Opening Statements and Presentation of Evidence**

  Learning Objective 24.3: Differentiate the types of evidence that may be used in the presentation of the evidence.

- **Closing Arguments and Judge's Charge to the Jury**

  Learning Objective 24.4: Explain the purposes of closing arguments and judge's charges to the jury.

- **Jury Deliberations and the Verdict**

  Learning Objective 24.5: Describe the procedures involved with jury deliberations and the controversial nature of jury nullification.

The Hardships of Jury Duty

8 Trial

In 2017, actor and comedian Bill Cosby went to trial after being charged with three counts of felony aggravated indecent assault. The 12-member jury deliberated for 52 hours before it was determined by a judge that they were not going to come to a unanimous decision regarding any of the three counts against Cosby. In an interview following the trial, one juror in the Cosby case provided insight regarding jury duty and demonstrated

lived in a designated hotel during the trial, away from their jobs, friends, and families, with limited access to the outside world. The juror who discussed the case noted that tensions were very high during the course of deliberations, adding that one juror punched the wall out of frustration. Jurors were crying because of the difficulties of the situation, including the challenges of deciding on the case and being placed in a small room in which to deliberate (Francescani & Puckett, 2017). Legal analyst Danny Cervallos (2017) noted that jurors deliberated until around 9:00 p.m. on most nights and added that "deliberations in the Cosby trial were a textbook example of how tortuous jury duty can be, and how inherently oppressive the decision making process is for a high-profile jury." The challenges faced by the jurors during the trial were compounded by the fact that they failed to attain unanimity; thus, the case was retried. In the retrial, Cosby was found guilty on all three counts.

1 Criminal Act

the challenges that can be associated with being on a trial (Francescani & Puckett, 2017).

Jurors in the Cosby trial, which lasted 6 days, were sequestered, which means they

Picture yourself serving as a jury in a similar case. For days and perhaps weeks, you are prevented from living at home; restricted in what you can read, watch, or listen to; prevented from going to work or seeing family members; and are doing this essentially because you have been chosen to. Is there some way we could ease the burdens of jury duty? Should we pay jurors more than we do or ease the restrictions we place on sequestered jurors (e.g., let them see family members)?

Bench Trials

● **Learning Objective 24.1:** Discuss the benefits and disadvantages of bench trials.

Defendants are presumed innocent until proven guilty. However, not all defendants are entitled to a trial by jury. Juvenile defendants generally do not have the right to a jury trial (although some states permit them under certain conditions; see Module 26), nor do adult defendants charged with **petty offenses** or **infractions**, which are violations of a regulation, ordinance, or municipal code or minor crimes that warrant short terms of incarceration or fines (e.g., public intoxication).

In cases involving petty offenses or misdemeanors, the right to a trial by a jury varies among states. In *Baldwin v. New York* (1970), the Supreme Court ruled that jury trials are provided only to defendants charged with serious crimes, where the associated penalty is beyond 6 months. For lesser offenses, most states provide only **bench trials**, in which judges replace jurors in determining guilt at a trial. The exceptions to that are Vermont and Virginia, which provide defendants with the right to a jury trial in all cases.

Bench trials may also be used when a defendant waives the right to a jury trial. Among the benefits of a bench trial are:

- speedier and less expensive case processing,
- greater likelihood of cases being assessed on merit as opposed to emotion,
- judges being less likely to consider extralegal factors (e.g., the defendant's race, ethnicity, etc.), and
- judges being less likely to be influenced by the media (Champion et al., 2012).

The disadvantages of bench trials include:

- judges possibly imposing more severe penalties for particular offenses (e.g., drug offenses),
- the greater likelihood of corruption in cases where judges act alone, and
- judges being less likely to consider a defendant's emotional appeal (Champion et al., 2012).

Bench trials proceed through the same steps as a jury trial, with the exception of jury selection, judge's instructions to the jury, and jury deliberations. Bench trials are generally more informal than jury trials, because there is less of a need to explain legal terminology and the trial procedures to the participants (as is the case with jury trials), and the prosecutor, defense attorney, and judge may even be closely familiar with one another. Figure 24.1 depicts the steps of a jury trial, to which the remainder of this module turns.

8 Trial

petty offenses
Violations of a regulation, ordinance, or municipal code or minor crime that warrant short terms of incarceration or fines

infractions The lowest level of criminal behavior that is usually not punishable by confinement; instead, offenders are often given a citation or traffic ticket

bench trials Trials in which judges assess the facts of the case, apply the law, and offer verdicts and sentences; judges replace jurors in determining guilt

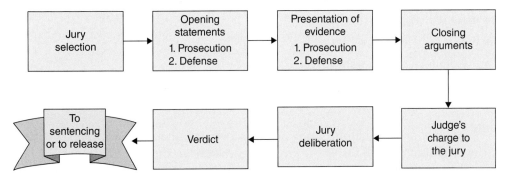

FIGURE 24.1. Steps of a Jury Trial. Trials proceed through a series of events, beginning with the selection of jurors. This is followed by opening statements, the presentation of evidence, and closing arguments. Once both sides have closed, the judge issues directions and guidance to the jurors, who deliberate and offer a verdict.

Which of these steps do you believe has the most significant impact on the outcome of trials? Why?

● **Learning Objective 24.2:** Explain how potential jurors are identified and removed from consideration from serving on a jury.

Fair Labor Standards Act Legislation which states that jurors do not have to be paid by employers for time not worked, including time spent at jury duty

Jury Selection

The selection of jurors is one of the most important steps of the trial process. The Sixth Amendment to the U.S. Constitution holds that defendants are entitled to a public trial by an impartial jury of their peers. Assembling trial juries requires careful consideration and consumes much court time and many resources.

Jury Sizes

All states require 12-member juries in capital offense cases. A few states allow for juries of 6 to 8 in some or all felony cases, including Alabama, Connecticut, Florida, Indiana, Massachusetts, and Utah. With respect to misdemeanor cases, some states allow the use of only 6 jurors, while others will conduct trials with 7 or 8 jurors (Banks, 2017).

Juror Compensation

A hardship for some jury members is the time they miss away from work. Trials may last a day or several weeks. The **Fair Labor Standards Act** does not require jurors to be paid by employers for time not worked, including time spent at jury duty. However, some state laws require employers to pay employees who serve jury duty, and most people (an estimated 62%) are paid by employers (Bureau of Labor Statistics, 2016).

Federal jurors receive $50 per day from the government and an extra $10 per day after jurors have served 10 days on a trial. Each state pays jurors for their time; however, the pay is relatively low. For example, the national average pay for jurors is roughly $22 per day (see Table 24.1). Most jurors serve only a short period of time.

Sources of a Jury

Potential jurors are selected from several sources. A combination is generally preferable, because each source is limited with regard to reaching all potential jurors. Potential juror sources include:

- voter registration lists,
- motor vehicle registration lists,
- unemployment and welfare rolls,
- water service customer lists, and
- tax-related information.

venire A group of potential jurors; jury pool

A group of potential jurors, also known as a **venire**, should reflect a cross-section of the community. With respect to this issue, the racial composition of juries is important in many respects. For example, researchers examining the racial composition of juries on trial outcomes found that juries formed from all-White jury pools convicted Black defendants more often (16 percentage points) than White defendants. The same study noted that the gap in conviction rates disappeared when the jury pool included at least one Black member (Anwar et al., 2012).

Disqualification or Dismissal of Jurors

Certain individuals are not permitted to serve on juries, including:

- ex-felons,
- individuals below a specified age,

TABLE 24.1. Juror Pay

JUROR PAY IS A FLAT RATE FOR ALL SERVICE DAYS		JUROR PAY IS GRADUATED (THIRD DAY PAY RATE)	
STATE	**PAY**	**STATE**	**PAY**
New York	$40.00	Colorado	$50.00
West Virginia	$40.00	Massachusetts	$50.00
Nebraska	$35.00	North Dakota	$50.00
Mississippi[a]	$28.50	South Dakota	$50.00
District of Columbia	$30.00	Wyoming[a]	$50.00
Hawaii	$30.00	Utah	$49.00
Virginia	$30.00	Indiana[a]	$40.68
Georgia[a]	$24.27	Michigan	$40.19
National average flat rate	$21.95	New Jersey	$40.00
New Hampshire	$21.29	Nevada	$40.00
Minnesota	$20.59	Arkansas	$35.00
Oklahoma	$20.00	National average graduated rate	$32.34
Maryland	$17.50	Arizona	$30.00
South Carolina[a]	$16.16	Florida	$30.00
Wisconsin	$16.00	North Carolina	$30.00
Rhode Island	$15.00	Vermont	$30.00
Illinois[a]	$13.15	Texas	$26.80
Kentucky	$12.50	Alaska	$25.00
Washington[a]	$11.59	Louisiana	$25.00
Tennessee	$11.55	Montana	$25.00
Alabama	$10.00	Oregon	$25.00
Idaho	$10.00	Pennsylvania	$25.00
Iowa	$10.00	Washington	$25.00
Kansas[a]	$10.00	Missouri	$20.40
Maine	$10.00	Delaware	$20.00
		Ohio[a]	$20.00
		Illinois	$16.50
		California	$15.00
		Connecticut[b]	$0.00

Source: Caseload Highlights, *by P. L. Hannaford-Agor and N. L. Waters, 2008, National Center for State Courts (http://www.courtstatistics.org/__data/assets/pdf_file/0023/30596/National-Jury-Improvement-Efforts.pdf).*

[a]*Localities may supplement state-mandated juror fees. Rate reflects average fee for counties reporting.*
[b]*Connecticut pays jurors $50 per day beginning on the 6th day of service; employers are required to pay jurors regular wages and salaries for the first 5 days of jury service.*

- nonresidents of the United States,
- individuals unable to understand English, and
- individuals with a personal connection to the case or the criminal justice system (e.g., judges, police officers).

Sometimes once a trial starts, it becomes necessary to dismiss a juror, or a juror must be replaced for various reasons, for example if they:

- become ill and cannot continue,
- engage in misconduct (e.g., failing to obey the court's instructions), or
- become biased or prejudiced as a result of some knowledge they obtained after the trial begins.

Therefore, alternate jurors are selected after attorneys choose a jury. These individuals sit in the jury box along with other jurors throughout the trial and listen to the cases; however, they do not participate in jury deliberations unless they replace a member of the jury. They are aware of their role as alternates and the importance of their responsibility of remaining engaged in the trial proceedings. Alternates help ensure that cases may proceed if jurors are dismissed.

Challenging Potential Jurors

Potential jurors are questioned during **voir dire**, which means "speak the truth." The process involves questioning potential jurors regarding any prejudices, knowledge, or opinions they may have regarding the case or the defendant. Essentially, voir dire is used to determine the qualifications of potential jurors to offer a fair and unbiased view of the case. Trial judges in the federal courts conduct the questioning during voir dire, although judges may permit attorneys to conduct the questioning or submit questions for the judge to ask. Attorneys conduct the questioning in most state courts (del Carmen & Hemmens, 2017).

The defense and prosecution use different challenges in efforts to select a jury from the jury pool. Eliminating potential jurors from the jury pool is done through several means:

- A **challenge to the array** may be submitted prior to jury selection by defense attorneys who believe the jury pool is not reflective of the community or is biased in some manner. A new jury pool is provided if the court agrees with the attorney's claim.
- A **challenge for cause** may be issued by attorneys if during voir dire they identify a particular reason why a potential juror may be unsuitable for the trial. For instance, a potential juror could be removed for cause if during voir dire it was determined that the individual is racist or if it was found that the potential juror was familiar with the defendant in the case. The potential juror is dismissed if the court agrees with the attorney's claim.
- A **peremptory challenge** may be offered during voir dire by attorneys who do not wish to have a potential juror impaneled. Attorneys are not required to offer a reason or justification, but the exclusion cannot be based on race (*Batson v. Kentucky*, 1986) or gender (*J.E.B. v. Alabama*, 1994), and attorneys may, through a **Batson challenge**, be required to provide a reason other than these to exclude a prospective juror through a peremptory challenge. Attorneys are permitted only a specified number of peremptory challenges; the number varies by state and depends on the seriousness of the charge. They are permitted an unlimited number of challenges for cause.

voir dire "Speak the truth"; the process involves questioning potential jurors regarding any prejudices, knowledge, or opinions they may have regarding the case or the defendant

challenge to the array A challenge offered prior to jury selection by defense attorneys who believe the jury pool is not reflective of the community or is biased in some manner; a new jury pool is provided if the court agrees with the attorney's claim

challenge for cause A challenge offered by attorneys if, during voir dire, they identify a particular reason why a potential juror may be unsuitable for the trial

peremptory challenge A challenge offered during voir dire by attorneys who do not wish to have a potential juror impaneled; attorneys are not required to offer a reason or justification, but the exclusion cannot be based on race or gender; attorneys are permitted only a specified number of peremptory challenges

Batson challenge A challenge requiring attorneys to provide a reason other than race or gender to exclude a prospective juror through a peremptory challenge

As noted in the "In the News" feature at the start of this module, actor and comedian Bill Cosby faced three charges of sexual assault. The jurors chosen for the two trials (the first resulted in a mistrial) were sequestered in efforts to avoid their decisions being influenced by the extensive media coverage of the case. After 6 days of testimony and arguments and 5 days of deliberations in the first case, the jurors were deadlocked and a mistrial was declared. The retrial involved new jurors and 13 days of testimony and arguments and a day and a half of deliberations. The lives of these jurors were essentially put on hold while they assisted the courts.

Do you believe serving on a jury that has been sequestered is an undue hardship? Why or why not?

More peremptory challenges are available in cases involving more serious offenses (del Carmen & Hemmens, 2017). Once attorneys have used all of the peremptory challenges, they must accept all jurors unless a challenge for cause can be offered.

1 Criminal Act

Sequestering Juries

Judges determine whether a jury should be **sequestered**, or isolated from the general public, during the trial. Jurors may be sequestered out of concern for publicity surrounding the trial or to prevent **jury tampering**. Tampering is a crime that involves attempts to persuade a juror to come to a particular decision regarding a case. It may involve an individual discussing the case with a juror or a threat to harm the juror if they do not vote in a specific manner. Most juries are not sequestered, but they are also not permitted to discuss the case with anyone.

sequestered juries Juries that are isolated from the general public during the trial

jury tampering A crime that involves attempts to persuade a juror's decision regarding a case

Opening Statements and Presentation of Evidence

The opening statements portion of a trial and the presentation of the evidence are where the prosecution and defense primarily make their case. Their opening statements introduce their case to the court, making the judge, jury, and all others aware of how they generally plan to approach the case. Their presentation of evidence is

● **Learning Objective 24.3:** Differentiate the types of evidence that may be used in the presentation of the evidence.

where they provide support for their arguments and perhaps attempt to discredit the arguments put forth by the opposing side.

Opening Statements

8 Trial

Attorneys may begin the trial with an opening statement to the judge and jury, although they are not required to do so. Attorneys are less likely to use opening statements in bench trials, since judges are typically exposed to numerous trials and do not require them.

During opening statements, attorneys identify the evidence they intend to introduce at trial. Opening statements help jurors understand the evidence and testimony, as well as the nature of the case, but jurors are instructed that the information provided during opening statements is not to be considered as evidence. This first impression that the jury receives of the attorney's case can be very important, and the opening statement has been referred to as "arguably the most critical part of any trial" (Brook, 2013, p. 181).

The prosecution typically provides the first opening statement and is followed by the defense attorney. Some judges permit attorneys to speak at length during opening statements, while other judges impose a time limit.

Under a "good faith" requirement, the content of attorneys' opening statements may include only information about evidence that they believe will be permitted by the court during trial. Trial judges assess whether a statement is permissible. The following are not permitted during opening statements (del Carmen & Hemmens, 2017, p. 53):

- opinions
- conclusions
- references to the character of the accused
- argumentative statements
- references to matters that will not be supported by evidence in the trial

Presentation of Evidence

Following opening statements, the prosecution is the first to present evidence at trial. Of particular concern are the types of evidence that may be introduced and the procedures surrounding the presentation of evidence by both sides.

TYPES OF EVIDENCE

Evidence must be *competent*, or legally permissible; *material*, or having a direct bearing on the case; and *relevant*, or applicable to the case. There are different types of evidence introduced at trial: circumstantial, direct, testimonial, and real.

circumstantial evidence Also known as indirect evidence, it is evidence that does not directly link defendants and the crime and can be interpreted in various ways; it involves probabilities and possibilities, which leaves juries to determine whether circumstances are favorable or unfavorable to the defendant

direct evidence Evidence that provides an identifiable link between the defendant and the crime and can include eyewitness testimony

- **Circumstantial evidence**, or indirect evidence, does not directly link defendants and the crime and can be interpreted in various ways. Circumstantial evidence involves probabilities and possibilities, which leaves juries to determine whether circumstances are favorable or unfavorable to the defendant. An example would be assuming that the accused is guilty of murder because the gun used to kill the victim belonged to the accused. A judge's decision to permit this type of evidence is based on the strength of the evidence or the probability.

- **Direct evidence** provides an identifiable link between the defendant and the crime and can include eyewitness testimony. An example would be an eyewitness to a shooting testifying that they personally witnessed the accused pull the trigger and harm the victim.

- **Testimonial evidence** is a type of direct evidence that provides the bulk of evidence in court cases and may be provided by *lay witnesses* or *expert witnesses*. Lay witnesses are restricted to providing testimony based solely on what they witnessed with regard to the incident in question. Expert witnesses must have the appropriate credentials and be recognized by the court as an expert in a particular field to offer expert opinions. For instance, physicians may be called into court to offer an opinion regarding a cause of death. Expert witnesses are used to offer assistance in other areas, including fingerprint identification, ballistics tests, and handwriting and DNA analyses (see Module 22).

- **Real evidence** is physical evidence that can be circumstantial or direct, and it is presented to the jury in the form of exhibits. Fingerprints, notes, blood samples, and weapons are examples of real evidence.

Attorneys introduce several types of evidence during trials. A gun believed to have been used in a crime would be considered real evidence, because it is a tangible exhibit that can be physically held.

What type of evidence do you believe is most influential to a jury? Why?

PROSECUTION'S PRESENTATION OF EVIDENCE

The presentation of evidence at trial begins with the prosecution's **direct examination** of their witnesses and is followed by the defense's **cross-examination** of witnesses. The prosecution may ask their witness additional questions following cross-examination, in what is known as **redirect examination**. The defense may then ask the witness questions in **recross-examination**. Defense attorneys are not required to question the prosecution's witnesses, and the prosecution has no opportunity to ask additional questions of their witnesses if the defense does not cross or recross. The prosecution rests after presenting all of its evidence, and the defense then presents its case.

DEFENSE'S PRESENTATION OF EVIDENCE

The presentation of the defense's evidence occurs in the same manner as it does for the prosecution, although the defense is not required to present any evidence, given that the burden of proof is on the prosecution. Defense attorneys offer evidence in efforts to refute the prosecutor's case. For example, they may introduce a witness who provides testimony that the accused was in a location other than where the crime in question occurred. Or, they may provide evidence to support claims that the defendant acted in self-defense, out of necessity, or while under duress or being coerced (see Module 8).

REBUTTALS AND SURREBUTTALS

Following the defense's case, the prosecution can introduce witness testimony to refute testimony given from a defense witness in what is known as **rebuttal**. This testimony may be followed by testimony from the defense in attempts to discredit testimony offered during rebuttal, in what is known as **surrebuttal**. The defense rests after it presents all of its evidence.

OBJECTIONS

At any point during the presentation of the evidence, the attorneys may object to the questions asked and responses given, if they believe the information is *inadmissible* (unacceptable). The judge then *sustains* (permits) or *overrules* (denies) the objections. Only evidence that is legally permissible, has a direct bearing on the case, and is relevant to the case will be considered. For instance, evidence obtained from an illegal search by police officers will not be permitted at trial.

testimonial evidence A type of direct evidence that provides the bulk of evidence in court cases and may be provided by lay witnesses or expert witnesses

real evidence Physical evidence that can be circumstantial or direct; it is presented to the jury in the form of exhibits

8 Trial

direct examination Attorneys questioning their witnesses during a trial

cross-examination Attorneys questioning the opposition's witnesses after direct examination

redirect examination Attorneys questioning their witnesses following cross-examination

recross-examination
Attorneys questioning the opposition's witnesses following redirect examination

rebuttal The practice of prosecutors introducing witness testimony to refute testimony given from a defense witness

surrebuttal
Testimony from the defense in attempts to discredit testimony offered during rebuttal

● **Learning Objective 24.4:** Explain the purposes of closing arguments and judge's charges to the jury.

8 Trial

summation Closing arguments of a trial

Closing Arguments and Judge's Charge to the Jury

The closing arguments offered by the prosecution and the defense and the judge's charge to the jury signify the conclusion of the trial. Closing arguments enable both sides to summarize their cases and connect their presentation of evidence with what they proposed they would do during opening statements. These arguments are followed by the judge's charge to the jury, which involves judges providing guidance or directions for jurors as they set off to deliberate.

Closing Arguments

During closing arguments, or **summation**, attorneys review their case. Closing arguments assist jurors in recalling and considering the evidence provided at trial. Summations typically highlight the evidence presented, the strength of the arguments, and the weaknesses of the opposition's case. Attorneys are not permitted to enter personal opinions or new evidence at closing, and jurors are not supposed to consider the information shared at closing arguments as evidence (similar to opening statements).

States vary in the order in which closing arguments are made, although the prosecution typically closes first, followed by the defense. The prosecution may then have the option of rebuttal, or making the final closing statement. Closing arguments are considered the "final word," or parting information provided to jurors who will soon deliberate on the case. Accordingly, prosecutors must be organized and persuasive. The content of what is shared at closing arguments is particularly important. In one study, researchers found that the evidence summarized in attorneys' closing arguments in child sexual abuse cases influenced whether the accused was convicted (Stolzenberg & Lyon, 2014).

Judge's Charge to the Jury

Closing arguments are followed by a judge's instructions to the jury. At this stage, the judge prepares a **charge to the jury**, which is a written document that explains how the law applies to the case and other information to assist jurors. The charges are typically prepared in an informal conference between the judge and the attorneys and must be written in a neutral manner, meaning that they cannot sway juror decisions. A judge's charge to the jury is subject to appellate review and may include:

- identification of the crime for which the defendant is accused,
- definitions of legal concepts pertaining to the case,
- a reminder of the need for the prosecution to prove guilt beyond a reasonable doubt,
- an explanation of what evidence may be considered,
- a list of potential verdicts, and
- procedural instructions, including guidance for jurors should they wish to contact the judge with questions.

Ensuring that jurors understand the directions provided by judges prior to deliberations is an important aspect of the trial. Because of our increasingly diverse society, judges must make efforts to address cultural differences, language barriers, and a lack of familiarity with the legal system to ensure that all jurors clearly understand their charges.

What, specifically, could judges do to ensure that jurors from all backgrounds clearly understand the instructions?

Jurors as a group are not always familiar with the law; thus, the directions can be highly influential. Some researchers have questioned whether juries always understand the instructions (e.g., Dattu, 1998; Foglia, 2003) and whether the instructions have any impact on how prepared juries are to render a decision (e.g., Steele & Thornburg, 1991). One study surveyed jurors who had recently served on a jury and found that a substantial portion of them were mistaken about the directions pertaining to "burden of proof" and "beyond a reasonable doubt" (McKimmie et al., 2014). Our increasingly diverse society requires that charges to the jury be presented in easy-to-understand language (e.g., absent much legal terminology that would make it difficult for jurors to understand) to assist jurors who may have difficulty grasping written jury instructions (Dattu, 1998).

charge to the jury A written document that explains how the law applies to the case and other information to assist jurors

Jury Deliberations and the Verdict

Jurors deliberate after receiving instructions from the judge and do so with no outside parties in the deliberation room. Researchers are limited in their ability to fully understand what occurs during this stage of the trial proceedings, given the secretive nature of deliberations. Our knowledge regarding jury deliberations is largely a result of studies of mock juries and interviews of jurors following cases. The length of deliberations may be short, for instance when there is either overwhelming or sparse evidence. Or, deliberations may take several days or sometimes weeks.

Procedures for Deliberation

Juries elect a **foreperson** or one is selected by the judge prior to formal deliberations. The foreperson presides over the deliberations and reads the verdict in the courtroom. Jurors may examine evidence introduced at trial and request portions of the transcript during deliberations because they are often prevented from taking notes during trial. Although the Supreme Court ruled that unanimity, or complete agreement among jurors, is not required in noncapital cases, most jurisdictions require a unanimous decision. Federal cases require 12-member juries and unanimity. An **Allen charge** is issued to juries that appear unable to reach agreement on a verdict. In these instances, judges recharge the jury with new instructions designed to encourage agreement.

In some instances, jurors cannot reach the required number of votes to come to a verdict. This is referred to as a **hung jury** or **deadlocked jury**; when this happens, the case may be retried with a new jury. Approximately 6% of criminal cases result in

- **Learning Objective 24.5:** Describe the procedures involved with jury deliberations and the controversial nature of jury nullification.

8 Trial

foreperson The leader of the jury either elected by fellow jurors or selected by a judge to preside over the deliberations and read the verdict in the courtroom

Allen charge A charge issued to juries that appear unable to reach agreement; judges use them to recharge the jury with new instructions designed to encourage agreement

hung jury Also known as a **deadlocked jury**, it occurs when jurors cannot reach the required number of votes to come to a verdict; the case may be retried with a new jury when this happens

jury nullification The practice of jurors dismissing the facts of a case and basing their decisions on other factors, such as their opinion of the participants in the crime or the appropriateness of the law

11 Appeal

a jury being unable to come to a verdict (Waters & Hans, 2009). There is no limit regarding how many times a case may be retried following a hung jury.

Following the announcement of a verdict in the courtroom, jurors may be polled by the trial attorneys. Polling jurors enables the attorneys to ensure that all (or the necessary number of) jurors agree with the verdict.

Jury Nullification

The right of a jury to decide a criminal case without fear of reprisal or much oversight has been a cornerstone of the U.S. system of justice. One of the more controversial aspects of criminal courts involves **jury nullification**, or the practice of jurors dismissing the facts of a case and basing their decisions on other factors, such as their opinion of the participants in the crime or the appropriateness of the law. For instance, jurors may vote to acquit when they believe the offender, while guilty, has suffered enough or when a juror perceives a law as being overly punitive.

Jury members are primarily tasked with considering the facts of a case presented before them and providing a verdict. They are given much freedom in their decision-making: No court officials are permitted in jury deliberations and no explanation or justification is required for a jury's decision. Accordingly, they may, and sometimes do, acquit defendants when the evidence presented would strongly suggest they vote to convict. Conversely, they may also vote to convict a defendant despite strong evidence that would suggest that they acquit the defendant, although their decision may be overturned at appeal. Acquittals, in contrast, cannot be overturned because of protections against double jeopardy, as provided in the Fifth Amendment. Jury nullification empowers jurors to become active participants in enforcing criminal laws.

The System in Perspective

As noted in the "In the News" feature at the start of this module, jury members in the initial Bill Cosby trial struggled to come to an agreement. They were sequestered during the length of the trial, and their lives were disrupted. Because they were unable to come to an agreement, it may seem that their efforts were of little value, but this is not the case. All juror participation, regardless of case outcome, is vital to the proper functioning of our justice system. Criminal trials, in general, require the systematic cooperation, input, and practices of many individuals. Trials proceed through a series of steps guided by constitutional requirements and protections and reflect society's concern for being fair and just with regard to actual and accused criminal behavior.

Summary

1. Learning Objective 24.1: *Discuss the benefits and disadvantages of bench trials.*

- Bench trials are speedier and less expensive than jury trials, and they provide a greater likelihood of cases being assessed on merit as opposed to emotion. Judges are less likely than

juries to consider extralegal factors and less likely than juries to be influenced by the media. The disadvantages of bench trials include judges possibly imposing more severe penalties than juries for particular offenses, the greater likelihood of corruption in cases where judges act alone, and juries being more likely than judges to consider a defendant's emotional appeal.

2. **Learning Objective 24.2:** *Explain how potential jurors are identified and removed from consideration from serving on a jury.*

- The defense and prosecution use different challenges in efforts to select a jury from the jury pool, including a challenge to the array, which is submitted prior to jury selection and may be offered by a defense attorney who believes the jury pool is not reflective of the community or is biased in some manner. Attorneys may issue a challenge for cause if they identify a particular reason why a potential juror may be unsuitable for the trial, and they may use peremptory challenges when they do not wish to have a potential juror impaneled, although the attorney is not required to offer a reason or justification. The latter type of exclusion cannot be based on race or gender, and attorneys have a set number of peremptory challenges.

3. **Learning Objective 24.3:** *Differentiate the types of evidence that may be used in the presentation of the evidence.*

- Attorneys present different types of evidence to make their cases at trial. Among the types of evidence are circumstantial evidence, which does not directly link defendants and the crime and can be interpreted in various ways. It involves probabilities and possibilities, which leaves juries to determine whether circumstances are favorable or unfavorable to the defendant. Direct evidence provides an identifiable link between the defendant and the crime and often includes eyewitness testimony, which is also known as testimonial evidence. Real evidence is physical evidence that is presented to the jury in the form of exhibits and includes fingerprints, notes, blood samples, and weapons.

4. **Learning Objective 24.4:** *Explain the purposes of closing arguments and judge's charges to the jury.*

- Closing arguments enable the prosecution and defense to summarize their case, primarily through recapping their presentation of the evidence and demonstrating how their efforts related to what they proposed to do in their opening statements. The judge's charge to the jury involves judges providing guidance or directions for jurors as they set off to deliberate.

5. **Learning Objective 24.5:** *Describe the procedures involved with jury deliberations and the controversial nature of jury nullification.*

- Juries elect a foreperson or one is selected prior to formal deliberations. The foreperson presides over the deliberations and reads the verdict in the courtroom. Jurors may examine evidence introduced at trial and request portions of the transcript during deliberations. Although the Supreme Court ruled that unanimity, or complete agreement among jurors, is not required in noncapital cases, most jurisdictions require a unanimous decision. In cases when agreement is not reached, judges recharge the jury with new instructions designed to encourage agreement. A hung jury is declared in cases when agreement is still not found, and the case may be retried. Jury nullification is controversial because jurors who engage in it are arguably neglecting to evaluate a case on the facts presented to them.

Questions for Critical Thinking

1. Should all defendants have a right to trial, including those who have committed relatively minor offenses? Why or why not?
2. What additional steps could be taken to further ensure that fair, objective jurors are selected for trials?
3. Is it fair for the prosecution to be the first to present its evidence to the jury? Does the prosecution have an unfair advantage? Or does the defense have an advantage because it follows and is the last to present evidence? Why?

4. How could judges and the courts in general better ensure that jurors are best prepared for jury deliberations? Should we include a court representative in deliberation rooms to ensure that all legal questions are properly addressed? Why or why not?

5. Should jury nullification be permitted, or should jurors be required to strictly evaluate cases on the legal merits of the case? Discuss.

Key Terms

Allen charge
Batson challenge
bench trials
challenge for cause
challenge to the array
charge to the jury
circumstantial evidence
cross-examination
deadlocked jury
direct evidence
direct examination
Fair Labor Standards Act
foreperson
hung jury
infractions

jury nullification
jury tampering
peremptory challenges
petty offenses
real evidence
rebuttal
recross-examination
redirect examination
sequestered juries
summation
surrebuttal
testimonial evidence
venire
voir dire

For digital learning resources, please go to
https://www.oup.com/he/burns1e

Sentencing and Appeals

Some inmates may begin serving their sentences immediately after the sentences are imposed. Others may be sentenced at a later point. Many offenders maintain the hope that their cases will be overturned by an appellate court. This photo depicts a man being escorted out of court who was convicted of sexually assaulting a 7-year-old girl and sentenced to 7.5 years in prison.

Should all offenders be immediately taken into custody to begin their sentences? Why or why not?

Upon being found guilty or admitting guilt, offenders are sentenced. Once a sentence is imposed, some offenders have the option of appealing their case to higher level courts. Appellate courts review the transcripts of the trial courts and consider areas of potential error. This module addresses both sentencing and appeals, beginning with a look at approaches to sentencing, the sentencing process, and disparities in sentencing. It includes a directed examination of capital punishment, given the controversial nature and seriousness of the penalty. This module ends with a look at appeals and postconviction review.

MODULE OUTLINE

- **The Purposes of Sentencing**

  Learning Objective 25.1: Summarize the primary purposes of criminal sanctions.

- **Approaches to Sentencing**

  Learning Objective 25.2: Characterize the approaches to sentencing.

- **The Sentencing Process**

  Learning Objective 25.3: Describe how sentences are imposed.

- **Capital Punishment**

  Learning Objective 25.4: Explain why capital punishment cases cost more than other cases.

- **Disparities in Sentencing**

  Learning Objective 25.5: Discuss why some groups generally receive tougher sentences than others.

- **Appeals and Postconviction Review**

  Learning Objective 25.6: Identify the possible outcomes of appellate court hearings.

IN THE NEWS

9 Sentencing

Sentencing Controversies

"Three strikes" refers to the mandate in many states that an individual's third felony conviction (regardless of type of felony) results in an extended prison sentence (perhaps 20 years), and a significant portion of that time (e.g., 75% of the sentence) must be served. California went so far as to include misdemeanors in its count of strikes against an offender. In 2014, a ballot initiative known

PRISON PROGRAMS GIVING INMATES HOPE FOR FUTURE
PROP 57 LATEST ATTEMPT TO LOWER PRISON POPULATION

as Proposition 47 passed, which lightened the notably strong "Three Strikes law." It

was estimated that roughly 1,000 California prisoners were released early as a result (Miles, 2013).

Then, in September 2018, a California appellate court ruled that a state constitutional amendment, Proposition 57, would apply to prisoners sentenced under three strikes legislation. Proposition 57 requires that any person convicted of a nonviolent felony offense be considered for parole, regardless of California's Three Strikes law. The state's parole board estimated that up to 4,000 nonviolent third strikers could be affected ("California Rethinks," 2018).

Since their passage, three strikes penalties have been somewhat controversial. Supporters of three strikes legislation argue that the penalties help ensure the punishment appropriately fits the crime, save prison space for dangerous felons, and conserve money while ensuring that dangerous criminals remain incarcerated. Opponents argue that the penalties are too severe and not flexible enough to address the many variables associated with each crime. Do you believe three strikes and similar mandatory penalties for repeat offenders should be used, or should each case be evaluated on its own merits?

● **Learning Objective 25.1:** Summarize the primary purposes of criminal sanctions.

9 Sentencing

The Purposes of Sentencing

The reasons for a particular sentence are not always explicitly announced upon sentencing. However, in general, sentences seek to either *rehabilitate* (or "cure" offenders), *incapacitate* (physically prevent offenders from committing crimes again), offer *retribution* (revenge), *deter* (dissuade offenders from committing crimes again), or *restore* (return offenders and society to their prior conditions). To be sure, these goals of criminal sentencing are not mutually exclusive, and multiple goals can be addressed with one sentence. For instance, an offender may receive jail time and anger-management counseling—sentences that seek to achieve multiple goals (retribution, incapacitation, and rehabilitation). Emphases on particular goals of criminal sanctioning have changed over time.

Rehabilitation

Convicted offenders sometimes receive sentences with the underlying goal of **rehabilitation**. Such sentences begin with efforts to understand why an offender broke the law and proceed to treat, counsel, and educate them so they refrain from doing so in the future (Allen et al., 2013). Rehabilitation seeks to "correct" the individual without substantial punishment. Rehabilitation as a goal is found in sentences such as drug and/or alcohol rehabilitation, counseling, job skills training, and education.

Incapacitation

Some criminal sentences involve **incapacitation**, or physically restraining individuals from committing additional crimes. Efforts to incapacitate offenders in the United States primarily involve prison or jail sentences (Scott & Holmberg, 2003). However, some countries (e.g., Saudi Arabia and Nigeria) under Islamic law chop off the hand or hands of individuals convicted of theft ("The World's Most Barbaric," 2010).

Selective incapacitation is the practice of identifying and incarcerating dangerous and/or repeat offenders for extended periods. Sentences of life in prison are obvious examples of attempts to incapacitate offenders.

Retribution

Sentences with a goal of retribution seek to punish offenders. **Retribution** is based on retaliation, or the "eye for an eye" or "just deserts" approach, which has been particularly popular throughout history (Burns, 2007). It seeks to punish offenders with as much pain as they inflicted on their victims. Capital punishment is primarily based on retribution, and individuals in most states can be executed for taking the life of another. Sentences with the goal of retribution aim to directly associate punishment with the criminal event and they consider an offender's criminal history.

Retributive efforts have generated controversy, however, because some believe that inflicting punishment in response to wrongful behavior amounts to "two wrongs not making a right." There is also concern about the appropriateness of punishment in relation to the harms committed. In particular, it is difficult to determine what level of punishment is appropriate, or just, for particular offenses.

Deterrence

Retribution as a goal of criminal sentences is often combined with **deterrence**, because sentencing officials often hope that the punishment imposed will dissuade the individual and/or others from committing a similar harm. Lengthy prison sentences and large fines are examples of criminal sentences that seek to deter. There are two types of deterrence: specific and general.

Specific deterrence, sometimes referred to as special deterrence, includes sanctions designed to deter particular individuals from committing additional crimes. A judge telling an offender that they must remain drug free or they will go to jail is an example. Efforts directed toward **general deterrence** seek to discourage a general audience from engaging in a particular behavior. Having offenders pick up trash along highways is an example of general deterrence, because those who drive by will assumedly associate criminal behavior with the punishment of picking up trash.

Imposing sentences that seek to dissuade individuals from committing crime is based on the early works of the classical school of criminological thought, in which it was believed that criminals rationally consider the costs and benefits of committing crime. It was and is believed that the goal of governing bodies should be to create and impose penalties that discourage individuals from trying to obtain the benefits associated with criminal behavior (Kleck & Barnes, 2014).

10
Corrections

rehabilitation A goal of criminal sentencing that begins with understanding why an offender broke the law and proceeds to help them refrain from doing so in the future through education, counseling, and other forms of treatment

incapacitation A goal of criminal sentencing that seeks to physically prevent offenders from committing additional crimes; incarceration is an example

selective incapacitation The practice of identifying and incarcerating dangerous and/or repeat offenders for extended periods

retribution A goal of criminal sentencing that seeks to punish offenders; it is based on retaliation, or the "eye for an eye" or "just deserts" approach

deterrence A goal of sentencing that seeks to discourage or dissuade individuals or everyone from committing various behaviors

10
Corrections

specific deterrence A goal of sentencing that seeks to discourage or dissuade specific individuals from committing various behaviors

---

---

general deterrence A goal of sentencing that seeks to discourage or dissuade everyone from committing harmful behaviors

restoration A goal of sentencing that focuses on restoring offenders and victims to where they were physically and/or mentally prior to the crime, with an emphasis on betterment

Restoration

Some criminal sentences focus on restoring offenders and victims back to where they were physically and/or mentally prior to the crime, with an emphasis on betterment. The belief is that with some offenders, and under some conditions, it would be possible and helpful to reintegrate offenders as opposed to casting them out from society. **Restoration** is grounded, in part, in the belief that human lives should not be discarded simply because of criminal behavior, and it often involves restitution (or repayment in some form to the victim) and victim–offender mediation.

Restoration is a primary component of restorative justice, which views crime as an offense against another person as opposed to a crime against the state (see Module 7). It more directly involves victims and the community in efforts to repair the harms associated with the crime. The emphasis with regard to restoration is on addressing harms, as opposed to punishing offenders for their current and previous actions (Van Ness & Strong, 1997, pp. 32–36).

● **Learning Objective 25.2:** Characterize the approaches to sentencing.

9 Sentencing

Approaches to Sentencing

Some sentences are determined by legislation passed in the jurisdiction in which the crime was committed; others involve discretion on behalf of sentencing bodies and correctional agencies. Jurisdictions use various approaches in sentencing to help ensure greater consistency and justice. These approaches include indeterminate sentences, determinate sentences, structured sentences, and mandatory sentences.

Indeterminate Sentences

Indeterminate sentences involve a minimum and maximum time an inmate will serve. The amount of time is decided by a parole board, which determines the offender's suitability for release from prison. This approach is generally more focused on rehabilitation than other approaches. Indeterminate sentencing involves much discretion and, therefore, inconsistency.

Determinate Sentences

Some jurisdictions responded to the inconsistency of indeterminate sentences, beginning in the 1970s, by imposing various structured sentencing processes, including determinate sentencing. **Determinate sentences** involve offenders receiving a maximum period of incarceration, which can be reduced if they earn good time credits, for instance by not misbehaving and through participation in betterment programs. So, for example, an inmate who receives a 10-year sentence will be released after about 5 years, if they earn enough good time credit. The use of good time credits encourages inmates to behave and better themselves while incarcerated.

Structured Sentences

Structured sentences, in the form of sentencing guidelines, emerged in the 1980s in some states. **Sentencing guidelines** seek to reduce disparity and promote uniformity in sentencing primarily through consideration of an offender's criminal history and current offense. States that use the guidelines typically have a list of all offenses in relation to several risk levels. Each offense corresponds with a particular length or range of incarceration time. Figure 25.1 depicts a partial view of the sentencing guidelines worksheet used in Virginia.

Sentencing guidelines were used by the federal government until 2005 when the Supreme Court ruled that the Sixth Amendment right to trial by jury requires that aside from a prior conviction, only facts introduced by a defendant or proved beyond a reasonable doubt to a jury at the trial may be used to calculate a sentence. The court further ruled that the federal guidelines would be considered (in an advisory capacity) but not directly followed by federal judges (*U.S. v. Booker*, 2005).

Some states mandate that judges stay within the proposed guidelines; other states use the guidelines in an advisory manner and do not require judges to conform to them. Still, other states permit judges to sentence offenders below or above the guidelines, although they must provide written explanations for doing so.

Mandatory Sentences

Mandatory sentences were first introduced in 1951 with the passage of the Boggs Act, which stipulated penalties associated with possession of marijuana. They were a result of judicial and parole board discretion and the desire for more punitive responses to crime. Mandatory penalties largely limit judicial decision-making to legislatively prescribed, required penalties for particular offenses. Similar to sentencing guidelines, mandatory sentences are viewed as being less biased because they do not consider race, gender, age, and other extralegal variables.

Examples of mandatory sentences include **habitual offender laws** and **three strikes penalties**, which mandate that offenders with specific types and numbers of prior convictions receive extended penalties. The laws and penalties are designed to ensure that repeat offenders are imprisoned for extended periods. About half of all states (28) and the federal government currently use habitual offender or three strikes penalties, and the statutes vary among the states. Some states refer to those who fall under the law as "persistent offenders," and most states mandate that only serious (felony) cases count as strikes.

The federal government implemented a "three strikes" statute following passage of the Violent Crime Control and Law Enforcement Act of 1994. It provided a mandatory life in prison sentence for a convicted felon who had been previously convicted in federal court of a serious violent felony (e.g., murder, kidnapping) and had two or more previous convictions in federal or state courts, at least one of which was a serious violent felony.

Also during the 1990s, reform efforts tried to ensure that inmates serve a greater percentage of their sentences. One approach to doing so was the creation of

9 Sentencing

indeterminate sentences Sentences that involve a minimum and maximum time an inmate will serve; the amount of time is decided by a parole board, which determines the offender's suitability for release from prison

determinate sentences Sentences that involve offenders receiving a maximum period of incarceration, which can be reduced if they earn good time credits

structured sentences Sentences imposed under the direction of sentencing guidelines that seek to reduce disparity and promote uniformity in sentencing, primarily through consideration of an offender's criminal history and current offense

sentencing guidelines Guidelines used in sentencing that seek to reduce disparity and promote uniformity in sentencing, primarily through consideration of an offender's criminal history and current offense

mandatory sentences Sentences that require offenders to serve a predetermined amount of time

habitual offender laws Legislation that mandates offenders with extensive criminal backgrounds receive extended penalties

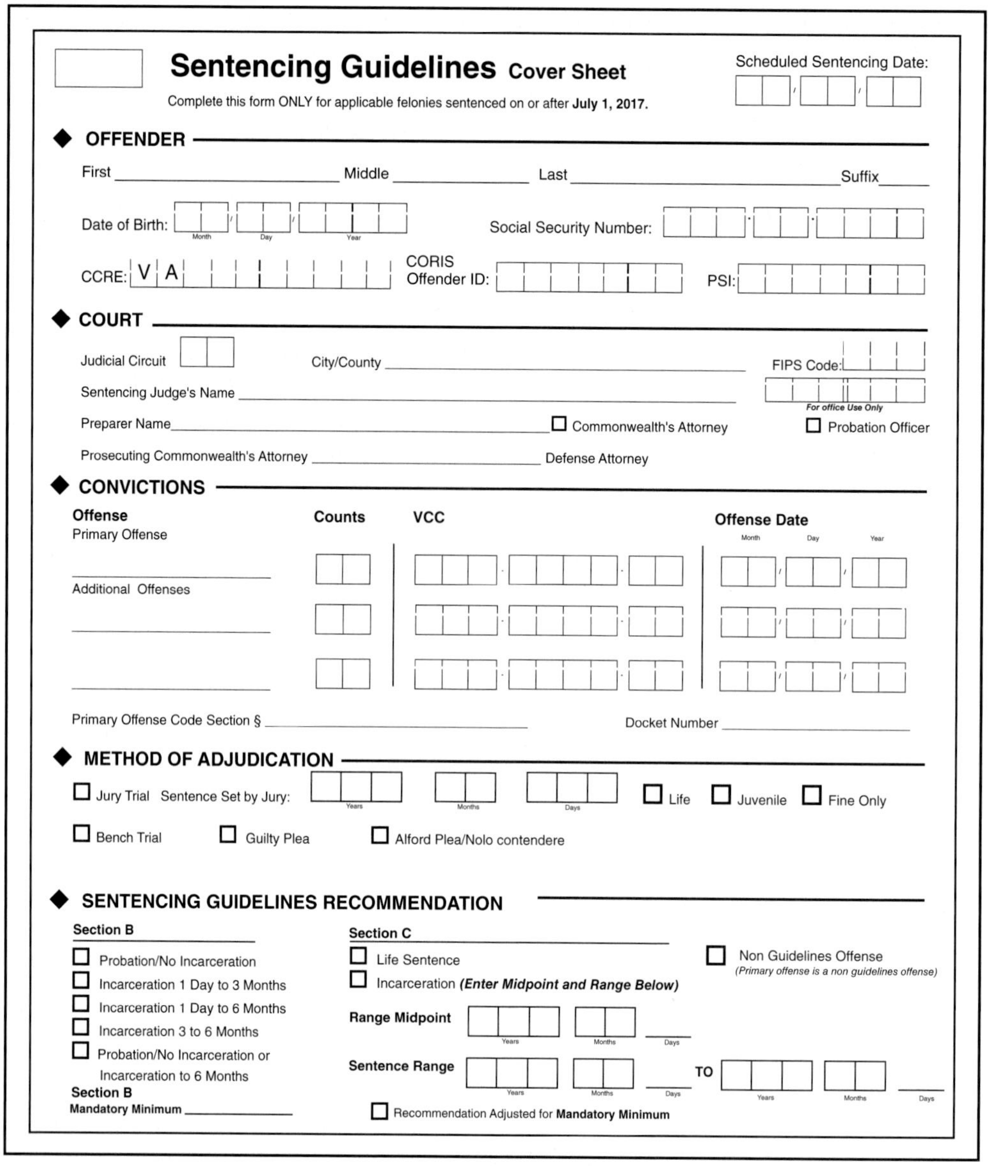
Sentencing Guidelines Cover Sheet

Complete this form ONLY for applicable felonies sentenced on or after **July 1, 2017.**

Scheduled Sentencing Date:

OFFENDER

First ______ Middle ______ Last ______ Suffix ______

Date of Birth: Month / Day / Year

Social Security Number:

CCRE: V A

CORIS Offender ID:

PSI:

COURT

Judicial Circuit

City/County ______

FIPS Code:

Sentencing Judge's Name ______

For office Use Only

Preparer Name ______ ☐ Commonwealth's Attorney ☐ Probation Officer

Prosecuting Commonwealth's Attorney ______ Defense Attorney

CONVICTIONS

Offense	**Counts**	**VCC**	**Offense Date** (Month / Day / Year)
Primary Offense			
Additional Offenses			

Primary Offense Code Section § ______ Docket Number ______

METHOD OF ADJUDICATION

☐ Jury Trial Sentence Set by Jury: Years Months Days ☐ Life ☐ Juvenile ☐ Fine Only

☐ Bench Trial ☐ Guilty Plea ☐ Alford Plea/Nolo contendere

SENTENCING GUIDELINES RECOMMENDATION

Section B

☐ Probation/No Incarceration

☐ Incarceration 1 Day to 3 Months

☐ Incarceration 1 Day to 6 Months

☐ Incarceration 3 to 6 Months

☐ Probation/No Incarceration or Incarceration to 6 Months

Section B Mandatory Minimum ______

Section C

☐ Life Sentence

☐ Incarceration ***(Enter Midpoint and Range Below)***

Range Midpoint Years Months Days

Sentence Range Years Months Days TO Years Months Days

☐ Recommendation Adjusted for **Mandatory Minimum**

☐ Non Guidelines Offense *(Primary offense is a non guidelines offense)*

FIGURE 25.1. Partial Sentencing Guidelines Score Sheet for Virginia. This form depicts some of the information that is compiled and considered with regard to sentencing guidelines. The guidelines were created and are used in some states to promote consistency in sentencing. ***Source:*** *Virginia Criminal Sentencing Commission (n.d.). Sentencing guidelines cover sheet. http://www.vcsc.virginia.gov/worksheets_2017/worksheet_covernotRA.pdf*

What would be some strengths and weaknesses of using sentencing guidelines?

three strikes penalties Legislation that mandates offenders with specific types and numbers of prior convictions to receive extended penalties

truth-in-sentencing laws Legislation that sought to ensure that inmates serve a greater percentage of the sentence imposed

First Step Act Federal prison reform legislation that passed in 2018 with the goal of reducing recidivism and the severity of some federal sentencing practices

truth-in-sentencing laws, which were used in most jurisdictions (29) and required offenders to serve at least 85% of their imposed sentence. Fourteen other states had related truth-in-sentencing requirements. The states differed in determining which offenses were subject to truth-in-sentencing laws. In 1996, the federal government offered federal incentive grants for states to adopt and use truth-in-sentencing legislation (Sabol et al., 2002).

In 2018, the federal government passed the Formerly Incarcerated Reenter Society Transformed Safely Transitioning Every Person Act, or **First Step Act**, which contained many prison reforms and efforts to reduce recidivism. Among other provisions, the act permitted roughly 2,600 offenders serving life sentences for crack cocaine convictions the opportunity to petition the court for a reduced sentence and allowed federal judges to not adhere to mandatory minimum sentencing guidelines for offenders with no criminal history. It also eased the severity of the federal three strikes rule. In particular, the mandatory life sentence penalty was changed to a 25-year sentence, and serious drug felonies that previously warranted an automatic 20-year minimum sentence were reduced to 15 years (J. George, 2018; Schallhorn, 2019).

The Sentencing Process

Sentencing convicted offenders is one of the most controversial aspects of criminal case processing, primarily because of differing perceptions of justice. Some judges have reputations for imposing more punitive sentences than others. The power to remove freedoms from an individual is absent in most other fields, and discretion plays a large role.

Responsibility for Sentences

Sentences may be imposed by judges, juries, or legislative bodies, but in most states judges determine sentences. Some jurisdictions have sentencing structures (e.g., mandatory sentences) that are defined by law, while others use guidelines that provide a range of penalties from which the sentencing body can choose. This prevents the imposition of particularly lenient or restrictive penalties. A few states permit defendants to choose if they wish to be sentenced by a judge or a jury following their trial.

Speed of Sentencing

In less serious cases, or cases in which the penalty is legally defined, sentences may be offered immediately following a guilty plea or guilty verdict. The sentencing process occurs relatively quickly compared to the adjudication process in general. For example, the median time from arrest to adjudication was 111 days with regard to felony sentencing in large urban courts in the United States in 2009. However, about two thirds of defendants (65%) received their sentence within 1 day of the conviction date. Sentences for misdemeanors (83%) were more likely than sentences for felonies (60%) to occur within 1 day. Most sentences (93%) were imposed within 2 months of the conviction date (Reaves, 2013).

Presentence Investigation Report

In cases involving more serious crimes, many states require the preparation of a **presentence investigation report** (PSIR) prior to imposing a penalty. The PSIR is either requested by a judge or required by law and is often prepared by a probation or parole officer who provides background information on the offender and recommends a sentence. The information included in the PSIR addresses the offender's:

- needs,
- risk level,
- past criminal behavior,
- family circumstances, and
- educational and employment histories.

The PSIR also provides a plan of supervision for the offender. Judges are not required to impose the recommended sentence in the PSIR.

● **Learning Objective 25.3:** Explain how sentences are imposed.

9 Sentencing

3 Arrest

presentence investigation report A report containing information that is either requested by a judge or required by law and is often prepared by a probation or parole officer who provides background information on the offender and offers a recommended sentence

10
Corrections

Types of Sentences

Many types of sentences are given to those convicted of crimes, and sentencing bodies may use a combination of sentences for a particular offender. Various factors are considered with regard to the type of sentences imposed, including the nature of the offense, the offender's prior record, available resources (e.g., how crowded the jails are), and the suitability of the sentence for the offender; for instance, a judge who sentences a drug offender may wish to include some type of drug treatment in the sentence. Among the types of sentences are:

- *capital punishment*, or the death penalty;
- *incarceration*, which involves confinement in prison or jail;
- *probation*, or supervision in the community;
- *home confinement*, which is typically used in conjunction with electronic monitoring and involves offenders being confined to their home during certain times;
- *restitution*, or repayment to the victim for the harms associated with the crime;
- *fines*, which involve offenders paying money to the state for their crime(s); and
- *community service*, in which offenders perform work (e.g., pick up trash) for the community as repayment for their crime(s).

There are many other types of sentences, and several types of sentences may be imposed on an offender at the same time. For instance, drug users who burglarize homes may be required to serve jail time, pay restitution, and receive counseling.

Capital Punishment

● **Learning Objective 25.4:** Explain why capital punishment cases cost more than other cases.

10
Corrections

9 Sentencing

1 Criminal Act

Capital punishment cases draw much more scrutiny and consume far more resources than other cases because of the severity of the potential penalty imposed. Accordingly, these cases are treated somewhat differently than other cases, and the use of the death penalty has historically been controversial.

The modern era of capital punishment began following the Supreme Court's decision in *Furman v. Georgia* (1972) to nullify the death penalty based on the belief that capital punishment was being applied in an arbitrary and capricious manner. Following the *Furman* decision, most states revised their statutes. A few years later in *Gregg v. Georgia* (1976), the court ruled that death penalty laws are not considered cruel and unusual under all circumstances; this decision essentially opened the door for states to revise their laws further and reintroduce the death penalty. Most states reserve the death penalty for only the most serious offenses.

Types of Offenses for Which Capital Punishment Is an Option

Capital punishment was used much more freely in earlier times than it is in the early 21st century. Prior to the American Revolution, English courts had declared over 200 felonies as being punishable by death (Neubauer & Fradella, 2017). Today, only a handful of crimes are punishable by execution, and states vary with regard to the offenses for which the death penalty is an option. Generally, the variation among states pertains to the nature and extent of aggravating circumstances accompanying a homicide. In addition, certain individuals are exempt from receiving capital punishment, including offenders who commit crimes while under the age of 18 (*Roper v. Simmons*, 2005) and the developmentally disabled (*Atkins v. Virginia*, 2002). Table 25.1 depicts the offenses for which the death penalty is an option in each state.

Methods of Execution

As of 2018, all states with the death penalty authorized lethal injection as a method of execution, and all of the executions during that year were by lethal injection (Davis & Snell, 2018). Lethal injection was initially believed to be more humane than other methods of execution; however, more recent reports that some victims suffer "excruciating pain" and paralysis of breathing mechanisms during the process (Amnesty International, 2019) have led to debate over whether injection is indeed a humane means of execution. Fifteen states also authorize an alternative method of execution and generally permit the condemned prisoner to select the method to be used. Alternative methods include:

- electrocution (eight states),
- lethal gas (three states),
- hanging (three states),
- firing squad (two states), and
- nitrogen hypoxia (one state).

TABLE 25.1.   Capital Offenses by State

STATE	OFFENSE
Alabama	Intentional murder (Ala. Stat. Ann. § 13A-5-40(a)(1)-(20)) with 12 aggravating factors (Ala. Stat. Ann. § 13A-5-49)
Arizona	First-degree murder, including premeditated murder and felony murder, accompanied by at least 1 of 14 aggravating factors (A.R.S. § 13-703(F))
Arkansas	Capital murder (Ark. Code Ann. § 5-10-101) with a finding of at least 1 of 10 aggravating circumstances; and treason (Ark. Code Ann. § 5-51-201)
California	First-degree murder with special circumstances; military sabotage; train-wreck causing death; treason; perjury resulting in execution of an innocent person; and fatal assault by a prisoner serving a life sentence
Colorado	First-degree murder with at least 1 of 17 aggravating factors; first-degree kidnapping resulting in death; and treason
Delaware[a]	First-degree murder (11 Del. C. § 636) with at least 1 statutory aggravating circumstance (11 Del. C. § 4209)
Florida	First-degree murder with aggravating factors; felony murder; and capital drug-trafficking felonies
Georgia	Murder with aggravating circumstances; rape, armed robbery, or kidnapping with bodily injury or ransom when the victim dies; aircraft hijacking; and treason (O.C.G.A. § 17-10-30)
Idaho	First-degree murder with aggravating factors; first-degree kidnapping; and perjury resulting in the execution of an innocent person
Indiana	Murder with 18 aggravating circumstances (I.C. 35-50-2-9)
Kansas	Intentional and premeditated killing of a person in 1 or more of 7 different circumstances (K.S.A. 21-5401)

(Continued)

TABLE 25.1. *(Continued)*

STATE	OFFENSE
Kentucky	Capital murder with the presence of at least 1 statutory aggravating circumstance; and capital kidnapping (K.R.S. 532.025)
Louisiana	First-degree murder with aggravating circumstances (La. R.S. 14:30); and treason (La. R.S. 14:113)
Mississippi	Capital murder with aggravating circumstances (Miss. Code Ann. § 97-3-19(2)); and aircraft piracy (Miss. Code Ann. § 97-25-55(1))
Missouri	First-degree murder with at least 1 statutory aggravating circumstance (565.020 R.S.M.O. 2000)
Montana	Capital murder with 1 of 9 aggravating circumstances (Mont. Code Ann. § 46-18-303); aggravated kidnapping resulting in death of victim or rescuer; felony murder; aggravated assault or aggravated kidnapping while in detention; and capital sexual intercourse without consent (Mont. Code Ann. § 45-5-503)
Nebraska	First-degree murder with a finding of 1 or more statutory aggravating circumstances
Nevada	First-degree murder with at least 1 of 15 aggravating circumstances (N.R.S. 200.030, 200.033, 200.035)
New Hampshire	Murder committed in the course of rape, kidnapping, drug crimes, or home invasion; killing of a police officer, judge, or prosecutor; murder for hire; and murder by a prisoner while serving a sentence of life without parole (R.S.A. 630:1, R.S.A. 630:5)
New Mexico[b]	First-degree murder with at least 1 of 7 aggravating factors (N.M.S.A. 1978 § 31-20A-5)
New York[c]	First-degree murder with 1 of 13 aggravating factors (NY Penal Law §125.27)
North Carolina	First-degree murder (N.C.G.S. §14-17) with the finding of at least 1 of 11 statutory aggravating circumstances (N.C.G.S. § 15A-2000)
Ohio	Aggravated murder with at least 1 of 10 aggravating circumstances (O.R.C. 2903.01, 2929.02, and 2929.04)
Oklahoma	First-degree murder (21 O.S. § 701.7) in conjunction with a finding of at least 1 of 8 statutorily defined aggravating circumstances (21 O.S. § 701.12)
Oregon	Aggravated murder (O.R.S. 163.095)
Pennsylvania	First-degree murder (18 Pa.C.S.A § 2502(a)) with 18 aggravating circumstances (42 Pa.C.S.A § 9711)
South Carolina	Murder with at least 1 of 12 aggravating circumstances (§ 16-3-20(C)(a))

TABLE 25.1. *(Continued)*

STATE	OFFENSE
South Dakota	First-degree murder (S.D.C.L. 22-16-4) with 1 of 10 aggravating circumstances (S.D.C.L. 23A-27A-1)
Tennessee	First-degree murder (Tenn. Code Ann. § 39-13-202) with 1 of 15 aggravating circumstances (Tenn. Code Ann. § 39-13-204)
Texas	Criminal homicide with 1 of 9 statutory aggravators (Tex. Penal Code § 19.03)
Utah	Aggravated murder (Utah Code Ann. § 76-5-202)
Virginia	Premeditated murder with 1 of 15 aggravating circumstances (VA Code § 18.2-31(1-15))
Washington[d]	Aggravated first-degree murder
Wyoming	First-degree murder; and murder during the commission of sexual assault, sexual abuse of a minor, arson, robbery, burglary, escape, resisting arrest, kidnapping, or abuse of a minor younger than age 16 (W.S.A. § 6-2-101(a))

Source: National Prisoner Statistics program (NPS-8), Bureau of Justice Statistics, 2018; and Capital Punishment, 2018—Statistical Tables (NCJ 254786), by T. L. Snell, 2020, U.S. Department of Justice, Bureau of Justice Statistics.

[a]The Delaware Supreme Court held that a portion of Delaware's death-penalty-sentencing statute (11 Del. C. § 4209) was unconstitutional (Rauf v. State, 145 A.3d 430 (Del. 2016)). No legislative action has been taken to amend the statute. As a result, capital cases are no longer pursued in Delaware.
[b]New Mexico enacted a prospective repeal of its capital statute as of July 1, 2009. Offenders who committed capital offenses on or before that date are eligible for the death penalty.
[c]The New York Court of Appeals held that a portion of New York's death-penalty-sentencing statute (CPL 400.27) was unconstitutional (People v. Taylor, 9 N.Y. 3d 129 (2007)). No legislative action has been taken to amend the statute. As a result, capital cases are no longer pursued in New York.
[d]The Washington Supreme Court has declared the state's death-penalty statute unconstitutional (State v. Gregory, 192 Wash. 2d 1, 427 P.3d 621 (2018)). No legislative action has been taken to repeal the statute.

Use of Capital Punishment by States

The use of the death penalty is heavily concentrated in certain states. In 2019, 22 inmates were executed, with all of the executions occurring in just seven states. Texas executed the largest number of prisoners (9 executions; Snell, 2020). Figure 25.2 notes the states in which offenders were executed in 2019 and the number of prisoners executed. Not all states use the death penalty. As of 2018, 34 states authorized the use of capital punishment.

Costs and Other Factors Associated With Capital Punishment

Several factors, including cost, influence a prosecutor's decision to seek death in those states where capital punishment is used. The costs associated with capital punishment cases are substantially higher than they are for non–death

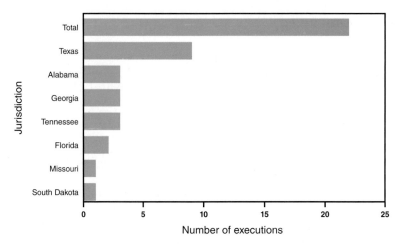

FIGURE 25.2. Use of the Death Penalty, 2019. *Source:* National Prisoner Statistics Program (NPS-8), *by the Bureau of Justice Statistics, 2018.*

Lethal injection is the most commonly used form of execution in the United States. All states that have the death penalty authorize its use, and it is viewed as the most humane means by which to execute an inmate.

Why do you think lethal injection is considered the most humane among the methods available?

8 Trial

penalty murder cases. For example, from 1978 to 2010, California taxpayers paid $4 billion more on capital murder cases than they would have if the state's most severe penalty was life in prison without the possibility of parole (Alarcon & Mitchell, 2011). Others have noted that North Carolina would have spent an estimated $11 million less annually on criminal justice activities if capital punishment had been abolished (Cook, 2009). Other states face similar financial costs. For example, it has been estimated that the annual cost of capital punishment in California is $137 million, which is far more than the cost of lifetime incarceration, which is $11.5 million. In New York, it is estimated that the trial and initial appeal for each death penalty case costs the state $1.8 million (Erb, 2014).

Many of the expenses incurred pertain to trials. Among the more costly aspects of a capital murder trial are the following:

- *length of time required for jury selection*, which can last a month or longer, compared to just a few days for a non–death penalty capital murder trial
- *appointment of a second attorney* to assist the defense in capital murder cases
- *separate sentencing phase* required in capital murder cases
- *expert testimony and other mitigating information* that would not be allowed in non–death penalty trials; expert witnesses are also more likely to be involved in all aspects of the case, given the seriousness of the charges and potential punishment
- *jury costs*, because the juries are often sequestered, which costs the state in terms of housing, feeding, and protecting jurors
- *investigations into a defendant's life history* to help jurors determine whether death is an appropriate penalty

- *housing of a death row inmate* through the lengthy appeals process; appeals are mandatory
- *backlogged cases* as attorneys devote substantial time and resources to death penalty cases at the expense of others

Beyond cost, other considerations play a role in a prosecutor's decision to seek the death penalty. These include :

- *the egregiousness of the offense*, for example murdering someone who is particularly vulnerable, such as a child;
- *the quality of evidence*; for instance, prosecutors want to be very certain that they will win the case and that strong evidence will support their cause;
- *the wishes of the victims' families*; for instance, some victims' families may be morally opposed to the death penalty and/or they may not wish to wait for the lengthy appeals and the extended time it takes to execute the offender; and
- *the background of the offender*; for instance, defendants with long criminal records or violent histories are more likely to face capital charges (Douglas & Stockstill, 2008).

Jury Composition in Capital Punishment Cases

Jury composition is particularly important in capital offense cases, given people's strong opinions about the issue. In 1968, the Supreme Court noted that states cannot exclude opponents to the death penalty from juries in capital cases (*Witherspoon v. Illinois*). However, in 1986 the court overturned that decision and noted that prospective jurors who oppose the death penalty may be excluded if their opinions too heavily influence their performance as jurors during sentencing (*Lockhart v. McCree*).

8 Trial

Death-qualified juries consist of jury members in capital punishment cases who are not opposed to imposing the death penalty. Research regarding the differences between death-qualified juries and regular juries suggests notable differences between the groups, including in demographics and perceptions of a just world. Members of death-qualified juries were more likely to find capital defendants guilty and have higher levels of homophobia, racism, and sexism (B. Butler, 2007).

death-qualified juries Jury members in capital punishment cases who are not opposed to imposing the death penalty

Capital Punishment and Controversy

Capital punishment has generated much debate. Critics of the death penalty put forward several arguments against the practice.

9 Sentencing

- *It is "cruel and unusual" and thus in violation of the Eighth Amendment.* Amnesty International reported that the United States was 1 of only 20 countries that executed an inmate in 2018 (Death Penalty Information Center, 2020a).
- *It denies due process of the law.* The finality associated with the penalty results in executed individuals not being able to benefit from new evidence that might exonerate them. A total of 172 individuals were **exonerated**, or removed from death row, between 1973 and November 2020 as a result of being acquitted of all charges related to the crime that placed them on death row, having all charges that placed them on death row dismissed by the prosecution, or having

exonerated Being released from prison as a result of the discovery of new evidence suggesting that the individual did not commit the crime for which they were sentenced

been granted a complete pardon based on evidence of innocence (Death Penalty Information Center, 2020b).

- *It is an ineffective form of crime control.* Common sense would suggest that the imposition of the death penalty would reduce crime, because the threat of death would seemingly deter individuals from killing others. Nevertheless, research suggests that the death penalty does not serve as an effective deterrent (e.g., Kovandzic et al., 2009). Despite this finding, about one-third (32%) of respondents to a Gallup poll believed it does (Gallup, 2014).

- *It is morally wrong.* Capital punishment involves a society intentionally killing humans. An estimated 40% of Americans believe that the death penalty is morally wrong (Brenan, 2020), and many individuals who do not support capital punishment most commonly note that their lack of support is based on their belief that it is wrong to take a life (Gallup, 2014).

- *It is imposed in an arbitrary and sometimes discriminatory manner.* Certain groups (e.g., poor minorities) remain more likely to receive the penalty, especially when their crimes involve White and female victims. For instance, one study found that the death penalty was more often sought and used in cases involving high-status victims who were sophisticated, conventional, respectable, and integrated into the community (Phillips, 2009). Other studies suggested that defendants found guilty of murdering Black victims were less likely to receive a death sentence than those found guilty of murdering White victims (Baldus et al., 1990; M. R. Williams & Holcomb, 2001), and defendants in capital cases involving female victims were more likely to receive a death sentence than defendants in cases involving male victims (M. R. Williams et al., 2007; M. R. Williams & Holcomb, 2001). Researchers also noted the importance of considering the joint effect of victim characteristics and found that White female victim cases differed from other cases in that they were more likely to involve the death penalty (Holcomb et al., 2004).

Numerous variables impact the inconsistency with which the death penalty is applied (Foster, 2001):

- scope of the state's death penalty laws and whether a state uses capital punishment
- prosecutors' attitudes regarding the death penalty
- competency of the defense and the resources available to them
- attitude of the victims' families
- willingness of the jury to impose the penalty
- class and race of the victim
- number of victims
- heinousness of the crime
- offenders' criminal history
- strength of the evidence
- level of remorse on the part of the offender
- residency status of the offender (transients are more likely to receive the penalty)

Support for the death penalty in general has fluctuated over time, although it reached a high of 80% in support of its use in the mid-1980s (Gallup, 2014). Support for its use has been trending downward since that time, and an estimated 56% in 2019 supported its use for a person convicted of murder. Americans in 2018 were also more likely to believe that the death penalty is applied fairly (49%) than unfairly (45%), although the gap between the percentage who believe it is applied fairly has steadily dropped (Jones, 2019).

Disparities in Sentencing

Perceptions differ regarding whether our justice system treats all groups fairly. In 2016, non-Whites, who constitute a disproportionate percentage of offenders under correctional supervision, were over twice as likely (23%) as Whites (10%) to believe that our justice system is too tough (McCarthy, 2016). Perceptions of justice are often based on the sentences given to offenders, and those most impacted by sentencing practices are the ones who most often disapprove of justice-based practices. However, evidence suggests that sentencing practices contribute much to the disparity, or overrepresentation of certain groups within our justice systems. And, in some cases, this disparity involves discriminatory or biased actions (e.g., Walker et al., 2018).

Evidence of Disparity

It is well documented in the research literature that some groups receive longer and tougher sentences than other groups (e.g., Walker et al., 2018; McNamara & Burns, 2020). In particular, Blacks have been the target of more punitive sentences than other groups. For example, a study that examined sentencing outcomes for Black and White men who were first-time offenders found that Black men received statistically significant longer sentences (Burch, 2015). A report by the Sentencing Project (Nellis, 2016) highlighted the disparity, or disproportionality, of African Americans and Latinos being sentenced to prison. Among other findings, the report noted that:

- in state prisons, Blacks were incarcerated at a rate that was 5.1 times the imprisonment of Whites and Latinos at a rate 1.4 times that of Whites;
- in 12 states, over half of the prison population was Black; and
- in 11 states, at least 1 in 20 adult Black males were in prison.

The disparities in sentencing are further evidenced in the most severe punishment: the death penalty. Evidence strongly suggests that racial minorities have been more likely to receive capital punishment compared to other groups (Walker et al., 2018).

Why the Disparity?

There are several proposed reasons that explain why some racial and ethnic minority groups (e.g., African Americans and Hispanic Americans) generally receive harsher sentences than others. While the majority of sentences are arguably not discriminatory in nature, history suggests that there are times when certain groups receive more punitive sentences than others.

ECONOMICS

To begin, harsher sentences may be attributable to economics. Individuals with financial means can hire private counsel who will generally devote more time and resources toward representing their clients (M. R. Williams, 2013).

● **Learning Objective 25.5:** Explain why some groups generally receive tougher sentences than others.

9 Sentencing

African American males are incarcerated at a disproportionate and alarming rate. It is argued that the disparity is a result of overinvolvement in crime coupled with biased and discriminatory practices on behalf of law enforcement and the courts.

What role do you think discrimination plays in the racial disparities apparent in the criminal justice system?

As a result, those with economic means are more likely to receive less harsh sentences than those who are poor. Racial and ethnic minorities generally have lower household incomes than other groups. For example, in 2019 the median income for African American ($45,438) and Hispanic ($56,113) households was notably lower than the median household income for all races ($68,703) (Semega et al., 2020).

DISCRIMINATION BY SENTENCING BODIES

The discrepancy in sentencing may also be attributable to racism and discrimination on behalf of sentencing bodies (McNamara & Burns, 2020). Discretion with regard to sentencing makes it possible for discriminatory sentencing to occur. Sentencing practices are influenced by many individuals with differing opinions, backgrounds, and life experiences, although the extent to which each impacts sentencing differs. Many key individuals involved in the adjudication process have decision-making powers that could influence the sentences offenders receive, including judges, jurors, defense attorneys, and prosecutors (B. Kim et al., 2015).

CRIMES COMMITTED BY DIFFERENT GROUPS

Finally, the differences in sentences could be explained by members of some racial and ethnic minority groups committing more serious crimes and/or having lengthier criminal records than members from other groups (McNamara & Burns, 2020). Having a lengthier criminal record results in offenders being more likely to be sentenced as habitual offenders and more likely to receive extended periods of incarceration.

● **Learning Objective 25.6:** Identify the possible outcomes of appellate court hearings.

Appeals and Postconviction Review

An appeal may be filed following a trial, which provides an example of how our system is designed to ensure justice. **Appeals** are requests for higher courts to review trial court proceedings to ensure that proper procedures were followed and the punishment was just. The denial of an appeal does not signify the end of the appellate process for an inmate, because state and federal inmates may challenge their conviction after all opportunities for appeal are exhausted through a postconviction review process, particularly if they believe their constitutional rights were violated.

Appeals

Defendants are not required to appeal their cases, but capital cases undergo mandatory appeal at the highest level state court in most states. Cases are not retried at the appellate level; instead, appellate court judges hear brief oral arguments from the prosecution and defense and review the trial court transcript. Because they have been convicted and are no longer presumed innocent, defendants have the burden of proof at the appellate level and must demonstrate why the lower court ruling should be reversed or otherwise altered.

appeals Requests for higher courts to review trial court proceedings to ensure that proper procedures were followed and the punishment was just

After hearing both sides' cases, appellate courts may:

11 Appeal

- *uphold (i.e., affirm) the lower court decision.* An appellate court may uphold a lower court ruling even if it finds an error in the trial court proceedings. The **harmless error doctrine** holds that small, insignificant errors that likely had little or no effect on the outcome of a case are not grounds for a reversal.

- *reverse the lower court decision.* An appellate court overturns, or sets aside, the decision of the lower court and no further court action is required.

- *reverse and remand (order a retrial of) the lower court decision*. If this happens, the case is returned to trial court for further arguments and another verdict. A reverse and remand decision does not violate a defendant's Fifth Amendment protection against **double jeopardy**—being tried twice for the same offense—because defendants waive that protection upon filing an appeal.

Appellate courts hear far fewer cases than trial courts, and most appellate court decisions support the lower courts' findings, but reversals or alterations occasionally occur (Waters et al., 2015).

PROSECUTORIAL APPEALS

Most states do not allow the prosecution to appeal a case once an acquittal is rendered. However, prior to or during a trial, some jurisdictions permit prosecutors to appeal certain rulings. For example, if a judge refused the introduction of some evidence (suppressed evidence), then a prosecutor could appeal such a decision. In such instances, appellate courts review the case to determine if the judge acted properly.

POSTCONVICTION BAIL

Some offenders are detained while their case is under appellate review, because they have no constitutional right to bail following a conviction. Postconviction bail is at the discretion of the trial court judge, who considers several factors including the defendant's prior record, the defendant's ties to family and community, and the severity of the sentence (Scheb & Scheb, 2009).

INTERMEDIATE APPELLATE COURTS AND COURTS OF LAST RESORT

Most states (41) have an intermediate appellate court, and all states have a court of last resort (often called the state's supreme court). They are called courts of last resort because there is no higher *state* court to review appeals. In the states that use them, intermediate appellate courts hear appeals of cases heard in the trial courts. In other states, the courts of last resort hear appeals. While courts of last resort can hear appeals from intermediate appellate courts, it is discretionary, because defendants are entitled to having only one appeal heard (see Module 21).

Beyond the state supreme courts is the U.S. Supreme Court, which is accessible to defendants having their case tried in either federal or state court. The U.S. Supreme Court, however, hears a very small percentage of cases and does not have to hear all cases for which it receives requests.

THE ROLE OF APPELLATE COURTS

Appellate courts help ensure that a defendant's rights were recognized at trial by reviewing the case with particular consideration of the issue or issues under appeal. Some states permit defendants to request review of their sentence, and some permit prosecutors to appeal sentences they believe are too lenient. Among the issues commonly raised in appeals are:

- *concerns regarding jury selection*, for instance if a judge permits the inclusion of a perceived or professed racist on a jury;

harmless error doctrine The standard holding that small, insignificant errors made by prosecutors during trial with likely little or no effect on the outcome of a case are not grounds for a reversal

double jeopardy Being tried for the same crime twice; it is prohibited by the Fifth Amendment

The U.S. Supreme Court is the highest court in the land and provides review of cases heard in trial and appellate courts. The court is selective in the cases it reviews, because state appellate courts and the U.S. courts of appeal hear initial appeals. The court receives roughly 7,000–8,000 petitions each term and hears only about 80 cases.

Given that there is no higher court, should the U.S. Supreme Court be required to hear more cases than it does? Why or why not?

- *ineffective assistance of public counsel*, for instance if the public defender assigned to a case provides inadequate representation;
- *introduction of improperly obtained evidence*, for instance if a judge permits the introduction of a piece of evidence that was obtained through an illegal police search; and
- *coercion on behalf of law enforcement*, for instance, if police officers use physical force to encourage a suspect to admit guilt.

Appellate courts mainly address the legal issues involved at trial, leaving factual issues to judges and juries in the lower courts. Through providing oversight and promoting accountability, appellate courts encourage consistency in the lower courts and discourage judicial and attorney misconduct.

Postconviction Review

11 Appeal

writ of habeas corpus Petitions that claim an inmate's constitutional rights were violated and challenge the fact or duration of confinement

In addition to appeals, most states permit inmates to file **writ of habeas corpus** petitions for postconviction relief. These petitions claim that the inmate's constitutional rights were violated and challenge the fact or duration of confinement. However, they are rarely successful, because the courts typically uphold the trial court's decision.

The low percentage of outcomes favorable to prisoners who file habeas corpus petitions is expected given the late stage in criminal case processing at which postconviction review occurs. Nevertheless, the option for those whose cases were upheld in appellate courts provides another avenue of accountability to ensure that justice is served.

Postconviction remedies differ from appeals in several ways (Neubauer & Fradella, 2017):

- only prisoners may file for postconviction review
- the disputes raised in a petition must address constitutional, not technical, concerns
- the issues raised in filing for postconviction review may be broader than those addressed during appeal (e.g., claiming constitutional protections that emerged since the trial verdict)
- inmates can file an unlimited number of postconviction petitions

The System in Perspective

As noted in the "In the News" feature at the start of this module, the perceived injustices associated with California's three strikes penalties resulted in the state altering its laws. California took initiative in addressing what it saw as inherent problems in its original laws. Both sentencing and appeals require input from various parties, and both are symbolic of our concern for justice. Sentencing an offender requires consideration of what constitutes justice and is largely viewed as the culmination of a sequence of events that began with the investigation of a crime and arrest of a suspect. Appeals reflect our concern for finding justice, as they exist to review earlier court proceedings and ensure that no constitutional rights have been violated.

Summary

1. Learning Objective 25.1: *Summarize the primary purposes of criminal sanctions.*

- The primary purposes of criminal sanctions are rehabilitation, which involves attempts to "correct" criminals; incapacitation, or physically restraining offenders from committing additional harms; retribution, or punishment; deterrence, or discouraging criminal behavior; and restoration, or efforts to repair the harms done by crime and restore offenders into law-abiding citizens.

2. Learning Objective 25.2: *Characterize the approaches to sentencing.*

- Approaches to sentencing include indeterminate, determinate, structured, and mandatory sentences. Indeterminate sentences include a minimum and maximum time an inmate will serve, with a parole board determining the date of release. Determinate sentences involve a maximum period of incarceration, which the inmate can reduce through good behavior. Structured sentences involve sentencing guidelines. Mandatory sentences limit judicial discretion to legislatively prescribed, fixed penalties for specific offenses.

3. Learning Objective 25.3: *Describe how sentences are imposed.*

- Sentences may be imposed by judges, juries, or legislative bodies, although judges determine an offender's sentence in most states. Some jurisdictions have sentencing structures through which sentences are statutorily defined. Some states allow defendants to choose if they wish to be sentenced by a judge or a jury following their trial. Sentences may be imposed immediately following a guilty plea or guilty verdict in less serious cases or in cases in which the sentence is legislatively defined. Some states use guidelines that seek to ensure fairness in sentencing.

4. Learning Objective 25.4: *Explain why capital punishment cases cost more than other cases.*

- Capital punishment cases cost substantially more than typical court cases for several reasons. Among the more costly aspects of a capital murder trial are the length of time required for jury selection, the requirement that judges appoint a second attorney to assist the defense in capital murder cases, and the separate sentencing phase required in capital murder cases. Another costly aspect of capital punishment pertains to defendants being permitted to add mitigating information that would not be allowed in non–death penalty trials and the more likely use of expert witnesses. Jury costs also often increase in death penalty cases because the juries are often sequestered. Investigation costs, the costs associated with multiple appeals, and the cost to house a death row inmate also add to the cost of capital cases.

5. Learning Objective 25.5: *Discuss why some groups generally receive tougher sentences than others.*

- The differences in sentences received by different groups can arguably be explained by a combination of factors, including economic issues, racism and discrimination on behalf of sentencing bodies, and the fact that members of some racial and ethnic minority groups commit more serious crimes and/or have lengthier criminal records.

6. Learning Objective 25.6: *Identify the possible outcomes of appellate court hearings.*

- Appellate courts may uphold, reverse, or reverse and remand (require a retrial of) the lower court decision. Appellate courts also hear habeas corpus petitions (petitions that claim a violation of constitutional rights), in which they uphold or deny the trial court's decision to detain the offender.

Questions for Critical Thinking

1. Based on the relatively recent increases in the correctional population beginning in the 1980s, what do you believe has been the primary goal(s) of sentencing practices? Discuss your answer.

2. Should all states be required to adopt and abide by sentencing guidelines? Why or why not?

3. What types of information do you believe should be included in a presentence investigation report?

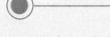

4. What factors do you believe are most strongly related to the conviction of individuals on trial for a capital crime?

5. What steps could be taken to better ensure that there are no disparities among groups with regard to sentencing?

6. What improvements could be made to appellate court procedures to better ensure that defendants' constitutional rights are not violated?

Key Terms

appeal
death-qualified juries
determinate sentences
deterrence
double jeopardy
exonerated
First Step Act
general deterrence
habitual offender laws
harmless error doctrine
incapacitation
indeterminate sentences

mandatory sentences
presentence investigation report
rehabilitation
restoration
retribution
selective incapacitation
sentencing guidelines
specific deterrence
structured sentences
three strikes penalties
truth-in-sentencing laws
writ of habeas corpus

For digital learning resources, please go to
https://www.oup.com/he/burns1e

Juvenile Courts

The juvenile justice system is distinct from the criminal justice system, which processes adults. Much like there is no single criminal justice system, there is no single juvenile justice system. States have their own distinct systems of justice for juveniles, and the practices vary within each one.

What do you believe are the benefits and drawbacks of having a different system of justice to process juveniles?

Adults are responsible for protecting children; this is an ideal recognized in the earliest juvenile courts. At some point, however, the belief that children should be held accountable, particularly for serious crimes, began to gain momentum. This module addresses several key components of juvenile courts, beginning with an examination of the history of the courts, followed by a discussion of case processing in the juvenile justice system. Then this module discusses juvenile justice practices as they relate to adult courts and ends with a look toward the future of juvenile courts.

MODULE OUTLINE

• **History of Juvenile Courts**

Learning Objective 26.1: Trace the development of juvenile courts.

• **Case Processing in the Juvenile Justice System**

Learning Objective 26.2: Describe the primary steps involved in case processing in the juvenile justice system.

• **Differences Between the Juvenile Justice System and the Criminal Justice System**

Learning Objective 26.3: Distinguish the juvenile justice system from the criminal justice system.

• **Future of Juvenile Courts**

Learning Objective 26.4: Summarize the arguments of those who wish to abolish and those who wish to preserve the juvenile justice system.

Teen Courts

1 Criminal Act

10 Corrections

In Indiana, a Tippecanoe County youth was caught stealing $300 worth of clothing from a mall. Another youth punched a fellow student in the face after an argument. Both individuals appeared before the county's teen court program, in which a group of teens sentenced the young man caught shoplifting to serve on six teen court juries, complete 57 hours of community service work, write two essays, and attend a shoplifting workshop. The youth who committed the battery was sentenced to 25 hours of community service and had to serve on a

jury at four teen court hearings. He also had to write a one-page essay on anger management (D. P. McCoy, 2015).

Communities are increasingly using teen courts, also known as youth courts, peer courts, and student courts, as alternatives to juvenile court. There are roughly 1,050 youth court programs in just about all states (National Association of Youth Courts, 2020). The courts are designed to provide peer-driven, positive influences on troubled youth and operate at a lower cost compared to traditional juvenile courts. Teen courts offer informal proceedings in which trained teenagers may serve as jurors and decide minor cases. The majority of youth court programs in the United States (93%) require juveniles to admit guilt prior to becoming involved in the youth court; thus, the courts largely serve as sentencing bodies (Global Youth Justice, 2021). Juvenile court judges may divert cases to teen courts, where the focus is on rehabilitation, and victim input is encouraged.

Aside from serving as jurors, teens also serve active roles as lawyers, bailiffs, and clerks. Some courts empower these teens to serve as judges and may use panels of judges including three to six teens. Adult volunteers serve as trainers, advisors, and coordinators of the courts, although some courts have small paid staffs that help facilitate the operations. Participants in teen courts must sign an oath of confidentiality regarding the proceedings to protect the interests of the parties involved in the cases. Do you believe it is appropriate for teens to make sentencing decisions for other teens? Why or why not?

History of Juvenile Courts

Juvenile justice in the United States is largely grounded in the policies of early England. Of particular importance with regard to juvenile courts is the concept of **parens patriae**, which literally means "the father of the country." This concept originated with the king of England during the 12th century and essentially meant that the king made decisions for all matters regarding juveniles. It applies in the early 21st century, because the government, via the juvenile justice system, has the power to formally and informally process youths who misbehave.

Juvenile cases in early England often came before **chancery courts**, which were created in the 15th century to hear cases that could not be heard in common law courts (Seymour, 1994). The courts primarily dealt with issues concerning equity

● **Learning Objective 26.1:** Trace the development of juvenile courts.

(e.g., property boundary disputes), and parens patriae was a major guiding principle. Chancery courts and **poor laws**—introduced throughout the 16th century to assist destitute individuals, including children, in finding work or apprenticeships—largely characterize the early roots of juvenile justice in America (Champion et al., 2013).

Juvenile Justice in Early America

The English model of handling wayward youth continued in the American colonies, as colonists adopted the British approach with regard to laws, processes, and sanctions. Then, the population growth of many large cities during the early 1800s, particularly as individuals moved to the cities to find work, led to concentrated areas of poverty and many unsupervised children. Working parents in the urban, industrial areas often could not afford child care and largely relied on others in their community to monitor their children.

CHILD SAVERS

Various groups often intervened to assist children, for instance by providing them with work programs, healthy living conditions, assistance with educational endeavors, and general supervision. Members of one such group that emerged during the 19th century primarily came from the middle and upper classes. Collectively they were known as the **child savers** (Platt, 1969) and often created temporary homes or shelters for children in need of protection from the streets.

HOUSES OF REFUGE

Houses of refuge were established to manage and generally assist those who committed status offenses. **Status offenses** are legal violations based on age that apply to juveniles and not adults (e.g., running away from home, being undisciplined). The New York House of Refuge, created in 1825, is considered the first juvenile reformatory in America (Pickett, 1969). Other houses of refuge soon emerged in other cities. Children at these facilities received a basic education, worked, and learned trades, but the houses resembled prisons, and conditions were generally poor (Siegel et al., 2011).

Establishment of a Distinct Juvenile Court System

In addition to the child savers movement and the creation of houses of refuge, legislation was regularly passed to address truancy and other types of juvenile misconduct and to establish juvenile courts (Champion et al., 2013). These and other efforts contributed to the establishment of a juvenile justice system and the recognition of juvenile offenders as distinct from adult criminals.

ILLINOIS JUVENILE COURT ACT OF 1899

The concept of parens patriae was formalized by the court case *Ex parte Crouse* (1839), which provided the courts with the legal power to intervene in the lives of children. The first juvenile court was established in 1899 when the Illinois legislature passed the Act to Regulate the Treatment and Control of Dependent, Neglected, and Delinquent Children, or the **Illinois Juvenile Court Act**. The jurisdiction of the court was all children under age 16 who violated any state or local law or ordinance, and the provisions of the act sought to deal with both delinquency and child neglect (Fox, 1998). The following principles guided the court (Bartollas & Miller, 2014):

- Operations were informal; for instance, children, judges, parents, and probation officers would sit around a table instead of in a formal courtroom to adjudicate cases.
- Youth could be brought into court based on complaints.
- The hearings were not public and records were kept confidential.

parens patriae "The father of the country"; the concept originated during the 12th century and essentially meant that the king made decisions for all matters regarding juveniles; it applies in the early 21st century because the government, via the juvenile justice system, has the power to process unruly youths

chancery courts Courts created in the 15th century in England that heard cases that could not be heard in common law courts, including juvenile cases; the courts primarily dealt with issues concerning equity, as opposed to law

10
Corrections

poor laws Laws introduced in the 16th century to assist destitute individuals, including children, in finding work or apprenticeships; they largely characterize the early roots of juvenile justice in the United States

child savers The collective name for the groups of individuals who often intervened to assist children beginning in the 19th century

houses of refuge Homes that were established to manage status offenders and generally assist them in the 19th century

status offenses Violations of the law by juveniles that would not be an offense if committed by adults (e.g., truancy, drinking alcohol)

illinois Juvenile Court Act The legislation responsible for establishing the first juvenile court

- Proof of the child's criminality was not required for the youth to be considered in need of court services.
- The court had much discretion in sentencing and providing services.
- Lawyers were not permitted.
- Legal standards were relaxed; for instance, hearsay evidence was permitted, and proof beyond a reasonable doubt was not required.

The Illinois court largely set the stage for subsequent juvenile courts with its emphasis on rehabilitation over punishment. The attractiveness of the Illinois court contributed to all states having juvenile courts by the 1940s (Champion et al., 2012).

SUPREME COURT DECISIONS OF THE 1960S AND 1970S

Early juvenile courts provided limited legal protections for juveniles. Several Supreme Court decisions in the 1960s and 1970s reshaped juvenile courts and reflected the court's overall concern with providing due process protections. Among the important Supreme Court cases that helped ensure the protection of juvenile rights in court were the following:

- *Kent v. United States* (1966) provided basic due process rights in transferring juveniles to the adult courts.
- *In re Gault* (1967) required due process and constitutional procedures in juvenile courts and made the courts more accountable.
- *In re Winship* (1970) required the state to prove its case beyond a reasonable doubt in juvenile matters.
- *Breed v. Jones* (1975) ruled that trying a juvenile in adult court after adjudicating them in juvenile court constitutes double jeopardy.

GETTING TOUGH ON JUVENILES IN THE 1980S AND 1990S

Beginning in the late 1980s and 1990s, there was a dramatic shift toward becoming increasingly punitive toward juveniles (e.g., Sickmund, 2009; Webb, 2008). Laws pertaining to the transfer of juveniles to adult court became more stringent, despite the beginning of a decline in the juvenile offending rate. This was largely in response to concerns regarding increased juvenile violence, school and other types of shootings involving juveniles, and general delinquency. The trend toward getting tough on juveniles was reflected in (Puzzanchera & Hockenberry, 2013):

- *tougher punishments*, including longer periods of incarceration;
- *easier access to juvenile records and proceedings*, which historically were sealed to protect the interests and identities of juveniles;
- *states lowering the age at which youth are considered adults*, which meant that more juveniles would be processed in adult court; and
- *more frequent use of transfers to the adult system*, where juveniles found guilty could receive longer, tougher penalties. For instance, only 14 states had automatic transfer laws mandating that certain juvenile offenders be tried as adults in 1995. By 2003, 31 states had such laws (Steiner & Hemmens, 2003).

The more punitive approach primarily involved the expansion of both the list of crimes for which a juvenile could be transferred to the adult system (e.g., offenses committed with the use of a firearm or carjacking that results in serious injury) and offender eligibility, for example as it pertains to age or criminal history (Redding,

2010). The stricter approach contrasted historical efforts that recognized children as different from adults
and in need of adult guidance, as well as the belief that
juveniles were more amenable to rehabilitation, treatment, and therapeutic approaches.

A SHIFT BACK FROM "GETTING TOUGH" IN THE 21ST CENTURY

There is some evidence that the "get tough" approach
may be diminishing in the early 21st century. Some recent developments suggest that the system is returning
to an approach that seeks to protect and treat children
(Benekos et al., 2013). Part of the reason for the apparent shift has been the lack of effectiveness of more severe punishments. For example, research suggests that
treating an increasing number of juveniles as adults
failed to make communities safer and resulted in worse
outcomes for the youth (Rubin, 2013).

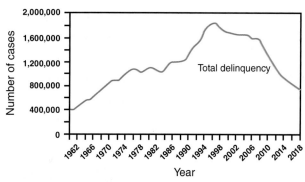

FIGURE 26.1. Delinquency Cases in Juvenile Court, 1960–2018.
The number of delinquency caseloads increased substantively
from 1960 to 1996 and then dropped from 1997 to 2018. ***Source:***
Juvenile Court Statistics 2018 *(p. 6), by S. Hockenberry and*
C. Puzzanchera, 2020, National Center for Juvenile Justice.

What factors might be impacting these trends in
delinquency caseloads?

Further evidence of a possible shift back toward a more rehabilitative, nurturing
approach is seen in an assessment of enacted legislative proposals that addressed juvenile jurisdiction, records, treatment programming, transfer, and sentencing from
2005 to 2007 (Willison et al., 2009). Rates of transfer to criminal court have declined;
for instance, just under 4,000 delinquency cases were waived to adult courts in 2018,
which was 47% below the 2006 level (Hockenberry & Puzzanchera, 2020). Part of the
decrease is attributable to decreases in juvenile delinquency cases (see Figure 26.1;
Hockenberry & Puzzanchera, 2020; Puzzanchera & Addie, 2014).

Case Processing in the Juvenile Justice System

Police officers use discretion when handling cases involving juveniles, with only the
more serious cases leading to an arrest. Upon encountering youths who have violated
the law, agents decide if they wish to **refer** (send) the case to the justice system or
choose some other option, such as a warning or releasing the juvenile to parents or
guardians. The decision to refer is often based on the following:

- the seriousness of the offense in question
- victims' input
- conversations with the juveniles and their parents or guardians
- consideration of the juveniles' prior contacts with the justice system

Each jurisdiction in the United States has a policy regarding the handling of referrals. Upon being referred, juveniles are screened by an intake department, which
ensures that there is justification to process the case and may send the case for further processing or handle the case more informally, for instance by referring it to a
social service agency. Law enforcement referred the majority of all delinquency cases
in 2018 (82%), although many others can make referrals, including relatives, school
officials, probation officers, concerned neighbors, victims, social service providers,
and truant officers (Hockenberry & Puzzanchera, 2020).

● **Learning
Objective 26.2:**
Describe the
primary steps
involved in case
processing in the
juvenile justice
system.

3 Arrest

refer Sending a case to
the juvenile justice system
for formal processing

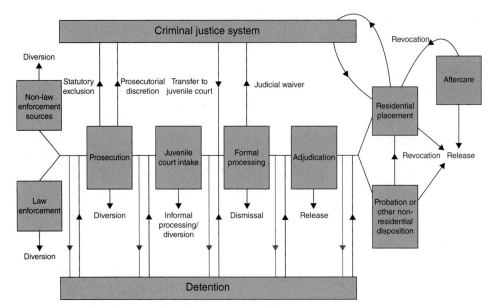

FIGURE 26.2. The Stages of Delinquency Case Processing in the Juvenile Justice System. The objectives of the juvenile justice system are similar to those of the criminal justice system, although the stages of case processing in the two systems differ slightly. For instance, consider that one enters the juvenile justice system through law enforcement and non–law enforcement sources. The terminology used also differs to a large extent. ***Source:*** *Office of Juvenile Justice and Delinquency Prevention. (n.d.). Juvenile justice system structure & process. https://www.ojjdp.gov/ojstatbb/structure_process/case.html*

What stages found in the processing of adults are not depicted in this figure?

Juvenile court proceedings can be categorized according to three stages: preadjudication procedures, adjudicatory hearings, and dispositional hearings. It is also possible during the proceedings that a case is **waived** (transferred) to the adult system for processing. Figure 26.2 depicts the stages of delinquency case processing in the juvenile justice system.

Preadjudication Procedures

Preadjudication procedures are akin to pretrial procedures in the adult system. The primary steps at these stages involve detention hearings, intake, and decisions regarding whether to transfer juveniles to the adult system, divert them from formal processing, or release them from the system, for instance because of a lack of evidence.

DETENTION OF JUVENILES

Detention may occur after the youth is taken into custody, during the time in which juveniles are considered for case processing, or after the adjudicatory hearing. The police typically make the first decision regarding detention. All states require that a detention hearing be held within a few days after a juvenile is detained, although the requirement is typically 24 hours. Judges review the case at the hearing and determine if continued detention is warranted. Juveniles may be held in a secure detention facility if the court believes they will be a risk to the community, will be at risk if they return to the community, or may fail to appear at an upcoming hearing. They may also be detained for diagnostic evaluation purposes.

Federal regulations discourage detaining arrested juveniles in adult lockups and jails, although there are instances when securing a juvenile in a facility with adults may be necessary, for instance when arranging transportation to a juvenile detention facility. In such cases, federal regulations mandate that juveniles be secured in an area out of the sight and sound of adult inmates. Six states prohibit juveniles from being detained or locked up in facilities that house adult inmates (Office of Juvenile

waived Transferring a juvenile case to the adult (criminal) justice system for processing

preadjudication procedures The proceedings that occur in juvenile case processing prior to adjudication; they are akin to pretrial procedures in the adult system and involve detention hearings, intake, and decisions regarding the next step for juveniles

detention Taking a juvenile into custody; it is akin to placing an adult in jail in the criminal justice system

Justice and Delinquency Prevention, 2015). Bail is permitted for juveniles in nine states (Bartollas & Miller, 2014). For the most part, however, juveniles are released to the custody of their parents or guardians.

INTAKE IN JUVENILE COURTS

The **intake** function within juvenile courts is typically the responsibility of the juvenile probation department and/or the prosecutor's office. The intake process serves multiple purposes, which include:

- screening cases to assess whether individuals need the court's assistance,
- controlling the use of detention,
- reducing the court's caseloads,
- keeping minor cases out of the courts, and
- directing youth to appropriate community services and agencies (Griffin & Torget, 2002).

Screening is usually the first and most important process that happens during intake. During screening, authorized officials must decide whether to handle the case informally, dismiss the case, or request formal intervention of the juvenile court. This decision is largely based on the facts of the case, although intake personnel consider other factors, including prior contact with the system, interviews with the suspect and others (e.g., parents and police), and the best interests of society and the youth. Jurisdictions may use intake screenings or intake hearings to assess information provided by involved parties such as the police, parents, and/or victims. Or, the procedure may be less formal and simply involve a conversation between an intake officer and the accused.

Intake results in various outcomes in most jurisdictions, including:

- dismissal of the case,
- turning over the youth to their parents or guardians (either with or without referrals for counseling or particular services),
- placing the youth on informal probation or supervision,
- securing the youth in detention until their next court appearance, or
- referring the youth to the juvenile prosecutor for additional action and perhaps the filing of a **petition**, which is a legal document that alleges that a youth is delinquent, a status offender, or in need of assistance.

CONSENT DECREES AND INFORMAL PROBATION

Juveniles may agree to a **consent decree**, which is an agreement to meet specific conditions without the court formally finding them guilty. The conditions may include victim restitution, drug counseling, a curfew, or school attendance. Most jurisdictions require juveniles to admit to committing the act to be eligible for consent decrees. A probation officer often monitors the juvenile's behavior to determine whether they meet the conditions, or what is often known as **informal probation**. A case is dismissed if the juvenile successfully complies with the informal conditions. Failure to meet the conditions may result in the formal prosecution of the case.

Adjudicatory Hearings

Adjudication refers to judging or acting in response to a petition filed in juvenile court. **Adjudication hearings** are the equivalent of adult criminal trials. Generally, the hearings determine if the accused is to be held responsible for the delinquent act. An adjudicated delinquent is analogous to a convicted offender in criminal court.

---

intake The step in juvenile case processing that involves screening cases to assess whether individuals need the court's assistance; at this stage, authorized officials decide whether to handle the case informally, dismiss the case, or request formal intervention of the juvenile court

petition Legal documents filed by involved parties who allege that a youth is delinquent, a status offender, or in need of assistance; it is akin to charging in the criminal justice system

consent decree (juveniles) An agreement that a youth who has violated the law will meet specific conditions without the court formally finding them guilty

informal probation The monitoring of an individual who has agreed to meet specific requirements in return for not having their case formally processed by the court

10
Corrections

8 Trial

adjudication Judging or acting in response to a petition filed in juvenile court

adjudication hearings Proceedings in juvenile court that are akin to trials in criminal court

Prosecutors are the first to present their case in adjudication hearings, followed by the defense (presenting the juvenile's arguments). Parents, probation officers, and victims may also offer input during the hearings. The adjudication process is notably less structured than criminal court trials, and juvenile court judges typically have discretion in how proceedings occur. Judges are responsible for making the determination that the juvenile was responsible for the offense(s) in most cases, although some states grant juveniles the right to a jury trial.

Adjudication hearings have traditionally been closed to the public in efforts to protect the identity and reputation of the youth. However, that has been changing in recent years, and there is variation among the states. Twenty-one states open the hearings, but with specific requirements (Bartollas & Miller, 2014).

EVIDENCE FOR DETERMINING GUILT IN JUVENILE COURT

The standard of evidence required for determining guilt in juvenile court is generally the same as it is in the adult court: proof beyond a reasonable doubt (*In re Winship*, 1970). In cases involving status offenses, however, the Supreme Court has permitted the less stringent requirement of a preponderance of the evidence (reflecting the fact that the juvenile court is a civil as opposed to criminal court). Most jurisdictions use the stricter burden of proof in all juvenile proceedings.

Judges who hear the evidence presented by the defense and prosecution may decide that the facts do not support the petition filed, and the youth is free to leave the court with no further action required. If, however, the judge finds evidence to support the petition, they issue a ruling, which is akin to sentencing in criminal courts.

LEGAL PROTECTIONS FOR JUVENILES

Per various Supreme Court decisions passed in the 1960s and 1970s, juveniles maintain many of the same legal safeguards as adults, but juveniles have increasingly been granted numerous legal protections and constitutional rights. The 1967 U.S. Supreme Court case *In re Gault* (1967) held that juveniles required safeguards in court:

- the right to receive notice of the charges
- the right to confront and cross-examine witnesses
- the right to remain silent and protect themselves from self-incrimination
- access to counsel

Other examples of legal protections provided to juveniles in court include:

- prohibition of hearsay evidence, which is information or evidence offered by individuals who are not testifying in court,
- protection from double jeopardy, and
- the need for prosecutors to establish proof beyond a reasonable doubt to demonstrate guilt.

disposition hearing Similar to a sentencing hearing in criminal court, it is held once a juvenile has been adjudicated

Dispositional Hearings

Disposition hearings are similar to sentencing hearings in criminal court and are held once a juvenile has been adjudicated (sometimes immediately after). In these instances, judges will discuss the findings with the youth, their parents or guardians, and the attorneys and will review any social service reports offered by a probation officer. The judge will then decide a **disposition**, which is a sentence imposed on a juvenile and may include paying a fine, restitution, probation, confinement, or participation in substance abuse or other form of treatment program.

9 Sentencing

disposition A sentence imposed on a juvenile

It was not until 1967 that juveniles were granted the right to counsel. The U.S. Supreme Court's decision in *In re Gault* granted juveniles various protections that they historically lacked in the courts.

What might explain why it took much longer to provide juveniles with the same rights provided to adults?

TYPES OF DISPOSITIONS

There are three main types of dispositions. Dispositions may be nominal, conditional, or custodial (Champion et al., 2012):

- **Nominal dispositions** are the least punitive and typically involve warnings, reprimands, and/or release to the custody of the juvenile's parents or guardians.
- **Conditional dispositions** include probationary options, such as a set of requirements that must be met. These conditions may include restitution, community service, and completion of substance abuse programs.
- **Custodial dispositions** are the most severe and involve some type of confinement. These dispositions may be nonsecure or secure.
  - Nonsecure custody may include sending juveniles to a group home, a camp, or specific schools where the youths can maintain some level of freedom, albeit with restrictions.
  - Secure custody is the more severe form of the two and is used for the most serious offenders who are sent to detention facilities.

TRENDS TOWARD A BIFURCATED SYSTEM

An increasing number of courts are waiting a period of time, often 10 days to 2 weeks, after the adjudication hearing to hold a disposition hearing. The **bifurcated system**, as it is sometimes called, proposes to provide judges more information regarding the disposition of youth offenders. In particular, the rules regarding the consideration of evidence are less restrictive in disposition hearings, allowing for the introduction of information that would have been prevented at the adjudicatory hearing (Bartollas & Miller, 2014).

nominal dispositions The least punitive dispositions used by juvenile courts; they typically involve warnings, reprimands, and/or release to the custody of the juvenile's parents or guardians

conditional dispositions Probationary options, including a set of requirements that must be met; such requirements may include restitution, community service, and completion of substance abuse programs

custodial dispositions Confinement in secure or nonsecure facilities, such as detention centers or group homes

bifurcated system The practice of courts waiting a period of time after the adjudication hearing to hold a disposition hearing, often in efforts to provide judges more information regarding the disposition of youth offenders

predisposition report A report containing information about the juvenile offender and their offense, which is used by juvenile court judges at the disposition hearing

Separating the disposition hearing from the adjudication hearing also permits the probation department to more thoroughly prepare a **predisposition report**, which includes information regarding the referral incident, prior behavior, previous contacts with the police and courts, family concerns, employment history, and school records. It may also include input regarding available programs and support systems, as well as various assessments, including psychological evaluations and/or diagnostic tests. The dispositional recommendations are presented to the judge at the disposition hearing and may also be offered by the prosecution and the youth. The judge has the final say regarding the disposition. Probation was the most restrictive disposition imposed in 59% of juvenile cases in 2018; 28% of cases involved out-of-home placement in a facility (Hockenberry & Puzzanchera, 2020).

11 Appeal

APPEALS

Juveniles do not have a constitutional right to appeal the court's decision; however, almost all states have statutes that grant juveniles the right to have their case reviewed or retried. The court noted in *In re Gault* that the equal protection clause of the Constitution should provide juveniles with the same rights as adults to appeal, and most states have responded by offering the right to appeal. State statutes typically require juvenile cases on appeal to be heard in an appellate court, although a few require a new trial (Bartollas & Miller, 2014).

Waiver to Adult Court

judicial waiver laws Legislation that grants judges the power to waive juvenile cases to the criminal justice system

statutory exclusion laws Laws that automatically exclude particular types of cases from the jurisdiction of juvenile courts, meaning that they will automatically be considered in criminal court

concurrent jurisdiction laws Legislation that grants prosecutors the power to waive juvenile cases to the criminal justice system

Juvenile court judges in most states are permitted to waive juvenile court jurisdiction in certain cases and transfer jurisdiction to criminal court for the juvenile to be tried as an adult. In some cases, juveniles are automatically waived because of legislation that requires a transfer. The court's decision to transfer or waive a case is often based on the seriousness of the offense, the juvenile's likelihood of rehabilitation, and the accused's involvement in the justice system. Waiving juveniles to adult court is used in the most serious cases, and is done in efforts to secure longer sentences for the most troubled youth. Sentences in criminal (adult) court can be much longer than they are in juvenile court. Juveniles who are sentenced to extended periods of incarceration in adult court will remain in custody in a juvenile facility until they reach the age of adulthood, at which point they will be transferred to an adult facility (e.g., prison). States vary with regard to the processes and requirements involved with transferring juvenile cases to adult court:

- Forty-five states have **judicial waiver laws**, in which juvenile court judges use their discretion to transfer juveniles to adult court.
- Twenty-nine states have **statutory exclusion laws** that automatically exclude particular types of cases from the jurisdiction of juvenile courts, meaning that they will automatically be considered in criminal court.
- Fifteen states have **concurrent jurisdiction laws** that grant prosecutors the authority to waive cases.

Legislatures in almost every state made it much easier to transfer juvenile court jurisdiction to the adult system beginning in the 1980s and 1990s (Puzzanchera & Addie, 2014).

demand waivers The means by which juveniles demonstrate that they wish to have their case heard in adult court, where they are entitled to more legal protections

Juveniles may also request, via **demand waivers**, that their case be heard in criminal court, where they are entitled to more legal protections. All juveniles who have their case waived to adult court are entitled to have a waiver hearing to determine the appropriateness of the order to send their case to criminal court. Some states mandate that juveniles tried in adult court will be tried in adult court for any subsequent actions. Figure 26.3 depicts the number of cases judicially waived to criminal court.

As of 2020, 22 states had no specified minimum age at which a juvenile could be transferred to adult court. Those that specified a minimum age most commonly require youths to be at least 14 years of age, although 2 states had a minimum age of 10 years (Office of Juvenile Justice and Delinquency Prevention, 2020). There is some criticism with transferring children at such a young age, and some have deemed it "inconsistent with common sense" (Ruddell & Mays, 2012, p. 31).

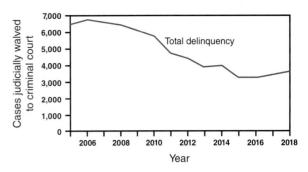

FIGURE 26.3. Delinquency Cases Judicially Waived to Criminal Court, 2005–2018. Roughly 3,800 delinquency cases were waived to criminal court in 2018, which represents a very small percentage of all delinquency cases processed. The percentage of waived cases has declined since the 1990s, returning to the rates witnessed in the mid-1980s. *Source:* Juvenile Court Statistics 2018, *by S. Hockenberry and C. Puzzanchera, 2020, National Center for Juvenile Justice.*

What factors could explain the decrease in the number of cases waived to adult court?

Differences Between the Juvenile Justice System and the Criminal Justice System

States vary with regard to the manner in which they process juveniles. Each state has a juvenile justice system, as does the District of Columbia, but there is no juvenile court at the federal level. The handful of delinquency cases at the federal level are heard in district courts, and adjudicated juveniles are placed in state or local facilities when the **commitment** decision, or judge's ruling to incarcerate, is made. Several characteristics distinguish states' juvenile justice systems from their criminal justice systems, including:

- limited age jurisdiction, meaning that juvenile courts only have jurisdiction over juveniles until they reach a specified age;
- informal proceedings;
- parents or guardians involved in the process;
- records of juveniles sealed once they are adults;
- confidentiality; and
- they are civil courts instead of criminal ones.

Structure of Juvenile Courts

The structures of juvenile courts vary a great deal among jurisdictions. For instance, distinct juvenile courts in urban areas address the legal concerns of children, while juveniles in smaller cities and rural areas are typically tried by adult court judges using juvenile justice guidelines. Juveniles may also have their cases heard by **family court judges**, who primarily hear domestic relations cases. A small number of states use stand-alone juvenile courts, which have their own staff, judges, administration, and other court personnel. The jurisdiction of juvenile courts generally includes cases involving delinquency, neglect, and dependency (e.g., cases in which juveniles do not have a relative or someone else to care for them).

- **Delinquent juveniles** are those who have violated the law and are subject to some type of sanction or treatment.
- **Neglected juveniles** are those whose parents or guardians are not providing adequate care and warrant state intervention.
- **Dependent juveniles** are those who have no parent or guardian to care for them or nobody capable of providing adequate supervision.

● **Learning Objective 26.3:** Distinguish the juvenile justice system from the criminal justice system.

commitment Assigning a juvenile to a period of incarceration

family court judges Judges who primarily hear domestic relations cases

8 Trial

delinquent juveniles Children who have violated the law and are subject to some type of sanction or treatment

neglected juveniles Children who warrant state intervention because their parents or guardians are not providing adequate care

In 1993, Christopher Simmons and a friend bound a woman in duct tape and electrical wire, beat her, and threw her body into a river from a bridge. Simmons was later found guilty and sentenced to death. Upon review of his case, the Supreme Court ruled that it is a violation of the Eighth Amendment to impose the death penalty for crimes committed by individuals under the age of 18.

Do you agree with the court's decision? Or do you think there are cases in which the death penalty would be an appropriate sentence for juveniles?

Neglected and dependent juveniles have not violated laws, but they are in need of assistance, and the courts will typically seek to provide foster care for these youth.

Primary Actors in Juvenile Courts

The primary actors in criminal court are found in juvenile court, although there are some differences. Compared to adult courts:

- juvenile courts are more likely to include input from parents or guardians and representatives from social service agencies;

- probation officers are more involved and typically work more closely with juveniles, providing background information, supervising youth on probation, advising probationers regarding the conditions of their probation, and maintaining case files; and

- juvenile courts generally use a **referee**, commissioner, or master, to hear the facts of the case and oversee detention hearings, as well as adjudicate in some cases on approval of the juvenile court judge (Bartollas & Schmallager, 2014).

Jury Trials and Penalties in Juvenile Courts

Other primary differences between the criminal and juvenile court systems pertain to jury trials and the range of penalties that can be imposed. The Supreme Court ruled in 1971 that juveniles are not entitled to a jury trial (*McKeiver v. Pennsylvania*), although states could grant the right to trial through their state constitutions. States vary with regard to offering them; for example, 10 states provide jury trials for juveniles who request them and others offer them under specified conditions (Bartollas & Schmalleger, 2014).

Penalties in the criminal justice system can be imposed for the duration of an offender's life, whereas the jurisdiction of juvenile court judges typically concludes when the youth reaches adulthood. In *Graham v. Florida* (2010), the Supreme Court ruled that sentencing offenders under age 18 to life without the possibility of parole (which would involve a transfer to adult court) for nonhomicidal offenses violated the Eighth Amendment's protection from cruel and unusual punishment. In addition, in *Roper v. Simmons* (2005), the court eliminated the death penalty for juveniles.

MYTHBUSTING

Everyone Is Entitled to a Trial by Jury

It is often believed that anyone who has committed a crime is entitled to a jury trial. However, this is not the case. Not all adult offenders are, and even fewer juveniles are entitled to a trial by jury. Less than one-fourth of states allow jury trials for juveniles, and in 11 states they are permitted only if the judge allows them (Champion et al., 2013).

Terminology Differences

Another notable difference between the criminal justice system and the juvenile justice system is the terminology sometimes used. The different terminology used with juveniles compared to adults is designed to protect youthful offenders from being labeled or stigmatized by the terms used for adult offenders, or criminals (Hess et al., 2013) Table 26.1 includes some examples of the differences in terminology.

TABLE 26.1. Differences in Terminology Used in Juvenile Versus Adult Court Systems

JUVENILE TERM	EQUIVALENT ADULT TERM
Adjudication hearing	Trial
Disposition	Sentence
Disposition hearing	Sentencing hearing
Commitment	Incarceration
Detention	Jail
Delinquency	Crime
Petition	Indictment or charge

Age

The age at which a youth is considered an adult varies among the states and is established by state legislation. As shown in Figure 26.4, most states classify juveniles as youth who are at or below 17 years old, and juvenile courts have jurisdiction over these individuals. Youth under the age of 7 are considered incapable of creating criminal intent, and thus they are not culpable under the law. Offenders below the

8 Trial

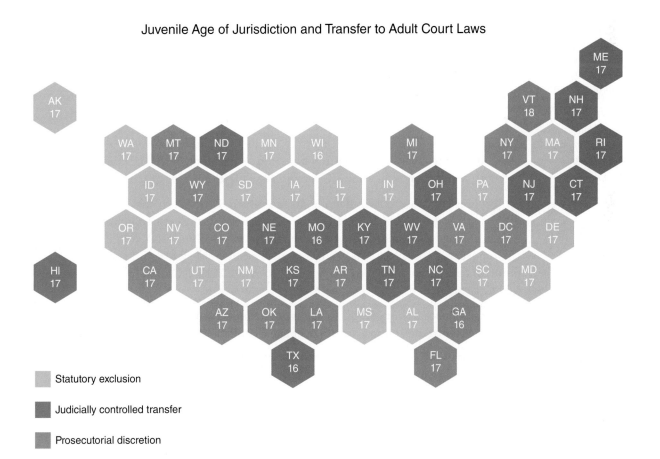

FIGURE 26.4. Juvenile Age of Jurisdiction and Transfer to Adult Court Laws. The majority of states require that juveniles be at least 17 years old to be eligible for transfer to adult court. The laws differ among states with regard to how and when juveniles are to be transferred. *Source:* Juvenile Age of Jurisdiction and Transfer to Adult Court, *by the National Conference of State Legislatures, 2020 (http://www.ncsl.org/research/civil-and-criminal-justice/juvenile-age-of-jurisdiction-and-transfer-to-adult-court-laws.aspx).*

Do you believe that 16-year-olds are too young to be treated as adults? Why or why not?

8 Trial

9 Sentencing

10 Corrections

9 Sentencing

dependent juveniles Children who have no parent or guardian to care for them or nobody capable of providing adequate supervision

referee A juvenile court official who hears the facts of the case and oversees detention hearings, as well as adjudicates in some cases on approval of a juvenile court judge

● **Learning Objective 26.4:** Summarize the arguments of those who wish to abolish and those who wish to preserve the juvenile justice system.

minimum age of juvenile court jurisdiction are often placed under the supervision of human services or social welfare and are assessed and treated.

Criticisms of the Juvenile Justice System and Reform

A survey of adult prisoners who had previously been in some form of placement as a juvenile sheds light on the perceptions of the juvenile justice system from an offender's perspective. Researchers asked a sample of adult inmates to comment on their experiences in the juvenile justice system and noted that among the primary concerns were their lack of understanding of the juvenile and/or adult court processes, the ineffectiveness and poor quality of defense counsel in the juvenile justice system, and their belief that judges behaved improperly in their cases (F. Butler, 2011). This and related work highlight the need for continued development and reform.

The current juvenile justice system is criticized for a number of reasons including:

● lack of effectiveness in rehabilitating youth,

● inconsistencies in punishment, and

● poor legal representation in the following forms (Drizin & Luloff, 2007):

  ● poor investigative work

  ● infrequent use of motions in court

  ● juggling of large caseloads

  ● overreliance on plea bargaining

  ● general lack of training

In light of these and other concerns, several policy reforms have been offered to improve the system, including:

● restructuring the courts to more effectively meet their therapeutic goals,

● accepting punishment as a primary component of juvenile justice, and

● eliminating juvenile courts altogether and processing youths in criminal courts, with required modifications (Champion et al., 2013).

Progress with regard to juvenile justice reform is noted in the "Juvenile Justice 2018 Year-End Report" by the National Conference of State Legislatures (2019), which highlighted some of the efforts made in various states. A common theme in the report was the efforts to grant juveniles additional rights and soften the more punitive approach adopted in the latter part of the 20th century. The following were among the reform efforts:

● Massachusetts changed the lower age of juvenile court jurisdiction to 12 years of age. Prior to the change, a child over age 6 could be charged in juvenile court.

● Nebraska restricted children under the age of 12 from being placed in detention.

● Delaware required that juveniles under age 18 who are charged as adults remain in juvenile facilities prior to trial.

● California prohibited the transfer of all children younger than 16 to adult court.

● Washington prohibited the automatic transfer to adult court for 16- and 17-year-olds who commit specific crimes (e.g., robbery).

Future of Juvenile Courts

The future of juvenile courts is uncertain. While the entire elimination of the juvenile court system is unlikely to occur soon, some critics argue that it should be abolished in favor of one court system that would process both adults and juveniles. However, those who support the continued use of juvenile courts cite the greater likelihood of rehabilitation on the part of juveniles if the two courts are kept separate.

Abolitionists

Those who support the abolition of the juvenile justice system are known as **abolitionists**. They believe the current juvenile justice system has failed to reach its goals of preventing delinquency and rehabilitating juveniles who break the law. They maintain that juveniles are maturing much more quickly these days, committing adult crimes, and therefore should be processed in criminal (adult) courts. Abolitionists further argue that abolishing the juvenile justice system would:

- save court resources,
- reduce the monetary costs of justice,
- provide greater continuity of services,
- result in juveniles having greater due process rights in court, and
- address the flaws associated with the juvenile courts (e.g., Dawson, 1990; Feld, 1997; Jackson & Knepper, 2003).

abolitionists Those who support the abolition of the juvenile justice system

Preservationists

Those who support the continued use of juvenile courts, or **preservationists**, cite the long-standing recognition of children as being less responsible for their actions than adults and the greater likelihood of rehabilitation on the part of juveniles (e.g., Dawson, 1990). Preservationists argue that the problems associated with the juvenile justice system are attributable to implementation issues and not the court structure. They add that juvenile courts work well for many who enter them, and processing youth in adult courts would not be a more effective solution (e.g., Jackson & Knepper, 2003). The abolition of the juvenile courts, they argue, would likely result in less of a concern for treating or rehabilitating troubled youth and a greater focus on punishment, which contrasts with the original thought behind creating a distinct court system for juveniles.

preservationists Those who support the continued use of juvenile courts

Future Directions

While many scholars have weighed in on the future of juvenile justice, there remains no consensus regarding the best approach for moving forward. Some suggest that the community will become increasingly involved in confronting delinquency, in much the same manner that the community has become increasingly involved in fighting crime as part of community-oriented policing approaches (Burns, 2007). Futurist Gene Stephens (1997) earlier cited the importance of establishing community–school partnerships, tutoring programs, peer counseling hotlines, and proactive police–community programs to best address delinquency and ease the burden on juvenile courts. These efforts have certainly helped and are expected to continue doing so in the future.

In addition, many signs point to a less punitive juvenile justice system in the future that focuses more on prevention and treatment and less on detention and transfers to adult court. Evidence of this is found in federal legislation passed in 2018, known as the **Juvenile Justice Reform Act of 2018**, which reauthorized and improved the Juvenile Justice and Delinquency Prevention Act of 1974. Among other requirements, the act:

- bans the shackling of pregnant girls,
- provides funding for tutoring,
- includes drug and alcohol treatment programs for youth,
- provides for mental health treatment, and
- requires states that receive federal funding to collect data on racial disparities in their juvenile justice system and create plans for correcting any inequalities.

Juvenile Justice Reform Act of 2018 Legislation that reauthorized and improved the Juvenile Justice and Delinquency Prevention Act of 1974; the act banned the shackling of pregnant girls; provided funding for tutoring, drug and alcohol programs for youth, and mental health treatment; and required states that receive federal funding to collect data on racial disparities in their juvenile justice system and create plans for correcting any inequalities

In addition, the First Step Act (see Module 25), which also passed in 2018, included a provision that ends the practice of placing juveniles in solitary confinement.

The System in Perspective

As noted in the "In the News" feature at the beginning of this module, teen courts offer promise in efforts to prevent young adults from future involvement in the criminal justice system. They were created based on the belief that a juvenile's contemporaries may be best able to determine the most appropriate punishments that will lead to better behavior by young adults in the future. While it is unlikely that these courts will replace the more formal juvenile courts, they do offer some real benefits by potentially saving resources, providing an arena for educating young adults, and perhaps offering a more appropriate means of finding justice. These courts, with the contributions of law enforcement, juvenile and adult courts, and corrections officials, should decrease the likelihood of troubled youth ending up in the criminal justice system.

Juvenile courts became more punitive in their approaches toward delinquency beginning in the 1980s. The use of detention became more common as juveniles were increasingly being treated as adults.

Should we abolish the juvenile justice system and process juveniles through our criminal justice systems? Why or why not?

Summary

1. Learning Objective 26.1: *Trace the development of juvenile courts.*

- Juvenile courts in the United States are grounded in English practices. The concept of parens patriae gives the state power to formally process troubled youth and was adopted in the United States after originating in England. The use of houses of refuge and the accomplishments of the child savers helped shape the current practices of the juvenile court. The Illinois Juvenile Court Act set the stage for the development of juvenile courts in the United States. Several Supreme Court decisions in the 1960s and 1970s provided juveniles additional legal protections in the courts.

2. Learning Objective 26.2: *Describe the primary steps involved in case processing in the juvenile justice system.*

- The primary steps involved in case processing in the juvenile justice system include preadjudication procedures, the adjudicatory hearing, and disposition hearings. The preadjudication procedures are similar to the pretrial procedures in the adult system. The adjudicatory hearing is akin to adult criminal trials. Disposition hearings follow the adjudication of a juvenile and are similar to sentencing hearings in the adult system.

3. Learning Objective 26.3: *Distinguish the juvenile justice system from the criminal justice system.*

- The juvenile justice system is similar to the criminal justice system in that it consists of various agencies, institutions, and personnel who process individuals who are accused of violating the law. The primary actors in criminal court are also found in juvenile court, although there are some differences. Compared to adult courts, juvenile courts are more likely to include input from parents and representatives from social service agencies. Some other differences include the juvenile justice system having limited age jurisdiction; emphasizing informal proceedings; sealing the records of juveniles; emphasizing confidentiality; and operating in civil, instead of criminal, courts.

4. Learning Objective 26.4: *Summarize the arguments of those who wish to abolish and those who wish to preserve the juvenile justice system.*

• Those who support the abolition of the juvenile justice system, or abolitionists, argue that doing so would save court resources, reduce the monetary costs of justice, provide greater continuity of services, contribute to juveniles having greater due process rights in court, and address the proposed flaws associated with the juvenile courts. Preservationists cite the long-standing recognition of children as less responsible for their actions than adults and the greater likelihood of rehabilitation on the part of juveniles. They argue that the problems associated with the juvenile justice system are attributable to implementation issues and not the court structure, and processing youth in adult courts would not be a more effective solution.

Questions for Critical Thinking

1. What are the similarities between the first juvenile court (which was created in 1899) and juvenile courts in the early 21st century? What are the differences?

2. What are some of the benefits and drawbacks of waiving juvenile cases to adult court? Discuss your responses.

3. Is it in the best interests of society for juvenile courts to shift from the "get tough" approach to delinquency toward one that focuses on protecting, nurturing, and rehabilitating troubled youth? Why or why not?

4. With regard to the future of juvenile courts, who do you believe will prevail: preservationists or abolitionists? Discuss your selection.

Key Terms

abolitionists
adjudication
adjudication hearings
bifurcated system
chancery courts
child savers
commitment
concurrent jurisdiction laws
conditional dispositions
consent decree
custodial dispositions
delinquent juveniles
demand waivers
dependent juveniles
detention
disposition
disposition hearing
family court judges
houses of refuge

Illinois Juvenile Court Act
informal probation
intake
judicial waiver laws
Juvenile Justice Reform Act of 2018
neglected juveniles
nominal dispositions
parens patriae
petition
poor laws
preadjudication procedures
predisposition report
preservationists
refer
referee
status offenses
statutory exclusion laws
waived

For digital learning resources, please go to
https://www.oup.com/he/burns1e

Future of Courts

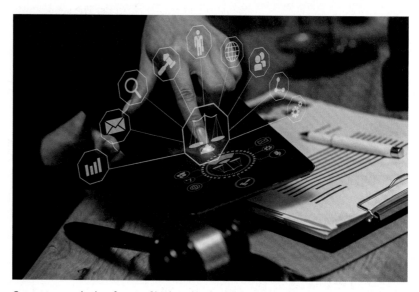

Computers and other forms of high technology have changed our courts.
Advancements such as the ability to provide detailed imagery of evidence help jurors,
judges, and all others involved in courtroom proceedings ensure justice. The ability
to search legal databases, create graphic presentations of evidence, and simply
schedule court hearings also helps with efficiencies in the courts.

What are some limitations of technology use in the courts?

Based on historical and recent trends and factors, both internal and
external to the court, we can anticipate what tomorrow's courts will
look like and aspects of how they will operate. Courtroom procedures
have historically evolved and are anticipated to continue doing so
as technology changes. In addition, globalization and new types of
crimes will undoubtedly shape tomorrow's courts. This module starts
with a look at technology and changes in crime-fighting before examining the influences of globalism on the courts. This module ends
with a discussion of likely changes in courtrooms and courtroom
procedures.

Justice for High-Technology Crimes

In April 2017, Roman Seleznev, a Russian hacker, who has homes in Indonesia and Russia, was given a 27-year prison sentence by a federal district court for his role in operating a vast credit card and identity theft operation. His crimes contributed to the theft and resale of over 2 million credit card numbers, which contributed to losses of at least $70 million but possibly as much as $1 billion. The sentence for Seleznev was the longest ever imposed in the United States for hacking-related practices (Perlroth, 2017).

Law enforcement authorities in the United States have for years tried to capture Russian hackers believed to be victimizing businesses and individuals in the United States. However, Russian hackers often have protection from the Russian government as long as they do not target victims in their own country and as long as they assist Russian intelligence agencies. Seleznev was caught while vacationing in the Maldives, where he thought he was safe because the country does not have an extradition agreement with the United States. However, the U.S. Department of State persuaded officials in the Maldives to cooperate with them (Perlroth, 2017).

Judges sometimes face difficulties in determining sentences for high-technology crimes, particularly when the extent of the harms may be difficult to ascertain or the judges may not be clear on how the technology functions. The sentence imposed on Seleznev was in part based on the harms committed and in part to send a message to other hackers that these types of crimes will result in serious consequences. Do you believe the sentence given to Seleznev is appropriate? Or should he have received a more or less severe penalty? Why?

Technology

Technology is changing the world and is no doubt changing the courts. Many 21st-century courtrooms, including the more progressive ones known as **wired courts**, or technology-enabled courts, feature technologies that have improved the adjudication process. However. the constant development of technological advances suggests that tomorrow's courts will look and function differently. Among the primary areas of development to enhance the quality and efficiency of courtroom practices are electronic case filing, database integration, and enhanced audio/visual recordings.

Electronic Case Filing

Federal courts now use a digital, paperless filing method with each pleading submitted via the electronic case filing system. Such filing is also used in an increasing number of state courts because of its benefits, which include:

- the defense and prosecution both having easy access to the materials,
- all parties being notified via email of the filing, and
- reduced costs.

● **Learning Objective 27.1:** Explain how technology will change courts in the future.

wired courts
Progressive courts that feature technologies that have improved the adjudication process; they are also known as technology-enabled courts

Litigation support software is also assisting attorneys with regard to managing court transcripts and documents, providing document imaging, and accessing evidence.

Database Integration

database integration The storage of various types of information that can be accessed by multiple users; it helps various branches of the criminal justice system share information with each other

Database integration, which involves the storage of various types of information that can be accessed by multiple users, helps branches of the criminal justice system share information with each other (Siegal et al., 2011). For instance, the Federal Judicial Center, which is the education and research agency of the judicial branch of the U.S. government, provides public access to its integrated database, which contains data on criminal defendant filings, civil cases, and terminations in district courts (Federal Judicial Center, n.d.b). The database is regularly updated and allows users to access information in an efficient and timely manner.

Enhanced Audio/Visual

Primary among the technological advancements in the courtroom has been improved audio and video. High-resolution cameras and monitors, both within the court and, in some cases, in the jury boxes, enable jurors and other participants to more clearly see the evidence. In addition, the ability to be involved in the proceedings from outside the court has provided more efficiency. As a result, witnesses can often testify from afar, thus reducing transportation and other costs.

The enhanced audio/visual capabilities in the courtroom have been largely augmented by the increased use of smart phones and other recording devices by police personnel and the public:

- An estimated 96% of Americans own smart phones (Pew Research Center, 2020), which makes recording video and audio of crimes and other incidents more common.
- Increases in the numbers of officers wearing body cameras and cameras in patrol cars make it easy for courtroom personnel to watch accounts of events as opposed to or in addition to witness testimony (McDonald & Bachelder, 2017).
- Animation or virtual reality displays of events in question enable involved parties to more clearly experience what has been or will be discussed in court.
- Telephone interpreting systems enable courtroom personnel to overcome language barriers.
- Digital audio reporting enables courtroom reporters to better create transcripts of courtroom activities.

Online Courts and Future Innovations

online courts Courts in which all proceedings are carried out through technology and participants may engage virtually

It is possible that in the future **online courts**, in which all proceedings are carried out through technology and participants (including jurors) may contribute virtually, may become a reality in the United States. Such courts could be facilitated by audio, video, electronic conferencing, and whatever new developments emerge in the future. Judge Herbert Dixon has noted that continued and additional use of video hearings will result in the general acceptance of virtual hearings and trials, despite the resistance of some attorneys and judges who fear that technology might provide an unfair advantage to one side or the other or affect juror objectivity (Carpenter, 2001; Dixon, 2013a). In fact, some countries, including China and Canada, have already introduced online legal proceedings. For example, in 2017, China introduced its online cybercourt. The court enables those involved in the case to participate online and primarily hears cases involving civil disputes as they relate to online commerce, for instance when consumers receive an item other than what they expected when they purchased it (BBC, 2017).

Other technology that will become increasingly important for the courts includes geospatial data (e.g., information from phones, global positioning system devices, tablets, and related devices) and technology to detect deception (e.g., devices that assess fidgeting and changes in vocal pitch or that use three-dimensional cameras to track movements of a person's entire body) (Dixon, 2013a).

Implementation

Technology has the potential to enhance the courts, but its acceptance is not universal, and there is also often lack of agreement regarding which technologies should be used. For instance, courts have to determine if they wish to provide video monitors in the jury box or if one large video display will suffice (Dixon, 2013b). The benefits of providing a monitor for each juror are obvious; however, the costs are significant. Implementing technology into the courts and other areas of the criminal justice system involves:

- consideration of the law,
- operational needs,
- the capacity to service and maintain the technology,
- training required to use technology, and
- costs.

Many technological advances have improved court practices, and many developments in the field are expected. The associated costs of advancing our courts and ensuring that technology is implemented and used appropriately will challenge court officials in the years ahead.

How long do you believe it will be until we have online trials in the United States?

8 Trial

MYTHBUSTING

There are no Downsides to Using Technology in the Courts

Many people believe that technology has changed, and will continue to change our court systems for the better. There are, however, some limitations associated with technological advancements as they pertain to the courts. Primary among the challenges are costs, including those associated with purchasing and maintaining the equipment. Courts must also consider how to incorporate new forms of technology into the proceedings. For instance, they must consider if a video depiction (a simu-

lation) of a crime occurring would unfairly influence jurors and would be admissible. Some jurisdictions finance the use of technology in the courts, in part, through adding a special fee to tickets issued by the police. Violators in Geauga County, Ohio, for instance, pay an extra $10 in fees that is directed toward computers and information technology in the clerk's office (Farkas, 2016). While there are certainly benefits to using technology in the courts, there are disadvantages as well.

Changes in Crime and Crime-Fighting

Crime has been around for quite some time and, barring any major changes, will persist. What has changed with regard to crime has been the extent to which it occurs and the nature of the crimes committed. Crime has increasingly become electronic in nature, and laws and the courts must address these new types of high-technology crime. In addition, crime-fighting has evolved as technological developments have assisted law enforcement efforts. This in turn influences courtroom practices, especially with regard to laws concerning searches, seizures, and privacy rights.

● **Learning Objective 27.2:** Describe the primary changes in crime and crime-fighting that will affect the courts.

Types of High-Technology Crimes

Roughly 90% of the U.S. population used the internet at some point in 2020. It is also estimated that there are over 4.9 billion users of the internet worldwide (Internet World Stats, 2020). Such a large number of users provide many targets for criminals, and evidence suggests that high-technology crime (cybercrime) is increasing. The Internet Crime Complaint Center was created by the Federal Bureau of Investigation in 2000 in efforts to enable the public to report suspected internet-facilitated crime. The center provides reports and general information based on citizen complaints of the types of high-technology crime victimization that occurs. In 2019, the center noted that the most common types of victimization involved were:

- *nonpayment/nondelivery*, which involves goods and services being shipped and payment not being received (nonpayment) or payment for goods that are never shipped (nondelivery);
- *personal data breach*, which involves the sharing of personal information from a secure location to an untrusted one;
- *extortion*, which involves the unlawful extraction of goods or money though undue use of authority or intimidation and could involve threats of physical harm; and
- *phishing/vishing/smishing/pharming*, which involves the use of unsolicited emails, texts, and/or telephone calls purportedly from a legitimate business requesting financial, personal, or login credentials (Internet Crime Complaint Center, 2020) (see Module 3 for a discussion of cybercrime).

Differences Between High-Technology and Traditional Crime

The differences between cybercrime and traditional forms of crime will result in the continuous need to create and update legislation, and courtroom personnel will need to keep pace with technological developments. Among the differences between cybercrime and traditional crime are the following:

- anonymity associated with cybercrime
- openness and underregulation of the internet
- abstract nature of the evidence involved in cybercrime (e.g., information, knowledge)
- greater likelihood of interjurisdictional and international issues associated with cybercrime
- limited body of existing legislation directed toward cybercrime

Lack of Precedent and Established Laws

Courts have had to increasingly address a wide array of high-technology crimes without the benefit of having many years of precedent and established laws that could guide their decision-making. With regard to the latter, lawmakers must regularly pass laws that effectively keep pace with the rapid technological advancements and associated crime, even though they may not be fully aware of the capacity and nature of some of the technologies. This lack of established legislation and precedent, as well as differences in laws and concerns for high-technology crimes of an international nature, is among the difficulties expected to continue troubling the courts.

Interjurisdiction of Cybercrime

Most computer crime is cross-jurisdictional, which means that cooperative efforts are required from officials at the local, county, state, federal, and international levels. There are, however, varying levels of defined laws across jurisdictions. In attempts to better address this and related challenges, in 2007, the United States became a participant in the **Convention on Cybercrime**, a treaty created by the Council of Europe in an attempt to address internet and other computer crimes by synchronizing national laws, enhancing investigations into such crimes, and promoting cooperation among countries (Council of Europe, n.d.). The interjurisdictional nature of cybercrimes will continue to challenge the courts.

Use of High-Technology and Forensic Science in Crime-Fighting

Related to the increase in cybercrime is the way that high technology will largely shape future crime-fighting efforts and, by extension, the courts. Police departments generally seek new technology and view analytics, biometrics, and other high-technology advancements as important for effectively fighting crime (Daly, 2013). Such developments have legal ramifications as they pertain to procedural law, and the courts will have to continue creating legal boundaries for their use both by law enforcement and by attorneys in the courts.

Forensic science involves the use of scientific methods to address crime and related problems (see online resources for a more complete discussion of forensic science). With forensic science, law enforcement agents are able to better collect and analyze criminalistics evidence. The use of more conclusive evidence assists with decisions regarding culpability and gives more credibility to the criminal justice system, and the courts in particular, because jurors can base their decisions on stronger evidence than was collected and presented in the past. However, the acceptance and rules for introduction of such evidence in court need to be continuously established. In addition, errors and misconduct by scientists can, and do, result in wrongful convictions. Errors with regard to the handling and storage of DNA evidence or law enforcement personnel acting illegally, for example by placing DNA samples at crime scenes, may have negative ramifications for justice in the courts (Burns, 2013; Shaer, 2016).

Convention on Cybercrime A treaty created by the Council of Europe in an attempt to address internet and other computer crimes by synchronizing national laws, enhancing investigations into such crimes, and promoting cooperation among countries

1 Criminal Act

The enhanced incorporation of forensic sciences into the courtroom has many benefits. For instance, the certainty with which we can link evidence collected from a crime scene to the accused or exonerate those who have been wrongfully accused has advanced to unprecedented levels.

To what extent do you believe the continued use of forensic sciences will enhance our confidence in the criminal justice system?

Influences of Globalism

Crime is becoming more international, as communication, travel, and commerce are becoming increasingly global in nature. **Globalism** refers to the transnational integration of cultural, social, and economic issues and the international integration and interaction of agents, agencies, countries, and others that have historically been relatively isolated from one another (Burns, 2013). Countries across the globe have become increasingly intertwined with one another as a result of advances in technology, communications, travel, trade, and commerce. The increasingly international

● **Learning Objective 27.3:** Explain how globalism will impact the future of the courts.

globalism The transnational integration of cultural, social, and economic issues and the international integration and interaction of agents, agencies, countries, and others that have historically been relatively isolated from one another

1 Criminal Act

3 Arrest

human trafficking Moving people across and within borders without their consent; it is often done through the use of violence, coercion, and/or deception and is a modern-day form of slavery often used to obtain labor or sex

nature of crime results in courts having to ensure that they are legally and procedurally prepared to confront such crimes.

International Crime and Human Trafficking

International crimes are traditional forms of crime that cross borders of countries. They are difficult to detect, apprehend, and adjudicate because of the various countries involved. Crimes such as drug and human trafficking, environmental harms, illegal weapons trafficking, and gang crime, which were once viewed primarily as domestic concerns, have increasingly become international in nature, and the courts must adapt to the changes.

Organized crime groups, terrorists, drug cartels, and others will continue to challenge the courts with the complexity, frequency, and international nature of their activities. For instance, various organized crime groups, including the Chinese triads, the Yakuza, La Cosa Nostra, Russian gangs, and Mexican and Colombian drug cartels, are among the many groups that have engaged in international crime and provided difficulties for international justice–based efforts. Figure 27.1 depicts the international nature of heroin trafficking as it emerges from Asia.

Among the more troubling forms of international crime is **human trafficking**, which is not legal anywhere in the world (K. Williams, 2014). Human trafficking involves moving people across and within borders without their consent. It is often done through the use of violence, coercion, and/or deception and has been deemed "a major worldwide concern" and "likely one of the most egregious acts violating the most basic and fundamental human rights" (Sciarabba & Sullivan, 2010, p. 227).

Global human trafficking is estimated to be the third largest illicit global trade (behind drugs and guns), involving over 4 million people annually, and is believed to generate annual revenues of $7 billion to $10 billion (Aguilar-Milan et al., 2008).

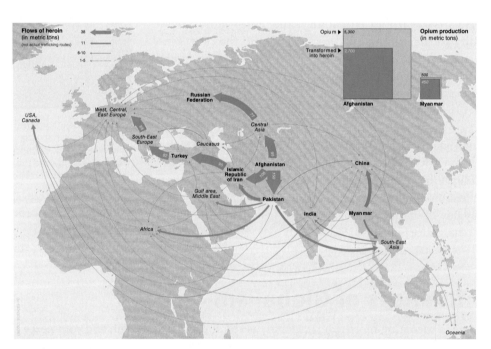

FIGURE 27.1. Global Heroin Flows From Asian Points of Origin. Drug trafficking is among the most significant international crimes. As depicted here, heroin emerging from Asia is transported through, and to, many countries. The transport of other drugs (e.g., cocaine) follows equally elaborate chains that make the tracking and related enforcement efforts difficult. Greater cooperation between countries with regard to international drug offenses is required and expected in the future, particularly with regard to the prosecution of these crimes. ***Source:*** *UNODC, World Drug Report 2010 (United Nations Publication, Sales No. E.10.XI.13).*

What do you believe are the most significant challenges confronting the international drug trade?

The International Labour Organization estimates that there are roughly 21 million adults and children in forced labor, being trafficked, held in debt bondage, or working in slave-like conditions. The organization estimates the annual profits for forced labor to be around $150 billion (International Labour Organization, 2020).

Courts in some areas have taken proactive efforts to address human trafficking through the creation of specialized courts (see Module 21) that focus directly on these types of cases. For example, in 2013, New York State established a statewide system of specialized courts designed to address prostitution cases and help rescue human and sex trafficking victims from continued exploitation and arrests. The Human Trafficking Intervention Courts address cases involving prostitution-related crimes that proceed past arraignment. The cases are evaluated by the judge, defense lawyer, and prosecutor, and upon agreement, the court refers defendants to protective services such as drug treatment, shelter, healthcare, job training, and education in efforts to prevent them from returning to the sex trade. The program is modeled after specialized courts that address domestic violence and low-level drug offenses (Rashbaum, 2013).

7
Arraignment

Benefits and Drawbacks of Globalism

Despite the differences among court systems and laws, courts can learn from one another, which is a benefit of globalism. Greater interaction among countries and court systems will likely perpetuate the sharing of ideas regarding the best ways to adjudicate cases (Ritter, 2006). Such learning is not restricted to the courts, and globalism has increased the range of vulnerable targets for criminals and facilitated the sharing of criminal tactics.

Among the challenges with regard to the courts and globalism are the differences in laws and justice systems across countries. While increased globalism has, to some extent, enhanced levels of cooperation among different countries, conflict exists as well. Changes influence justice-based practices at differing rates and in various forms because some countries are more advanced than others (Andreas & Nadelmann, 2006).

The International Criminal Court

Several incidents in the 1970s brought new focus to the need for courts to better address global crimes. Further, the expansion of the illegal drug trade, concerns about human trafficking and exploitation of humans, and several terrorist attacks, including the attacks on the United States in 2001, highlighted the increasingly international nature of crime (Andreas & Nadelmann, 2006).

1 Criminal Act

The idea of having an international court had long existed; for example, the United Nations General Assembly noted the need for a permanent international court to address the types of crimes witnessed in World War II. Negotiations to create such a court were under way in the mid-1990s, when atrocities in the former Yugoslavia and Rwanda emerged and added a sense of urgency and immediacy.

In 1998, a conference of 160 nations established the first treaty-based international criminal court. The treaty adopted at the conference is known as the **Rome Statute of the International Criminal Court** (International Criminal Court, n.d.), and in 2002 the **International Criminal Court (ICC)** was created, which is a court of last resort. Its funding comes from participating countries and voluntary contributions from governments, international organizations, individuals, corporations, and others. There were 123 member countries as of October 2020 (International Criminal Court, 2020).

Rome Statute of the International Criminal Court The treaty adopted at a 1998 conference of 160 nations; it established the first treaty-based international criminal court

The ICC is a permanent international court that investigates, prosecutes, and tries individuals accused of committing the most serious crimes that are of concern

International Criminal Court (ICC) A treaty-based international court of last resort; it investigates, prosecutes, and tries individuals accused of committing the most serious crimes that are of concern to the international community

to the international community, in particular, genocide, crimes against humanity, war crimes, and aggression. Participating nations in the ICC assemble at least once a year to:

- set policies for the court,
- review the court's activities,
- address budgeting issues, and
- consider new projects.

The creation of the ICC is certainly a positive step toward addressing international crime, but it has jurisdiction only over the most serious offenses. Many other international crimes occur outside the jurisdiction of the ICC.

Adjudication of International Crimes and Extradition

Adjudicating international crimes is difficult for various reasons, including the following:

- jurisdictional issues
- legal issues
- nationalistic mindsets
- politics
- cultural differences
- troubled international relations

Many of these same issues challenge courts in the United States with regard to domestic crimes.

extradition A state surrendering an individual accused of a crime to the state in which the individual is accused

Extradition, which involves a state surrendering an individual accused of a crime to the state in which the individual is accused, will become increasingly used as globalism increases. The U.S. Secretary of State is responsible for requesting the return of individuals from the United States who commit crimes and flee to another country under the terms of extradition treaties the United States has with other countries. The United States has extradition treaties with over 100 countries. Among the countries with which it does not have a treaty are China, North Korea, and Russia.

Changes to Courtroom Procedures

Envision the courts in the year 2050. What does the courtroom look like? Are the judges still wearing gowns, striking a gavel, and exuding authority? Is there a courtroom? Are the courtrooms crowded? Has technology replaced traditional means of adjudicating cases? These and other questions will be answered over time, and current practices are among the many factors that will affect future developments. Nobody can definitively tell us what the future holds for the courts, but we can make educated projections that help us better prepare for what is ahead.

- **Learning Objective 27.4:** Summarize the projections for the future of the courts, and describe how courtroom procedures may be different in the future.

Future of Courts in General

Several scholars have offered input regarding what they believe lies ahead for the courts. They suggest that the courts will:

- serve as instruments of social change,
- be held accountable for transparency and performance,

- experience greater expectations and demands for access to information,
- be subject to additional media coverage and public scrutiny,
- confront language problems resulting from increasing levels of diversity,
- upgrade or replace aging court infrastructure (e.g., facilities, technology),
- be affected by technological changes (e.g., conducting business from remote locations via technology and increased litigation for electronic crimes),
- face funding challenges,
- see federal courts become increasingly involved in local criminal justice issues,
- see state and local courts increasingly adjudicate federal issues (e.g., immigration),
- continue to be politicized and experience attacks on judicial independence, and
- encounter changing demographics, including an aging workforce and increased racial and ethnic diversity among those who enter the courts (Martin & Wagenknecht-Ivey, 2011; Roberson & DiMarino, 2012).

In citing the need for courts in all countries to prepare for the future, one researcher noted that "there's no question that terrorism, the growth of multicultural populations, massive migration, upheaval in age-composition demographics, technological developments, and globalization over the next three or more decades will affect the world's criminal justice systems" (Ritter, 2006, p. 8).

1 Criminal Act

Future of Courtroom Procedures

Generally speaking, courtroom procedure has remained somewhat consistent throughout its history. Trials have been conducted in much the same manner for hundreds of years. In the future, however, we may see new developments that radically change courts and courtroom proceedings. Among the most anticipated are the influence of the media and entertainment on the courts, juror practices as they pertain to taking notes and being more active during trials, language services to overcome language barriers, the increased use of alternative dispute resolution, the increased use of specialized courts, and concerns related to court security.

8 Trial

INFLUENCE OF MEDIA AND ENTERTAINMENT

The media have often been criticized for sensationalizing crime, increasing fear of crime, and encouraging unsubstantiated crime waves (e.g., Kappeler & Potter, 2018). Of particular importance is the media's influence on juror expectations in the courtroom. Consumers of media are often influenced by the content to which they are exposed.

One show in particular that has influenced courtrooms is *CSI: Crime Scene Investigation* and its derivatives (*CSI: New York* and *CSI: Miami*). The shows distort the reality of crime and its investigation, which has influenced some jurors' expectations regarding the presentation of evidence in court, or what is known as the *CSI* effect.

Research regarding the influences of the shows on jurors used mock jurors consisting of *CSI* viewers and non-*CSI* viewers who were presented a fictitious case. *CSI* viewers were more critical than their counterparts of the forensic evidence presented at trial and found the evidence less believable. Further, a greater percentage of non-*CSI* viewers voted to convict (29%, compared to 18% of *CSI* viewers), although it was not a statistically significant difference (Schweitzer & Saks, 2007). Despite these and related findings, there is some debate regarding whether *CSI* and other crime-related shows affect viewer behavior in the courts (e.g., Y. S. Kim et al., 2009).

8 Trial

JURORS TAKING NOTES AND ASKING QUESTIONS

In the future, there may also be greater leniency with regard to jurors taking notes during trials and playing a more active role in trials, for instance through permitting jurors to ask questions during the trial. Jurors in some states are permitted to question witnesses, and some states provide notebooks containing exhibits and legal papers designed to assist the estimated 4 million jurors who serve each year with jury deliberations. Research in the area has suggested that jurors who took notes during a mock trial were better able to recall the events of the trial, and the notes enabled jurors to more correctly recall information (Thorley, 2016).

However, the practice of allowing jurors to ask questions has been criticized by defense attorneys. Many argue that doing so enables prosecutors to redirect, or change their case, in response to juror questions that may provide a preview of how jurors view the case (Willing, 2005).

LANGUAGE SERVICES

Increased levels of diversity within the United States mean the courts will be more accountable for providing assistance with language barriers. Courts primarily use interpreters to help ensure proper communications. A study by the National Center for State Courts found that over 86% of respondents reported that court personnel are providing language services in courtroom proceedings often on a daily or weekly basis, with Spanish (97%) being the most frequently requested language. The noted that when dealing with less frequently spoken languages, most courts seek support from neighboring jurisdictions, use bilingual individuals who are certified translators, or use commercial telephonic services (National Center for State Courts, 2013).

telephone interpreting systems Devices that enable individuals in the courtroom who do not speak or understand the dominant language to hear and communicate via a translator participating through a telephone

Some jurisdictions use **telephone interpreting systems**, which enable individuals in the courtroom who do not speak or understand the dominant language to hear and communicate via a translator participating through a telephone. The systems connect human interpreters to people who want to speak to each other but do not speak or understand a common language. This service is particularly helpful when individuals in court speak an uncommon foreign language and no interpreters are in close proximity to the court.

The challenges associated with increasing levels of diversity are not restricted to the United States; for instance, the court system in South Africa recognizes 11 official languages, which means they heavily rely on the use and accuracy of interpreters (Siemer, 2001).

8 Trial

ALTERNATIVE DISPUTE RESOLUTION

The fact that a large majority of cases are resolved via plea bargaining in the courts suggests that trials have become rarer. It is unlikely that trials will be eliminated from the courts entirely, although alternative methods of adjudication may become increasingly common in the future. Siegel and colleagues (2011) cited the recent increase in alternative methods of adjudication. In particular, they noted **alternative dispute resolution**, or the various means of settling disputes away from courtrooms, as alternatives to costly trials. **Arbitration**, or settling disputes outside the courts via the use of a trained third party whose decision is legally binding, is one of the more popular forms of alternative dispute resolution. A less formal method is **mediation**, in which a trained mediator (similar to the arbitrator) helps both parties come to some agreement. Mediators, unlike arbitrators, are not empowered to impose decisions on the involved parties (Siegel et al., 2011).

alternative dispute resolution The various means of settling disputes away from courtrooms; they are alternatives to trials

arbitration Settling disputes outside the courts via the use of a trained third party whose decision is legally binding

SPECIALIZED COURTS

The popularity of specialized courts (e.g., drug courts or human trafficking courts) provides evidence that the role of the courts is shifting. Courts are increasingly engaging in problem-solving in efforts to address the root of the problems facing the individuals who enter the courts. Specialized courts require many resources from outside the courts (e.g., social service agencies, probation officers), which must be available for problem-solving to be successful (see Module 21).

mediation A method of alternative dispute resolution in which a trained mediator helps both parties come to some agreement

COURT SECURITY

Court security has become a concern (Roberson & DiMarino, 2012) as security threats and violent incidents increase in frequency, and funding to protect the courts has diminished (Fatusko et al., 2013). Additional officers are needed to protect the courts, additional training of the security officers is needed, and smaller courthouses generally lack the funds to implement basic security screening devices (Fatusko et al., 2013).

Within the realm of security threats within courtrooms has been protecting courtroom personnel from the spread of COVID-19. Courts have taken general precautions in handling cases (see Module 20); however, threats to the overall well-being of all who enter the courtroom requires close attention. Among the protocols taken to address those in the courtroom for any reason (e.g., as a juror, worker, or defendant) were:

- redesigning courtrooms to permit and ensure social distancing,
- requiring masks or face shields,
- using plexiglass barriers,
- vetting prospective jurors for health vulnerabilities,
- using technology to conduct business, and
- regularly cleaning furniture and surfaces.

These and other precautions were used to limit exposure and the spread of the deadly virus and demonstrate the wide array of security concerns inherent in courtrooms.

The System in Perspective

The "In the News" feature at the start of this module noted the 27-year prison sentence imposed on a man responsible for up to possibly $1 billion in losses resulting from hacking and credit card and identity theft. These types of crimes were not possible before technology made them so. While Roman Seleznev did not physically harm anyone, the financial costs associated with his crimes are substantial. Our courts, akin to the other components of the criminal justice system, must be prepared for increased harms caused by new types of crime. Strong arguments could be made that Seleznev deserved a much longer sentence given the substantial financial losses associated with his crimes or, conversely, a shorter sentence because his crimes were nonviolent. Courts in the future will have to discern what constitutes justice for new types of crime, and they will also have to understand new technology and be able to present laws pertaining to it to jurors and others in the courtroom.

Long-term planning is essential for the longevity of any agency, institution, or organization. Accordingly, each component within the criminal justice system must proactively address changes. Unfortunately, many criminal justice agencies, including those associated with the courts, are burdened with current challenges, and planning is often overlooked. The uncertainty of the future leads some officials to be fearful of wasting resources. Nevertheless, careful planning and consideration of various factors undoubtedly will assist the courts in not only keeping pace with changes, but also staying ahead of them.

Summary

1. Learning Objective 27.1: *Explain how technology will change courts in the future.*

- Technology will continue to change the courts with regard to the presentation of evidence, the filing of paperwork, attorney access to files and documents, the potential for jury members to serve via teleconferencing, and the need for court personnel to understand how to use and interpret technological advancements and keep pace with technological changes.

2. Learning Objective 27.2: *Describe the primary changes in crime and crime-fighting that will affect the courts.*

- Crime is becoming increasingly technology-based, as is crime-fighting. The courts will need to keep pace with the changes with regard to how these cases will be presented in court and applying the laws pertaining to the advanced forms of crime. The increasing international nature of crime will contribute to additional concerns regarding jurisdictional issues, particularly as they apply to the different laws that exist in different countries. The use of forensic science in crime-fighting will require courts to become well versed in some hard sciences that have largely been absent from court proceedings in the past.

3. Learning Objective 27.3: *Explain how globalism will impact the future of the courts.*

- Globalism will impact the courts as countries become further intertwined with respect to crime and related legal issues. International crimes such as human trafficking, terrorism, drug trafficking, and other organized crime-related activities impact many countries. Globalism will help the courts, because it offers increased opportunities for countries to learn from one another and share information. The International Criminal Court was created, in part, to address the increasingly international nature of crime attributable to globalism.

4. Learning Objective 27.4: *Summarize the projections for the future of the courts, and describe how courtroom procedures may be different in the future.*

- Projections for the future of the courts involve issues pertaining to courts serving as instruments of social change, media coverage, language problems, political pressures, technological changes, expansion of federal courts, funding, aging court structures, changing demographics, transparency in the courts, sharing information, and state and local courts addressing federal issues.

  Courtroom procedures in the future may be different in the sense that we may see greater juror expectations of the use of forensic sciences in presenting cases, jurors being allowed to take notes during trials and generally granted assistance with their role, the increased need to address language barriers, and alternatives to plea bargaining and trials becoming increasingly common, for instance in the form of alternative dispute resolution. The increased use of specialized courts and concerns for various safety-related threats are also anticipated to impact the future of courtroom procedures.

Questions for Critical Thinking

1. Do you expect that jurors will someday be able to participate in trials (via teleconferencing) from their homes? Why or why not?

2. Given the major influences of technology on our society and its impact on crime, do you believe that within 10 years we will have specialized courts that focus primarily on high-technology crimes? Why or why not?

3. What are some of the primary difficulties associated with adjudicating international crime? Are these difficulties similar to those faced with regard to technology-based crimes? Discuss your response.

4. How could our courts better prepare for our increasingly diverse society?

Key Terms

alternative dispute resolution
arbitration
Convention on Cybercrime
database integration
extradition
globalism
human trafficking

International Criminal Court
mediation
online courts
Rome Statute of the International Criminal Court
telephone interpreting systems
wired courts

For digital learning resources, please go to
https://www.oup.com/he/burns1e

Module

28

History of Corrections

MODULE OUTLINE

- **European Correctional Practices (1760 B.C.–1779)**

  Learning Objective 28.1: Identify the early European correctional practices.

- **Corrections During the Colonial Period (1607–1776)**

  Learning Objective 28.2: Summarize the developments in corrections during colonial times in the United States.

- **Corrections Following the American Revolution (1777–1865)**

  Learning Objective 28.3: Explain the significance of the contributions of Dr. Benjamin Rush and the Pennsylvania and Auburn prison systems.

- **Corrections Following the Civil War (1866–1899)**

  Learning Objective 28.4: Describe the developments in corrections in the United States following the Civil War.

- **Corrections in the United States in the 20th and Early 21st Centuries (1900–Present)**

  Learning Objective 28.5: Trace the development of corrections beginning in the 20th century until today.

The roots of corrections in the United States were established in early England. Public shaming, for instance through securing offenders in devices (pillories) for the public to see and ridicule, was among the correctional practices brought to the United States from England.

Do you believe public shaming can serve as valuable punishment and deterrent for offenders? Why or why not?

Correctional practices in the United States are heavily influenced by early English systems, as colonists brought with them many of the same practices that were used in England. We have reformed and refined correctional practices throughout history, with the goals of ensuring that justice is served and human rights are respected. This module traces the history of corrections, beginning with a consideration of early European influences. The focus then shifts to corrections during colonial times, following the American Revolution, after the Civil War, and then finally in the 20th and early 21st centuries.

Budget Cuts and Corrections

In February 2017, inmates at the James T. Vaughn Correctional Center in Delaware rioted and killed a correctional officer and injured others. Over 100 prison officers quit or retired early following the riot, which placed the facility at a higher risk of violent outbursts. The riot was one of several recent riots in prisons across the United States. The Delaware prison, like many others, was overcrowded and understaffed (Galvin, 2017).

Many correctional agencies are feeling the effects of reduced or insufficient funding to provide correctional services. Economic pressures on state legislators have contributed to reduced budgets for correctional services in many states, resulting in overcrowded and understaffed prisons that increase the likelihood of violence among inmates, lead to turnover among staff, and reduce the opportunities for rehabilitating inmates.

Although state prison populations have decreased in recent years, housing prisoners is costly, and states will continue to struggle to find the financial means to adequately house prisoners or seek alternatives. What alternatives to prison do you believe states should consider?

1 Criminal Act

European Correctional Practices (1760 B.C.–1779)

Corrections in the United States was heavily influenced by correctional practices in Europe. Some of these practices were appalling by 21st-century standards, while others provided a foundation on which current correctional practices are based. Modules 8 and 20 discuss the **Code of Hammurabi**, which dates back to 1760 B.C. and sought to:

- identify crimes,
- note punishments for criminal behavior, and
- provide settlements for common conflicts.

The code also incorporated the term **lex talionis**, which refers to the law of retaliation, or punishment that corresponds with the harms caused. It is sometimes referred to as "an eye for an eye" justice. Lex talionis became an integral part of

● **Learning Objective 28.1:** Identify the early European correctional practices.

10 Corrections

corrections worldwide (Clear et al., 2016). Many early European correctional practices were brutal by early 21st-century standards (Peters, 1995).

Torture, Branding, and Mutilation

Early English responses to crime included torture, branding, and mutilation. The punishments were designed to be related closely to the seriousness and nature of the crime. For instance, thieves had their fingers or hands removed, liars had their tongues removed, and adulterers were branded with an "A" to their head to signify their behavior and reduce their attractiveness. Branding was also used on other areas of offenders' bodies; for instance, a "T" would be carved into the hands of thieves or a "B" would be stamped on blasphemers (those who spoke poorly about God).

Banishment and Transportation

In addition to torture, branding, and mutilation, other sanctions were used, including banishment and **transportation**, which involved removing individuals from communities. The use of banishment in primitive societies meant that the offender was released to the wilderness to fend for themselves, which often resulted in death (Allen et al., 2013).

Transportation began in England in 1596 and was used in the 17th and 18th centuries to send undesirables to the American colonies. Relocating offenders helped England alleviate the problems of increasing crime rates and overcrowded jails. The American Revolution in 1776 brought an end to the practice, however, and England then had to find another location for transporting its unwanted persons (Allen et al., 2013). In the interim, England used **prison hulks**, which were old merchant and naval ships that were essentially floating prisons, where conditions were deplorable (Alarid & Reichel, 2013).

Gaols and Workhouses

Imprisonment as a sanction was not particularly common in earlier times. English **gaols** were used for detaining defendants or those awaiting their punishment. King Henry II ordered the construction of jails in England in 1166 for detaining offenders who awaited trial. Jails were also used to extract confessions or coerce the payment of debts. Detainees could avoid jail via the **fee system**, which enabled those with the financial means to pay to avoid serving jail time. The practice of using long-term incarceration as a form of punishment for convicted offenders did not fully emerge until the 19th century (Alarid & Reichel, 2013).

Workhouses, which were sometimes referred to as poorhouses, were used to house individuals who committed minor law violations. These facilities were designed to be places for training and caring for the poor, although they evolved into penal institutions (Allen et al., 2013).

John Howard's Reforms and the Penitentiary Act of 1779

Early jail conditions were poor. Among the more significant early jail reformers was John Howard, who was a sheriff in England. Howard had been imprisoned by the French and later paroled to England, and he recognized the horrendous jail conditions and deplorable conditions on prison hulks, in particular.

John Howard sought to improve jails and various other correctional practices. He published a book in 1777, *The State of Prisons in England and Wales*, which drew attention to the harms associated with incarceration. His work was based on his travels throughout Europe, during which he sought alternatives to the English jail model. He introduced the term **penitentiary**, which refers to institutions that emphasize offenders doing penance and reflecting on their behaviors, as opposed to places

---

Code of Hammurabi The first known legal code; it identified crimes, noted punishments for criminal behavior, and provided settlements for common conflicts

lex talionis a latin term that means "an eye for an eye"; it is the law of retaliation, or punishment that corresponds with the harms caused

1 Criminal Act

transportation Removing individuals from communities; it began in England and was used in the 17th and 18th centuries to send undesirables to the American colonies

10 Corrections

prison hulks Old merchant and naval ships that were essentially floating prisons

gaols Early English jails that were used for detaining defendants or those awaiting their punishment

fee system A system that enabled those with the financial means to pay to avoid serving jail time

workhouses Sometimes referred to as poorhouses, they were used as houses of correction for individuals who committed minor law violations

where inmates were brutally punished for their behaviors. England soon passed the **Penitentiary Act of 1779**, which, among other reform-oriented contributions, required English prisons and jails to:

- become secure and sanitary structures,
- undergo systematic inspections,
- abolish fees charged to inmates, and
- reform inmates in solitary cells after they worked in common areas during the day (Seiter, 2014).

Howard's work was also influential in removing insane inmates from British prisons and separating women and children from men (Roth, 2005).

Corrections During the Colonial Period (1607–1776)

Colonial America was largely rural, and the clergy and wealthy primarily maintained social control (Clear et al., 2016). Responses to crime in the colonies were largely based on English criminal codes and involved the Puritans' association of crime with sin. Colonists seldom used institutions for confinement, instead choosing fines, death, and other punishments, some of which would be illegal by early 21st-century standards, to sanction criminal behavior (Rothman, 1995).

Pillories and Stocks

During the colonial period, corporal and capital punishment were used for many offenses and often to serve as a deterrent. **Corporal punishment** involves physically harming offenders as punishment for their actions. Stocks and pillories were perhaps the most commonly used forms of corporal punishment in the colonies (Oliver & Hilgenberg, 2006). **Pillories** were wooden frames with holes for offenders' hands and head, and they were used to ridicule and restrain offenders. **Stocks** were similar to pillories, although they permitted offenders to sit while undergoing punishment. Citizens who passed by would ridicule and throw objects at the offenders, which added to the punishment (Seiter, 2014).

Jails

Colonists used jails modeled after English gaols. Jail conditions in the colonies were deplorable. They were often unsanitary, lacked food, and housed women, children, and men all together (Seiter, 2014). The Massachusetts Bay Colony built its first prison in 1836 in Boston, and numerous jails were built as the population expanded. By the time of the American Revolution, each of the 12 counties in Massachusetts was required to have its own jail (Roth, 2005).

The Quakers and Correctional Reform

William Penn was the chief proprietor (or governor) of Pennsylvania from 1681 until 1712, when he became ill and his wife assumed the role. Penn was a major prison reformer whose influence was noted prior to the American Revolution. He was also a Quaker. The

penitentiary Institutions that emphasize offenders doing penance and reflecting on their behaviors

Penitentiary Act of 1779 An act that reformed English prisons and jails, such that they became more secure and sanitary and subject to systematic inspections; the act also abolished fees charged to inmates

● **Learning Objective 28.2:** Summarize the developments in corrections during colonial times in the United States.

10
Corrections

corporal punishment Physically harming offenders as punishment for their actions; it was also designed to deter the offender and others

Capital and corporal punishment were used relatively commonly in colonial America. The punishments were imposed in open spaces to punish and shame offenders and serve as a deterrent for others.

Do you believe public shaming would be effective in the United States in the early 21st century?

pillories Wooden frames with holes for offenders' hands and feet that were used to punish, ridicule, and restrain offenders

stocks Structures that were similar to pillories, although they permitted offenders to sit while undergoing punishment and ridicule

Quakers had suffered religious persecution in their home country (England), and many came to America in search of freedom to choose their way of life (Seiter, 2014). They had largely settled in Pennsylvania and recognized the inhumane and inefficient application of the criminal codes. Under the governance of Penn, the Quakers established a system of justice that included the following (American Correctional Association, 1983):

- abolition of capital punishment except for the crime of homicide
- replacement of bloody corporal punishment with imprisonment and hard labor
- provision of free food and lodging to prisoners
- replacement of stocks and pillories with detention houses

● **Learning Objective 28.3:** Explain the significance of the contributions of Dr. Benjamin Rush and the Pennsylvania and Auburn prison systems.

Corrections Following the American Revolution (1777–1865)

Correctional practices lacked many standards and a sense of professionalism in colonial America. For example, jailers during the 18th century often supplemented their incomes through selling alcohol to inmates, and wealthier inmates paid for comfort and temporary leaves from incarceration. Correctional practices underwent many changes following the American Revolution, as the new country gained freedom from English control and increasingly structured its correctional systems and practices in the manner the citizens viewed as most appropriate.

The Contributions of Dr. Benjamin Rush

Dr. Benjamin Rush became leader of the Philadelphia Society for Alleviating the Miseries of Public Prisons in the late 1700s and revived the Quaker code, which had been repealed when William Penn died in 1718. Rush proposed the following:

10
Corrections

- classifying inmates for housing by separating females from males, and with consideration of the seriousness of the offense
- a system of labor that would contribute to institutions being self-supporting
- incorporation of gardens for producing prison food
- outdoor exercise for inmates
- indeterminate periods of incarceration for prisoners, which meant that inmates were released when prison officials believed they were ready to reenter society
- individualized treatment based on the types of crimes committed (Roth, 2005)

Rush's efforts contributed much toward the reform of correctional practices, and many of his ideas are still evident in early 21st-century prisons.

The Walnut Street Jail Becomes the First Prison

10
Corrections

The Philadelphia Society created the first prison in the United States in 1790 when a wing of the Walnut Street Jail (which had been created in 1776 as the first jail in America) was converted into a space for housing convicted offenders in lieu of corporal punishment. In accord with John Howard's idea of the penitentiary, the Walnut Street Jail emphasized hard work and penance in response to criminal behavior (Seiter, 2014). Inmates at the jail were not permitted to converse with one another, and efforts were made to restrict interaction among inmates out of concern that they would encounter each other after release (Seiter, 2014).

The Walnut Street Jail, including the prison wing, closed in 1835 for a number of reasons, including a riot involving over 200 inmates in 1820 that signified the troubles found in the jail (Teeters, 1955). However, it served as the model for design and operation of the first two prisons opened in Philadelphia: the Western State Penitentiary (opened in 1826) and the Eastern State Penitentiary (1829).

The Pennsylvania and Auburn Systems of Incarceration

The emphasis that the Walnut Street Jail and other penitentiaries in the area placed on inmates being separate and silent was characteristic of what became known as the **Pennsylvania system**, which stressed reformation and the prevention of interaction among inmates out of concern that they would learn criminal behaviors from one another (Seiter, 2014). The Pennsylvania system was popular, although it faced several challenges, including:

- difficulty in preventing inmates from interacting with one another,
- high costs of operation,
- inmates being unproductive, and
- critiques that solitary confinement was detrimental to inmates' psychological health.

In response to these challenges and critiques, modifications were made to prison facilities around the United States. One of the more influential early prison approaches implementing these modifications was the **Auburn system**, which emerged in New York State in 1817. The Auburn system separated inmates at night, although it permitted them to congregate during the day because inmates provided labor that offset some of the prison costs. The Auburn system provided a model for prisons throughout the United States, primarily because of the lower costs and less harmful psychological effects on inmates compared to the Pennsylvania system (Seiter, 2014).

Origins of Parole

Prison overcrowding was an increasing concern in the United States by the late 1860s, and additional prisons were built in response. There was also a shift in thinking that emphasized prisoner reform, for instance in the form of education, vocational training, and early release for good behavior and self-improvement. Prison officials looked outside the United States for guidance in efforts to become less punitive and more reform oriented (Roth, 2005).

Prison reformers took notice of the efforts of Captain Alexander Maconochie, who was instrumental in reforming the Australian prison system, and Sir Walter Crofton, who heavily influenced the Irish penal system in making it more humane and also more likely to provide inmates with better chances for success upon release compared to earlier approaches (Seiter, 2014). Referred to as the **Irish system**, Maconochie and Crofton introduced the ideas of indeterminate sentencing (see Module 25), which involves providing a less restrictive environment, preparing inmates for release, and then releasing inmates on a conditional basis.

Maconochie promoted a **mark system** in which inmates earned credits for good behavior and work or lost them for bad behavior. Upon earning enough marks, prisoners received a **ticket of leave**, which was a conditional pardon as they were released to the community. The system provided the roots for parole.

As director of the Irish prison system, Crofton incorporated many of Maconochie's ideas and created a four-stage process that resulted in an inmate's return to the community. The system involved:

- solitary confinement for roughly 9 months;
- special prison, in which inmates worked with other inmates and took classes;

Pennsylvania system An approach to prisons that stressed reformation and the prevention of interaction among inmates out of concern that they would learn criminal behaviors from one another

Auburn system An approach to prisons that separated inmates at night, yet permitted them to congregate during the day

10
Corrections

9 Sentencing

Irish system An approach to prisons that involved the use of indeterminate sentencing, emphasizing the preparation of inmates for release, providing a less restrictive environment, and releasing inmates on a conditional basis

---

CAREERS

Parole officers are responsible for the legal custody of offenders after they are released from incarceration. They ensure that ex-prisoners abide by the conditions of their parole and help them reintegrate into society. They also investigate parole violations.

- a transitional stage, in which inmates must provide evidence of being reformed; and
- a ticket of leave, which was conditional release—parole as it is currently recognized (Seiter, 2014).

These developments became ingrained to various degrees in correctional practices in the United States. In 1836, Tennessee became the first state to implement a good time reduction of prison sentences. By 1900, over half of the states had some form of parole or independent sentencing option (Roth, 2005).

mark system The system by which inmates could earn credits through good behavior and work that permitted them to be released early from their sentences

Origins of Probation

Probation, the oldest form of community corrections in the United States, appeared in 1841 when shoemaker John Augustus provided bail for a man charged with public drunkenness (Roth, 2005). Augustus had become concerned about individuals having to spend time in the harsh conditions in jails and persuaded the court to release the man into his custody. Augustus soon helped roughly 1,800 other offenders in the same manner and became the country's first probation officer. In 1878, Massachusetts passed the first probation law for juveniles, and New York passed the first statute authorizing probation for adults in 1901. Other states soon followed.

ticket of leave A document of release from institutionalization that was received by inmates upon earning enough marks; it was part of the Irish system

● **Learning Objective 28.4:** Describe the developments in corrections in the United States following the Civil War.

10
Corrections

Corrections Following the Civil War (1866–1899)

The United States experienced a civil war that was fought from 1861 to 1865. Few developments in corrections occurred during the time of battle. However, following the war, notable regional differences emerged among the states with regard to correctional practices. By the end of the 19th century, most cities across the United States had jails that were primarily controlled by sheriffs (Schmalleger & Smykla, 2009).

Zebulon Brockway and the First Reformatory

The **American Correctional Association** is the oldest and largest international correctional association in the world and has supported the professional development of corrections since 1870. A precursor to the American Correctional Association, the National Prison Association, met in 1870 and adopted the principles of the Irish system, which emphasized inmate rehabilitation and preparing inmates for return to society as opposed to focusing on punishment of inmates. The emphasis in prisons was on education, reformation, and vocational training (Seiter, 2014).

The first reformatory in the United States, the Elmira Reformatory, was constructed in Elmira, New York, and opened in 1876. It housed inmates ranging from ages 16 to 30 who were serving their first prison term. Zebulon Brockway, a former director of the Detroit House of Correction, became an influential administrator at the institution. The reformatory:

- used indeterminate sentences with fixed minimum terms,
- allowed for the early release of inmates on parole,
- emphasized reforming inmates,
- provided greater vocational training, and
- offered increased opportunities for education.

American Correctional Association The oldest and largest international correctional association in the world; it has supported the professional development of corrections since 1870

Corrections in the South: Black Codes and the Lease System

The history of corrections in the southern and western portions of the United States is often overlooked, although many significant developments occurred in these areas. For example, **Black Codes** passed in Southern states were created to control newly freed slaves, making offenders subject to harsh punishments. The codes were created to nullify the rights granted to slaves following passage of the 13th Amendment in 1865. Among other prohibitions, Black Codes, which included **vagrancy laws**, restricted newly freed slaves from:

- intermarrying with Whites,
- renting land in urban areas,
- assuming an occupation other than servant or farmer unless they paid a tax,
- being unemployed,
- preaching the gospel without a license, and
- lacking a permanent residence (McNamara & Burns, 2020).

The punishments for Blacks who violated the codes were notably severe. For instance, the penalty for intermarriage in Mississippi was life in prison (Oshinsky, 1996).

Many Southern states were recovering from the effects of the Civil War and were not economically capable of building prisons. Instead, they created a **lease system** in which inmates were leased by the state to contractors who fed and clothed inmates in return for their labor, which often came in the form of building railroads, mining, and working on farms. Southern states used prisoners as field laborers, who provided

Black Codes Laws passed in Southern states designed to control newly freed slaves, making offenders subject to harsh punishments

vagrancy laws Laws that were central to the Black Codes; they were used to punish Blacks who were unemployed and had no residence

lease system The practice of states leasing inmates to contractors who fed and clothed inmates in return for their labor

Inmate labor, including labor provided through the use of the lease system, helped many Southern states in the absence of slave labor. Southern states leased inmates to contractors who paid the state for the inmate services.

What are some of the consequences of states leasing inmates to private businesses?

prison farms
Correctional facilities where inmates perform some type of manual labor that provides economic benefit for the prison

assistance in the absence of slave labor. The large majority of the convicts leased were African American males (Litwack, 1999). **Prison farms**, which are correctional facilities where inmates perform some type of manual labor (e.g., farming, logging) that provides economic benefit for the prison, were created in many Southern areas and remain a part of correctional practices in some places (Clear et al., 2016).

The leasing of inmates concluded largely as a result of humanitarian concerns and reduced profits. By the end of the 19th century, states began realizing that other types of labor systems were more beneficial than leasing (Alarid & Reichel, 2013). Abusive living and working conditions for inmates leased to private companies and the fact that using inmate labor took jobs from law-abiding citizens contributed to the demise of the leasing system. Southern prisons responded by creating prison plantations, or farms on which inmates could work and provide food for the prison (Oliver & Hilgenberg, 2006).

The First Female Prisons

Although some institutions housed females in separated sections, female prisoners were located in institutions designed for males until the early 19th century (see Module 33 for a discussion of the special needs of female inmates). In response to claims by female reformers that female inmates should be treated different from males, women's facilities began to open (Alarid & Reichel, 2013).

Beginning in the 20th century, females were incarcerated exclusively in female prisons, which were less threatening and smaller than male prisons. The relatively small number of female inmates compared to males resulted in fewer facilities for female inmates (Adler et al., 2012). Following are some key dates related to the introduction of female prisons:

- 1835—Mount Pleasant, New York, Female Prison is attached to Sing Sing, a male prison
- 1873—Women's Prison opens in Indiana
- 1877—Reformatory Prison for Women opens in Massachusetts

Early correctional facilities for female offenders differed from male prisons largely in the sense that there was more of an emphasis on reform in female prisons. The facilities were often titled "reformatories" and emphasized education and preparation for return to society. The design of female facilities often differed from male prisons, because female inmates were often housed in small, cottage-like facilities that had kitchens, living rooms, and sometimes nurseries for prisoners with children. The design was used to help train females for their domestic role as mother and caregiver and to provide vocational training with regard to sewing, cooking, and cleaning (Feinman, 1983).

Federal Corrections

Prisoners convicted of federal offenses prior to the late 19th century were housed in state prisons and local jails, depending on the length of their stay. The prisons were given housing fees by the federal government, and federal inmates in some states were part of the leasing system. By 1887, Congress was uncomfortable with the leasing system and no longer permitted the contracting of inmates.

Three Penitentiary Act Legislation that authorized the construction of three penitentiaries to house federal offenders

In 1891, Congress passed the **Three Penitentiary Act**, which authorized the construction of three penitentiaries to house federal offenders. The first was built in Leavenworth, Kansas, followed by the construction of facilities in Washington and Georgia. Poor record keeping, the increased number of facilities, and overcrowding in the federal prison system over time contributed to the need for an agency to provide oversight and accountability of the federal prisons. Accordingly, the Federal Bureau of Prisons was created in 1929 (Roth, 2005; Seiter, 2014). The bureau is still in operation in the early 21st century and remains responsible for housing and managing federal prisons.

Corrections in the United States in the 20th and 21st Centuries (1900–Present)

Increased imprisonment throughout the United States during the early decades of the 20th century resulted in a shift in approach within prisons. The number of inmates in U.S. prisons increased by over 170% during the first 3 decades (Cahalan, 1986), which created a substantial burden for prison administrators (Seiter, 2014). A record number of individuals, roughly 6.5 million, were under correctional supervision at the close of the 20th century, and the United States had the highest incarceration rate of any country in the world by the beginning of the 21st century. The emphasis on incarceration has shown signs of slowing in recent years, however, largely in response to budgetary concerns and greater use of alternatives to incarceration.

War, Capital Punishment, the Great Depression, and Inmate Labor: 1920s Through 1940s

During the period from the 1920s to the 1940s, the United States experienced two major events: the Great Depression and World War II. These events impacted corrections in the country in many ways; for instance, inmates donated blood for the soldiers and were required to register for the draft. Many inmates who were eligible to enlist in the military did so. As many men went off to fight the war, including some prisoners, the number of prisoners declined from roughly 190,000 in 1940 to about 120,000 in 1943 (Christianson, 1998; Roth, 2005).

Increasing crime in the 1920s contributed to a shift in thinking about capital punishment and correctional practices in general. The **abolition movement**, which promoted the abolition of capital punishment, was becoming less powerful, and the number of executions began to climb during this time (Death Penalty Information Center, 2014). Over 5,000 offenders were executed between 1918 and 1959, as crime and public support for the death penalty increased. The first Gallup poll, administered in 1937, noted that the vast majority of Americans supported capital punishment (Roth, 2005).

The Great Depression (1929–1933) resulted in economic problems throughout the United States and an increased prison population. The development of **"big house" prisons**, or institutions that hold over 2,500 inmates, emerged during the late 1920s to accommodate these increases (Roth, 2005).

The perception that prisoners should be more productive, particularly from an economic standpoint, contributed to inmates working to offset the costs of incarceration. While the use of inmate labor to produce goods became increasingly popular, private industry, which sold competing goods and materials, suffered as a result. The effects of the Depression compounded these problems. In response, the U.S. government passed the **Hawes–Cooper Act of 1929** and the **Ashurst–Sumners Act** (1935 and later amended in 1940), which limited the sale of inmate-produced goods on the open market (Seiter, 2014).

Restrictions limiting inmate industry meant that many prisons designed to provide goods and materials were underutilized, and the influx of new immigrants, the Great Depression, and the increased amount of crime in the 1920s and 1930s weakened support for inmate rehabilitation (Allen et al., 2013).

● **Learning Objective 28.5:** Trace the development of corrections beginning in the 20th century until today.

10 Corrections

10 Corrections

abolition movement A movement in the 1920s that promoted the abolition of capital punishment

"big house" prisons Institutions that hold over 2,500 inmates

Hawes–Cooper Act of 1929 and the Ashurst–Sumners Act Legislation that limited the sale of inmate-produced goods on the open market

10
Corrections

"Curing" Offenders: 1930s Through 1960s

Beginning in the 1930s, reformers believed that criminal behavior was pathological and inmates could be medically "cured" of their assumed illnesses. They proposed that corrections officials should seek to examine, diagnose, and treat offenders, after which professionals could identify and respond to the primary causes of their behavior (Abadinsky, 2015). Accordingly, various types of treatment and rehabilitative programs for inmates were implemented during the 1950s and 1960s. Economic prosperity and declining crime rates in the 1950s generated optimism with regard to prisoner rehabilitation (Roth, 2005). Offenders were perceived to be "curable" through correctional programming, and prisoner reintegration became increasingly important. Helping inmates make successful life adjustments upon leaving institutions was emphasized, and community corrections became increasingly popular, particularly in the form of probation, halfway houses, and parole (see Module 31 for further discussion of probation and parole and Modules 31 and 34 for elaboration on halfway houses).

Increased Accountability in Prisons: 1960s Through 1970s

Until the 1960s, prisons were generally permitted to operate absent judicial interference primarily as a result of: (a) the U.S. Constitution's concern for the separation of powers, which would mean that the judicial branch of government should not interfere with the operations of prisons run by the executive branch, and (b) the belief that judges should let correctional experts operate and administer prisons (F. Cole, 1987). This lack of accountability, or **"hands-off" doctrine**, abruptly changed with the U.S. Supreme Court's decision in *Cooper v. Pate* (1964), which largely influenced the accountability and oversight of prisons. The decision:

"hands-off" doctrine The practice of permitting prisons to operate absent judicial interference

- permitted greater judicial intervention in the operations of prisons,
- gave inmates greater access to the courts, and
- led to an increase in the number of inmate-filed claims of inhumane punishment.

As a result of this and other decisions, prisoners increasingly received their due process rights in the 1960s and 1970s. For example, a federal district court judge ruled in *Holt v. Sarver* (1970) that the entire Arkansas prison system was inhumane and violated the Eighth Amendment protection from cruel and unusual punishment. The judge issued guidelines for administrators to correct the problems. This case, among others, signified the need for judicial intervention and seemingly ended the hands-off doctrine.

Questioning Rehabilitation: 1970s Through 1980s

10
Corrections

The emphasis on rehabilitation during the 1960s and 1970s was challenged by several scholars, particularly by Robert Martinson (1974), who reviewed 231 studies to determine which rehabilitation programs worked in corrections. Martinson found that very few treatment programs were correlated with reductions in recidivism (reoffending). Some scholars (e.g., Palmer, 1975) criticized Martinson's work by noting that many treatment programs did work, and Martinson (1979) later recanted his "nothing works" position. However, public officials had already taken notice of Martinson's initial findings.

Increased crime, especially violent crime, in the 1980s and the proposed limitations of the rehabilitative approach to corrections generated a shift in correctional focus. The public and government officials became more supportive of a punitive approach. Accordingly, funding for rehabilitation decreased, and parole was eliminated in several states (Seiter, 2014).

Getting Tough on Criminals: 1980s Through 1990s

The correctional population grew substantially beginning in the 1980s. For instance, federal prisons underwent substantial growth beginning in the 1980s following passage of the **Sentencing Reform Act of 1984**, which:

- created determinate sentencing,
- abolished parole, and
- reduced opportunities to earn time for good behavior in prison to a maximum reduction of 15% per year.

Correctional practices at both the state and the federal levels beginning in the 1980s sought to hold offenders more accountable for their actions. Offenders received longer sentences, and the focus was on incapacitation rather than rehabilitation. Mass incarceration occurred based on the belief that deterrence, incapacitation, and retribution were the best approaches to address criminal behavior.

Several mandatory minimum sentencing provisions (see Module 25 for discussion of mandatory and other types of sentencing) were enacted, all of which contributed to the federal inmate population expanding from approximately 24,000 to almost 58,000 from 1980 to 1989. The U.S. prison population in general doubled between 1970 and 1980 and doubled once again between 1981 and 1995 (Roth, 2005). Concerns for illegal drugs and illegal immigration resulted in the inmate population reaching roughly 136,000 by the end of 1999 (Federal Bureau of Prisons, 2020a). All told, between 1980 and 2009, there was a 500% increase in prison populations fueled by various factors, including:

- increased fear of crime,
- politicians' emphasis on a "get tough" approach on crime,
- the war on drugs,
- rising crime rates in the 1980s and early 1990s,
- more conservative public values, and
- disenchantment with correctional practices (Allen et al., 2013).

Using Private Prisons and Intermediate Sanctions: 1980s Through 1990s

The increased costs associated with incarcerating a large number of offenders at both the state and the federal levels contributed to government officials eventually

9 Sentencing

Sentencing Reform Act of 1984 Legislation that created determinate sentencing, abolished parole, and reduced opportunities for earning time for good behavior

---

MYTHBUSTING

Rehabilitation Doesn't Work

The "get tough" on crime approach adopted beginning in the 1980s was spurred by beliefs that rehabilitation efforts were ineffective. However, much research suggests that inmates are susceptible to treatment, and correcting the wayward behaviors of some individuals is more cost-effective and preferred over warehousing inmates in prisons for lengthy periods (e.g., Ross, 2012).

With regard to public attitudes toward our justice systems, in 2016 Americans were 7 times more likely to say that our systems were "too tough" than they were in 1992 (J. McCarthy, 2016). Changes in attitudes toward justice coupled with positive results regarding rehabilitation could lead to a dynamic shift in corrections in the near future.

The correctional population began to increase steadily beginning in the 1980s. Governments at all levels were impacted, as additional funding was required to provide correctional services.

Do you believe getting tough on offenders through incarceration is an effective use of taxpayer money? Why or why not?

seeking alternatives. The privatization of prisons was among the proposed means to ease the government's financial burden of warehousing prisoners. The use of private prisons (see Module 32) increased by 500% between 1985 and 1995, and at least 30 states were contracting out prison labor to private companies by the mid-1990s (Roth, 2005). Intermediate sanctions, such as house arrest/electronic monitoring, intensive supervision probation, and boot camps, were introduced during this time and became increasingly popular as well. Module 31 addresses intermediate sanctions.

Decreasing Correctional Supervision: The Early Part of the 21st Century

At year-end 2019, the United States had roughly 1,430,805 inmates in state and federal prisons. This represents a decrease of about 33,500 prisoners from 2018 and a decrease of 11.4% from 2009, when the U.S. prison population peaked at 1,615,487. The imprisonment rate in 2019 was the lowest since 1995, with 419 prisoners per 100,000 U.S. residents (Carson, 2020a). Further, the correctional population in general decreased for the 11th consecutive year, and there were just over 6.4 million persons under the supervision of U.S. adult correctional systems in 2018 (Maruschak & Minton, 2020). Correctional populations have also decreased in light of many states releasing inmates early out of concerns for the spread of COVID-19 (Prison Policy Initiative, 2020).

After three decades of consistent prison building and tougher laws, states began to restrict their spending on corrections, in part because of budget deficits and other economic concerns. Regardless, there remain a large number of individuals under correctional supervision. As noted in Table 28.1, roughly 1 in every 40 U.S. adult residents were under correctional supervision in 2018 (Maruschak & Minton, 2020).

Correctional Reform: 2018 and Beyond

Several signs point to continued correctional reform in the years ahead. The aforementioned decreases in the adult correctional population suggest that we may be relying less on formal punishments to address crime, as do the reform efforts evident in our juvenile justice systems (see Module 26). The most obvious examples of correctional reform are found in legislation and actions taken by the federal government and several states. The First Step Act (see Module 25) was deemed the most significant correctional reform bill in over a decade and is expected to reduce the sentences of roughly 9,000 federal inmates. The bill also reduced mandatory sentences for drug crimes and provided millions of dollars for prison programming (George, 2018).

Perhaps most important for correctional reform, the widespread support for the legislation from both Republicans and Democrats suggested that this may be the first of several laws designed to enhance correctional practices. This act by Congress signified that the federal government is willing to focus on correctional reform in much the same manner as several states have in recent years. Some traditionally "tough on crime states" such as Texas, Georgia, and Louisiana have made efforts to reduce prison crowding and provide more options for rehabilitation (George, 2018).

TABLE 28.1. Rate of Persons Supervised by U.S. Adult Correctional Systems

| YEAR | TOTAL CORRECTIONAL POPULATION[a] | | COMMUNITY-SUPERVISION POPULATION | INCARCERATED POPULATION[b] | |
	ADULTS SUPERVISED PER 100,000 U.S. ADULT RESIDENTS[c]	U.S. ADULT RESIDENTS UNDER CORRECTIONAL SUPERVISION	ADULTS ON PROBATION/PAROLE PER 100,000 U.S. RESIDENTS OF ALL AGES[c]	ADULTS IN PRISON/LOCAL JAIL PER 100,000 U.S. ADULT RESIDENTS[d]	ADULTS IN PRISON/LOCAL JAIL PER 100,000 U.S. RESIDENTS OF ALL AGES[c]
2008	3160	1 in 32	1,670	1,000	760
2009	3100	1 in 32	1,630	980	750
2010	3000	1 in 33	1,570	960	730
2011	2930	1 in 34	1,540	940	720
2012	2880	1 in 35	1,520	920	710
2013	2830	1 in 35	1,490	910	700
2014	2780	1 in 36	1,470	900	690
2015	2710	1 in 37	1,440	870	680
2016	2640	1 in 38	1,400	860	670
2017	2590	1 in 39	1,380	850	660
2018	2510	1 in 40	1,340	830	650

Note. Rates are estimated to the nearest 10. Rates include a small number of persons age 17 or younger who were under adult correctional supervision.
Source: Annual Probation Survey, Annual Parole Survey, Annual Survey of Jails, and National Prisoner Statistics program, 2008–2018, *by the Bureau of Justice Statistics; U.S. Census Bureau, postcensal estimated resident populations for January 1 of each year, 2009–2019; and* Correctional Populations in the United States, 2017–2018 *(NCJ 252157), by L. M. Maruschak and T. D. Minton, 2020, U.S. Department of Justice, Bureau of Justice Statistics.*

[a]*Offenders who were supervised in the community by probation or parole agencies, were under the jurisdiction of state or federal prisons, or were in the custody of local jails.*
[b]*Offenders who were under the jurisdiction of state or federal prisons or were held in local jails.*
[c]*Rates were calculated using U.S. Census Bureau estimates of the U.S. resident population of persons of all ages for January 1 of the following year.*
[d]*Rates were calculated using U.S. Census Bureau estimates of the U.S. resident population of persons age 18 or older for January 1 of the following year.*

The System in Perspective

As discussed in the "In the News" feature at the start of this module, the prison riot, a prison officer death, prison officers injuries, and the departure of over 100 prison officers who quit or retired in Delaware highlight the continuous challenges faced by prisons and those who work in them. Budget cuts, an increasing correctional population, and changing public values have all provided obstacles to the successful functioning of correctional institutions throughout history. Despite these and related challenges, the goals of all correctional systems have and will continue to center around punishing offenders, discouraging them from committing additional crimes, removing dangerous persons from society, and addressing whatever issues encouraged them to become involved in crime.

Summary

1. Learning Objective 28.1: *Identify the early European correctional practices.*

- The early European correctional practices were punitive by 21st-century standards and included killing, imprisonment, corporal punishment, public shaming, torture, branding, mutilation, banishment, and transportation.

2. Learning Objective 28.2: *Summarize the developments in corrections during colonial times in the United States.*

- The developments in corrections during colonial times in the United States were largely influenced by English practices and Puritanism. Corporal and capital punishment and the stocks and pillories were primary among the correctional practices. Jails were used for detaining defendants or for those awaiting their punishment. The Massachusetts Bay Colony built its first prison in 1836 in Boston and others followed. Correctional practices lacked many standards and a sense of professionalism.

3. Learning Objective 28.3: *Explain the significance of the contributions of Dr. Benjamin Rush and the Pennsylvania and Auburn prison systems.*

- Dr. Rush was instrumental in the classification of inmates, creating a system of labor that contributed to institutions being self-supporting, incorporating gardens for producing prison food, encouraging outdoor exercise for inmates, creating indeterminate periods of incarceration for prisoners, and providing individualized treatment based on the types of crimes committed. The Pennsylvania system stressed reformation and the prevention of interaction among inmates through separating inmates. The Auburn system separated inmates at night, although it permitted them to congregate during the day because inmates provided labor that offset some of the prison costs.

4. Learning Objective 28.4: *Describe the developments in corrections in the United States following the Civil War.*

- Several important developments in corrections occurred following the Civil War, including the passage of Black Codes in the South and the use of a lease system and penal farms. The first reformatory in the United States opened in 1876, and the introduction of distinct prisons or reformatories for women occurred in 1873.

5. Learning Objective 28.5: *Trace the development of corrections beginning in the 20th century until today.*

- The crime rate increased in the 1920s, which drew attention to correctional practices. During the 1920s and 1930s, the use of capital punishment increased, and the Great Depression contributed to increasing crime rates and a growing prison population. Beginning in the 1930s, prison reformers were influential in generating the belief that criminal behavior was pathological and inmates could be medically "cured" of their assumed illnesses. As a result, the 1960s and 1970s ushered in changes regarding many aspects of the criminal justice system, largely in response to the prisoner rights movement and Supreme Court decisions that began protecting due process rights. However, increased crime in the 1980s and the proposed limitations of the rehabilitative approach to corrections generated a shift in correctional focus toward holding offenders accountable for their actions, the increased use of incarceration, and the imposition of longer sentences. More recently, states have begun to restrict their spending on corrections, which has led to a growth in alternatives to traditional incarceration, including private prisons and intermediate sanctions. Several signs point to continued correctional reform, including the passage and support of the First Step Act.

Questions for Critical Thinking

1. What aspects of early European correctional practices do you see in modern-day correctional practices?

2. How are correctional practices in the early 21st century similar to those used during colonial times? In what ways have we progressed far beyond earlier practices?

3. Which prison system, the Pennsylvania prison system or the Auburn system, do you believe was most effective? Why?

4. What humanitarian concerns do you see with regard to the lease system?

5. Do you believe getting tough on offenders through the increased use of incarceration is the most effective approach to addressing crime problems? Why or why not?

Key Terms

abolition movement
American Correctional Association
Ashurst–Sumners Act
Auburn system
"big house" prisons
Black Codes
Code of Hammurabi
corporal punishment
fee system
gaols
"hands-off" doctrine
Hawes–Cooper Act of 1929
Irish system
lease system
lex talionis

mark system
penitentiary
Penitentiary Act of 1779
Pennsylvania system
pillories
prison farms
prison hulks
Sentencing Reform Act of 1984
stocks
Three Penitentiary Act
ticket of leave
transportation
vagrancy laws
workhouses

For digital learning resources, please go to
https://www.oup.com/he/burns1e

Module

29

Current Organization of Corrections

The many types of correctional services are administered at various levels of government with the goals to incarcerate, help, punish, and/or deter offenders.

What might be some of the benefits of centralizing corrections in the United States to include one national correctional agency that would oversee all types of correctional services? What might be some drawbacks?

Corrections in the United States is decentralized, meaning that there is no single correctional system. Instead, correctional systems exist at the federal, state, and local levels. The various types of correctional services are administered at different levels of government, and by the private sector in some cases, which results in many inconsistencies with regard to administration and organization among jurisdictions. In an effort to bring clarity to the confusion, this module begins with coverage of the organization of probation, followed by a discussion of how intermediate sanctions are organized and administered and the organization of institutional corrections in the form of jails and prisons. This module concludes with a look at the three models used to administer parole services.

O. J. Simpson on Parole

In October 2017, former professional football player and actor O. J. Simpson left a Nevada prison to begin life as a parolee. He had served 9 years for an armed robbery conviction in 2007. However, he is perhaps most well known for a 1995 criminal court trial in which he was found not guilty after being charged with the double murder of his ex-wife and her friend. In 2017, Simpson was released to the Nevada Division of Parole and Probation, with the conditions of his parole including abstinence from consuming alcohol in large amounts, associating with convicted felons and those who engage in criminal activity, and possessing firearms and drugs (Vercammen & Karimi, 2017).

Upon Mr. Simpson's release, it was speculated that he would seek a move to Florida, where two of his children resided. Relocation for parolees is a bit more difficult than it is for others, because there must be agreement among the involved jurisdictions or states to transfer the supervision. After hearing of Simpson's initial interest in possibly relocating to her state (he later decided to not relocate to Florida), Florida's attorney general wrote a letter to the Florida Department of Corrections stating that she did not want to allow him to relocate

there; she noted that Mr. Simpson would burden local law enforcement and might risk the safety of Floridians (Rossman, 2017). Such relocations are not guaranteed, but instead are considered a privilege for the parolee (Vercammen & Karimi, 2017). Should parolees be permitted to relocate

1 Criminal Act

as they choose, or should they be restricted to staying in the jurisdiction in which they served prison time?

10 Corrections

Probation

Probation typically involves a sentence of incarceration that is suspended with the offender's agreement to meet specific conditions while being supervised in the community. Failure to meet the specified conditions may result in probation being revoked and the offender serving the original sentence. Probation is primarily used for:

● enabling offenders to remain in and reintegrate into the community,

● helping offenders avoid the stigmatization and effects of institutionalization,

● saving governments money because it is less expensive than incarceration,

● **Learning Objective 29.1:** Summarize the arguments for the centralized and decentralized administration of probation.

- offering offenders another option when institutionalization is not the appropriate sanction, and

- providing offenders with an opportunity to remain in the community where they may be more likely to get treatment and related services.

The Administration of Probation Services

10
Corrections

Probation originated in the courts and became units of the judicial branches of city and county governments. Although probation is administered at the local, state, and federal levels of government in the United States, most probation departments are located in county governments. The large number of counties in the United States results in a wide array of organizational structures among probation agencies. Figure 29.1 depicts the organization chart of probation services in Alameda County, California. At the top of the organizational chart is the chief probation officer, under which there is an assistant chief probation officer and several divisions: Adult Services, Juvenile Services, Juvenile Facilities, and Administrative Services.

The recent trend has been toward moving probation out of the judiciary because some believe the judiciary is not well prepared to manage human service operations (Clear et al., 2016) and that budgeting is better coordinated in the executive branch (Whitehead et al., 2013). However, there are also strong arguments for keeping probation in the courts so that judges can more closely monitor the progress of probationers and note more promptly any failures by probationers to

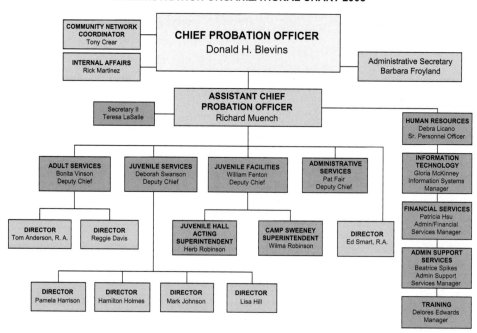

FIGURE 29.1. The Organization of Probation Services in Alameda County, California. This figure provides an example of how probation services are offered at the county level. As noted, a chief probation officer oversees various areas, including Adult Services, Juvenile Services, Juvenile Facilities, and Administrative Services.

In which of these areas would you most prefer to work? Why?

comply with conditions. Adult probation is located in the executive branch of state government in about three quarters of states, where it is combined with parole (Abadinski, 2015).

Probation is administered in six ways, as noted by author Howard Abadinsky, in his book *Probation and Parole* (Abadinsky, 2015):

- *juvenile*: distinct probation services for juveniles, which are administered on a municipal or county level or on a state-wide basis
- *municipal*: independent probation units administered by the lower courts of the municipality
- *county*: a county operating its own probation agency under state laws and guidelines
- *state*: one agency administering a central system of probation and providing probation services throughout the state
- *state combined*: a state agency in the executive branch (e.g., a department of corrections) administering combined probation and parole services
- *nationally*: federal probation officers, as part of the courts, supervising parolees

The system used to administer probation depends on the jurisdiction of the offenders—for example, juvenile offenders will be supervised by a juvenile probation agency and federal offenders will be monitored by federal probation officers—or the type of approach adopted by the respective states. For example, probation may be administered at the municipal, county, or state levels.

Debate Over Centralization Versus Decentralization

There is debate regarding whether the administration of probation should be centralized or decentralized. In the early 21st century, probation services are highly decentralized, with over 2,000 different agencies supervising the roughly 4 million probationers in the United States (Abadinski, 2015). Supporters for decentralizing probation services argue that cities or counties, more than their counterparts in centralized systems, can better:

10
Corrections

- administer probation services,
- respond to specific issues involving the community,
- employ more flexible policies, and
- make use of community resources (Clear et al., 2016).

Supporters for centralizing probation services argue that a single, statewide probation agency, more than local probation authorities, can:

- offer more professionalism and use the most updated and best practices,
- provide broader programs that promote consistency and uniformity of policies and service across areas, and
- train their personnel to assume a variety of roles (Clear et al., 2016).

Ultimately, each state must consider the strengths and weakness and determine which structure works best for them. States that have experience and success in providing human services via one state-level agency may opt for a centralized approach, while states that have successfully provided such services at smaller levels of government may opt for a decentralized approach. Module 31 provides further discussion of probation.

● **Learning Objective 29.2:** Describe the intermediate sanctions administered by the judiciary, probation agencies, and correctional departments.

10
Corrections

Intermediate Sanctions

Intermediate sanctions provide sentencing options that are more severe than probation, yet less severe and less costly than incarceration. Examples include house arrest, electronic monitoring, and day reporting centers. Offenders selected for intermediate sanctions are generally low risk and nonviolent.

There is some debate regarding who should administer intermediate sanctions. Some argue that officials from prisons, jails, probation, and parole should administer the sanctions because they have the staff, experience, and knowledge to create programs to meet offender needs. Others argue that new public and private agencies should be created to administer intermediate sanctions, because the traditional agencies have their hands full with administering their services (Clear et al., 2016).

Intermediate sanctions are organized according to the agencies that administer the sanctions (Clear et al., 2016). Module 31 provides more in-depth coverage of specific types of intermediate sanctions, but what follows is a brief overview of the types of intermediate sanctions administered by the judiciary, probation agencies, and correctional departments.

Administration by the Judiciary

The introduction and increased popularity of intermediate sanctions largely resulted from judges who were dissatisfied with their sentencing options and interested in using programs over which they would have greater levels of control. The intermediate sanctions administered by the judiciary include:

- *pretrial diversion*: redirecting offenders from formal processing with the expectation that they will meet specified requirements;
- *fines*: paying a sum of money to the government as punishment for offending;
- *community service*: providing unpaid labor as punishment for offending; and
- *restitution*: making amends for misbehavior and assuming responsibility for actions through repayment to victims in the form of money or services.

Administration by Probation Agencies

Intermediate sanctions administered by probation agencies primarily involve supervision in the community, including:

- *day reporting and treatment centers*: facilities that provide treatment and supervision to offenders residing in the community;
- *intensive supervision probation*: probation that involves closer and stricter supervision than regular probation;
- *home confinement*: restriction of offenders to the confines of their home; and
- *electronic monitoring*: an electronic device that tracks offenders' locations.

Boot camps are considered an intermediate sanction because they are less punitive and sometimes less costly than incarceration in prison or jail, yet more punitive than probation. They are administered by correctional departments.

Which agencies or departments do you believe should administer intermediate sanctions? Why?

Administration by Correctional Departments

Correctional departments are involved with the short-term institutionalization of offenders undergoing intermediate sanctions. The sanctions administered by correctional departments primarily include:

- *shock probation*: offenders are sentenced to incarceration but are released after a short period and placed on probation per the order of a judge; and

- *boot camps*: offenders undergo strict military-like discipline, including physical training, team skills development, and education.

Jails

Jails are full-service institutions that provide many of the same services as prisons, including security, medical care, and programming. Vocational and educational programs in jail are designed to manage inmates and prepare them for release (Schmalleger & Smykla, 2009). Jails are primarily operated by a county government, although counties that incorporate large metropolitan areas may collaborate with the city, and both levels of government may contribute to the budget and management of the jail. The Federal Bureau of Prisons operates jails at the federal level.

Jails differ from lockups, which are often found in police stations, typically only have a few cells, and hold individuals for a short while until they are transported to another facility. By contrast, jails house many different individuals, including:

- accused offenders who are unable to make bail or are not granted pretrial release;

- individuals awaiting arraignment, trial, conviction, or sentencing;

- violators of probation, parole, and bail or bond;

- federal and state inmates when prisons are overcrowded;

- some mentally ill persons who are awaiting transfer to mental health facilities;

- some juveniles who are awaiting transfer to another facility; and

- persons convicted of a misdemeanor who are sentenced to 1 year or less of incarceration.

Jails vary quite a bit in terms of size and inmate population:

- *Size*: Some rural facilities may hold only 3 or 4 inmates, while large municipal facilities may hold 20,000 inmates and employ thousands of correctional officers and staff. Jails admitted roughly 10.7 million arrestees in 2018, and an estimated 738,400 inmates were confined in city and county jails as of mid-year 2018. They employ roughly 221,600 full-time staff (about 80% of whom are correctional officers) to oversee them (Zeng, 2020).

- *Gender*: Most jails are authorized to house both male and female inmates; only about 13% were authorized to house men only, and about 1% housed only women (Stephan & Walsh, 2011). Males and females are separated within the jails that house both. Males have historically been overrepresented among jail inmates; for instance, they constituted roughly 84% of the jail inmate population in 2018 (Zeng, 2020).

Budgetary concerns are primary influences in the administration and organization of jails and have led to some local jails charging inmates housing fees and medical copays (Birzer & Craig-Moreland, 2006). Some states offer **pay-to-stay jails**, in which some offenders convicted of minor offenses can stay instead of serving their time in county jail. Pay-to-stay jails offer inmates some privileges not found in other

● Learning Objective 29.3: Identify the agencies responsible for operating jails.

10
Corrections

pay-to-stay jails An alternative approach to traditional jails; they allow some offenders convicted of minor offenses to serve their time in these facilities instead of county jail and offer inmates some privileges not found in other jails

jails, including access to a private cell, bathroom, and shower, as well as cell phones and other electronic devices. The benefits of these types of jails include cost savings and inmate safety, although they have been criticized for providing a different, more lenient form of punishment and justice for those who can afford it.

Jail Management

regional jails Two or more jail jurisdictions having a formal agreement to operate jails collectively

Jail management in rural areas is primarily the responsibility of sheriff's departments. **Regional jails**, in which two or more jail jurisdictions have a formal agreement to operate jails collectively, have become increasingly popular, because counties sometimes find it difficult to operate a jail on their own. These facilities are typically managed by a regional jail commission (Stephan & Walsh, 2011). The recent trend toward consolidation among jurisdictions and the use of regional jails resulted in a reduction in the number of jails.

Jail Accreditation

accreditation A system of accountability in which an oversight body assesses and evaluates agencies and organizations to ensure that they are competent, credible, and/or in compliance with a set of standards

Accreditation is a system of accountability in which an oversight body assesses and evaluates agencies and organizations to ensure that they are competent, credible, and/or in compliance with a set of standards. The American Correctional Association provides accreditation for jails and other correctional facilities in the United States through a series of evaluations, audits, reviews, and hearings. Other groups, such as the American Jail Association and the National Institute of Corrections, also provide standards and technical assistance for jails. Although it is not required in all states, jail accreditation serves several important purposes, including:

- ensuring that jails abide by strict standards;
- helping jails protect against lawsuits over the conditions of confinement;
- enabling the operating agency to better evaluate jail operations, policies, and procedures, which contributes to better management of the facilities; and
- enhancing professional recognition of the many contributions of jails (Schmalleger & Smykla, 2009).

Jails are covered in much greater depth in Module 32.

● **Learning Objective 29.4:** Describe the services provided by each primary component of the prison organization.

10
Corrections

Prisons

Prisons are considered **total institutions** in which the same people work, eat, and socialize every day (Goffman, 1961). Accordingly, control and regulation within prisons are needed to meet inmate needs. State and federal prisons had jurisdiction over roughly 1.4 million persons sentenced to more than 1 year of incarceration at the end of 2019 (Carson, 2020a).

The General Organization of Prison Facilities

Prisons are often organized according to the services needed to operate the facility. A warden or superintendent is at the top of the organizational structure, and directly under them are deputy wardens who oversee specific areas, such as management, custody, and programming (see Module 30).

Management consists of many of the administrative functions required to operate prisons, including the following:

- budgeting
- planning

- food services
- clothing and laundry
- landscaping
- purchasing
- the canteen

Custodial staff account for over 60% of prison personnel (Schmalleger & Smykla, 2009). Custody involves:

- institutional security,
- officer forces,
- prisoner discipline,
- investigations, and
- visitation.

Programming involves:

- medical and dental services,
- education,
- recreation,
- counseling,
- religion, and
- inmate classification (Clear et al., 2016).

Deputy wardens may also be assigned to prison industry and agriculture, depending on the ability of each facility to provide work opportunities for inmates. These areas require special attention from prison officials because inmates are typically provided with tools and a sense of freedom when working in a shop or in the fields. Some states created **specialized work camps**, which are low-security facilities centered on working outside the prison facility. For instance, inmates may work at forestry camps or on ranches.

Federal Prisons

The Federal Bureau of Prisons (BOP) manages all federal correctional institutions. It is housed within the U.S. Department of Justice. As of 2020, the federal prison

> **CAREERS**
>
> **Wardens**, or superintendents, oversee the administration of prisons. They plan, direct, and coordinate institutional programs and are responsible for the administrative and organizational control of prisons through the supervision, security, and training of inmates.

total institutions Facilities in which the same people work, eat, and recreate every day

specialized work camps Low-security facilities centered on working outside the prison facility

---

MYTHBUSTING

Prisoners Are Well Taken Care Of

As administrators of total institutions, prison officials must ensure that prisoners receive the healthcare they need. Many people believe that inmates receive above-average and completely free medical and dental care that is not provided to most people outside prison (Ross, 2012). The truth is that while healthcare in prison is provided, the quality of the care is below average, which leads many inmates to worry about catching serious and perhaps fatal diseases (e.g., Murphy, 2003; Ross, 2012). Information about disease prevention is rarely distributed in an effective manner, the prison infirmary is often poorly staffed, and inmates are rarely taken outside the prison to receive help in a civilian hospital.

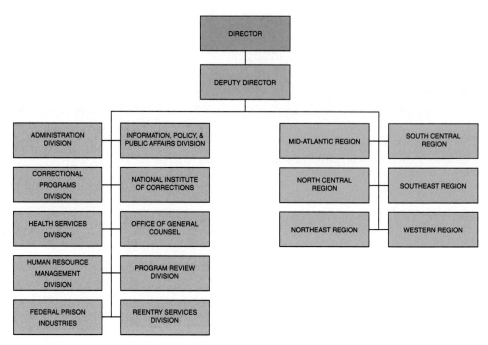

FIGURE 29.2. The Organization of the Federal Bureau of Prisons. The Federal Bureau of Prisons is headed by a director and deputy director who oversee various branches of the bureau.

What value comes from having a governing body that oversees the organizational designs of all prisons?

population was roughly 155,000 (Federal Bureau of Prisons, 2020b). Figure 29.2 depicts the organizational chart of the BOP.

Most federal inmates (81%) are housed in BOP-operated facilities. The BOP also contracts with private corporations, which oversee 9% of the inmates (Federal Bureau of Prisons, 2020b). The remaining inmates are confined in other areas, such as offenders' homes per their sentence of home confinement, although most inmates who fall in this category are housed in residential reentry centers as they prepare for release from incarceration.

The BOP employs over 37,000 personnel who provide a variety of correctional services. The bureau operates institutions at five security levels: minimum, low, medium, high, and administrative. The administrative facilities address special missions, including the detention of pretrial defendants, the treatment of inmates with serious or chronic medical issues, and incarcerating notably dangerous or violent inmates (Federal Bureau of Prisons, 2020c).

State Prisons

Prior to the early 1930s and 1940s, state prison operations were not centrally controlled, and state legislatures were minimally involved. Prison wardens were largely in control and had a great degree of discretion and little oversight. In the early 21st century, the power of wardens has decreased with legislative oversight, the intervention of the courts, and centralized state correctional agencies.

The executive branch of government in each state administers each prison. States typically have a department of corrections or similar agency that oversees the prison operations within each state. These state agencies are organized in different ways; for instance, some have a director, secretary, or commission of corrections who is appointed by and reports directly to the governor. Other states use separate boards or commissions designed to avoid direct connections between politics and corrections.

Members of the boards or commissions, however, may be appointed by the governor and usually must be composed of individuals from different political parties (e.g., Seiter, 2014). State governors often appoint commissioners of corrections, who are tasked with overseeing the prisons. Each prison is administered by a warden or superintendent who reports directly to the commissioner's office.

The size, type, and location of prison facilities vary among the states. Most states house all female inmates in one prison, given the relatively small number of female prisoners. In addition, most prisons are located in rural areas, in part as a result of costs, because land is cheaper in rural areas compared to urban locations (Clear et al., 2016).

Security Levels

In 2017, Frederick Darren Berg, also known as "Mini Madoff" for his role in defrauding investors of $150 million, escaped from a federal minimum-security camp in California. In contrast to the elaborate prison escapes often highlighted in popular culture, and the media, Mr. Berg simply left the camp. Critics have questioned why the inmate was placed in such a low-security correctional institution given the seriousness of his crimes, the length of his sentence (18 years), and the amount of restitution he owes ($140 million) (Carter, 2017).

1 Criminal Act

9 Sentencing

Prisoners are classified primarily according to their risk level and their treatment needs. The classification process begins after the offender has been sentenced to prison and transferred to the custody of the state. Initial classification occurs at this point, which involves the state's reception center receiving, diagnosing, and orientating the inmate. Testing and interviewing are used to determine the inmate's risk threat and plan a treatment approach. These events typically occur at facilities external to the prison where the inmate will serve their time. The inmate is transferred to the prison upon completion of the initial, external classification.

New inmates are further assessed shortly after entering the prison. These assessments are used to help determine appropriate housing, work assignments, and programming for the inmate. Reclassification is used throughout an offender's time in prison to make any adjustments to prior classification. For instance, inmates may be moved to a more secure unit, a different treatment program, or a different work assignment. The need for reclassification is important because inmates change in behavior over time, and recognition of their accomplishments or failures may be important for safety and/or programming needs.

Some states do not have institutions designed for specific security levels and may divide a facility into different sections for the different categories of inmates (Clear et al., 2016). Most states use four levels of security classification: minimum, medium, maximum, and supermax.

MINIMUM SECURITY

Minimum-security prisons typically house nonviolent offenders. Inmates at these prisons have much more freedom, and the facilities resemble college dormitories. There are typically few, if any, preventive walls, fences, guard towers, or other restrictive barriers because minimum-security facilities are used for low-risk inmates and those who are close to completing their incarceration.

MEDIUM SECURITY

Inmates in medium-security facilities may have committed serious offenses (e.g., robbery); however, they are not

CAREERS

Classification and treatment directors plan correctional programs, assign inmates to particular programs, and review inmate case reports. In some facilities, the responsibilities of classification and treatment director are distinct.

Shown here is Alcatraz Island, which housed a maximum-security prison known as "the Rock" from 1934 to 1963. Maximum-security prisons are very secure facilities designed to negate any possibility of escape. The facilities are highly regimented. They house those convicted of the most serious crimes.

Do you believe housing the most serious offenders together encourages criminal behavior or discourages it? Why?

perceived by prison officials to be hardened criminals who are immune to rehabilitative efforts, as is the case with many inmates in maximum-security facilities (Clear et al., 2016). Inmates in medium-security prisons are granted some contact with the outside world, with emphasis on work and rehabilitative programs. Some of the more recently constructed medium-security facilities are more campus-like in their design, meaning that small housing units are scattered among the various units of the prison (e.g., the dining hall, classrooms). However, guard towers, razor-wire fences, and other security devices are part of the design.

MAXIMUM SECURITY

Maximum-security prisons house offenders who pose serious threats. Inmate behaviors in these institutions are highly regimented, and the facilities typically contain high walls and armed guards protecting the perimeter. The perimeters of these facilities typically consist of high fencing, electronic sensing devices, and video surveillance. Inmates in maximum-security facilities are provided little contact with the outside world.

SUPERMAX

Upon receiving the death penalty for his role in the 2013 Boston Marathon bombings, Dzhokhar Tsarnaev was placed in a federal Administrative Maximum facility in Colorado. The supermax-security prison opened in 1994 and is considered the highest-security prison in the United States; it was designed for the most dangerous federal inmates.

supermax prisons
Facilities that provide a greater level of security than maximum-security prisons by isolating inmates from society, other inmates, and prison staff

Supermaximum or **supermax prisons** provide a greater level of security than maximum-security prisons by isolating inmates from society, other inmates, and prison staff. They generally house the most dangerous offenders in their cells for 23 hours per day and provide few services or privileges for inmates, although there are some variations as to how they are operated and exist.

The use of supermax prisons has generated controversy regarding whether they violate human rights or are effective (Mears et al., 2013), although they are assuming an increasingly prominent role in American corrections (Mears, 2008). Some inmates have volunteered for supermax confinement as a source of protection, to be alone, or to avoid work assignments (Pizzaro & Narag, 2008).

The use of supermax prisons reflects a return to earlier correctional practices in which the primary purpose was to control the most dangerous offenders. The BOP's use of Alcatraz Island in the San Francisco Bay as a prison, which opened in 1934 and closed in 1963, demonstrated the government's concern for heavily securing dangerous inmates. Module 32 includes much more specific information on the operation of prisons.

● **Learning Objective 29.5:** Differentiate between the three models used to administer parole services.

Parole

The two primary functions of parole authorities include community supervision of inmates released from incarceration and the decision to release inmates from prison. Some states use two distinct agencies to perform these functions; other states use a state department of corrections that is responsible for both tasks.

Each state is responsible for administering parole within its boundaries and has its own paroling authority that falls under the jurisdiction of the executive office. Compared to probation, the administration of parole at the state level is less complex because parole services are typically administered centrally on a statewide basis. Some states, however, use county-level probation and parole officers (Abadinski, 2015).

U.S. Parole Commission

The organization and administration of parole services at the federal level is less complex than it is at the state level because there is only one federal government. The U.S. Parole Commission is the paroling authority at the federal level. It is located in the U.S. Department of Justice. The supervisory responsibilities of parole officers at the federal level are similar to those at the state level. The organizational design of the U.S. Parole Commission is noted in Figure 29.3.

Parole Boards

Parole board members have power to grant parole, set the conditions of parole, supervise parolees, revoke parole, and discharge offenders from parole. In jurisdictions with determinate sentencing (see Module 25) in which there is no discretion in the timing of the release, they may retain the power to determine the conditions of release (Schmalleger & Smykla, 2009). Inmates who wish to be granted parole must provide an acceptable parole release plan to parole boards. The failure to do so is the most common reason for denial of parole (Clear & Dammer, 2000).

Parole officers perform many of the same functions as probation officers, primarily as they relate to supervision in the community and providing guidance for former inmates to live a crime-free life. Parole officers, however, face added challenges in working with a population (former inmates) that is being released from incarceration and facing the difficulties of adjusting to life outside prison.

How would this make the responsibilities of parole officers more difficult than the challenges faced by probation officers?

10
Corrections

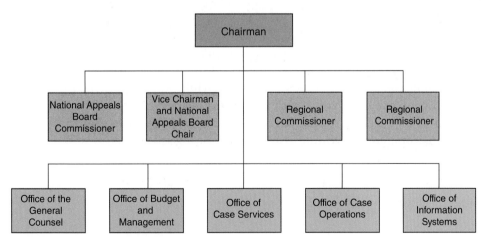

United States Parole Commission

FIGURE 29.3. **The Organizational Design of the U.S. Parole Commission.** The U.S. Parole Commission is responsible for parole services at the federal level. The agency is headed by a chairman, who is supported by four executive offices, including the Office of Case Services and the Office of Case Operations, which conduct parole hearings and monitor the progress of parolees, respectively.

What would be one of the most significant challenges associated with providing parole services across the entire United States?

9 Sentencing

institutional model (parole) A model of parole that uses members from within the inmate's institution to determine parole eligibility

autonomous model (parole) A model of parole in which parole decisions are made by individuals outside the inmate's institution

consolidated model (parole) A model of parole that has individuals from both within and outside the inmate's institution assess inmates' suitability for parole

Three organizational models are used to administer parole services: the institutional, autonomous, and consolidated models.

THE INSTITUTIONAL MODEL OF PAROLE

The **institutional model** uses members from within the inmate's institution to determine parole eligibility. Familiarity with the inmate is a primary benefit of this model, but factors unrelated to the offender's suitability for release (e.g., institutional factors such as overcrowding) may influence the decisions of institutional members. The institutional model is more commonly used in the juvenile justice system than in adult corrections (B. R. McCarthy et al., 2001).

THE AUTONOMOUS MODEL OF PAROLE

Parole decisions are made by individuals outside the inmate's institution in the **autonomous model**. A primary benefit of this model includes the potential for greater objectivity in decision-making because individuals outside the inmate's institution assess the inmate's suitability for parole. A concern with the autonomous model is the lack of familiarity between parole board members and inmates (B. R. McCarthy et al., 2001).

THE CONSOLIDATED MODEL OF PAROLE

The **consolidated model** of parole proposes to address the limitations of the autonomous and institutional models by having individuals from both within and outside the inmate's institution assess inmates' suitability for parole. Institutional members in the consolidated model do not maintain the authority to release inmates; however, they offer input to parole officials from outside the institution who also sit on the board (B. R. McCarthy et al., 2001).

Parole board members in almost all states are full-time employees of the state and in most states are appointed by the governor (Seiter, 2014). They serve several primary functions, including assessing inmate suitability for parole, determining a release date, and parole policy development. Module 31 includes more in-depth coverage of parole.

The System in Perspective

As noted in the "In the News" feature at the start of this module, upon being released from prison, O. J. Simpson was put on parole until 2022 in his Nevada community. Simpson has undergone both institutional and community corrections while serving time in prison and being closely monitored while on parole. Given his high profile, many people in various agencies and levels of government have had an interest in and/or effect on his case. The goal of corrections is to ensure that those treated both in the community and in institutions are processed efficiently and monitored properly and that humane and appropriate services are provided to those under correctional supervision.

Summary

1. Learning Objective 29.1: *Summarize the arguments for the centralized and decentralized administration of probation.*

- Probation services are highly decentralized in the early 21st century. Supporters for decentralizing probation services argue that cities or counties can more effectively administer probation services because they can better respond to specific issues pertaining to the community and are more flexible. Further, agencies operating under a decentralized approach can make better use of community resources than their counterparts in centralized systems. Supporters for centralizing probation services argue that local probation authorities often lack professionalism and use outdated practices. They argue that a single, statewide probation agency can provide broader programs that promote consistency and uniformity of policies and service across areas. They further argue that centralized agencies are larger and can train their personnel to assume a variety of roles.

2. Learning Objective 29.2: *Describe the intermediate sanctions administered by the judiciary, probation agencies, and correctional departments.*

- Intermediate sanctions have been categorized according to the agencies that administer the sanctions: the judiciary, probation agencies, and correctional departments. The intermediate sanctions administered by the judiciary include pretrial diversion, fines, forfeiture, community service, and restitution. Sanctions administered by probation agencies include day reporting and treatment centers, intensive supervision probation, home confinement, and electronic monitoring. Intermediate sanctions administered by correctional departments primarily include shock probation and boot camps.

3. Learning Objective 29.3: *Identify the agencies responsible for operating jails.*

- Jails are primarily operated by a county government, although counties that incorporate large metropolitan areas may collaborate with the city, and both levels of government may contribute to management of the jail. The Federal Bureau of Prisons operates jails at the federal level.

4. Learning Objective 29.4: *Describe the services provided by each primary component of the prison organization.*

- Prisons are often organized according to the services needed to run the facility. A warden or superintendent is at the top of the organizational structure, and directly under the warden are deputy wardens who may oversee specific areas such as management, custody, programming, industry, and agriculture. Management consists of many of the administrative functions required to operate prisons, including budgeting, planning, food services, clothing and laundry, landscaping, purchasing, and the canteen. Custody involves institutional security, officer forces, prisoner discipline, investigations, and visitation. Programming involves medical and dental services, education, recreation, counseling, religion, and classification.

5. Learning Objective 29.5: *Differentiate between the three models used to administer parole board services.*

- Three organizational models are used to administer parole services. The institutional model uses members from within the inmate's institution to determine parole eligibility. Familiarity with the inmate is a primary benefit of this model, but factors unrelated to the offender's suitability for release may influence the decisions of institutional members. Parole decisions are made by individuals outside the inmate's institution in the autonomous model. A primary benefit of this model is the potential for greater objectivity in decision-making because individuals outside the inmate's institution assess the inmate's suitability for parole. A concern with the autonomous model is the lack of familiarity between parole board members and inmates. The consolidated model of parole proposes to address the limitations of the autonomous and institutional models by having individuals from both within and outside the inmate's institution assess suitability for parole.

Questions for Critical Thinking

1. Does it make sense to you to combine probation and parole services? Should all states combine responsibility for both forms of community supervision into one agency, or should they remain separated, as they are in some states?

2. What would be the benefit of creating a centralized state agency that oversaw the administration of all intermediate sanctions? What would be the drawbacks?

3. Do you believe sheriff's departments, which are tasked with providing traditional law enforcement services, should operate jails? Why or why not?

4. Are the strict conditions associated with supermax prisons a violation of human rights? Why or why not?

5. Which organizational model do you believe would be most effective with regard to the administration of parole services? Why?

Key Terms

accreditation
autonomous model (parole)
consolidated model (parole)
institutional model (parole)
pay-to-stay jails

regional jails
specialized work camps
supermax prisons
total institutions

For digital learning resources, please go to
https://www.oup.com/he/burns1e

Corrections Personnel

Corrections officers typically work closely with sometimes dangerous individuals. Low pay, low prestige, and difficult working conditions make this a tough job. Their work, however, is vital to our safety.

Do you believe corrections officers should receive greater recognition for their work through higher financial rewards? Why or why not?

Correctional employees provide many important services that rehabilitate and secure offenders and keep society safe. Working in corrections can be rewarding, dangerous, and stressful. Individuals with an interest in learning more about human behavior, helping troubled individuals, and/or addressing crime are often drawn to careers in corrections. This module begins with a look at working in probation and parole, followed by consideration of what it is like to be a corrections officer. The discussion then turns to the responsibilities of offender treatment and education specialists, as well as prison wardens and administrators. This module concludes with a look at diversity among corrections personnel.

MODULE OUTLINE

- **Probation and Parole**

  Learning Objective 30.1: Identify the primary responsibilities of probation and parole officers and parole board members.

- **Correctional Officers**

  Learning Objective 30.2: Identify the primary responsibilities of corrections officers.

- **Offender Treatment and Education Specialists**

  Learning Objective 30.3: Identify the primary responsibilities of offender treatment and education personnel.

- **Wardens and Institutional Administration**

  Learning Objective 30.4: Identify the primary responsibilities of prison wardens.

- **Diversity Among Corrections Personnel**

  Learning Objective 30.5: Discuss the benefits of diversifying correctional staffs.

10
Corrections

Inmate Abuse

In April 2015, a prison inmate in New York with a history of erratic behavior associated with bipolar disorder packed his bags and stated that he was going home, even though he still had several years left on the sentence he was serving. Soon after his announcement, he got into a confrontation with prison officers and was repeatedly kicked and punched, jumped on, and thrown or dragged down a staircase, according to inmate accounts. Prison officials called for an ambulance but

that the inmate had likely overdosed on K2, a synthetic marijuana (Winerip & Schwirtz, 2015). An autopsy concluded that the inmate had sustained bruises and cuts to the head and extremities and had died of a cardiac arrhythmia. No illicit drugs were found in his system.

No officers were disciplined following the incident. Several inmates at the facility claimed they were punished for speaking with the inmate's family, lawyers, and news reporters by being placed in solitary confinement and threatened with violence after they spoke. Similar allegations of inmate abuse emerged from another prison in New York, where inmates claimed they were beaten and choked by corrections officers seeking information about escapees. Some of the inmates were placed in solitary confinement (Winerip & Schwirtz, 2015).

Inmate abuse, whether it comes from prison officers or other prisoners, has been problematic in prisons throughout history. The relationship between officers and inmates is often unpleasant because of several factors, including inmate misbehavior and mistreatment of prison officers. These factors and others contribute to inmates sometimes being recipients of abuse. Is there ever justification to mistreat an inmate? What steps could be taken to better prevent inmate abuse?

SAMUEL HARRELL

mentioned nothing about the physical altercation. Instead, they told the ambulance crew

Probation and Parole

Probation and parole officers are more extensively involved with offenders and their cases than any other criminal justice professionals (Schmalleger & Smykla, 2009). The jobs can be stressful because of regular interaction with known offenders, extensive amounts of paperwork, high caseloads, and deadlines that are beyond officers' control (Finn & Kuck, 2005). The positions can also be rewarding, however, because of the variety of tasks and opportunities associated with the job, along with the stability of working for the government and the many opportunities to help offenders and protect society.

The specific tasks performed by probation and parole officers include the following (Abadinsky, 2015):

- monitoring and enforcing offender compliance
- investigating suspicions of client misbehavior

● **Learning Objective 30.1:** Identify the primary responsibilities of probation and parole officers and parole board members.

- assisting with sentencing practices
- analyzing and making recommendations regarding probation or parole revocation or imposing stricter conditions
- report writing and documenting information
- interacting and communicating with offenders
- interacting with non-offenders (e.g., school and work officials, families)
- working with fellow probation or parole agencies
- working with other components of the justice system

Some states place probation and parole services under a single agency since many of the services they provide are the same. Doing so facilitates hiring and training personnel; however, there are differences between probationers and parolees. Probationers continue to reside in their community and face many of the same challenges that contributed to their involvement in crime, while parolees leave institutions and are faced with the various problems associated with reentry (Clear et al., 2016).

The responsibilities of probation and parole officers became more difficult in 2020 among widespread concerns for COVID-19. In-person and office check-ins were suspended in many jurisdictions, and communication via telephones and computers became increasingly common (Prison Policy Initiative, 2020). Community supervision officers were required to practice social distancing and use protective gear such as gloves, masks, and/or face shields when interacting with the individuals in their caseloads.

9 Sentencing

10 Corrections

Primary Functions of Probation Officers

Probation officers provide the primary functions of investigation and supervision. **Investigations** involve gathering information to assist with sentencing practices, including the preparation of presentence investigation reports, which (as noted in Module 25) provide information that assists with sentencing decisions and contains a plan of supervision. **Supervision** involves monitoring and overseeing offenders during the course of their probation period. The primary components of supervision as it pertains to probation include:

- **resource mediation:** providing probationers with guidance and services to facilitate their success; this may include assistance in finding substance abuse counseling, employment, and education;
- **surveillance:** monitoring the activities of probationers; this may occur at the probationers' home or work; and
- **enforcement:** taking the proper steps to ensure that probationers are aware of the need to abide by their probation agreement and properly responding to those who violate their agreement (Schmalleger & Smykla, 2009).

Probation caseloads have expanded as the correctional population has increased, and it is generally believed that larger caseloads result in reduced levels of quality supervision. Caseloads vary among jurisdictions, although most are high (e.g., over 100 cases per officer), which means that monthly visits to probationers are brief (Whitehead et al., 2013). The American Probation and Parole Association earlier established a case-to-staff ratio of 200:1 for minimum supervision, 50:1 for medium supervision, and 20:1 for intensive supervision (B. Burrell, 2006). Ultimately, there is no accepted level of probation officer caseload.

Probation officers sometimes struggle to find balance between their need to enforce the law and provide assistance to probationers. For instance, officers must

investigations (probation) Gathering information to assist with sentencing practices, including the preparation of presentence investigation reports

supervision (probation) Monitoring and overseeing offenders during the course of their probation sentences

resource mediation Providing probationers with guidance and services to facilitate their success on probation; it may include assistance in finding substance abuse counseling, employment, and education

surveillance (probation) Monitoring the activities of probationers

enforcement (probation) Taking the proper steps to ensure that probationers are aware of the need to abide by their probation agreement and properly responding to those who violate their agreement

10
Corrections

enforce the law when probationers violate the terms of their probation, but doing so may conflict with or hamper rehabilitative efforts. As a result, probation officers must use their discretion in balancing these efforts.

Primary Functions of Parole Officers

Inmates who are released early remain under the supervision of a parole officer, who ensures that the parolees abide by the terms of their parole agreement. Parole officer responsibilities are similar to those of probation officers, with the primary difference being that parolees face particular challenges as they reenter society. Upon leaving an institution, they may suffer from the ill-effects of incarceration and face difficulties getting reestablished in society. With regard to the latter, parole officers must often help parolees with:

- finding residences,
- maintaining jobs,
- managing money,
- reestablishing ties with family members and friends, and
- adjusting to living under direct supervision by a parole officer.

Parole Boards

pre-parole investigation reports Reports that provide helpful information that is used to determine one's suitability for and the associated conditions of parole

Some states use parole boards to determine whether inmates are granted parole, the conditions of parole, when parole should be revoked, and when parolees may be discharged from parole (see Module 29). They are typically assisted by **pre-parole investigation reports**, which are similar to presentence investigation reports and provide helpful information that is used to determine one's suitability for and the associated conditions of parole (Clear & Dammer, 2000).

Governors in most states appoint members of the parole board or parole commission; these members are full-time employees of the state. Statutes and some state constitutions define the size (most consist of five to nine members), basic qualifications for parole board members, and terms of service (Whitehead et al., 2013). Parole board members have been criticized for lacking relevant background or education, and political patronage has, on occasion, hampered the selection process (Abadinski, 2015).

● Learning Objective 30.2: Identify the primary responsibilities of corrections officers.

Correctional Officers

In 2015, two prison inmates escaped from the Clinton Correctional Facility in New York, resulting in a manhunt for the individuals that took almost 3 weeks and cost the state roughly $23 million. One of the inmates was killed while evading capture. The other was captured. The escape drew national attention and was facilitated by two prison employees who were later arrested for their actions. One employee provided the inmates with the tools to escape and planned to join them after they killed her husband. The other employee smuggled tools into the prison and provided other favors for one of the escapees in exchange for paintings and drawings (Katersky, 2015). This unfortunate account highlights the importance of corrections officers doing their job properly.

1 Criminal Act

Primary Responsibilities and Assignments of Correctional Officers

Correctional officers provide many services within institutions. Primarily, they enforce rules and regulations, ensure that inmates are confined to the institution, and keep inmates and staff secure. They oversee the control, movement, and surveillance of inmates. Their responsibilities include:

- providing security through detaining offenders,
- inspecting the institutional facilities to ensure that they meet standards and are orderly,
- reporting on inmate conduct,
- searching inmates for contraband,
- ensuring that incarceration is secure and humane,
- providing inmates with the opportunities to better themselves, and
- preparing inmates for release.

Prison officers are assigned particular duties that vary according to their location within the institution and the extent and nature of contact with inmates. These positions include the following (Clear et al., 2016):

- **block officers:** working directly with inmates in housing units
- **work detail supervisors:** overseeing the work details of inmates, for instance as they pertain to cleaning and maintaining the institution
- **industrial shop and school officers:** providing security for civilians who provide services to inmates, including teachers, counselors, and trainers
- **yard officers:** overseeing inmates recreating in the prison yard
- **administration building assignments:** providing safety and security in the administrative building(s), including the visitors' room and prison gates
- **wall posts:** standing post at towers aligned along the prison walls
- **relief officers:** providing a variety of tasks to assist with vacancies in the staff

Challenges Facing Correctional Officers

Regularly dealing with individuals who are deemed in need of constant monitoring and direction makes the work of corrections officers unique in many aspects. On a regular day, prison officers may interact with more felons than many police officers will engage with in an entire year. Corrections officers generally face many distinct challenges in relation to their position, including the following (Conover, 2000):

- securing uncooperative inmates who violate or attempt to break the prison rules
- addressing the gap between training and what truly occurs on the job
- dealing with the stress associated with the job
- experiencing hostility and lack of support from senior coworkers and administrators
- being paid low wages for a job with limited prestige

In May 2017, the Florida Department of Corrections Secretary encouraged legislators to pass a bill that would increase the pay (which was about $30,900 a year for new

3 Arrest

10
Corrections

Prison officers perform various functions. Officers do not carry guns except for on wall posts out of fear of the weapons falling into the hands of prisoners.

What weapons do you believe would be most effective for prison officers to control unruly inmate behavior?

block officers Prison officers who work directly with inmates in housing units

work detail supervisors Prison officers who oversee the work details of inmates

industrial shop and school officers Prison officers who protect civilians who provide services to inmates, including teachers, counselors, and trainers

yard officers Prison officers who oversee inmates recreating in the prison yard

administration building assignments Prison officer assignments that involve providing safety and security in the administrative building, including the visitors' room and prison gates

wall posts Correctional officers who stand post at towers aligned along the prison walls

relief officers Prison officers who provide a variety of tasks to assist with vacancies in the staff

officers) for those who work in prisons. She noted that it was difficult to hire staff, and many prison officers were inexperienced, young, and tired from working overtime. The latter, she noted, costs the state more than it would to fully staff the prison system (Mueller, 2017).

Aside from the low pay, the nature of corrections work, in terms of exposure to violence and communicable diseases (see Module 32), can be a challenge. The COVID-19 pandemic that spread across the world in 2020 greatly impacted prisons and jails, where social isolation was difficult and correctional workers interact closely with inmates. The fear of catching the infectious disease was prominent among correctional workers, and many were diagnosed with it (Cook, 2020). Legislators and prison officials responded in many ways to the pandemic, in part by reducing prison and jail populations by releasing some low-risk inmates, older inmates, and those with preexisting conditions that made them vulnerable to the virus (Prison Policy Initiative, 2020).

Assembling and retaining a quality staff is important for corrections agencies. Employee turnover has been problematic in terms of costs and the ability to effectively operate. The financial costs include the need to recruit, select, and train new employees and the overtime costs required to pay current employees who fill voids in the workforce. The loss of experienced staff members hampers correctional agencies in terms of consistency and continuity.

Correctional Officer Requirements and Selection Processes

Correctional officers are required to be well trained and have strong interpersonal skills. They are not paid well relative to the work they do. The U.S. Bureau of Labor noted that the mean annual salary for correctional officers and jailers was $50,130 in 2019 (U.S. Bureau of Labor Statistics, 2020a). Employment in these areas is expected to decline from 2019 to 2029 (U.S. Bureau of Labor Statistics, 2020b), arguably because of budget constraints and decreases in the crime rate.

A high school diploma or General Educational Development certificate is required in most states for becoming a correctional officer, although some states will waive the educational requirement for years of experience. The relatively low level of educational background is a result of the need to attract a large body of applicants. Background checks and various assessments are used in selecting correctional officers, including the following (Schmalleger & Smykla, 2009):

- evaluations of physical agility
- reading comprehension
- psychological well-being
- oral interviews

- report writing
- drug testing

States vary widely with regard to their requirements for the number of classroom hours for trainees, although since the 1970s, the trend has been toward increased training and professionalization in the field. Most commonly, states require between 200 and 299 hours of academy training before someone can become a corrections officer. Most states operate extensive training academies that are similar to those provided for law enforcement personnel, but that also address issues relevant to institutionalization. An assessment of correctional officer training academies found that almost all states trained officers in the following areas (Burton et al., 2018):

- prison programs and services
- inmate supervision
- security counting procedures
- inmate discipline
- cell and body searches
- use of force
- controlling contraband
- firearms basics
- grievances

10
Corrections

Jailers

Whereas correctional officers work in prisons, jailers (local correctional workers) operate in jails. They deal with some of the most volatile individuals in the system and are perhaps the least equipped to deal with them. Jailers have been described as "among the most poorly trained, least-educated, and worst-paid employees in the criminal justice system" (Clear et al., 2016, p. 181).

Jailers face some distinct challenges that prison correctional officers do not:

- Many individuals who enter jails have not been medically screened—which may lead to the spread of communicable diseases—or psychologically evaluated, which means inmate behavior may be more volatile or dangerous.
- Jails are understaffed and overcrowded, particularly in urban areas (Lambert et al., 2004).
- It is harder to classify and diagnose inmates because of the transient nature of jail populations and the fact that some individuals may only be in jail for a few hours or days.

Offender Treatment and Education Specialists

● **Learning Objective 30.3:** Identify the primary responsibilities of offender treatment and education personnel.

Prisons and other correctional institutions employ various treatment personnel, such as psychologists, psychiatrists, and social workers, who provide inmates with treatment and rehabilitative services. These professionals may provide counseling, self-help, and medical treatment, as well as vocational and educational assistance by teaching inmates new skills that will better prepare them for life outside the correctional institutions.

Treatment Personnel

Each offender enters corrections with a unique background and specific needs. Understanding which correctional approach works best for each offender can be challenging. In addition, treatment personnel must contend with a lack of resources devoted toward rehabilitating inmates (because of the high cost and the belief by some that treatments are ineffective). Of particular concern in corrections is assisting those with substance abuse problems and/or mental health issues, as well as the challenge of rehabilitating sex offenders (see Module 33 for discussion of special inmate populations). Those who treat inmates know that they are dealing with a difficult population, and treatment in general is never an exact science. Treatment personnel must be prepared to provide programming and treatment as they pertain to:

10
Corrections

- psychological issues,
- behavioral concerns,
- social skills,
- education, and
- vocational preparedness.

SUBSTANCE ABUSE SERVICES

According to the Bureau of Justice Statistics, only 28% of state prison and jail inmates who met the criteria for drug dependence or abuse noted that they had received drug treatment or participated in a related program since their admission to jail or prison (Bronson et al., 2017). Self-help groups such as Alcoholics Anonymous and Narcotics Anonymous are the most commonly used programs in prisons and jails to help offenders with substance abuse problems. A benefit of these programs is that inmates can continue to participate in them after their release (Boyes-Watson & Krumholz, 2018).

Substance abuse counselors in prisons and jails assess clients and provide both group and individual therapy. They also provide educational programming to the institutions in general and report to administrators regarding treatment needs and progress for inmates. However, counselors must deal with increasing workloads, in large part because of a high turnover rate and lack of new counselors entering the field, and the large number of offenders who require treatment (Perkins & Oser, 2014).

The high turnover rate and limited numbers of new counselors working in the field have been attributed to the following factors (Fahy, 2007; Knudsen et al., 2006):

- poor compensation for the work
- counselors becoming frustrated with the work because of emotional exhaustion and feeling a lack of professional accomplishment
- the low professional prestige associated with the position

Research comparing job frustration levels among substance abuse counselors who worked with offenders in prison and those who worked with offenders in the community found that counselors employed in the community setting reported higher levels of perceived organizational support. This discrepancy was explained, in part, by the lack of resources for rehabilitation often found in prisons and the bureaucratic nature of many prison administrations, which could make counselors feel isolated (Perkins & Oser, 2014).

MENTAL ILLNESS

It is estimated that over half of all prison and jail inmates have a mental health problem. The Bureau of Justice Statistics reported that an estimated 37% of state and federal prisoners and 44% of jail inmates had been told in the past by a mental health professional that they had a mental disorder (Bronson & Berzofsky, 2017). Mentally ill inmates face numerous challenges while incarcerated, and untreated inmates struggle with their disease(s) and confinement, which affects other inmates and prison staff. Module 33 addresses the incarceration of the mentally ill.

Treatment personnel use various means to assist the wide range of problems facing many inmates. For instance, they attempt to rehabilitate inmates with psychological problems by addressing the underlying mental or emotional issues that contributed to the offender's criminal behavior. Some treatment personnel seek to correct offender behavior through behavior therapy, for instance through the use of positive and negative reinforcements and role modeling.

- **Positive reinforcements** reward inmates for prosocial behavior, such as reducing the length of an inmate's sentence if they successfully complete an anger-management course.
- **Negative reinforcements** are designed to punish inmates for antisocial behavior, for instance by taking away an offender's "good time."
- **Role modeling** involves patients assuming the role of others, for instance the victim of domestic violence.

Treatment staff may focus on creating an institutional environment that supports prosocial behavior in efforts to rehabilitate offenders, and those who provide educational and vocational programs focus on educating offenders and teaching new skills that will better prepare them for life outside the institution.

positive reinforcements Rewards for inmates who engage in prosocial behavior

negative reinforcements Punishments for inmates engaging in antisocial behavior

role modeling A treatment approach that involves patients assuming the role of others

10
Corrections

Education Personnel

Providing various types of education is important in the rehabilitation of offenders, especially because about 65% of inmates in state and federal prisons and jails have not received a high school diploma or its equivalent, and 14% have less than an 8th-grade education ("Economic Perspectives," 2016). Correctional educators:

- teach vocational training programs,
- provide academic counseling,
- offer in-service training for correctional employees, and
- serve on institutional boards (Whitehead et al., 2013).

Correctional educators must have a bachelor's degree and be certified to teach. Relevant work and/or teaching experience in one's area of specialization is also often required. In addition, familiarity with a variety of teaching techniques designed to assist individuals with

Offender treatment and education programs are provided in jails and prisons to help prepare inmates for successful reentry into society. Shown here, an inmate participates in a cosmetology class that includes training in many cosmetology procedures. Upon successful completion of the program, inmates can take a written exam and obtain a cosmetology license.

Do you believe greater funding should be allocated to provide education and treatment for offenders, or should funding be used to build additional prisons and jails?

● **Learning Objective 30.4:** Identify the primary responsibilities of prison wardens.

10
Corrections

wardens Also known as superintendents, they are the chief executive officers of prisons

attitudinal, behavioral, and learning difficulties is particularly important in the correctional setting.

Wardens and Institutional Administration

Correctional agencies have historically relied less on policy and more on the instincts and common-sense experience of individuals who worked their way through the ranks to manage prisons. In the 1980s, however, with the vast expansion of prisons and the correctional population and the influx of new staff, it became particularly important for newly appointed managers and hired officers to have a strong policy foundation on which they could operate (Phillips & Roberts, 2000). The correctional workforce increased from roughly 27,000 in 1950 (Cahalan, 1986) to an estimated 714,000 full-time employees in 2016 (Hyland, 2019). Ultimately, there was a move toward increasing the professionalism of correctional staff and administration.

The correctional staff are supervised by administrators, and none is perhaps more powerful than prison wardens, or superintendents. As noted in Module 29, there are many other administrative positions within corrections. Each plays a significant role in ensuring that particular divisions or units, and correctional agencies in general, operate in an efficient and effective manner.

Prison Wardens and Superintendents

Wardens are the chief executive officers of prisons. They manage prisons and are responsible for ensuring facilities meet their goals. They primarily oversee:

- operations of the prison,
- supervisory staff,
- support staff, and
- inmates.

Wardens are their institutions' primary point of contact with the nonprison world and typically report to the deputy commissioner for institutions in a central state office. They may also interact with the state legislature on matters pertaining to proposed or enacted legislation and with parole boards with regard to release decisions.

Within the institution, wardens are typically assisted by deputy wardens who oversee specific areas of the facility, such as management, custody, industry, and treatment programs. Figure 30.1 depicts an advertisement that highlights the responsibilities, salary, and expectations of a prison warden.

Wardens in the early 21st century have less authority and control than in years past. Extensive prison litigation beginning in the early 1970s helped curb the power maintained by wardens. Wardens had to adjust to operating prisons with increased accountability and decreased autonomy (Clear et al., 2016). State-level administrators have assumed some of the responsibilities typically assigned to wardens, particularly as they relate to:

- budgeting,
- research,
- program development,

WARDEN MIKE DURFEE STATE PRISON

South Dakota Department of Corrections - Sioux Falls, South Dakota

SALARY INFORMATION

Entry Level Salary:

$87,000.00 annual

JOB DESCRIPTION

Open Warden position at Mike Durfee State Prison in Springfield South Dakota. The Warden is responsible for the planning, operation, direction, and management of the Mike Durfee State Prison, Rapid City Community Work Center and Yankton Community Work Center. The position will involve occasional overnight travel to the DOC Administrative Office in Pierre, other state prisons, and out-of-state conferences.

The Ideal Candidate Will Have: A bachelor's degree in criminal justice, sociology, or a related field, and at least three years of experience in corrections or law enforcement administration is preferred.

Knowledge of: Human behavior, institutional psychology, operational management and the criminal justice system.

Ability to:

Display High Integrity—Create an environment that fosters high ethical standards.

Exercise Due Diligence—Manage resources and day-to-day responsibilities in a manner that instills public trust. This includes security of facilities to ensure the safety of the public, staff and inmates.

Act Decisively—Use vision, creativity, reasoning and experience to reach conclusions and make effective decisions.

Critically Think—Make good decisions even under a great deal of stress.

Organizational Change—Proactively and successfully bring about change based on evidence-based practices to improve public safety.

Focus on Offenders Programming—Anticipate and meet the needs of offenders by delivering and continuously improving quality programming to lower recidivism.

Take Entrepreneurial Risks—Identify opportunities to develop new evidence-based practices and encourages resourceful and innovative solutions to problems.

Build Strong Alliances—Develop networks and uses them to strengthen internal and external organizational support.

Turn Vision into Strategy—Think and act strategically to ensure the agency moves towards its mission.

JOB REQUIREMENTS

Age: 18+

Education: Bachelors Degree

Experience: 3+ years

FIGURE 30.1. Warden Job Description. As noted in the requirements for a position as warden, experience in correctional supervision is important. Also of importance is the ability to establish and maintain relationships with a wide array of people and groups.

Should the education level required for the position be higher than it is in this advertisement? Why or why not?

- public information, and
- legislative relations.

10
Corrections

deputy wardens of management Prison administrators who oversee many housekeeping responsibilities such as those pertaining to financial records, providing food and supplies, and maintaining the buildings and grounds

deputy wardens of custodial personnel Prison administrators who oversee correctional officers and the overall security of the institution

deputy wardens of program personnel Prison officials who administer treatment, educational, and vocational programs

deputy wardens of industry and agriculture Prison administrators who oversee the individuals who manage machine shops and/or farms

● **Learning Objective 30.5:** Discuss the benefits of diversifying correctional staffs.

Other Prison Administrators

Wardens are assisted by various institutional administrators who specialize in particular areas of importance to prison and jail management. They may work in offices away from the main plant, and many have very little contact with inmates (Clear et al., 2016). Some common administrative positions include the following:

- **Deputy wardens of management** oversee many of the day-to-day operations necessary in prisons, including managing the financial records, providing food and supplies, and maintaining the buildings and grounds.
- **Deputy wardens of custodial personnel** oversee correctional officers and the overall security of the institution.
- **Deputy wardens of program personnel** administer treatment, educational, and vocational programs.
- **Deputy wardens of industry and agriculture** oversee the individuals who manage machine shops and/or farms.

Diversity Among Corrections Personnel

Changes in workforce demographics have shaped current correctional practices (Hunt, 2004). Historically, employment positions within all areas of corrections were mostly filled by White males. Beginning in the 1970s and 1980s, females and racial and ethnic minorities increasingly assumed roles in corrections (McNamara & Burns, 2020). In addition, the infamous 1971 prison riot at the Attica Correctional Facility in New York, which resulted in the deaths of 10 correctional officers and civilian employees and 33 inmates, occurred in part because inmates perceived that correctional staff did not respect cultural and religious differences (Abadinski, 2015; Booker, 1999). Closer consideration of correctional staff demographics and tolerance for difference soon followed the riot.

Generally, the benefits of having a diverse correctional staff include the following (McNamara & Burns, 2020):

- the opportunity for staff members from different cultures, races, and ethnicities to learn from one another
- more understanding from corrections officials regarding offender behaviors and beliefs
- the message sent to inmates that not all who work in the criminal justice system are White males

Racial and Ethnic Minorities

Prisons are often built in rural areas, where the populations are typically homogeneous. In turn, correctional staffs have largely consisted of White males. Inmates, however, often come from more heterogeneous urban areas (Booker, 1999), and African Americans are overrepresented as inmates. This situation has contributed to cultural differences impacting staff–inmate relations. However, legislation and court decisions over the years have slowly introduced improvements in this area.

Diversifying correctional staffs has been difficult because of the perception by some that the justice system is racist or biased (Camp et al., 2001). A series of **affirmative action programs** that began in the 1960s were designed to address the historical mistreatment of racial and ethnic minorities with regard to employment. They have contributed to the increased representation of historically underrepresented groups in correctional workforces.

In the early 21st century, the percentage of African Americans employed in corrections surpassed their percentage in the U.S. population overall. Roughly 13% of the U.S. population is African American, but in 2020 over 12% of the Federal Bureau of Prisons staff was African American (Federal Bureau of Prisons, 2020d), and about 33% of those employed as correctional officers or jailers in 2020 were African American. Further, 26.9% of probation officers or correctional treatment specialists were Black or African American (U.S. Bureau of Labor Statistics, 2020b). These numbers suggest that African Americans are no longer underrepresented in at least some correctional positions.

Other groups remain underrepresented among correctional staffs; for instance, Hispanic or Latinos (who constitute about 18% of the U.S. population) comprised 12.8% of the correctional officers and jailers in 2020 and 12.8% of probation officers and correctional treatment specialists. Asians constituted 2.7% of those employed as correctional officers or jailers in 2020, yet represent 5.4% of the U.S. population (U.S. Bureau of Labor Statistics, 2020b).

Females

Females have also faced obstacles in gaining acceptance as correctional officers. Historically, many male correctional officers believed that female officers:

- lacked the physical strength necessary to protect themselves from attack and to adequately support fellow officers,
- could be easily manipulated by inmates,
- would incite sexually motivated attacks or sexual harassment,
- would engage in inappropriate relationships with inmates, and
- would be unable to supervise inmates in all areas of a housing unit, such as a shower or bathroom (Nicholas, 2012/2013).

Despite these beliefs, female officers have assumed an increasing and important role in prisons and throughout corrections. **Title VII of the Civil Rights Act of 1964**, which was amended in 1972, prohibited sex-based discrimination by public employers. And since the 1980s, states have abandoned requirements that female officers may only supervise female probationers, parolees, or inmates.

Today, correctional staffs include more women than ever before. In 2020, more females (50.7%) than males (49.3%) worked as probation officers or correctional treatment specialists (U.S. Bureau of Labor Statistics, 2020b). Further, females comprised roughly 28.5% of the staff in the Federal Bureau of Prisons in 2020, a percentage that has steadily increased through the years (Federal Bureau of Prisons, 2020d), and females comprised about 31% of all jailers in 2018 (Zeng, 2020).

10
Corrections

affirmative action programs Programs designed to promote the hiring of disadvantaged groups who have suffered from discrimination

Title VII of the Civil Rights Act of 1964 Legislation passed in 1964 that prevents governments, unions, employment agencies, and private employers with 15 or more employees from discriminating based on color, race, sex, religion, or national origin

Many efforts were made to diversify the ranks of correctional officers beginning in the 1970s and 1980s. Overall increased involvement of females in the workforce and affirmative action programs largely contributed to correctional agency workforces becoming increasingly diverse.

What do you believe would be the most successful means to increasingly diversify correctional agencies?

The System in Perspective

Place yourself in the position of the correctional officers described in the "In the News" feature at the beginning of this module. You have to respond to a confrontational inmate with a history of erratic behavior associated with bipolar disorder who has packed his bags and claimed he is going home despite the fact that he still has several years left to serve. How would you respond? Corrections officials generally face situations that are uncommon in other occupations. They regularly interact with troubled individuals who have lost many of their freedoms. The individuals may need help with addiction, anger management, mental illness, and other problems that have negatively affected their lives. Ultimately, it takes the efforts of many individuals to secure and treat offenders. The process of doing so starts with the police who make the arrests, the attorneys who prosecute and defend, and the juries and judges who make important decisions. Securing justice for those who break the law cannot occur without the efforts of all of these individuals, the groups highlighted in this module, and many others who work in corrections. Each individual who works in the field contributes in various ways that combined help meet the goals of corrections and our justice systems in general.

Summary

1. Learning Objective 30.1: *Identify the primary responsibilities of probation and parole officers and parole board members.*

- Probation and parole officers provide the primary functions of investigation and supervision. Parole boards determine when an individual is believed to be suitable for parole and have statutory power to grant parole, set the conditions of parole, supervise parolees, revoke parole, and discharge offenders from parole.

2. Learning Objective 30.2: *Identify the primary responsibilities of corrections officers.*

- Correctional officers provide a variety of services within institutions. Primarily, they enforce rules and regulations and are responsible for ensuring that inmates are confined to the institution and that inmates and staff are secure. They oversee the control, movement, and surveillance of inmates. Their goals include providing security through detaining offenders, inspecting the institutional facilities to ensure that they meet standards and are orderly, reporting on inmate conduct, searching inmates for contraband, ensuring that incarceration is secure and humane, providing inmates the opportunities to better themselves, and preparing inmates for release.

3. Learning Objective 30.3: *Identify the primary responsibilities of offender treatment and education personnel.*

- Treatment personnel attempt to rehabilitate inmates with various problems by addressing the underlying social, mental, or emotional issues that contributed to the offender's criminal behavior. Correctional educators provide instruction for inmates who wish to further their education and may teach vocational training programs, provide academic counseling, offer in-service training for correctional employees, and serve on an institutional board.

4. Learning Objective 30.4: *Identify the primary responsibilities of prison wardens.*

- Wardens, or superintendents, are the chief executive officers of prisons. They manage prisons and are responsible for the facility meeting its goals. They primarily oversee all institutional personnel and are the institutions' primary point of contact with the nonprison world. They may also interact with the legislature and parole boards.

5. Learning Objective 30.5: *Discuss the benefits of diversifying correctional staffs.*

- The benefits of diversifying correctional staffs include presenting opportunities for staff members from different genders, cultures, races, and ethnicities to learn from one another; corrections officials being more understanding of offender behaviors and beliefs; and the message sent to inmates that not all who work in the criminal justice system are White males.

Questions for Critical Thinking

1. How are probation and parole services both similar and different?

2. Which prison officer assignments do you believe would be most dangerous? Which would be the safest? Which would you choose if you were a prison officer?

3. What types of offender treatment services are particularly important in prisons?

4. Do you believe wardens maintain too much power in prisons? Would you someday like to be a warden? Discuss your answer.

5. Should we strive to have prison staffs that reflect the demographics of the inmate population or the demographics of society in general? Or, should we not be concerned with employee demographics and simply hire the best available people? Why?

Key Terms

administration building assignments
block officers
deputy wardens of management
deputy wardens of custodial personnel
deputy wardens of industry and agriculture
deputy wardens of program personnel
enforcement (probation)
industrial shop and school officers
investigations (probation)
negative reinforcements
positive reinforcements

pre-parole investigation reports
relief officers
resource mediation
role modeling
supervision (probation)
surveillance (probation)
Title VII of the 1964 Civil Rights Act
wall posts
wardens
work detail supervisors
yard officers

For digital learning resources, please go to
https://www.oup.com/he/burns1e

Module

31

Community Corrections

There are many forms of community corrections. Some offenders live in halfway houses such as the one depicted here, where they are closely supervised while living in the community.

Do you think the dangers of letting offenders live in the community outweigh the benefits to offenders who are permitted to live outside prison?

Determining an appropriate sentence for an offender involves consideration of various issues, particularly with regard to the type of sentence imposed and the duration of the sentence. Some in society view sentences served in the community as not particularly punitive or effective; however, supervising and treating offenders in the community has many benefits. This module starts with a discussion of probation, before moving on to discuss intermediate sanctions and parole/reentry. Each of these areas of community corrections provides communities with viable options other than incarceration.

Medical Parole

In July 2017, a former New Hampshire priest was granted parole much earlier than prison officials anticipated. The man had received a 30- to 60-year sentence in 1998 for multiple sex crimes involving two altar boys in the 1990s. He was 71 at the time of his release and was granted medical parole after doctors confirmed that cancer was spreading throughout his body. He was required to wear an electronic monitoring device while on parole. State law allows for his return to prison if his condition improves (Hayward, 2017).

Inmates in New Hampshire and 46 other states, as well as those in the federal system, may be granted early release if it is felt that their medical conditions are severe enough that they pose no reasonable risk to society (Randall et al., 2017). Three conditions must be met for offenders to be eligible for medical parole in New Hampshire: The inmate is certified by a doctor to have a terminal, debilitating, incapacitating, or incurable medical condition; the cost of treating the condition is excessive; and the inmate likely will not break any laws and will act as a good citizen while released (Randall et al., 2017).

There is some concern that medical parole may result in nursing homes and related assisted-care living facilities resembling halfway houses for the elderly or ill and that residents will be at a higher risk of victimization. This concern is tempered by the requirements of states that inmates have notable physical ailments that restrict them

 1 Criminal Act

BREAKING NEWS
Former Priest Convicted Of
Sexual Assault Granted Parole
WMUR9

from harming others. Do you support the increased use of medical parole? Why or why not? Aside from cost savings, what are the benefits of medical parole?

 10 Corrections

Probation

Probation is conditional freedom granted to an offender, allowing an offender to be supervised in the community under the conditions specified in the probation agreement. These conditions may include submitting to random drug tests, obeying curfews, and avoiding particular individuals or locations.

Probationers account for the majority of adults (55.2% in 2018) under correctional supervision (roughly 3.54 million adults) (Maruschak & Minton, 2020). The use of probation as a sanction has increased over time because of overcrowded prisons and the costs associated with incarceration. Judges who impose a jail or prison sentence following a guilty verdict may suspend the sentence and allow the offender to reside in the community on probation in lieu of incarceration. Should probation be revoked, the offender generally serves the original jail or prison sentence. Offenders are accountable for their actions and subject to additional penalties if they violate the terms of their probation.

● **Learning Objective 31.1:** Explain some of the benefits of probation.

10 Corrections

probation Conditional freedom granted to an offender, allowing the offender to be supervised in the community under the conditions specified in the probation agreement

9 Sentencing

10 Corrections

Benefits of Probation

Probation may be combined with other sanctions and provides sentencing authorities with flexibility in addressing the needs of offenders. Rehabilitating offenders is easier with probation than it is in prison or jail because probationers are not surrounded by the negative influences of incarceration (Glaser, 1995). Benefits of probation include:

- judges being given flexibility in sentencing;
- probationers being able to live in the community and maintain employment and family ties;
- probationers being better able than inmates to make restitution;
- probationers being able to use the treatment, counseling, and other services available in their community; and
- communities being able to save on costs, because the costs associated with probation are lower compared to many other sanctions.

Investigation and Supervision

The primary functions of probation officers are investigation and supervision. Investigation refers to the preparation and presentation of a presentence investigation report for judges to use in sentencing hearings (see Modules 25 and 30). Supervision involves monitoring offenders in the community. The supervision function of probation has three components (Clear & Dammer, 2000):

technical violations Noncriminal behaviors that violate the terms of a probation or parole agreement

- written conditions of probation
- probationer reporting (probationers and probation officers making contact with one another in an office, in the field, or via technology)
- enforcing the orders of the court

Probation officers must properly handle cases in which probationers commit either new offenses or **technical violations**, which are noncriminal behaviors (e.g., failing a drug test) that violate the terms of the probation. Probation officers can avoid involving a judge in minor infractions, although their level of discretion decreases as the seriousness of the violation increases.

standard conditions (probation) General constraints imposed on all probationers

FORMAL CONSTRAINTS

Probation supervision involves enforcing informal and formal conditions placed on probationers. Formal constraints are guided by courts and/or the law and placed within three categories (Clear et al., 2016):

punitive conditions (probation) Conditions imposed on probationers to increase the severity or restrictiveness of their sentence

- **Standard conditions** are general constraints imposed on all probationers (e.g., accountability to probation officers, remaining employed, notifying their probation officer regarding any change of address).
- **Punitive conditions** are imposed on probationers to increase the severity or restrictiveness of their sentence (e.g., fines, restitution, community service).
- **Treatment conditions** target particular needs of the probationer and add a rehabilitative approach to probation (e.g., substance abuse treatment, anger-management courses, and general counseling requirements).

treatment conditions (probation) Conditions of probation that target particular needs of the probationer and add a rehabilitative approach to probation

CASELOAD SIZE

Probation officer caseloads have increased substantially over the years, despite calls for smaller caseloads to ensure that probationers are more adequately supervised

Probation officers are expected to provide supervision for probationers and presentence investigation reports for judges. Part of the supervisory responsibilities of probation officers is to visit probationers at their home or place of work to ensure they are performing well.

What do you believe would be the most difficult and rewarding aspects of being a probation officer?

MYTHBUSTING

Probation Is Too Lenient

It is often believed that probation is not restrictive enough. However, probationers forfeit many individual rights, such as protections from searches without a warrant. They are also required to submit to alcohol and drug testing and have to gain approval from their probation officer to sign a contract, leave the county, and take various other actions. Recent probation practices have become increasingly punitive in nature, as more numerous and/or stringent conditions have been placed on probationers by judges. This, in turn, increases the likelihood of probationers violating the terms of their probation agreement. Jurisdictions have also increasingly charged fees for probation supervision; most states have laws permitting authorities to make probationers and parolees pay for being supervised in the community.

Yes, some offenders and others in society may view probation as lenient and preferable to incarceration. However, probation can be as tough as judges and probation officers want it to be. This flexibility is one of the benefits of probation.

and receive the necessary services. Some researchers suggest that smaller caseloads improve probation outcomes (e.g., Jalbert & Rhodes, 2012), although there is some debate regarding whether smaller probation caseloads truly are more effective (Clear et al., 2016). As noted in Module 30, there is no accepted level of probation officer caseload.

LEVELS OF SUPERVISION

Caseload size is largely influenced by the level of supervision probationers require. Probation officers may be asked to oversee:

- regular caseloads with standard probationers who need no special attention,
- intensive supervision caseloads with high-risk offenders who need extra supervision and attention, and
- special caseloads that consist of probationers with particular types of problems, such as substance abuse or mental illness.

Each group provides distinct challenges for probation officers. For example, probation officers are generally undertrained or underprepared to work with sex offenders because of the time-intensive, complex, and expensive training required (Allen et al., 2013). Mentally ill probationers also provide challenges for probation officers, given the need for officers to be concerned with ensuring clients take medications regularly, probationers committing suicide or harming others, and the generally unstable behavior of mentally ill probationers (see Module 33).

Jurisdictions classify supervision as minimum, medium, high, and maximum (Abadinsky, 2015; Whitehead et al., 2013). Minimum supervision is the least restrictive and may require probationers to report to their probation officer once a month and have telephone contact. Probationers at this level are typically low-risk offenders who have committed minor offenses. The number of required contacts (which may be in person, by computer, or by phone) increases as the security level moves toward maximum supervision, which requires the most surveillance and control.

Probation concludes with the probationer either successfully completing the terms of probation or misbehaving and having probation revoked. Roughly one-third of probationers fail to successfully complete the terms of their probation or parole, for reasons such as committing new crimes, committing technical violations, or absconding (Pew Charitable Trusts, 2018).

10
Corrections

6 Hearing

probation revocation hearings
Hearings used to determine whether probationers who are caught committing a new offense or a technical violation should be subject to whatever penalty of incarceration the judge originally ordered but suspended in favor of probation

Probation Revocation

Probation revocation hearings are held to determine whether probationers who are caught committing a new offense or a technical violation should be subject to whatever penalty of incarceration the judge originally ordered. Probationers have several due process protections during probation revocation hearings. In *Mempa v. Rhay* (1967), the U.S. Supreme Court held that defendants could not receive a sentence after probation revocation without the assistance of an attorney to represent them. In *Gagnon v. Scarpelli* (1973), the Supreme Court clarified the probation revocation hearing process, which involves three steps (Seiter, 2014):

- In a *preliminary hearing*, the facts of the case are reviewed to determine if there is probable cause to believe a violation occurred.
- In a *hearing*, the facts of the case are heard and a decision is rendered. The probation department presents evidence to support the allegation of misbehavior, and the probationer has an opportunity to refute the evidence.

- In *sentencing*, a judge decides how to respond to the probation violation(s). In cases involving violations, judges can simply reprimand the probationer and restore them to supervision, add conditions to the probation agreement and restore them to probation, or revoke the probation and incarcerate the offender under the original sentence.

Intermediate Sanctions

Intermediate sanctions are a series of penalties that are more punitive than probation, yet less severe and less costly than incarceration (See Module 29 for discussion of administering these sanctions). They are intended to:

- reduce prison overcrowding,
- save government resources,
- offer flexibility with regard to sentencing options,
- protect public safety, and
- keep offenders in the community where they can continue to work and remain with family members (B. R. McCarthy et al., 2001).

Corrections officials use risk assessments to determine an offender's suitability for various intermediate sanctions, and the sanctions can be used in combination with one another. For instance, an offender may receive intensive supervision probation with electronic monitoring.

The popularity of intermediate sanctions has been encouraged by several factors, including:

- displeasure with traditional probation services,
- prison overcrowding,
- budgetary concerns associated with incarceration,
- the belief that intermediate sanctions are more effective with regard to rehabilitating some offenders,
- recognition of the importance of community resources in assisting offenders, and
- flexibility of the sanctions to meet the needs of various offenders (Seiter, 2014).

The use of intermediate sanctions is not consistent across jurisdictions in the United States, and not all states use all forms of intermediate sanctions. Among the more commonly used intermediate sanctions are day reporting centers, shock probation, shock incarceration, intensive probation supervision, and home confinement with electronic monitoring. Determining which sanction best suits an offender has been challenging, because each sanction has strengths and weaknesses, and each offender is unique.

Day Reporting Centers

Day reporting centers (DRCs) provide services such as treatment and surveillance to offenders living at home. They enable offenders to avoid incarceration and attend self-help programs in the community. Offenders sentenced to DRCs must report regularly (e.g., daily) to a designated center to help ensure that they are meeting the requirements of their sentence. The requirements may range from remaining at the

---

● **Learning Objective 31.2:** Describe intermediate sanctions and the reasons for their popularity.

10
Corrections

intermediate sanctions A series of penalties that are more punitive than probation, yet less severe and less costly than incarceration

10
Corrections

day reporting centers An intermediate sanction that provides services such as treatment and surveillance to offenders living at home; offenders sentenced to these centers must report regularly to a designated center to help ensure that they are meeting the requirements of their sentence

center for a set number of hours per day to merely reporting to the center daily for drug or alcohol testing (see Module 34 for discussion of day treatment centers and juveniles).

SERVICES AND BENEFITS

DRCs provide various correctional programs and services, such as:

- classes on parenting and life skills,
- counseling,
- educational programs,
- drug testing, and
- meetings with probation officers.

They have become increasingly popular in jurisdictions that rely more on community-based alternatives to incarceration. They also emphasize rehabilitation and help reduce prison and jail crowding (Kim et al., 2008).

A recent study of a DRC in Las Vegas found that compared to offenders on probation or parole, those who attended the local DRC:

- had lower levels of new charges or violations,
- were more likely to be successfully discharged from the program, and
- were more likely to obtain and maintain employment and a stable residence (West et al., 2019).

These positive results highlight the many objectives associated with DRCs.

NIMBY

Despite the benefits of DRCs, they are not universally well liked, particularly by the communities in which they are located. The term **NIMBY** ("not in my backyard") has been used to describe the approach taken by some community members who do not wish to have the facilities located in their neighborhoods out of fear of the potential harmful effects. Group homes and other community-based facilities often feel the effects of NIMBY. In 2017, city council members in San Diego, California, faced strong opposition from community members when they proposed the placement of an 84-bed drug treatment center for homeless individuals who had a history of repeatedly committing nonviolent, less serious crimes. Critics of the plan, which involved renovating a hotel, argued that it would attract criminals to the area, reduce the number of locations for tourists to stay, and hamper revitalization efforts in the area (Garrick, 2017).

Shock Probation

Some states use **shock probation** as a means of scaring offenders into a life free of crime. Those receiving shock probation are unaware that they will be placed on probation shortly after being incarcerated. The goal is to "shock" the offender into law-abiding behavior through the scare associated with prison time. Shock probation is similar to **split sentencing**, in which an offender is given a short period of incarceration, followed by probation. The primary difference between the two is that the offender who receives a split sentence *knows* that they will be released to probation after a designated period of time, while those receiving shock probation do not.

Generally, offenders are not sentenced to shock probation. Instead, they are sentenced to a period of incarceration and are released after a short period and placed on probation based on a judge's discretion. Judges primarily consider the offender's

NIMBY "Not in my backyard"; it refers to the approach taken by some community members who do not wish to have correctional facilities located in their neighborhoods out of fear of the potential harmful effects

shock probation An intermediate sanction in which offenders are sentenced to a period of incarceration, although they are released after a short time and placed on probation

split sentencing A sentence in which an offender is given a short period of incarceration, followed by probation

9 Sentencing

behavior while incarcerated and their suitability for probation. Shock probation is not used in all states and typically applies to first-time offenders.

This sanction is more rehabilitative than is incarceration, because offenders can avoid continued exposure to the harms associated with prison life and can benefit from community resources, including the treatment, educational, and counseling opportunities not necessarily available to inmates.

Shock Incarceration

Shock incarceration is more commonly known as **boot camp** and typically involves young, first-time offenders undergoing strict, military-like discipline, including physical training, team skills development, and education for approximately 90–180 days. Campers may also receive job training, counseling, and treatment. Some boot camps are reserved for adults, although many are used for juveniles. Boot camp programs vary, but they are all based on the belief that individuals can be shocked out of a life of crime and deterred from further wrongdoing.

The goal of many boot camps is to establish respect for authority and fear of becoming further involved in the justice system. Further, they often seek to "break" offenders' psyches and then rebuild them with positive attributes such as self-discipline and respect for themselves and others.

Boot camps for offenders were introduced and became popular in the 1980s because they fit the "tough on crime" approach that emerged during that time. Research on boot camps, however, suggests that the camps have limited effectiveness in preventing further criminal behavior. They are less prevalent in the early 21st century than they were in the 1990s, and they typically do not reduce participants' odds of reoffending (Meade & Steiner, 2010).

State-run boot camps are often located on the grounds of larger correctional facilities (e.g., prisons), which permits the sharing of services and programs. Offenders in boot camps, however, are segregated from the other inmate populations.

Intensive Supervision Probation

Intensive supervision probation (ISP) features a greater number of and more frequent face-to-face contacts between the probationer and probation officer than traditional probation. Those sentenced to ISP have greater restrictions and are monitored by officers who have smaller caseloads. ISP has become popular because it:

- helps alleviate prison overcrowding,
- is tougher than regular probation, and
- is more cost-effective than incarceration.

Despite these advantages, ISP is more costly than traditional probation, and some research has suggested that it is no more successful than standard probation in preventing individuals from offending (e.g., Hyatt & Barnes, 2014).

Home Confinement and Electronic Monitoring

Home confinement, which is sometimes referred to as house arrest, requires offenders to remain within the confines of their home during designated hours of each day. Those hours vary from an evening curfew, to detention

shock incarceration
Also known as **boot camp**; programs that involve offenders undergoing strict military-like discipline, including physical training, team skills development, and education

10
Corrections

intensive supervision probation A type of probation in which officers have smaller caseloads, probationers have greater restrictions, and there are a greater number of and more frequent face-to-face contacts between the probationer and probation officer

Shock incarceration, or boot camp, is an intermediate sanction that seeks to encourage offender conformity through the use of military-style drill instruction accompanied by skills and character-building programming.

What potential dangers are associated with this type of correctional approach?

10
Corrections

home confinement
Also known as house arrest;
it is an intermediate sanction
that requires offenders to
remain within the confines
of their home during designated hours of each day

1 Criminal
Act

3 Arrest

at home during all nonworking hours, to nearly continuous incarceration at home. Offenders on house arrest typically face the same restrictions as probationers and may be permitted to leave the confines of their home to attend work, school, counseling, and other approved places. Offenders are monitored at home in several ways that may include telephone calls, visits, and electronic devices.

The use of electronic monitoring in conjunction with home confinement steadily grew throughout the 1980s and 1990s, but electronic devices are also used with individuals at various states of case processing (e.g., with individuals being supervised pretrial, probationers, and parolees). A common form of electronic monitoring is through an ankle bracelet that sends an electronic message when an offender enters or leaves their home.

The active version of electronic monitoring uses a surveillance device that transmits a constant signal to a probation office, enabling the probation officer to know if the offender leaves the designated premises. The passive version of electronic monitoring requires the offender to place the device into a verifier box that, often along with voice identification, confirms the offender's identity. Traditionally, electronic monitoring involved radiofrequency, although technological advances have resulted in offenders also being monitored through global positioning systems.

Offenders who are monitored in the community are not permitted to remove the device. Doing so sends an alert to their supervising officer, and the offender will be sought and punished. One Massachusetts offender, who had been allowed to work during the day and return to jail at night, unlawfully removed his device and left the minimum-security prerelease program in which he was enrolled. The offender was arrested and charged with escape from a penal institution and wanton destruction of property over $250 (Spencer, 2017).

● **Learning Objective 31.3:** Compare mandatory and discretionary parole and identify the primary challenges inmates face upon leaving prison.

10
Corrections

maxing out Prisoners
serving their entire sentence

Parole, Release, and Reentry

Prisoners generally do not spend relatively long periods in prison. The average time served by state prisoners released in 2016 was 2.6 years. Those serving time for violent offenses served an average of 4.7 years, while property and drug offenders served an average of 21 months (Kaeble, 2018). The large majority of those released from prison are supervised in the community for a period of time after their release. The others, or those who "max out," undergo no supervision.

Maxing out refers to prisoners serving their entire sentence. Inmates who "max out" their sentences are generally released from prison at the expiration of their sentence and have no conditions placed on them at release. They are typically offenders who received and served short periods of incarceration. All other inmates, particularly those who receive a mandatory or discretionary release from prison, are often subject to parole upon exiting prison. Parole involves conditional supervision in the community. The primary function of parole is to reintegrate former inmates from incarceration in a productive manner. Release from prison can be difficult for offenders for many reasons, and preparation for reentry is particularly important to ensure former inmates do not return to incarceration.

Discretionary and Mandatory Parole

Parolees are expected to abide by conditions set forth in a parole contract until a specified date per the agreement. States use one of two methods in granting parole: discretionary and mandatory parole.

Discretionary parole is associated with the rehabilitation model and indeterminate sentencing (minimum and maximum periods of incarceration with offenders being released by parole boards—see Module 25). Parole board members use their discretionary authority to release or continue to detain an inmate following a defined period of time. Inmates seeking parole in jurisdictions using discretionary parole must demonstrate that they are "ready" or "prepared" for reentry to a parole board and may do so through taking advantage of counseling, educational, and general rehabilitative opportunities. Discretionary release was in use throughout much of the 20th century.

Research generally suggests that the most significant factors that influence parole board decision-making (i.e., discretionary parole) include the following (Caplan, 2007):

- institutional behavior
- incarceration length
- the severity of the crime
- the inmate's criminal history
- the presence of mental illness
- victim input

Mandatory parole is generally used in states with determinate sentencing structures, in which offenders receive a maximum period of incarceration with an early and conditional release based on time served and earned good time (see Module 25). For instance, if an offender received a 10-year prison sentence, each day they served would earn time off of their sentence. They would also earn time off of their sentence each day for good behavior, or good time. The accumulated time served and time earned for good behavior would reduce their prison sentence from 10 years, resulting in the early, mandatory release of the inmate, perhaps after 5 to 6 years.

In 2015, the greatest percentage (about 44%) of the cases entering parole involved discretionary entry (Kaeble & Alper, 2020). Regardless of which type of parole is used, parolees are subject to parole revocation if they fail to meet the terms of the parole agreement.

Parole Revocation

Similar to the hearings that occur when probationers violate the terms of their probation agreement, parolees face a hearing if they commit a crime or technical violation (an act that is not criminal but violates the terms of the parole agreement) while on parole. **Parole revocation hearings** are used to determine if parolees who violate the terms of their release agreement should be returned to incarceration. Parole officers play an important role in the parole revocation process, which begins with a parole board assessing whether there is reasonable cause to believe a legal or technical violation occurred. Evidence of a violation may prompt a hearing to determine whether the offender will return to prison.

9 Sentencing

10
Corrections

discretionary parole   A means by which inmates are released from prison; it involves the use of parole boards making a determination of whether the inmate appears ready to be released

mandatory parole   Generally used in states with determinate sentencing structures, it involves the early, conditional release of inmates whose sentence was reduced as a result of time served and earned good time

In 2006, Cyntoia Brown was convicted of murdering a man who picked her up with the intention of having sex with her. Although she was only 16 years old at the time, she received a life sentence for the crime. She was to be eligible for parole after serving 51 years. However, in 2019, she was released to 10 years of parole after the Tennessee governor granted her clemency based on his belief that the penalty was too severe and that Brown had been a victim of sex trafficking. Several celebrities, including National Basketball Association star LeBron James and musical artist Rihanna, openly supported the early release of Cyntoia Brown.

Based on her having served over a dozen years in prison, what challenges do you foresee for Brown following her release?

Parolees have particular due process rights at revocation hearings (e.g., *Morrissey v. Brewer*, 1972) including the right to:

- confront witnesses;
- receive written notice of the charges against them;
- present testimony, witnesses, and evidence on their own behalf; and
- receive a written statement justifying the reasoning behind the final decision.

In *Gagnon v. Scarpelli* (1973), the U.S. Supreme Court ruled that defendants have a limited right to counsel and the court will determine whether representation shall be provided to the parolee.

The commission of a new offense or a technical violation does not necessarily result in parole revocation, and overcrowded prisons have reduced the likelihood of parole violators returning to prison (O'Leary, 2010). Parole officers have used their discretion at times to overlook some technical violations or rely on alternatives to incarceration (e.g., intensive supervision or electronic monitoring) to address them.

Aside from incarceration, alternative sanctions for parole violations include the loss of parole time (meaning the offender must spend a greater amount of time on parole) and an enhanced level of supervision (e.g., more stringent conditions or more frequent visits from a parole officer). Although most inmates are released on parole, there are other conditions under which they reenter society.

Other Forms of Release

Aside from receiving discretionary release, mandatory release, and maxing out, prisoners reenter society in other ways, sometimes on a temporary basis. **Clemency** is "a pardon, reduction of sentence, or release of an inmate by the governor or pardoning authority" (Allen, Latessa, & Ponder, 2013, p. 254). It is sometimes used in cases where evidence emerges post-conviction and exonerates a prisoner. The four forms of clemency are:

- Pardons involve a government official restoring the rights and privileges of convicted individuals, for instance to correct a miscarriage of justice. For instance, in 2015 the Virginia governor pardoned a man who had served 29 years in prison for rape and kidnapping, after another man, who closely resembled the pardoned inmate, admitted to the crimes.
- **Amnesty** is similar to a pardon, although it applies to a group or class of offenders (e.g., when the U.S. grants amnesty to undocumented immigrants).
- **Commutations** involve the shortening or changing of prison sentences, for instance, when inmates become terminally ill or when death sentences are reduced to sentences of life in prison.
- **Reprieves** are often associated with capital punishment, and typically do not result in the release of the offender, but a reduction in the severity of the punishment or a delay in its imposition (Allen, Latessa, & Ponder, 2013).

Clemency is used relatively infrequently compared to discretionary and mandatory release, primarily because most situations involving offenders do not warrant the special considerations inherent in clemency.

Inmates are sometimes released as a result of extraordinary circumstances, as was the case following the outbreak of the COVID-19 pandemic in 2020. Corrections officials throughout the United States released thousands of inmates in an

parole revocation hearings Hearings that are used to determine if parolees who violate the terms of their release agreement should be returned to incarceration

clemency A pardon, reduction of sentence, or release of an inmate by the governor or pardoning authority

10
Corrections

amnesty A type of clemency that is similar to a pardon, although it applies to a group or class of offenders

commutations A type of clemency that involves the shortening or changing of prison sentences, for instance, when inmates become terminally ill or when death sentences are reduced to sentences of life in prison

reprieves A type of clemency; they are often associated with capital punishment, and typically do not result in the release of the offender, but a reduction in the severity of the punishment or a delay in its imposition

unprecedented effort to reduce the spread of the communicable virus. Low-level offenders, the elderly, and sickly inmates in jails and prisons were released in efforts to protect corrections officers and inmates (Elinson & Paul, 2020).

Some jurisdictions also offer temporary release programs through which inmates can slowly readjust to life outside prison:

- **Work release programs** provide inmates with an opportunity to reorient themselves with life and work outside prison as they gain job skills.

- **Study release programs** provide offenders with time outside prison to attend classes and further their education or learn job skills. Inmates are expected to return to prison each day following their student-related obligations.

- **Furloughs** enable offenders to leave prison for extended periods (typically 24 to 72 hours) for various reasons, such as reestablishing family ties or searching for housing or employment in anticipation of an upcoming release from incarceration.

The benefits of these types of release were noted in research on a work release program in Minnesota which found that, despite the increased likelihood of participants in the program getting caught for technical violations while on work release, they were less likely to reoffend with a new crime. The program helped participants find jobs and saved the state an estimated $1.25 million, or roughly $700 per inmate (Duwe, 2015).

Reentry

Offenders leaving incarceration must overcome various hurdles and readjust to environments that may be very different from the ones they left previously. The societies they enter will also differ greatly from the prison society they leave behind. Offenders face the added difficulties of reestablishing social and family ties, finding housing and employment, and doing so with the status as a former inmate. In addition, offenders with substance abuse or mental health concerns must also ensure that they find the treatment they need.

BARRIERS ASSOCIATED WITH REENTRY

Among the challenges associated with reentry are the civil disabilities imposed on convicted felons, including the limitations on the right to vote or hold public office. States vary in the restrictions placed on felons with regard to voting. For instance, in 2020 only 2 states (Maine and Vermont) and the District of Columbia permitted felons to vote from prison, and only 16 states permitted felons to vote upon being released from incarceration. Other states had stricter laws that can prevent felons from ever voting again (National Conference of State Legislatures, 2020; ProCon, 2017). An estimated 6.1 million Americans were prohibited from voting in 2016 because of **felon disenfranchisement laws** that restrict voting privileges for felons (Uggen et al., 2016). Such legislatively defined restrictions of former inmates, known as **invisible punishments** (e.g., Mauer & Chesney-Lind, 2002), provide numerous obstacles for individuals returning from incarceration.

Other legal barriers to reentry include restrictions in some states regarding:

- eligibility for public assistance and food stamps
- public housing
- driver's licenses

work release programs Programs that provide inmates an opportunity to reorient themselves with life and work outside prison as they gain particular job skills

study release programs Programs that provide offenders time outside prison to attend classes and further their education or learn job skills

furloughs Permitting inmates to leave prison for extended periods for various reasons

10
Corrections

felon disenfranchisement laws Legislation that restricts or removes voting privileges for felons

invisible punishments Legislatively defined restrictions of former inmates

- adoptions and foster care
- student loans (*After Prison*, 2004)

EMPLOYMENT

Finding employment upon leaving a correctional institution can be difficult because both formal and informal barriers challenge offenders. For instance, various state statutes prevent former offenders from obtaining select positions such as:

- barbers (even though many prisons provide inmates training in this area),
- beauticians,
- bus drivers,
- firefighters,
- child-care workers, and
- nurses (Clear et al., 2016; Ispa-Landa & Loefler, 2016).

Informally, employers are often hesitant to hire former inmates or offenders in general, and thus ex-offenders generally obtain low-paying positions. One study noted that the median hourly wage for ex-offenders was $9. The same study cited the importance of obtaining gainful employment upon release, as evidenced by the finding that individuals who earned more than $10 per hour were half as likely to return to prison as those who made less than $7 per hour (Visher et al., 2008).

EXPUNGEMENT AND SEALINGS

Offenders may seek an expungement or pardon to assist with their reentry efforts. **Expungement** involves completely deleting an offender's criminal record; thus, it is no longer visible to anyone, including the police and other government officials. Offenders can also petition a judge for a **partial sealing**, in which only certain portions of the record are restricted, or a **complete sealing**, which removes an offender's record from public access (although police agencies and some other government entities may have access to it) (Ispa-Landa & Loefler, 2016).

The laws regarding expungement and sealings vary widely among the 45 states that permit them. For instance, 5 states do not allow arrest (i.e., nonconviction) records to be expunged, and 18 states permit conviction records to be sealed (Ispa-Landa & Loefler, 2016). Convictions for select offenses (e.g., rape, murder, sexual battery) are typically not eligible for expungement.

As referenced above, a **pardon** is an act by the executive branch of the state or federal government that excuses an offense and absolves the offender from the consequences of the crime. Pardons are used to address miscarriages of justice, remove the stigma of a conviction, and mitigate penalties (Clear et al., 2016). In 2020, President Trump issued a series of pardons for various reasons. For instance, he pardoned former New York City Police Commissioner Bernard Kerik, who pleaded guilty in 2009 to tax fraud and lying to the government. The president explained his action by suggesting that he had received many good recommendations about Kerik's character (Toobin, 2020).

REINTEGRATION PROGRAMS

Several reintegration programs are offered to assist with prisoner reentry. Among them are **halfway houses**, which offer homelike atmospheres with community

expungement
Legally removing a conviction from an individual's state official records

partial sealing Restricting only certain portions of an offender's criminal record

complete sealing Removing an offender's record from public access, although police agencies and some other government entities may have access to it

pardon An act by the executive branch of the state or federal government that excuses an offense and absolves the offender from the consequences of the crime

halfway houses Facilities that provide many of the same services as group homes, although they are more commonly used with offenders who have served some period of incarceration and are readjusting to life outside confinement; they provide transitional residences for individuals who may struggle with entering the same environment that contributed to the earlier misbehavior

supervision. The facilities help inmates transition from institutionalization and provide programming that can meet inmate needs while they reenter society. They assist individuals who may struggle with entering the same environment that contributed to their earlier misbehavior and provide an alternative to strict institutionalization. Halfway houses are also sometimes used to assist probationers who struggle with the terms of their probation.

Community resources can be particularly helpful with regard to inmate reentry; for instance, community-based organizations, faith-based organizations, and local businesses assist inmates with their transition from incarceration (Petersilia, 2003). The federal government recently recognized the importance of reentry; for instance, in April 2018, Congress signed into law the **Second Chance Act**, designed to assist individuals leaving prison. The unique legislative act authorized federal grants to nonprofit and government agencies to provide support and design services to reduce recidivism through assisting those leaving prison.

The federal government and some other jurisdictions have been supportive of reentry partnerships between corrections agencies, community agencies, and police departments. Some jurisdictions created **reentry courts**, a type of problem-solving court, to assist inmates exiting prison. The courts facilitate reentry because they provide parolees with close supervision, links to social services, and intensive case management.

> **CAREERS**
>
> **Halfway house managers** perform the duties of both correctional officers and prison administrators. They maintain custodial responsibility for halfway houses and are accountable for the residents. They may perform personal searches, dispense medications and supplies, and oversee the residents' daily domestic responsibilities.

Second Chance Act Legislation designed to assist individuals leaving prison; it authorized federal grants to nonprofit and government agencies to provide support and design services to reduce recidivism through assisting those leaving prison

reentry courts Problem-solving courts that are designed to assist inmates exiting prison

The System in Perspective

As discussed in the "In the News" feature at the start of this module, the case involving a priest who was released from prison early because of medical concerns demonstrates some of the benefits of community corrections. Enabling low-risk, notably ill offenders to receive medical parole reduces the burden (in terms of costs and care) on prison officials and enables offenders to serve their time outside prison walls and with family and friends while they battle their medical issues. However, the practice is also controversial because some people see it as the system being "too soft."

Administering community corrections requires the efforts of many individuals and agencies that are not necessarily part of the criminal justice system but play an important role in its functioning. An offender's friends and family members, community treatment programs, and employers are among the many groups who contribute to supervising offenders in the community. They help offenders stay trouble free and provide necessary healthcare, education, and employment resources. There are also groups within the criminal justice system that contribute. Community corrections personnel such as probation and parole officers must work closely with others in our justice systems, including judges, halfway house managers, and law enforcement. Ultimately, it takes efforts from many individuals to ensure that the different forms of community corrections are effective.

Summary

1. Learning Objective 31.1: *Explain some of the benefits of probation.*

- Probation is helpful in the sense that it provides an alternative to incarceration, and it can be tailored to meet the probationers' needs. It permits offenders to remain in the community and maintain family ties, facilitates the payments that may be associated with restitution, promotes rehabilitation through enabling offenders to receive treatment in the community, reduces the negative impacts associated with incarceration, and is one of the least expensive correctional sanctions.

2. Learning Objective 31.2: *Describe intermediate sanctions and the reasons for their popularity.*

- Intermediate sanctions are designed to be more punitive than probation, yet not as costly or severe as incarceration. Their popularity has been encouraged by displeasure with traditional correctional services, prison overcrowding, budget constraints, the belief that intermediate sanctions can be more effective than traditional sanctions, recognition of the need to better integrate the community to assist offenders, and the flexibility inherent in their use.

3. Learning Objective 31.3: *Compare mandatory and discretionary parole and identify the primary challenges inmates face upon leaving prison.*

- Parole can be discretionary or mandatory. Discretionary parole involves parole board members using their discretionary authority to release or continue to detain an inmate. Mandatory parole involves the early, conditional release of inmates whose sentence was reduced as a result of time served and earned good time.

- Offenders often face a series of barriers that hamper their efforts to succeed outside prison or jail. Among the challenges are the civil disabilities imposed on convicted felons, including the limitations on the right to vote or hold public office and the restrictions regarding eligibility for public assistance and food stamps, public housing, driver's licenses, adoptions and foster care, and student loans. Finding housing and employment upon leaving prison can be difficult, as can overcoming various hurdles and readjusting to life outside the institution. Offenders face the added difficulties of reestablishing social and family ties and doing so with the status as a former inmate.

Questions for Critical Thinking

1. In what ways do you believe probation could be enhanced?

2. Do you believe we will see new forms of intermediate sanctions in the future? If so, what might they be like? If not, why not?

3. What actions could be taken to ensure that former inmates have greater levels of success upon their exit from prison?

Key Terms

amnesty
boot camp
clemency
complete sealing
commutation

day reporting centers
discretionary parole
expungement
felon disenfranchisement laws
furloughs

halfway houses
home confinement
intensive supervision probation
intermediate sanctions
invisible punishments
mandatory parole
maxing out
NIMBY
pardon
parole revocation hearings
partial sealing
probation
probation revocation hearings

punitive conditions (probation)
reentry courts
reprieves
Second Chance Act
shock incarceration
shock probation
split sentencing
standard conditions (probation)
study release
technical violations
treatment conditions (probation)
work release programs

For digital learning resources, please go to
https://www.oup.com/he/burns1e

Module

32

MODULE OUTLINE

- **Functions of Jails and Prisons**

  Learning Objective 32.1: Distinguish jails from prisons in terms of the functions they serve.

- **Growth in the Prison Population**

  Learning Objective 32.2: Identify the factors that contributed to the increased growth in the prison population beginning in the 1980s.

- **Privatization**

  Learning Objective 32.3: Summarize the arguments in support of and against the use of private prisons.

- **Prison Life**

  Learning Objective 32.4: Describe the formal rules and informal aspects of prison life that affect the experience of inmates.

- **Violence in Prisons**

  Learning Objective 32.5: Explain the dynamics of prison violence and the theoretical reasons for prison riots.

Institutional Corrections

Incarceration poses many challenges for inmates and serves many important purposes for society in general. The United States has experienced significant growth in the number of people incarcerated.

Do you believe we should continue heavily relying on incarceration to solve our crime problems? Why or why not?

Institutionalization in the form of jails and prisons was designed with several purposes in mind. Primarily, it punishes offenders, deters potential offenders, removes dangerous individuals from society, and provides opportunities for rehabilitating troubled individuals. This module closely examines institutional corrections, beginning with a comparison of jails and prisons. This is followed by coverage of the substantial growth we have witnessed with regard to the prison population and the use of privately operated facilities to address this growth. The module concludes with consideration of life inside prison, with special attention devoted to violence in correctional facilities.

Restorative Justice and You

In April 2015, Sharletta Evans wrote an op-ed piece during Victim Rights Awareness Week in which she discussed how she supported restorative justice for the individual who killed her 3-year-old son. In 1995, Evans's son was caught in the crossfire of a drive-by shooting in Denver. Initially, Evans wanted the three teenagers involved in the shooting to spend their lives in prison, but she eventually had a change of heart. About 10 years later, she wished for her son's killers to be rehabilitated and returned to society when they were ready. She was in contact with one of the offenders and told him about her pain and that she had forgiven him. Members of Ms. Evans's nonprofit organization, Victim Offender Mitigation Initiative, visit prisons and speak with inmates as part of a faith-based restorative justice curriculum.

After decades of increasing incarceration rates and a general reliance on punishment to address crime, alternative, potentially more effective approaches are becoming more popular. Among them is restorative justice, which aims to repair the damage done by crime, with consideration of the needs of victims, offenders, and the community. Restorative justice seeks to protect the community, hold offenders accountable for their actions, and encourage them to become law-abiding citizens. This approach may involve forgiveness, which can be difficult considering the traumatic, destructive nature of some criminal acts. Do you believe there will be a time when restorative justice replaces punishment as a primary goal of sentencing? What would be needed to prompt such a change?

1 Criminal Act

9 Sentencing

SHARLETTA EVANS

10 Corrections

Functions of Jails and Prisons

Offenders who receive sentences of 12 months or more of incarceration are placed in prison, while jails typically house those who receive sentences of less than 12 months and some individuals awaiting case processing. Incarceration is one of the most punitive and costly sentences.

Compared to jails, prisons have a less transient population and thus provide greater opportunities for prison officials to become familiar with inmates. Greater efforts are directed toward assessing inmates in prison compared to jails, given their long-term stay and the fact that they have all been convicted of crimes serious enough to warrant incarceration. Prisons also offer more programming for inmates, such as counseling and other forms of treatment. Figure 32.1 depicts the number of individuals in prisons and jails in the United States and the offenses for which they were incarcerated.

9 Sentencing

● **Learning Objective 32.1:** Distinguish jails from prisons in terms of the functions they serve.

10
Corrections

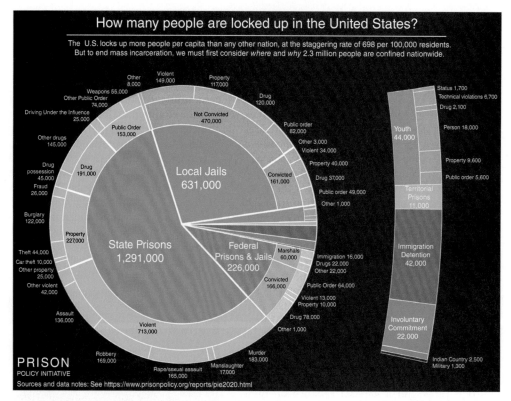

FIGURE 32.1. Correctional Populations in the United States. Over 2 million offenders convicted of a variety of crimes are incarcerated in the United States. Most prison inmates were incarcerated for committing a violent crime, and most jail inmates were not convicted, meaning they were being detained prior to trial. ***Source:*** *Sawyer, W. & Wagner, P. (2020). Mass Incarceration: The Whole Pie 2020. Prison Policy Initiative. https://www.prisonpolicy.org/reports/pie2020.html*

Do you believe the United States relies too heavily on incarceration? Why or why not?

10
Corrections

Importance and Functions of Jails

There are over 2,800 jails scattered across the United States. They represent one of the most underappreciated components of the criminal justice system and have been described as "poorhouses of the twentieth century" (Goldfarb, 1975, p. 29), dumping grounds for officers engaged in social sanitation (Welch, 1994), and "the ultimate ghetto" (Thompson, 1986, p. 205). Despite being underappreciated, jails are particularly important with regard to justice-based practices given that:

● more people go through jails than prisons,

● numerous critical decisions are made while inmates are detained in jail, and

● jail-based experiences greatly influence inmates (Irwin, 1985).

Jails serve several important functions, including:

● detaining those who cannot make bail or are not granted pretrial release,

● detaining probation and parole violators while they await a hearing,

● holding mentally ill offenders who are awaiting assessment,

● holding convicted offenders who are awaiting sentencing,

● housing inmates sentenced to incarceration for less than a year, and

● housing felons when state prisons are overcrowded.

Challenges of Jails

Jails face a number of challenges regardless of size. They have historically struggled with issues such as the following (May et al., 2014):

10
Corrections

- *overcrowding*: An estimated 20% of all jail jurisdictions in the United States were operating at or above 100% of their rated capacity (Zeng, 2020).
- *suicide*: Suicide was the leading cause of deaths in jails in 2016, accounting for 31% of all jail deaths (Carson & Cowhig, 2020).
- *high levels of violence*: An estimated 1.6% of jail inmates reported an incident involving sexual violence by another inmate, and 1.8% reported an incident with jail staff (Beck et al., 2013).
- *high rates of staff turnover*: County jails in Texas reported an annual average turnover rate of 29.5% (Wood, 2017).
- *limited resources*: An estimated 26% of jail inmates reported experiences that met the threshold for serious psychological distress (Bronson & Berzofsky, 2017), and jails typically do not have the resources to provide adequate services.
- *influences of local politics*: Sheriffs are elected in 46 states, which introduces politics into the administration and operation of jails. Module 29 addresses jail administration.

Prison Models

10
Corrections

In commenting on his life in a Siberian labor camp, Russian novelist Fyodor Dostoevsky noted that "the degree of civilization in a society can be judged by entering its prisons." This quote was taken from Dostoevsky's book *The House of the Dead*, published in 1862, and his insight remains relevant in the early 21st century.

Jails serve several important functions within the criminal justice system, but are underappreciated by most in society. Jail conditions may be problematic because of limited funding and scarce programming.

Why might offenders rate jail time as tougher than time spent in prison?

custodial model
A model of incarceration that dominates most maximum-security prisons in the early 21st century through its emphasis on incapacitation, deterrence, and retribution

rehabilitation model A model of incarceration that seeks to treat or rehabilitate offenders

reintegration model A model of incarceration that emphasizes offenders maintaining ties with the community

Current prison practices emphasize individual responsibility and rely heavily on punishment in response to criminal behavior. The primary goals of prisons are to rehabilitate, punish, and prevent inmates from further harming society. Three models of incarceration have dominated corrections since the early 1940s (G. F. Cole et al., 2013):

- The **custodial model** emphasizes incapacitation, deterrence, and retribution and is the model evident in most maximum-security prisons in the early 21st century. The focus in these institutions is on security, discipline, and order.
- The **rehabilitation model** seeks to treat or rehabilitate offenders. While popular from the 1950s through the 1970s, this model has largely been replaced given concerns for incapacitation, deterrence, and retribution beginning in the 1980s.
- The **reintegration model** strives to help offenders maintain ties with the community and is akin to community corrections. The belief is that one should remain in contact with the outside world while incarcerated for the sake of easing the transition from prisoner to citizen.

● **Learning Objective 32.2:** Identify the factors that contributed to the increased growth in the prison population beginning in the 1980s.

Growth in the Prison Population

The prison population has increased substantially over the past 100 years. In placing the growth in corrections into some historical perspective, a report from the Sentencing Project noted that between 1920 and 1970, the overall population in the United States nearly doubled, while the number of prisoners increased at just a slightly higher pace. However, between 1970 and 2000, while the general population increased by less than 40%, the number of individuals in jails and prisons increased by over 500% (King et al., 2005). In the early 21st century, the United States has roughly 5% of the world's population, yet it has roughly 20% of the world's prisoners (Sawyer & Wagner, 2020). Figure 32.2 depicts the substantial increase in the prison population from 1978 to 2017.

10
Corrections

Reasons for the Growth

A rehabilitative model that focused on providing education and job skills to offenders and treating them in the community dominated sentencing practices for much of the 20th century. Beginning in the 1970s, however, critics saw flaws with the emphasis on rehabilitation. Some believed that indeterminate sentencing was soft on criminals, while others believed it contributed to unjust and biased penalties because of heavy reliance on the discretion maintained by judges and parole boards (Belbot, 2012). These and related arguments, along with a general public that in the 1980s became increasingly fearful of crime, less tolerant of criminals, and more supportive of "get tough" approaches, contributed to a shift in policies and practices and an increase in the prison population.

Politicians responded to the concerns and passed numerous legislative acts that supported a more punitive approach to crime, for instance through:

- imparting tougher sentences,
- hiring more police officers,
- building more prisons, and
- increasing the penalties associated with drug crimes, including longer sentences, as part of the "war on drugs" introduced by President Nixon in 1971 (Stone & Scharf, 2011).

All of these actions led to an increase in the prison population. Hiring more police officers results in officers being better able to appropriately respond to and investigate crimes. In addition, the construction of new prisons meant that prison overcrowding would not prompt the use of alternatives to incarceration (e.g., probation).

Overcrowding

Wisconsin's prison population tripled between 1990 and 2017, and legislators noted that the state was not equipped to address the increase. Building a new prison would cost roughly $309 million—money that the state was not prepared to allocate. In response, several pieces of legislation were passed in efforts to reduce overcrowding, including one bill that provided shorter periods of incarceration for those who violate the terms of their probation or parole (not including the commission of another crime). Another bill proposed to increase the number of inmates eligible for

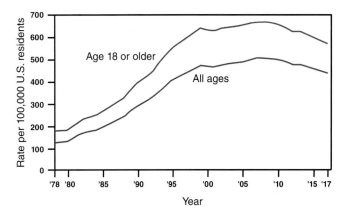

FIGURE 32.2. U.S. Prison Population Change, 1978–2017. The number and rate of prisoners increased steadily from 1978 until 2010. Since 2010 there have been slight decreases. *Source:* Prisoners in 2017 *(NCJ 252156), by J. Bronson and E. A. Carson, 2019, U.S. Department of Justice, Bureau of Justice Statistics.*

Do you believe that our prison population rate will return to pre-1980s levels? Why or why not?

the state's early release program, which releases inmates with drug or alcohol addictions early to receive treatment (Brown, 2017). Wisconsin is not the only state seeking to address problems related to prison overcrowding. The Bureau of Justice Statistics noted that at year-end 2019, 21 states and the Federal Bureau of Prisons had a number of prisoners in custody that met or exceeded the maximum number of their prison facilities' capacity (Carson, 2020a).

10
Corrections

Overcrowded correctional facilities contribute to various health and safety concerns for inmates and staff, including:

- increased discipline problems,
- the accelerated spread of communicable diseases,
- limited treatment and programming opportunities,
- increased healthcare concerns, and
- a general decreased quality of life.

Addressing Overcrowding

In 2011, the U.S. Supreme Court upheld a lower court ruling that the state of California needed to reduce its prison population by 30,000 inmates to alleviate overcrowding (*Brown v. Plata*, 2011). The court ruled that the overcrowded prisons in California violated the Eighth Amendment's ban on cruel and unusual punishment, primarily because it was claimed that the state was unable to provide basic care for inmates with serious medical and mental health issues. The state was able to reduce its prison population in part through moving many lower level felons and parole violators to county jails and offering financial incentives for counties to reduce the number of felony probationers they sent to state prison (Lofstro & Martin, 2015).

10
Corrections

Other states have also taken steps to address overcrowded prisons through:

- legalizing drugs or reducing the penalties associated with drugs,
- eliminating mandatory minimum sentencing statutes,
- modifying truth-in-sentencing calculations to allow shorter sentences (see Module 25 for discussion of sentencing practices), and

- adopting parole supervision reforms that have reduced the number of individuals sent back to prison for parole violations (Travis & Crayton, 2009) (see Module 31 for a discussion of parole violations).

The First Step Act, passed in 2018, also addressed prison overcrowding by moving away from the historically punitive approaches designed to keep inmates in prisons and jails for a longer time. The act eases punitive prison sentences at the federal level. Among other provisions, the legislation increased the number of good conduct time credits inmates can receive from 47 days per year to 54 days, which means that inmates will be serving shorter sentences on average. It also expanded the use of compassionate release for terminally ill inmates, which eases prison overcrowding. Combined, these actions should result in reduced prison overcrowding, because some sentences will be shorter and inmates will be serving reduced portions of their sentences.

● **Learning Objective 32.3:** Summarize the arguments in support of and against the use of private prisons.

10
Corrections

privatization Private contractors operating correctional facilities and contracting to provide services in others

private prisons Institutions operated by private companies that contract with federal or state authorities to provide correctional services

Privatization

Most prisons are state operated. However, akin to the incorporation of the private sector assuming some traditional law enforcement services (see Module 11) and in the courts (e.g., in the form of privately secured bail via bonding agencies; see Module 23), private, for-profit companies exist in corrections as well. In what is referred to as **privatization**, private companies may oversee all, or only some, aspects of prison operations and other correctional practices. In addition to prisons, private groups or companies have been involved in operating halfway houses, juvenile facilities, probation services, and jails (Allen et al., 1978; Carson & Anderson, 2016).

Private prisons are institutions operated by for-profit private companies that contract with federal or state authorities. They provide the same correctional services as government-run prisons, including:

- managing facilities;
- developing, designing, and leasing facilities to jurisdictions; and
- providing services such as dental care and healthcare, substance abuse treatment, and training.

The federal government housed over 14,000 inmates in privately operated facilities in 2020 (Federal Bureau of Prisons, 2020e). Some states rely on private prisons as well. Five states (Hawaii, Montana, Tennessee, New Mexico, and Oklahoma) housed at least 20% of their prison population in privately operated facilities at year-end 2019. Private prisons held 7% of the total U.S. prison population in 2019, including 16% of all federal prisoners (Carson, 2020a). Figure 32.3 depicts the extent to which each state used private prisons in 2017.

The Benefits of Private Prisons

Private prisons are being used by states and the federal government to alleviate overcrowding and address other issues. Private prisons have several benefits (Alarid & Reichel, 2013; Schmalleger & Smykla, 2009):

- *flexibility*: Private prisons are less affected by the bureaucratic challenges often associated with government-operated agencies and institutions and are thus more flexible in responding to problems and opportunities that may arise.

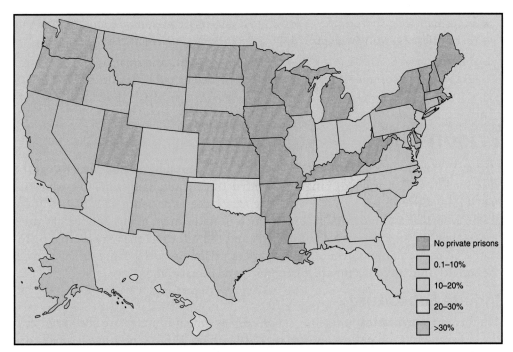

FIGURE 32.3. Proportion of Inmates in Private Prisons. Not all states use private prisons and jails, and states vary greatly regarding the extent to which they do. Two states (Montana and New Mexico) housed over 30% of their incarcerated population in private prisons or jails. The average percentage for all states in 2019 was 7%. *Source:* Private Prisons in the United States, *by the Sentencing Project, 2019 (https://www. sentencingproject.org/publications/private-prisons-united-states/).*

Do you believe we should restrict the use of private prisons? Why or why not?

- *eases government pressure*: Private prisons take the burden off governments to provide day-to-day prison services, and they may be motivated to provide effective and efficient services given their need to receive new contracts and remain in business.

- *creativity*: Private prisons can be more creative and innovative in solving problems because they are not burdened by all of the same restrictions and rules as government-run prisons.

The Criticisms of Private Prisons

Despite the benefits of private prisons, they are not universally well liked. Ultimately, states must weigh the advantages along with the disadvantages to determine what is best for their state. Some of the concerns regarding private prisons include the following (Champion et al., 2013):

10
Corrections

- *unjust*: It is believed by some in society that punishing offenders should be left to the government, which would have more oversight and accountability. The concern is that private prisons will place profits over justice and equity.

- *expensive*: Contracting with private agencies can be more expensive because of the profit margin added to the costs of providing correctional services.

- *less quality*: Private industries may seek to cut corners and provide less quality supervision and services in efforts to maximize profits.

- *less accountable*: There are few entities to hold private prisons accountable and uncertainties regarding who provides oversight for private facilities.
- *staff turnover*: Staff turnover is costly because benefits and salaries in the private sector are not commensurate with those provided by public facilities.

Learning Objective 32.4: Describe the formal rules and informal aspects of prison life that affect the experience of inmates.

10
Corrections

Prison Life

Life in prison is much different from life on the outside. Prison society can be described by a host of terms ranging from frustrating and dangerous to boring and controlling. Several aspects of prison life affect the experience of inmates. There are both formal and informal rules by which inmates must abide. The formal rules are established by correctional authorities, and the informal ones are created by inmates. Of particular importance with regard to prison life are the inmate subculture, the convict/inmate code, inmate misconduct, and inmate labor.

Inmate Subculture

The term **prisonization** refers to the process by which inmates are socialized into the prison world, or **prison subculture** (Clemmer, 1966). The prison subculture consists of the distinct values, norms, and beliefs identified among prison inmates. Prisoners construct their own rules, terminology, economic system, and groups that heavily influence the prison atmosphere (Santos, 2004). The extent to which inmates subscribe to the prison subculture is largely influenced by the length of time they spend in prison and the custody level of the institution (Terry, 2003).

Prison argot, or the language or gestures used by inmates to communicate, helps distinguish the inmate subculture from life outside prison. The use of prison argot:

- helps inmates feel different and unique,
- facilitates social interactions and relationships,
- provides a sense of secrecy, and
- enables inmates to declare allegiance to a group or subgroups (Einat & Einat, 2000).

Inmates create slang terms to describe various aspects of life. The terms generally vary among institutions and groups of inmates. Figure 32.4 highlights some of the terminology used by inmates.

The Convict/Inmate Code

Inmates adjust to prison life largely through understanding and adapting to the **convict code**, which is a set of informal rules guiding inmate behavior. It includes the following (Ross & Richards, 2002):

- minding your own business
- being tough
- being loyal to convicts as a group
- paying debts
- not attracting attention
- sticking by your words
- not snitching on other inmates
- not exploiting other inmates
- showing strong solidarity among the inmates with whom one associates
- exhibiting disdain for prison staff

prisonization
The process by which inmates are socialized into the prison world or prison subculture

prison subculture
The distinct values, norms, and beliefs identified among prison inmates

10
Corrections

prison argot
The language or gestures used by inmates to communicate; it helps distinguish the inmate subculture from life outside prison

---

Prison Argot—Examples

Bug—An insane person

Croaker—Correctional staff who diagnoses illness

Fish—First-time inmates who have yet to be indoctrinated into prison life

Gunned down—To be covered in urine or feces by another inmate

Hole—Isolation cell

Juice card—Favors provided by prison officers

Kill zone—The prohibited area next to an outside prison wall or fence

Nickel—Five-year sentence

Pulling a train—Serving consecutive sentences

Rabbit—Escaped inmate

Screw, hack, or pig—Correctional officer

Shank—A prison knife

Squares—Inmates who oppose the prison subculture, are well-behaved, and seek to improve themselves

---

FIGURE 32.4. Prison Argot: Examples. Prisoners create various words to describe events, people, and all else in prison. The terms are not universal across prisons, and inmates at different institutions use different terms. *Source:* Corrections: The Fundamentals, *by B. Foster, 2006, Pearson;* Behind Bars: Surviving Prison, *by J. I. Ross and S. C. Richards, 2002, Alpha; and* Corrections: An Introduction *(4th ed.), by R. P. Seiter, 2014, Pearson.*

Should prison officials prohibit the use of prison argot, for instance to demonstrate their control over inmates? Why or why not?

convict code Also known as the inmate code, it is the set of rules created and enforced by inmates that guides inmate behavior

Inmate codes and subcultures have been identified in both male and female prisons, although female inmates have a somewhat different code. Module 33 includes a discussion of the female subculture.

Inmate Misconduct

In 2016, the Federal Bureau of Prisons, which housed roughly 185,000 inmates, confiscated over 5,000 cell phones from inmates (Saul, 2018). The illegal use of cell phones by inmates is but one example of the many types of prisoner misconduct that persists on a regular basis. Research shows that inmates who engage in misconduct are more likely than those who do not to continue offending in the community upon their release (Trulson et al., 2011). Thus, it is important for prison officials to be aware of which inmates engage in misconduct and provide them the appropriate counseling or prolong their punishment.

10
Corrections

TYPES OF MISCONDUCT

Among the most common types of institutional misconduct are:

- entering unauthorized areas;
- using violence;
- profiting (e.g., via gambling, loansharking, or selling services);
- possessing illegal goods;
- inciting violent behavior;
- refusing to adhere to instructions of correctional staff;
- destroying property; and
- interacting improperly with correctional staff.

As an example with regard to profiting, a **sub rosa economy** exists in many jails and prisons in which inmates barter and negotiate goods and services. Although this

1 Criminal Act

sub rosa economy
An underground economy in which inmates barter and negotiate various goods and services

Artists illegally provide tattoos for inmates in prison. They must perform their services outside the view of prison officials and use makeshift tools (e.g., pen ink mixed with other ingredients and paper clips) to perform their art.

Should tattooing be permitted in prisons? What might be some of the concerns associated with tattoos?

merchants Inmates who sell other inmates various goods and services

jailhouse lawyers Inmates who sell their legal services to other inmates, for instance by conducting legal research or writing writs

artists Prisoners who illegally create and sell artwork or tattoos

deprivation theory Explains prisoner misconduct with consideration of how inmates adapt and cope with the pains and deprivations of imprisonment

importation theory Explains prisoner misconduct as a product of the behaviors, beliefs, and experiences of inmates prior to their institutionalization

administrative control theory Proposes that prison disorder is more likely to occur when prison management is provided in a weak, unstable, and/or divided manner

type of underground economy is prohibited, inmates sometimes run underground commissaries out of their cells, in which inmates known as **merchants** sell other inmates various goods and services (e.g., contraband smuggled into the prison). **Jailhouse lawyers** may sell their legal services to other inmates, for instance by conducting legal research or writing writs. **Artists** may sell artwork or tattoos.

EXPLAINING PRISONER MISCONDUCT

Research focused on prison inmate misconduct has helped explain why it occurs and who is most likely to engage in it. Three theoretical perspectives have been offered to explain the cause of inmate misconduct, including:

- **deprivation theory**, which centers on how inmates adapt and cope with the pains and deprivations of imprisonment (Clemmer, 1966; Sykes, 1958). For instance, an inmate may act violently against prison staff out of frustration at being incarcerated.
- **importation theory**, which proposes that inmate behaviors in prison are shaped by experiences and beliefs held prior to institutionalization (Irwin & Cressey, 1962). For example, an inmate may regularly get into fights with other inmates because that is how they behaved prior to their incarceration.
- **administrative control theory** and **inmate balance theory**, which suggest that prison management practices influence inmate behaviors. For instance, prison officials who unfairly restrict the number of hours of recreation per week that inmates get may encourage inmate misbehavior.

Measurements of the extent of prisoner misconduct are difficult to attain given that inmate misbehavior is largely unreported and undetected. However, a review of the research literature identified inmates with the following characteristics as being more likely than their counterparts to engage in misconduct. Such inmates generally:

- are younger (ages 21–35),
- are classified as a medium- or maximum-security risk,
- are associated with antisocial peers or are involved in a gang,
- have mental health problems,
- are from disadvantaged neighborhoods, and
- were sentenced to 5 years or more of incarceration (Steiner et al., 2014).

Inmate Labor

One way to address prisoner misconduct is by giving inmates the opportunity to work within the prison. Inmates are often assigned to institutional maintenance jobs that assist with operating and maintaining the prison. Whether inmates should or should not be able to work has been controversial since the origins of prisons. Among the benefits of prisoner labor are that it:

- helps maintain facility operations,
- saves government resources,
- enables prisoners to pay money they owe (e.g., for restitution or child support),

- reduces prisoner idleness,
- reduces inmate misbehavior in some cases as prisoners seek to maintain or attain valued employment positions, and
- teaches inmates skills (Alarid & Reichel, 2013).

Critics of prisoner labor argue that:

- prison-made goods can be produced and sold at a lower cost than in the private sector, thus creating an unfair market advantage for prisons. Non–prison industries may not be able to compete with prison industries that are not bound by the same labor law restrictions (e.g., minimum wage laws);
- prison labor generates safety concerns because inmates are granted more freedoms and access to items that could be used as weapons; and
- correctional institutions exploit inmates through having them work for low wages.

It is common for inmates to work in laundry services, food preparation, landscaping, and industry. Prison industry jobs are popular among many inmates because they often provide the most pay and a longer work environment. Prison industry systems produce a variety of goods, including traffic signs, license plates, furniture, and dairy products. The extent to which industry and agriculture employment opportunities exist varies among institutions.

Federal Prison Industries, also known as UNICOR, is a federal government corporation that was created in 1934 and uses inmate labor from the Federal Bureau of Prisons to produce services and goods. It is restricted to selling products to federal government agencies. The agency recently expanded its services to the private sector, albeit on a limited basis.

10
Corrections

inmate balance theory A theory which proposes that prisons operate more effectively when officials tolerate minor infractions, allow inmate leaders to maintain order, and relax security measures to an acceptable level

CAREERS

Vocational counselors provide educational programs in vocational specialties within various correctional institutions. They help inmates understand their capabilities and develop goals for employment upon release from prison.

Violence in Prisons

The challenges of prison life, the conditions of confinement, and the violent nature of some prison inmates result in prisons being the setting for various types of violence. Prison gangs are also a concern, as are prison riots. The dynamics of prison violence can be categorized according to:

- inmate-on-inmate violence,
- inmate-on-prison officer violence, and
- prison officer-on-inmate violence.

● **Learning Objective 32.5:** *Explain the dynamics of prison violence and the theoretical reasons for prison riots.*

Inmate-on-Inmate Violence

Inmate-on-inmate violence is the most common form of prison violence. Researchers found that about 21% of male prisoners were physically assaulted in the 6-month period under study. An estimated 2%–5% were sexually assaulted (Wolff & Shi, 2009). Further, correctional officials reported 8,763 allegations of sexual victimization in prisons in 2011, 10% of which were substantiated following an investigation (Beck et al., 2014). These numbers do not reflect the unreported acts of violence that occur in prisons.

10
Corrections

The structured nature of prisons, including inmates being closely supervised and restricted from having weapons, results in the most serious form of violence, homicide, occurring relatively infrequently in prison. For instance, researchers noted that there were an average of 4 homicides per 100,000 inmates annually, and prison homicide rates have declined over 90% over the past 30 years (Cunningham et al., 2010). Research from the U.S. Bureau of Justice Statistics noted that 2% of all state and federal prison inmate deaths from 2001 to 2014 were the result of homicide (Noonan, 2016).

10
Corrections

Inmate-on-Prison Officer Violence

Correctional officers work in an environment filled with tension and conflict, and they are often vulnerable to attack (see Module 30). An assessment of inmate assaults on prison staff suggested that serious assaults (attacks that required more than first aid) on prison staff were generally infrequent (there were 53 per 100,000 inmates annually), and inmates serving sentences for violent offenses were over four times more likely than nonviolent offenders to commit serious assaults (Sorensen et al., 2011). In 2018, there were 1,270 physical attacks against Federal Bureau of Prisons staff by prisoners. A small number of those attacks (21) resulted in serious injury to the staff member (Carson, 2020b).

Prison Officer-on-Inmate Violence

Prison officers are permitted and expected to use force in certain situations. There are limits on their use of force, much like there are with regard to police officers using force. However, prisoners regularly challenge the authority of prison staff, and so it is particularly important for correctional officers to be properly trained and understand the threshold at which violence is warranted and permitted.

Prison officers are generally permitted to use physical force against prisoners in the following circumstances (C. R. Smith, 1999):

- self-defense
- defense of others
- upholding prison rules
- preventing a crime
- preventing escapes

The use of guns in prison is primarily restricted to protecting the perimeter of the facility or for protection when transporting inmates outside the facility. Firearms may also be stored in a secured armory in case of a riot, but they are not used for everyday inmate management out of fear that inmates will overpower the officers and gain control of the guns. Instead, officers use various less lethal weapons, including:

- **oleoresin capsicum spray** (also known as pepper spray), which causes a temporary loss of vision (up to 45 minutes) in those who are sprayed;

- **noise flash diversionary devices** (also known as stun munitions or flash-bangs), which are similar to powerful firecrackers that disorient threatening inmates and permit the officers time to rush and subdue them;

- impact and blunt-force tools, such as shotguns that fire beanbags, which harm but do not kill threatening inmates;

- **conducted-energy devices** (also known as stun guns), which can be fired at threatening inmates and send electricity through their bodies; the electricity causes involuntary muscle contractions and enables the officer to gain control; and

- light, particularly bright light, which when shined in inmates' eyes can confuse and disable them (Mann, 2015).

Officers are trained to use these weapons along with verbal commands based on the perceived threats posed by inmates (Module 30 addresses correctional officer training). Verbal communication, including commands, is believed to be the most important tool for prison officers (Mann, 2015), given that they wish to avoid violent encounters. Less lethal weapons are ultimately used to disorient, incapacitate, and/or distract threatening inmates (Mann, 2015).

Prison Riots

Prison riots are an extreme form of prison violence that have declined in frequency in recent years. They involve 30 or more inmates taking control of a prison, or a section of a prison, or taking hostages for a period of 30 minutes or longer, which results in significant property damage or serious injury (Useem & Piehl, 2006). There are many explanations for prison riots, although they can be broadly categorized according to natural responses to poor prison conditions and the social context of prisons (Boin & Rattray, 2004).

POOR PRISON CONDITIONS

The causes of riots are explained, in part, by the conditions under which inmates live. Several aspects of prison life in particular contribute to the increased likelihood of rioting, including the following (e.g., Alarid & Reichel, 2013; Seiter, 2014):

- temperature (in particular very hot weather)
- overcrowding
- prison staff shortages that result in reduced levels of security
- poor security measures
- poor food service
- inadequate medical care
- lack of recreation equipment

SOCIAL CONTEXT OF PRISONS

Riots have also been explained through the social context of prisons, which involves a breakdown in the precarious relationship between prisoners and prison administrators (e.g., Useem, 1985). Several researchers earlier commented on the inmate balance theory, which holds that prisons operate more effectively when officials:

- tolerate minor infractions,
- allow inmate leaders to maintain some sense of order, and
- relax security measures to an acceptable level (Clemmer, 1966; Sykes, 1958).

oleoresin capsicum spray (pepper spray) A less lethal weapon that causes a temporary loss of vision (up to 45 minutes) in those who are sprayed

noise flash diversionary devices Also known as "stun-munitions" or "flash-bangs"; similar to powerful firecrackers, these nonlethal devices disorient threatening inmates and permit officers time to rush and subdue them

conducted-energy devices Less-lethal weapons that deliver an electrical charge that disrupts an individual's central nervous system for a moment so that an officer may gain control of an individual without causing injury

10
Corrections

According to the inmate balance theory, overenforcement of the rules and regulations creates an environment conducive to disorder and collective violence (Useem & Reisig, 1999).

Other, related theories offer insight regarding the occurrence of institutional disorder, including the administrative control theory. This theory holds that prison disorder is more likely to occur when prison management is provided in a weak, unstable, and/or divided manner (DiIulio, 1987; Useem & Reisig, 1999). Examples of poor management contributing to prison disorder include:

- inmate perceptions of unjust or poor conditions of confinement,
- prison management and officials becoming indifferent to the necessary security and daily tasks of prison management, and
- management neglecting to control gangs and permitting them to flourish (Useem & Reisig, 1999).

Other entities that can cause order or disorder depending on the context are prison gangs. Gangs are particularly powerful and prominent in some prisons and significantly impact the social context and environment of those institutions.

Prison Gangs

Prison gangs are criminal groups that exist within corrections systems and typically have existing ties to gangs outside our justice systems. Gang affiliation leads to increased prison misconduct, including violence. Known gang members in prison are more likely than nongang inmates to behave violently while incarcerated (e.g., Griffin & Hepburn, 2006; Worrall & Morris, 2012). The increased likelihood of gang members engaging in violence outside prison does not disappear once they are incarcerated. Researchers found that both the victims and the perpetrators of homicides in prison were often gang affiliated, with gang members more often being the perpetrators (Cunningham et al., 2010).

10
Corrections

Prison gangs grew in number in the 1960s and 1970s as race relations caused instability in prisons, much as it did on the outside (Alarid & Reichel, 2013). The proliferation of gangs outside prisons contributed to their growth within prisons because gang members on the outside were incarcerated and recruited members during their stay. Estimates of gang membership in prison range from less than 5% (Trulson et al., 2006) to 25% (Knox, 2005). Some examples of prison gangs are shown in Figure 32.5. Members of prison gangs commit a disproportionate amount of crime, including violent crime both within and outside prison (Kelley, 2014).

Gang leaders and organized crime figures are among the most respected prison inmates, followed by gang members because of their association with a protective group (Terry, 2003). Heads of gangs earn that respect largely through their ability to use violence to meet their needs. These and other gang members require additional supervision by prison staff given their propensity for violence.

prison gangs Criminal groups that exist within corrections systems and typically have existing ties to gangs outside our justice systems

Preventing Prison Violence

One aspect of prisons that makes them unique from other institutions is that every part of prison life contains the enhanced potential for violence. As a result, careful consideration must be given at all times to prevention. Some methods for addressing prison violence are:

- carefully classifying inmates and housing them accordingly (e.g., not placing weaker inmates in a cell with known violent offenders),
- providing recreational opportunities,
- increasing the accountability and oversight of prison operations by government officials (e.g., legislators),
- providing early release incentives, counseling, treatment, and
- enhancing correctional officer and administrator training.

- **Barrio Azteca**—The roughly 2,000 members (and many associates) are often linked to Mexican drug cartels, and their main source of income is through drug smuggling.
- **Black Guerrilla Family**—Founded in 1966 in the California prison systems by Black Panther George Jackson, the roughly 1,000 black members (and many associates) promote an anti-government philosophy.
- **Aryan Brotherhood**—A White supremacist, neo-Nazi group of roughly 20,000 inmates who are mainly White males.
- **Dead Man Incorporated**—Created in the 1980s, the group operates mainly in the Maryland Division of Corrections and has an estimated membership of over 370 inmates. They consist primarily of White males who are anti-government.
- **Mexican Mafia** (or **La Eme**)—Formed in the 1950s, the group has an estimated membership of 350 to 400. Membership is largely comprised of Mexican-American males who previously belonged to a Southern California street gang.
- **Nazi Low Riders**—A California-based gang that subscribes to a White-supremacist philosophy, the gang is estimated to have 800-1,000 members, most of whom are White males.
- **Neta**—The gang began in Puerto Rico and spread to the United States. It is now one of the most violent prison gangs. It's comprised of about 7,000 members in Puerto Rico and 5,000 members in the rest of the United States.
- **Texas Syndicate**—Believed to have a membership of 1,300 members, the gang consists largely of Mexican-American males between the ages of 20-40. It is one of the largest and most violent prison gangs active on both sides of the U.S.-Mexico border.

FIGURE 32.5. Examples and Sizes of Prison Gangs. The relationship between race and ethnicity and gangs is evident in the characteristics of these and other prison gangs. Prison gangs vary in size, with some having tens of thousands of members. The negative aspects of gangs in prison are well documented (e.g., increased levels of violence).

What would be a benefit of prison gangs?

The System in Perspective

The use of incarceration to punish offenders can be controversial. As noted in the "In the News" feature at the start of this module, Sharletta Evans, whose young son was killed in a drive-by shooting, eventually had a change of heart regarding the perpetrators of the crime and argued that those responsible for the death should have been released from prison ahead of schedule. Among other issues, this case generates discussion regarding the length of prison sentences and justice. How do we know that a particular number of years is appropriate for a specific crime? And how should we address cases in which a victim's family argues strongly to reduce the penalties imposed on the offender? Regardless, prisons and jails will continue to be used to secure the most dangerous and troublesome offenders.

Compared to all other institutions, prisons and jails are unique in many ways. They house individuals deemed unfit to live in our free society and must provide treatment, care, recreation, security, and all else for inmates. No other institution faces such tasks. The interesting and sometimes secretive nature of incarceration

Prison violence consists of violent acts by officers and prisoners. Having to regularly control a dangerous population places prison officers at a high risk of victimization.

Should prison officers be permitted to carry firearms? Why or why not?

has resulted in it regularly being addressed in popular culture. What is often missing from the movies, books, films, and other offerings are the many contributions from and influences of individuals who work in the institution, in corrections in general, and in our justice systems even more generally. Many individuals are involved with the daily operations of prisons, and their contributions are vital because prisons serve as an important piece of our justice-based practices. Aside from capital punishment, prisons reflect our most serious form of punishment.

Summary

1. Learning Objective 32.1: *Distinguish jails from prisons in terms of the functions they serve.*

- Jails differ from prisons in several ways, because jails generally house both inmates serving less than a year incarceration and individuals who are being detained prior to trial. Jails are also used to incarcerate or detain individuals who cannot afford bail or are not granted pretrial release, convicted offenders prior to their sentencing, felons when state prisons become overcrowded, probation and parole violators while they await a hearing, and mentally ill offenders who are awaiting assessment. Prisons generally hold inmates serving sentences of a year or more and are more likely than jails to offer vocational, educational, and other opportunities for rehabilitation given that inmates are housed for longer periods.

2. Learning Objective 32.2: *Identify the factors that contributed to the increased growth in the prison population beginning in the 1980s.*

- Various factors contributed to the growth in the prison population, including the increased use of mandatory sentencing and other "get tough on crime" legislative acts, the war on drugs, the growth in law enforcement, prison construction, politics, and fear of crime.

3. Learning Objective 32.3: *Summarize the arguments in support of and against the use of private prisons.*

- The benefits of private prisons include the greater level of flexibility they maintain in responding to opportunities and problems, their ability to reduce the pressures and costs of prison overcrowding, their potential to be creative and innovative, and the potential for

prison officials to be highly motivated to provide strong, quality services with the goal of securing additional contracts. Privately run facilities are generally less influenced by politics than government-run facilities. Private prisons also face criticism, because it is argued that punishing offenders should be left to the government, contracting with private agencies can be more expensive, and private industries may seek to cut corners and provide fewer quality supervision services in efforts to maximize profits. Further, there are concerns regarding the accountability of private prisons and uncertainties regarding who provides oversight for private facilities. Staff turnover is also a concern with privatization.

4. Learning Objective 32.4: *Describe the formal rules and informal aspects of prison life that affect the experience of inmates.*

- The formal rules and informal aspects of prison life are heavily impacted by the prison subculture. The subculture consists of distinct values, norms, and beliefs identified among prison inmates and largely shapes the experiences of prison inmates. Prison argot is used by inmates to facilitate inmate communication, and the convict code provides guidelines for inmates to adjust to and navigate prison life. Prisoner misconduct is a notable informal aspect of prison life, and inmates often break prison rules for a variety of reasons. Prison labor can be used to counteract prisoner misconduct by enabling inmates to make money, learn new skills, and take their minds off the difficulties of being in prison.

5. Learning Objective 32.5: *Explain the dynamics of prison violence and the theoretical reasons for prison riots.*

- The dynamics of prison violence include inmate-on-inmate violence, inmate-on-prison officer violence, and prison officer-on-inmate violence. The inmate balance theory proposes that prisons operate more effectively when officials tolerate minor infractions, allow inmate leaders to maintain some sense of order, and relax security measures to an acceptable level. The administrative control theory holds that prison disorder is more likely to occur when prison management is provided in a weak, unstable, and/or divided manner.

Questions for Critical Thinking

1. Would you support the idea of combining jails and prisons to have one facility that would house offenders serving short- and long-term sentences? What would be the benefits? What about the drawbacks?

2. What do you believe would be the most effective means by which we could reduce prison overcrowding?

3. Do you support or oppose the increased privatization of correctional services? Further, do you believe that at some point in the near future most correctional services will be provided by the private sector? Discuss your responses.

4. What do you believe would be the most difficult aspect of being in prison?

5. What do you believe is the most effective means to prevent prison violence, both among inmates and in relation to prison officers?

Key Terms

administrative control theory
artists
conducted-energy devices
convict code
custodial model
deprivation theory
importation theory
inmate balance theory
jailhouse lawyers
merchants
noise flash diversionary devices

oleoresin capsicum spray
prison argot
prison gangs
prisonization
prison subculture
private prisons
privatization
rehabilitation model
reintegration model
sub rosa economy

For digital learning resources, please go to
https://www.oup.com/he/burns1e

Module

33

Diversity, Female Inmates, and Special Category Prisoners

Corrections officials must be prepared to address a diverse population that has many special needs. An increasing number of females and aging offenders and those with mental illnesses and infectious diseases are but a few of the many issues that require additional considerations for correctional officials.

Do you believe we should build separate prisons to house offenders with specific needs, for instance with regard to elderly inmates or the mentally ill?

Diversity abounds in prison. Corrections officials are tasked with supervising, controlling, and helping each offender, all with limited resources. They must do so with consideration of the cultural and demographic differences and special needs of inmates. This module addresses diversity among prisoners and focuses on specific inmate groups. The discussion of diversity in general with regard to inmate populations is followed by coverage of female inmates, our aging correctional population, and inmates with HIV/AIDS. This module concludes with a look at mental illness in relation to incarceration.

Controlling Inmates by Banning Books

IN THE NEWS

In January 2018, the North Carolina Department of Public Safety removed the book *The New Jim Crow: Mass Incarceration in the Age of Colorblindness* from its list of books banned from state prisons (Fain, 2018). The book, written by author Michelle Alexander, has sold over a million copies and has received public attention for its coverage of racial disparities in sentencing policies and the manner in which mass incarceration has disproportionately impacted African Americans. It presents mass incarceration as a continuation of the tradition of racial discrimination in the United States. In 2019, Paul Butler's *Chokehold: Policing Black Men* was banned by Arizona prison officials because of its criticism of U.S. justice systems. Prison officials later rescinded the ban after pressure from various interest groups such as the American Civil Liberties Union.

State prison systems maintain lists of books that they prohibit inmates from reading. The considerations for banning materials vary by state, although they generally center around whether the content would provoke violence, contains sexually explicit material, or provides instruction on how to conceal contraband or make weapons (Fain, 2018). The decision by the North Carolina officials to allow Alexander's book left the state of Florida as the only prison system to ban her

work as of February 2018. A recurring reason for banning the book has been that it could pose a security threat that generates conflict between racial groups (Bromwich, 2018).

Prison officials maintain control over inmates, and for good reason. There are times, however, when the nature and extent of that control are questioned. Do you believe prison officials violate the rights of inmates by not

9 Sentencing

allowing them to read certain books such as those by Alexander and Butler, or are they justified in doing so given the potential for racially motivated tension and violence in prison?

10 Corrections

Diversity Among the Prison Population

The word **diversity** refers to a variation of different qualities, and it may pertain to gender, race, ethnicity, age, culture, and related issues. Jails and prisons are particularly impacted by diversity because of the overrepresentation of racial and ethnic minorities—in particular African Americans—institutionalized across the United States. Prison and jail officials have had to increasingly respond to cultural differences while ensuring that the goals of their institution are being met.

Consider eye contact as an example. Maintaining eye contact while conversing is a sign of respect within prisons, but in Native American culture maintaining eye contact is a sign of disrespect (Cesarz & Madrid-Bustos, 1991). Failure by correctional officials or prisoners to recognize this cultural practice could result in a misinterpretation of behavior and lead to problems (Cesarz & Madrid-Bustos, 1991).

● **Learning Objective 33.1:** Describe the racial disparity in the prison population.

10 Corrections

diversity A variation of different qualities; it may pertain to gender, race, ethnicity, age, or culture, as well as other issues

Native American inmates in Alabama used the court system to fight for the right to have long hair in prison, because they claimed it was part of their sacred and ancestral core religious traditions. Prison officials claimed it was a hygiene and security risk, for instance because inmates could hide weapons in their long hair (Chandler, 2015). An appellate court ruled against the Native Americans.

In what other ways could cultural practices conflict with prison operations?

10
Corrections

Overrepresentation of African Americans and Hispanics in Prison

The overrepresentation of African Americans and to some extent Hispanics at all stages of our justice systems, including incarceration, is well documented in government reports and the research literature. Figure 33.1 depicts the extent to which Blacks and Hispanics are overrepresented in prisons when compared with Whites.

A 2016 report by the Sentencing Project highlights diversity and disparity as it relates to prisons. Among the key findings from the report were the following (Nellis, 2016):

- Incarceration of African Americans in state prisons occurs at a rate 5.1 times the imprisonment of Whites.
- Incarceration of Latinos occurs at a rate 1.4 times the rate of Whites.
- In 12 states, more than half of the prison population is Black. Maryland has the highest percentage of Black inmates (72%).
- In 11 states, at least 1 in 20 adult Black males is in prison.
- Oklahoma is the state with the highest overall Black incarceration rate; 1 in 15 Black males ages 18 and older is in prison.

Further, data from the Bureau of Justice Statistics suggests that even though Blacks comprise only 13% of the U.S. population, they account for roughly 32% of state and federal prisoners. Hispanics, which comprise roughly 18% of the U.S. population, are also disproportionately imprisoned, particularly in federal prisons, where they represent 30.3% of all federal prisoners, largely because of the federal government's illegal immigration enforcement practices. By contrast, Whites are notably underrepresented in prison (30.6%) compared to the U.S. population in general (60%) (Carson, 2020a; Federal Bureau of Prisons, 2020d).

The reasons for the overrepresentation of Hispanics and African Americans in prisons, and more generally under correctional supervision, is largely the result of events that occurred prior to this stage of criminal case processing. Those events may pertain to the extent to which groups engage in criminal behavior and/or they may involve the differential treatment of groups by law enforcement and court personnel. The extent to which the disparity is attributable to one or the other and how much each impacts the overrepresentation of racial and ethnic minorities in prisons is difficult to discern.

Effect of Diversity on Prison Operations

Social groups (including prison gangs, see Module 32) are largely formed along racial and ethnic lines in prison. Accordingly, prison administrators must consider diversity, race, and ethnicity with regard to issues such as determining who shares a cell, who is placed in particular cell blocks, and who eats or recreates together. Failure to properly consider diversity contributes to a disruptive prison. Prison administrators must address whether they should separate inmates of different backgrounds to enhance prison safety and whether doing so discourages inmates from being tolerant and accepting of individuals from races and ethnicities other than their own.

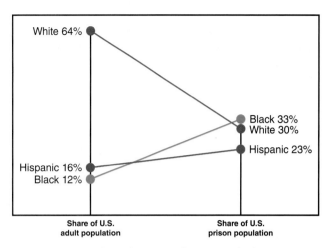

FIGURE 33.1. Imprisonment Rate of Sentenced Prisoners by Race and Ethnicity, 2017. Despite recent declines in the rate of African Americans (and other groups) in prisons, they remain largely overrepresented compared to other groups. Note. Whites and Blacks include those who report being only one race and are non-Hispanic. Hispanics are of any race. Prison population is defined as inmates sentenced to more than a year in federal or state prison. ***Source:*** *The Gap Between the Number of Blacks and Whites in Prison Is Shrinking, by J. Gramlich, April 30, 2019, Pew Research Center (https://www.pewresearch.org/fact-tank/2019/04/30/shrinking-gap-between-number-of-blacks-and-whites-in-prison).*

Do you believe the overrepresentation is a result of overinvolvement in crime or bias on behalf of criminal justice officials and/or others (e.g., jurors)?

10
Corrections

● **Learning Objective 33.2:** Contrast incarceration for females with incarceration of males.

Female Inmates

Most states house all female inmates in one prison and often do not have distinct female prisons for each security level (Clear et al., 2016). The reason for the limited number of female prisons is that there are a relatively small number of female inmates compared to males, given that males are more likely than females to commit crimes, especially the more serious crimes that warrant incarceration. Females made up only 7.5% (*n* = 107,955) of the total U.S. prison population in 2019 (Carson, 2020a).

Increased Female Incarceration

Historically, the number of males under correctional supervision has been greater than the number of females. In recent years, the rate of growth for both groups has declined, although as noted in Table 33.1, the number of male prisoners decreased at a faster rate than that of females.

As the number of females in prison has grown in the past few decades, so has the female jail population. The female local jail population increased by 48% from 1999

3 Arrest

TABLE 33.1. Prisoners Under the Jurisdiction of State or Federal Correctional Authorities, by Jurisdiction and Sex, 2008–2018

10
Corrections

YEAR[a]	TOTAL	FEDERAL[b]	STATE	MALE	FEMALE
2008	1,608,282	201,280	1,407,002	1,493,670	114,612
2009	1,615,487	208,118	1,407,369	1,502,002	113,485
2010	1,613,803	209,771	1,404,032	1,500,936	112,867
2011	1,598,968	216,362	1,382,606	1,487,561	111,407
2012	1,570,397	217,815	1,352,582	1,461,625	108,772
2013	1,576,950	215,866	1,361,084	1,465,592	111,358
2014	1,562,319	210,567	1,351,752	1,449,291	113,028
2015	1,526,603	196,455	1,330,148	1,415,112	111,491
2016	1,508,129	189,192	1,318,937	1,396,296	111,833
2017	1,489,189	183,058	1,306,131	1,377,815	111,374
2018	1,465,158	179,898	1,285,260	1,354,313	110,845
Percent change					
	–8.90%	–10.60%	–8.70%	–9.30%	–3.30%
	–1.6	–1.7	–1.6	–1.7	–0.5

Note. Overall, there are far more males than females in prison, but the decline in the female prison population has been slower than it has been for males. Jurisdiction refers to the legal authority of state or federal correctional officials over a prisoner, regardless of where the prisoner is held. Counts are for December 31 of each year. As of December 31, 2001, sentenced felons from the District of Columbia were the responsibility of the Federal Bureau of Prisons. *Source:* National Prisoner Statistics, 2008–2018, by the Bureau of Justice Statistics; and Prisoners in 2018 (NCJ 253516), Table 1, by E. A. Carson, 2020c, U.S. Department of Justice, Bureau of Justice Statistics (https://www.bjs.gov/content/pub/pdf/p18.pdf).

[a]Total and state counts for 2018 include imputed counts for New Hampshire and Oregon, which did not submit 2018 National Prisoner Statistics (NPS) data. Total and state estimates for 2017 include imputed counts for New Mexico and North Dakota, which did not submit 2017 NPS data. For years prior to 2017, data for one to two states per year were imputed and included in total and state counts but have since been confirmed by state respondents. Counts for 2017 and earlier may have been revised based on updated reporting and may differ from numbers in past reports.
[b]Includes adult prisoners held in nonsecure community corrections facilities and adults and persons age 17 or younger held in privately operated facilities.

to year-end 2013 (Minton et al., 2015) and by 15% from 2008 to 2019 (Zeng, 2020). Females accounted for 15.6% of the jail population at mid-year 2018, compared to 11.4% in 2000 (Zeng, 2018, 2020).

Female Inmate Subculture

The social structure of male prisons emphasizes masculinity, manhood, and homophobia (see Module 32). Female prisons, however, are more structured around kinship, open expression of affection, and family structures (Van Wormer & Bartollas, 2007). Female inmates are more likely than male prisoners to have **prison play-families** or **pseudo-families**, which involve inmates assuming the roles of different family members, such as a mother, father, sister, brother, or grandparent. The pseudo-families can be as large as 15–20 members and are a coping mechanism for inmates who miss the family support and kinship they had outside prison (Bedard, 2009).

In addition, compared to inmates in male prisons, inmates in female prisons are:

- less likely to join a gang for protection,
- less likely to engage in violence,

prison play-families
Also known as **pseudo-families**; they involve inmates assuming the roles of different family members

- more likely to become involved in other inmates' problems, and
- more likely to interact with the staff (McGuire, 2011; Pollock, 2002).

Despite the reduced likelihood of violence in female prisons, research suggests that the following were discouraged and more likely to generate violent responses by female inmates (McGuire, 2011):

- snitching
- gossiping
- failing to maintain standards of cleanliness
- commenting on other inmates' time in prison

Concerns Regarding Treatment

Historically, the same treatment, counseling, and other therapeutic approaches were offered in both male and female correctional facilities. The need for changes became apparent as more females entered prisons and jails. While female inmates require many of the same treatment services as their male counterparts (e.g., substance abuse counseling, anger management, and mental health assistance), they are more likely than males to need treatment and counseling as it relates to:

- child care,
- family reunification programs,
- childhood sexual abuse, and
- family violence.

Of particular importance is child care, given that females are more often than males to be responsible for the supervision of their children.

Female Inmates With Children

About two-thirds of the women in prison in the United States have a child under age 18 (NPR, 2015). The increased number of females under correctional supervision has prompted corrections officials to respond to the distinct issues and concerns pertaining to female offenders. The U.S. Department of Justice noted that among parents who lived with children prior to their incarceration, mothers (77%) were almost 3 times more likely than fathers (26%) to note that they had provided most of the daily care for their children (Glaze & Maruschak, 2008). Accordingly, females are more likely than males to have to locate care for their children while they undergo correctional supervision, and efforts are needed to prevent the **collateral damage**, which are the harms suffered by children whose parents are incarcerated (Crawford, 2003).

collateral damage
The harms suffered by children whose parents are incarcerated

EFFECTS ON CHILDREN AND INMATES

Given that mothers are often the primary caregivers, the effects of having an incarcerated mother may often be more impactful on children than the effects of an incarcerated father. The children are more likely to experience problems associated with being separated from their primary caregiver (Bloom & Steinhart, 1993; L. Davis & Shlafer, 2017; Smyth, 2012). Among the concerns are the social, psychological, and economic effects of the increased number of children with incarcerated mothers and the long-term effects they will have on children, including the

Maintaining the bond between a mother and her children is important for both groups. Providing opportunities for female inmates to care for their children may be considered part of rehabilitative efforts within prisons.

Should female inmates who are parents be granted special privileges to see their children, and should those privileges be extended to male inmates who are primary caregivers?

10
Corrections

● **Learning Objective 33.3:** Describe the special considerations associated with elderly inmates.

9 Sentencing

10
Corrections

increased likelihood of them also becoming involved in the criminal justice system themselves (McGee et al., 2007), as well as mental health problems (L. Davis & Shlafer, 2017).

The benefits of enabling inmates, in particular females, to maintain ties to their children impact both the children and the inmate parent. Enabling inmates to keep close family ties during the inmate's incarceration is related to:

- lower recidivism rates,
- improved mental health of inmates,
- stronger families ties and connections following release, and
- enhanced success on parole (Hariston, 1991; Schaefer, 1991).

EFFORTS TO MAINTAIN STRONG FAMILY TIES

Efforts toward enabling inmates to maintain strong family ties include:

- providing convenient visiting hours and more regular contact for inmates and their children,
- incarcerating parents as close as possible to their children, and
- ensuring that mothers of newborns have opportunities to bond with their child.

With regard to newborns, establishing and maintaining the bond between mothers and newborn children is particularly important because the infant is in a dependent and impressionable state. Accordingly, about 20% of states allow mothers with infant children to care for them in prison nurseries (NPR, 2015). Most prisons, however, require that the baby be taken away from the mother within 48 to 72 hours and placed with a relative or foster care. Bedford Hills Prison in New York is one of eight prison nurseries in the United States. It can accommodate up to 26 mothers and serves about 40 each year. Pregnant inmates who qualify are sent to the facility, where they are able to spend about a year with their newborn and sometimes longer (Hasty, 2018).

Aging Inmates

The average life expectancy in the United States has increased steadily over time and is currently around 79 years. Longer prison sentences imposed in previous decades have contributed to an increasingly older prison inmate population. As noted in Figure 33.2, the percentage of prisoners age 55 and older increased by 280% between 1999 and 2016, while the percentage of prisoners under age 55 increased by only 3% (McKillop & Boucher, 2018).

Another consideration with regard to prisoners and aging is that prisoners also tend to age faster than noninmates because of their:

- risky past behavior,
- increased likelihood of past substance abuse,
- stressful lifestyles, and
- inadequate medical care.

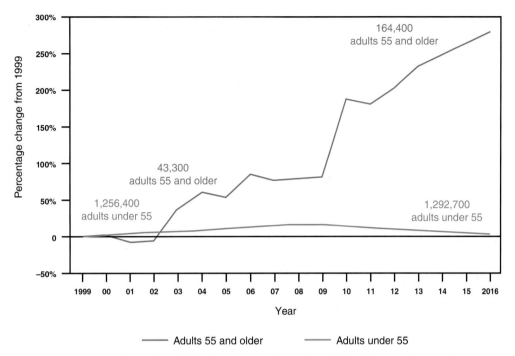

FIGURE 33.2. **Increased Number of Elderly Inmates.** The number of elderly inmates increased substantially between 1999 and 2016. Longer prison sentences and people living longer lives are primary reasons for the increase. *Source: Pew Charitable Trusts.*

What else might explain the relatively large increase in the number of elderly inmates?

Note. *The Bureau of Justice Statistics estimates the age distribution of prisoners using data from the Federal Justice Statistics Program and statistics that states voluntarily submit to the National Corrections Reporting Program. State participation in this program has varied, which may have caused year-to-year fluctuations in the bureau's national estimates, but this does not affect long-term trend comparisons. From 2009 to 2010, the number of states submitting data increased substantially, which might have contributed to the year-over-year increase in the national estimate between those years.* ***Source:*** *Aging Prison Populations Drive Up Costs, by M. McKillop and A. Boucher, 2018, Pew Charitable Trusts (http://www.pewtrusts.org/en/research-and-analysis/articles/2018/02/20/aging-prison-populations-drive-up-costs).*

Costs Associated With Aging Inmates

The costs to house aging inmates are on average three times as much as housing younger inmates, primarily because healthcare costs increase with age (Aging Inmate Committee, 2012). Of particular importance with regard to housing an increasing number of older inmates are:

10
Corrections

- protecting them from victimization,
- addressing their potential mental deterioration as they age, and
- providing healthcare services for various ailments.

Older inmates are more likely than their younger counterparts to require costly structural changes to institutions, including wheelchair ramps, bedrails, and bathing equipment, and are more likely to have special dietary needs (Aging Inmate Committee, 2012). They are also more likely to suffer from chronic healthcare problems that are costly to treat, such as diabetes, cancer, emphysema, kidney problems, heart problems, and hypertension (Stal, 2012). Older inmates became of particular concern to prison officials in 2020, as the COVID-19 pandemic spread globally. The effects of the virus were particularly impactful on the elderly. The close quarters inherent in institutionalization and the lack of the ability to social distance resulted in this group being more at risk than many others in the prison population. In response, several institutions provided early release for older inmates (Prison Policy Initiative, 2020).

Laws Pertaining to Aging Inmates

10
Corrections

Americans with Disabilities Act of 1990 A civil rights law that prohibits discrimination with regard to disability; further, it requires employers to provide reasonable accommodations to employees with disabilities and establishes accessibility requirements for public facilities

The **Americans with Disabilities Act of 1990** is a civil rights law that prohibits discrimination with regard to disability. Further, it requires employers to provide reasonable accommodations to employees with disabilities and established accessibility requirements for public facilities. In 2006, the U.S. Supreme Court ruled that the protections of the act extend to prison inmates and prevents discrimination of those with disabilities (*United States v. Georgia*, 2006). This legislation required substantial changes in prisons, such as providing ramps and increased lighting. These alterations have also benefited aging inmates.

Many states have responded to the special needs of older prison populations by providing geriatric housing facilities or separate wings or units. Such areas cater to the specific needs of the elderly, for example with wheelchair and walker accommodations and recreational opportunities designed with the elderly in mind (e.g., board games as opposed to volleyball) (Aging Inmate Committee, 2012). The staffs at these facilities are often trained in caring for the aging and the elderly (Schmalleger & Smykla, 2009).

The likelihood of offending decreases with age, so prisons can save substantial resources by releasing some elderly, less-threatening inmates early. Some states have introduced early release programs to reduce prison populations, and elderly inmates are among those targeted groups for the programs (Mikle, 2013).

● **Learning Objective 33.4:** Describe the special considerations associated with inmates with HIV or AIDS.

Inmates With HIV/AIDS

Prisons and jails struggle with finding ways to prevent the spread of diseases and to treat and house those who are infected with highly communicable diseases such as tuberculosis, hepatitis, and HIV/AIDS. Consider how quickly the common cold spreads in dorms and classrooms, and now imagine that happening in the close, confined quarters of correctional institutions. **Human immunodeficiency virus (HIV)** and the **acquired immune deficiency syndrome (AIDS)** are communicable and harm one's immune system by destroying white blood cells that help fight infections. Those with the virus are at a greater risk for serious infections and certain cancers. AIDS is the final stage of infection associated with HIV, when one's ability to fight off infections has notably diminished. HIV/AIDS are of particular concern in prisons and jails given the nature of activities in which some inmates engage and the close quarters in which they live.

Increased Risks to Inmates

10
Corrections

HIV is transmitted from one person to another via contaminated blood and semen, primarily through the use of dirty needles and unprotected sex. The use of dirty needles to inject drugs or make tattoos both within and outside prisons and jails places inmates at an increased risk of obtaining and spreading the disease. Further, having unprotected consensual or nonconsensual sex in prisons and jails places inmates at risk, particularly since condoms are not readily available to inmates.

The Extent of HIV/AIDS in the Prison Population

Concerns for HIV/AIDS in prison remain despite recent declines both in prison and in the larger outside population. For instance, the rate of HIV among state and federal prison inmates peaked in 1992, when it reached 2,471 cases per 100,000 inmates. At year-end 2015, the rate was 1,297. Figure 33.3 depicts the decrease in the number and rate of prisoners who had HIV in state and federal institutions between 1991 and 2015.

Accompanying the declines in the number and rate of HIV-infected inmates has been a decline in the number of AIDS-related deaths. In 1999, there were 520 AIDS-related deaths in state prisons, however there were only 45 in 2015 (Maruschak & Bronson, 2017). The Bureau of Justice Statistics began collecting data on AIDS-related deaths in federal prisons in 1999, when there were 16 deaths. In 2014 there were no such deaths, and in 2015 there was 1 in federal prison. Figure 33.4 depicts the decreases in the number of AIDS-related deaths and mortality rate among state prisoners from 1991 to 2015.

Testing for HIV/AIDS in Correctional Institutions

Identifying inmates who have HIV and AIDS is vital in controlling the spread of the diseases. The long incubation period associated with HIV and AIDS, or the time between when the inmate contracted HIV and the inmate displays signs of having AIDS (10–15 years in some cases), generates a need for adequate HIV testing in prisons. In 2015, 15 states had mandatory HIV testing for all prisoners upon their entrance, and 17 states offered the test to inmates and administered it if they approved. These numbers have increased from 2011, when 14 states had mandatory testing and 13 gave inmates the option (Maruschak & Bronson, 2017).

Mandatory testing for HIV among inmates is controversial and widely debated. Opponents of mandatory testing in correctional institutions note the following (Clear et al., 2016):

- Privacy and confidentiality issues will be problematic, because infected inmates may be stigmatized and mistreated by other inmates.

Human immunodeficiency virus (HIV) A communicable virus that harms one's immune system by destroying white blood cells that help fight infections, which places those with the virus at a greater risk for serious infections and certain cancers

Acquired immune deficiency syndrome (AIDS) The final stage of infection associated with HIV, when one's ability to fight off infections has notably diminished

10
Corrections

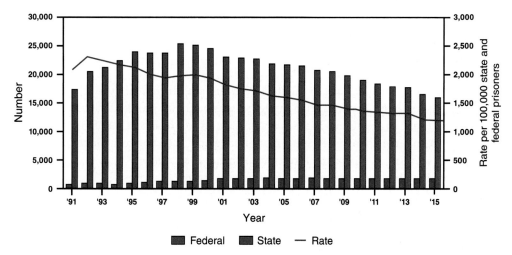

FIGURE 33.3. Number of Prisoners Who Had HIV and Rate of HIV per 100,000 in State and Federal Correctional Institutions, 1991–2015. The number and rate of HIV-infected inmates in state and federal facilities peaked around the turn of the century and has steadily declined since. *Note. Includes inmates in the custody of state and federal prison authorities that were known to be HIV-positive or had confirmed AIDS.*

Source: HIV in Prisons, 2015—Statistical Tables *(NCJ 250641), by L. M. Maruschak and J. Bronson, 2017, U.S. Department of Justice, Bureau of Justice Statistics.*

What might be some of the reasons for the decline?

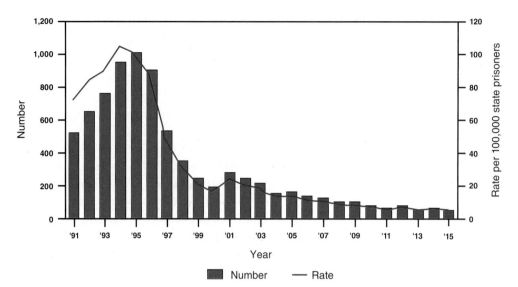

FIGURE 33.4. The Number of AIDS-Related Deaths and Mortality Rate Among State Prisoners From 1991 to 2015. The number and rate of AIDS-related deaths in state prisons peaked in the mid-1990s and has largely dropped since. The drops are related to the decreased number and rate of HIV-infected inmates in state prisons. *Source:* HIV in Prisons, 2015—Statistical Tables (NCJ 250641), by L. M. Maruschak and J. Bronson, 2017, U.S. Department of Justice, Bureau of Justice Statistics.

Note. AIDS-related deaths were based on the jurisdiction population from 1991 to 2000 and the custody population from 2001 to 2015. Use caution when comparing data prior to 2001 to data from 2001 and beyond. Jurisdiction refers to the legal authority of state and federal correctional officials over a prisoner, regardless of where the prisoner is held.

What steps could be taken to continue to reduce the extent to which HIV/AIDS is addressed in prisons and jails?

- There is no evidence that the rate of transmission of the disease in prison is higher than it is in the free community, and thus there is no need to screen inmates.
- Policies exist to ensure that correctional officials do not become infected with HIV or any communicable diseases transmitted through bodily fluids.

Housing Infected Inmates

10
Corrections

Correctional institutions have struggled with housing inmates with HIV or AIDS. They require costly treatments that range between $50,000 and $145,000 annually per patient (Clear et al., 2016). There is also the need to protect others from contracting HIV and ensuring that infected inmates have access to the same level of correctional programming and treatment options as other inmates.

Various housing options are used among the states to address HIV and AIDS in prison. The decisions are primarily based on the number of inmate patients a state has, as well as cost and resources considerations. Most states segregate inmates with AIDS, but not necessarily those with HIV. Inmates with AIDS are usually placed in a correctional hospital or infirmary, although some states place them in a hospital in the community (Clear et al., 2016).

In 2013, South Carolina became the final state in the United States to abolish its policy of segregating HIV-positive prisoners. Segregating HIV-infected inmates in efforts to prevent its spread had been controversial. Aside from restricting inmates from programming, vocational, educational, and other rehabilitative opportunities, segregation resulted in the "outing" of infected inmates, which stigmatizes the prisoners. The practice was discouraged by the American Civil Liberties Union and the Centers for Disease Control. Most prisons instead focus on preventative actions, such as educating all inmates about the diseases and how they spread.

Inmates With Mental Illness

Identifying, treating, and controlling inmates with mental illnesses has long challenged jail and prison officials. The term **mental illness** refers to a variety of mind disorders that impact one's behavior, mood, and thinking and increase the likelihood of antisocial behavior and institutionalization. Inmates with mental health problems generally do not do well while incarcerated. They are perceived by staff and other inmates to be disruptive, potentially dangerous, and unpredictable. Such perceptions, in addition to the effects of the mental illnesses, result in inmates being stigmatized, neglected, and targeted (e.g., for an assault) by other inmates (Schmalleger & Smykla, 2009).

The increased likelihood of inmates having a mental illness, compared to the general public, highlights the need for a more holistic approach to corrections, including the services of mental health professionals who can identify, diagnose, and help treat those who are affected.

Types and Effects of Mental Illness

Among the more common types of mental illnesses identified among inmates are:

- **depression**—constant feelings of dejection;
- **anxiety disorders**—excessive feelings of panic or worry;
- **schizophrenia**—breakdowns in the way one thinks, feels, and acts; affected individuals may have difficulty determining what is real and what is not, and they may be withdrawn or have difficulty expressing normal emotions;
- **bipolar disorder**—may involve alternating periods of depression and elation;
- **post-traumatic stress disorder**—exposure to a traumatic event may cause an individual to mentally relive the event and experience extended periods of nervousness and being "on edge" (see Module 13 for discussion of how it affects police officers); and
- various addictive behaviors, such as drug addiction and eating disorders.

Many people suffer from varying degrees of mental disorders, most of which do not significantly impact their everyday lives. Some individuals, however, are heavily impacted by their illness, which could contribute to behaviors that increase their likelihood of being incarcerated. For example, having schizophrenia may cause someone to act in an irrational manner toward others. Some mental illnesses appear after one has been incarcerated, as a result of the difficulties of prison life (see Module 32) Depending on the type and severity of their illness, inmates may exhibit the following signs (Schmalleger & Smykla, 2009):

- neglecting to practice proper hygiene
- disobeying prison officials' orders
- screaming
- physically harming themselves

● **Learning Objective 33.5:** Explain the extent to which inmates suffer from mental illnesses.

10 Corrections

mental illness A variety of mind disorders that impact one's behavior, mood, and thinking

depression A mental illness involving feelings of dejection, isolation, and hopelessness; it can be hereditary or brought on by other factors

anxiety disorders Mental illnesses involving excessive feelings of panic or worry

schizophrenia A mental illness involving breakdowns in the way one thinks, feels, and acts

bipolar disorder A mental disorder involving alternating periods of depression and elation

1 Criminal Act

Many inmates suffer from mental illnesses that can negatively affect their behavior while incarcerated and may have contributed to their incarceration.

Should all corrections officers be required to take extensive training with regard to interacting with mentally ill inmates?

post–traumatic stress disorder

A mental illness in individuals exposed to a traumatic event that causes them to relive the event and experience extended periods of nervousness and being "on edge"; it is sometimes used as a defense in which defendants claim that their behavior was attributed to the mental effects of having suffered from some traumatic incident

10
Corrections

10
Corrections

The Extent of Mental Health Problems in Jails and Prisons

Compared to the general public, prisons and jails house a disproportionate percentage of inmates with mental health problems. A study conducted by the Bureau of Justice Statistics highlighted some of the mental health problems found among the incarcerated. The study found that about 14% of state and federal prisoners and 26% of jail inmates reported experiences that met the threshold for serious psychological distress. The same report noted that 37% of prisoners and 44% of jail inmates were told in the past by a mental health professional that they had a mental disorder (Bronson & Berzofsky, 2017). Table 33.2 highlights these and other findings regarding the prevalence of mental health indicators among jail and prison inmates.

Reasons for the Increased Likelihood of Mental Illness in Prisons and Jails

The relatively high percentages of inmates with mental illnesses may be attributable to the sometimes irrational behavior exhibited by mentally ill individuals. The behavior that leads to a person's incarceration may be the result of their illness, or the illness may be amplified by the failure to take proper medications and/or substance use or abuse.

In addition, the high rate of mental illnesses among inmates has also been impacted by the deinstitutionalization of psychiatric patients beginning in the 1950s and 1960s. Around this time, it was widely believed that many individuals with mental illnesses would receive better treatment in the community instead of within a therapeutic institution. The practice of deinstitutionalization has largely continued, and those with mental illnesses have increasingly become homeless or institutionalized in prisons and jails (e.g., Raphelson, 2017).

Jails and the Mentally Ill

As evidenced in Table 33.2, jails are more likely than prisons to house inmates with mental health problems. The number of inmates with mental illnesses has increased since the 1970s when states closed psychiatric hospitals without providing adequate community treatment programs (Geller, 2014). However, jail inmates with mental illnesses are less likely to receive treatment and programming compared to inmates in prisons. This is largely because of the higher turnover of the jail population compared to the prison population.

Among the problems of jailing the mentally ill are the lack of treatment provided in jails and the troubles jail inmates face from often being kept isolated in small cells for long periods, sometimes with minimal treatment or human interaction. The isolation is often imposed out of concern for the inmate being victimized or harming others (Geller, 2014).

Jail administrators address concerns regarding the mentally ill in jails in part by diverting them to community-based services or providing jail-based treatment programs. With regard to the former, researchers found that individuals with serious mental illness who were diverted to community-based services had fewer arrests and spent fewer days in jail in the year following their diversion than in the 12 months prior (Case et al., 2009). With regard to the latter, research

TABLE 33.2. Prevalence of Mental Health Indicators Among Prisoners and Jail Inmates

MENTAL HEALTH INDICATOR	PRISONERS (%)*	JAIL INMATES (%)
No indication of a mental health problem[a]	49.90	36.0**
Current indicator of a mental health problem[b]		
Serious psychological distress[c]	14.50	26.4**
History of a mental health problem		
Ever told by mental health professional they had a mental disorder	36.90	44.3**
Major depressive disorder	24.20	30.6**
Bipolar disorder	17.50	24.9**
Schizophrenia/other psychotic disorder	8.70	11.7**
Post-traumatic stress disorder	12.50	15.9**
Anxiety disorder[d]	11.70	18.4**
Personality disorder[e]	13.00	13.5

Note. Roughly half of all prisoners and the majority of jail inmates have indicated some type of mental illness. These percentages highlight the need for diagnosing and treating the various mental illnesses in prisons and jails. *Source:* National Inmate Survey, 2011–2012, by the Bureau of Justice Statistics; and Indicators of Mental Health Problems Reported by Prisoners and Jail Inmates, 2011–12 (NCJ 250612), by J. Bronson and M. Berzofsky, 2017, U.S. Department of Justice, Bureau of Justice Statistics (https://www.bjs.gov/content/pub/pdf/imhprpji1112.pdf).
*Comparison group.
**Difference with the comparison group is significant at the 95% confidence level.
[a]Includes persons with a score of 7 or less on the K6 scale and who had never been told by a mental health professional they had a mental disorder.
[b]Current at time of the interview.
[c]Includes persons with a score of 13 or more on the K6 scale.
[d]Includes panic disorder and obsessive compulsive disorder and excludes post-traumatic stress disorder.
[e]Includes antisocial and borderline personality disorder.

1 Criminal Act

3 Arrest

generally suggests that mental health programming services within institutions can help address psychiatric symptoms and assist with prison and jail operations (Hagar et al., 2008).

MYTHBUSTING
Mental Illnesses Cause Violent Crime

Many people believe that individuals with mental illnesses are far more likely than others to commit violent crimes. This perception has been shaped by many factors, including the public's enhanced exposure to many sensationalized crimes that are more likely to involve offenders who are mentally ill and the disproportionate depiction of criminals as being mentally ill in media accounts of crime (Parrott & Parrott, 2015). Research in the area, however, notes that most people who have mental illnesses are not at an increased risk of committing violence when compared to those without illnesses, but they may be more likely to become violent if they abuse alcohol or drugs (Corrigan, 2005; Van Dorn et al., 2012). While inappropriate behavior on the part of those with mental illnesses may draw the attention of the criminal justice system, this does not necessarily mean that the mentally ill are more violent than others.

The System in Perspective

Racial disparity is evident in our prison systems and correctional systems in general. It is also the topic of the book *The New Jim Crow*, which was banned by some state prison systems from the list of books inmates are permitted to read (as noted in the "In the News" feature at the start of this module). Prison officials believed the book posed a security threat and could incite violence among different racial groups within prisons. The fear that reading about racial disparities in prison could result in violence highlights the volatile nature of prison life, as well as the need to address issues regarding diversity, multiculturalism, and tolerance within institutions.

Prisons and jails cannot choose whom they will house. They are responsible for supervising individuals sentenced to incarceration, regardless of the offender's gender, race, ethnicity, socioeconomic status, physical ability, sexual preference, age, and related issues. While those who work in law enforcement and the courts also deal with many types of individuals, corrections officials are regularly exposed to individuals from all walks of life for prolonged periods. As the United States becomes increasingly diverse, our justice systems must respond appropriately to the changes.

Summary

1. **Learning Objective 33.1:** *Describe the racial disparity in the prison population.*

   • Relative to their presence in the U.S. general population, Blacks are notably overrepresented in prisons, while Hispanics are somewhat overrepresented. Whites are underrepresented.

2. **Learning Objective 33.2:** *Contrast incarceration for females with incarceration of males.*

   • The prison subculture in female prisons differs from that found in male prisons, for instance in relation to the establishment of play-families and the lack of emphasis on gang involvement or violence. Treatment needs and consideration of parental responsibilities also differ in female prisons, because there is a more pronounced need for females (often the primary caregivers) to have access to or interact with their children.

3. **Learning Objective 33.3:** *Describe the special considerations associated with elderly inmates.*

   • The increasing number of elderly inmates has generated special considerations for prison and jail officials. It is more costly to house elderly inmates than younger inmates. In part, this is because elderly inmates have more health and safety-related issues to address, as well as recreational and structural issues and special dietary needs.

4. **Learning Objective 33.4:** *Describe the special considerations associated with inmates with HIV or AIDS.*

   • The close, confined quarters of correctional institutions are among the special considerations associated with inmates with HIV or AIDS. Other considerations include preventing the spread of the disease, testing procedures, and providing treatment and housing for those who are infected. Corrections officials must consider the need to protect all inmates and staff from acquiring the diseases.

5. **Learning Objective 33.5:** *Explain the extent to which inmates suffer from mental illnesses.*

   • It is estimated that about 14% of state and federal prisoners and 26% of jail inmates reported experiences that met the threshold for serious psychological distress, and 37% of prisoners and 44% of jail inmates were told in the past by a mental health professional that they had a mental disorder. Jails are more likely than prisons to house inmates with mental health problems and face particular challenges because jail inmates with mental illnesses are at a higher risk of not receiving treatment and programming.

Questions for Critical Thinking

1. Do you believe our prisons will become more diverse than they currently are? Why or why not? If so, in what ways will they become increasingly diverse? If not, why not?

2. Assume you are the warden of a women's prison in which the inmates are complaining that they wish to see more of their children. How would you respond to the complaints?

3. Should the costly prison space taken by elderly inmates who no longer pose much of a threat to society be used to house younger, more dangerous offenders? Why or why not?

4. What reasons could be offered for the decreased rates of HIV and AIDS in prisons?

5. Should inmates with mental illnesses be treated in prisons or jails, or do you believe they would be more responsive to treatment in a noncustodial setting?

Key Terms

Acquired immune deficiency syndrome (AIDS)
Americans with Disabilities Act of 1990
anxiety disorders
bipolar disorder
collateral damage
depression
diversity

Human immunodeficiency virus (HIV)
mental illness
post–traumatic stress disorder
prison play-families
pseudo-families
schizophrenia

For digital learning resources, please go to
https://www.oup.com/he/burns1e

Juvenile Corrections

Various custodial and noncustodial options are available for troubled youth. Determining which facility or sanction works best with juveniles is as difficult as it is with adults.

Do you believe we treat juvenile offenders too leniently, too harshly, or just right?

An online search of the term *juvenile corrections* on a random day generated news stories pertaining to a teen accused of assault and sexual abuse, a young man charged with assaulting an officer at a juvenile correctional facility, a juvenile fleeing from a facility and charged with resisting arrest and criminal mischief, and the increasing costs of an investigation of misconduct among juvenile detention staff. These headlines shed some light on the nature of juvenile justice in the United States, but they fail to show the many positive contributions in the field and the variety of options available and practices used to address delinquent and related behaviors. This module covers these and related issues, beginning with an overview of juvenile corrections, which sets the stage for a discussion of juvenile probation, intermediate sanctions as they are used with juveniles, custodial juvenile corrections, and issues related to security and aftercare.

A Nontraditional Reason to Close a Boot Camp

Following their popularity in the 1980s and 1990s, several boot camps around the United States closed out of concerns for camper deaths/injuries and a lack of promising evaluations. In 2015, Camp Outlook in Washington closed, in part, for a different reason: a decline in juvenile arrests. The camp, unlike boot camps in many other states, helped reduce recidivism rates and saved the state money. However, a decline in juvenile arrests resulted in shrinking class sizes, which came at an increased cost to the state. There were roughly 39,000 juvenile arrests in 2004, yet only about 13,000 in 2014, which amounts to a roughly 67% decline over the decade (O'Sullivan, 2015). The last class at the camp had 6 graduates.

Each day at the camp would begin at 5 a.m. and include physical training, therapy programs, and educational and vocational training. Camp Outlook was one of the more effective boot camps; it appeared to lower rates of recidivism for violent felonies among campers, compared to those with similar backgrounds who did not attend the camp. Closing the camp saved the state roughly $1.7 million over a 2-year budget cycle. Do you think boot camps for troubled juveniles, such as Camp Outlook, are a good idea?

3 Arrest

10
Corrections

An Overview of Juvenile Corrections

Various legislative acts have sought to refine juvenile corrections. In 1974, Congress enacted the **Juvenile Justice and Delinquency Prevention Act**, which encouraged states to remove status offenders (i.e., youths who commit offenses that are based on age and are not applicable to adults, for instance running away from home) from institutions. The act was not binding on the states, although it encouraged them to place status offenders with community social service or welfare agencies as alternatives to institutionalization. The act, as later amended in 1980, encouraged the removal of all juveniles from adult facilities. The primary concerns with placing juveniles in adult jails or lockups include the following (Champion et al., 2013):

- the risk of assault by staff and/or other inmates
- the facilities not being designed to confine youth or offer appropriate services or programming
- the criminogenic effects of being incarcerated with adult offenders
- the reality of being confined in a jail

● **Learning Objective 34.1:** Outline what happens to juveniles after they are taken into custody.

10
Corrections

Placing juveniles in jail, even if only temporarily, has generated criticism because of the many potential harms and limitations associated with doing so.

Should we use jails to detain some troubled youth? Why or why not?

8 Trial

Juvenile Justice and Delinquency Prevention Act of 1974 Legislation that encouraged states to remove status offenders from institutions; the act was not binding on the states, although it encouraged them to place status offenders with community social service or welfare agencies as alternatives to institutionalization

8 Trial

10 Corrections

Despite these legislative actions, in 2018 there were 3,400 juveniles held in local jails, most of whom were being held while they were on or awaiting their trial as an adult. However, the number of juvenile jail inmates dropped from a peak of 7,700 in 2008 (Zeng, 2020). Most juveniles taken into custody are not placed in adult facilities. Instead, they and their cases are evaluated by juvenile justice officials who determine the most appropriate means to process the case.

Entering Juvenile Corrections

Many of the same sanctions used for adults are used with juveniles. Among the distinctions between adult and juvenile corrections are the enhanced focus on rehabilitating juveniles compared to adults, the terminology used (see Module 26), and the steps that occur when juveniles enter the system.

When youths are taken into custody, important decisions must be made in terms of whether they should be released to the custody of their parents or guardian, warned, detained, committed, or diverted from the system. **Detained youths** are held prior to adjudication or disposition. They are detained out of concern that they may be a risk to the community or may fail to appear at a later court hearing, much like adults are placed in jail and may be granted pretrial release. **Committed youths** have been adjudicated delinquent and ordered to be held under correctional supervision, much like adults sentenced to incarceration.

Diversion involves redirecting juveniles from formal case processing. It can involve simply halting the official processing of the case or referring juveniles to programs designed to meet their specific needs. With regard to the latter, juveniles may be diverted from formal processing, for example pending their completion of a mental health or substance abuse program.

Juveniles who are found to be or plead guilty receive some type of disposition from the court. As noted in Module 26, a disposition is akin to a sentence in adult courts. The most commonly imposed disposition is juvenile probation for adjudicated delinquents (see Figure 34.1).

Noncustodial and Custodial Options

Juvenile corrections is often discussed in terms of noncustodial and custodial options. Noncustodial options are less punitive and generally involve treating and supervising offenders in the community. They include:

- probation,
- intensive supervision probation,
- restitution,
- community service,
- house arrest with electronic monitoring,
- day treatment programs, and
- aftercare.

The more secure forms of juvenile corrections, the custodial options, are often designed for offenders who typically have committed a more serious offense (e.g., robbery) or have a history of delinquent behavior. These options include:

- reception and diagnostic centers,
- detention centers,

Case flow for a typical 1,000 delinquency cases in 2017

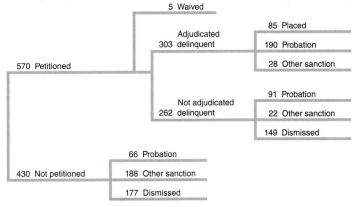

Case flow for 818,900 delinquency cases in 2017

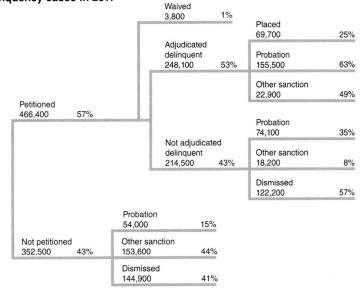

FIGURE 34.1. Case Flow for Delinquency Cases. Probation is most commonly used to address juveniles adjudicated delinquent. Roughly 28% of adjudicated delinquents were placed in confinement in 2017. *Source:* Delinquency Cases in Juvenile Court, 2017 *(NCJ 253105), by S. Hockenberry, 2019, U.S. Department of Justice, Office of Juvenile Justice and Delinquency Prevention.*

Why do you think probation is used so frequently to address delinquency?

detained youths
Youths who are held prior to adjudication or disposition; they are detained out of concern that they may be a risk to the community or may fail to appear at a later court hearing

committed youths Youths who have been adjudicated delinquent and ordered to be held under correctional supervision

diversion Halting or suspending formal proceedings with the agreement that the defendant will meet some agreed-on obligation

- foster homes and shelter care,
- group homes/halfway houses,
- camps and ranches,
- residential treatment centers, and
- training schools and juvenile correctional facilities.

Adjudicated youths may receive both custodial and noncustodial sanctions. For example, an offender may receive restitution along with being required to serve time at a group home.

● **Learning Objective 34.2:** Discuss the extent to which probation is used with juveniles and the functions it serves.

Juvenile Probation

Given that most juvenile offenders do not warrant secure confinement, various non-custodial correctional options are often used. The most commonly used sanction is juvenile probation. The percentage of adjudicated cases in which probation was imposed has been generally around 63% for the past two decades (Figure 34.2).

Juveniles sentenced to probation remain in the community under the supervision of a juvenile probation officer and may face other requirements such as drug counseling, restitution, community service, or weekend confinement (Livsey, 2012). In addition to being used as a formal sanction, probation is also used as a form of diversion. Some diverted youths voluntarily agree to abide by specific probation conditions, typically with the understanding that their case will not be adjudicated if they successfully meet the agreed-on requirements.

Nature of Juvenile Probation

Juvenile and adult probation are similar in nature (see Module 31). However, juvenile probation officers often seek to build a bond with juvenile offenders and develop a sense of trust that is often absent at the adult level. Probation officers may bring in mentors and/or engage in recreational opportunities with the youth and often try to work closely with community services, schools, and families. In particular, juvenile probation officers must remain in contact with school officials to monitor attendance, behavior, and performance, and so they sometimes create or work within school-based programs.

10
Corrections

Probation Restrictions

Similar to adults on probation, juvenile probationers are restricted in the community and must agree to a series of terms designed to best address their rehabilitative needs while protecting society. The restrictions placed on juveniles on probation typically include:

- being drug and alcohol free,
- remaining in school,
- obeying the law,
- being home or with parents/guardians at designated times,
- refraining from weapons possession or use, and
- meeting treatment or counseling requirements.

FIGURE 34.2. Percentage of Cases Adjudicated Delinquent, Resulting in Probation. Probation has been used in roughly 60%–65% of cases adjudicated delinquent in recent years. It is the most likely sanction imposed by juvenile courts. *Source:* Juvenile Court Statistics 2018, *by S. Hockenberry and C. Puzzanchera, 2020, National Center for Juvenile Justice.*

Would you support the idea of placing all juvenile offenders on probation, with varying degrees of supervision based on the seriousness of the offense for which they were adjudicated?

Primary Functions of Juvenile Probation Officers

Similar to probation officers who supervise adults, juvenile probation officers have a variety of responsibilities when supervising juveniles. Their primary functions include the following (Bartollas & Schmalleger, 2014):

- **intake:** processing the juvenile offender; a probation officer conducts a preliminary investigation, interviews the offender, and develops a course of action for the offender

- **caseload management:** maintaining a file for the juvenile offender; this also includes an assortment of administrative functions related to ensuring accountability and effective probation supervision

- **investigation**/supervision: the actual supervision of the offender, surveillance, monitoring, counseling, and guidance; the probation officer compiles and assesses information pertaining to the juvenile offender's performance

- **reporting:** keeping the court apprised regarding various issues, including violations of probation conditions and recommendations for continued community supervision or release from community corrections

---

CAREERS

Juvenile probation officers supervise juveniles on probation. They mentor juvenile probationers and enforce the laws and regulations regarding the probation agreement. They may work closely with the families or caregivers of probationers to provide accountability and rehabilitate offenders and may accompany their clients at court hearings, therapy sessions, or volunteer work.

Intermediate Sanctions and Juveniles

Juvenile judges historically were largely restricted to imposing sentences of confinement or probation. The array of options expanded around the 1980s with the introduction of various intermediate sanctions that gave juvenile court judges greater flexibility in sentencing. Among the more commonly used intermediate sanctions in juvenile corrections are intensive supervision probation, restitution, community service, house arrest with electronic monitoring, and day treatment programs.

● **Learning Objective 34.3:** Describe the intermediate sanctions used with juveniles.

Intensive Supervision Probation

As noted in Module 31, intensive supervision probation is a more restrictive form of probation. It provides greater accountability of youths when traditional probation is not restrictive enough but the offenders' actions do not warrant confinement. Intensive supervision probation for juveniles may consist of a single probation officer overseeing a relatively small caseload (e.g., 15 offenders) or a team of officers working to supervise a larger number of offenders.

10 Corrections

The supervision includes frequent meetings with the juvenile (e.g., four times per week) and various other forms of accountability, such as regular meetings or contacts with parents, teachers, guardians, treatment supervisors, employers, and others. Weekend and evening activities are monitored, and probation officers ensure that restitution and/or supervision fees are being paid, if required. The close supervision and small caseloads result in higher costs for this type of probation.

4 Booking

Restitution

Restitution is often imposed as a condition of juvenile probation and requires offenders to make amends for their misbehavior and assume responsibility for their actions. Restitution may consist of financial repayment to victims or some other form of repayment, primarily because juveniles do not typically have the financial means to repay victims. Probation officers may help offenders find employment to assist with restitution requirements, and jurisdictions have established programs that provide juveniles with opportunities to perform community service, with their payment going to their victims.

An example of a restitution program for juveniles is the Juvenile Community Offender Restitution and Public Service program in Maricopa County, Arizona,

Intake The step in juvenile case processing that involves screening cases to assess whether individuals need the court's assistance; at this stage, authorized officials decide whether to handle the case informally, dismiss the case, or request formal intervention of the juvenile court

10
Corrections

caseload management (juvenile probation) Maintaining files for offenders and an assortment of administrative functions related to ensuring accountability and effective probation supervision

10
Corrections

investigation (juvenile probation) Supervision of the offender, surveillance, monitoring, counseling, and guidance on behalf of the probation officer, who compiles and assesses information pertaining to the probationer's performance and reports to the court regarding various issues

Reporting A responsibility of juvenile probation officers; it involves keeping the court apprised regarding various issues

which provides youthful offenders with employment opportunities and directs their pay to their victims. Offenders enrolled in the program also participate in educational and counseling programs that encourage personal responsibility and develop job skills (Judicial Branch of Arizona, 2014).

Community Service

Juvenile offenders may be required to perform some form of community service in which they engage in unpaid work or their payment is given to their victims as restitution or donated to a victim compensation fund. Community service may include:

- picking up trash,
- landscaping public areas,
- washing government vehicles, or
- performing other volunteer work.

Community service is designed to help offenders recognize the significance of their actions and promote responsibility while offenders repay society and/or victims for their behavior. Along with restitution, it is a primary component of restorative justice, which involves repayment to society and victims for the harms done.

Community service benefits society in that free labor eases government budgets. However, critics of community service argue that the use of free labor eliminates job opportunities for law-abiding citizens. Accordingly, it is important for the courts to identify and use community service activities that minimize the negative effects and maximize the benefits to the offender, victim, and society.

House Arrest With Electronic Monitoring

Juveniles placed on house arrest, or home confinement, are required to be home at specific times. They are often only permitted to leave for specific purposes, such as attending school, counseling, or work. House arrest proposes to:

- reduce institutional overcrowding,
- enable juvenile offenders to remain in the community where they can attend school and/or work, and
- reduce the costs associated with incarceration.

Critics argue that house arrest:

- is not a severe enough punishment,
- focuses primarily on surveillance,
- is intrusive, and
- may compromise public safety because offenders remain in the community (Champion et al., 2013).

House arrest is typically used with electronic monitoring in efforts to better secure the whereabouts of the offender. The monitoring is 24 hours a day. Juveniles assigned to electronic monitoring, along with their parents, must agree to the terms of the sanction. House arrest with electronic monitoring for juveniles is used in the same manner as it is for adults (see Module 31).

Electronic monitoring costs between $5 and $25 per day, per offender, to use (Champion et al., 2013), and it is anticipated that the costs will decrease as technology advances. The costs vary depending on the intensity of the surveillance, and the devices used. While the costs of electronic monitoring remain much lower than the costs of confinement, juveniles, as compared to adults, are much less likely to be able to pay the costs associated with this sanction.

Day Treatment Programs

Residential day treatment programs provide various services to delinquent and at-risk youth, who typically report to the centers once or twice a day for programming, classes, and general accountability. Attendees may receive assistance in finding employment, life skills training, substance abuse counseling, and related services designed to rehabilitate them and help them to adjust and behave. These facilities are generally less restrictive than many other forms of juvenile corrections.

Experiential education, which is a philosophical approach to teaching in which students directly engage in and learn from experiences and reflections (e.g., working on a ranch), is sometimes included as a component of day treatment programs (see Module 31 for discussion of day reporting centers as they are used with adults).

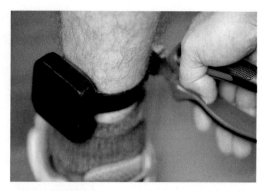

Electronic monitoring through the use of ankle bracelets is sometimes used to track juvenile (and adult) offenders who reside in the community.

What risks are associated with the use of electronic monitoring?

Custodial Placement for Juveniles

Out-of-home, or custodial, placement is used for offenders who are deemed unsuitable for community supervision. These offenders have typically committed serious and/or numerous offenses and are believed to warrant confinement. Proponents of confining juveniles argue that the separation from their troubling environments will better serve them, and certain actions should be punished by incarceration. Confinement arguably also serves as a deterrent. Critics argue that confinement results in youth more closely interacting with more and a wider array of delinquents, and research suggests that confinement is not related to decreases in future criminal behavior (e.g., Loughran et al., 2009). Figure 34.3 depicts the breakdown and extent to which these types of facilities house juvenile offenders.

Custodial placement for juveniles is categorized by length of time and security level. While there is much variation in the amount of time youths spend at facilities, long-term secure facilities on average hold juveniles for about 6 months and short-term facilities for about a month. In terms of security, nonsecure facilities enable youth to freely leave during the day, although they must abide by curfews and other rules and restrictions. Among the more commonly used facilities are reception and diagnostic centers, detention centers, foster homes and shelter care, group homes and halfway houses, camps and ranches, residential treatment centers, and training schools and juvenile correctional facilities.

● **Learning Objective 34.4:** Describe the custodial placement options for juveniles.

experiential education A philosophical approach to teaching in which students directly engage in and learn from experiences and reflections

10
Corrections

Reception and Diagnostic Centers

Some states have specific reception and diagnostic centers that detain juveniles while they undergo evaluation prior to being assigned to a juvenile correctional center. Officials at **reception and diagnostic centers** assess juveniles and diagnose any problems they may have. They then create treatment plans and identify training schools that best suit adjudicated juveniles.

The diagnosis at these centers may consist of psychologists evaluating intelligence, maturity, attitudes, and emotional problems. Social workers also work on cases in these centers to assist with the evaluations and diagnoses. Physical and dental evaluations may also be conducted. The evaluations last from roughly 4 to 6 weeks (Bartollas & Schmalleger, 2014), after which the youth is transferred to what

---

reception and diagnostic centers
Facilities that create treatment plans, identify training schools that best suit adjudicated juveniles, and assess juveniles and diagnose any problems they may have

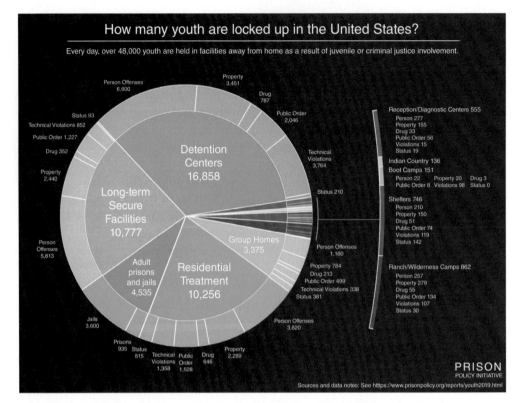

FIGURE 34.3. Juvenile Correctional Facilities by Facility Type. Various types of facilities are used to house juveniles. Detention centers and long-term secure facilities housed the largest number of juveniles. A notable number of youths (4,535) are housed in adult prisons and jails, despite the arguments in opposition to such placement. **Source:** Youth Confinement: The Whole Pie, *by W. Sawyer, 2019, Prison Policy Initiative (https://www.prisonpolicy.org/reports/youth2019.html).*

Should juveniles be housed in adult facilities, even though they are separated from adult inmates? Why or why not?

10
Corrections

detention centers
Short-term facilities that house juveniles awaiting resolution of their cases in court

is believed to be the most appropriate juvenile correctional facility. Most states do not have specific reception and diagnostic centers. Instead, the diagnostic process and evaluation takes place upon the offender's arrival at a training school (Bartollas & Miller, 2014).

Detention Centers

Detention centers, sometimes called juvenile halls, were created at the end of the 19th century as alternatives to jail for juveniles. They are temporary holding facilities that house juveniles awaiting resolution of their cases in court (Bartollas & Schmalleger, 2014). Most detention centers are secure custodial facilities that offer diagnostic, educational, counseling, and recreational programs. Suicide by inmates is of particular concern at these facilities because they house some offenders who are experiencing their first encounter with incarceration (Champion et al., 2013). Detainees live in dormitory-style housing or single cells that may resemble what is found in the adult system. The emphasis in the facilities is on custody, much like it is in adult facilities, and many are located in urban areas and sealed off from the community via their physical structure and other security measures (Allen et al., 2013).

Foster Homes and Shelter Care

Foster homes are used with both offenders (often those who commit minor offenses or status offenses) and children in need of supervision. The latter have not violated the law, however they require supervision. These homes provide youth with a substitute family for a temporary period that varies. The average time of placement in these facilities was about 20 months in 2017 (U.S. Department of Health and Human Services, 2018).

The majority of youth who enter foster homes (49%) return to their parents or their principal caregiver (U.S. Department of Health and Human Services, 2018). Juveniles in foster homes are emancipated at age 18 in most states and are no longer required to live under foster care.

Shelter care is similar to foster care, although shelter care facilities are used on a much more temporary basis, for instance for a few hours or weeks. They are primarily used for youth awaiting placement in foster or group homes.

Group Homes/Halfway Houses

Group homes are operated by public correctional agencies and some private agencies that contract with local or state governments. The homes typically accommodate 6–30 residents and provide kitchens, recreational areas, meeting rooms, and living quarters. Residents attend school in the community, take field trips, and may be granted special permission to leave the facility for other reasons, such as visiting family or attending religious services.

The homes provide a variety of services depending on the needs of the residents, with some homes being particularly focused on treatment. Residents have daily chores to assist with the operation of the home and typically attend group counseling sessions. There is no single model of group home; each facility determines what works best with regard to context and resources.

Halfway houses, as discussed in Module 31, are considered group homes and are used with juveniles as well as adults. Halfway homes provide many of the same services as group homes, although they are more commonly used with offenders who have served some period of incarceration and are readjusting to life outside confinement.

Camps and Ranches

Various types of camps or experiential learning are used within the realm of juvenile corrections, including boot camps, wilderness and forestry camps, and ranches. Boot camps are typically used for individuals who struggle with probation or for whom long-term incarceration is too severe (see Module 31). Boot camps emphasize military-style discipline, structured activity, and physical training for periods generally ranging from 60 to 180 days. Boot camps, sometimes referred to as shock incarceration, are designed to:

- shock offenders into abandoning their wrongful behaviors,
- break down the offenders and build them back up with strong values and discipline,
- provide educational and vocational training,
- ease jail and prison overcrowding, and
- deter at-risk and other youths.

Wilderness camps or **forestry camps** have been used to rehabilitate at-risk youth, juvenile probationers, and adjudicated youth. They encompass experiential education designed to offer youth means by which they can grow personally, socially, and emotionally (Fuentes & Burns, 2002).

10
Corrections

foster homes
Nonsecure facilities that are used with both offenders and children in need of supervision; they provide youth with a substitute family for a temporary period

shelter care Care that is often provided for youth awaiting placement in foster or group homes; it is similar to foster care, although shelter care facilities are used on a much more temporary basis

10
Corrections

group homes
Facilities that typically accommodate 6–30 residents under correctional supervision and provide kitchens, recreational areas, meeting rooms, and living quarters; they provide a variety of services depending on the needs of the residents, with some homes being particularly focused on treatment

10
Corrections

wilderness camps
Programs that involve counselors taking small groups of troubled youth into the wilderness where they will have to overcome challenges while learning positive values

forestry camps
Minimum-security placements that generally involve youths working outdoors, perhaps by assisting with conservation- and preservation-based activities

The concept emerged as early as 1932, when the Los Angeles County Probation Department established the first forestry camp program (Roberts, 1998). The camps are largely based on the Outward Bound model, created by Kurt Hahn, which proposes that exposure to particular experiences can generate positive behavior (Berman & Anton, 1988). The camps involve counselors taking small groups of troubled youth into the wilderness, where they will have to overcome challenges while learning the following values:

- teamwork
- survival
- trust
- self-worth
- pride
- commitment

Juveniles may also be required to work on a ranch or in a state park; for instance, they may mow lawns, perform general maintenance on the facility, or generally assist with conservation- and preservation-based activities. The programs are minimum-security custodial placements typically reserved for first-time offenders or those who committed minor offenses. The hands-on work offenders provide is supplemented by counseling, education, and vocational training. For instance, the Log Cabin Ranch is a 640-acre residential facility for juveniles adjudicated delinquent in San Francisco, California. The 12-month program provided by the ranch provides the following services (City and County of San Francisco, n.d.):

- academics (e.g., attendees can work toward a General Education Development certificate)
- mental health, medical, and dental services
- vocational training
- substance abuse counseling
- behavior management programming

10
Corrections

The goals of this and related ranch programs are to rehabilitate, train, and educate troubled youth and use nature and counseling in doing so.

Residential Treatment Centers

residential treatment centers
Facilities that provide residential care for juveniles supplemented with focused treatment services

Residential treatment centers are similar to group homes, although there is a much greater focus on treatment efforts. Residential treatment centers provide residential care for juveniles and are supplemented with focused treatment services. They help youthful offenders with various behavioral and substance abuse problems, and residents receive treatment without experiencing the negative effects of heavily secured correctional facilities. The facilities house youths with psychiatric, psychological, behavioral, and/or substance abuse issues who have been deemed unsuitable for day treatment or other nonsecure confinement, yet found to be unsuitable for placement in a heavily secured facility or psychiatric hospital (Greenwood, 2008).

10
Corrections

Training Schools and Juvenile Correctional Facilities

The long-term confinement of juvenile delinquents historically involved placement in a reform school, which resembled prisons for juveniles. These facilities offered few amenities and limited educational and other opportunities for rehabilitation. In the early 21st century, long-term secure confinement facilities include **training schools**, reformatories, and juvenile correctional facilities, and we no longer use the term *reform school* or refer to long-term juvenile facilities as *prison*. Training school are used to incarcerate juvenile offenders (typically for a year or more) and provide many opportunities for rehabilitation, including the following (Champion et al., 2013):

- education
- substance abuse counseling
- social and coping skills
- vocational training
- mental health counseling

Some training schools resemble prisons in their architecture (e.g., locked cell blocks, high walls), procedures, and use of solitary confinement for unruly inmates, while others use less restrictive facilities such as dormitories (Whitehead et al., 2013).

The primary goals among training schools and related facilities have been con- formity/obedience, treatment, and reeducation/development (Street et al., 1966). Institutions may be state accredited for granting high school diplomas, and they may help juveniles prepare for a General Educational Development exam. Some facilities are equipped to offer vocational training in areas that will help juveniles to succeed upon release. The training may focus on the following (Bartollas & Schmalleger, 2014):

- automobile repair
- welding
- carpentry
- barbering
- machine shop skills
- food service
- sewing and beauty care
- administrative skills

training schools

Facilities used to incarcerate juvenile offenders, typically for a year or more; they pro- vide many opportunities for rehabilitation, particularly with regard to education and vocational training

10
Corrections

● **Learning Objective 34.5:** Identify the security concerns related to the custodial placement of juveniles.

Security Issues With Custodial Placement for Juveniles

Custodial placement for juveniles involves the same security-related concerns as for adults. The goals of keeping offenders safe and confined while providing rehabilitative ser- vices challenge those who work in juvenile corrections on a regular basis. Security issues such as gangs and overcrowding are problematic at some juvenile residential facilities.

10
Corrections

Gangs and Overcrowding

Among the primary contributors to victimization of juveniles in custodial placement are gangs and overcrowding. Gang activity, in particular, has been problematic in secure facilities, because institutionalized gang members may recruit and teach other troubled youth about gang life. The close confinement and regular contact among inmates facilitates the interactions. The concerns regarding gang members in juvenile confinement facilities include:

- gang-involved behavior that threatens staff and residents,
- the negative effects on programming efforts, and
- the potential harms to institutional security (Howell & Roush, 1999).

Overcrowding is also problematic in juvenile facilities; an estimated 22% of juvenile residential facilities reported that the number of residents they housed put them at or above the capacity of their standard beds in 2016 (Hockenberry & Sladky, 2018). Overcrowded facilities increase the likelihood of various forms of victimization and the strained resources for corrections officials to provide adequate treatment.

Violence and Victimization

10
Corrections

Violence and victimization are problematic in some secure facilities, and aside from the direct harms, their presence can hinder efforts directed toward rehabilitation and treatment. The Office of Juvenile Justice and Delinquency Prevention noted that 46% of youths in custody had their property stolen in their absence, 10% were robbed, and 29% were threatened or beaten (Sedlak et al., 2013). An estimated 7.1% were sexually victimized within the past year of their confinement, with 5.8% of youths reporting that the sexual assault was committed by the facility staff (Smith & Stroop, 2019). The individuals at greatest risk of being violently victimized were:

- those who were among the most serious offenders,
- youth with prior sexual or physical abuse,
- youths in custody with a learning disability, and
- youths who had experienced more incidents involving physical control by facility staff (Sedlak et al., 2013).

The Need for Security

10
Corrections

With regard to security, roughly 46% of all juvenile residential facilities lock youth in their sleeping rooms at least some of the time, most often at night (89%) or when a youth is notably misbehaving (76%). An estimated 27% of facilities use external gates in fences or walls with razor wire to detain juveniles (Hockenberry & Sladky, 2018). As noted in Table 34.1, shelters were more likely than other types of facilities to report unauthorized departures (escapes).

Aftercare for Juveniles

● Learning Objective 34.6: Explain what aftercare is and the benefits it provides for juveniles.

Aftercare is provided to juveniles after they have been released from some form of custody. It is akin to adult parole and involves supervision and guidance in the community. Juveniles who return to the same families, communities, schools, and/or friends after being incarcerated typically face various problems readjusting. As a result, effective aftercare is often important to a juvenile offender's success. Among other benefits, aftercare:

- rewards juveniles for good behavior during their confinement,
- alleviates overcrowding,

TABLE 34.1. Unauthorized Departures by Juvenile Facility Type

FACILITY TYPE	NUMBER OF FACILITIES		PERCENTAGE OF REPORTING FACILITIES WITH UNAUTHORIZED DEPARTURES
	TOTAL	REPORTING	
Total facilities	1,772	1,567	19
Detention center	662	611	4
Shelter	31	124	47
Reception/diagnostic center	58	46	17
Group home	344	289	29
Ranch/wilderness camp	30	28	21
Training school	189	178	7
Residential treatment center	678	591	26

Note. An estimated 20% of facilities reported an unauthorized departure in 2016. Shelters and groups homes had the highest percentage of departures, while detention centers and training schools had the lowest. One fifth of facilities reported unauthorized departures in the month before the census date. Detail may sum to more than the totals because facilities could select more than one facility type. ***Source:*** *From authors' analysis of Juvenile Residential Facility Census 2016 [machine-readable data file]; and Juvenile Residential Facility Census, 2016: Selected Findings (NCJ 251785), by S. Hockenberry and A. Sladky, 2018, U.S. Department of Justice, Office of Juvenile Justice and Delinquency Prevention (https://ojjdp.ojp.gov/sites/g/files/xyckuh176/files/pubs/251785.pdf).*

- helps reintegrate individuals back into the community,
- enhances offenders' potential for rehabilitation, and
- helps deter youth from offending through providing regular supervision (Champion et al., 2013).

Placing Youths on Aftercare

10
Corrections

Jurisdictions vary with regard to the decision to place a youth on aftercare and the administration of the supervision. A few states use determinate sentencing, in which the decision to release to aftercare is determined by a youth's time served and their behavior while confined. Most states use indeterminate sentencing, in which the decision to release is made by:

- juvenile correctional agencies (the most common),
- boards (similar to parole boards) that determine a youth's suitability for aftercare, or
- sentencing judges.

Aftercare officers may meet with youths in the facility in which they are housed prior to their release to help develop a plan for success in the community.

Requirements of Aftercare

10
Corrections

As part of the placement plan, the officer will ensure that the juvenile has a suitable home in which to reside and develop a program or plan that will facilitate the youth's readjustment to society. Among the requirements commonly found in the plans are the following:

- obeying parents and teachers
- adjusting to school or work

Akin to adult parolees, juveniles on aftercare are monitored in the community for some time after their incarceration. Restrictions are placed on them, and they work with officials who monitor their progress upon release.

What challenges do juveniles on aftercare face that adults on parole do not?

- abiding by a curfew
- avoiding contact with specific individuals
- avoiding the use of illegal substances
- reporting to the aftercare officer as designated

Violating the terms of the agreement may result in the offender returning to a secure setting or receiving more restrictive community supervision. Most youths are placed on aftercare for at least 1 year (Bartollas & Schmalleger, 2014).

The System in Perspective

As discussed in the "In the News" feature at the start of this module, the closing of Camp Outlook, a boot camp in Washington, because of decreasing juvenile delinquency highlights a very important shift in juvenile corrections. Delinquency and juvenile arrest rates have declined in recent years, and officials have responded in many cases by reallocating funding that was used to support boot camps to delinquency prevention programs. However, decreases do not signify the elimination of delinquency or arrests.

Determining how to best address juveniles who misbehave has long challenged politicians, juvenile justice professionals, social workers, and other officials. Juveniles are often viewed as young and impressionable, and yet their behavior sometimes contradicts this view. Getting too tough on troubled youth could be viewed as giving up on a juvenile, while being too soft may not send the message that behavior changes are needed. Providing appropriate juvenile services at the right moment is crucial to stopping young offenders from later becoming involved in the criminal justice system.

Summary

1. Learning Objective 34.1: *Outline what happens to juveniles after they are taken into custody.*

- Youths in custody are considered either detained or committed. Detained youths are held prior to being adjudicated or disposed. Committed youths have been adjudicated delinquent and ordered to be held under correctional supervision. Other approaches are taken with regard to juvenile offenders; for instance, they may be released to the custody of their parents or guardian, warned, or diverted from the system. Juveniles who are found to be or plead guilty receive some type of disposition from the court. The more commonly imposed dispositions include juvenile probation and commitment to group homes, juvenile correctional institutions, and residential treatment centers.

2. Learning Objective 34.2: *Discuss the extent to which probation is used with juveniles and the functions it serves.*

- The percentage of cases in which probation was imposed has been generally around 63% in the past two decades. Probation is a formal sanction, although it can also be used as a form of diversion. Juveniles sentenced to probation remain in the community under the supervision of a juvenile probation officer and may face other requirements, such as drug counseling, restitution, community service, or weekend confinement.

3. Learning Objective 34.3: *Describe the intermediate sanctions used with juveniles.*

- Among the intermediate sanctions used with juveniles are intensive supervision probation, restitution, community service, house arrest with electronic monitoring, community service, and day treatment programs. Intensive supervision probation for juveniles may consist of a single probation officer overseeing a relatively small caseload or a team that supervises a larger number of offenders. Restitution requires offenders to make amends for their misbehavior and assume responsibility for their actions. Offenders may also receive community service, through which they engage in unpaid work or their payment is given to their victims as restitution or donated to a victim compensation fund. Juveniles placed on house arrest, or home confinement, are required to be home at specific times. House arrest is typically used with electronic monitoring. Various residential day treatment programs provide assorted services to delinquent and at-risk youth, who typically report to the centers once or twice a day for programming, classes, and general accountability.

4. Learning Objective 34.4: *Describe the custodial placement options for juveniles.*

- Various types of facilities are used for the custodial placement of juveniles. Among them are reception and diagnostic centers, which create treatment plans and identify training schools that best suit adjudicated juveniles. Detention centers are short-term facilities that house juveniles awaiting resolution of their cases in court, and foster homes provide youth with a substitute family for a temporary period. Shelter care is similar to foster care, although shelter care facilities are used on a much more temporary basis. Group homes and halfway houses provide a variety of services depending on the needs of the residents, with some homes being particularly focused on treatment. Further, various types of camps or experiential learning are used within the realm of juvenile corrections, including boot camps, wilderness camps, and working on ranches or spending time in a forestry camp. Residential treatment centers are similar to group homes, although there is a much greater focus on treatment efforts. Training schools and other secure correctional facilities are used to incarcerate juvenile offenders, but they provide many opportunities for rehabilitation.

5. Learning Objective 34.5: *Identify the security concerns related to the custodial placement of juveniles.*

- There are concerns about overcrowding and gang members in juvenile confinement facilities. Gang-involved behavior threatens staff and residents, negatively affects programming efforts, and potentially harms institutional security. The individuals at greatest risk of being violently victimized in juvenile confinement facilities are the most serious offenders, youths with prior sexual or physical abuse, youths with a learning disability, and youths who have experienced more incidents involving physical control by facility staff.

6. Learning Objective 34.6: *Explain what aftercare is and the benefits it provides for juveniles.*

- Aftercare is provided to juveniles upon their release from some form of custody. It is akin to adult parole and involves supervision and guidance in the community. Among the benefits of aftercare are that it rewards juveniles for good behavior during their confinement, helps alleviate overcrowding, helps reintegrate individuals back into the community, enhances offenders' potential for rehabilitation, and helps deter youth from offending by providing regular supervision.

Questions for Critical Thinking

1. What are the pros and cons of using diversion to address delinquency?

2. Given the differences between adult and juvenile probation, which do you believe would be most effective in helping offenders refrain from committing crime?

3. What type of intermediate sanction do you believe would be most suitable for a juvenile offender with a substance abuse problem? Why?

4. What form of custodial placement would you prefer if you were sentenced to one? Why?

5. What could be done to better secure juvenile correctional facilities?

6. How could we improve aftercare services?

Key Terms

caseload management (juvenile probation)
committed youths
detained youths
detention centers
diversion
experiential education
forestry camps
foster homes
group homes

intake (juvenile probation)
investigation (juvenile probation)
Juvenile Justice and Delinquency Prevention Act of 1974
reception and diagnostic centers
reporting
residential treatment centers
shelter care
training schools
wilderness camps

For digital learning resources, please go to
https://www.oup.com/he/burns1e

Future of Corrections

While the idea of floating prisons in the future seems a bit far-fetched, so did the idea of computers being an integral part of our lives. The future of corrections is filled with projections of both idealistic and gloomy scenarios and everything in between.

How do you envision prisons in 30 years?

Imagine life without prisoners, prisons, jails, or other correctional facilities. Instead of being institutionalized, offenders are medically treated or medically incapacitated for a designated time. Consider the potential of advanced medicines and science that could directly address and correct each criminal behavior and prevent future offending. Or, consider a drug that could mentally and physically incapacitate offenders so that they would lose a portion of their lives while unconscious, forego the hardships and negative influences of incarceration, and be kept from harming others. Could these considerations become reality in the next 10 years? In the next 25 years? This module starts with a look at the effectiveness of current correctional practices, followed by a discussion of technological advancements and the future of both institutional and community corrections.

MODULE OUTLINE

- **Evaluating Current Correctional Practices**
  Learning Objective 35.1: Identify the means by which correctional programs are evaluated.

- **Technology**
  Learning Objective 35.2: Describe how technological developments will likely impact corrections in the future.

- **Community and Institutional Corrections**
  Learning Objective 35.3: Evaluate the suggestions offered to improve prisons in the future.

IN THE NEWS

Prisons and Drone Drops

1 Criminal Act

In March 2020, two men were charged with using drones, which are unmanned flying aircraft, to drop drugs, cell phones, SIM cards, and syringes into a federal prison in New Jersey. Federal authorities noted that there had been at least seven other illegal drone deliveries since July 2018 (Setty, 2020). Drones were also used to drop drugs and other contraband in multiple Ohio prison yards. In one instance, a drop sparked a brawl among the inmates because the items were intended for the inmate member of one gang, but

10 Corrections

a member from a rival gang retrieved them (Otte, 2017). Although it was not a crime to fly a drone over Ohio's state prisons or to record

over the facilities, it is a crime to drop contraband (Ludlow, 2015).

The use of drones to smuggle contraband into prisons is not unique to Ohio and New Jersey; drones have been used for this purpose in other states as well. Using drones demonstrates the creativity and lengths to which individuals will go to assist friends and family members in prisons. It also demonstrates the potential for technology to pose additional challenges.

Officials at all prisons will have to consider methods by which they can prevent the use of drones to deliver contraband, including means to identify and respond to the devices. New antidrone technology is being considered by prison officials. Among the developments is a mechanism that has the capability of detecting drones and disrupting the signal between the user and the drone, thus diverting the drone from the prison facility. Other antidrone technology includes the creation of geoperimeters that would be set up around prisons and force any detected drones to land or turn around prior to entering the perimeter (Otte, 2017). The costs of the technology and the fact that some of it is still in its testing phase have prohibited its widespread use (Otte, 2017). Besides dropping contraband, what other threats could drones pose for prisons? How could prison officials use drones to assist with prison responsibilities?

● **Learning Objective 35.1:** Identify the means by which correctional programs are evaluated.

Evaluating Current Correctional Practices

The effectiveness of current correctional practices will impact the future of corrections. We are likely to build on correctional programs that appear to be successful and alter or abandon seemingly ineffective approaches. Assessing the effectiveness of correctional programs is complex, because there are different goals involved in the various sanctions, and many variations exist among the types of programs implemented. However, we can evaluate many community and institutional corrections programs in terms of costs, recidivism rates, deterrence, incapacitation, retribution, and rehabilitation.

Costs

Correctional options are often evaluated in terms of their costs. Governments spend a substantial portion of their budgets and many resources on corrections. State and local expenditures for correctional institutions are estimated to cost over $80 billion annually (Kyckelhahn, 2015).

One study by the Vera Institute of Justice found that state prison costs were roughly $43 billion in the 45 states under study and that the average annual cost per inmate was $33,274, ranging from $14,780 per inmate in Kentucky to over $69,000 in New York (Mai & Subramanian, 2017). The National Association of State Budget Officers (2019) noted that correctional expenditures constituted 3% of total state expenditures in fiscal year 2019. Figure 35.1 provides the costs of corrections and compares them to the costs of law enforcement and the courts. Corrections consumes over 44% of the costs associated with the three primary areas of criminal justice.

Economic pragmatism with regard to correctional practices emphasizes cost savings. With respect to community supervision, cost savings are measured in terms of the financial resources spent on probation and parole, for example in lieu of incarceration. In 2016, the annual cost of imprisonment in the Bureau of Prisons ($34,770 annually) was almost 8 times the costs of placing the same offender under postconviction supervision ($4,392) in the federal system (U.S. Courts, 2017). Community supervision is less costly than incarceration, and the cost savings increase when offenders are required to pay for supervision services.

Recidivism Rates and Deterrence

Another common way to evaluate the effectiveness of correctional programs is to look at recidivism rates. These rates can be evaluated for both community corrections and institutional corrections.

COMMUNITY CORRECTIONS

The success of community correction programs can be measured by examining the following:

- the percentage of arrests or technical violations while on community supervision
- the percentage of convictions while on community supervision
- the percentage of probationers or parolees who are incarcerated (with regard to probation) or reincarcerated (parole)
- general offender success in the community, including stable employment and adequate housing

Almost a third of the roughly 2.3 million individuals who exit probation or parole each year fail to successfully complete the terms imposed on them when they received community supervision (Pew Charitable Trusts, 2018). They may fail because they commit a crime while on supervision, violate the terms of their agreement, or flee. An assessment of federal offenders placed on community supervision sheds additional light. The study followed 43,000 offenders who received probation or were supervised upon release from incarceration. The researchers found that 35% of those supervised in the community were arrested within 3 years, and 43% were arrested within 5 years of placement (Markman et al., 2016). These percentages could be considered optimistically in that less than half were arrested within 5 years, or the percentages could be considered more pessimistically, because well over one-third of offenders were arrested. Regardless, the arrest rates for those on community corrections are lower than they are for those strictly released from prison.

10
Corrections

economic pragmatism An approach to correctional practices that emphasizes cost savings

3 Arrest

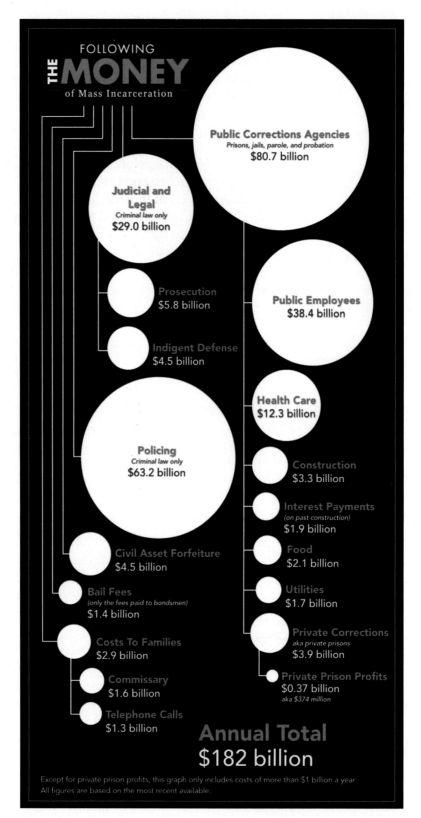

FIGURE 35.1. Costs of Corrections. The United States spends over $80 billion on corrections annually. The costs of corrections outweigh those associated with both law enforcement and the courts. The largest portion of correctional spending goes toward employees. *Source: Prison Policy Initiative. https://www.prisonpolicy.org/reports/money.html.*

What do you believe would be the most effective way to reduce the extensive amount of money spent on corrections?

INSTITUTIONAL CORRECTIONS

Recidivism rates are also among the more common means by which institutional corrections programs are evaluated. Prisons generally seem to struggle with meeting the goal of being a deterrent (Pollock et al., 2012). Researchers analyzed the recidivism of prisoners released in 30 states in 2005 and found that 68% of state prisoners released from these states in 2005 were arrested within 3 years of release, 79% were arrested within 6 years of release, and 83% were rearrested within 9 years (Alper et al., 2018).

3 Arrest

However, these numbers must be considered in light of the fact that arrestees are innocent until proven guilty. As such, researchers assessed recidivism based on conviction rates and found that an estimated 45.2% of inmates had an arrest that resulted in a conviction in court within 3 years of release, and 55.4% of inmates had an arrest within 5 years that resulted in a conviction (Durose et al., 2014).

1 Criminal Act

These data are somewhat discouraging given that over half of released prisoners were convicted of a crime within 5 years of their release. As noted earlier, offenders sentenced to community corrections have lower rates of rearrest, which may be a result of the type of offender who is on probation compared to those who are incarcerated. In particular, incarcerated individuals are most likely to have committed a more serious offense (or more offenses in general) than probationers. As such, one would logically expect that they would have higher rearrest rates than probationers. However, the argument could be made that those leaving prison should be reformed given the rehabilitative services they have access to that help prepare them for reentry and adjustment in the community.

While it is difficult to discern exactly why those released from prison have higher rates of recidivism than those on community corrections, it may be the case that they are not receiving adequate rehabilitation services while incarcerated. Further, the effects of being in prison, surrounded by criminals, may also influence inmate behavior upon release.

Incapacitation and Retribution

Correctional institutions incapacitate offenders by physically preventing them from committing harm outside the institution, and they are undoubtedly punitive in nature. However, prison escapes do happen. There were roughly 2,353 prisoner escapes from state and federal prisons in 2018, which was a much lower number than in the early part of the 21st century: The number of escapes reached over 5,100 in 2000 (Statista, 2020). The decrease occurred even though the number of inmates increased. Many of the incidents considered escapes occur outside institutions, for instance when inmates absconded while on work release or during an off-site hospital visit (Kutner, 2015). Between 2009 and 2013, only 1 inmate escaped from a maximum-security prison, and only 9 others escaped from medium- or minimum-security facilities. All were captured within 1 day (Toppo, 2015). Better prison designs that enable inmates to be monitored more effectively, improved leadership, and greater control of inmates have contributed to the decreased number of escapes (Kutner, 2015).

10 Corrections

The goal of retribution, or punishing offenders, is largely met through the restriction of freedoms faced by inmates. The structured, closely monitored prison and jail environments and the challenges that accompany living with other inmates under stressful conditions go far toward meeting the goal of retribution. In addition, solitary confinement is used to incapacitate and punish the most dangerous offenders and deter others, despite the fact that researchers noted no reductions in the levels of inmate-on-inmate violence in supermax prisons in the three states they studied (Pizzaro & Narag, 2008). Those opposed to solitary confinement argue that it is

9 Sentencing

overly expensive, does not rehabilitate offenders, and generates or exacerbates mental illnesses (American Civil Liberties Union, 2018).

10
Corrections

Rehabilitation

The types of rehabilitation programs found in jails and prisons vary and generally include:

- treatment (e.g., to address alcohol and drug abuse),
- counseling and therapy (e.g., to assist with anger management and provide conflict resolution skills),
- educational programming (e.g., to assist with living a crime-free life in the community), and
- vocational programming (e.g., to provide job skills for greater success upon return to society).

Rehabilitation is designed to "fix" or "correct" offender behaviors, which can be difficult. It is an area in which disciplines other than criminal justice (e.g., psychology and social work) assist with the goal of preparing offenders for return to society. The approaches have had varying levels of success; however, innovations in medicine and treatment, as well as our advanced understanding of how the brain and body operate, provide promise for the future.

An analysis of studies between 1980 and 2011 examined the relationship between correctional education and inmate outcomes. Results from the study suggested that, on average, inmates who received correctional education had 43% lower odds of recidivating than their counterparts. Those who received education were also more likely to find employment postrelease (L. M. Davis et al., 2013).

Vocational training also increases the effectiveness of prisons because inmates learn practical skills and necessary work habits to assist them in finding and maintaining employment after incarceration. While there is not enough recent research regarding the impact of vocational training on recidivism rates to offer significant conclusions (Newton et al., 2018), it would seem logical that providing inmates with work skills would help them locate jobs upon release and help keep them from engaging in crime. Unfortunately, vocational training in prison suffers from several limitations, including the following (Clear et al., 2016):

- The training typically centers on the least desirable jobs that already have large labor pools (e.g., barbering, welding).
- Inmates are often trained using outdated or inadequate equipment, because prisons typically lack the resources to upgrade.
- The regimen of prison life involves regularly telling inmates what to do, which can hamper their creativity or initiative.
- There are not always enough job training programs in prison.

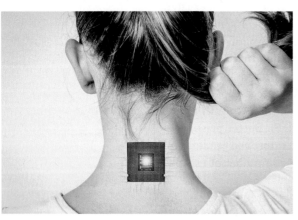

Some projections of the future include the use of certain drugs or the implantation of microchips to monitor and control offenders.

What would be some of the concerns with implanting offenders with trackers in efforts to control their behavior and monitor them?

Vocational training has the potential to enhance the prison experience for inmates, but it appears that several obstacles must first be overcome.

Other Areas of Evaluation

In addition to costs, recidivism rates, retribution, and rehabilitation, correctional institutions are also evaluated based on other criteria, including:

10
Corrections

- administration quality,
- ability to keep inmates active,
- respect for inmate rights, and
- provision of a safe and secure facility.

With regard to the provision of a safe and secure facility, the Texas Department of Criminal Justice noted that 22 people died as a result of indoor weather conditions at 15 state prisons between 1998 and 2017. Most prisons in Texas do not have air conditioning (Banks, 2017). In 2017, the situation escalated to the point that a federal judge gave state prison officials 15 days to create a plan that would lower the temperature to 88 degrees inside a state prison where it was believed that the heat was endangering the health of inmates (Associated Press, 2017).

Technology

The use of technology in prisons generally began in the 1970s with cameras to supervise inmates. As the cameras became less costly, more effective, and more durable, their use for surveillance increased (Stone & Scharf, 2011). Among other innovations, closed-circuit television has proven effective in preventing prisoner escapes (Vachiradath, 2013).

Correctional agencies have increasingly relied on various technological advancements to assist with their day-to-day operations. For example, toilet flushing can be controlled via computers that inform correctional officers of multiple flushes and enable them to shut off control valves. This technology helps address the problems associated with inmates stuffing items into their toilets or attempting to flood the area (Dotson, 2012). What follows is merely a sampling of the influences of technology on corrections, and as technology changes, so will its role in corrections.

● **Learning Objective 35.2:** Describe how technological developments will likely impact corrections in the future.

Software and Mapping

In the early 21st century, technological developments affect all aspects of corrections. For example, probation officers have benefited from developments that enable them to quickly generate presentence investigation reports and risk assessment scores that use data gathered from official reports and interviews of offenders. Software programs have also assisted probation officers with monitoring payments, for instance with regard to the fines the offender received or for restitution (Schmalleger & Smykla, 2009).

10
Corrections

Mapping programs have assisted probation agencies with regard to allocating probation officers. Being able to visually assess the areas in which probationers are located facilitates more effective supervision. Crime mapping enables probation and parole agencies to better recognize high-crime areas that could pose challenges for individuals on community supervision, and it alerts officers to probationers or parolees in restricted areas.

Global Positioning Systems

The **Global Positioning System (GPS)** is a global navigation satellite system, owned by the U.S. Air Force, which provides location and time information to

Global Positioning System A global navigation satellite system, owned by the U.S. Air Force, that provides location and time information to users with a receiving device

active GPS monitoring Monitoring that enables constant notification of an offender's whereabouts at all times

passive GPS monitoring Monitoring that provides a signal when an offender is within the confines of a particular location

users with a receiving device. GPS has been increasingly used in tracking offenders in the community. Earlier technology involved an ankle bracelet that provided a signal to officials when an individual on community supervision entered or left a specified location. Today, however, GPS enables officials to pinpoint all of the specific locations at which an offender has been. **Active GPS monitoring** enables constant notification of the offender's whereabouts; however, it is costly because of cellular charges. **Passive GPS monitoring** simply provides a signal that an offender is within the confines of a particular location, and so it is less costly (Downing, 2006).

Despite the relatively high costs for active monitoring, GPS monitoring is still less expensive than incarceration. Active GPS monitoring costs roughly $13–$36 per day, and offenders sometimes help cover the fees (Meloy, 2014; Payne & DeMichele, 2011). The benefits and weaknesses of GPS monitoring follow (Downing, 2006).

Advantages of GPS monitoring:

- constantly tracks offenders
- sounds an alarm if the device is tampered with or removed
- allows for creation of inclusion and exclusion zones
- is accepted as accurate by the judicial and scientific communities
- does not require offenders to have a landline in their residence
- protects potential crime victims
- permits offenders to use community services and be employed
- has been shown to improve offender behavior (for those who comply with rules)

Disadvantages of GPS monitoring:

- cannot track individuals inside or at certain locations
- requires cellular coverage, which is costly
- initial and replacement costs are high
- requires timely responses by corrections officials regarding offender violations
- requires timely training for offenders and monitoring staff
- data must be processed on a regular basis
- sends notification even if an offender enters an exclusion area accidently, for instance when a bus passes through the zone

GPS AND COMMUNITY CORRECTIONS

GPS tracking is used in many capacities with regard to community corrections. The technology is used to protect victims of domestic abuse (because abusers can be tracked) and to generally oversee some individuals being supervised in the community. Further, jurisdictions are increasingly requiring the lifetime supervision of sex offenders, and GPS surveillance systems are being used to better track these offenders (W. D. Burrell & Gable, 2008). GPS technologies enable the creation of inclusion (e.g., home, work, school) and exclusion zones (e.g., bars, particular residences), which enable victims, community supervision officers, and others to be immediately notified if an offender enters or leaves the defined range.

GPS AND INSTITUTIONAL CORRECTIONS

Although they are primarily used in community corrections, tracking devices worn by prison and jail inmates help corrections officials better control inmate populations. Being able to identify the immediate location of an inmate and where they have been provides numerous benefits to institutional officials. Tracking devices within institutions:

- may deter inmates from violating the rules out of fear of being tracked,
- can help investigators solve cases involving prisoner misconduct, and
- facilitate inmate counts.

Tracking devices can also be used to determine when there is an unusual concentration of inmates in a particular area, which could be a sign of existing or potential trouble (Bulman, 2009). In the future, individuals on community corrections may be tracked via implanted monitoring devices that are placed within one's skin.

Videoconference Visitation and Enhanced Visitor Screening

Videoconference visitation allows inmates to visit with individuals outside the institution through the use of technology and is increasingly replacing personal visitations. In doing so, it:

- helps increase the number of visits that can occur each day,
- reduces staff time in checking visitors and escorting inmates to visitation areas, and
- reduces the amount of contraband smuggled in by visitors (Ducker, 2004).

The use of technology to facilitate visits benefits children as well; for instance, some facilities will not permit children into visitation areas for security reasons, and children may be frightened by visitation rooms (St. Pierre, 2011). Videoconferencing will likely increase in popularity as the technology improves and costs decrease (Rogers, 2013).

In addition to benefiting visitation, technology has enhanced screening practices in prisons and jails. Officials can better detect weapons, cell phones, and other forms of contraband. Some of the screening technologies used by the Transportation Security Administration in its efforts to screen airline passengers are being incorporated into prisons for the purposes of scanning visitors, employees, and inmates (Bulman, 2009).

The use of videoconferencing in lieu of in-person visitation became particularly important following the spread of COVID-19 in 2020. Most prisons and jails across the United States suspended or reduced in-person visits out of concern for the transmission of the virus. They instead relied on teleconferencing and phone calls, with some jails and prisons waiving or reducing the high fees often associated with such visitations (Prison Policy Initiative, 2020).

Telemedicine

Telemedicine, which permits healthcare professionals to consult with institutional medical personnel via videoconferencing, is also enhancing corrections and is expected to continue doing so. Inmates may ultimately receive better healthcare treatment via telemedicine, and staff benefit from not having to take an inmate to a specialist in the community. Telemedicine is particularly helpful for remote correctional facilities because it reduces the risks associated with moving inmates or bringing specialists to the facility (St. Pierre, 2011).

Automated Kiosks

Automated kiosks are booths containing electronic devices that are located in public areas. Individuals on community supervision may be required to report to a

videoconference visitation Inmates visiting with individuals outside the institution through the use of technology

10
Corrections

telemedicine Healthcare professionals consulting with institutional medical personnel via videoconferencing

It is anticipated that kiosks will continue to facilitate offender reporting. Such automation reduces the reliance on correctional workers to monitor offenders in the community.

What are the limitations of using kiosks for offender reporting?

automated kiosks
Booths containing electronic devices that are located in public areas; they enable those on community supervision to more easily report to corrections officials

10
Corrections

specified kiosk, at which point they may be interviewed and/or tested for drugs and/or alcohol. Biometrics facilitates community supervision by ensuring that the interviews and/or tests conducted at the kiosks involve the correct person. These kiosks:

- enable those on community supervision to more easily report to corrections officials,
- facilitate community supervision practices, and
- save resources on behalf of those being supervised and community supervision officials.

Challenges Associated With Technology

While technology has certainly assisted the correctional field, particularly in light of the pandemic pertaining to COVID-19, it also provides a host of challenges. For instance, the compilation of personal information in electronic databases requires that the data be securely protected. Further, mobile phones and the chargers used to power them have become increasingly popular forms of contraband confiscated in prisons and jails.

Among other areas of concern related to technology are the following (Stone & Scharf, 2011):

- legal issues (e.g., respecting rights to privacy)
- implementation (e.g., determining the most effective means by which technology can be introduced)
- cost (e.g., ensuring that funding is available to use the technology)
- maintenance (e.g., ensuring the technology works efficiently and effectively)
- training (e.g., ensuring that all employees know how to use the technology)

Community and Institutional Corrections

● **Learning Objective 35.3:** Evaluate the suggestions offered to improve prisons in the future.

10
Corrections

All types of correctional practices have undergone growth and development historically, in particular since the 1970s. In commenting on the current need to take action to better influence the future of corrections, researchers argued that just as we expect offenders to reform and better themselves, we should expect corrections personnel to move forward. They added that continued development in corrections must include the following (Lutze et al., 2012):

- reducing prison and community corrections populations to manageable levels
- ensuring that agencies support and participate in **evidence-based practices**—policies that emphasize thorough empirical evaluation and rely on scientific evidence that is objective, provides consistent results, and is applicable to individuals or groups other than those used in the production of the original evidence
- considering corrections as a human service profession that supports the individual needs of offenders and the professional needs of officers

The Future of Community Corrections

In commenting on the future of community corrections, researchers have suggested the following needs (Clear et al., 2016):

- Address the tendency of criminal justice officials to dismiss less restrictive sentencing options in favor of more punitive ones.

- Increase community support for intermediate sanctions.

- Clarify the purposes of community corrections and intermediate sanctions, because it is argued there is too much confusion clouding the objectives of various sanctions, including concerns about rehabilitation, easing prison overcrowding, punishment, cost-effectiveness, and other issues.

The future of community corrections will likely involve the continued incorporation of technological advancements designed to facilitate community supervision and reduce correctional costs. However, technology reduces the need for human interaction, which is particularly important in community corrections. Technological devices and products may become preferred over human contact, which could negatively influence the establishment of relationships, networking and employment opportunities, and personal, helpful insight provided by community corrections personnel. Careful consideration of all technological advancements in community corrections should include not only cost savings, but also the uniqueness of each client.

The Future of Incarceration

Until the 1970s, prison space was reserved for the most serious offenders. That changed in the 1980s when prisons began to be viewed as "an infinite resource that could be expanded continuously to meet capacity without regard to monetary expense or human cost" (Lutze et al., 2012, p. 44). The increased use of prisons beginning around this time was largely influenced by:

- rising crime rates in the 1970s,
- more conservative public values that emphasized law and order, and

evidence-based practices Policies and practices that emphasize thorough empirical evaluation and rely on scientific evidence that is objective, provides consistent results, and is applicable to individuals or groups other than those used in the production of the original evidence

9 Sentencing

10 Corrections

Technological advancements and the study of human behavior will continue impacting both institutional and community corrections. We know much more about brain functioning, DNA, and human behavior than ever before, and progress in this area continues.

Would we be better off if scientists and doctors could analyze a person's brain waves and body chemistry to determine who is best suited for community corrections and who should be incarcerated? What would be the drawbacks of this development?

- the belief that rehabilitation was ineffective with regarding to preventing criminal behavior (see Module 32).

In light of the challenges generally facing prisons in the early 21st century, researchers have offered suggestions for improvement, some of which relate to the criminal justice system as a whole (Austin & Irwin, 2001; Pollock et al., 2012):

- committing to the principles of rehabilitation and restorative justice
- reforming recruiting, training, and retaining staff to encourage employees to be committed to organizational goals
- improving the social, psychological, moral/ethical, and physical safety aspects of prisons to enable inmates to focus on rehabilitation instead of survival
- ensuring that rehabilitation practices are evidence based
- considering the barriers to improving prisons, including the profits from mass prison construction, budgetary restraints, and public opinion
- reforming sentencing practices toward using alternatives to incarceration for nonviolent drug offenders
- granting inmates adequate healthcare
- providing greater assistance for reentry

Creating the perfect prison is not possible, but adherence to these suggestions will vastly improve tomorrow's prisons (Pollock et al., 2012). There are also signs suggesting that the United States may be reducing its heavy reliance on incarceration. For example, the prison population at the end of 2019 was the smallest since 2002 and had declined 11% from its all-time peak in 2009 (Carson, 2020a). Further, many of the provisions included in the First Step Act (see Module 25), which passed in 2018, may serve to reform sentencing and further decrease incarceration rates and overcrowding.

Despite the challenges historically associated with jails, their future appears promising in several respects. Jails in many jurisdictions have been replaced or renovated since the 1970s. Further, many small jurisdictions are starting to combine their resources and build jails that serve the needs of multiple communities. However, such arrangements may generate some political struggles, for instance in relation to budgeting. Despite some political resistance, the movement appears to be toward improving jails and sharing jails among jurisdictions (Clear et al., 2016).

MYTHBUSTING
Assessing Reading Levels Helps With Prison Planning

While meeting with the mayors of several large cities, a National Public Radio host commented that prison administrators consider the test scores of third graders to determine if they will have to start building more prisons. The NPR host was not the only person to comment that prison space in the future is determined by elementary school grades, for instance as a mayoral candidate in St. Petersburg, Florida, and others have noted the relationship between children's educational performances and the likelihood of ending up in prison (Hudson, 2012; Sanders, 2013). While the educational level of prisoners is below the national average, prisons do not consider elementary reading levels in determining future prison space. Instead, they use formulas that consider arrest rates and demographic data, including the anticipated number of 18- to 25-year-old men in their state (Hudson, 2012).

The System in Perspective

The use of drones to drop contraband in prison yards (as discussed in the "In the News" feature at the start of this module) is but one of the many issues relating to technological advances that corrections officials will have to address. Technology and related changes will undoubtedly shape corrections in the future; however, not all of the changes will negatively impact corrections. For instance, drones could also be used to monitor inmates while they recreate in open air spaces, thus reducing the reliance on prison officers to do so.

Projecting the future of corrections involves consideration of many variables. Among the issues for consideration are changes in other aspects of our justice system. Correctional agencies provide unique services, but they are all impacted by the other primary components of the justice system (law enforcement and the courts). For instance, an enhanced "get tough on crime" approach adopted by law enforcement and/ or the courts will impact the resources required by correctional agencies. A more rehabilitative, or softer, approach adopted by law enforcement and/or the courts will also impact the direction of and resources required by correctional agencies.

Staying abreast of developments both within and outside the criminal justice system is required for effective correctional programming, as are communication and cooperation. Some projections for the future see correctional agencies more heavily relying on medications and behavioral therapy, and the onus is on correctional agencies to monitor developments in these and related areas to stay ahead of the curve. Similarly, correctional agencies need to continuously be mindful of proposed and enacted legislation as it pertains to corrections. Being proactive, as opposed to simply reacting to changes in other aspects of our justice system and other areas, will help ensure the effectiveness of all correctional programs and agencies.

Summary

1. Learning Objective 35.1: *Identify the means by which correctional programs are evaluated.*

- Assessing the effectiveness of correctional programs is complex because there are different goals involved in the various sanctions, and many variations exist among the types of programs used. Nevertheless, correctional options are often evaluated in terms of their costs, cost savings, the success of offenders in the community and within institutions, and their ability to incapacitate, deter, punish, and rehabilitate offenders.

2. Learning Objective 35.2: *Describe how technological developments will likely impact corrections in the future.*

- Technology will continue to impact corrections, particularly in relation to cameras to provide supervision, software to assist probation officers and others, offender tracking through GPS, mapping programs to better monitor individuals in the community, videoconferencing to assist with visitation, screening practices to detect contraband, telemedicine, and automated kiosks for reporting practices.

3. Learning Objective 35.3: *Identify the suggestions offered to improve prisons in the future.*

- It has been argued that prisons in the future could be improved by committing to the principles of rehabilitation and restorative justice; improving the recruitment, training, and retention of staff and encouraging employees to be committed to organizational goals; improving the social, psychological, moral/ethical, and physical safety aspects of prisons in efforts to enable inmates to focus on rehabilitation; using evidence-based rehabilitation practices; and considering the barriers to improving prisons.

Questions for Critical Thinking

1. How would you rate the overall effectiveness of both community and institutional corrections? Discuss whether you believe one is more effective than the other.

2. Envision prisons in 30 years. What technological devices will be used to house inmates? What threats will prisons face as a result of technological advancements?

3. Assume you have unlimited resources to improve correctional practices. What three changes would you initially make to ensure that prisons in the future more effectively meet their goals? What three changes would you make to probation practices?

Key Terms

active GPS monitoring
automated kiosks
economic pragmatism
evidence-based practices

Global Positioning System
passive GPS monitoring
telemedicine
videoconference visitation

For digital learning resources, please go to
https://www.oup.com/he/burns1e

Glossary

Abolitionists Those who support the abolition of the juvenile justice system

Abolition movement A movement in the 1920s that promoted the abolition of capital punishment

Abuses of authority Acts of police misconduct that include intentional actions in the course of police work that are designed to inflict harm upon others or violate individual rights

Accreditation A system of accountability in which an oversight body assesses and evaluates agencies and organizations to ensure that they are competent, credible, and/or in compliance with a set of standards

Acquired immune deficiency syndrome (AIDS) The final stage of infection associated with HIV, when one's ability to fight off infections has notably diminished

Active GPS monitoring Monitoring that enables constant notification of an offender's whereabouts at all times

Acts of commission Actions that occurred or were committed

Acts of omission Incidents in which a harm occurred by the failure of an individual to meet a designated responsibility

Actus reus Actions, and in some cases inactions, on behalf of individuals

Adjudication Judging or acting in response to a petition filed in juvenile court

Adjudication hearings Proceedings in juvenile court that are akin to trials in criminal court

Administration building assignments Prison officer assignments that involve providing safety and security in the administrative building, including the visitors' room and prison gates

Administrative control theory Proposes that prison disorder is more likely to occur when prison management is provided in a weak, unstable, and/or divided manner

Administrative law Laws, rules, and regulations that address issues such as environmental, consumer, workplace, and public health protections

Administrative Office of the U.S. Courts Created in 1939, this office performs administrative support functions for the federal judiciary, including administrative, legal, financial, management, and information technology support

Administrative searches Searches conducted by government investigators to assess whether there are violations of government regulations

Adversarial legal system The legal system used in the United States, which involves the prosecution and defense presenting their cases before a judge and perhaps a jury; the burden of proof is on the prosecution to demonstrate beyond a reasonable doubt that the defendant is culpable for the crime in question

Affidavit A written statement establishing probable cause to conduct a search

Affirmative action programs Programs designed to promote the hiring of disadvantaged groups who have suffered from discrimination

Affirmative defense A defense offered by defendants who claim responsibility for the actions that caused the harm in a crime, although they provide reasons (defenses) for why they are not criminally responsible

Age Discrimination in Employment Act of 1967 Legislation passed in 1967 that was designed to prevent maximum age limits for employment and address discrimination against older Americans; the act initially applied to law enforcement agencies, but Congress has since exempted them

Aggressive patrol A type of patrol in which officers proactively address specific types of crimes and infractions

Alibi A defense through which defendants claim that they were physically somewhere other than the crime scene at the time of the crime and therefore could not have committed the offense

Allen charge A charge issued to juries that appear unable to reach agreement; judges use them to recharge the jury with new instructions designed to encourage agreement

Alternative dispute resolution The various means of settling disputes away from courtrooms; they are alternatives to trials

AMBER Alert system A program that uses media outlets to assist in recovering abducted children

American Correctional Association The oldest and largest international correctional association in the world; it has supported the professional development of corrections since 1870

Americans With Disabilities Act of 1990 A civil rights law that prohibits discrimination with regard to disability; further, it requires employers to provide reasonable accommodations to employees with disabilities and establishes accessibility requirements for public facilities

Amnesty A type of clemency that is similar to a pardon, although it applies to a group or class of offenders

Anomie A sense of normlessness, in which a breakdown in society's norms results in a feeling of strain

Anti-Drug Abuse Act of 1986 Legislation that mandated a minimum sentence of 5 years in prison without parole for possession of 5 grams of crack cocaine

Anti-Federalists States' rights supporters who believed that a strong federal court system would restrict individual liberties and viewed the creation of a federal court system as a threat to the power maintained by state courts

Antisocial behavior Behaviors that contrast with the customs or expectations of a society

Antisocial personality disorder A disorder in which the afflicted often are short-sighted, are hedonistic, and lack empathy for others; they show a lack of concern for their actions and the consequences their actions have on others

Anxiety disorders Mental illnesses involving excessive feelings of panic or worry

Appeals Requests for higher courts to review trial court proceedings to ensure that proper procedures were followed and the punishment was just

Appellate courts Courts that hear cases that originated and were decided in trial courts; their primary purposes are to provide accountability for the trial courts and ensure that proper procedures were followed and the law was correctly applied and interpreted

Arbitration Settling disputes outside the courts via the use of a trained third party whose decision is legally binding

Arraignment Court hearings in which the accused again hears the charges against them and enters a plea

Arrest Seizing and restricting the freedoms of individuals believed to have committed a crime

Article I tribunals Legislative federal courts that were created by legislature as opposed to courts that were created by the Constitution; they address specialized issues, including taxes and veterans' claims

Article III courts Federal courts that hear cases that fall under Article III of the Constitution (e.g., the U.S. Court of International Trade and the Foreign Intelligence Surveillance Court)

Artists Prisoners who illegally create and sell artwork or tattoos

Ashurst–Sumners Act Legislation that limited the sale of inmate-produced goods on the open market

Assault Unlawfully attacking someone for the purpose of inflicting harm

Assigned counsel systems A means of providing indigent defense in which the courts appoint attorneys as needed to represent the poor; the attorneys are selected from a list of available attorneys; this approach is often used in small cities and rural areas

Assize of Clarendon Passed in 1166, it established that 12 men from each hundred and 4 others from each township would determine who was responsible for a crime and order the sheriff to bring them to the court; it was a precursor to grand juries

Attendant circumstances Situations, actions, or characteristics that render particular behaviors criminal

Attorney–client privilege A standard that protects attorneys from having to disclose information their clients share with them

Automated Fingerprint Identification Systems Systems used by many police departments in efforts to match fingerprints stored electronically; they are accessible to multiple departments

Auburn system An approach to prisons that separated inmates at night, yet permitted them to congregate during the day

Automated kiosks Booths containing electronic devices that are located in public areas; they enable those on community supervision to more easily report to corrections officials

Autonomous model (parole) A model of parole in which parole decisions are made by individuals outside the inmate's institution

Avocational crimes A type of white-collar crime that involves illegal but nonconventional offenses committed outside an organization or occupation

Bail An agreement requiring the accused to post a predetermined amount of money and/or meet other conditions to be released from custody; it is used to ensure that they will return for later court proceedings

Bailiffs Sometimes called "marshals" or "court officers," they provide a law enforcement presence in the courtroom; they are typically an armed peace officer who is expected to maintain safety in the courts

"Bait and switch" scams Scams in which consumers are lured into a store by low prices, only to find out that the store does not have the product; consumers are then offered a more expensive product

Ballistics The examination of firearms, bullets, and other projectiles

Basic training Training that takes place at the police academy and is designed to instill in new officers the skills and knowledge relevant to police work; it occurs at the beginning of officers' careers and largely shapes their overall practices and effectiveness

Batson challenge A challenge requiring attorneys to provide a reason other than race or gender to exclude a prospective juror through a peremptory challenge

Battered spouse syndrome defense A defense in which defendants claim that they were justified in killing or seriously injuring their spouse in light of the abuses they regularly sustained at the hands of their partner and the belief that their life was in danger

Bench trials Trials in which judges assess the facts of the case, apply the law, and offer verdicts and sentences; judges replace jurors in determining guilt

Bench warrant Warrants issued by a judge requesting the arrest of an individual who violated a court order

Bifurcated system The practice of courts waiting a period of time after the adjudication hearing to hold a disposition hearing, often in efforts to provide judges more information regarding the disposition of youth offenders

"Big house" prisons Institutions that hold over 2,500 inmates

Bill of Rights The first 10 amendments added to the U.S. Constitution

Biometrics The use of an individual's physical characteristics to distinguish them from others through technology programmed to recognize differences among individuals

Bipolar disorder A mental disorder involving alternating periods of depression and elation

Black Codes Laws passed in Southern states designed to control newly freed slaves, making offenders subject to harsh punishments

Black Lives Matter An activist movement that campaigns against violence and racism directed toward African Americans

Block officers Prison officers who work directly with inmates in housing units

Blood feuds One of the earliest means of resolving disputes or seeking justice, they were used in some primitive cultures whereby the family members of a victim killed by another person had the right and obligation to kill the murderer or a member of the offender's family

Bobbies The name given to officers in the London Metropolitan Police Force in recognition of Sir Robert Peel

Booking Also known as processing; it involves making or updating an administrative record of an arrestee

Booking officers Officials who work in jails and process arrestees

Boot camp Shock incarceration; programs that typically involve first-time offenders undergoing strict military-like discipline, including physical training, team skills development, and education

Bow Street Runners A group of men who proactively searched for lawbreakers in the Bow Street region of London and were paid a sum of money for each individual they brought to court

Broken windows hypothesis The belief that offenders perceive order maintenance problems as opportunities to commit crimes primarily because it appears citizens in the area do not care about their community

Buie sweep Officers conducting a warrantless sweep of an arrestee's premises following a lawful arrest; it is permitted and done to help ensure the safety of the officers

Bureau of Social Hygiene An organization that received grants and donations and was created to address issues pertaining to sex, crime, and delinquency

Burglary Unlawfully entering a structure to commit a felony or a theft

Burnout Officers losing their enthusiasm for the job, which leaves them incapable of performing up to standards

Capital punishment Also known as the death penalty; it involves taking the life of an offender in response to their actions

Carnival mirror of crime A reference to media misrepresentation of crime

Case law Law that stipulates decisions rendered in earlier cases set precedent for future cases that are similar in nature

Caseload management (juvenile probation) Maintaining files for offenders and an assortment of administrative functions related to ensuring accountability and effective probation supervision

Caseloads The number of new cases filed, cases reopened, and cases reactivated in court

Causation The relationship between the act and the harms incurred within crimes

Challenge for cause A challenge offered by attorneys if, during voir dire, they identify a particular reason why a potential juror may be unsuitable for the trial

Challenge to the array A challenge offered prior to jury selection by defense attorneys who believe the jury pool is not reflective of the community or is biased in some manner; a new jury pool is provided if the court agrees with the attorney's claim

Chancery courts Courts created in the 15th century in England that heard cases that could not be heard in common law courts, including juvenile cases; the courts primarily dealt with issues concerning equity, as opposed to law

Character witnesses Witnesses who provide information regarding the demeanor, nature, character, behavior, and other traits of the defendant to assist the court in determining whether the individual would be likely to commit the crime for which they are accused

Charge bargaining Defendants pleading guilty to a less serious charge than the one originally filed, which may ultimately reduce the penalty involved

Charge to the jury A written document that explains how the law applies to the case and other information to assist jurors

Child savers The collective name for the groups of individuals who often intervened to assist children beginning in the 19th century

Christopher Commission A commission assembled in 1991 that argued that the Los Angeles Police Department's failure to control police brutality largely contributed to the civil unrest that occurred in Los Angeles

Circumstantial evidence Also known as indirect evidence, it is evidence that does not directly link defendants and the crime and can be interpreted in various ways; it involves probabilities and possibilities, which leaves juries to determine whether circumstances are favorable or unfavorable to the defendant

Citizen patrols Community outreach programs in which citizens undergo a period of training prior to being equipped with a radio and set out to patrol particular areas; these volunteers are expected to contact the police as warranted and provide additional surveillance for departments

Citizen police academies Community outreach programs that offer citizens the opportunity to train in various areas of police work

Civic duty A responsibility that citizens have to their government; jury duty is an example

Civilian review boards Community outreach programs offered by police departments that involve community members offering input regarding questionable police practices

Civil law A body of law that addresses disputes between individuals, businesses, and government agencies

Civil service commissions Commissions throughout the United States that provide oversight by ensuring that bias, political influence, and favoritism do not impact personnel decisions

Classical school A school of criminological thought holding that individuals freely decide on their own actions and do so by rationally weighing the consequences of their actions, in order to avoid pain and seek pleasure

Classical theory A school of criminological thought proposing that people make rational decisions with regard to committing or not committing crime and that fear of painful repercussions will discourage criminal behavior

Clearance rates Data found in the Uniform Crime Report that notes the rate of crimes in which an arrest was made and charges were filed

Clemency A pardon, reduction of sentence, or release of an inmate by the governor or pardoning authority

Clerks of court Employees of the court who provide administrative services to the courts; they largely assist with the immediate needs of the events occurring in courtrooms

Code of Hammurabi The first known legal code; it identified crimes, noted punishments for criminal behavior, and provided settlements for common conflicts

Collateral damage The harms suffered by children whose parents are incarcerated

Commitment Assigning a juvenile to a period of incarceration

Committed youths Youths who have been adjudicated delinquent and ordered to be held under correctional supervision

Common law Laws adopted by colonists; the laws originated from the early and unwritten laws of England and are derived from ancient practices and customs that have been adopted throughout history

Community corrections Sanctions that are imposed in the community

Community courts Courts that address many quality-of-life crimes such as prostitution, trespassing, and vandalism; they use various community services to address the root causes of problems in the community

Community era of policing The era of policing beginning in the 1980s that has been characterized by proactive police efforts to better involve the community and address crime and crime-related problems

Community Oriented Policing Services A component within the U.S. Department of Justice that promotes community policing

Community policing A philosophical approach to policing that promotes partnerships with various groups, emphasizes problem-solving techniques to address the underlying causes of crime, and encourages officers and other personnel to better use and interact with the public

Community prosecution As an alternative to traditional prosecutorial practices, it involves greater efforts to engage the community in crime-fighting, solving problems, and generally enhancing citizens' quality of life; it requires cooperation and collaboration between prosecutors and individuals both within and outside the criminal justice system

Community service A sanction in which offenders are required to perform some type of labor that benefits the community

Commutations A type of clemency that involves the shortening or changing of prison sentences, for instance, when inmates become terminally ill or when death sentences are reduced to sentences of life in prison

Companion cases Two or more court cases that have been consolidated by an appellate court because they involve a common legal issue

Complaint A charge, which requires support by oath or affirmation of the victim or arresting officer, that an offense was committed by a particular person

Complete sealing Removing an offender's record from public access, although police agencies and some other government entities may have access to it

Compurgation A method for clearing an individual accused of a crime through a series of oaths and by others attesting to the innocence of the accused; it would occur if the evidence was unconvincing or if an individual refused to confess or lacked witnesses

Computer-assisted instruction Also known as computer-based training, it enables police personnel to undergo training via computers that also provide evaluation

Concurrence The requirement that actus reus and mens rea occur simultaneously for the commission of a crime

Concurrent jurisdiction The power of both state and federal courts to hear a case; officials work together to decide in which level of court the accused should stand trial

Concurrent jurisdiction laws Legislation that grants prosecutors the power to waive juvenile cases to the criminal justice system

Conditional dispositions Probationary options, including a set of requirements that must be met; such requirements may include restitution, community service, and completion of substance abuse programs

Conditional release Defendants having to meet specific requirements if they wish to be released prior to trial

Conducted-energy devices Less-lethal weapons that deliver an electrical charge that disrupts an individual's central nervous system for a moment so that an officer may gain control of an individual without suffering injury

Confederation A system of government in which states are sovereign

Conflict theory Theory that is grounded in the belief that power differences in society influence who is viewed as delinquent or criminal and how those individuals are treated

Consensual crimes Crimes involving individuals who willingly engage in acts that they may not view as harmful or arguably have no direct victims

Consent A defense in which the defendant claims that a harmful act should not be considered a crime because the victim consented

Consent decree (juveniles) An agreement that a youth who has violated the law will meet specific conditions without the court formally finding them guilty

Consent decrees Agreements between parties involved in a case to cease the alleged improper or illegal activity

Consolidated model (parole) A model of parole that has individuals from both within and outside the inmate's institution assess inmates' suitability for parole

Constitutional Convention Held in 1787, it was the convening of officials to frame the U.S. Constitution; among other accomplishments, they established the structure of U.S. courts; the debate largely centered on whether there should be a federal court system distinct from state courts

Continuum of force A guideline for the escalation in police use of force, which dictates the levels of force officers should use in relation to a suspect's behavior

Contract systems A means of providing indigent representation in which governments and private attorneys, bar associations, or law firms contract with the state to represent indigent clients in a jurisdiction for a specified time and at a designated rate

Contreprenurial crime A type of white-collar crime that involves scams, swindles, and frauds that appear to be legitimate business

Controlled Substances Act The statute prescribing federal U.S. drug policy regarding the manufacturing, importation, possession, use, and distribution of drugs in the United States

Control theories Theories that propose people will misbehave if no controls on their behaviors are in place

Convenience samples Subjects in research studies who are easy to reach and include

Conventional crimes The most common types of crime committed; refers to acts that come to mind when most people think of crime

Convention on Cybercrime A treaty created by the Council of Europe in an attempt to address internet and other computer crimes by synchronizing national laws, enhancing investigations into such crimes, and promoting cooperation among countries

Convict code Also known as the inmate code, it is the set of rules created and enforced by inmates that guides inmate behavior

Corporal punishment Physically harming offenders as punishment for their actions; it was also designed to deter the offender and others

Corporate crime A type of white-collar crime in which illegal and harmful acts are committed by individuals to promote corporate and/or personal interests

Corporate paralegals Paralegals who provide legal assistance for corporations, for example by preparing employee contracts, shareholder agreements, companies' annual financial reports, and stock-option plans

Corruption A type of police misconduct that includes the misuse of authority for an officer's personal gain or that of others

Count bargaining Defendants pleading guilty to some, but not all of the charges filed against them; this may reduce the potential penalties defendants face

Court administrators Court officials who ensure that cases flow in an efficient and timely manner; among other responsibilities, they oversee the scheduling of hearings and cases, maintain court records, oversee budgeting, plan space utilization, and manage courtroom personnel

Court of Appeals Act of 1891 Legislation that created new courts known as circuit courts of appeals, which released the burden of the Supreme Court from hearing many types of minor offenses so it could instead focus on more substantive cases

Court of the Star Chamber A court used in the 15th century as a tool of oppression by the king, it was composed of the king's councilors, who met in a room with stars painted on a ceiling in the palace of Westminster Abbey to address particular offenses such as rioting, perjury, and conspiracy; the court engaged in serious acts of repression before it was abolished in 1641

Court reporters Also known as stenographers, they document the courtroom proceedings by preparing written transcripts of courtroom proceedings

Courts of record Courts in which formal transcripts of the actions are created for use at the appellate level

Credit card theft Illegally obtaining and/or using credit card information through the use of computers

Crime A violation of criminal law that is subject to punishment by the state

Crime control model A model of criminal justice, which assumes that suppressing crime is the most important aspect of justice-based actions

Crime Index A single statistic found in the Uniform Crime Report believed to be representative of the crime rate based on the population in each jurisdiction in the United States

Crimes of globalization Illegal acts that occur in or involve different countries

Crime Stoppers program A media-based program that offers cash rewards to people who come forward with information about a crime

Criminal codes Definitions of crimes and their associated penalties as passed by elected legislatures

Criminal Division Prosecutes some nationally significant criminal cases and provides some supervision over U.S. attorneys

Criminal homicide The willful and illegal killing of one person by another

Criminalistics The use of scientific principles and techniques to examine evidence and ultimately solve crimes

Criminal justice The practices and procedures by which individuals who violate the law are identified and held accountable

Criminal Justice Act Legislation that required the federal judicial districts to establish a system to provide indigent defense

Criminal justice system The practices of groups within law enforcement, the courts, and corrections designed to bring offenders to justice

Criminologists Scientists who study crime, criminal behavior, and justice-based practices

Criminology The study of the extent, causes, control, and nature of criminal behavior

Cross-examination Attorneys questioning the opposition's witnesses after direct examination

Crystal Judson Domestic Violence Protocol Program A program passed by Congress in 2005 that provides funding to police departments that adopt protocols to address domestic violence cases involving officers

CSI effect A term that refers to the effects of images portrayed on the television show *CSI* in relation to viewers' perceptions of "real-world" criminal justice

Culture Values, behaviors, beliefs, and material objects that collectively identify a people's way of life; it shapes behaviors, personalities, and outlooks

Custodial dispositions Confinement in secure or nonsecure facilities, such as detention centers or group homes

Custodial model A model of incarceration that dominates most maximum-security prisons in the early 21st century through its emphasis on incapacitation, deterrence, and retribution

Cybercrimes Crimes committed through the use of a computer (or other related technological device) and a network, in which the computer may be used for the commission of or as the target of the offense

Cyberterrorism The use of technology to engage in terrorism

Dark figure of crime Crimes not reported to the police or found in the Uniform Crime Report; they are included in the National Crime Victimization Survey

Database integration The storage of various types of information that can be accessed by multiple users; it helps various branches of the criminal justice system share information with each other

Data-Driven Approaches to Crime and Traffic Safety Initiatives to merge crime and traffic data to lower crime rates and traffic accident violations with limited or no additional funding

Day reporting centers An intermediate sanction that provides services such as treatment and surveillance to offenders living at home; offenders sentenced to these centers must report regularly to a designated center to help ensure that they are meeting the requirements of their sentence

Deadlocked jury Also known as a hung jury, it occurs when jurors cannot reach the required number of votes to come to a verdict; the case may be retried with a new jury when this happens

Dealing in stolen property Buying, receiving, possessing, selling, concealing, or transporting any property while being aware that it was illegally taken

Death in Custody Reporting Act of 2013 Legislation passed by Congress that mandates that states receiving federal criminal justice assistance grants report all deaths in law enforcement custody

Death-qualified juries Jury members in capital punishment cases who are not opposed to imposing the death penalty

Decentralized With regard to law enforcement, it refers to the absence of a central unified law enforcement agency

Decertification A punishment for police misconduct in which police administrators work with state accreditation and regulatory boards to remove an officer of their state certification to be a police officer

Decoy units Police units used in criminal investigations to provide opportunities for individuals to engage in criminal acts; either the undercover officers or officers located nearby respond to the crime if and when it occurs

Defendant rehabilitation (prosecutors) A prosecutorial policy of foregoing prosecution in favor of diversion if there is an acceptable perceived likelihood of rehabilitation

Defense attorneys Lawyers who provide representation for the accused; they may be secured privately or provided by the state

Defenses Responses offered by defendants who seek to demonstrate that they are not legally liable for the crime in question

Delinquency Behavior that violates the criminal code and is committed by youth who have not reached a statutorily prescribed age

Delinquent juveniles Children who have violated the law and are subject to some type of sanction or treatment

Demand waivers The means by which juveniles demonstrate that they wish to have their case heard in adult court, where they are entitled to more legal protections

Democracy A system of government in which power is delegated to the people

Department of Homeland Security A cabinet-level department created with the Homeland Security Act of 2002 whose mission is to protect the American people, its homeland, and its values

Dependent juveniles Children who have no parent or guardian to care for them or nobody capable of providing adequate supervision

Deposit bail Requires defendants to pay a percentage of the bail that is set; however, they are responsible for the full amount of the bond if they do not return to court as expected

Depression A mental illness involving feelings of dejection, isolation, and hopelessness; it can be hereditary or brought on by other factors

Deprivation theory Explains prisoner misconduct with consideration of how inmates adapt and cope with the pains and deprivations of imprisonment

Deputy wardens of management Prison administrators who oversee many housekeeping responsibilities such as those pertaining to financial records, providing food and supplies, and maintaining the buildings and grounds

Deputy wardens of custodial personnel Prison administrators who oversee correctional officers and the overall security of the institution

Deputy wardens of industry and agriculture Prison administrators who oversee the individuals who manage machine shops and/or farms

Deputy wardens of program personnel Prison officials who administer treatment, educational, and vocational programs

Detained youths Youths who are held prior to adjudication or disposition; they are detained out of concern that they may be a risk to the community or may fail to appear at a later court hearing

Detention Taking a juvenile into custody; it is akin to placing an adult in jail in the criminal justice system

Detention centers Short-term facilities that house juveniles awaiting resolution of their cases in court

Detention officers Officials who work in jails and are responsible for keeping arrestees safe in custody until they appear before a judge

Determinate sentences Sentences that involve offenders receiving a maximum period of incarceration, which can be reduced if they earn good time credits

Deterrence A goal of sentencing that seeks to discourage or dissuade individuals or everyone from committing various behaviors

Diabetes A life-threatening disease in which one's body does not produce or respond to the hormone insulin properly and results in the abnormal processing of carbohydrates and high levels of glucose; it can be brought on by regularly consuming a diet high in fat, calories, and cholesterol and a lack of physical exercise

Dictatorship A system of government in which one individual maintains power

Differential association theory A criminological theory proposing that people's exposure to negative influences encourages them to engage in negative behaviors, including crime

Directed patrol A proactive approach to patrolling in which officers use uncommitted time to address particular issues or locations

Direct evidence Evidence that provides an identifiable link between the defendant and the crime and can include eyewitness testimony

Direct examination Attorneys questioning their witnesses during a trial

Discovery The disclosure of information between prosecutors and defense attorneys; it is primarily used to prevent one side from introducing unexpected evidence at trial

Discretionary parole A means by which inmates are released from prison; it involves the use of parole boards making a determination of whether the inmate appears ready to be released

Disposition A sentence imposed on a juvenile

Disposition hearing Similar to a sentencing hearing in criminal court, it is held once a juvenile has been adjudicated

Diversion Halting or suspending formal proceedings with the agreement that the defendant will meet some agreed-on obligation

Diversity A variation of different qualities; it may pertain to gender, race, ethnicity, age, or culture, as well as other issues

DNA profiling The practice of gathering DNA from a crime scene or victim and comparing it to DNA collected from suspects to help build cases

Domestic violence A specific type of violent crime that involves behaviors that cause physical harm, create fear, prevent a partner from doing as they wish, or force them to behave in manners they do not wish to

Domestic violence court Specialized courts that address cases related to domestic violence; the emphasis in these courts is often on protecting victims and offering offender accountability over offender treatment

Domestic Violence Offender Gun Ban Also known as the Lautenberg Amendment; it was an amendment to the Omnibus Consolidated Appropriations Act of 1997 and bans access to firearms by individuals who are convicted of domestic violence

Double jeopardy Being tried for the same crime twice; it is prohibited by the Fifth Amendment

Downtime Gaps of inactivity between the times officers respond to citizens' calls for service

Drug Abuse Resistance Education One of the most popular efforts offered by police and targeted toward juveniles; the program involves officers encouraging children to resist drugs through classroom-based instruction

Drug courts Specialized courts that typically address adult felony drug cases involving nonviolent offenders with substance abuse problems

Drunkenness Drinking alcoholic beverages to the extent that a person's mental faculties and physical coordination are substantially impaired

Due process The legal safeguard that ensures individuals are treated in a fair and just manner during legal proceedings

Due process model A model of criminal justice that emphasizes certainty and diligence; it is primarily concerned with recognizing due process rights and freedoms

Due process protections Efforts to ensure that individual rights and freedoms are not violated

Duress Sometimes referred to as coercion; it involves an individual committing a harm based on a threat of harm from another person or persons

Durham test A test for insanity holding that a defendant is not criminally responsible if their actions were part of a mental disease or defect

Early warning systems Also known as early intervention systems, they are systems that facilitate the identification of problem police officers through the use of computer programs that permit supervisors to closely monitor officers who regularly receive complaints

Economic pragmatism An approach to correctional practices that emphasizes cost savings

Eighth Amendment An amendment to the U.S. Constitution that prohibits cruel and unusual punishment, excessive bail, and excessive fines

Electronic monitoring Electronic tracking devices that allow officials to locate offenders; it is often used in conjunction with home confinement

Electronic reporting The use of audio equipment by court reporters to record courtroom proceedings

Employee Protection Act of 1988 Legislation passed in 1988 that prohibited the use of polygraph examinations in the private sector, but not for government agencies

Enforcement (probation) Taking the proper steps to ensure that probationers are aware of the need to abide by their probation agreement and properly responding to those who violate their agreement

Enterprise crime Criminal enterprises that profit from illegal activities that are typically in great public demand; also known as organized crime

Entrapment A defense in which defendants claim that government agents induced them into committing a crime

Environmental equity The fair distribution of environmental risks across all demographic groups

Environmental justice A type of justice that is concerned with the fact that the poor and other less powerful groups are most likely to be affected by environmental harms

Environmental racism Policies, practices, or directives pertaining to environmental harms that disproportionately affect individuals, groups, or communities because of race

Equal Employment Opportunity Act of 1972 Legislation that extended the Civil Rights Act of 1964 to state and local governments

Europol Also known as the European Police Office, this organization was created in 1998 to confront international crime, address the removal of border controls in the European Union, and serve as a clearinghouse of information

Evidence-based practices Policies and practices that emphasize thorough empirical evaluation and rely on scientific evidence that is objective, provides consistent results, and is applicable to individuals or groups other than those used in the production of the original evidence

Exclusionary rule Prohibits the introduction of illegally seized evidence into courtroom proceedings

Exculpatory evidence Evidence obtained by the prosecution during investigations that is favorable to the defense; the Supreme Court ruled that such evidence must be shared with the defense

Excuses Defenses in which the accused admits to the act in question but states that they are not criminally responsible for doing so because extraordinary circumstances caused them to commit the crime

Executive branch The branch of government that primarily enforces the law

Exonerated Being released from prison as a result of the discovery of new evidence suggesting that the individual did not commit the crime for which they were sentenced

Experiential education A philosophical approach to teaching in which students directly engage in and learn from experiences and reflections

Expert witnesses Witnesses who are called into court to offer their expert opinion regarding various issues; they have specialized skills and knowledge in particular areas that may be relevant to the courtroom proceedings

Expungement Legally removing a conviction from an individual's state official records

Extradition A state surrendering an individual accused of a crime to the state in which the individual is accused

Fair Labor Standards Act Legislation which states that jurors do not have to be paid by employers for time not worked, including time spent at jury duty

Family court judges Judges who primarily hear domestic relations cases

Federal crime A violation of federal laws

Federalism The division of government power between a central government and its constituents

Federalist A system of government in which the powers are distributed to national, state, county, and local levels

Federalists Also known as Nationalists, they distrusted the prejudices of the states and believed a strong national government would support economic and political cohesiveness for the new country; they supported the creation of federal courts

Federal Judicial Center Provides training and research for federal judges; its responsibilities include recommending improvements in the administration and management of the federal courts

Federal Magistrate Act of 1968 Legislation creating U.S. magistrate judges who have limited jurisdiction to assist district court judges, for instance through setting bail and overseeing initial appearances

Fee system A system that enabled those with the financial means to pay to avoid serving jail time

Felon disenfranchisement laws Legislation that restricts or removes voting privileges for felons

Felonies Crimes that are more serious in nature than misdemeanors and are punished in a variety of ways, including a penalty of a year or more of incarceration or the death penalty

Felony murders Deaths that result during the commission of a felony; punishment for murder applies even if there was no intent by the offender to commit murder

Field citations More commonly known as "tickets," they are citations that require a person to appear in court on a specific time and day to answer charges

Field training Training designed to reinforce what officers learned during basic training, provide additional information about specific aspects of the job, and ensure that officers can apply what they learned at the academy; it involves new officers working closely with field training officers

Field training officers Skilled and experienced officers who, in providing field training, assist rookie officers as they move from the academy to the streets and evaluate new officers' performances

Fifth Amendment An amendment to the U.S. Constitution that protects individuals from double jeopardy and self-incrimination; it also provides for the right to a grand jury in serious crimes and ensures that the accused is provided due process

Finance crimes Large-scale crimes that occur in the world of finance and financial institutions

Fines Payment of money to the government for violating the law

First Amendment Protects several basic liberties, including the freedom of religion, of speech, of the press, to petition the government, and to assemble in groups

First Step Act Federal prison reform legislation that passed in 2018 with the goal of reducing recidivism and the severity of some federal sentencing practices

Fleeing felon rule An earlier standard regarding police use of deadly force which noted that deadly force could be used to subdue an offender who committed a felony and was attempting to escape from the police

Forcible rape The penetration of the vagina or anus with any body part or object, or oral penetration by a sex organ of another person, without the victim's consent

Forensic anthropologists Professionals who assist with investigations through the identification and examination of skeletal remains of decomposed or dismembered bodies

Forensic entomologists Professionals who study the science of insects and assist criminal investigations by identifying the time or date of a death based on examination of the characteristics of the insects living within a decomposing body

Forensic odontologists Professionals who assist with the identification of victims through analyses of teeth

Forensic pathology The science of dead bodies and autopsies; it involves the investigation of violent, sudden, unnatural, or unexplained deaths

Forensic science Applying science to police-enforced laws

Foreperson The leader of the jury either elected by fellow jurors or selected by a judge to preside over the deliberations and read the verdict in the courtroom

Forgery and counterfeiting Altering, copying, or imitating something without legal permission to do so, with the intent to present the altered item as the original

Forestry camps Minimum-security placements that generally involve youths working outdoors, perhaps by generally assisting with conservation- and preservation-based activities

Foster homes Nonsecure facilities that are used with both offenders and children in need of supervision; they provide youth with a substitute family for a temporary period

14th Amendment An amendment to the U.S. Constitution that provides due process of law

Fourth Amendment An amendment to the U.S. Constitution that protects individuals from unreasonable searches and seizures and notes that no warrants will be issued without probable cause, supported by oath or affirmation and describing the place to be searched and the persons or items to be seized

Frankpledge system Informal social control in which multiple families lived in close proximity and protected one another. As part of the approach, citizens agreed to respect the law, help maintain order, and bring offenders to court.

Freedom of Information Act Legislation that requires government agencies to share their records with the public

Frisks The practice of police patting down or running their hands along the clothes of suspects to check for weapons

"Fruit of the poisonous tree" doctrine An extension of the exclusionary rule which holds that any secondary information or evidence collected as a result of an illegal search is also inadmissible in court

Fully secured bail A type of pretrial release in which defendants post the full amount of the bail that is set; defendants who return to court at all specified times will receive the bail they posted

Furloughs Permitting inmates to leave prison for extended periods for various reasons

Gambling Unlawfully betting or wagering money or something else of value; it also includes offering opportunities to gamble and tampering with the outcome of a contest to gain a gambling advantage

Gang intervention units Specialized police units that address delinquency and related behaviors through targeting gangs and gang-related activity

Gang Resistance Education and Training Program (G.R.E.A.T.) Established in 1991 and modeled after the Drug Abuse Resistance Education program, it involves law enforcement officers providing classroom content to children and young adults covering topics such as life skills, problem-solving, and alternatives to delinquency

Gaols Early English jails that were used for detaining defendants or those awaiting their punishment

General deterrence A goal of sentencing that seeks to discourage or dissuade everyone from committing harmful behaviors

General strain theory An expansion of strain theory, which proposes that obtaining material goods is not the only motivation for committing crime; instead, strain perpetuates anger, depression, or frustration, which encourage some criminal behavior

General theory of crime A developmental theory of crime that modifies social control theory to incorporate biosocial, psychological, routine activities, and rational choice theories

Globalism The transnational integration of cultural, social, and economic issues and the international integration and interaction of agents, agencies, countries, and others that have historically been relatively isolated from one another

Globalization The interaction and integration of ideas and practices among different countries

Global Positioning System A global navigation satellite system, owned by the U.S. Air Force, that provides location and time information to users with a receiving device

Good faith exception An exception to the exclusionary rule that permits the introduction of illegally seized evidence if an officer makes an honest and reasonable error

Government crime Illegal activities on behalf of government itself, government agencies, or government leaders

Grand jury hearings Court hearings in which prosecutors appear before grand jurors to explain why the case should continue to be prosecuted; the standard of proof is probable cause

Graveyard shift The overnight shift for police officers; typically the 12 a.m. to 8 a.m. shift when many businesses are closed and it is also often eerily quiet

Group homes Facilities that typically accommodate 6–30 residents under correctional supervision and provide kitchens, recreational areas, meeting rooms, and living quarters; they provide a variety of services depending on the needs of the residents, with some homes being particularly focused on treatment

Habeas Corpus Act of 1679 An act that permitted imprisoned individuals to request a hearing before a judge to make the charges against them public; judges determined whether the confinement was justified or the accused should be released or remain imprisoned before trial

Habeas corpus petitions Writs filed by prisoners contesting the constitutionality of their confinement

Habitual offender laws Legislation that mandates offenders with extensive criminal backgrounds receive extended penalties

Halfway houses Facilities that provide many of the same services as group homes, although they are more commonly used with offenders who have served some period of incarceration and are readjusting to life outside confinement; they provide transitional residences for individuals who may struggle with entering the same environment that contributed to the earlier misbehavior

"Hands-off" doctrine The practice of permitting prisons to operate absent judicial interference

Harassment Repeated actions or words that serve no legitimate purpose and are directed at a specific person with the intent to annoy or alarm them

Harmless error doctrine The standard holding that small, insignificant errors made by prosecutors during trial with likely little or no effect on the outcome of a case are not grounds for a reversal

Harrison Narcotics Tax Act Legislation that outlaws opium and cocaine; it is often recognized as the first drug control policy

Hate crimes Offenses that are motivated, in whole or in part, by an offender's bias against a race, religion, sexual orientation, ethnicity/national origin, or disability

Hate Crime Statistics Act Legislation that requires the U.S. attorney general to collect data on hate crimes

Hate speech Verbal attacks against a person or group based on a dislike of their attributes such as race, sexual orientation, and other factors

Hawes–Cooper Act of 1929 Legislation that limited the sale of inmate-produced goods on the open market

Hearsay testimony Evidence offered not from someone with personal knowledge of the situation in question, but from someone who heard information from others

Hierarchy rule A limitation of the Uniform Crime Report that applies when multiple offenses occur in the same event; according to the rule, reporting agencies only identify the offense highest on the priority list they receive and do not score the other, less serious, offense(s)

Holding facilities Detention facilities similar to jails, although they generally do not hold individuals who have been sentenced; they temporarily hold arrestees who are awaiting court hearings

Home confinement Also known as house arrest; it is an intermediate sanction that requires offenders to remain within the confines of their home during designated hours of each day

Homicide Killing another person

Hot pursuit exception Permits officers to enter places otherwise protected by the Fourth Amendment without a search warrant if they are in pursuit of a suspect based on probable cause

Houses of refuge Homes that were established to manage status offenders and generally assist them in the 19th century

Human immunodeficiency virus (HIV) A communicable virus that harms one's immune system by destroying white blood cells that help fight infections, which places those with the virus at a greater risk for serious infections and certain cancers

Human trafficking Moving people across and within borders without their consent; it is often done through the use of violence, coercion, and/ or deception and is a modern-day form of slavery often used to obtain labor or sex

Hundreds Early England living arrangements that consisted of roughly 10 tythings (or roughly 100 families), an appointed leader, and perhaps assistants to organize any law enforcement and justice efforts

Hung jury Also known as a deadlocked jury, it occurs when jurors cannot reach the required number of votes to come to a verdict; the case may be retried with a new jury when this happens

Identity-theft fraud Illegally obtaining and/or using the identity of another person via the use of computers

Illinois Juvenile Court Act The legislation responsible for establishing the first juvenile court

Importation theory Explains prisoner misconduct as a product of the behaviors, beliefs, and experiences of inmates prior to their institutionalization

Incapacitation A goal of criminal sentencing that seeks to physically prevent offenders from committing additional crimes; incarceration is an example

Incarceration Being physically confined or detained in a jail or prison

Inchoate crimes Offenses that were not completed, but for which there was evidence that the individuals involved were preparing, conspiring, or attempting to commit a crime

Independent source exception An exception to the exclusionary rule that permits the introduction of illegally seized evidence if the police are able to demonstrate that the information was obtained from a source unrelated to the illegal search or seizure

Indeterminate sentences Sentences that involve a minimum and maximum time an inmate will serve; the amount of time is decided by a parole board, which determines the offender's suitability for release from prison

Indictment A charging document that is issued by grand juries when they believe that the prosecution has provided probable cause to believe a crime was committed and the accused was responsible

Indigency The state of being poor or needy

Individualized justice Justice-based approaches designed to best meet an offender's need; they are often associated with problem-solving courts

Industrial shop and school officers Prison officers who protect civilians who provide services to inmates, including teachers, counselors, and trainers

Inevitable discovery exception An exception to the exclusionary rule that permits the introduction of illegally seized evidence if it can be shown that the evidence would have or might have been obtained even if the officer had not illegally seized it

Informal probation The monitoring of an individual who has agreed to meet specific requirements in return for not having their case formally processed by the court

Informants Individuals who provide information in expectation of some benefit or reward from police or prosecutors; they may be rewarded for their input through money or a reduced sentence or penalty for their cooperation

Information A charging document that is issued when judges rule in preliminary hearings that probable cause exists to believe a crime was committed and the accused was responsible

Infractions The lowest level of criminal behavior that is usually not punishable by confinement; instead, offenders are often given a citation or traffic ticket

Initial appearance A defendant's first appearance before a judge; it is used to resolve less serious cases and address a series of issues pertaining to case processing in more serious cases

Inmate balance theory A theory which proposes that prisons operate more effectively when officials tolerate minor infractions, allow inmate leaders to maintain order, and relax security measures to an acceptable level

Insanity As it pertains to the courts, it is a legal, as opposed to medical, issue that is interpreted differently among the states with regard to whether they use the defense, how to define insanity, and the burden of proof needed to demonstrate insanity

In-service training Training provided to officers in efforts to keep them abreast of changes in the field, developments regarding laws and ordinances, changes in technology, and new department policies; some officers must also undergo such training if they are promoted or if they change or plan to change job assignments

Institutional model (parole) A model of parole that uses members from within the inmate's institution to determine parole eligibility

Intake The step in juvenile case processing that involves screening cases to assess whether individuals need the court's assistance; at this stage, authorized officials decide whether to handle the case informally, dismiss the case, or request formal intervention of the juvenile court

Intelligence-led policing A type of policing that uses real-time crime and data analyses to direct regular patrol and specialized units; it is supported by surveillance and intelligence-gathering practices

Intensive supervision probation A type of probation in which officers have smaller caseloads, probationers have greater restrictions, and there are a greater number of and more frequent face-to-face contacts between the probationer and probation officer

Intent (mens rea) An offender meaning or intending to commit a crime

Interfering with and disrupting computer services Illegally altering the computer services of another to prevent them from operating properly

Intermediate appellate courts A second level of courts that hear appeals; in the early 21st century, 41 states have intermediate courts of appeal

Intermediate sanctions A series of penalties that are more punitive than probation, yet less severe and less costly than incarceration

Internal affairs Sometimes referred to as Offices of Professional Standards, it is an internal police unit that evaluates and investigates allegations of questionable police conduct; internal affairs units typically report directly to the chief or deputy chief

International Association of the Chiefs of Police A professional association for law enforcement worldwide

International Criminal Court A treaty-based international court of last resort; it investigates, prosecutes, and tries individuals accused of committing the most serious crimes that are of concern to the international community

Interpersonal crimes Crimes in which one person uses, or threatens to use, force against another person; also known as violent crimes

INTERPOL The world's largest international police organization; it facilitates international police cooperation and supports and assists all organizations, authorities, and services that seek to prevent or confront international crime

Interrogations The practice of questioning suspects or persons of interest in a case to test information and hopefully obtain a confession and conviction; those being questioned must be informed of their rights

Interviewer effects The influences or biases that those who administer assessments may have on the respondents and responses

Interviewing The practice of gathering information through questioning individuals who are familiar with a case; those being questioned do not need to be informed of their rights

Investigation (juvenile probation) Supervision of the offender, surveillance, monitoring, counseling, and guidance on behalf of the probation officer, who compiles and assesses information pertaining to the probationer's performance and reports to the court regarding various issues

Investigations Studying evidence and facts to identify, find, and ultimately prove the guilt of individuals believed to have committed a crime

Investigations (probation) Gathering information to assist with sentencing practices, including the preparation of presentence investigation reports

Invisible punishments Legislatively defined restrictions of former inmates

Irish system An approach to prisons that involved the use of indeterminate sentencing, emphasizing the preparation of inmates for release, providing a less restrictive environment, and releasing inmates on a conditional basis

Irresistible impulse test An insanity defense that is used when defendants suffer from a mental illness that prevented them from controlling their actions

Jailhouse lawyers Inmates who sell their legal services to other inmates, for instance by conducting legal research or writing writs

Jails Correctional facilities that house inmates serving less than a year incarceration, those who cannot make bail or are denied release, and those who are awaiting sentencing, evaluation, or a parole or probation violation hearing

"John Doe" warrant A type of arrest warrant requested by officers when they do not know the name of the individual they wish to arrest

Joint terrorism task forces Small groups of highly trained investigators, analysts, and law enforcement specialists that are designed to combine the resources of federal, state, and local law enforcement to address terrorism and related issues

Judges Court officials who are responsible for ensuring that courtroom proceedings operate in a fair manner

Judges Bill of 1925 Legislation that gave the Supreme Court greater control over the cases it heard

Judicial branch The branch of government that primarily interprets the law

Judicial Conference of the United States The principal policymaking body with regard to the administration of the federal courts; the group considers and proposes improvements with regard to various areas of the federal court system, including civil procedure, criminal procedure, bankruptcy procedure, appellate procedure, and rules of evidence

Judicial waiver laws Legislation that grants judges the power to waive juvenile cases to the criminal justice system

Judiciary Act of 1789 Legislation that sought to clarify uncertainties regarding the structure of the courts and provided a foundation on which our current court system exists; the act established a federal judicial system

Judiciary Act of 1801 Legislation that created many new judgeships and expanded the jurisdiction of the lower federal courts; this change, however, lasted only briefly

Jurisdiction The power or right to exert one's legal power over another; it can be considered in terms of geography, subject matter, and the functions and responsibilities of a court

Jury nullification The practice of jurors dismissing the facts of a case and basing their decisions on other factors, such as their opinion of the participants in the crime or the appropriateness of the law

Jury tampering A crime that involves attempts to persuade a juror's decision regarding a case

Jury trials Formal hearings in which laypersons (jurors) hear the evidence presented by the prosecution and defense and make a determination of whether the accused should be found guilty or not guilty

Justice Actions that are considered fair, equitable, and morally appropriate

Justices of the peace Also known as magistrates, they were responsible for hearing cases and preserving the king's peace; they remain in use to a limited extent in the early 21st century, particularly in rural areas

Justification defenses A series of defenses that are used when defendants claim that they are responsible for the act in question, but their actions were acceptable or permitted based on the situation and circumstances

Juvenile Justice and Delinquency Prevention Act of 1974 Legislation that encouraged states to remove status offenders from institutions; the act was not binding on the states, although it encouraged them to place status offenders with community social service or welfare agencies as alternatives to institutionalization

Juvenile Justice Reform Act of 2018 Legislation that reauthorized and improved the Juvenile Justice and Delinquency Prevention Act of 1974; the act banned the shackling of pregnant girls; provided funding for tutoring, drug and alcohol programs for youth, and mental health treatment; and required states that receive federal

funding to collect data on racial disparities in their juvenile justice system and create plans for correcting any inequalities

Kerner Commission Also known as the National Advisory Commission on Civil Disorders, the commission noted that police practices contributed to the civil unrest occurring in the 1960s; it suggested that the officers engaged in unprofessional conduct particularly through aggressive enforcement practices, inadequate training, poor supervision, and overzealous patrol practices

Kin policing An early form of informal social control that involved a victim's family members bringing an offender to justice

Knapp Commission A commission assembled in 1970 which speculated that half of the New York City Police Department engaged in corruption

Labeling theory A theoretical explanation of crime that focuses on individuals' reactions to the social judgments or labels placed on them

Larceny-theft Unlawfully taking property from the possession of another

Latent trait theories Theories proposing that a master trait that is present at birth or is attained shortly thereafter predisposes individuals to engage in crime

Lay judges Judges who are nonlawyers and are sometimes referred to as magistrates, justices of the peace, or associate judges; they serve on state courts of limited jurisdiction in most states and a small number serve on state courts of general jurisdiction

Lay witnesses Eyewitnesses to a crime considered in court

Lease system The practice of states leasing inmates to contractors who fed and clothed inmates in return for their labor

Legal sufficiency The prosecutorial use of discretion that favors only proceeding with cases in which all legal elements are present

Legislative courts Courts created by legislature as opposed to courts created by the Constitution; they are established for some specialized purpose

Legislatures Legislative bodies that have the power to enact laws

Letter of the law Typically associated with officer responses to more serious offenses, it refers to officers having limited discretion and being more likely to enforce the law

Lex talionis A Latin term that means "an eye for an eye"; it is the law of retaliation, or punishment that corresponds with the harms caused

Life course theories Theories that consider how criminal careers occur throughout one's life; they recognize that changes in one's life can affect whether individuals may ultimately engage in crime or antisocial behavior

Lifestyle-exposure theory A theory that considers an individual's lifestyle in attempts to explain why some groups or individuals are victimized more than others

Litigation paralegals Paralegals who conduct research for lawyers, maintain documents received from clients, and retrieve and organize evidence for use at trial

London Metropolitan Police Act The act that essentially created the London Metropolitan Police, which was the first urban police department in the Western world

Major Crimes Act Passed in 1885, it attempted to clarify law enforcement jurisdiction in Native American lands by noting that most serious crimes fall under the jurisdiction of federal authorities, while tribal authorities have jurisdiction over less serious crimes

Mala en se Acts that are considered to be wrong in themselves

Mala prohibita Acts that are considered wrong because they are prohibited

Mandatory parole Generally used in states with determinate sentencing structures, it involves the early, conditional release of inmates whose sentence was reduced as a result of time served and earned good time

Mandatory sentences Sentences that require offenders to serve a predetermined amount of time

Mark system The system by which inmates could earn credits through good behavior and work that permitted them to be released early from their sentences

Matthew Shepard and James Byrd Hates Crime Prevention Act Legislation that extended the 1960 federal hate crime law to cover offenses motivated by a victim's actual or perceived gender, sexual orientation, gender identity, or disability; it provided more money to investigate and prosecute hate crimes and required the Federal Bureau of Investigation to track statistics on hate crimes committed against transgender people

Maxing out Prisoners serving their entire sentence

Mediation A method of alternative dispute resolution in which a trained mediator helps both parties come to some agreement

Mens rea (intent) An offender meaning or intending to commit a crime

Mental health courts Specialized courts that contain dockets of mentally ill individuals who are assessed and processed by court personnel and clinical specialists

Mental illness A variety of mind disorders that impact one's behavior, mood, and thinking

Merchants Inmates who sell other inmates various goods and services

Merit selection or Missouri Bar Plan A means of selecting judges that is a hybrid approach incorporating various judicial selection approaches, including appointment and election

Misdemeanors Crimes that are less serious than felonies and are punishable by various means, including fines, probation, or less than 1 year of incarceration in jail

M'Naghten test The oldest test for insanity; it considers a defendant's intellectual capacity at the time of the offense to understand what they were doing was right or wrong

Mobile digital terminals High-powered laptops that are mounted and wired into a police car that allow officers to obtain necessary information in the field

Model Code of Judicial Conduct A set of ethical guidelines created by the American Bar Association; the goals of the guidelines are to promote ethical judicial behavior and encourage confidence in the courts

Model Penal Code and Commentaries A guideline for states to follow with regard to rational, effective criminal law

Mollen Commission A commission which in 1992 investigated police corruption in New York and found that officers who engaged in the most serious forms of corruption began to engage in misconduct through beating and abuse of suspects

Monarchies Governments headed by royalty in the form of a king or queen

Money laundering The transfer of illegally obtained funds among financial institutions in different countries

Monitoring the Future A survey that asks youths about their viewpoints, attitudes, and experiences with regard to various issues including drug use, views about drugs, delinquency, and victimization

Motor vehicle theft The theft or attempted theft of a motor vehicle, including boats, cars, motorcycles, and related vehicles

National Advisory Commission on Civil Disorders Also known as the **Kerner Commission** (1967–1968), the commission noted that police practices contributed to the civil unrest occurring in the 1960s; it suggested that the officers engaged in unprofessional conduct particularly through aggressive enforcement practices, inadequate training, poor supervision, and overzealous patrol practices

National Crime Victimization Survey A national survey that provides an estimate of crime in the United States by asking a representative sample of residents living throughout the country about their roles as a victim in a crime

National Incident-Based Reporting System A part of the Uniform Crime Report Program; it improved the quality of crime data collected by law enforcement agencies because it provides more detailed and helpful information than does the Summary Reporting System

Nationalists Also known as Federalists, they distrusted the prejudices of the states and believed a strong national government would support economic and political cohesiveness for the new country; they supported the creation of federal courts

National Survey on Drug Use and Health A survey that measures the prevalence of alcohol and drug use among household members over age 11

Necessity A defense in which defendants claim that their harmful behavior should not be considered criminal because they were acting out of need

Negative reinforcements Punishments for inmates engaging in antisocial behavior

Neglected juveniles Children who warrant state intervention because their parents or guardians are not providing adequate care

Negligence Someone neglecting to do something when they are responsible to do so; or failing to know the laws in a particular jurisdiction

Neurophysiology The study of brain activity

NIMBY "Not in my backyard"; it refers to the approach taken by some community members who do not wish to have correctional facilities located in their neighborhoods out of fear of the potential harmful effects

No bill An outcome of grand jury hearings which signifies that the grand jury failed to find probable cause, at which point the case is dismissed

Noble cause corruption A type of corruption in which officers misuse their powers for the sake of what they believe is "justice"

Noise flash diversionary devices Also known as "stun-munitions" or "flash-bangs"; similar to powerful firecrackers, these nonlethal devices disorient threatening inmates and permit the officers time to rush and subdue them

No-knock searches Police searches that do not require an announcement; they are permitted by state statute and require judicial approval

Nolle prosequi A notice by the prosecutor stating that the government is foregoing prosecution of a case

Nolo contendere "No contest"; a plea that is legally recognized as guilty and is offered by defendants who do not wish to admit guilt; it protects defendants from having an admission of guilt used against them in any subsequent civil trial

Nominal dispositions The least punitive dispositions used by juvenile courts; they typically involve warnings, reprimands, and/or release to the custody of the juvenile's parents or guardians

Nongovernmental organizations Typically not for profit, they are organizations set up by groups that are run independent of governments, although they may receive funding from governments, businesses, foundations, or individuals; they provide a wide range of services, including efforts to address various types of human rights violations and crimes

Oath-helper Individuals who assisted both plaintiffs and the accused in compurgation by swearing under oath that the accused was innocent or guilty

Objective standard of reasonableness The criteria for assessing the quality of representation provided to indigent defendants

Occupational crime Crimes committed within the context of one's employment or occupation

Office of the Solicitor General The office responsible for representing the U.S. government before the U.S. Supreme Court in federal appeals

Offices of Inspector General Offices charged with preventing and detecting fraud, abuse, waste, and other criminal violations pertaining to federal programs, employees, and operations

Oleoresin capsicum spray (pepper spray) A less lethal weapon that causes a temporary loss of vision (up to 45 minutes) in those who are sprayed

Oligarchies Systems of government in which power is maintained by a small group of powerful individuals

Online courts Courts in which all proceedings are carried out through technology and participants may engage virtually

Online harassment Using a computer to harass others, for instance through sending disturbing images or emails

Order maintenance The role of the police in keeping the peace

Ordinance of 1787 Also known as the Northwest Ordinance, it was an attempt by the national government to address the lawlessness in the West; it prescribed the law for most of the western territories

Ordinance violations Violations of rules, laws, or regulations that apply to a specific village, city, or town

Organized crime Criminal enterprises that profit from illegal activities that are typically in great public demand

Paralegals Also known as legal assistants, they perform administrative and clerical tasks for lawyers, research and prepare cases, research laws, investigate the facts of a case, obtain and draft legal documents, interview defendants and witnesses, attend and schedule hearings, and generally support attorneys as needed

Pardon An act by the executive branch of the state or federal government that excuses an offense and absolves the offender from the consequences of the crime

Parens patriae "The father of the country"; the concept originated during the 12th century and essentially meant that the king made decisions for all matters regarding juveniles; it applies in the early 21st century because the government, via the juvenile justice system, has the power to process unruly youths

Parole The supervision of ex-inmates in the community after they are released early from jail or prison

Parole boards Officials who evaluate inmates after they have served a period of incarceration; they make determinations of whether inmates appear ready to be released

Parole revocation hearings Hearings that are used to determine if parolees who violate the terms of their release agreement should be returned to incarceration

Part I offenses A category of crimes in the Uniform Crime Report that consists of criminal homicide, rape, robbery, aggravated assault, burglary, larceny-theft, arson, and motor vehicle theft

Part II offenses A category of crimes in the Uniform Crime Report that consists of 21 crimes other than those designated in Part I

Partial sealing Restricting only certain portions of an offender's criminal record

Passive GPS monitoring Monitoring that provides a signal when an offender is within the confines of a particular location

Pay-to-stay jails An alternative approach to traditional jails; they allow some offenders convicted of minor offenses to serve their time in these facilities instead of county jail and offer inmates some privileges not found in other jails

Peace Officer Standards and Training Commission State agencies that regulate the minimum police training standards set by each state and help ensure that training curricula are in accord with training standards

Penitentiary Institutions that emphasize offenders doing penance and reflecting on their behaviors

Penitentiary Act of 1779 An act that reformed English prisons and jails, such that they became more secure and sanitary and subject to systematic inspections; the act also abolished fees charged to inmates

Pennsylvania system An approach to prisons that stressed reformation and the prevention of interaction among inmates out of concern that they would learn criminal behaviors from one another

Peremptory challenge A challenge offered during voir dire by attorneys who do not wish to have a potential juror impaneled; attorneys are not required to offer a reason or justification, but the exclusion cannot be based on race or gender; attorneys are permitted only a specified number of peremptory challenges

Petition Legal documents filed by involved parties who allege that a youth is delinquent, a status offender, or in need of assistance; it is akin to charging in the criminal justice system

Petty offenses Violations of a regulation, ordinance, or municipal code or minor crime that warrant short terms of incarceration or fines

Pillories Wooden frames with holes for offenders' hands and feet that were used to punish, ridicule, and restrain offenders

Plain view doctrine An exception to the warrant requirement that permits officers to seize evidence without a warrant if it is in view of the officer, although the police must have justification for being present to view the evidence

Plea bargaining Informal negotiations between the prosecution and defense in efforts to expedite criminal cases; as part of the process, defendants may admit guilt in exchange for a more favorable outcome of their case

Police athletic leagues Outreach programs by the police in which officers host various types of sports leagues that enable them to more closely and positively interact with youth and generally discourage delinquency

Police crime Criminal behavior committed by police officers while on duty

Police deviance Unethical activities committed by police officers; the acts do not conform to the high standards expected of members of the criminal justice system

Police Explorer programs Programs that enable juveniles to better understand the law and police work; they are experience- and education-based programs that facilitate police–youth relations

Police lineups A method of investigation in which an eyewitness is asked if they can identify a suspect from either photographs or individuals lined up along a wall at the police station

Police public information officers Police personnel who are the spokespersons for police agencies and provide information to media and other sources

Police violence Violence by and against the police; it can be justified or unjustified, legal or illegal, and deadly or nondeadly

Policymaking A planned course of action designed to affect persons or issues

Political era of policing The period of time during which politicians heavily influenced officers, departments, and police practices (1840–1930); members of law enforcement also had close personal relationships with the communities they served and often provided non-crime-fighting services for the general public

Political threat explanations The argument that police use of deadly force is most likely to occur in areas where there are notable racial or economic differences, largely in response to the divisions between groups

Polygraph examinations Tests that measure one's heart rate, blood pressure, breathing rate, and perspiration in response to a series of questions and statements; the goals of the examination are to ensure accuracy of the background information and note any psychological irregularities

Ponzi scheme A scam in which investors are promised large financial returns as more investors join

Poor laws Laws introduced in the 16th century to assist destitute individuals, including children, in finding work or apprenticeships; they largely characterize the early roots of juvenile justice in the United States

Positive reinforcements Rewards for inmates who engage in prosocial behavior

Positivist school of criminology A school of criminological thought that emphasizes the scientific study of crime and the belief that criminal behavior is influenced by factors beyond the control of the individual

Post–traumatic stress disorder A mental illness in individuals exposed to a traumatic event that causes them to relive the event and experience extended periods of nervousness and being "on edge"; it is sometimes used as a defense in which defendants claim that their behavior was attributed to the mental effects of having suffered from some traumatic incident

Pre-adjudication procedures The proceedings that occur in juvenile case processing prior to adjudication; they are akin to pretrial procedures in the adult system and involve detention hearings, intake, and decisions regarding the next step for juveniles

Predictive policing An approach to policing that incorporates software that uses algorithms to anticipate the time, location, and suspects involved in a crime

Predisposition report A report containing information about the juvenile offender and their offense, which is used by juvenile court judges at the disposition hearing

Preliminary hearings Hearings in which prosecutors appear before a judge to explain why a case should continue to be pursued or prosecuted; the standard of proof is probable cause

Premenstrual dysphoric disorder A defense used by some women who claim that the effects of menstruation contributed to their violent behavior

Pre-parole investigation reports Reports that provide helpful information that is used to determine one's suitability for and the associated conditions of parole

Preponderance of evidence The standard typically used to win in civil courts; it requires greater than 50% of the evidence supporting one side or the other

Presentence investigation report A report containing information that is either requested by a judge or required by law and is often prepared by a probation or parole officer who provides background information on the offender and offers a recommended sentence

Presentment An outcome of a grand jury investigation in which they found probable cause and the need for further case processing

Preservationists Those who support the continued use of juvenile courts

Pretrial motions Requests offered by the prosecution and/or defense prior to trial; they seek to ensure that proper procedures are being followed and defendants' rights are respected

Pretrial release The release of defendants prior to trial with special conditions or requirements

Pretrial service programs Programs used in some jurisdictions that gather and share with the court information about defendants, particularly with regard to their level of risk upon being released prior to trial

Preventive patrol Also known as routine patrol, it primarily involves officers driving around their beats, responding to calls, and observing citizen behavior

Prison argot The language or gestures used by inmates to communicate; it helps distinguish the inmate subculture from life outside prison

Prison farms Correctional facilities where inmates perform some type of manual labor that provides economic benefit for the prison

Prison gangs Criminal groups that exist within corrections systems and typically have existing ties to gangs outside our justice systems

Prison hulks Old merchant and naval ships that were essentially floating prisons

Prisonization The process by which inmates are socialized into the prison world or prison subculture

Prison play-families Also known as pseudo-families; they involve inmates assuming the roles of different family members

Prisons Correctional facilities that house offenders sentenced to incarceration for a year or longer

Prison subculture The distinct values, norms, and beliefs identified among prison inmates

Private prisons Institutions operated by private companies that contract with federal or state authorities to provide correctional services

Private security industry Individuals, agencies, organizations, and services other than public law enforcement agencies that primarily engage in preventing loss or harm to others

Privatization Private contractors operating correctional facilities and contracting to provide services in others

Probable cause The standard of proof required in searches and seizures of property without a warrant, searches and seizures of property with a warrant, arrests with a warrant, and arrests without a warrant

Probation Conditional freedom granted to an offender, allowing the offender to be supervised in the community under the conditions specified in the probation agreement

Probation revocation hearings Hearings used to determine whether probationers who are caught committing a new offense or a technical violation should be subject to whatever penalty of incarceration the judge originally ordered but suspended in favor of probation

Problem-oriented policing A style of policing that seeks to address the causes of crime and disorder, as opposed to reacting to crime; the problem-solving process involves scanning, analysis, response, and assessment

Problem-solving courts Also known as specialized or specialty courts, they include various courts that focus directly on particular types of crime or adjudicate certain types of offenders

Pro bono Legal services offered on a volunteer basis

Procedural defense A defense in which a defendant claims that a government official failed to follow procedural law

Procedural justice A type of justice that ensures justice-based processes are fair and just, regardless of individual differences or circumstances

Procedural law Laws that address the legal methods by which substantive law must be enforced or applied

Progressive era The period when several important justice-related developments emerged (1900–1920), including the proliferation of juvenile courts, the establishment of probation and parole, and efforts to ensure that defendants were afforded their Sixth Amendment right to an attorney

Prohibition The time when the selling, transporting, and manufacturing of alcohol was illegal (1919–1933); police corruption became particularly widespread during this period as organized crime grew

Proof beyond a reasonable doubt The highest standard of proof used in criminal courts; it requires much certainty that the accused is responsible for the act(s) in question

Property crime Crimes that involve wrongfully taking something from someone else without the use or threat of force

Pro se The practice of individuals representing themselves in court

Prosecutors As representatives of the state primarily responsible for ensuring justice, their responsibilities include being actively involved in courtroom proceedings and providing a key link between law enforcement and the courts

Prostitution and commercialized vice Unlawfully promoting or participating in sexual activities for profit

Pseudo-families Also known as prison play-families: inmates assuming the roles of different family members

Psychoanalysis A set of theories regarding the impact of the mind on human behavior; also a treatment technique

Public defender programs A means by which indigent representation is provided; they include salaried staff attorneys who represent the poor and are most often found in large cities

Public offenses Felonies or misdemeanors committed in the presence of law enforcement

Public-order crimes Crimes that threaten or challenge the moral order, norms, or customs of society

Public safety exception An exception to the Miranda warning requirement that permits officers to question individuals in custody without reading them their rights if the need for answers is imperative for public safety

Punitive conditions (probation) Conditions imposed on probationers to increase the severity or restrictiveness of their sentence

Punitive probation A sanction for police misconduct that involves closely monitoring and assessing the actions of problematic officers over a period of time

Purged taint exceptions An exception to the exclusionary rule that permits the introduction of illegally obtained evidence if suspects willfully offer the information

Pyromania A pathological disorder that results in the affected individual feeling the impulsive need to set fires

Questioned document analysis The comparison of handwriting samples, computer printouts, typewriters, paper, and ink in efforts to analyze evidence and ultimately solve crimes

Racial profiling The practice of targeting or suspecting individuals based not on behavior but on race or ethnicity

Ransomware Software that harms computer files when it is downloaded

Rape The penetration of the vagina or anus with any body part or object, or oral penetration by a sex organ of another person, without the victim's consent

Rape shield laws Laws that are designed to limit the ability of a defendant's counsel to introduce evidence regarding the accuser's sexual history during a rape trial; they also protect a victim's identity

Rational choice theory A theory proposing that individuals decide whether to commit a crime by considering the potential payoffs in relation to the likelihood of getting caught and the associated punishments

Reactive explanations The argument that police killings are more prominent in areas with high violent crime rates or where officers are working under difficult conditions

Real evidence Physical evidence that can be circumstantial or direct; it is presented to the jury in the form of exhibits

Reasonable suspicion The standard of proof required for officers to stop individuals acting in an unusual manner which may suggest that a crime is taking or has taken place and the individual acting suspiciously may be dangerous and/or responsible

Rebuttal The practice of prosecutors introducing witness testimony to refute testimony given from a defense witness

Recalls Special elections in which voters note their support or disapproval for specific judges

Reception and diagnostic centers Facilities that create treatment plans, identify training schools that best suit adjudicated juveniles, and assess juveniles and diagnose any problems they may have

Recklessness Individuals acting in a carefree, atypical manner

Recross-examination Attorneys questioning the opposition's witnesses following redirect examination

Recruitment The practice of generating a pool of interested job candidates from which individuals will be selected for further evaluation and consideration

Redirect examination Attorneys questioning their witnesses following cross-examination

Reentry courts Problem-solving courts that are designed to assist inmates exiting prison

Refer Sending a case to the juvenile justice system for formal processing

Referee, A juvenile court official who hears the facts of the case and oversees detention hearings, as well as adjudicates in some cases on approval of a juvenile court judge

Reform era of policing Also known as the "progressive era" or the "professional era"; it was a period during which the goal was to reform, advance, and generally professionalize policing (1930–1980); it was characterized by an emphasis on crime-fighting

Regional jails Two or more jail jurisdictions having a formal agreement to operate jails collectively

Rehabilitation A goal of criminal sentencing that begins with understanding why an offender broke the law and proceeds to help them refrain from doing so in the future through education, counseling, and other forms of treatment

Rehabilitation model A model of incarceration that seeks to treat or rehabilitate offenders

Reintegration model A model of incarceration that emphasizes offenders maintaining ties with the community

Release on recognizance Pretrial release on the promise from defendants that they will return to court

Relief officers Prison officers who provide a variety of tasks to assist with vacancies in the staff

Reporting A responsibility of juvenile probation officers; it involves keeping the court apprised regarding various issues

Representative sample A segment of a larger group that shares or reflects the characteristics of the larger group

Reprieves A type of clemency; they are often associated with capital punishment, and typically do not result in the release of the offender, but a reduction in the severity of the punishment or a delay in its imposition

Reprimands Written citations and accounts of infractions that are kept in officers' personnel files

Residency requirements Regulations which mandate that police officers live within a prescribed distance from the department for which they are employed

Residential treatment centers Facilities that provide residential care for juveniles supplemented with focused treatment services

Resource mediation Providing probationers with guidance and services to facilitate their success on probation; it may include assistance in finding substance abuse counseling, employment, and education

Restitution A sanction whereby offenders repay the victims of their crimes for any hardships incurred

Restoration A goal of sentencing that focuses on restoring offenders and victims to where they were physically and/or mentally prior to the crime, with an emphasis on betterment

Restorative justice A type of justice that proposes victims and the community should be more involved in repairing the harms resulting from criminal behavior and efforts should be made to ensure that offenders no longer choose to break the law

Retribution A goal of criminal sentencing that seeks to punish offenders; it is based on retaliation, or the "eye for an eye" or "just deserts" approach

Retributive justice A type of justice that is based on the belief that individuals should be treated as they treat others

Ride-along programs Community outreach programs that enable citizens to better understand police work by allowing participants to accompany officers on their shifts

Robbery Taking or attempting to take anything of value from another person or persons through the use of force or threat of use of violence and/or by putting the victim in fear

Robotics The use of robotic devices to perform functions traditionally performed by humans

Role modeling A treatment approach that involves patients assuming the role of others

Rome Statute of the International Criminal Court The treaty adopted at a 1998 conference of 160 nations; it established the first treaty-based international criminal court

Routine activities theory A theory that helps explain victimization in relation to the activities of individuals within their everyday lives; it argues that people commit crimes when motivated offenders, suitable targets, and a lack of guardianship are present

Routine patrol Also known as preventive patrol, it primarily involves officers driving around their beats, responding to calls, and observing citizen behavior

Saturation patrol A patrol strategy in which police departments allocate a larger-than-typical number of police officers to a hot spot

Schizophrenia A mental illness involving breakdowns in the way one thinks, feels, and acts

School resource officers Sworn officers who work in schools to prevent disorder and enhance police–community relations

School-to-prison pipeline A term that refers to the increasing patterns of students having contact with the justice system as a result of more punitive approaches to addressing school-related problems

Second Amendment Provides the right for people to keep and bear arms; it has been and is the focus of much analysis with regard to gun control

Second Chance Act Legislation designed to assist individuals leaving prison; it authorized federal grants to nonprofit and government agencies to provide support and design services to reduce recidivism through assisting those leaving prison

Selective enforcement The practice of police officers whereby they enforce some of the laws some of the time

Selective incapacitation The practice of identifying and incarcerating dangerous and/or repeat offenders for extended periods

Self-defense A defense in which defendants claim that their actions were necessary to repel an imminent harm

Self-report studies An approach to research in which subjects share their feelings, opinions, behaviors, and beliefs in response to queries or prompts without interference from the researcher

Sentence bargaining Defendants pleading guilty and receiving an agreed-on sentence that is less than the maximum

Sentencing guidelines Guidelines used in sentencing that seek to reduce disparity and promote uniformity in sentencing, primarily through consideration of an offender's criminal history and current offense

Sentencing Reform Act of 1984 Legislation that created determinate sentencing, abolished parole, and reduced opportunities for earning time for good behavior

Sequestered juries Juries that are isolated from the general public during the trial

Serology Also known as biology screening, it involves the examination of blood, semen, and other bodily fluids

Shelter care Care that is often provided for youth awaiting placement in foster or group homes; it is similar to foster care, although shelter care facilities are used on a much more temporary basis

Shire A group of several hundreds; Early English families living communally

Shock incarceration Boot camp; programs that involve offenders undergoing strict military-like discipline, including physical training, team skills development, and education

Shock probation An intermediate sanction in which offenders are sentenced to a period of incarceration, although they are released after a short time and placed on probation

Situational crime prevention An approach based on rational choice theory that involves reducing opportunities to commit crimes and the likelihood of victimization

Sixth Amendment Provides various rights to defendants at trial

Social disorganization theory A theory that considers the crime-related effects of the disintegration of conventional values and beliefs

Socialization The process by which people learn from one another; people acquiring knowledge, attitudes, values, and habits that are deemed acceptable or normal by a group or the larger society

Social justice A type of justice that considers how societies provide for the needs of their members

Social learning theories Theories proposing that crime is learned, often from criminal peers; it begins with the belief that people are born good, but over time learn to be bad

Social process theories Theories of criminal behavior that stress the importance of socialization and interactions between individuals in society

Social structure theories Theories of criminal behavior proposing that a lack of power in society and living in poverty and deprivation encourage involvement in crime

Sociology The study of social relationships and institutions; it focuses on issues such as religion, family, social classes, cultures, and related topics

Solicitors A historical term used to refer to lawyers

Specialized courts Also known as problem-solving or specialty courts, they include various courts that focus directly on particular types of crime or adjudicate certain types of offenders

Specialized work camps Low-security facilities centered on working outside the prison facility

Specific deterrence A goal of sentencing that seeks to discourage or dissuade specific individuals from committing various behaviors

Speedy Trial Act Legislation designed to ensure that federal defendants are promptly brought to trial per their Sixth Amendment right to a speedy trial

Spirit of the law Typically associated with officer responses to less serious offenses, it refers to officers having much more discretion and being more likely to act in a less punitive manner

Split sentencing A sentence in which an offender is given a short period of incarceration, followed by probation

Spoils system The practice of politicians rewarding individuals who support their candidacy with employment; it was quite evident during the political era of policing

Standard conditions (probation) General constraints imposed on all probationers

Stare decisis A Latin term for "stand by the decision"; it is the concept on which case law is based

State attorney general A state's chief legal officer

State-corporate crimes Hybrid forms of white-collar crime that involve some combination of governmental and corporate criminals

State courts of general jurisdiction The group of courts responsible for the major trials in the state systems

State courts of limited jurisdiction The most common among the courts, they are the lower level trial courts; they hear the bulk of court cases

State crimes Violations of laws created by states

State judicial conduct commissions State commissions that evaluate complaints regarding judges

State supreme courts Also known as state courts of last resort, they are the highest appellate court in each state

Status offenses Violations of the law by juveniles that would not be an offense if committed by adults (e.g., truancy, drinking alcohol)

Statute of limitations A maximum time frame during which criminal charges can be filed

Statutory exclusion laws Laws that automatically exclude particular types of cases from the jurisdiction of juvenile courts, meaning that they will automatically be considered in criminal court

Sting operations An investigative technique in which officers pose as criminals with the intent to gain access to offenders

Stocks Structures that were similar to pillories, although they permitted offenders to sit while undergoing punishment and ridicule

Stop and frisk Also known as a threshold inquiry or field inquiry; it involves officers briefly detaining and patting down individuals they believe may pose a risk

Strain theory A theoretical explanation of crime which proposes that crime results from individuals' frustration at their apparent lack of legitimate opportunities for economic and social advancement

Stress An uncomfortable state of arousal in which individuals perceive the demands of an incident as difficult or beyond their ability to satisfy or alter those demands

Strict liability offenses Offenses that do not require criminal intent

Structured sentences Sentences imposed under the direction of sentencing guidelines that seek to reduce disparity and promote uniformity in sentencing, primarily through consideration of an offender's criminal history and current offense

Study release Programs that provide offenders time outside prison to attend classes and further their education or learn job skills

Subcultural deviance theories Criminological theories that focus on the effects of subcultures having values and norms that conflict with those of the larger society; the theories propose that individuals who grow up in or are influenced by the values of those subcultures act in accordance with those influences

Subculture Cultural patterns, including values, meanings, and behavioral patterns, that identify some segments in the population as distinct from other groups

Subpoena A written document that is used to summon witnesses to court

Subpoena duces tecum A court order requiring the person named in the document to produce documents such as records, computer files, books, or other tangible items for the courts

Sub rosa economy An underground economy in which inmates barter and negotiate various goods and services

Substantial capacity test A test for insanity that focuses on whether the defendant had substantial capacity, as opposed to total capacity, to understand the rightfulness of their actions

Substantive law Laws that dictate our everyday behavior; they define criminal behaviors and identify the punishments associated with them

Summary trial A trial conducted by magistrates for a petty offense or infraction

Summation Closing arguments of a trial

Supermax prisons Facilities that provide a greater level of security than maximum-security prisons by isolating inmates from society, other inmates, and prison staff

Supervision (probation) Monitoring and overseeing offenders during the course of their probation sentences

Surety bond The means by which defendants without the financial resources to post bail secure their release through the use of a bail bonding agency

Surrebuttal Testimony from the defense in attempts to discredit testimony offered during rebuttal

Surveillance (probation) Monitoring the activities of probationers

Surveillance An investigative technique in which suspects are observed to gain information and can be used in three manners: fixed, moving, or electronic

System efficiency The manner by which prosecutors' offices consider their caseloads in light of a high volume of cases and lack of resources for prosecution

Technical violations Noncriminal behaviors that violate the terms of a probation or parole agreement

Telemedicine Healthcare professionals consulting with institutional medical personnel via videoconferencing

Telephone interpreting systems Devices that enable individuals in the courtroom who do not speak or understand the dominant language to hear and communicate via a translator participating through a telephone

Terrorism Unlawfully using force and violence to intimidate or coerce others in furtherance of political or social objectives

Testimonial evidence A type of direct evidence that provides the bulk of evidence in court cases and may be provided by lay witnesses or expert witnesses

Theories Means by which we explain natural occurrences by observing and measuring relationships regarding observable phenomena

Third-party custody A means of pretrial release in which a third party assumes responsibility for the defendant's future attendance in court

Three Penitentiary Act Legislation that authorized the construction of three penitentiaries to house federal offenders

Three strikes penalties Legislation that mandates offenders with specific types and numbers of prior convictions to receive extended penalties

Ticket of leave A document of release from institutionalization that was received by inmates upon earning enough marks; it was part of the Irish system

Title VII of the Civil Rights Act of 1964 Legislation passed in 1964 that prevents governments, unions, employment agencies, and private employers with 15 or more employees from discriminating based on color, race, sex, religion, or national origin

Tort law Laws that address wrongs between individuals and the associated damages

Total institutions Facilities in which the same people work, eat, and recreate every day

Toxicology Analyzing biological samples for drugs and other toxic substances

Training schools Facilities used to incarcerate juvenile offenders, typically for a year or more; they provide many opportunities for rehabilitation, particularly with regard to education and vocational training

Trajectory An aspect of life course theory that refers to the path of behavior that individuals assume throughout life

Transition An aspect of life course theory that refers to influential instances, or turning points that encourage or discourage individuals from engaging in crime

Transnational crimes Offenses that impact more than one country

Transportation Removing individuals from communities; it began in England and was used in the 17th and 18th centuries to send undesirables to the American colonies

Treason A crime that involves betraying one's country

Treatment conditions (probation) Conditions of probation that target particular needs of the probationer and add a rehabilitative approach to probation

Trial by battle An early means of litigation that emerged in England following the 11th-century Norman Conquest; it involved plaintiffs and defendants agreeing to settle their differences via an agreed-on location and weapon, such as a battle-axe

Trial by ordeal Used in early English cases in which the plaintiff could not obtain enough oaths, it involved the accused being required to perform particular dangerous acts, and their survival was viewed as fate determining their innocence

Trial courts Courts that decide matters of fact and determine whether a defendant is found guilty; they host various types of court-related hearings in addition to conducting trials

Trial sufficiency The manner by which prosecutors' offices consider their caseloads by prosecuting cases primarily when there is a strong likelihood of winning at trial

True bill Also known as a bill of indictment, it is issued by grand juries when they find probable cause for the continued prosecution of a defendant

Truth-in-sentencing laws Legislation that sought to ensure that inmates serve a greater percentage of the sentence imposed

Twelve Tables Early Roman law created around 450 B.C. that consolidated earlier rules, customs, and traditions into codified law; each table addressed particular aspects of justice

Tythings Early England living arrangements that consisted of 10 families living communally

Unauthorized and illegal file sharing Illegally distributing information such as music, software, and movie files through the use of a computer

Unified court system Court systems that use a single-tiered organization of trial courts, thus eliminating the distinction between courts of limited jurisdiction and courts of general jurisdiction

Uniform Crime Reporting Program A program that includes crime-related data based on reports submitted to the Federal Bureau of Investigation by law enforcement agencies

Unitary system of government A system of government in which all control is allocated to a national government

Unmanned aerial vehicles Also known as drones, they are unmanned aircraft increasingly used for various law enforcement purposes

United Nations An international organization that was founded in 1945 and addresses issues including human rights, sustainable development, terrorism, disarmament, health emergencies, and gender equality

United States Code The official compilation of federal laws in the United States

Unsecured bond A means of pretrial release that involves the setting of a bail amount, although no monetary payment is required for release; defendants are responsible for the full bail amount should they fail to return to court

USA PATRIOT Act Passed in 2001, it provided funding for local law enforcement to protect the homeland; it enabled law enforcement agents to use greater levels of surveillance, enhanced the punishments associated with terrorist acts, and facilitated better relationships and communication among levels of law enforcement

U.S. attorney general A member of the president's cabinet who heads the U.S. Department of Justice and oversees prosecutions in the federal government

U.S. attorneys The primary litigators for the federal government

U.S. Congress The legislative branch of the federal government; it consists of the U.S. Senate and the U.S. House of Representatives

U.S. Constitution The supreme law in the United States; it identifies the powers of government, the limitations associated with those powers, and the protections granted to individuals

U.S. courts of appeals Federal appellate courts that hear appeals from cases first tried in the U.S. district courts within their circuit

U.S. Department of Justice A department in the federal government that includes the Federal Bureau of Prisons, the USMS, the FBI, the DEA, and the ATF

U.S. district courts The trial courts of the federal judicial system

U.S. magistrate judges Judges who assist federal judges through performing all of the same tasks as district court judges with the exception of trying and sentencing felony defendants

U.S. Sentencing Commission An independent agency in the judicial branch of the U.S. government that establishes sentencing policies for the federal government, advises Congress regarding crime policies, and provides information on federal crime and sentencing issues

U.S. Supreme Court The highest court in the land; it has authority over the 51 distinct legal systems in the United States

Utilitarianism The assumption that human behaviors are associated with pain and pleasure

Vagrancy laws Laws that were central to the Black Codes; they were used to punish Blacks who were unemployed and had no residence

Vandalism Willfully destroying or defacing property without the consent of the owner

Vehicle tracking systems An investigative technique in which investigators track vehicles using devices placed on a suspect's vehicle and global positioning systems

Venire A group of potential jurors; jury pool

Victim impact statements Written or oral information offered by crime victims that address how the crime has impacted them; they assist sentencing bodies with their decision-making

"Victimless" crimes Crimes in which no victim is directly involved

Victimology The study of victims

Victim precipitation Acts in which victims provoke or instigate criminal behavior

Victim Rights and Restitution Act Legislation through which Congress gave crime victims rights, including the right to be present at court proceedings, notification of the proceedings involving the crime of which they were a victim, and consultation with prosecutors

Victims' bills of rights A series of legislative acts designed to protect and assist victims of crime

Victims of Crime Act Legislation that allocated funds for research on victim needs, for victim compensation, and for victim assistance programs in eligible states that had programs designed to assist victims of sexual assault, spousal abuse, or child abuse

Victims' rights movement A movement during the 1970s and 1980s that helped put an end to blaming individuals for being victimized and gave victims a larger role in criminal case processing

Victim Witness Protection Act Legislation that required the use of victim impact statements in federal trials and encouraged states to adopt a similar approach

Videoconference visitation Inmates visiting with individuals outside the institution through the use of technology

Violent Crime Control and Law Enforcement Act of 1994 The largest crime bill in the history of the United States; the act addressed many issues pertaining to crime and justice, including the allocation of over $50 million for the expansion of drug courts, providing victims in federal courts with permission to speak at sentencing hearings, and expanding victim services; it also made restitution mandatory in sexual assault cases

Violent crimes Crimes in which one person uses, or threatens to use, force against another person; also known as interpersonal crimes

Voice stress analyzers Devices that measure small frequency modulations heard in human voices that are believed to happen when someone is lying

Voice writing A means by which transcripts are made in court; it involves court reporters speaking directly into a voice silencer; reporters repeat the testimony offered in court into the silencer

Voir dire "Speak the truth"; the process involves questioning potential jurors regarding any prejudices, knowledge, or opinions they may have regarding the case or the defendant

Waived Transferring a juvenile case to the adult (criminal) justice system for processing

Wall posts Correctional officers who stand post at towers aligned along the prison walls

Wardens Also known as superintendents, they are the chief executive officers of prisons

Weapons offenses Violations of laws prohibiting the manufacture, sale, purchase, transportation, possession, concealment, or use of firearms or other weapons

Weregild An early means of settling disputes among Germanic tribes of Europe, it was the practice of offenders paying an amount of money to the deceased victim's family; the amount paid was based on the social status of the victim

White-collar crime Illegal acts that violate an individual or group's legal responsibility or trust, which often occur during the course of occupational activity; it is typically committed by individuals of high social status for organizational or personal gain

Wickersham Commission In 1931, it criticized the police for widespread corruption and misconduct, including accusations of officers engaging in unprofessional conduct with regard to interrogating suspects and the use of force

Wilderness camps Programs that involve counselors taking small groups of troubled youth into the wilderness where they will have to overcome challenges while learning positive values

Wired courts Progressive courts that feature technologies that have improved the adjudication process; they are also known as technology-enabled courts

Work detail supervisors Prison officers who oversee the work details of inmates

Workhouses Sometimes referred to as poorhouses, they were used as houses of correction for individuals who committed minor law violations

Work release programs Programs that provide inmates an opportunity to reorient themselves with life and work outside prison as they gain particular job skills

Writing and distributing malicious code The creation and spread of viruses and other harmful information that destroys or alters the information contained in the computers of those who are victimized

Writ of certiorari An order from a superior court to the lower courts to send the case records forward for review

Writ of habeas corpus Petitions that claim an inmate's constitutional rights were violated and challenge the fact or duration of confinement

Yard officers Prison officers who oversee inmates recreating in the prison yard

Zero-tolerance policing A style of policing that is rooted in the broken windows hypothesis and seeks to aggressively address small infractions that could lead to larger ones

References

UNIT I

Adler, F., Laufer, W., & Mueller, G. O. (2018). *LooseLeaf for criminology* (9th ed.). McGraw–Hill.

Adler, F., Mueller, G. O. W., & Laufer, W. S. (2007). *Criminology* (6th ed.). McGraw–Hill.

Agnew, R. (1992). Foundation for a general strain theory of crime and delinquency. *Criminology*, 28, 535–566.

Aichorn, A. (1963). *Wayward youth*. Viking.

Albanese, J. S. (2011). *Organized crime in our times* (6th ed.). Anderson.

American Civil Liberties Union. (2013). *Cell phone location tracking public record requests*. https://www.aclu.org/cases/cell-phone-location-tracking-public-records-request.

Arrigo, B. (1999). *Social justice/criminal justice: The maturation of critical theory in law, crime, and deviance*. West/Wadsworth.

Beaver, K. M., Hoffman, T., Shields, R. T., Vaughn, M. G., DeLisi, M., & Wright, J. P. (2010). Gender differences in genetic and environmental influences on gambling: Results from a sample of twins from the National Longitudinal Study of Adolescent Health. *Addiction*, 105, 536–542.

Beccaria, C. (1963). *On crimes and punishments*. Prentice Hall. (Original work published 1764)

Becker, H. S. (1963). *Outsiders: Studies in the sociology of deviance*. Free Press.

Bird, D. (1982, November 4). Defense linked to menstruation dropped in case. *New York Times*. https://www.nytimes.com/1982/11/04/nyregion/defense-linked-to-menstruation-dropped-in-case.html

Boetig, B. P., & Parrish, P. A. (2008). Proactive media relations: The visual library initiative. *FBI Law Enforcement Bulletin*, 77(11), 7–9.

Borum, R., & Fulero, S. M. (1999). Empirical research on the insanity defense and attempted reforms: Evidence toward informed policy. *Law and Human Behavior*, 23(1), 117–135.

Bronson, J. (2018). *Justice expenditure and employment extracts 2015* (NCJ 251780). U.S. Department of Justice, Bureau of Justice Statistics.

Bronson, J. (2019). *Justice expenditure and employment extracts 2016* (NCJ 254126). U.S. Department of Justice, Bureau of Justice Statistics.

Bronson, J., & Berzofsky, M. (2017). *Indicators of mental health problems reported by prisoners and jail inmates, 2011–12* (NCJ 250612). U.S. Department of Justice, Bureau of Justice Statistics.

Brown v. Board of Education, 347 *U.S.* 483 (1954).

Bullard, R. (1990). *Dumping in Dixie: Race, class and environmental quality*. Westview.

Bullard, R. (1996). Environmental justice: It's more than waste facility siting. *Social Science Quarterly*, 77, 493–499.

Bumgarner, J., Crawford, C., & Burns, R. (2018). *Federal law enforcement: A primer* (2nd ed.). Carolina Academic Press.

Burns, R., & Crawford, C. (1999). School shootings, the media, and public fear: Ingredients for a moral panic. *Crime, Law and Social Change*, 32(2), 147–168.

Cassell, P. G. (2009). In defense of victim impact statements. *Ohio State Journal of Criminal Law*, 6(2), 611–648.

Center for Strategic and International Studies. (2018). *Economic impact of cybercrime—no slowing down*. https://www.mcafee.com/enterprise/en-us/assets/reports/restricted/rp-economic-impact-cybercrime.pdf?utm_source=Press&utm_campaign=bb9303ae70-EMAIL_CAMPAIGN_2018_02_21&utm_medium=email

Chalfin, A. (2016). Economic costs of crime. In W. Jennings (Ed.), *The encyclopedia of crime and punishment*. https://onlinelibrary.wiley.com/doi/epdf/10.1002/9781118519639.wbecpx193

Chammah, M. (2017). *What's behind the decline in the death penalty?* The Marshall Project. https://www.themarshallproject.org/2017/10/02/what-s-behind-the-decline-in-the-death-penalty

Christiansen, K. O. (1970). Crime in a Danish twin population. *Acta Geneticae Medical Gemellologial*, 19, 323–326.

Clark, M. (2013, July 15). Zimmerman verdict renews focus on "stand your ground" laws. *USA Today*. https://www.usatoday.com/story/news/nation/2013/07/15/stateline-zimmerman-stand-your-ground/2517507/

Clarke, R., & Homel, R. (1997). A revised classification of situational crime prevention techniques. In S. Lab (Ed.), *Crime prevention at a crossroads* (pp. 17–27). Anderson.

Clear, T., & Cadora, E. (2003). *Community justice*. Wadsworth.

Cloward, R. A., & Ohlin, L. E. (1960). *Delinquency and opportunity: A theory of delinquent gangs*. Free Press.

CNN. (2016, August 17). *Adam Gadahn fast facts*. https://www.cnn.com/2013/03/23/us/adam-gadahn-fast-facts/index.html

Cohen, A. K. (1955). *Delinquent boys: The culture of the gang*. Free Press.

Cohen, L., & Felson, M. (1979). Social change and crime rate trends: A routine activities approach. *American Sociological Review*, 44, 588–608.

Coker, K. L., Smith, P. H., Westphal, A., Zonana, H. V., & McKee, S. A. (2014). Crime and psychiatric disorders among youth in the US population: An analysis of the National Comorbidity Survey-Adolescent Supplement. *Journal of the American Academy of Child & Adolescent Psychiatry*, 53(8), 888–899.

Conklin, J. E. (2003). *Why crime rates fell*. Allyn & Bacon.

Conklin, J. E. (2013). *Criminology* (11th ed.). Pearson.

Connor, T. (2018). *Death of Keeven Robinson in custody is ruled homicide by asphyxiation*. NBC News. https://www.nbcnews.com/news/crime-courts/death-keeven-robinson-custody-was-homicide-asphyxiation-n873976

Damphousse, K. (2009). The dark side of the web: Terrorists' use of the internet. In F. Schmalleger & M. Pittaro (Eds.), *Crimes of the internet* (pp. 573–592). Pearson Prentice Hall.

Davis, R. C., & Mulford, C. (2008). Victim rights and new remedies: Finally getting victims their due. *Journal of Contemporary Criminal Justice*, 24(2), 198–208.

Davis, R. C., & Smith, B. E. (1994). The effects of victim impact statements on sentencing decisions: A test in an urban setting. *Justice Quarterly*, 11, 453–469.

Dempsey, J. S. (2011). *Introduction to private security* (2nd ed.) Wadsworth/Cengage.

Dent, M. (2016). *Crime costs the global economy a staggering $870 billion*. The Fiscal Times. https://www.thefiscaltimes.com/2016/03/02/Crime-Costs-Global-Economy-Staggering-870-Billion

Doerner, W. G., & Lab, S. P. (2002). *Victimology* (3rd ed.). Anderson.

Dolliver, M. J., Kenney, J. L., Williams Reid, L., & Prohaska, A. (2018). Examining the relationship between media consumption, fear of crime, and support for controversial criminal justice policies using a nationally representative sample. *Journal of Contemporary Criminal Justice*, 34(4), 399–420.

Durkheim, E. (1951). *Suicide: A study in sociology* (J. A. Spaulding & G. Simpson, Trans.). Free Press. (Original work published 1897).

Eligon, J. (2016, January 21). A question of environmental racism in Flint. *New York Times*. https://www.nytimes.com/2016/01/22/us/a-question-of-environmental-racism-in-flint.html

Ellis, L. (1988). Neurohormonal bases of varying tendencies to learn delinquent and criminal behavior. In E. Morris & C. Braukmann (Eds.), *Behavioral approaches to crime and delinquency* (pp. 499–518). Plenum.

Federal Bureau of Investigation. (2018). *2017 Crime in the United States*. https://ucr.fbi.gov/crime-in-the-u.s/2018/crime-in-the-u.s.-2018/topic-pages/tables/table-1

Federal Bureau of Investigation. (n.d.a). *UCR home—NIBRS quick facts*. https://www.fbi.gov/file-repository/ucr/nibrs-quick-facts.pdf/view

Federal Bureau of Investigation. (n.d.b). *2018 Hate crime statistics*. https://ucr.fbi.gov/hate-crime/2018/topic-pages/incidents-and-offenses

Federal Bureau of Investigation. (2019). *National data—clearance figure*. https://ucr.fbi.gov/crime-in-the-u.s/2018/crime-in-the-u.s.-2018/topic-pages/clearance-browse-by/national-data

Federal Bureau of Investigation. (2020a). *2019 crime in the United States—estimated number of arrests—Table 29*. https://ucr.fbi.gov/crime-in-the-u.s/2019/crime-in-the-u.s.-2019/tables/table-29

Federal Bureau of Investigation. (2020b). *Uniform Crime Report—crime in the United States: Offense definitions*. https://www.ucrdatatool.gov/offenses.cfm

Federal Bureau of Investigation. (2021). *Internet crime report*. https://www.ic3.gov/Media/PDF/AnnualReport/2020_IC3Report.pdf

Federal Bureau of Prisons. (2021). *Offenses*. https://www.bop.gov/about/statistics/statistics_inmate_offenses.jsp

Feinberg, S. L. (2002). Media effects: The influence of local newspaper coverage on municipal police size. *American Journal of Criminal Justice*, 26(2), 249–268.

Freud, S. (1927). *The ego and the id*. Hogarth.

Friedrichs, D. O. (2010). *Trusted criminals: White collar crime in contemporary society* (4th ed.). Cengage/Wadsworth.

Gaines, L. K., & Kappeler, V. E. (2012). *Homeland security*. Pearson.

Garrett, B. L. (2017). *End of its rope: How killing the death penalty can revive criminal justice*. Harvard University Press.

Gelb, A., & Stevenson, P. (2017). *Share of population behind bars falls back to 1998 level. Pew Charitable Trusts*. https://www.pewtrusts.org/en/research-and-analysis/articles/2017/01/12/us-adult-incarceration-rate-declines-13-percent-in-8-years

Glueck, S., & Glueck, E. T. (1950). *Unraveling juvenile delinquency*. Commonwealth Fund.

Goddard, H. H. (1914). *Feeblemindedness: Its causes and consequences*. Macmillan.

Goddard, H. H. (1915). *The criminal imbecile*. Macmillan.

Gottfredson, M. R., & Hirschi, T. (1990). *A general theory of crime*. Stanford University Press.

Greife, M., Stretesky, P. B., O'Connor Shelley, T., & Pogrebin, M. (2015). Corporate environmental crime and environmental justice. *Criminal Justice Policy Review, 28*(4), 327–346.

Hall, J. (1960). *General principles of criminal law* (2nd ed.). Bobbs–Merrill.

Hanson, R. F., & Self-Brown, S. (2010). Screening and assessment of crime victimization and its effects. *Journal of Traumatic Stress, 23*(2), 207–214.

Harrell, E. (2012). *Violent victimization committed by strangers, 1993–2010* (NCJ 239424). U.S. Department of Justice, Bureau of Justice Statistics.

Heath, B. (2015). New police radars can "see" inside homes. *USA Today*. https://www.usatoday.com/story/news/2015/01/19/police-radar-see-through-walls/22007615/

Helmkamp, J., Ball, J., & Townsend, K. (Eds.). (1996). *Definitional dilemma: Can and should there be a universal definition of white collar crime?* National White Collar Crime Center.

Herd, D. (2014). Changes in the prevalence of alcohol in rap music lyrics 1979–2009. *Substance Use & Misuse, 49*(3), 333–342.

Herrnstein, R. J., & Murray, C. (1994). *The bell curve: Intelligence and class structure in American life*. Free Press.

Hindelang, M. J., Gottfredson, M. R., & Garofalo, J. (1978). *Victims of personal crime: An empirical foundation for a theory of personal crime*. Ballinger.

Hindelang, M. J., Gottfredson, M. R., & Flanagan, T. J. (Eds.). (1981). *Sourcebook of criminal justice statistics—1980*. U.S. Government Printing Office.

Hirschi, T. (1969). *Causes of delinquency*. University of California Press.

Hirschi, T., & Hindelang, M. J. (1977). Intelligence and delinquency: A revisionist review. *American Sociological Review, 42*, 571–586.

Hobijn, B., & Sager, E. (2007). What has homeland security cost? An assessment: 2001–2005. *Current Issues in Economics and Finance, 13*(2), 1–7.

Howley, S., & Dorris, C. (2007). Legal rights for crime victims in the criminal justice system. In R. C. Davis & A. J. Lurigio (Eds.), *Victims of crime* (3rd ed., pp. 299–314). Sage.

Husak, D. (2008). *Overcriminalization: The limits of the criminal law*. Oxford University Press.

INTERPOL. (2019). *Cybercrime*. https://www.interpol.int/Crimes/Cybercrime

Jerin, R. A., & Fields, C. (2009). Murder and mayhem in the media: Media misrepresentation of crime and criminality. In R. Muraskin & A. R. Roberts (Eds.), *Visions for change: Crime and justice in the twenty-first century* (5th ed., pp. 217–229). Pearson Prentice Hall.

Jones, J. M. (2019). *U.S. support for legal marijuana steady in past year. Gallup*. https://news.gallup.com/poll/267698/support-legal-marijuana-steady-past-year.aspx

Jones, J. M. (2020). *Black, White adults' confidence diverges most on police. Gallup*. https://news.gallup.com/poll/317114/black-white-adults-confidence-diverges-police.aspx

Jones, M., & Bonner, H. S. (2016). What should criminal justice interns know? Comparing the opinions of student interns and criminal justice practitioners. *Journal of Criminal Justice Education, 27*(3), 381–409.

Kaeble, D., & Cowhig, M. (2018). *Correctional populations in the United States, 2016* (NCJ 251211). U.S. Department of Justice, Bureau of Justice Statistics.

Kappeler, V. E., Blumberg, M., & Potter, G. W. (2018). *The mythology of crime and criminal justice* (5th ed.). Waveland Press.

Keck, N. (2018, April 13). *Alleged Vermont school shooting plot spurs debate about when intent becomes a crime. NPR*. https://www.npr.org/2018/04/13/602237899/alleged-vermont-school-shooting-plot-spurs-debate-about-when-intent-becomes-a-cr

Kelly, T. K. (1984). Where offenders pay for their crimes: Victim restitution and its constitutionality. *Notre Dame Law Review, 59*(3), 685–716.

Kilgore, A. (2017, November 9). *Aaron Hernandez suffered from the most severe CTE ever found in a person his age. Washington Post*. https://www.washingtonpost.com/sports/aaron-hernandez-suffered-from-most-severe-cte-ever-found-in-a-person-his-age/2017/11/09/fa7cd204-c57b-11e7-afe9-4f60b5a6c4a0_story.html?noredirect=on&utm_term=.84ba36b286ac

Kilpatrick, D. G., Beatty, D., & Howley, S. S. (1998). *The rights of crime victims: Does legal protection make a difference?* U.S. Department of Justice, National Institute of Justice.

Krohn, M. D., Thornberry, T. P., Gibson, C. L., & Baldwin, J. M. (2010). The development and impact of self-report measures of crime and delinquency. *Journal of Quantitative Criminology, 26*, 509–525.

Lange, J. (1930). *Crime and destiny* (C. Haldane, Trans.). Charles Boni. (Original work published 1919)

Langton, L., Berzofsky, M., Krebs, C., & Smiley-McDonald, H. (2012). *Victimizations not reported to the police, 2006–2010* (NCJ 238536). U.S. Department of Justice, Bureau of Justice Statistics.

Lawserver. (2018). *Texas Penal Code 9.42—deadly force to protect property*. https://www.lawserver.com/law/state/texas/tx-codes/texas_penal_code_9-42

Lee, J. J., Gino, F., Jin, E. S., Rice, L. K., & Josephs, R. A. (2015). Hormones and ethics: Understanding the biological basis of unethical conduct. *Journal of Experimental Psychology, 144*(5), 891–897.

Lemert, E. M. (1967). *Human deviance, social problems, and social control*. Prentice Hall.

Lurigio, A. J. (1987). Are all victims alike? The adverse, generalized, and differential impact of crime. *Crime & Delinquency, 33*, 452–467.

Lyman, M. D., & Potter, G. W. (2011). *Organized crime* (5th ed.). Pearson Prentice Hall.

Lynch, M. J., Burns, R. G., & Stretesky, P. B. (2014). *Environmental law, crime and justice* (2nd ed.). LFB Scholarly Publishing.

Mao, F. (2018, September 23). *Australian strawberries: Why would someone hide a needle in fruit? BBC News*. https://www.bbc.com/news/world-australia-45555835

Marsh, J. (2018, November 12). *Strawberry needle scare: Woman allegedly spiked punnets for revenge. CNN*. https://www.cnn.com/2018/11/12/australia/australia-strawberry-needle-intl/index.html

Martschenko, D. (2017, October 11). *IQ tests have a dark, controversial history—but they're finally being used for good. Business Insider*. https://www.businessinsider.com/iq-tests-dark-history-finally-being-used-for-good-2017-10

McCarthy, A. (2014, June 18). *Bro country's sexism is ruining country music. Dallas Observer*. https://www.dallasobserver.com/music/bro-countrys-sexism-is-ruining-country-music-7070740

McCarthy, J. (2019). *52% describe problem of crime in the U.S. as serious. Gallup*. https://news.gallup.com/poll/268283/describe-problem-crime-serious.aspx

McCollister, K. E., French, M. T., & Fang, H. (2010). The cost of crime to society: New crime-specific estimates for policy and program evaluation. *Drug and Alcohol Dependence, 108*(1–2), 98–109.

McDonald, S. (2009). Understanding restitution. *Victims of Crime Research Digest, 2*. http://www.justice.gc.ca/eng/rp-pr/cj-jp/victim/rd09_2-rr09_2/p2.html#ftn1

McQuade, S. C., III. (2006). *Understanding and managing cybercrime*. Pearson Allyn & Bacon.

Merton, R. K. (1968). *Social theory and social structure*. Free Press.

Miller, H. A., & Kim, B. (2009). Hate crime. In J. M. Miller (Ed.), *21st century criminology: A reference handbook* (Vol. 2, pp. 490–498). Sage.

Mills, C. W. (1956). *The power elite*. Oxford University.

Moffit, T., Lynam, D., & Silva, P. (1994). Neuropsychological tests predicting persistent male delinquency. *Criminology, 32*, 277–300.

Montgomery, D. (2020). *COVID-19 curbs community policing at a time of diminishing trust. Pew Trusts*. https://www.pewtrusts.org/en/research-and-analysis/blogs/stateline/2020/10/01/covid-19-curbs-community-policing-at-a-time-of-diminishing-trust

Morgan, A. M. (1987). Victim rights: Criminal law: Remembering the "forgotten person" in the criminal justice system. *Marquette Law Review, 70*(3), 572–597.

Morgan, R. E., & Kena, G. (2017). *Criminal victimization, 2016* (NCJ 251150). U.S. Department of Justice, Bureau of Justice Statistics.

Morgan, R. E., & Truman, J. L. (2020). *Criminal victimization, 2019* (NCJ 255113). U.S. Department of Justice, Bureau of Justice Statistics.

Motivans, M. (2019). *Federal justice statistics, 2015–2016* (NCJ 251770). U.S. Department of Justice, Bureau of Justice Statistics.

Muftić, L. R., Bouffard, L. E., & Bouffard, J. A. (2007). An exploratory analysis of victim precipitation among men and women arrested for intimate partner violence. *Feminist Criminology, 2*, 327–346.

Murphy, R. (2011). Realistic simulated training. *Law & Order, 59*(9), 46–51.

Murray, E. (2018, April 25). Fair Haven school shooting plot: What we know. *Burlington Free Press*. https://www.burlingtonfreepress.com/story/news/local/2018/04/25/fair-haven-school-shooting-plot-what-we-know-now/549728002/

National Registry of Exonerations. (2020). *Exonerations by year: DNA and Non-DNA*. https://www.law.umich.edu/special/exoneration/Pages/Exoneration-by-Year.aspx

Neubauer, D. W., & Fradella, H. F. (2019). *America's courts and the criminal justice system* (13th ed.). Cengage.

Newmark, L. C. (2004). *Crime victims' needs and VOCA-funded services: Findings and* recommendations from two national studies. National Institute of Justice.

Newport, F. (2017, November 2). *Americans' fear of walking alone ties 52-year low*. Gallup. http://news.gallup.com/poll/221183/americans-fear-walking-alone-ties-year-low.aspx

New York Times. (2021, March 28). What to know about the death of George Floyd in Minneapolis. https://www.nytimes.com/article/george-floyd.html

Oleson, J. C., & Chappell, R. (2012). Self-reported violent offending among subjects with genius-level IQ scores. *Journal of Family Violence*, 27(8), 715–730.

Oliver, W. M., & Hilgenberg, J. F., Jr. (2018). *A history of crime and criminal justice in America* (3rd ed.). Carolina Academic Press.

Oudekerk, B. A., Warnken, H., & Langton, L. (2019). *Victim service providers in the United States, 2017* (NCJ 252648). U.S. Department of Justice, Bureau of Justice Statistics.

Owen, S. S., Fradella, H. F., Burke, T. W., & Joplin, J. W. (2015). *Foundations of criminal justice*. Oxford University Press.

Packer, H. L. (1968). *The limits of the criminal sanction*. Stanford University Press.

Paresh, D. (2018, October 24). *Facebook removes 8.7 million sexual photos of kids in last three months*. Technology News. https://www.reuters.com/article/us-facebook-child-safety/facebook-removes-8-7-million-sexual-photos-of-kids-in-last-three-months-idUSKCN1MY1SE

Pew Research Center. (2019). *Internet use*. https://www.pewinternet.org/chart/internet-use/

Piquero, A., & Mazerolle, P. (2001). *Life-course criminology contemporary and class readings*. Wadsworth.

Planty, M., Burch, A. M., Banks, D., Couzens, L., Blanton, C., & Cribb, D. (2015). *Arrest-Related Deaths Program: Data quality profile* (NCJ 248544). Bureau of Justice Statistics, U.S. Department of Justice.

Prosecuting Attorneys' Council of Georgia. (n.d.). *Crime victims bill of rights*. https://pacga.org/resources/victim-assistance/georgia-crime-victims-bill-of-rights//

Pulido, L. (2016) Flint, environmental racism, and racial capitalism. *Capitalism Nature Socialism*, 27(3), 1–16

Reichel, P. L. (2013). *Comparative criminal justice systems: A topical approach*. Pearson.

Reiman, J., & Leighton, P. (2013). *The rich get richer and the poor get prison* (10th ed.). Pearson.

Reiss, A. J., Jr. (1971). *The police and the public*. Yale University Press.

Richey, W. (2012, November 26). Supreme Court rejects Idaho case on prohibiting the insanity defense. *Christian Science Monitor*. https://www.csmonitor.com/USA/Justice/2012/1126/Supreme-Court-rejects-Idaho-case-on-prohibiting-the-insanity-defense

Robbins, G. (2017, April 17). Soaring number of computers being hijacked for ransom. *San Diego Union-Tribune*. http://www.sandiegouniontribune.com/news/cyber-life/sd-me-connected-ransomware-20170421-story.html#

Roberson, C., Wallace, H., & Stuckey, G. B. (2013). *Procedures in the justice system* (10th ed.). Pearson.

Robinson, M. B. (2009). *Justice blind? Ideals and realities of American criminal justice* (3rd ed.). Pearson.

Roeder, O., Eisen, L.-B., & Bowling, J. (2015). *What caused the crime decline? Brennan Center for Justice, New York University School of Law*. https://www.brennancenter.org/sites/default/files/analysis/What_Caused_The_Crime_Decline.pdf

Roman, E. (2018, May 2). *Man arrested for soliciting sexual acts from a minor on social media*. WCTI12. http://wcti12.com/news/local-crime/man-arrested-for-soliciting-sexual-acts-from-a-minor-on-social-media

Rosen, L. (1995). The creation of the Uniform Crime Report. *Social Science History*, 19(2), 215–238.

Roth, M. P. (2011). *Crime and punishment: A history of the criminal justice system* (2nd ed.). Cengage.

Rowe, D., Osgood, D. W., & Nicewander, W. A. (1990). A latent trait approach to unifying criminal careers. *Criminology*, 28, 237–270.

Sacks, E., & Zambrano, J. (2017, June 1). *Massachusetts man accused of kidnapping, torture*. NBC News. https://www.nbcnews.com/news/crime-courts/3-bodies-found-home-massachusetts-man-accused-kidnapping-torture-n879236

Sampson, R. J., & Laub, J. H. (1993). *Crime in the making*. Harvard University Press.

Schouten, R. (2012). The insanity defense: An intersection of morality, public policy, and science. *Psychology Today*. https://www.psychologytoday.com/us/blog/almost-psychopath/201208/the-insanity-defense

Schur, E. (1965). *Crimes without victims: Deviant behavior and public policy*. Prentice Hall.

Schwark, S. (2017). Visual representations of sexual violence in online news outlets. *Frontiers in Psychology*, 8, 774. https://doi.org/10.3389/fpsyg.2017.00774

Sgarzi, J. M., & McDevitt, J. (2003). *Victimology: A study of crime victims and their roles*. Prentice Hall.

Shaw, C. R., & McKay, H. D. (1942). *Juvenile delinquency and urban areas: A study of rates of delinquents in relation to differential characteristics of local communities in American cities*. University of Chicago Press.

Sheldon, W. H. (1949). *Varieties of delinquency youth: An introduction to constitutional psychiatry*. Harper & Bros.

Sims, B., Yost, B., & Abbott, C. (2005). Use and non-use of victim services programs: Implications from a statewide survey of crime victims. *Criminology & Public Policy*, 4(2), 361–384.

Steadman, H. J. (1985). Insanity defense research and treatment of insanity acquittees. *Behavioral Sciences & the Law*, 3(1), 37–48.

Stretesky, P. B., & Lynch, M. J. (2004). The relationship between lead and crime. *Journal of Health and Social Behavior*, 45(2), 214–229.

Stohr, M. K. (2005). Victim services programming: If it is efficacious, they will come. *Criminology & Public Policy*, 4(2), 391–398.

Sutherland, E. (1931). Mental deficiency and crime. In K. Young (Ed.), *Social attitudes* (pp. 357–375). Henry Holt.

Sutherland, E. H. (1939). *Principles of criminology*. Lippincott.

Sutherland, E. H. (1940). White-collar criminality. *American Sociological Review*, 5, 1–12.

Thompson, M. (2011, June 29). The $5 trillion war on terror. *Time*. http://nation.time.com/2011/06/29/the-5-trillion-war-on-terror/

Trulson, C. R. (2005). Victims' rights and services: Eligibility, exclusion, and victim worth. *Criminology & Public Policy*, 4(2), 399–414.

Unnever, J. D., Gabbidon, S. L., & Higgins, G. E. (2011). The election of Barack Obama and perceptions of criminal injustice. *Justice Quarterly*, 28(1), 23–45.

Urban Institute. (n.d.). *Police and corrections expenditures*. https://www.urban.org/policy-centers/cross-center-initiatives/state-and-local-finance-initiative/state-and-local-backgrounders/police-and-corrections-expenditures

United Church of Christ. (1987). *Toxic wastes and race in the United States: A national report on the racial and socio-economic characteristics with hazardous waste sites*. United Church of Christ, Commission for Racial Justice.

United States v. Grimaud, 220 *U.S.* 506 (1911).

U.S. Department of Homeland Security. (2016). *Our mission*. https://www.dhs.gov/our-mission

U.S. Department of Justice. (2018, April 13). *Justice Department honors Asset Forfeiture Program team with the Crimes (sic) Victims' Financial Restoration Award*. https://www.justice.gov/opa/pr/justice-department-honors-asset-forfeiture-program-team-crimes-victims-financial-restoration

U.S. Government Accounting Office. (2017). *Costs of crime: Experts report challenges estimating costs and suggest improvements to better inform policy decisions*. https://www.gao.gov/assets/690/687353.pdf

Utah State Courts. (2018). *Criminal penalties*. http://www.utcourts.gov/howto/criminallaw/penalties.asp

Van Brocklin, V. (2012, June 20). *Fudge factor: Cooking the book on crime stats*. Police1. https://www.policeone.com/patrol-issues/articles/5736845-Fudge-factor-Cooking-the-books-on-crime-stats/

Van Dijk, J. (2008). *The world of crime: Breaking the silence on problems of security, justice, and development across the world*. Sage.

Van Ness, D., & Strong, K. H. (1997). *Restoring justice*. Anderson.

Vaughn, M. G., Salas-Wright, C. P., Delisi, M., & Perron, B. (2014). Correlates of traumatic brain injury among juvenile offenders: A multi-site study. *Criminal Behavior and Mental Health*, 24, 188–203.

Vold, G. (1958). *Theoretical criminology*. Oxford University Press.

Vold, G. B., & Bernard, T. J. (1986). *Theoretical criminology* (3rd ed.). Oxford University Press.

Waitt, T. (2017, December 14). *FBI releases 2016 NIBRS Crime Reporting Data*. American Security Today. https://americansecuritytoday.com/fbi-releases-2016-nibrs-crime-reporting-data-learn-video/

Walker, S. (1998). *Popular justice: A history of American criminal justice* (2nd ed.). Oxford University Press.

Walker, S. (2006). *Sense and nonsense about crime and drugs* (6th ed.). Wadsworth.

Wallace, H., & Roberson, C. (2006). *Principles of criminal law* (3rd ed.). Pearson Allyn & Bacon.

WDSU News. (2019, May 10). *Family of Keeven Robinson files suit one year after death*. https://www.wdsu.com/article/family-of-keeven-robinson-files-suit-one-year-after-death/27435241

Weed, F. J. (1995). *Certainty of justice: Reform in the crime victim movement*. Aldine de Gruyter.

Wevodau, A. L., Cramer, R. J., Clark, J. W., III, & Kehn, A. (2014). The role of emotion and cognition in juror perceptions of victim impact statements. *Social Justice Research*, 27(1), 45–66.

Williams, F. P., III, & McShane, M. D. (2014). *Criminological theory* (6th ed.). Pearson.

Wilson, J. Q., & Dilulio, J. J., Jr. (2006). *American government* (10th ed.). Houghton Mifflin.

Wilson, J. Q., & Herrnstein, R. (1985). *Crime and human nature*. Simon & Schuster.

Wolfgang, M. (1958). *Patterns in criminal homicide*. University of Pennsylvania Press.

Wong, C. M. (2018, April 27). *Texas man who killed neighbor uses "gay panic" defense and avoids murder charge*. HuffPost. https://www.huffingtonpost.com/entry/texas-james-miller-gay-panic_us_5ae35296e4b04aa23f22efe8

Worley, R. M., & Worley, V. B. (2013). Games guards play: A self-report study of the institutional deviance within the Texas Department of Criminal Justice. *Criminal Justice Studies*, 26(1), 115–132.

Worrall, J. L., & Moore, J. L. (2014). *Criminal law and procedure*. Pearson.

Zhao, J. S., Lawton, B., & Longmire, D. (2015). An examination of the micro-level crime-fear of crime link. *Crime & Delinquency*, 61, 19–44.

UNIT II

Aamodt, M. G. (2008). Reducing misconceptions and false beliefs in police and criminal psychology. *Criminal Justice and Behavior*, 35(10), 1231–1240.

Adams, T. (2001). *Police field operations* (5th ed.). Prentice Hall.

Adelman, M., & Morgan, P. (2006). Law enforcement versus battered women: The conflict over the Lautenberg Amendment. *Affilia: Journal of Women and Social Work*, 21(1), 28–45.

Aguilar-Millan, S., Foltz, J. E., Jackson, J., & Oberg, A. (2008). Global crime case: The modern slave trade. *The Futurist*, 45.

Ainsworth, A. (2017, February 22). *Detroit police officers convicted of stealing, selling drugs to be sentenced*. Click on Detroit. https://www.cabq.gov/cpoa/documents/cpoa-english-complaint-and-commendation-form.pdf

Alcindor, Y., & Penzenstadler, N. (2015, January 21). Police redouble efforts to recruit diverse officers. *USA Today*. http://www.usatoday.com/story/news/2015/01/21/police-redoubling-efforts-to-recruit-diverse-officers/21574081/

Allen, K. (2017, March 13). *Miami police officer arrested after allegedly robbing people he pulled over*. ABC News. http://abcnews.go.com/US/miami-police-officer-arrested-allegedly-robbing-people-pulled-over/story?id=46046931

Alpert, G. P., Dunham, R. G., & Stroshine, M. S. (2015). *Policing: Continuity and change* (2nd ed.). Waveland.

American Civil Liberties Union. (2014, June). *War comes home: The excessive militarization of American policing*. https://www.aclu.org/sites/default/files/assets/jus14-warcomeshome-report-web-rel1.pdf

Amnesty International. (1996). *United States of America: Police brutality and excessive use of force in the New York City Police Department*.

Arizona v. Gant, 556 U.S. 332 (2009).

Associated Press. (2018, December 20). *Ex-Ohio cop accused of kicking handcuffed suspect pleads guilty*. https://www.apnews.com/b55cd7b2b6b942c4a4aa6a719b50bd1d

Ayers, R. M., & Flanagan, G. S. (1992). *Preventing law enforcement stress: The organization's role*. Bureau of Justice Assistance.

Ballenger, J. J., Best, S. R., Metzler, T. J., Wasserman, D. A., Mohr, D. C., Liberman, A., Delucchi, K., Weiss, D. S., Fagan, J. A., Waldrop, A. E., & Marmar, C. R. (2011). Patterns and predictors of alcohol use in male and female urban police officers. *American Journal on Addictions*, 20(1), 21–29.

Barkan, S. E., & Bryjak, G. J. (2014). *Myths and realities of crime and justice: What every American should know* (2nd ed.). Jones & Bartlett.

Barker, T., & Carter, D. L. (Eds.) (1994). *Police deviance* (2nd ed.). Anderson.

Barlow, D. E., & Barlow, M. H. (2013). The myth that the role of the police is to fight crime. In R. M. Bohm & J. T. Walker (Eds.), *Demystifying crime & criminal justice* (2nd ed., pp. 147–156). Oxford University Press.

Barr, L. (2020, January 2). *Record number of US police officers died by suicide in 2019, advocacy group says*. ABC News. https://abcnews.go.com/Politics/record-number-us-police-officers-died-suicide-2019/story?id=68031484

Baskin, D., & Sommers, I. (2010). The influence of forensic evidence on the case outcomes of homicide incidents. *Journal of Criminal Justice*, 38(6), 1141–1149.

Beck, E. (2016, June 28). Police respond to reports of armed citizen patrols. *Charleston Gazette-Mail*. http://www.wvgazettemail.com/apps/pbcs.dll/article?avis=CH&date=20160628&category=GZ0118&lopenr=160629583&Ref=AR

Becton, J. B., Meadows, L., Tears, R., Charles, M., & Ioimo, R. (2005). Can citizen police academies influence citizens' beliefs and perceptions? *Public Management*, 87(4), 20–23.

Ben-Zur, H. (2009). Coping styles and affect. *International Journal of Stress Management*, 16, 87–101.

Bersani, B. E., & Piquero, A. R. (2017). Examining systematic crime reporting bias across three immigrant generations: Prevalence, trends, and divergence in self-reported and official reported arrests. *Journal of Quantitative Criminology*, 33, 835–857.

Bloss, W. (2007). Escalating U.S. police surveillance after 9/11: An examination of causes and effects. *Surveillance & Society*, 4(3), 208–228.

Blue H.E.L.P. (2019). *Law enforcement suicides*. https://bluehelp.org/wp-content/uploads/2019/08/2016-to-2019-.pdf

Bopp, W. J., & Schultz, D. O. (1972). *A short history of American law enforcement*. Charles C. Thomas.

Braden-Perry, M., Wagner, M., Hensley, N., & Brown, S. R. (2016, July 18). *Extremist angry over death of Alton Sterling Kills three Baton Rouge cops before he's shot dead in gunfight with police*. Daily News. http://www.nydailynews.com/news/national/multiple-baton-rouge-police-officers-killed-shooting-attack-article-1.2714761

Braga, A. A., Welsh, B. C., & Schnell, C. (2015). Can policing disorder reduce crime? A systematic review and meta-analysis. *Journal of Research in Crime and Delinquency*, 52(4), 567–588.

Branson, R. (2012, December 7). *War on drugs a trillion-dollar failure*. CNN. http://www.cnn.com/2012/12/06/opinion/branson-end-war-on-drugs/

Brehm, S. S., Kassin, S. M., & Fein, S. (1999). *Social psychology* (4th ed.). Houghton Mifflin.

Brewster, J., Stoloff, M., & Sanders, N. (2005). Effectiveness of citizen police academies in changing the attitudes, beliefs, and behavior of citizen participants. *American Journal of Criminal Justice*, 30(1), 21–34.

Brinegar v. United States, 338 U.S. 160 (1949).

Broderick, J. (1987). *Police in time of change*. Waveland Press.

Brooks, C. (2019). *Federal law enforcement officers, 2016—statistical tables* (NCJ 251922). U.S. Department of Justice, Bureau of Justice Statistics.

Brooks, C. (2020). *Local police departments: Policies and procedures, 2016* (NCJ 254826). U.S. Department of Justice, Bureau of Justice Statistics.

Brooks, L. W. (2010). Police discretionary behavior: A study of style. In R. G. Dunham & G. P. Alpert (Eds.), *Critical issues in policing: Contemporary readings* (6th ed., pp. 71–89). Waveland.

Brower v. County of Inyo, 486 U.S. 593 (1989).

Brown v. Mississippi, 297 U.S. 278 (1936).

Bruggeman, W. (2002). Policing and accountability in a dynamic European context. *Policing & Society*, 12(4), 259–273.

Bud, T. (2016). The rise and risks of police body-worn cameras in Canada. *Surveillance & Society*, 14(1), 117–121.

Bumgarner, J. (2006). *The growth of federal law enforcement in America*. Praeger.

Burns, R. G. (2013). *Policing: A modular approach*. Pearson.

Cafferty, P., & Engstrom, D. (2000). *Hispanics in the United States*. Transaction Books.

California v. Hodari D, 499 U.S. 621, 626 (1991).

Canter, D., Hammond, L., & Youngs, D. (2013). Cognitive bias in line-up identifications: The impact of administrator knowledge. *Science & Justice*, 53(2), 83–88.

Carlier, J., Lamberts, R., & Gersons, B. (1997). Risk factors for posttraumatic stress symptomatology in police officers: A prospective analysis. *Journal of Nervous and Mental Disease*, 185, 498–506.

Carroll v. United States, 267 U.S. 132 (1925).

Carter, D. L. (2004). *Law enforcement intelligence: A guide for state, local, and tribal law enforcement agencies*. Office of Community Oriented Policing Services.

Carter, D. L., & Radelet, L. A. (1999). *The police and the community* (6th ed.). Prentice Hall.

Cavender, G., & Deutsch, S. K. (2007). CSI and moral authority: The police and science. *Crime, Media, Culture*, 3, 67–81.

CBS 46. (October 30, 2017). *Former police officer convicted for accepting bribes, computer fraud*. https://www.cbs46.com/news/former-police-officer-convicted-for-accepting-bribes-computer-fraud/article_392292f8-9612-5b02-9d8d-2c2d-36b9e14a.html

Cebulak, W. (2004). Why rural crime and justice really matter. *Journal of Police and Criminal Psychology*, 19(1), 71–81.

Chapman, R., Baker, S., Bezdikian, V., Cammarata, P., Cohen, D., Leach, N., Schapiro, A., Scheider, M., Varano, R., & Boba, R. (2002). *Local law enforcement responds to terrorism: Lessons in prevention and preparedness*. U.S. Department of Justice, Office of Community Oriented Policing Services.

Cheema, R. (2016). Black and blue bloods: Protecting police officer families from domestic violence. *Family Court Review*, 54(3), 487–500.

Chimel v. California, 395 U.S. 752 (1969).

Chiquillo, J. (2017). *Girl pinned down at McKinney pool party sues ex-cop, city for $5 million*. Dallas News. https://www.dallasnews.com/news/mckinney/2017/01/03/girl-pinned-mckinney-pool-party-sues-ex-cop-city-5-million

Chriss, J. J. (2011). *Beyond community policing: From early American beginnings to the 21st century*. Paradigm.

City of Canton, Ohio v. Harris, 489 U.S. 378 (1989).

Clark, S. E., Brower, G. L., Rosenthal, R., Hicks, J. M., & Moreland, M. B. (2013). Lineup administrator influences on eyewitness identification and eyewitness confidence. *Journal of Applied Research in Memory and Cognition*, 2(3), 158–165.

Cleveland. (2018, October 29). *Drunken driver hits parked police car: Brunswick Hills Township police blotter*. https://www.cleveland.com/brunswick/index.ssf/2018/10/drunken_driver_hits_parked_pol.html

Coburn, J. (2016, August 13). Justice Department report expands on earlier inquiries into Baltimore police. *The Baltimore Sun*. http://www.baltimoresun.com/news/maryland/investigations/bs-md-sun-investigates-0814-20160813-story.html

Cochran, J. K., & Bromley, M. L. (2003). The myth (?) of the police subculture. *Policing: An International Journal of Police Strategies & Management*, 26(1), 88–117.

Cohen, S., & Prendergast, D. (2015, June 16). Violent crime surges—even with more cops on the streets. *New York Post*. http://nypost.com/2015/06/16/violent-crime-surges-even-with-more-cops-on-the-streets/

Cohen, S., Ruiz, R. R., & Childress, S. (2013, November 23). Departments are too slow to police their own abusers. *New York Times*. http://www.nytimes.com/projects/2013/police-domestic-abuse/

Community Oriented Policing Services. (2014). *Community policing defined. U.S. Department of Justice.* http://www.cops.usdoj.gov/pdf/vets-to-cops/e030917193-CP-Defined.pdf

Corcoran, K., & Baker, S. (2018, October 1). *It has been one year since the Las Vegas shooting rocked the US. Here's exactly how the nation's worse modern gun massacre unfolded. Business Insider.* https://www.businessinsider.com/timeline-shows-exactly-how-the-las-vegas-massacre-unfolded-2018-9

Cordner, G. (2013). The myth that science solves crimes. In R. M. Bohm & J. T. Walker (Eds.), *Demystifying crime & criminal justice* (2nd ed., pp. 157–165). Oxford University Press.

Corsianos, M. (2003). Discretion in detectives' decision making and "high profile" cases. *Police Practice and Research*, 4(3), 301–314.

Crank, J., & Caldero, M. (1999). *Police ethics: The corruption of noble cause.* Anderson.

Crank, J., Kadleck, C., & Koski, C. M. (2010). The USA: The next big thing. *Police Practices and Research*, 11(5), 405–422.

Crawford, C., & Burns, R. (2008). Police use of force: Assessing the impact of time and space. *Policing & Society*, 18(3), 322–335.

Crawford, C., & Burns, R. (2016). Reducing school violence: Considering school characteristics and the impacts of law enforcement, school security, and environmental factors. *Policing: An International Journal of Police Strategies & Management*, 39(3), 456–477.

Cronin, J. M., & Ederheimer, J. A. (2006). *Conducted energy devices: Development of standards for consistency and guidance.* U.S. Department of Justice Office of Community Oriented Policing Services and Police Executive Research Forum.

Cross, C. L., & Ashley, L. (2004). Police trauma and addiction: Coping with the dangers. *FBI Law Enforcement Bulletin*, 73(10), 24–31.

Daly, G. (2013, September 19). Embracing the police force of the future. *CNN.* http://www.cnn.com/2013/09/18/tech/innovation/police-future-technology/

Davis, C., & Erez, E. (1998). *Immigrant populations as victims: Toward a multicultural criminal justice system.* U.S. Department of Justice, Bureau of Justice Statistics.

Davis, E., Whyde, A., & Langton, L. (2018). *Contacts between police and the public, 2015* (NCJ 251145). U.S. Department of Justice, Bureau of Justice Statistics.

De Angelis, J., Rosenthal, R., & Buchner, B. (2016). *Civilian oversight of law enforcement.* National Association for Civilian Oversight of Law Enforcement.

DeCicco, D. A. (2000). Police officer candidate assessment and selection. *FBI Law Enforcement Bulletin*, 69(12), 1–6.

Decker, L. K., & Huckabee, R. G. (2002). Raising the age and education requirements for policing: Will too many women and minority candidates be excluded? *Policing: An International Journal of Police Strategies and Management*, 25(4), 789–802.

Delattre, E. J. (1996). *Character and cops: Ethics in policing* (3rd ed.). American Enterprise Institute.

del Carmen, R. V., & Hemmens C. (2017). *Criminal procedure: Law and practice* (10th ed.). Cengage.

Dempsey, J. S. (2003). *Introduction to investigations* (2nd ed.). Wadsworth.

Dempsey, J. S., & Forst, L. S. (2014). *An introduction to policing* (7th ed.). Delmar Cengage.

Department of Homeland Security. (2016, May 11). *Secretary Johnson announces new DHS mission statement.* https://www.dhs.gov/news/2016/05/11/secretary-johnson-announces-new-dhs-mission-statement

Diaz, J. (2019). *Guns confuse police and get people killed. KERA News.* https://www.keranews.org/2019-05-13/how-realistic-looking-toy-guns-confuse-police-and-get-people-killed

Doerner, W. G. (1997). The utility of the oral interview board in selecting police academy admissions. *Policing: An International Journal of Police Strategy and Management*, 20(4), 777–785.

Doerner, W. G., & Hunter, R. D. (2006). Post FTO performance evaluations of rookie police officers. *Journal of Ethnicity in Criminal Justice*, 4(1/2), 113–128.

Drug Policy Alliance. (2016). *So far, so good.* Drug Policy Alliance. http://www.drugpolicy.org/sites/default/files/Marijuana_Legalization_Status_Report_101316.pdf

Dulaney, W. M. (1996). *Black police in America.* Indiana University Press.

Durose, M. R., Burch, A. M., Walsh, K., & Tiry, E. (2016). *Publicly funded forensic crime laboratories: Resources and services, 2014* (NCJ 250151). U.S. Department of Justice, Bureau of Justice Statistics.

Ebel, J. (2018, October 22). *Three men charged in undercover sex sting operation. KTIV.* https://ktiv.com/2018/10/22/three-men-charged-in-under-cover-sex-sting-operation/

Editorial Board. (2015, July 5). Editorial: Police perjury: It's called "testilying." *Chicago Tribune.* http://www.chicagotribune.com/news/opinion/editorials/ct-police-false-testimony-edit-20150702-story.html

Eichenwald, K. (2014, August 18). Why militarized police departments don't work. *Newsweek.* http://www.newsweek.com/2014/08/29/why-militarized-police-departments-dont-work-265214.html

Elfrink, T. (2018, November 30). "It's still a blast beating people": St. Louis police indicted in assault of undercover police officer posing as protestor. *Washington Post.* https://www.washingtonpost.com/nation/2018/11/30/its-still-blast-beating-people-st-louis-police-indicted-assault-undercover-officer-posing-protester/?utm_term=.62edf99870b9

Elmer-DeWitt, P., Constable, A., & Goodgame, D. (1985, October 14). Computers: Taking a byte out of crime. *Time.* http://content.time.com/time/magazine/article/0,9171,960128,00.html

Esbensen, F., Peterson, D., Taylor, T. J., Freng, A., Osgood, D. W., Carson, D. C., & Matsuda, K. N. (2011). Evaluation and evolution of the Gang Resistance Education and Training (G.R.E.A.T.) program. *Journal of School Violence*, 10, 53–70.

Ethington, P. J. (1987). Vigilantes and the police: The creation of a professional police bureaucracy in San Francisco. *Journal of Social History*, 21(2), 197–227.

Falcone, D. N., Wells, L. E., & Weisheit, R. A. (2002). The small-town police department. *Policing: An International Journal of Police Strategies & Management*, 25, 371–384.

Famega, C. N. (2005). Variation in officer downtime: A review of the research. *Policing: An International Journal of Police Strategies & Management*, 28(3), 388–414.

Federal Bureau of Investigation. (n.d.). *Joint terrorism task forces.* https://www.fbi.gov/investigate/terrorism/joint-terrorism-task-forces

Federal Bureau of Investigation. (2017). *Next generation identification.* https://www.fbi.gov/services/cjis/fingerprints-and-other-biometrics/ngi

Federal Bureau of Investigation. (2020a). *Crime in the United States—2018, Table 43: Arrests by race and ethnicity, 2018.* https://ucr.fbi.gov/crime-in-the-u.s/2018/crime-in-the-u.s.-2018/tables/table-43

Federal Bureau of Investigation. (2020b). *Officers feloniously killed.* https://ucr.fbi.gov/leoka/2019/topic-pages/officers-feloniously-killed

Fenton, J. (2018, December 6). Feds: Ex-Baltimore police officer admitted misconduct, expanding scope of Gun Trace Task Force corruption probe. *Baltimore Sun.* https://www.baltimoresun.com/news/maryland/investigations/bs-md-ci-gttf-ryckman-letter-20181204-story.html

Ferdik, F. V., Kaminski, R. J., Cooney, M. D., & Sevigny, E. L. (2014). The influence of agency policies on conducted energy device use and police use of lethal force. *Police Quarterly*, 17, 328–358.

Ferguson unrest: From shooting to nationwide protests. (2015, August 10). *BBC News.* http://www.bbc.com/news/world-us-canada-30193354

Fernandez, P. (2020). *Defunding the police will actually make us safer. American Civil Liberties Union.* https://www.aclu.org/news/criminal-law-reform/defunding-the-police-will-actually-make-us-safer/

Finn, P. (2010, September 22). Risk of small-scale attacks by al-Qaeda and its allies is rising, officials say. *Washington Post.* http://www.washington-post.com/wp-dyn/content/article/2010/09/22/AR2010092203807_pf.html

Fischer, R. J., Halibozek, E., & Green, G. (2008). *Introduction to security* (8th ed.). Butterworth-Heinemann.

Flynn, K. W. (2002). Training and police violence. In R. G. Burns & C. E. Crawford (Eds.), *Policing and violence* (pp. 127–146). Prentice Hall.

Folkart, B. A. (1986, December 25). Marquette Frye, whose arrest ignited the Watts riots in 1965, dies at age 42. *Los Angeles Times.* http://articles.latimes.com/1986-12-25/local/me-486_1_marquette-frye

Folkman, S. (2008). The case for positive emotions in the stress process. *Anxiety, Stress & Coping*, 21(1), 3–14.

Fort Lauderdale Police Department. (2013). *Hiring police officers.* http://www.flpd.org/home/showdocument?id=4168

Fort Worth Police Department. (2021). *About FWPD.* https://police.fortworthtexas.gov/About/

Francisco, T. (2018, August 21). *Chicago police take disciplinary action after photo of cops sleeping on the job goes viral. WGNTV.* https://wgntv.com/2018/08/20/chicago-police-take-disciplinary-action-after-photo-of-cops-sleeping-on-the-job-goes-viral/

Friend, Z. (2013, April 9). Predictive policing: Using technology to solve crime. *FBI Law Enforcement Bulletin.* https://leb.fbi.gov/2013/april/predictive-policing-using-technology-to-reduce-crime

Frum, D. (2017, April 24). How Trump is upending the conventional wisdom on illegal immigration. *The Atlantic.* https://www.theatlantic.com/politics/archive/2017/04/how-trump-is-upending-the-conventional-wisdom-on-illegal-immigration/524058/

Gaines, L. K., & Kappeler, V. E. (2011). *Policing in America* (7th ed.). Anderson.

Gaines, L. K., & Worrall, J. L. (2012). *Police administration* (3rd ed.). Delmar/Cengage.

Gang Resistance Education and Training. (2017). *What is G.R.E.A.T.?* https://www.great-online.org/About/What-Is-GREAT

Garrick, D. (2018, December 11). Police shortage prompts San Diego incentives, finder's fees. *San Diego Union–Tribune.* https://www.sandiegouniontribune.com/news/politics/sd-me-police-incentive-20181211-story.html

Gau, J. M., & Gaines, D. C. (2012). Top-down management and patrol officers' attitudes about the importance of public order maintenance: A research note. *Police Quarterly*, 15(1), 45–61.

Germann, A. C., Day, F. D., & Gallati, R. J. (1970). *Introduction to law enforcement and criminal justice.* Charles C. Thomas.

Gershon, R. R. M., Barocas, B., Canton, A. N., Li, X., & Vlahov, D. (2009). Mental, physical, and behavioral outcomes associated with perceived work stress in police officers. *Criminal Justice and Behavior*, 36(3), 275–289.

Gerspacher, N. (2008). The history of international police cooperation: A 150-year evolution in trends and approaches. *Global Crime*, 9(1–2), 169–184.

Gilberstadt, H. (2020, June 5). *A month before George Floyd's death, Black and White Americans differed sharply in confidence in the police. Pew Research.* https://www.pewresearch.org/fact-tank/2020/06/05/a-month-before-george-floyds-death-black-and-white-americans-differed-sharply-in-confidence-in-the-police/

Goldstein, H. (1990). *Problem-oriented policing.* McGraw-Hill.

Goldstein, H. (1997). Toward community-oriented policing: Potential, basic requirements and threshold questions. *Crime & Delinquency*, 33, 6–36.

Graham v. Connor, 490 U.S. 386 (1989).

Gray, M. (2013, October 22). Surveillance is so dope: Google Earth helps bust pot farm. *Time.* http://newsfeed.time.com/2013/10/22/surveillance-is-so-dope-google-earth-helps-bust-pot-farm/

Greenwood, P. W., & Turner, S. (2011). Juvenile crime and juvenile justice. In J. Q. Wilson & J. Petersilia (Eds.), *Crime and public policy* (pp. 88–129). Oxford University Press.

Guffey, J. E., Larson, J. G., Zimmerman, L., & Shook, B. (2007). The development of a Thurstone scale for identifying desirable police officer traits. *Journal of Police and Criminal Psychology*, 22, 1–9.

Haberfeld, M., MacDonald, W., & von Hassell, A. (2008). International cooperation in policing: A partial answer to the query? In M. R. Haberfeld & I. Cerrah (Eds.), *Comparative policing: The struggle for democratization* (pp. 341–375). Sage.

Harcourt, B. E. (2001). *Illusion of order: The false promise of broken windows policing.* Harvard University Press.

Harrell, E., & Davis, E. (2020). *Contacts between police and the public, 2018—statistical tables* (NCJ 25,57,30). U.S. Department of Justice, Bureau of Justice Statistics.

He, N., Zhao, J., & Archbold, C. (2002). Gender and police stress: The convergent and divergent impact of work environment, work–family conflict, and stress coping mechanisms of female and male police officers. *Policing: An International Journal of Police Strategies & Management*, 25(4), 687–708.

Hess, K. M., & Wrobleski, H. M. (1996). *Introduction to private security* (4th ed.). West.

Hickman, M. J. (2003). *Tribal law enforcement, 2000* (NCJ 197936). U.S. Department of Justice, Bureau of Justice Statistics.

Holley, P. (2016, March 9). The latest policing tool to monitor rowdy spring breakers: Drones. *Washington Post.* https://www.washingtonpost.com/news/innovations/wp/2016/03/09/the-latest-policing-tool-to-monitor-rowdy-spring-breakers-drones/

Ho, V. (2018, October 31). After third Taser death, California police officials reconsider "less-lethal" weapon. *The Guardian.* https://www.theguardian.com/world/2018/oct/31/san-mateo-county-taser-death-law-enforcement

Horowitz, J. M. (2019, April 9). *Race in America 2019. Pew Research.* https://www.pewsocialtrends.org/2019/04/09/race-in-america-2019/#majorities-of-black-and-white-adults-say-blacks-are-treated-less-fairly-than-whites-in-dealing-with-police-and-by-the-criminal-justice-system

Hsu, S. S. (2010, May 27). Arizona immigration law will boost crime, police chiefs tell U.S. attorney general. *Washington Post.* http://www.washingtonpost.com/wp-dyn/content/article/2010/05/26/AR2010052601200.html?nav=emailpage

Hsu, S. S. (2015, April 18). FBI admits flaws in hair analysis over decades. *Washington Post.* https://www.washingtonpost.com/local/crime/fbi-overstated-forensic-hair-matches-in-nearly-all-criminal-trials-for-decades/2015/04/18/39c8d8c6-e515-11e4-b510-962fcfabc310_story.html

Huff, J., White, M. D., & Decker S. H. (2018). Organizational correlates of police deviance. *Policing: An International Journal*, 41(4), 465–481.

Hyland, S. S. (2018). *Body-worn cameras in law enforcement agencies, 2016* (NCJ 251775). U.S. Department of Justice, Bureau of Justice Statistics.

Hyland, S. S., & Davis, E. (2019). *Local police departments, 2016: Personnel* (NCJ 252835). U.S. Department of Justice, Bureau of Justice Statistics.

Indeed. (2020). *How much does a police officer make in the United States?* https://www.indeed.com/career/police-officer/salaries

In re Gault, 387 U.S. 1 (1967).

International Association of Chiefs of Police. (2004). *Impact of video enhancement on modern policing: Research and best practices from the IACP study on in-car cameras.*

INTERPOL (2018, October 23). *Illicit online pharmaceuticals: 500 tonnes seized in global operation.* https://www.interpol.int/News-and-Events/News/2018/Illicit-online-pharmaceuticals-500-tonnes-seized-in-global-operation

Jacobs, D., & O'Brien, R. (1998). The determinants of deadly force: A structural analysis of police violence. *American Journal of Sociology*, 103, 837–862.

Jennings, W. G., Fridell, L. A., & Lynch, M. D. (2014). Cops and cameras: Officer perceptions of the use of body-worn cameras in law enforcement. *Journal of Criminal Justice*, 42(6), 549–556.

Johnson, B. D., Golub, A., & Dunlap, E. (2006). The rise and decline of hard drugs, drug markets, and violence in inner-city New York. In A. Blumstein & J. Wallman (Eds.), *The crime drop in America* (pp. 164–206). Cambridge University Press.

Johnson, K. (2006, October 2). Police, firefighters challenge residency rules. *USA Today.* http://usatoday30.usatoday.com/news/nation/2006-10-02-residency-rules_x.htm

Johnson, K. (2012, November 16). More police require body armor. *USA Today.* https://www.usatoday.com/story/news/nation/2012/11/15/more-law-enforcement-agencies-require-body-armor/1707913/

Johnson, R. R., & Rhodes, T. N. (2009). Urban and small town comparison of citizen demand for police services. *International Journal of Police Science & Management*, 11(1), 27–38.

Joseph, J. (2009). Technoprison: Technology and prisons. In R. Muraskin & A. R. Roberts (Eds.), *Visions for change: Crime and justice in the twenty-first century* (5th ed., pp. 13–33). Pearson Prentice Hall.

Kappeler, V., Sluder, R. D., & Alpert, G. (1998). *Forces of deviance: Understanding the dark side of policing.* Waveland.

Kerrigan, H. (2011). Data-driven policing. *Governing*, 24(8), 54–55.

Kim, Y. S., Barak, G., & Shelton, D. E. (2009). Examining the "CSI-effect" in the cases of circumstantial evidence and eyewitness testimony: Multivariate and path analyses. *Journal of Criminal Justice*, 37, 452–460.

King, M. J. (2005, October). "Deliberate indifference": Liability for failure to train. *FBI Law Enforcement Bulletin*, 74(10), 22–31.

King, W. R., & Matusiak, M. C. (2013). The myth that police use of force is widespread. In R. M. Bohm & J. T. Walker (Eds.), *Demystifying crime & criminal justice* (2nd ed., pp. 178–184). Oxford University Press.

Kirschman, E. (2007). *I love a cop: What police families need to know.* Guilford Press.

Kirschman, E. (2018). Cops and PTSD. *Psychology Today.* https://www.psychologytoday.com/us/blog/cop-doc/201811/cops-and-ptsd

Kleck, G., & Barnes, J. C. (2014). Do more police lead to more crime deterrence? *Crime & Delinquency*, 60(5), 716–738.

Kochel, T. R., Wilson, D. B., & Mastrofski, S. D. (2011). Effect of suspect race on officers' arrest decisions. *Criminology*, 49(2), 473–512.

Kopan, T., & de Vogue, A. (2016, June 23). *Supreme Court oks warrant-less breathalyzer tests in drunk driving arrests. CNN Today.* http://www.cnn.com/2016/06/23/politics/supreme-court-drunk-driving-breathalyzers-birchfield/

Langton, L. (2010). *Women in law enforcement, 1987–2008* (NCJ 2,30,521). U.S. Department of Justice, Bureau of Justice Statistics.

Lanier, M., & Jockin, K. (2009). Contemporary policewomen: A working typology. In R. Muraskin & A. R. Roberts (Eds.), *Visions for change: Crime and justice in the twenty-first century* (5th ed., pp. 314–327). Pearson Prentice Hall.

Larned, J. G. (2010). Understanding police suicide. *The Forensic Examiner, Fall*, 64–71.

LaTourrette, T. (2010). The life-saving effectiveness of body armor for police officers. *Journal of Occupational and Environmental Hygiene*, 7, 557–562.

Laythe, J. (2002). "Trouble on the outside, trouble on the inside"; Growing pains, social change, and small town policing—the Eugene Police Department, 1862–1932. *Police Quarterly*, 5(1), 96–112.

Lee, T. L. (2016). Tennessee citizen police academies: Program and participant characteristics. *American Journal of Criminal Justice*, 41(2), 236–254.

Leger, D. L. (2014, January 30). Police carry special drug to reverse heroin overdoses. *USA Today.* https://www.usatoday.com/story/news/nation/2014/01/30/police-use-narcan-to-reverse-heroin-overdoses/5063587/

Lersch, K. (2013). The myths surrounding policewomen on patrol. In R. M. Bohm & J. T. Walker (Eds.), *Demystifying crime & criminal justice* (2nd ed., pp. 166–177). Oxford University Press.

Lersch, K. M., & Mieczkowski, T. (2005). Drug testing sworn law enforcement officers: One agency's experience. *Journal of Criminal Justice*, 33(3), 289–297.

Levitt, S. D. (2004). Understanding why crime fell in the 1990s: Four factors that explain the decline and six that do not. *Journal of Economic Perspectives*, 18(1), 163–190.

Lindsay, V., & Shelley, K. (2009). Social and stress-related influences on police officers' alcohol consumption. *Journal of Police Criminal Psychology*, 24, 87–92.

Lonon, S. (2016, March 7). Clearwater crime map now available. *Clearwater Patch.* https://patch.com/florida/clearwater/clearwater-crime-map-now-available-0

Lonsway, K., Moore, M., Harrington, P., Smeal, E., & Spillar, K. (2003). *Hiring & retaining more women: The advantages to law enforcement agencies.* National Center for Women & Policing. http://womenandpolicing.com/pdf/newadvantagesreport.pdf

Lowry, L. (2014, September 8). Polygraph tests help in Oklahoma criminal investigations. *News 9.* http://www.news9.com/story/26479726/

polygraph-tests-help-in-oklahoma-criminal-investigations

Lyman, M. D. (2010). *The police: An introduction* (4th ed.). Pearson.

Lynch, J., Boyette, C. & Simon, D. (2017, March 3). What is MS-13? The "transnational" street gang on the FBI's radar. *CNN*. http://www.cnn.com/2017/03/03/us/ms-13-gang-explained-street-gang-international/

Ma, C. C., Andrew, M. E., Fekedulegn, D., Gu, J. K., Hartley, T. A., Charles, L. E., Violanti, J. M., & Burchfiel, C. M. (2015). Shift work and occupational stress in police officers. *Safety and Health at Work*, 6, 25–29.

MacDonald, H. (2004). *Crime & the illegal alien: The fallout from crippled immigration enforcement.* Center for Immigration Studies.

Madani, D., & Li, D. K. (2019, August 23). *Ex-Houston police officer charged with murder after deadly drug trial. NBC News.* https://www.nbcnews.com/news/us-news/ex-houston-police-officer-charged-murder-after-deadly-drug-raid-n1006196

Maher, T. M. (2003). Police sexual misconduct: Officers' perceptions of its extent and causality. *Criminal Justice Review*, 28(2), 355–381.

Mapp v. Ohio, 367 U.S. 643 (1961).

Marmar, C. R., McCaslin, S. E., Metzler, T. J., Best, S., Weiss, D. S., Fagan, J., & Neylan, T. (2006). Predictors of posttraumatic stress in police officers and other first responders. *Annals of the New York Academy of Sciences*, 1071(1), 1–18.

Martinez, L. (2006, August). Real-life recruiting. *Law Enforcement Technology*, 33(8), 10–16.

Maryland v. Buie, 494 U.S. 325 (1990).

Maryland v. King, 569 U.S. 435 (2013).

McCarty, W. P., Zhao, J., & Garland, B. E. (2007). Occupational stress and burnout between male and female police officers: Are there any gender differences? *Policing: An International Journal of Police Strategies & Management*, 30, 672–685.

McCoy, S. P., & Aamodt, M. G. (2010). A comparison of law enforcement divorce rates with those of other occupations. *Journal of Police and Criminal Psychology*, 25, 1–16.

McNamara, R., & Burns, R. (2020). *Multiculturalism, crime, and criminal justice* (2nd ed.). Oxford University Press.

Menton, C. (2008). Bicycle patrols: An underutilized resource. *Policing: An International Journal of Police Strategies & Management*, 31(1), 93–108.

Merica, D. (2013, May 9). *Boston's top cop asked if bombing was preventable. CNN.* http://www.cnn.com/2013/05/09/politics/boston-bombing-hearing/

Mieczkowski, T. (2002). Drug abuse, corruption, and officer drug testing: An overview. In K. M. Lersch (Ed.), *Policing and misconduct* (pp. 157–192). Prentice Hall.

Mieczkowski, T. (2004). Drug testing the police: Some results of urinalysis and hair analysis in a major U.S. metropolitan police force. *Journal of Forensic Medicine*, 3, 115–122.

Miller, M. R. (1995). *Police patrol operations.* Copperhouse.

Miller, L. S., & Hess, K. M. (2005). *Community policing: Partnerships for problem solving* (4th edition). Wadsworth.

Minnesota v. Dickerson, 508 U.S. 366 (1993).

Miranda v. Arizona, 384 U.S. 436 (1966).

Mitchell, M. (2014, February 23). Bedford police work to keep residents out of jail, hospital. *Fort Worth Star–Telegram.* http://www.startelegram.com/news/local/crime/article3846924.html

Montgomery, D. (2020). *COVID-19 curbs community policing at a time of diminishing trust. Pew Trusts.* https://www.pewtrusts.org/en/research-and-analysis/blogs/stateline/2020/10/01/covid-19-curbs-community-policing-at-a-time-of-diminishing-trust

Morgan, R. E. (2014). *Crimes against the elderly, 2003–2013* (NCJ 2,48,339). U.S. Department of Justice, Bureau of Justice Statistics.

Mount Lebanon Police Department. (2019). *Now accepting applications – MLPD is hiring police officers.* http://mtlebanonpd.org/now-accepting-applications-mlpd-is-hiring-police-officers/

Muir, W. (1977). *Police: Streetcorner politicians.* University of Chicago Press.

Na, C., & Gottfredson, D. C. (2013). Police officers in schools: Effects on school crime and the processing of offending behaviors. *Justice Quarterly*, 30(4), 619–650.

Nalla, M. K. (2001). Designing an introductory survey course in private security. *Journal of Criminal Justice Education*, 12, 35–52.

Nashville. (2018). *Police department—family support groups.* https://www.nashville.gov/Police-Department/Administrative-Services/Behavioral-Health-Services/Family-Support-Groups.aspx

National Advisory Commission on Civil Disorders. (1967). *Report of the National Advisory Commission on Civil Disorders.* Bantam Books.

Newburn, T., & Jones, T. (2007). Symbolizing crime control: Reflections on zero tolerance. *Theoretical Criminology*, 11(2), 221–243.

Newport, F. (2016, July 28). *Americans offer solutions for problem of deadly shootings. Gallup.* http://www.gallup.com/poll/194012/americans-offer-solutions-problem-deadly-shootings.aspx?g_source=police%20and%20shootings&g_medium=search&g_campaign=tiles

New York City Police Department. (2019, May 22). *NYPD launches "Summer All-Out" with additional police officers to further reduce crime and violence.* https://www1.nyc.gov/site/nypd/news/pr0522/nypd-launches-summer-all-out-additional-police-officers-further-reduce-crime-violence

New York v. Belton, 453 U.S. 454 (1981).

New York v. Quarles, 467 U.S. 649 (1984).

Nix v. Williams, 467 U.S. 431 (1984).

Novak, K. J., Brown, R. A., & Frank, J. (2011). Women on patrol: An analysis of differences in officer arrest behavior. *Policing: An International Journal*, 34(4), 566–587.

O'Connell, P. E. (2008). The chess master's game: A model for incorporating local police agencies in the fight against global terrorism. *Policing: An International Journal of Police Strategies & Management*, 31(3), 456–465.

Officer Down Memorial Page. (2020). *Fallen officers from the COVID-19 pandemic.* https://www.odmp.org/search/incident/covid-19

O'Hara, A. F., Violanti, J. M., Levenson, R. L., & Clark, R. G. (2013). National police suicide estimates: Web surveillance study III. *International Journal of Emergency Mental Health and Human Resilience*, 15(1), 31–38.

Office of Juvenile Justice and Delinquency Prevention. (2018). *Statistical briefing book.* https://www.ojjdp.gov/ojstatbb/crime/faqs.asp

Office of Juvenile Justice and Delinquency Prevention. (2020). *Statistical briefing book.* https://www.ojjdp.gov/ojstatbb/crime/qa05101.asp?qaDate=2019

Oliver, W. M. (2006). The fourth era of policing: Homeland security. *International Review of Law, Computers & Technology*, 20(1/2), 49–62.

Oliver, W. M. (2007). *Homeland security for policing.* Prentice Hall.

Oliver, W. M. (2008). August Vollmer. In J. Bumgarner (Ed.), *Icons of crime fighting: Relentless pursuers of justice* (vol. 1, pp. 83–115). Greenwood Press.

Oliver, W. M., & Hilgenberg, J. F., Jr. (2006). *A history of crime and criminal justice in America.* Pearson Allyn & Bacon.

Paoline, E. A., III, Myers, S. M., & Worden, R. E. (2000). Police culture, individualism, and community policing: Evidence from two police departments. *Justice Quarterly*, 17(3), 575–605.

Peak, K. J., & Glensor, R. W. (2004). *Community policing and problem solving: Strategies and practices.* Pearson Prentice Hall.

Pearl, B. (2018, June 27). *Ending the war on drugs: By the numbers. Center for American Progress.* https://www.americanprogress.org/issues/criminal-justice/reports/2018/06/27/452819/ending-war-drugs-numbers/

Pearsall, B. (2010). Predictive policing: The future of law enforcement? *NIJ Journal*, 266.

Perez, A. D., Berg, K. M, & Myers, D. J. (2003). Police and riots, 1967–1969. *Journal of Black Studies*, 34(2), 153–182.

Perez, C., & McCluskey, J. D. (2004). Diversity in policing: Latino representation in law enforcement. *Journal of Ethnicity in Criminal Justice*, 2(3), 67–81.

Peterson, C., Stone, D. M., Marsh, S. M., Schumacher, P. K., Tiesman, H. M., McIntosh, W. L., Lokey, C. N., Trudeau, A.-R. T., Bartholow, B., & Luo, F. (2018). Suicide rates by major occupational group—17 states, 2012 and 2015. *Morbidity and Mortality Weekly Report*, 67, 1253–1260.

Pew Research Center. (2019, June 12). *Mobile fact sheet.* https://www.pewresearch.org/internet/fact-sheet/mobile/

Piza, E. L., & O'Hara, B. A. (2012). Saturation foot-patrol in a high-violence area: A quasi-experimental evaluation. *Justice Quarterly*, 31(4), 693–718.

Podlas, K. (2006). The "CSI effect": Exposing the media myth. *Fordham Intellectual Property, Media and Entertainment Law Journal*, 16, 429–465.

Police Foundation, the. (1981). *The Newark foot patrol experiment.*

Purpura, P. P. (2007). *Terrorism and homeland security: An introduction with applications.* Butterworth–Heinemann.

Rabe-Hemp, C. (2008). Female officers and the ethic of care: Does officer gender impact police behaviors? *Journal of Criminal Justice*, 36(5), 426–434.

Ratcliffe, J. H., Taniguchi, T., Groff, E. R., & Wood, J. D. (2011). The Philadelphia foot patrol experiment: A randomized controlled trial of police patrol effectiveness in violent crime hotspots. *Criminology*, 49(3), 795–831.

Ray, R. (2020). *What does "defund the police" mean and does it have merit? Brookings Institution.* https://www.brookings.edu/blog/fixgov/2020/06/19/what-does-defund-the-police-mean-and-does-it-have-merit/

Reaves, B. A. (2010). *Local police departments, 2007* (NCJ 2,31,174). U.S. Department of Justice, Bureau of Justice Statistics.

Reaves, B. A. (2011). *Census of state and local law enforcement agencies, 2008* (NCJ 2,33,982). U.S. Department of Justice, Bureau of Justice Statistics.

Reaves, B. A. (2012a). *Federal law enforcement officers, 2008* (NCJ 2,38,250). U.S. Department of Justice, Bureau of Justice Statistics.

Reaves, B. A. (2012b). *Hiring and retention of state and local law enforcement officers, 2009—statistical tables* (NCJ 2,38,251). U.S. Department of Justice, Bureau of Justice Statistics.

Reaves, B. A. (2015a). *Local police departments, 2013: Personnel, policies, and practices* (NCJ 2,48,677). U.S. Department of Justice, Bureau of Justice Statistics.

Reaves, B. A. (2015b). *Local police departments, 2013: Equipment and technology* (NCJ 2,48,767). U.S. Department of Justice, Bureau of Justice Statistics.

Reaves, B. A. (2016). *State and local law enforcement training academies, 2013* (NCJ 249784). U.S. Department of Justice, Bureau of Justice Statistics.

Rector, K. (2017, April 19). Justice investigation, police administrative review of Freddie Gray's arrest and death both remain open two years later. *Baltimore Sun*. http://www.baltimoresun.com/news/maryland/investigations/bs-md-ci-gray-investigations-20170419-story.html

Report of the Independent Commission on the Los Angeles Police Department. (1991, July 9). p. iii. https://archive.org/details/ChristopherCommissionLAPD/page/n21/mode/2up

Rice, G. E. (2015, June 17). Secondary trauma program helps Kansas City police cope with emotional toll of job experiences. *Kansas City Star*. http://www.kansascity.com/news/local/crime/article24826237.html

Richmond, R., Wodak, A., Kehoe, L., & Heather, N. (1998). How healthy are the police? A survey of lifestyle factors. *Addiction*, 93, 1729–1737.

Riksheim, E. C., & Chermak, S. M. (1993). Causes of police behavior revisited. *Journal of Criminal Justice*, 21(4), 353–382.

Roberg, R., & Bonn, S. (2004). Higher education and policing: Where are we now? *Policing: An International Journal of Police Strategies & Management*, 27(4), 469–486.

Roberg, R., Novak, K., Cordner, G., & Smith, B. (2015). *Police & society* (6th ed.). Oxford University Press.

Roberson, C., & Birzer, M. L. (2010). *Introduction to private security: Theory meets practice*. Pearson Prentice Hall.

Roberts, D. E. (1999). Race, vagueness, and the social meaning order-maintenance policing. *Journal of Criminal Law & Criminology*, 89(3), 775–836.

Roberts, K. (2019). Correlates of law enforcement suicide in the United States: A comparison with army and firefighter suicides using data from the national Violent Death Reporting System. *Police Practice and Research*, 20(1), 64–76.

Rogers, B. (2018, September 20). Houston's DPS crime lab investigated for mix-up in mailing blood sample. *Houston Chronicle*. https://www.houston-chronicle.com/news/houston-texas/houston/article/Houston-s-DPS-crime-lab-investigated-for-mix-up-13245980.php

Roman, J. K., Reid, S. E., Chalfin, A. J., & Knight, C. R. (2009). The DNA field experiment: A randomized trial of the cost-effectiveness of using DNA to solve property crimes. *Journal of Experimental Criminology*, 5, 345–369.

Ropero-Miller, J. (2016). *State forensic science commissions: Final report*. National Institute of Justice, Forensic Technology Center of Excellence.

Rosenbaum, D. P., & Hanson, G. S. (1998). Assessing the effects of school-based drug education: A six-year multilevel analysis of project D.A.R.E. *Journal of Research in Crime and Delinquency*, 35, 381–412.

Rosenfeld, R., Fornango, R., & Rengifo, A. F. (2007). The impact of order-maintenance policing on New York City homicide and robbery rates: 1988–2001. *Criminology*, 45(2), 355–384.

Rosenfeld, R., & Messner, S. F. (2010). The normal crime rate, the economy, and mass incarceration. In H. D. Barlow & S. H Decker (Eds.), *Criminology and public policy: Putting theory to work* (pp. 45–65). Temple University Press.

Roth, M. P. (2005). *Crime and punishment: A history of the criminal justice system*. Thomson/Wadsworth.

Rubin, R. (2016, November 16). Many states have legalized medical marijuana, so why does DEA still say it has no therapeutic use? *Forbes*. https://www.forbes.com/sites/ritarubin/2016/11/16/many-states-have-legalized-medical-marijuana-so-why-does-dea-still-say-it-has-no-therapeutic-use/#615190e67ec2

Saferstein, R. (2007). *Criminalistics: An introduction to forensic science* (9th ed.). Pearson Prentice Hall.

Sampson, R. J. (2008). Rethinking crime and immigration. *Contexts, Winter*, 28–33.

Schultz, P. D. (2008). The future is here: Technology in police departments. *The Police Chief*, 75(6), 20–22, 24–25.

Sciarabba, A. L., & Sullivan, C. G. (2010). Transnational crime and the law: An overview of current practices. In J. A. Eterno & D. K. Das (Eds.), *Police practices in global perspective* (pp. 225–250). Rowman & Littlefield.

Scrivner, E. (1991). Helping police families cope with stress. *Law Enforcement Bulletin*, 15, 6.

Silverthorne Lumber Co. v. United States, 251 U.S. 385 (1920).

Simpson, I. (2017, March 1). *Seven Baltimore police officers arrested on racketeering charges. Reuters*. http://www.reuters.com/article/us-baltimore-police-idUSKBN1685SC

Skolnick, J. (1966). *Justice without trial: Law enforcement in democratic society*. John Wiley & Sons.

Smalley, S. (2006, July 30). 75 officers failed city drug tests: Cocaine use more prevalent, raising concern. *Boston Globe*. http://archive.boston.com/news/local/articles/2006/07/30/75_officers_failed_city_drug_tests

Smith, M. R., & Petrocelli, M. (2001). Racial profiling? A multivariate analysis of police traffic stop data. *Police Quarterly*, 4(1), 4–27.

Sommers, R. (2016). Will putting cameras on police reduce polarization? *The Yale Law Journal*, 125(15), 1304–1356.

Sorcher, S. (2013, February 23). The backlash against drones. *National Journal*, p. 7.

Sousa, W., & Gauthier, J. F. (2008). Gender differences in officers' evaluations of police work: A survey of job satisfaction in the police workplace. *Justice Policy Journal*, 5(1), 1–24.

State v. Murphy, 465 p.2d 900, 902 (Or.App) (1970).

Statista. (2020). *Gender distribution of full-time law enforcement employees in the United States in 2019*. https://www.statista.com/statistics/195324/gender-distribution-of-full-time-law-enforcement-employees-in-the-us/

Stewart, D. S., & Morris, R. G. (2009). A new era of policing? An examination of Texas police chiefs' perceptions of homeland security. *Criminal Justice Policy Review*, 20(3), 290–309.

Stinson, P. M., Sr., Liederbach, J., Lab, S. P., & Brewer, S. L, Jr. (2016). *Police integrity lost: A study of law enforcement officers arrested*. National Institute of Justice, Office of Justice Programs, U.S. Department of Justice.

Substance Abuse and Mental Health Services Administration. (2019). *Key substance use and mental health indicators in the United States: Results from the 2018 National Survey on Drug Use and Health* (HHS Publication No. PEP19-5068, NSDUH Series H-54). Center for Behavioral Health Statistics and Quality, Substance Abuse and Mental Health Services Administration. https://www.samhsa.gov/data/sites/default/files/cbhsq-reports/NSDUHNationalFindingsReport2018/NSDUHNationalFindingsReport2018.pdf

Sullivan, J., Jenkins, J., Tate, J., Courtney, S., & Houston, J. (2016). In two years, police killed 86 people brandishing guns that look real—but aren't. *Washington Post*. https://www.washingtonpost.com/investigations/in-two-years-police-killed-86-people-brandishing-guns-that-look-real—but-arent/2016/12/18/ec005c3a-b025-11e6-be1c-8cec35b1ad25_story.html?noredirect=on&utm_term=.be383f0f5136

Swanson, C. R., Territo, L., & Taylor, R. W. (2012). *Police administration: Structures, processes, and behaviors* (8th ed.). Pearson.

Swatt, M. L., Gibson, C. L., & Piquero, N. L. (2007). Exploring the utility of general strain theory in explaining problematic alcohol consumption by police officers. *Journal of Criminal Justice*, 35, 596–611.

Taylor, B., Kubu, B., Fridell, L., Rees, C., Jordan, T., & Cheney, J. (2006). *Cop crunch: Identifying strategies for dealing with the recruiting and hiring crisis in law enforcement*. U.S. Department of Justice, Police Executive Research Forum.

Tennessee v. Garner, 471 U.S. 1 (1985).

Territo, L., & Sewell, J. D. (2007). *Stress management in policing* (2nd ed.). Carolina Academic Press.

Terrill, W., & Ingram, J. R. (2016). Citizen complaints against the police: An eight city examination. *Police Quarterly*, 19(2), 150–179.

Terrill, W., & Paoline, E. A., III. (2013). Less lethal force policy and police officer perceptions: A multi-site examination. *Criminal Justice and Behavior*, 40, 1109–1130.

Terrill, W., & Paoline, E. A., III. (2017). Police use of less lethal force: Does administrative policy matter? *Justice Quarterly*, 34(2), 193–216.

Terrill, W., & Reisig, M. D. (2003). Neighborhood context and police use of force. *Journal of Research in Crime and Delinquency*, 40(3), 291–323.

Terry, W. C. I. (1981). Police stress: The empirical evidence. *Journal of Police Science and Administration*, 9(1), 61–75.

Terry v. Ohio, 392 U.S. 1 (1968).

Test Country. (n.d.). *Drug testing for police officers and police departments*. https://abouttesting.testcountry.com/2009/10/drug-testing-for-police-officers-and-police-departments.html

Tewksbury, R., & West, A. (2001). Crime victims' satisfaction with police services: An assessment in one urban county. *The Justice Professional*, 14(4), 271–285.

Texas Forensic Science Commission. (2018). *About us*. http://www.txcourts.gov/fsc/about-us/

Theodore, N. (2013). *Insecure communities: Latino perceptions of police involvement in immigration enforcement*. https://greatcities.uic.edu/wp-content/uploads/2014/05/Insecure_Communities_Report_FINAL.pdf

Theriot, M. T. (2009). School resource officers and the criminalization of student behavior. *Journal of Criminal Justice*, 40, 257–273.

Uchida, C. (1993). The development of the American police: An historical overview. In R. Dunham & G. Alpert (Eds.), *Critical issues in policing: Contemporary readings* (2nd ed., pp. 16–32). Waveland Press.

United States v. Crews, 445 U.S. 463 (1980).

United States v. Scheffer, 523, U.S. 303 (1998).

U.S. Border Patrol. (2021). *USBP Weapons*, Part 5. http://www.usborderpatrol.com/Border_Patrol412e.htm

U.S. Bureau of Labor Statistics. (2021). *Police and detectives. Occupational outlook handbook*. https://www.bls.gov/ooh/protective-service/police-and-detectives.htm

U.S. Department of Justice. (2014). *Investigation of the Cleveland Division of Police*. https://www.justice.gov/sites/default/files/opa/press-releases/attachments/2014/12/04/cleveland_division_of_police_findings_letter.pdf

U.S. Department of Justice. (2017, January 13). *Justice Department announces findings of investigation into Chicago Police Department*. https://www.justice.gov/opa/pr/justice-department-announces-findings-investigation-chicago-police-department

U.S. Government Accountability Office. (2019). *DNA evidence: DOJ Should improve performance measurement and properly design controls for nationwide grant program*. GAO-19-216. https://www.gao.gov/assets/700/697768.pdf

U.S. Marshals. (2020). *Court security.* https://www.us-marshals.gov/judicial/court_security_officer.htm

Violanti, J. (1996). *Police suicide: Epidemic in blue.* Charles Thomas.

Violanti, J. M. (2004). Predictors of police suicide ideation. *Suicide & Life-Threatening Behavior, 34*(3), 277–283.

Violanti, J. M., Slaven, J. E., Charles, L. E., Burchfiel, C. M., Andrew, M. E., & Homish, G. G. (2011). Police and alcohol use: A descriptive analysis and associations with stress outcomes. *American Journal of Criminal Justice, 36,* 344–356.

von Hoffman, A. (1992). An officer of the neighborhood: A Boston patrolman on the beat in 1895. *Journal of Social History, 26*(2), 309–330.

Wadman, R. C., & Allison, W. T. (2004). *To protect and to serve: A history of police in America.* Pearson Prentice Hall.

Wakeling, S., Jorgensen, M., Michaelson, S., & Begay, M. (2001). *Policing on American Indian reservations: A report to the National Institute of Justice* (NCJ 1,88,095).

Walker, S., Spohn, C., & Delone, M. (2018). *The color of justice: Race, ethnicity, and crime in America* (6th ed.). Cengage.

Wallace-Wells, B. (2003). Bush's war on cops. *Washington Monthly, 35*(9), 30–37.

Ward, R. H., Kiernan, K. L., & Mabrey, D. (2006). *Homeland security: An introduction.* LexisNexis.

Weeks v. United States, 232 U.S. 383 (1914).

White, M. D. (2001). Controlling police decisions to use deadly force. Reexamining the importance of administrative policy. *Crime & Delinquency, 47,* 131–151.

White, M. D. (2007). *Current issues and controversies in policing.* Allyn & Bacon.

White, M. D. (2008). Identifying good cops early: Predicting recruit performance in the academy. *Police Quarterly, 11*(1), 27–49.

White, M. D., Cooper, J. A., Saunders, J., & Raganella, A. J. (2010). Motivations for becoming a police officer: Re-assessing officer attitudes and job satisfaction after six years on the street. *Journal of Criminal Justice, 38,* 520–530.

White, M. D., & Escobar, G. (2008). Making good cops in the twenty-first century: Emerging issues for the effective recruitment, selection, and training of police in the United States and abroad. *International Review of Law, Computers & Technology, 22*(1–2), 119–134.

White, S. (1972). A perspective on police professionalization. *Law and Society Review, 7*(1), 61–85.

Wilkinson, E. (2018, October 10). *David Stodden passes 3rd polygraph test in unsolved murders of wife and daughter.* King 5. https://www.king5.com/article/news/local/david-stodden-passes-3rd-polygraph-test-in-unsolved-murders-of-wife-and-daughter/281-603049836

Wilson, D. B., McClure, D., & Weisburd, D. A. (2010). Does forensic DNA help to solve crime? The benefit of sophisticated answers to naive questions. *Journal of Contemporary Criminal Justice, 26*(4), 458–469.

Wilson, J. Q. (1968). *Varieties of police behavior.* Harvard University Press.

Wilson, J. Q., & Kelling, G. (1982). Broken windows: The police and neighborhood safety. *Atlantic Monthly, 249,* 29–38.

Wilson v. Arkansas, 514 U.S. 927 (1995).

Wong Sun v. United States, 371 U.S. 471 (1963).

Wrobleski, H. M., & Hess, K. (2006). *Introduction to law enforcement and criminal justice.* Wadsworth.

UNIT III

Abadinski, H. (1988). *Law and justice.* Nelson–Hall.

Administrative Office of the U.S. Courts. (2020). *Federal judicial caseload statistics 2019.* https://www.uscourts.gov/statistics-reports/federal-judicial-caseload-statistics-2019

Aguilar-Millan, S., Foltz, J. E., Jackson, J., & Oberg, A. (2008). Global crime case: The modern slave trade. *The Futurist,* 45.

Alarcon, A. L., & Mitchell, P. M. (2011). Executing the will of the voters? A roadmap to mend or end the California legislature's multi-billion-dollar death penalty debacle. *Loyola of Los Angeles Law Review, 44*(3), S41–S224.

Allen, H. E., Latessa, E. J., & Ponder, B. S. (2013). *Corrections in America: An introduction* (13th ed.). Pearson.

American Bar Association. (2021). *ABA reports law school enrollment for 2020 remains stable.* https://www.americanbar.org/news/abanews/aba-news-archives/2020/12/law-school-enrollment/

American Bar Association. (n.d.b). *Homelessness courts: Taking the court to street.* https://www.americanbar.org/content/dam/aba/administrative/homelessness_poverty/one-pagers/homeless-court-one-pager.pdf#

American Bar Association. (2020). *ABA national lawyer population survey.* https://www.americanbar.org/content/dam/aba/administrative/market_research/national-lawyer-population-by-state-2020.pdf

Amnesty International. (2019). *Lethal injection.* https://www.amnestyusa.org/issues/death-penalty/lethal-injection/

Andreas, P., & Nadelmann, E. (2006). *Policing the globe.* Oxford University Press.

Anwar, S., Bayer, P., & Hjalmarsson, R. (2012). The impact of jury race in criminal trials. *Quarterly Journal of Economics, 127*(2), 1017–1055.

Arkowitz, H., & Lilienfeld, S. O. (2010, January 1). Why science tells us not to rely on eyewitness accounts. *Scientific American.* https://www.scientificamerican.com/article/do-the-eyes-have-it/#

Argersinger v. Hamlin, 407 U.S. 25 (1972).

Associated Press. (2017a, May 4). *7 Tennessee bounty hunters shot at wrong car, charged with murder.* NBC 4i. http://nbc4i.com/2017/05/04/7-tennessee-bounty-hunters-shot-at-wrong-car-charged-with-murder/

Associated Press. (2017b, August 9). Tiger Woods reaches plea deal in D.U.I. case, prosecutor says. *New York Times.* https://www.nytimes.com/2017/08/09/sports/golf/tiger-woods-dui-plea.html?mcubz=0

Atkins v. Virginia, 536 U.S. 304 (2002).

Autler, A. (2015, May 14). *Murfreesboro woman shaken after bounty hunters enter wrong apartment.* WSMV. http://www.wsmv.com/story/29070727/woman-shaken-after-bounty-hunters-enter-wrong-apartment

Babich, J. (2019, August 1). Bounty hunters not guilty on almost all counts in slaying of Jalen Johnson Milan. *Clarksville Leaf–Chronicle.* https://www.theleafchronicle.com/story/news/crime/2019/08/01/bounty-hunter-trial-verdict-jalen-johnson/1780526001/

Baker, J. H. (1990). *An introduction to English legal history* (3rd ed.). Butterworths.

Baldus, D. C., Woodworth, G., & Pulaski, C. A., Jr. (1990). *Equal justice and the death penalty: A legal and empirical analysis.* Northeastern University.

Baldwin v. New York, 399 U.S. 66 (1970).

Banks, C. P. (Ed.). (2017). *The state and federal courts: A complete guide to history, powers, and controversy.* ABC–CLIO.

Bartlett, R. (1986). *Trial by fire and water: The medieval judicial ordeal.* Clarendon Press.

Bartollas, C., & Miller, S. J. (2014). *Juvenile justice in America* (7th ed.). Pearson.

Bartollas, C., & Schmalleger, F. (2014). *Juvenile delinquency* (9th ed.). Pearson.

Batson v. Kentucky, 476 U.S. 79 (1986).

BBC. (2017, August 18). *Chinese "cyber-court" launched for online cases.* BBC News. http://www.bbc.com/news/technology-40980004

Benekos, P. J., Merlo, A. V., & Puzzanchera, C. M. (2013). In defence of children and youth: Reforming juvenile justice policies. *International Journal of Police Science & Management, 15*(2), 125–143.

Berger v. United States, 295 U.S. 78 (1935).

Berkson, L., & Carbon, S. (1978). *Court unification: History, politics, and implementation.* National Institute of Law Enforcement and Criminal Justice.

Berman, G., & Feinblatt, J. (2001). Problem-solving courts: A brief primer. *Law & Policy, 23*(2), 125–140.

Berman, G., Rempel, M., & Wolf, R. V. (Eds.). (2007). *Documenting results: Research on problem-solving justice.* Center for Court Innovation.

Bernstein, I. N., Kick, E., Leung, J. T., & Schulz, B. (1977). Charge reduction: An intermediary stage in the process of labeling criminal defendants. *Social Force, 56,* 362–384.

Betts v. Brady, 316 U.S. 455 (1942).

Boots, M. T. (2013, July 23). State puts an end to sentencing deals in serious crimes. *Anchorage Daily News.* http://www.adn.com/2013/07/23/2987774/law-department-puts-an-end-to.html

Borum, R., & Fulero, S. M. (1999). Empirical research on the insanity defense and attempted reforms: Evidence toward informed policy. *Law and Human Behavior, 23*(1), 117–135.

Boykin v. Alabama, 395 U.S. 238 (1969).

Brady v. Maryland, 373 U.S. 83 (1963).

Brady v. United States, 397 U.S. 742 (1970).

Breed v. Jones, 421 U.S. 519 (1975).

Brenan, M. (2020). *Record-low 54 percent in U.S. say death penalty morally acceptable.* Gallup. https://news.gallup.com/poll/312929/record-low-say-death-penalty-morally-acceptable.aspx

Brook, S. (2013). Opening statements: Persuasive advocacy without crossing the line. *FDCC Quarterly, 63*(3), 181–199.

Brown v. Board of Education of Topeka, 347 U.S. 483 (1954).

Burch, T. (2015). Skin color and the criminal justice system: Beyond Black–White disparities in sentencing. *Journal of Empirical Legal Studies, 12*(3), 395–420.

Bureau of Labor Statistics. (2016). *Employee benefits survey: Leave benefits.* U.S. Department of Labor. https://www.bls.gov/ncs/ebs/benefits/2016/ownership/civilian/table32a.htm

Burns, R. G. (2007). *The criminal justice system.* Pearson Prentice Hall.

Burns, R. G. (2013). *Policing: A modular approach.* Pearson.

Butler, B. (2007). Death qualification and prejudice: The effect of implicit racism, sexism, and homophobia on capital defendants' right to due process. *Behavioral Sciences and the Law, 25,* 857–867.

Butler, F. (2011). Rush to judgment: Prisoners' views of juvenile justice. *Western Criminology Review, 12*(3), 106–119.

California rethinks life sentences for thousands of non-violent third-strike offenders. (2018, October 18). *The Guardian.* https://www.theguardian.com/us-news/2018/oct/18/california-life-sentences-three-strikes

Camilletti, C. (2010). *Pretrial diversion programs.* U.S. Department of Justice, Bureau of Justice Assistance.

Carns, T. W., & Kruse, J. A. (1992). Alaska's ban on plea bargaining reevaluated. *Judicature, 75*(6), 310–317.

Carpenter, S. (2001). Technology gets its day in court. *Monitor on Psychology*, 32(9). http://www.apa.org/monitor/oct01/technology.aspx

Cervallos, D. (2017, June 23). *In Cosby trial, the awesome power of jurors*. CNN. http://www.cnn.com/2017/06/23/opinions/in-cosby-case-awesome-power-of-jurors-opinion-cevallos/index.html

Champion, D. J., Hartley, R. D., & Rabe, G. A. (2012). *Criminal courts: Structure, process, and issues*. Pearson.

Champion, D. J., Merlo, A. V., & Benekos, P. J. (2013). *The juvenile justice system: Delinquency, processing, and the law* (7th ed.). Pearson.

Chroust, A. (1965). *The rise of the legal profession in America* (Vol. 2.) University of Oklahoma Press.

Ciesco, T. (2018, August 28). *Tarrant County poised to launch first-of-its-kind diversion program for first responders*. NBC DFW. https://www.nbcdfw.com/news/local/Tarrant-County-Poised-to-Launch-First-of-Its-Kind-Diversion-Program-for-First-Responders-491867931.html

Cohen, T. (2014). Who's better at defending criminals? Does type of defense attorney matter in terms of producing favorable case outcomes. *Criminal Justice Policy Review*, 25(1), 29–58.

Cole, G. F., Gertz, M. G., & Bunger, A. (2004). *The criminal justice system: Politics and policies* (9th ed.). Wadsworth.

Colorado Commission on Judicial Discipline. (n.d.). *About us*. http://www.coloradojudicialdiscipline.com/About_us.html

Cook, P. J. (2009). Potential savings from abolition of the death penalty in North Carolina. *American Law and Economics Review*, 11(2), 498–529.

Cooper, J., & Neuhaus, I. M. (2000). The "hired gun" effect: Assessing the effect of pay, frequency of testifying, and credentials on the perception of expert testimony. *Law and Human Behavior*, 24(2), 149–171.

Council of Europe. (n.d.). *Details of Treaty No. 185: Convention on Cybercrime*. http://www.coe.int/en/web/conventions/full-list/-/conventions/treaty/185

Court Statistics Project. (2020). *State court caseload digest: 2018 data*. National Center for State Courts. http://www.courtstatistics.org/__data/assets/pdf_file/0014/40820/2018-Digest.pdf

Croft, J, & Smith, T. (2017, April 10). *Dylann Roof pleads guilty to state charges in church massacre*. CNN. http://www.cnn.com/2017/04/10/us/dylann-roof-guilty-plea-state-trial/index.html

Criminal trial publicity. (1936). *Journal of Criminal Law & Criminology*, 26(6), 950–951.

Daly, G. (2013, September 19). *Embracing the police force of the future*. CNN. http://www.cnn.com/2013/09/18/tech/innovation/police-future-technology/

Dattu, F. (1998). Illustrated jury instructions: A proposal. *Law & Psychology Review*, 22, 67–102.

Davis, E., & Snell, T. L. (2018). *Capital punishment, 2016* (NCJ 2,51,430). U.S. Department of Justice, Bureau of Justice Statistics.

Dawson, R. A. (1990). The future of juvenile justice: Is it time to abolish the system? *Journal of Criminal Law & Criminology*, 81(1), 136–155.

Death Penalty Information Center. (2020a). *Executions around the world*. https://deathpenaltyinfo.org/policy-issues/international/executions-around-the-world

Death Penalty Information Center. (2020b). *Innocence*. https://deathpenaltyinfo.org/policy-issues/innocence

del Carmen, R., & Hemmens, C. (2017). *Criminal procedure: Law and practice* (10th ed.). Cengage.

Diamond, D. (2011, May 27). Professional jurors: Has the time come? *Huffington Post*. http://www.huffingtonpost.com/diane-dimond/professional-jurors-has-t_b_867839.html

Dixon, H. B. (2013a). Technology and the courts: A futurist view. *The Judges Journal*, 52(3). http://www.americanbar.org/publications/judges_journal/2013/summer/technology_and_the_courts_a_futurist_view.html

Dixon, H. B. (2013b, December/January). The evolution of a high-technology courtroom. *Courts Today*, 22, 24–26.

Dorf, M. C., & Fagan, J. (2003). Problem-solving courts: From innovation to institutionalization. *American Criminal Law Review*, 40, 1501–1511.

Douglas, J. W., & Stockstill, H. K. (2008). Starving the death penalty: Do financial constraints limit its use? *The Justice System Journal*, 29(3), 326–337.

Drizin, S. A., & Luloff, G. (2007). Are juvenile courts a breeding ground for wrongful convictions? *Northern Kentucky Law Review*, 34, 257–322.

Duncan v. Louisiana, 391 U.S. 145 (1968).

Eisenstein, J., & Jacob, H. (1977). *Felony justice: An organizational analysis of criminal courts*. Little, Brown.

Ellis, R. (2016, July 12). *Michigan shooting: Inmate kills 2 bailiffs, sheriff says*. CNN. http://www.cnn.com/2016/07/11/us/michigan-courthouse-shooting/index.html

Erb, K. P. (2014, May 1). Considering the death penalty: Your tax dollars at work. *Forbes*. https://www.forbes.com/sites/kellyphillipserb/2014/05/01/considering-the-deathpenalty-your-tax-dollars-at-work/#11979e04664b

Escobedo v. Illinois, 378 U.S. 478 (1964).

Ex parte Crouse, 4, Whart. 9 (1839).

Farkas, K. (2016, November 30). *5 things your municipal court costs pay for: At any (court) cost*. Cleveland. http://www.cleveland.com/metro/index.ssf/2016/11/municipal_court_fees_fund_comp.html

Fatusko, T. F., Berson, S. V., & Swensen, S. K. (2013). *Status of court security in state courts: A national perspective*. National Center for State Courts.

Federal Judicial Center. (n.d.a). *Impeachments of federal judges*. https://www.fjc.gov/node/7496

Federal Judicial Center. (n.d.b). *Integrated database*. https://www.fjc.gov/research/idb

Federal Judicial Center. (2017). *Caseloads: Criminal cases, 1870–2016*. https://www.fjc.gov/history/courts/caseloads-criminal-cases-1870-2016

Feld, B. (1997). Abolish the juvenile court: Youthfulness, criminal responsibility, and sentencing policy. *Journal of Criminal Law and Criminology*, 88(1), 68–136.

Ferdico, J. N. (2005). *Criminal procedure for the criminal justice professional* (9th ed.). Wadsworth.

Foglia, W. D. (2003). They know not what they do: Unguided and misguided discretion in Pennsylvania capital cases. *Justice Quarterly*, 20(1), 187–211.

Foote, J. (1976). *Two hundred years of American criminal justice*. U.S. Government Printing Office.

Ford, M. (2017, February 5). When your judge isn't a lawyer. *The Atlantic*. https://www.theatlantic.com/politics/archive/2017/02/when-your-judge-isnt-a-lawyer/515568/

Foster, B. (2001). How the death penalty really works: Selecting death penalty offenders in America. In L. Nelson & B. Foster (Eds.), *Death watch: A death penalty anthology* (pp. 16–21). Prentice Hall.

Fox, S. J. (1998). A contribution to the history of the American juvenile court. *Juvenile and Family Court Journal*, 49, 7–16.

Francescani, C., & Puckett, J. (2017, June 21). *Inside the explosive Cosby jury deliberations that almost came to blows*. ABC News. http://abcnews.go.com/Entertainment/inside-explosive-cosby-jury-deliberations-blows/story?id=48195733

Frank, M. (2014, November 8). Marshall Frank: Time to switch to professional jurors. *USA Today*. https://www.usatoday.com/story/opinion/contributors/2014/11/17/marshall-frank-time-switch-professional-jurors/19165291/

Friedman, L. M. (1985). *A history of American law* (2nd ed.). Touchstone.

Friedman, L. M. (1993). *Crime and punishment in American history*. Basic Books.

Fuller, J. R. (2014). *Criminal justice: Mainstream and crosscurrents* (3rd ed.). Oxford University Press.

Furman v. Georgia, 408 U.S. 238 (1972).

Gallup. (n.d.). *Crime*. http://www.gallup.com/poll/1603/crime.aspx

Gallup. (2014). *Death penalty*. http://www.gallup.com/poll/1606/Death-Penalty.aspx

George, J. (November 16, 2018). *What's really in the First Step Act*. The Marshall Project. https://www.themarshallproject.org/2018/11/16/what-s-really-in-the-first-step-act

George, T. E., & Yoon, A. H. (2014). *The gavel gap: Who sits in judgment on state courts?* American Constitution Society for Law and Policy. http://gavel-gap.org/pdf/gavel-gap-report.pdf

Gideon v. Wainwright, 372 U.S. 335 (1963).

Global Youth Justice. (2021). *Statistics*. https://www.globalyouthjustice.org/resources/statistics/

Gottfredson, M. R., & Gottfredson, D. M. (1988). *Decision making in criminal justice: Toward the rational exercise of discretion* (2nd ed.). Plenum.

Graham v. Florida, 130 S. Ct. 2011 (2010).

Gramlich, J. (2017, March 28). *Federal criminal prosecutions fall to lowest level in nearly two decades*. Pew Research Center. http://www.pewresearch.org/fact-tank/2017/03/28/federal-criminal-prosecutions-fall-to-lowest-level-in-nearly-two-decades/

Green, T. A. (1985). *Verdict according to conscience: Perspectives on the English criminal jury trial*. University of Chicago Press.

Gregg v. Georgia, 428 U.S. 153 (1976).

Griffin, P., & Torget, P. (2002). *Desktop guide to good juvenile probation practice*. National Center for Juvenile Justice.

Gross, S., & Possley, M. (2016, June 16). Why do people confess to crimes they didn't commit? *Newsweek*. http://www.newsweek.com/why-people-confess-crimes-didnt-commit-470227

Harris, R. A., & Springer, J. F. (1984). Plea bargaining as a game: An empirical analysis of negotiated sentencing decisions. *Review of Policy Research*, 4, 245–258.

Hartley, R. D., Miller, H. V., & Spohn, C. (2010). Do you get what you pay for? Type of counsel and its effect on criminal court outcomes. *Journal of Criminal Justice*, 38, 1063–1070.

Hess, K. M., Orthmann, C. H., & Wright, J. P. (2013). *Juvenile justice* (6th ed.). Wadsworth.

Hockenberry, S., & Puzzanchera, C. (2020). *Juvenile court statistics 2018*. National Center for Juvenile Justice.

Holcomb, J., Williams, M., & Demuth, S. (2004). White female victims and death penalty research. *Justice Quarterly*, 21, 877–902.

Holder, E. (2013). *Memorandum to heads of Department of Justice components and United States attorneys*. Office of the Attorney General. https://www.justice.gov/sites/default/files/ag/legacy/2014/04/11/ag-memo-substantial-federal-interest.pdf

Holten, N. G., & Lamar, L. L. (1991). *The criminal courts: Structures, personnel, and processes*. McGraw–Hill.

Hull, E. (2010). Ignoring the crocodile: What's wrong with electing judges. *Social Policy*, 40(3), 43–47.

Hurtado v. California, 110 U.S. 516 (1884).

Imbler v. Pachtman, 424 U.S. 409 (1976).

Immarigeon, R. (2006). They myth that public attitudes are punitive. In R. M. Bohm & J. T. Walker (Eds.), *Demystifying crime and criminal justice* (pp. 149–157). Roxbury.

In re Gault, 387 U.S. 1 (1967).

In re Winship, 397 U.S. 358 (1970).

International Criminal Court. (2017). *The states parties to the Rome statute.* https://asp.icc-cpi.int/en_menus/asp/states%20parties/Pages/the%20states%20parties%20to%20the%20rome%20statute.aspx

International Labour Organization. (2020). *Statistics on forced labour, modern slavery and human trafficking.* https://www.ilo.org/global/topics/forced-labour/policy-areas/statistics/lang--en/index.htm

Internet Crime Complaint Center. (2020). *2019 internet crime report. Federal Bureau of Investigation.* https://www.ic3.gov/Media/PDF/AnnualReport/2019_IC3Report.pdf

Internet World Stats. (2020). *Internet usage statistics.* https://www.internetworldstats.com/stats14.htm#north

Jackson, M. S., & Knepper, P. (2003). *Delinquency and justice.* Allyn & Bacon.

Jacoby, J. E. (1980). *The American prosecutor: A search for identity.* Lexington Books.

J.E.B. v. Alabama ex rel. T.B., 511 U.S. 127 (1994).

Johnson v. Zerbst, 304 U.S. 458 (1938).

Jones, J. M. (2019). *Americans now support life in prison over death penalty. Gallup.* https://news.gallup.com/poll/268514/americans-support-life-prison-death-penalty.aspx

Judicial Counsel of California. (2018). *2018 Court statistics report: Statewide caseload trends.* https://www.courts.ca.gov/documents/2018-Court-Statistics-Report.pdf

Kappeler, V. E., & Potter, G. W. (2018). *The mythology of crime and criminal justice* (5th ed.). Waveland.

Keeton, G. (1966). *The Norman Conquest and the common law.* Ernest Benn.

Keith, D., Berry, P., & Velasco, E. (2019). *New report finds $39.7 million spent on campaigns for state supreme court judgeships in 2018, $10.8 million of it by special interest groups. Brennan Center for Justice.* https://www.brennancenter.org/our-work/analysis-opinion/new-report-finds-397-million-spent-campaigns-state-supreme-court

Kempin, F. G., Jr. (1973). *Historical introduction to Anglo-American law in a nutshell* (2nd ed.). West.

Kent v. United States, 383 U.S. 541 (1966).

Kessler, R. (2013). Why aren't cameras allowed at the Supreme Court again? *The Atlantic.* https://www.theatlantic.com/national/archive/2013/03/case-allowing-cameras-supreme-court-proceedings/316876/

Kim, B., Spohn, C., & Hedberg, E. C. (2015). Federal sentencing as a complex collaborative process: Judges, prosecutors, judge–prosecutor dyads, and disparity in sentencing. *Criminology, 53*(4), 597–623.

Kim, Y. S., Barak, G., & Shelton, D. E. (2009). Examining the "CSI-effect" in the cases of circumstantial evidence and eyewitness testimony: Multivariate and path analyses. *Journal of Criminal Justice, 37,* 452–460.

Kinnane, C. H. (1952). *A first book on Anglo-American law* (2nd ed.). Bobbs–Merrill.

Kleck, G., & Barnes, J. C. (2014). Do more police lead to more crime deterrence? *Crime & Delinquency, 60*(5), 716–738.

Komo Staff. (2017, June 15). Rowdy inmate attacks officers, assaults lawyer, tackles bailiffs in courtroom. *Komo News.* http://komonews.com/news/local/rowdy-inmate-attacks-officers-assaults-lawyer-tackles-bailiffs-in-yakima-courtroom

Kovandzic, T. V., Vieraitis, L. M., & Paquette Boots, D. (2009). Does the death penalty save lives? New evidence from state panel data, 1977 to 2006. *Criminology & Public Policy, 8*(4), 803–843.

Lafler v. Cooper, 566 U.S. 156 (2012).

LaFountain, R., Schauffler, R., Strickland, S., Holt, K., & Lewis, K. (2014). *Examining the work of state courts: An overview of 2012 state trial court caseloads.* National Center for State Courts.

Langton, L., & Farole, D., Jr. (2010). *State public defender programs, 2007* (NCJ 228229). U.S. Department of Justice, Bureau of Justice Statistics.

Lee, M. (2016, November 30). *Pressure mounts on public defenders amid funding crisis. Associated Press.* http://www.washingtontimes.com/news/2016/nov/30/new-mexico-judge-finds-public-defender-in-contempt/

Lockhart v. McCree, 476 U.S. 162 (1986).

Mahoney, B., Beaudin, B. D., Carver, J. A., III, Ryan, D. B., & Hoffman, R. B. (2001). *Pretrial services programs: Responsibilities and potential* (NCJ 1,81,939). U.S. Department of Justice, National Institute of Justice.

Malega, R., & Cohen, T. H. (2013). *State court organization* (NCJ 2,42,850). Bureau of Justice Statistics, U.S. Department of Justice.

Mapp v. Ohio, 367 U.S. 643 (1961).

Marble, D. H., & Worrall, J. L. (2009). Problem-solving courts. In M. Miller (Ed.), *21st century criminology: A reference handbook* (Vol. 2, pp. 771–779). Sage.

Marcham, F. (1937). *A history of England.* Macmillan.

Martin, J. A., & Wagenknecht-Ivey, B. J. (2011). It's a new day: Future trends require revolutionary changes in courts. In *Future trends in state courts 2011* (pp. 135–139). *National Center for State Courts.* http://ncsc.contentdm.oclc.org/cdm/ref/collection/ctadmin/id/1849

McCarthy, J. (2016, October 20). *Americans' views shift on toughness of justice system. Gallup.* https://news.gallup.com/poll/196568/americans-views-shift-toughness-justice-system.aspx

McCoy, D. P. (2015, July 4). Alternate reality: Teens run court for peers. *Journal & Courier.* http://www.jconline.com/story/news/2015/07/04/alternate-reality-teens-run-court-peers/29699599/

McCoy, K. (2019, February 22). El Chapo lawyers seek new trial, cite "misconduct" by jury that convicted the drug lord. *USA Today.* https://www.usatoday.com/story/news/nation/2019/02/22/joaquin-el-chapo-guzman-defense-motion-new-trial-jury-misconduct/2952241002/

McDonald, B., & Bachelder, H. (2017, January 6). With rise of body cameras, new tests of transparency and trust. *New York Times.* https://www.nytimes.com/2017/01/06/us/police-body-cameras.html?mcubz=0

McIntyre, L. J. (1987). *The public defender: The practice of law in the shadows of repute.* University of Chicago Press.

McKaskle v. Wiggins, 465 U.S. 168 (1984).

McKeiver v. Pennsylvania, 403 U.S. 528 (1971).

McKimmie, B. M., Antrobus, E., & Baguley, C. (2014). Objective and subjective comprehension of jury instructions in criminal trials. *New Criminal Law Review, 17*(2), 163–183.

McKinley, J. C., Jr., & Baker, A. (2014, December 7). Grand jury system, with exceptions, favors the police in fatalities. *New York Times.* http://www.nytimes.com/2014/12/08/nyregion

McNabb v. U.S., 318 U.S. 332 (1943).

McNamara, R., & Burns, R. (2020). *Multiculturalism, crime, and criminal justice* (2nd ed.). Oxford University Press.

McRae, M. A., & Nortman, K. (2012, September). Your witness. *The Los Angeles Lawyer.* http://www.gibsondunn.com/publications/Documents/McRaeNortman-YourWitness.pdf

Metcalfe, C. (2016). The role of courtroom workgroups in felony case dispositions: An analysis of workgroup familiarity and similarity. *Law & Society Review, 50*(3), 637–673.

Miles, K. (2013, September 11). Inmates released early in California under Prop 36 have low recidivism rates, report says. *Huffington Post.* http://www.huffingtonpost.com/2013/09/11/inmates-released-early-california_n_3901363.html

Miranda v. Arizona, 384 U.S. 436 (1966).

Missouri v. Frye, 566 U.S. 134 (2012).

Mueller, B., & Baker, A. (2014, December 20). 2 N.Y.P.D. officers killed in Brooklyn ambush; suspect commits suicide. *New York Times.* https://www.nytimes.com/2014/12/21/nyregion/two-police-officers-shot-in-their-patrol-car-in-brooklyn.html?mcubz=1&_r=0

National Association of Legal Assistants. (2017). *What do paralegals do?* https://www.nala.org/about-paralegals/what-do-paralegals-do

National Association of Youth Courts. (2020). *The significance of youth courts: The mission of the National Association of Youth Courts.* https://youthcourt.net/the-significance-of-youth-courts/

National Center for State Courts. (2013). *A national call to action: Access to justice for limited English proficient litigants.* National Center for State Courts.

National Center for State Courts. (2020a). *State court caseload digest, 2018 data. Court Statistics Project.* http://www.courtstatistics.org/__data/assets/pdf_file/0014/40820/2018-Digest.pdf

National Center for State Courts. (2020b). *Survey of judicial salaries.* https://www.ncsc.org/__data/assets/pdf_file/0017/51164/JSS-Handout-July-2020.pdf

National Center for State Courts. (2020c). *Coronavirus and the courts.* https://www.ncsc.org/newsroom/public-health-emergency

National Conference of State Legislatures. (2019). *Juvenile justice 2018 year-end report.* https://www.ncsl.org/research/civil-and-criminal-justice/juvenile-justice-2018-year-end-report.aspx

National Conference of State Legislatures. (2020). *Juvenile age of jurisdiction and transfer to adult court.* https://www.ncsl.org/research/civil-and-criminal-justice/juvenile-age-of-jurisdiction-and-transfer-to-adult-court-laws.aspx

Nellis, A. (2016). *The color of justice: Racial and ethnic disparity in state prisons.* The Sentencing Project.

Neubauer, D. W., & Fradella, H. F. (2017). *America's courts and the criminal justice system* (12th ed.). Wadsworth.

Neubauer, D. W., & Meinhold, S. S. (2013). *Judicial process: Law, courts, and politics in the United States* (6th ed.). Wadsworth.

The world's most barbaric punishments. (2010, July 8). *Newsweek.* http://www.newsweek.com/worlds-most-barbaric-punishments-74537

New York v. Quarles, 467 U.S. 649 (1984).

Office of Juvenile Justice and Delinquency Prevention. (2015). *OJJDP statistical briefing book.* http://www.ojjdp.gov/ojstatbb/structure_process/qa04306.asp?qaDate=2014

Office of Juvenile Justice and Delinquency Prevention. (2020). Juveniles tried as adults. *OJJDP statistical briefing book.* https://www.ojjdp.gov/ojstatbb/structure_process/qa04105.asp?qaDate=2018&text=no&maplink=link1

Office of Juvenile Justice and Delinquency Prevention. (n.d.). *Juvenile justice system structure & process.* https://www.ojjdp.gov/ojstatbb/structure_process/case.html

Office of the Fulton County District Attorney. (2014). *Community prosecution.* http://www.fultonda.org/

community_affairs/community_prosecution/index.php

Oliver, W. M., & Hilgenberg, J. F., Jr. (2006). *A history of crime and justice in America*. Pearson Allyn & Bacon.

Olson, D. E., Lurigio, A. J., & Albertson, S. (2001). Implementing the key components of specialized drug treatment courts: Practice and policy considerations. *Law & Policy, 23,* 171–196.

Palmer, C. A., & Hazelrigg, M. (2000). The guilty but mentally ill verdict: A review and conceptual analysis of intent and impact. *Journal of the American Academy of Psychiatry and the Law, 28,* 47–54.

Perlroth, N. (2017, April 21). Russian hacker sentenced to 27 years in credit card case. *New York Times.* https://www.nytimes.com/2017/04/21/technology/russian-hacker-sentenced.html

Pew Research Center. (2020, June 12). *Mobile fact sheet.* https://www.pewresearch.org/internet/fact-sheet/mobile/

Phillips, S. (2009). Status disparities in the capital of capital punishment. *Law & Society Review, 43*(4), 807–838.

Pickett, R. S. (1969). *House of refuge: Origins of juvenile reform in New York State, 1815–1857.* Syracuse University Press.

Platt, A. N. (1969). *The child savers: The invention of delinquency.* University of Chicago Press.

Plessy v. Ferguson, 163 US 537 (1896).

Pound, R. (1953). *The lawyer from antiquity to modern times.* West.

Puzzanchera, C., & Addie, S. (2014). *Delinquency cases waived to criminal court, 2010* (NCJ 2,43,042). U.S. Department of Justice, Office of Juvenile Justice and Delinquency Prevention.

Puzzanchera, C., & Hockenberry, S. (2013). *Juvenile court statistics, 2010.* National Center for Juvenile Justice.

Rashbaum, W. K. (2013, September 25). With special courts, state aims to steer women away from sex trade. *New York Times.* http://www.nytimes.com/2013/09/26/nyregion/special-courts-for-human-trafficking-and-prostitution-cases-are-planned-in-new-york.html?_r=0

Reaves, B. A. (2013). *Felony defendants in large urban counties, 2009—statistical tables* (NCJ 2,43,777). U.S. Department of Justice, Bureau of Justice Statistics.

Redding, R. E. (2010). *Juvenile transfer laws: An effective deterrent to delinquency?* (NCJ 2,20,595). U.S. Department of Justice, Office of Juvenile Justice and Delinquency Prevention.

Richardson, R., & Vines, K. (1970). *The politics of federal courts.* Little, Brown.

Ritter, N. (2006). Preparing for the future: Criminal justice in 2040. *National Institute of Justice Journal, 255,* 8–12.

Roach, M. A. (2014). Indigent defense counsel, attorney quality, and defendant outcomes. *American Law and Economics Review, 16*(2), 577–619.

Roberson, C., & DiMarino, F. J. (2012). *American criminal courts.* Pearson.

Roberson, C., Wallace, H., & Stuckey, G. B. (2013). *Procedures in the justice system* (10th ed.). Pearson.

Roper v. Simmons, 543 U.S. 551 (2005).

Roth, M. P. (2005). *Crime and punishment: A history of the criminal justice system.* Wadsworth.

Rubin, H. T. (2013, October/November). Extend jurisdiction to the eighteenth birthday and constrain the exceptions. *Juvenile Justice Update, 19*(5), 1–2, 6, 10–11.

Ruddell, R., & Mays, G. L. (2012). Transferring preteens to adult criminal courts: Searching for a justification. *Juvenile and Family Court Journal, 63*(4), 22–36.

Ruthhart, B. (2017, May 8). Police: Members of street gang identified suspects in cop shooting. *Chicago Tribune.* http://www.chicagotribune.com/news/local/breaking/ct-cop-shooting-la-raza-gang-20170507-story.html

Sabol, W. J., Rosich, K., Kane, K. M., Kirk, D., & Dubin, G. (2002). *Influence of truth-in-sentencing reforms on changes in states' sentencing practices and prison populations, executive summary.* U.S. Department of Justice. https://www.ncjrs.gov/pdffiles1/nij/grants/195163.pdf

Santobello v. New York, 404 U.S. 257 (1971).

Satter, L. (2017, August 26). *Attorney general to appeal ruling staying Arkansas abortion laws. Arkansas Online.* http://www.arkansasonline.com/news/2017/aug/26/state-asks-u-s-appellate-court-to-void--1/

Schallhorn, K. (2019, February 5). *What is the First Step Act? 5 things to know about the criminal justice reform law. Fox News.* https://www.foxnews.com/politics/what-is-first-step-act-5-things-to-know-about-the-criminal-justice-reform-law

Schauffler, R., LaFountain, R., Strickland, S., Holt, K., & Genthon, K. (2016). *Examining the work of state courts: An overview of 2015 state court caseloads.* National Center for State Courts. http://www.courtstatistics.org/~/media/Microsites/Files/CSP/EWSC%202015.ashx

Schauffler, R. Y., LaFountain, R. C., Strickland, S. M., Holt, K. A., Gibson, S. N., Mason, A. N., Otto, B. G., & Kauder, N. B. (2011). *Examining the work of state courts: An analysis of 2009 state court caseloads.* National Center for State Courts.

Scheb, J. M., & Scheb, J. M., II. (2009). *Criminal procedure* (5th ed.). Wadsworth.

Schmalleger, F., & Smykla, J. O. (2009). *Corrections in the 21st century* (4th ed.). McGraw-Hill.

Schweitzer, N. J., & Saks, M. J. (2007). The *CSI* effect: Popular fiction about the forensic science affects the public's expectations about real forensic science. *Jurimetrics, 47,* 357–364.

Sciarabba, A. L., & Sullivan, C. G. (2010). Transnational crime and the law: An overview of current practices. In J. A. Eterno & D. K. Das (Eds.), *Police practices in global perspective* (pp. 225–250). Rowman & Littlefield.

Scott, C. L., & Holmberg, T. (2003). Castration of sex offenders: Prisoners' rights versus public safety. *Journal of the American Academy of Psychiatry and the Law, 31,* 502–509.

Seelye, K. Q. (2016, August 9). Chicago Police Department warns of gangs' threats to attack officers. *New York Times.* https://www.nytimes.com/2016/08/10/us/chicago-police-department-warns-of-gangs-threats-to-attack-officers.html?mcubz=1&_r=0

Semega, J., Kollar, M., Shrider, E. A., & Creamer, J. (2020). *Income and poverty in the United States: 2019. U.S. Census Bureau.* https://www.census.gov/library/publications/2020/demo/p60-270.html

Seymour, J. (1994). *Parens patriae* and wardship powers: Their nature and origins. *Oxford Journal of Legal Studies, 14,* 159–188.

Shaer, M. (2016, June). The false promise of DNA testing. *The Atlantic.* https://www.theatlantic.com/magazine/archive/2016/06/a-reasonable-doubt/480747/

Sickmund, M. (2009). *Delinquency cases in juvenile court, 2005.* U.S. Department of Justice, Office of Juvenile Justice and Delinquency Prevention.

Siegel, L. J., Schmalleger, F., & Worrall, J. L. (2011). *Courts and criminal justice in America.* Pearson.

Siemer, D. C. (2001). *Effective use of courtroom technology: A judge's guide to pretrial and trial.* National Institute for Trial Advocacy. http://www.fjc.gov/public/pdf.nsf/lookup/cttech00.pdf/$file/cttech00.pdf

Snell, T. L. (2020). *Capital punishment, 2018—statistical tables* (NCJ 2,54,786). U.S. Department of Justice, Bureau of Justice Statistics.

Spohn, C., & Hemmens, C. (2009). *Courts: A text/reader.* Sage.

Steele, W. W., Jr., & Thornburg, E. G. (1991). Jury instructions: A persistent failure to communicate. *Judicature, 74*(5), 249–254.

Steiner, B., & Hemmens, C. (2003). Juvenile waiver 2003: Where are we now? *Juvenile and Family Court Journal, 54*(2), 1–24.

Stephens, G. (1997). Youth at risk: Saving the world's most precious resource. *The Futurist, 31,* 31–37.

Steury, E. H., & Frank, N. (1996). *Criminal court process.* West.

Stolzenberg, S. N., & Lyon, T. D. (2014). Evidence summarized in attorney's closing arguments predicts acquittals in criminal trials of child sexual abuse. *Child Maltreatment, 19*(2), 119–129.

Strickland v. Washington, 446 U.S. 668 (1984).

Strong, S. M. (2016). *State-administered indigent defense systems, 2013* (NCJ 2,50,249). U.S. Department of Justice, Bureau of Justice Statistics.

Strong, S. M., Rantala, R. R., & Kyckelhahn, T. (2016). *Census of problem-solving courts, 2012* (NCJ 2,49,803). U.S. Department of Justice, Bureau of Justice Statistics.

Supreme Court of the United States. (2021). *The court and its procedures.* https://www.supremecourt.gov/about/procedures.aspx

Surrency, E. C. (1967). The courts in the American colonies. *American Journal of Legal History, 11,* 252–276.

Tennessee v. Garner, 471 U.S. 1 (1985).

Thorley, C. (2016). Note taking and note reviewing enhance jurors' recall of trial information. *Applied Cognitive Psychology, 30*(5), 655–663.

U.S. Bureau of Labor Statistics. (2019). *U.S. Department of Labor, occupational employment statistics: bailiffs.* https://www.bls.gov/oes/2018/may/oes333011.htm

U.S. Bureau of Labor Statistics. (2020a). *U.S. Department of Labor, occupational employment statistics: court reporters.* https://www.bls.gov/ooh/legal/court-reporters.htm

U.S. Bureau of Labor Statistics. (2020b). *U.S. Department of Labor. Occupational employment statistics: paralegals and legal assistance.* https://www.bls.gov/ooh/legal/paralegals-and-legal-assistants.htm

U.S. Courts. (2020a). *Judicial vacancies.* https://www.uscourts.gov/judges-judgeships/judicial-vacancies

U.S. Courts. (2020b). Supreme Court procedures. https://www.uscourts.gov/about-federal-courts/educational-resources/about-educational-outreach/activity-resources/supreme-1

U.S. v. Booker, 543 U.S. 220 (2005).

U.S. v. Leon, 468 U.S. 897 (1984).

U.S. v. Salerno, 481 U.S. 739 (1987).

Van Ness, D., & Strong, K. H. (1997). *Restoring justice.* Anderson.

Vermont Office of the Attorney General (n.d.). *Office of the Vermont Attorney General.* https://ago.vermont.gov/about-the-attorney-generals-office/duties-responsibilities/

Virginia Criminal Sentencing Commission. (n.d.). *Sentencing guidelines cover sheet.* http://www.vcsc.virginia.gov/worksheets_2017/worksheet_covernotRA.pdf

Walker, S. (1998). *Popular justice* (2nd ed.). Oxford University Press.

Walker, S., Spohn, C., & DeLone, M. (2018). *The color of justice: Race, ethnicity, and crime in America* (6th ed.). Cengage.

Walsh, R. (1932). *A history of Anglo-American law.* Bobbs–Merrill.

Waters, N. L., Gallegos, A., Green, J., & Rozsi, M. (2015). *Criminal appeals in state courts* (NCJ 248874). U.S. Department of Justice, Bureau of Justice Statistics.

Waters, N. L., & Hans, V. P. (2009). A jury of one: Opinion formation, conformity and dissent on juries. *Journal of Empirical Legal Studies*, 6(3), 513–540.

Webb, P. (2008). Privacy or publicity: Media coverage and juvenile proceedings in the United States. *International Journal of Criminal Justice Studies*, 3(1), 1–14.

Williams, K. (2014, August). Human trafficking: The return of an ancient malaise and what law enforcement can do about it. *The Briefing*, 1–3.

Williams, M. R. (2013). The effectiveness of public defenders in four Florida counties. *Journal of Criminal Justice*, 41(4), 205–212.

Williams, M. R., Demuth, S., & Holcomb, J. E. (2007). Understanding the influence of victim gender in death penalty cases: The importance of victim race, sex-related victimization, and jury decision making. *Criminology*, 45(4), 865–891.

Williams, M. R., & Holcomb, J. E. (2001). Racial disparity and death sentences in Ohio. *Journal of Criminal Justice*, 29, 207–218.

Willing, R. (2005, March 17). Courts try to make jury duty less of a chore. *USA Today*, 17A–18A.

Willison, J. B., Mears, D. P., Shollenberger, T., Owens, C., & Butts, J. A. (2009). *Past, present, and future of juvenile justice: Assessing the policy options*. The Urban Institute.

Wilson, J. Q., & Kelling, G. (1982). Broken windows: The police and neighborhood safety. *Atlantic Monthly*, 249, 29–38.

Witherspoon v. Illinois, 391 U.S. 510 (1968).

Wolf, R. V. (2010). Community prosecution and serious crime: A guide for prosecutors. *U.S. Department of Justice, Bureau of Justice Assistance*. https://www.courtinnovation.org/sites/default/files/documents/CP_SC.pdf

Worrall, J. L. (2004). *Criminal procedure: From first contact to appeal*. Pearson Allyn & Bacon.

UNIT IV

Abadinsky, H. (2015). *Probation and parole: Theory and practice* (12th ed.). Pearson.

Adler, F., Mueller, G. O. W., & Laufer, W. S. (2012). *Criminal justice: An introduction* (6th ed.). McGraw-Hill.

Aging Inmate Committee. (2012, August/September). Aging inmates: Correctional issues and initiatives. *Corrections Today*, 84–87.

Alarid, L. F., & Reichel, P. L. (2013). *Corrections*. Pearson.

Allen, H., Parks, E., Carlson, E., & Seiter, R. (1978). *Program models, halfway houses*. U.S. Department of Justice.

Allen, H. E., Latessa, E. J., & Ponder, B. S. (2013). *Corrections in America: An introduction* (13th ed.). Pearson.

Alper, M., Durose, M. R., & Markman, J. (2018). *2018 update on prisoner recidivism: A 9-year follow-up period (2005–2014)* (NCJ 250975). U.S. Department of Justice, Bureau of Justice Statistics.

American Civil Liberties Union. (2018). *Solitary confinement*. https://www.aclu.org/issues/prisoners-rights/solitary-confinement

American Correctional Association. (1983). *The American prison: From the beginning … a pictorial history*. American Correctional Association.

Associated Press. (2017, July 19). *Judge orders Texas to lower temperature in sweltering prison*. ABC News. http://abcnews.go.com/amp/US/wireStory/judge-orders-texas-lower-temperature-sweltering-prison-48732697

Austin, J., & Irwin, J. (2001). *It's about time: America's imprisonment binge*. Wadsworth.

Banks, G. (2017, June 18). Heat-related prison deaths at issue in lawsuit. *Houston Chronicle*. https://www.houstonchronicle.com/news/houston-texas/houston/article/Heat-related-prison-deaths-at-issue-in-lawsuit-11229040.php

Bartollas, C., & Miller, S. J. (2014). *Juvenile justice in America* (7th ed.). Pearson.

Bartollas, C., & Schmalleger, F. (2014). *Juvenile delinquency* (9th ed.). Pearson.

Beck, A. J., Berzofsky, M., & Krebs, C. (2013). *Sexual victimization in prisons and jails reported by inmates, 2011–2012* (NCJ 241399). U.S. Department of Justice, Bureau of Justice Statistics.

Beck, A. J., Rantala, R. R., & Rexroat, J. (2014). *Sexual victimization reported by adult correctional authorities, 2009–11* (NCJ 243904). U.S. Department of Justice, Bureau of Justice Statistics.

Bedard, L. E. (2009, October 20). The pseudo-family phenomenon in women's prisons. *Corrections One*. https://www.correctionsone.com/women-in-corrections/articles/1956587-The-pseudo-family-phenomenon-in-womens-prisons/

Belbot, B. (2012). The sentencing revolution. In F. P. Reddington & G. Bonham, Jr. (Eds.), *Flawed criminal justice policies: At the intersection of the media, public fear and legislative response* (pp. 81–100). Carolina Academic Press.

Berman, D. S., & Anton, M. T. (1988). A wilderness therapy program as an alternative to adolescent psychiatric hospitalization. *Residential Treatment for Children & Youth*, 5(3), 41–53.

Birzer, M. L., & Craig-Moreland, D. (2006). Why do jails charge housing fees? *American Jails*, 20(1), 63–68.

Bloom, B., & Steinhart, D. (1993). *Why punish the children: A reappraisal of the children of incarcerated mothers in America*. National Council on Crime and Delinquency.

Boin, A., & Rattray, W. A. R. (2004). Understanding prison riots. *Punishment & Society*, 6(1), 47–65.

Booker, J. W., Jr. (1999). Staff equality: A welcomed addition to the correctional workplace. *Corrections Today*, 94–95.

Boyes-Watson, C., & Krumholz, S. T. (2018). *Crime and justice: Learning through cases* (3rd ed.). Rowman & Littlefield.

Bromwich, J. E. (2018, January 18). Why are American prisons so afraid of this book? *New York Times*. https://www.nytimes.com/2018/01/18/us/new-jim-crow-book-ban-prison.html

Bronson, J., & Berzofsky, M. (2017). *Indicators of mental health problems reported by prisoners and jail inmates, 2011–12* (NCJ 250612). U.S. Department of Justice, Bureau of Justice Statistics.

Bronson, J., & Carson, E. A. (2019). *Prisoners in 2017* (NCJ 252156). U.S. Department of Justice, Bureau of Justice Statistics.

Bronson, J., Stroop, J., Zimmer, S., & Berzofsky, M. (2017). *Drug use, dependence, and abuse among state prisoners and jail inmates, 2007–2009* (NCJ 250546). U.S. Department of Justice, Bureau of Justice Statistics.

Brown, G. (2017, December 13). *New set of bills aims to curb prison overcrowding in Wisconsin*. Wisconsin Public Radio. https://www.wpr.org/new-set-bills-aims-curb-prison-overcrowding-wisconsin

Brown v. Plata, 563 U.S. (2011).

Bulman, P. (2009, July/August). Using technology to make prisons and jails safer. *American Jails*, 9–12.

Burrell, B. (2006). *Caseload standards for probation and parole*. American Probation and Parole Association. http://www.colorado.gov/ccjjdir/Resources/Resources/Ref/APPA_Caseload_Standards_PP_0906.pdf

Burrell, W. D., & Gable, R. S. (2008). From B. F. Skinner to Spiderman to Martha Stewart: The past, present and future of electronic monitoring of offenders. *Journal of Offender Rehabilitation*, 46(3/4), 101–118.

Burton, A. L., Lux, J. L., Cullen, F. T., Miller, W. T., & Burton, V. S., Jr. (2018). Creating a model correctional officer training academy: Implications from a national study. *Federal Probation*, 82(1), 26–36.

Cahalan, M. W. (1986). *Historical corrections statistics in the United States: 1850–1984*. U.S. Department of Justice.

Camp, S., Saylor, W. G., & Wright, K. N. (2001). Racial diversity of correctional workers and inmates: Organizational commitment, teamwork, and workers' efficacy in prisons. *Justice Quarterly*, 18(2), 411–427.

Caplan, J. M. (2007). What factors affect parole: A review of empirical research. *Federal Probation*, 71(1), 16–19.

Carson, E. A. (2020a). *Prisoners in 2019* (NCJ 255115). U.S. Department of Justice, Bureau of Justice Statistics.

Carson, E. A. (2020b). *Data collected under the First Step Act, 2019* (NCJ 254268). U.S. Department of Justice, Bureau of Justice Statistics.

Carson, E. A. (2020c). *Prisoners in 2018* (NCJ 253516). U.S. Department of Justice, Bureau of Justice Statistics.

Carson, E. A., & Anderson, E. (2016). *Prisoners in 2015* (NCJ 250229). U.S. Department of Justice, Bureau of Justice Statistics.

Carson, E. A., & Cowhig, M. P. (2020). *Mortality in local jails, 2000–2016—statistical tables* (NCJ 251921). U.S. Department of Justice, Bureau of Justice Statistics.

Carter, M. (2017, December 14). Prison escape of Washington's "Mini Madoff" like *Shawshank Redemption* without sewer-pipe crawl, official says. *Seattle Times*. https://www.seattletimes.com/seattle-news/crime/official-prison-escape-of-washingtons-mini-madoff-like-shawshank-redemption-without-sewer-pipe-crawl/

Case, B., Steadman, H. J., Dupuis, S. A., & Morris, L. S. (2009). Who succeeds in jail diversion programs for persons with mental illness? A multi-site study. *Behavioral Sciences & the Law*, 27(5), 661–674.

Cesarz, G., & Madrid-Bustos, J. (1991, December). Taking a multicultural world view in today's corrections facilities. *Corrections Today*, 68, 70–71.

Champion, D. J., Merlo, A. V., & Benekos, P. J. (2013). *The juvenile justice system: Delinquency, processing, and the law* (7th ed.). Pearson.

Chandler, K. (2015, August 6). *Native American inmates lose fight for long hair in prison*. Associated Press. https://redpowermedia.wordpress.com/2015/08/10/native-americans-inmates-lose-fight-for-long-hair-in-prison/

Christianson, S. (1998). *With liberty for some*. Northeastern University Press.

City and County of San Francisco. (n.d.). *Juvenile probation department—Log Cabin Ranch School*. http://sfgov.org/juvprobation/log-cabin-ranch-school

Clear, T. R., & Dammer, H. R. (2000). *The offender in the community*. Wadsworth.

Clear, T. R., Reisig, M. D., & Cole, G. F. (2016). *American corrections* (11th ed.). Cengage.

Clemmer, D. (1966). *The prison community*. Holt.

Cole, F. (1987). The impact of *Bell v. Wolfish* upon prisoners' rights. *Journal of Crime and Justice*, 10, 47–70.

Cole, G. F., Smith, C. E., & DeJong, C. (2013). *The American system of criminal justice* (13th ed.). Wadsworth.

Conover, T. (2000). *Newjack: Guarding Sing Sing*. Random House.

Cook, J. (2020, April 5). Michigan prison guards concerned about dangers of COVID-19. *Macomb Daily.* https://www.macombdaily.com/news/coronavirus/michigan-prison-guards-concerned-about-dangers-of-covid-19/article_1e6c27f6-7604-11ea-a444-43bddcfab230.html

Cooper v. Pate, 378 U.S. 546 (1964).

Corrigan, P. W. (2005). *On the stigma of mental illness: Practical strategies for research and social change.* American Psychological Association.

Crawford, J. (2003, June). Alternative sentencing necessary for female inmates with children. *Corrections Today,* 8–10.

Cunningham, M. D., Sorensen, J. R., Vigen, M. P., & Woods, S. O. (2010). Inmate homicides: Killers, victims, motives, and circumstances. *Journal of Criminal Justice,* 38, 348–358.

Davis, L., & Shlafer, R. J. (2017). Mental health of adolescents with currently and formerly incarcerated parents. *Journal of Adolescence,* 54, 120–134.

Davis, L. M., Bozick, R., Steele, J. L., Saunders, J., & Miles, J. N. V. (2013). *Evaluating the effectiveness of correctional education: A meta-analysis of programs that provide education to incarcerated adults.* U.S. Department of Justice, Bureau of Justice Assistance.

Death Penalty Information Center. (2014). *Introduction to the death penalty.* http://www.deathpenaltyinfo.org/part-i-history-death-penalty#earlymid

DiIulio, J. J. (1987). *Governing prisons.* Free Press.

Dostoevsky, F. (1862). *The house of the dead.* Vremya.

Dotson, D. L. (2012, July/August). Using technology in the jail. *Sheriff,* 48–50.

Downing, H. (2006, October). The emergence of global positioning satellite (GPS) systems in correctional applications. *Corrections Today,* 42–45.

Ducker, T. T. (2004). Video visitation a boom in Omaha. *American Jails,* 18(5), 65–67.

Durose, M. R., Cooper, A. D., & Snyder, H. N. (2014). *Recidivism of prisoners released in 30 states in 2005: Patterns from 2005 to 2010* (NCJ 244205). U.S. Department of Justice, Bureau of Justice Statistics.

Duwe, G. (2015). An outcome evaluation of a prison work release program: Estimating its effect on recidivism, employment, and cost avoidance. *Criminal Justice Policy Review,* 26(6), 531–554.

Economic perspectives on incarceration and the criminal justice system. (2016). Executive Office of the President of the United States. https://obamawhitehouse.archives.gov/sites/whitehouse.gov/files/documents/CEA%2BCriminal%2BJustice%2BReport.pdf

Einat, T., & Einat, H. (2000). Inmate argot as an expression of prison subculture: The Israeli case. *Prison Journal,* 80(3), 309–325.

Elinson, Z., & Paul, D. (2020, March 22). Jails release prisoners, fearing Coronavirus outbreak. *Wall Street Journal.* https://www.wsj.com/articles/jails-release-prisoners-fearing-coronavirus-outbreak-11584885600

Fahy, A. (2007). The unbearable fatigue of compassion: Notes from a substance abuse counselor who dreams of working at Starbuck's. *Clinical Social Work Journal,* 35, 199–205.

Fain, T. (2018, January 23). *NC prisons un-ban book on race, mass incarceration after ACLU request.* WRAL. http://www.wral.com/nc-prisons-un-ban-book-on-race-mass-incarceration-after-aclu-request/17283409/

Federal Bureau of Prisons. (2020a). *About our facilities—statistic—past inmate totals.* U.S. Department of Justice. https://www.bop.gov/about/statistics/population_statistics.jsp#old_pops

Federal Bureau of Prisons. (2020b). *Population statistics.* https://www.bop.gov/mobile/about/population_statistics.jsp

Federal Bureau of Prisons. (2020c). *About our facilities.* https://www.bop.gov/about/facilities/federal_prisons.jsp

Federal Bureau of Prisons. (2020d). *Staff ethnicity/race.* https://www.bop.gov/about/statistics/statistics_staff_ethnicity_race.jsp

Federal Bureau of Prisons. (2020e). *Total federal inmates.* https://www.bop.gov/about/statistics/population_statistics.jsp

Feinman, C. (1983). A historical overview of the treatment of incarcerated women: Myths and realities of rehabilitation. *Prison Journal,* 63, 12–26.

Finn, P., & Kuck, S. (2005). *Stress among probation and parole officers and what can be done about it* (NCJ 205620). U.S. Department of Justice, National Institute of Justice.

Fleisher, M. S., & Krienert, J. L. (2009). *The myth of prison rape: Sexual culture in American prisons.* Rowman & Littlefield.

Foster, B. (2006). *Corrections: The fundamentals.* Pearson.

Fuentes, A. I., & Burns, R. (2002). Activities and staffing patterns in therapeutic wilderness camps: A national survey. *Journal of Offender Rehabilitation,* 35(1), 41–62.

Gagnon v. Scarpelli, 411 U.S. 778 (1973).

Galvin, G. (July 26, 2017). Underfunded, overcrowded state prisons struggle with reform. *U.S. News & World Report.* https://www.usnews.com/news/best-states/articles/2017-07-26/understaffed-and-overcrowded-state-prisons-crippled-by-budget-constraints-bad-leadership

Garrick, D. (2017, December 11). Homeless halfway house approved despite community opposition. *San Diego Union–Tribune.* http://www.sandiegouniontribune.com/news/politics/sd-me-motel-homeless-20171211-story.html

Geller, A. (2014, September 20). Jailed, some mentally ill inmates land in lockdown. *Associated Press.* http://bigstory.ap.org/article/jailed-some-mentally-ill-inmates-land-lockdown-0

George, J. (2018, December 19). *Okay, what's the second step? The Marshall Project.* https://www.themarshallproject.org/2018/12/19/okay-what-s-the-second-step

Glaser, D. F. (1995). *Preparing convicts for law-abiding lives: The pioneering penology of Richard A. McGee.* State University of New York Press.

Glaze, L. E., & L. M. Maruschak. (2008). *Parents in prison and their minor children* (NCJ 222984). U.S. Department of Justice, Bureau of Justice Statistics.

Goffman, E. (1961). *Asylums: Essays on the social situation of mental patients and other inmates.* Doubleday.

Goldfarb, R. (1975). *Jails: The ultimate ghetto.* Doubleday.

Gramlich, J. (2019, April 30). *The gap between the number of Blacks and Whites in prison is shrinking.* Pew Research Center. https://www.pewresearch.org/fact-tank/2019/04/30/shrinking-gap-between-number-of-blacks-and-whites-in-prison/

Greenwood, P. (2008). Prevention and intervention programs for juvenile offenders. *Juvenile Justice,* 18(2), 185–210. http://www.futureofchildren.org/futureofchildren/publications/docs/18_02_09.pdf

Griffin, M. L., & Hepburn, J. R. (2006). The effect of gang affiliation on violence misconduct among inmates during the early years of confinement. *Criminal Justice and Behavior,* 33, 419–448.

Hagar, G. M., Ludwig, T. E., & McGovern, K. (2008). Program evaluation for a jail-based mental health treatment program. *Journal of Correctional Health Care,* 14(3), 222–231.

Hariston, C. F. (1991). Family ties during imprisonment: Important to whom and for what? *Journal of Sociology and Social Welfare,* 18(1), 87–104.

Hasty, N. (2018). *Prison nurseries give incarcerated mothers a chance to raise their babies—behind bars. NBC News.* https://www.nbcnews.com/news/us-news/prison-nurseries-give-incarcerated-mothers-chance-raise-their-babies-behind-n894171

Hayward, M. (2017, July 6). Terminally ill ex-priest jailed for sex crimes granted parole. *New Hampshire Union Leader.* http://www.unionleader.com/crime/Terminally-ill-ex-priest-jailed-for-sex-crimes-granted-parole-07072017

Hockenberry, S. (2019). *Delinquency cases in juvenile court, 2017* (NCJ 253105). U.S. Department of Justice, Office of Juvenile Justice and Delinquency Prevention.

Hockenberry, S., & Puzzanchera, C. (2020). *Juvenile court statistics 2018.* National Center for Juvenile Justice.

Hockenberry, S, & Sladky, A. (2018). *Juvenile residential facility census, 2016: Selected findings* (NCJ 251785). U.S. Department of Justice, Office of Juvenile Justice and Delinquency Prevention.

Holt v. Sarver, 309 F. Supp. 362 (1970).

Howell, J. C., & Roush, D. W. (1999). Youth gang problems in juvenile detention and corrections facilities. *Journal for Juvenile Justice and Detention Services,* 14, 53–66.

Hudson, J. (2012, July 2). An urban myth that should be true. *The Atlantic.* https://www.theatlantic.com/business/archive/2012/07/an-urban-myth-that-should-be-true/259329/

Hunt, P. (2004). Correctional officers need cultural diversity training. In C. Smalls (Ed.), *The full spectrum: Essays on staff diversity in corrections* (pp. 127–155). American Correctional Association.

Hyatt, J. M., & Barnes, G. C. (2014). An experimental evaluation of the impact of intensive supervision on the recidivism of high-risk probationers. *Crime & Delinquency,* 63(1), 3–38.

Hyland, S. (2019). *Justice expenditure and employment extracts, 2016, Table 5* (NCJ 254126). U.S. Department of Justice, Bureau of Justice Statistics.

Irwin, J. (1985). *The jail: Managing the underclass in American society.* University of California Press.

Irwin, J., & Cressey, D. (1962) Thieves, convicts, and the inmate culture. *Social Problems,* 10, 145–157.

Ispa-Landa, S., & Loefler, C. E. (2016). Indefinite punishment and the criminal record: Stigma reports among expungement-seekers in Illinois. *Criminology,* 54(3), 387–412.

Jalbert, S. K., & Rhodes, W. (2012). Reduced caseloads improve probation outcomes. *Journal of Crime and Justice,* 35(2), 221–238.

Judicial Branch of Arizona, Maricopa County. (2014). *Juvenile probation: How can a juvenile be made to pay restitution?* http://www.superiorcourt.maricopa.gov/JuvenileProbation/payRestitution.asp

Kaeble, D. (2018). *Time served in state prison, 2016* (NCJ 252205). U.S. Department of Justice, Bureau of Justice Statistics.

Kaeble, D., & Alper, M. (2020). *Probation and parole in the United States, 2017–2018* (NCJ 252072). U.S. Department of Justice, Bureau of Justice Statistics.

Katersky, A. (2015, August 14). *NY prison escape: Manhunt cost the state $1 million a day, records show.* ABC News. http://abcnews.go.com/US/ny-prison-escape-manhunt-cost-state-million-day/story?id=33087504

Kelley, M. B. (2014, February 1). America's 11 most powerful prison gangs. *Business Insider.* http://www.businessinsider.com/most-dangerous-prison-gangs-in-the-us-2014-2

Kim, D.-Y., Joo, H.-J., & McCarty, W. P. (2008). Risk assessment and classification of day reporting center clients. *Criminal Justice and Behavior,* 35(6), 792–812.

King, R. S., Mauer, M., & Young, M. C. (2005). *Incarceration and crime: A complex relationship.* The Sentencing Project.

Knox, G. W. (2005). *The problem of gangs and security threat groups in American prisons today: Recent research findings from the 2004 Prison Gang Survey.* National Gang Crime Research Center.

Knudsen, H. K., Ducharme, L. J., & Roman, P. M. (2006). Counselor emotional exhaustion and turnover intention in therapeutic communities. *Journal of Substance Abuse Treatment, 31,* 173–180.

Kutner, M. (2015, April 5). Recent prisoner escapes have one common factor: Hospital visits. *Newsweek.* http://www.newsweek.com/recent-prisoner-escapes-have-one-common-factor-hospital-visits-319692

Kyckelhahn, T. (2015). *Justice expenditure and employment extracts, 2012—preliminary* (NCJ 251780). U.S. Department of Justice, Bureau of Justice Statistics.

Lambert, E., Reynolds, M., Paoline, E., & Watkins, C. (2004). The effects of occupational stressors on jail staff job satisfaction. *Journal of Crime and Justice, 27,* 1–32.

After prison: Roadblocks to reentry. (2004). Legal Action Center.

Litwack, L. F. (1999). *Trouble in mind: Black Southerners in the age of Jim Crow.* Vintage.

Livsey, S. (2012). *Juvenile delinquency probation caseload, 2009* (NCJ 239082). U.S. Department of Justice, Office of Juvenile Justice and Delinquency Prevention.

Lofstro, M., & Martin, B. (2015, February 6). *How California reduced its prison population.* Public Policy Institute of California. http://www.ppic.org/main/blog_detail.asp?i=1676

Loughran, T. A., Mulvey, E. P., Schubert, C. A., Fagan, J., Piquero, A. R., & Losoya, S. H. (2009). Estimating a dose–response relationship between length of stay and future recidivism in serious juvenile offenders. *Criminology, 47*(3), 699–740.

Ludlow, R. (2015). *High-tech smuggling: Drone drops drugs in Ohio Prison yard. Government Technology.* http://www.govtech.com/public-safety/High-Tech-Smuggling-Drone-Drops-Drugs-in-Ohio-Prison-Yard.html

Lutze, F., Johnson, W., Clear, T., Latessa, E., & Slate, R. (2012). The future of community corrections is now: Stop dreaming and take action. *Journal of Contemporary Criminal Justice, 28*(1), 42–49.

Mai, C., & Subramanian, R. (2017). *The price of prisons: Examining state spending trends, 2010–2015.* Vera Institute of Justice. https://storage.googleapis.com/vera-web-assets/downloads/Publications/price-of-prisons-2015-state-spending-trends/legacy_downloads/the-price-of-prisons-2015-state-spending-trends.pdf

Mann, M. (2015, December 14). *5 common non-lethal tools for the correctional officer. Corrections One.* https://www.correctionsone.com/less-lethal/articles/53899187-5-common-non-lethal-tools-for-the-correctional-officer/

Markman, J. A., Durose, M. R., Rantala, R. R., & Tiedt, A. D. (2016). *Recidivism of offenders placed on federal community supervision in 2005: Patterns from 2005 to 2010* (NCJ 249743). U.S. Department of Justice, Bureau of Justice Statistics.

Martinson, R. (1974). What works? Questions and answers about prison reform. *Public Interest, 35,* 22.

Martinson, R. (1979). New findings, new views, a note of caution regarding sentencing reform. *Hofstra Law Review, 7,* 243–258.

Maruschak, L. M., & Bronson, J. (2017). *HIV in prisons, 2015—statistical tables* (NCJ 250641). U.S. Department of Justice, Bureau of Justice Statistics.

Maruschak, L. M., & Minton, T. D. (2020). *Correctional populations in the United States, 2017–2018* (NCJ

252157). U.S. Department of Justice, Bureau of Justice Statistics.

Mauer, M., & Chesney-Lind, M. (Eds.). (2002). *Invisible punishment: The collateral consequences of mass incarceration.* Urban Institute.

May, D. C., Applegate, B. K., Ruddell, R., & Wood, P. B. (2014). Going to jail sucks (and it really doesn't matter who you ask). *American Journal of Criminal Justice, 39,* 250–266.

McCarthy, B. R., McCarthy, B. J., Jr., & Leone, M. C. (2001). *Community-based corrections* (4th ed.). Wadsworth.

McCarthy, J. (2016). *Americans' views shift on toughness of justice system.* Gallup. http://news.gallup.com/poll/196568/americans-views-shift-toughness-justice-system.aspx

McGee, Z. T., Joseph, E., Allicott, I., Gayle, T. A., Barber, A., & Smith, A. (2007). From the inside: Patterns of coping and adjustment among women in prison. In R. Muraskin (Ed.), *It's a crime: Women and justice* (pp. 507–527). Prentice Hall.

McGuire, M. D. (2011). Doing the life: An exploration of the connection between the inmate code and violence among female inmates. *Journal of the Institute of Justice & International Studies, 11,* 145–158.

McKillop, M., & Boucher, A. (2018). *Aging prison populations drive up costs.* Pew Charitable Trusts. https://www.pewtrusts.org/en/research-and-analysis/articles/2018/02/20/aging-prison-populations-drive-up-costs

McNamara, R., & Burns, R. (2020). *Multiculturalism, crime, and criminal justice* (2nd ed.). Oxford University Press.

Meade, B., & Steiner, B. (2010). The total effects of boot camps that house juveniles: A systematic review of the evidence. *Journal of Criminal Justice, 38*(5), 841–853.

Mears, D. P. (2008). An assessment of supermax prisons using an evaluation research framework. *The Prison Journal, 88,* 43–68.

Mears, D. P., Mancini, C., Beaver, K. M., & Gertz, M. (2013). Housing for the "worst of the worst" inmates: Public support for supermax prisons. *Crime & Delinquency, 59*(4), 587–615.

Meloy, M. L. (2014). You can run but you cannot hide: GPS electronic surveillance of sex offenders. In R. G. Wright (Ed.), *Sex offender laws: Failed policies, new directions* (2nd ed., pp. 165–179). Springer.

Mempa v. Rhay, 389 U.S. 128 (1967).

Mikle, J. (2013, March 31). Health care costs for older inmates skyrocket. *USA Today.* https://www.usatoday.com/story/news/nation/2013/03/31/health-care-costs-for-older-inmates-skyrocket/2038633/

Minton, T. D., Ginder, S., Brumbaugh, S. M., Smiley-McDonald, H., & Rohloff, H. (2015). *Census of jails: Population changes, 1999–2013* (NCJ 248627). U.S. Department of Justice, Bureau of Justice Statistics.

Morrissey v. Brewer, 408 U.S. 471 (1972).

Mueller, S. (2017, March 17). *Florida senators call staffing shortages in state prisons a crisis. WUSF News.* http://wusfnews.wusf.usf.edu/post/florida-senators-call-staffing-shortages-state-prisons-crisis#stream/0

Murphy, D. (2003). Aspirin ain't gonna help the kind of pain I'm in: Health care in the Federal Bureau of Prisons. In J. I. Ross & S. C. Richards (Eds.), *Convict criminology* (pp. 247–266). Wadsworth.

National Association of State Budget Officers. (2019). *2019 state expenditure report: Fiscal years 2017–2019.* https://higherlogicdownload.s3.amazonaws.com/NASBO/9d2d2db1-c943-4f1b-b750-0fca152d64c2/UploadedImages/SER%20Archive/2019_State_Expenditure_Report-S.pdf

National Conference of State Legislatures. (2020). *Felon voting rights.* https://www.ncsl.org/research/elections-and-campaigns/felon-voting-rights.aspx

National Public Radio. (2015, February 22). *For some mothers in prison, a sentence doesn't mean separation.* http://www.npr.org/2015/02/22/388262646/for-some-mothers-in-prison-a-sentence-doesnt-mean-separation

Nellis, A. (2016). *The color of justice: Racial and ethnic disparity in state prisons.* The Sentencing Project. http://www.sentencingproject.org/wp-content/uploads/2016/06/The-Color-of-Justice-Racial-and-Ethnic-Disparity-in-State-Prisons.pdf

Newton, D., Day, A., Giles, M., Wodak, J., Graffam, J., & Baldry, E. (2018). The impact of vocational education and training programs on recidivism: A systematic review of current experimental evidence. *International Journal of Offender Therapy and Comparative Criminology, 62*(1), 187–207.

Nicholas, L. A. L. (2012/2013, December/January). It's still a man's world ... or is it? Advice for women working in corrections. *Corrections Today,* 41–44.

Noonan, M. E. (2016). *Mortality in local jails, 2000–2014—statistics tables* (NCJ 250169). U.S. Department of Justice, Bureau of Justice Statistics.

O'Leary, J. (2010, November 9). *Corrections cost correction. Governing.* http://www.governing.com/blogs/bfc/corrections-cost-correction.html

Oliver, W. M., & Hilgenberg, J. F., Jr. (2006). *A history of crime and criminal justice in America.* Pearson Allyn & Bacon.

Oshinsky, D. M. (1996). *"Worse than slavery": Parchman Farm and the ordeal of Jim Crow justice.* Free Press.

O'Sullivan, J. (2015, July 25). Amid decline in juvenile arrests, state boot camp closes. *Seattle Times.* http://www.seattletimes.com/seattle-news/crime/amid-decline-in-juvenile-arrests-state-boot-camp-closes/

Otte, E. J. (2017, November 7). Drones dropping drugs into prisons; Ohio fights back. *Dayton Daily News.* https://www.daytondailynews.com/news/drones-dropping-drugs-into-prisons-ohio-fights-back/GSB3jLP3sy9VMVWiaO31KM/

Palmer, T. (1975). Martinson revisited. *Journal of Research in Crime and Delinquency, 12,* 123–152.

Parrott, S., & Parrott, C. T. (2015). Law & disorder: The portrayal of mental illness in U.S. crime dramas. *Journal of Broadcasting & Electronic Media, 594,* 640–657.

Payne, B. K., & DeMichele, M. (2011). Sex offender policies: Considering unanticipated con- sequences of GPS sex offender monitoring. *Aggression and Violent Behavior, 16,* 177–187.

Perkins, E. B., & Oser, C. B. (2014). Job frustration in substance abuse counselors working with offenders in prisons versus community settings. *International Journal of Offender Therapy and Comparative Criminology, 58*(6), 718–732.

Peters, E. W. (1995). Prison before the prison: The ancient and medieval worlds. In N. Morris & D. J. Rothman (Eds.), *The Oxford history of the prison: The practice of punishment in Western society* (pp. 3–47). Oxford University Press.

Petersilia, J. (2003). *When prisoners come home: Parole and prisoner reentry.* Oxford University Press.

Pew Charitable Trusts. (2015). *Re-examining juvenile incarceration.* http://www.pewtrusts.org/~/media/assets/2015/04/reexamining_juvenile_incarceration.pdf

Pew Charitable Trusts. (2018). *Probation and parole systems marked by high stakes, missed opportunities.* https://www.pewtrusts.org/research-and-analysis/issue-briefs/2018/09/probation-and-parole-systems-marked-by-high-stakes-missed-opportunities

Phillips, R. L., & Roberts, J. W. (2000). *Quick reference to correctional administration.* Aspen.

Pizzaro, J. M., & Narag, R. E. (2008). Supermax prisons: What we know, what we do not know, and where we are going. *Prison Journal, 88*(1), 23–42.

Pollock, J. M. (2002). *Women, prison & crime* (2nd ed.). Thomson/Wadsworth.

Pollock, J. M., Hogan, N. L., Lambert, E. G., Ross, J. I., & Sundt, J. L. (2012). A utopian prison: Contradiction in terms? *Journal of Contemporary Criminal Justice, 28*(1), 60–76.

Prison Policy Initiative. (2020). *Responses to the COVID-19 pandemic.* https://www.prisonpolicy.org/virus/virusresponse.html

ProCon. (2017). *State felon voting laws.* https://felonvoting.procon.org/view.resource.php?resourceID=000286#missouri

Randall, J., Pomerantz, A., & Fontanet, C. (2017, October 23). As I see it: Medical parole: Safe for communities, beneficial for taxpayers. *Worcester Telegram.* http://www.telegram.com/opinion/20171023/as-i-see-it-medical-parole-safe-for-communities-beneficial-for-taxpayers

Rantala, R. R. (2018). *Sexual victimization reported by adult correctional authorities, 2012–2015* (NCJ 251146). U.S. Department of Justice, Bureau of Justice Statistics.

Raphelson, S. (2017, November 30). *How the loss of U.S. psychiatric hospitals led to a mental health crisis.* NPR. https://www.npr.org/2017/11/30/567477160/how-the-loss-of-u-s-psychiatric-hospitals-led-to-a-mental-health-crisis

Roberts, A. R. (1998). Treating juveniles in institutional and open settings. In A.R. Roberts (Ed.), *Juvenile justice: Policies, programs, and services* (pp. 95–109). Dorsey Press.

Rogers, D. (2013, November/December). The surge in video visits: Is there a trade-off? If so, where is the balance? *Corrections Forum, 20*, 22, 24, 26.

Ross, J. I. (2012). Debunking the myths of corrections: An exploratory analysis. *Critical Criminology, 20*, 409–427.

Ross, J. I., & Richards, S. C. (2002). *Behind bars: Surviving prison.* Alpha.

Rossman, S. (2017, September 30). Florida attorney general doesn't want O. J. Simpson to move to her state. *USA Today.* https://www.usatoday.com/story/news/nation-now/2017/09/30/florida-attorney-general-doesnt-want-o-j-simpson-move-his-state/719483001/

Roth, M. P. (2005). *Crime and punishment: A history of the criminal justice system.* Wadsworth.

Rothman, D. J. (1995). Perfecting the prison: United States, 1789–1865. In N. Morris & D. J. Rothman (Eds.), *The Oxford history of the prison: The practice of punishment in Western society* (pp. 111–129). Oxford University Press.

Sanders, K. (July 17, 2013). PolitiFact Florida: Kathleen Ford says private prisons use third-grade data to plan for prison beds. *TampaBayTimes.com.* https://www.tampabay.com/news/politics/stateroundup/politifact-florida-kathleen-ford-says-private-prisons-use-third-grade-data/2131874/

Santos, M. G. (2004). *About prison.* Wadsworth/Thomson.

Saul, J. (January 8, 2018). Prisoners use smuggled phones and drones, but Justice Department plans to jam airwaves. *Newsweek.* http://www.newsweek.com/prison-cell-phone-drone-jam-justice-department-rosenstein-774330

Sawyer, W. (2019). *Youth confinement: The whole pie.* Prison Policy Initiative. https://www.prisonpolicy.org/reports/youth2019.html

Sawyer, W., & Wagner, P. (2020). *Mass incarceration: The whole pie 2020.* Prison Policy Initiative. https://www.prisonpolicy.org/reports/pie2020.html

Schaefer, N. E. (1991). Prison visiting policies and practices. *International Journal of Offender Therapy and Comparative Criminology, 35*(3), 263–275.

Schmalleger, F., & Smykla, J. O. (2009). *Corrections in the 21st Century* (4th ed.). McGraw–Hill.

Sedlak, A. J., McPherson, K. S., & Basena, M. (2013). *Nature and risk of victimization: Findings from the Survey of Youth in Residential Placement* (NCJ 240703). U.S. Department of Justice, Office of Juvenile Justice and Delinquency Prevention.

Seiter, R. P. (2014). *Corrections: An introduction* (4th ed.). Pearson.

The Sentencing Project. (2019). *Private prisons in the United States.* https://www.sentencingproject.org/publications/private-prisons-united-states/

Setty, G. (2020, March 15). *Two New Jersey men used drones to smuggle drugs and cell phones into a prison, federal authorities say.* CNN. https://www.cnn.com/2020/03/15/us/new-jersey-prison-drone/index.html

Smith, C. R. (1999). *Law and contemporary corrections.* Wadsworth.

Smith, E. L., & Stroop, J. (2019). *Sexual victimization reported by youth in juvenile facilities, 2018* (NCJ 253042). U.S. Department of Justice, Bureau of Justice Statistics.

Smyth, J. (2012). Dual punishment: Incarcerated mothers and their children. *Columbia Social Work Review, 3*, 33–45.

Sorensen, J. R., Cunningham, M. D., Vigen, M. P., & Woods, S. O. (2011). Serious assaults on prison staff: A descriptive analysis. *Journal of Criminal Justice, 39*, 143–150.

Spencer, B. (2017, November 17). *Jesse Craig gets a year in jail for cutting off electronic monitoring device, leaving prerelease program.* Fox 46 Charlotte. http://www.fox46charlotte.com/news/local-news/wanted-man-accused-of-breaking-into-a-car-cuts-off-electronic-monitoring-device

Stal, M. (2012). Treatment of older and elderly inmates within prisons. *Journal of Correctional Health Care, 19*(1), 69–73.

Statista. (2020). *Number of escapees from state and federal prisons in the United States from 2000 to 2018.* https://www.statista.com/statistics/624069/number-of-escapees-from-prisons-in-the-us/#statisticContainer

Steiner, B., Butler, H. D., & Ellison, J. M. (2014). Causes and correlates of prison inmate misconduct: A systematic review of the evidence. *Journal of Criminal Justice, 42*, 462–470.

Stephan, J., & Walsh, G. (2011). *Census of jail facilities, 2006* (NCJ 230188). U.S. Department of Justice, Bureau of Justice Statistics.

Stone, W. E., & Scharf, P. (2011). Examining the correctional technology paradox: Can correctional technologies save aggregate correctional costs? *The Journal of the Institute of Justice & International Studies, 11*, 171–184.

St. Pierre, C. (2011, May/June). Telejustice services cut costs. *Corrections Forum, 46*–48, 50.

Street, D., Vinter, R. D., & Perrow, C. (1966). *Organizations for treatment: A comparative study of institutions.* Free Press.

Sykes, G. M. (1958). *The society of captives.* Princeton University Press.

Teeters, N. K. (1955). *The cradle of the penitentiary: The Walnut Street Jail at Philadelphia, 1773–1835.* Temple University Press.

Terry, C. M. (2003). *The fellas: Overcoming prison and addiction.* Wadsworth.

Thompson, J. (1986). The American jail: Problems, politics, and prospects. *American Journal of Criminal Justice, 10*, 205–221.

Toobin, J. (2020, February 19). The trouble with Donald Trump's clemencies and pardons. *The New Yorker.* https://www.newyorker.com/news/daily-comment/the-trouble-with-donald-trumps-pardons

Toppo, G. (2015, June 9). Maximum-security prison breakouts "rare" even as populations rise. *USA Today.* https://www.sentencingproject.org/wp-content/uploads/2016/10/6-Million-Lost-Voters.pdf

United States v. Georgia, 546 U.S. 151 (2006)

U.S. Bureau of Labor Statistics. (2020a). *Occupational outlook statistics. Correctional officers and jailers.* U.S. Department of Labor. https://www.bls.gov/oes/current/oes333012.htm#nat

U.S. Bureau of Labor Statistics. (2020b). *Labor force statistics for the current population survey.* https://www.bls.gov/cps/cpsaat11.htm

U.S. Department of Labor. https://www.bls.gov/ooh/protective-service/correctional-officers.htm

U.S. Courts. (2017, August 17). *Incarceration costs significantly more than supervision.* http://www.uscourts.gov/news/2017/08/17/incarceration-costs-significantly-more-supervision

U.S. Department of Health and Human Services. (2018). *The AFCARS Report—Preliminary FY 2017 estimates as of August 10, 2018—No 25.* https://www.acf.hhs.gov/sites/default/files/cb/afcarsreport25.pdf

Useem, B. (1985). Disorganization and the New Mexico prison riot of 1980. *American Sociological Review, 50*(5), 677–688.

Useem, B., & Piehl, A. (2006). Prison buildup and disorder. *Punishment & Society, 8*(1), 87–115.

Useem, B., & Reisig, M. D. (1999). Collective action in prisons: Protests, disturbances, and riots. *Criminology, 37*(4), 735–760.

Vachiradath, C. (2013). The efficacy of technology in preventing the escape of inmates in prison. *Journal of Applied Security Research, 8*, 477–489.

Van Dorn, R., Volavka, J., & Johnson, N. (2012). Mental disorder and violence: Is there a relationship beyond substance use? *Social Psychiatry and Psychiatric Epidemiology, 47*, 487–503.

Van Wormer, K. S., & Bartollas, C. (2007). *Women and the criminal justice system* (2nd ed.). Allyn & Bacon.

Vercammen, P., & Karimi, F. (2017, October 2). *O. J. Simpson out of Nevada prison after 9 years, plans to stay in Vegas.* CNN. http://www.cnn.com/2017/10/01/us/oj-simpson-released-from-prison/index.html

Visher, C., Debus, S., & Yahner, J. (2008). *Employment after prison: A longitudinal study of releasees in three states.* Urban Institute, Justice Policy Center.

Wagner, P., & Rabuy, B. (2017). *Following the money of mass incarceration.* Prison Policy Initiative. https://www.prisonpolicy.org/reports/money.html

Welch, M. (1994). Jail overcrowding: Social sanitation and the warehousing of the underclass. In A. Roberts (Ed.), *Critical issues in crime and justice* (pp. 249–274). Sage.

West, M. P., Belisle, L. A., & Sousa, W. H. (2019). *Nevada's Day Reporting Center: Results from a randomized controlled trial.* UNLV Center for Crime and Justice Policy. https://www.unlv.edu/sites/default/files/page_files/27/CCJP-RIB-DRC.pdf

Whitehead, J. T., Dodson, K. D., & Edwards, B. D. (2013). *Corrections: Exploring crime, punishment, and justice in America* (3rd ed.). Anderson.

Winerip, M., & Schwirtz, M. (2015, August 18). Prison guard "Beat Up Squad" is blamed in New York inmate's death. *New York Times.* http://www.nytimes.com/2015/08/19/nyregion/fishkill-prison-inmate-died-after-fight-with-officers-records-show.html?_r=0

Wolff, N., & Shi, J. (2009). Contextualization of physical and sexual assault in male prisons: Incidents and their aftermaths. *Journal of Correctional Health Care, 15*(1), 58–82.

Wood, B. (2017). *Texas Commission on Jail Standards: 2016 annual report.* Texas Commission on Jail Standards. https://www.tcjs.state.tx.us/docs/2016AnnualJailReport.pdf

Worrall, J. L., & Morris, R. G. (2012). Prison gang integration and inmate violence. *Journal of Criminal Justice, 40*, 425–432.

Zeng, Z. (2018). *Jail inmates in 2016* (NCJ 251210). U.S. Department of Justice, Bureau of Justice Statistics.

Zeng, Z. (2020). *Jail inmates in 2018* (NCJ 253044). U.S. Department of Justice, Bureau of Justice Statistics.

Credits

Index

A reference that includes *d* indicates that the term is defined on that page. A *t* indicates that the information may be found in a table, and an *f* indicates that the information is located within a feature box.

private security: 168–169
state: 159–161
law enforcement, local: 155–159
marshals, tribal police, special jurisdiction: 158–159
organization of, 156
organizational design, 157f
responsibilities, 155
urban *vs.* rural agencies: 156, 158
lay witnesses, 326d
Laythe, J., 141
lease system, 423d
legal experts, 7
legislative courts, 299d
legislatures: 106, 107d
Lemert, Edwin, 74
lethal injection: 373, 376f
letter/spirit of the law, 260d
lex talionis: 97d, 105, 417, 418d
life course theories, 76d
lifestyle-exposure theory, 87d
The Limits of the Criminal Sanction (Packer), 99
litigation paralegals, 328
lobbying by corporations, 25
Lombroso, Cesare: 66, 67
London Metropolitan Police Act (1829), 138d
Los Angeles riots, 147

Madoff, Bernie: 33f, 80
Major Crimes Act (1885), 159
mandatory parole: 133d, 471
Mapp vs. Ohio (1961), 143
marijuana legalization: 26, 27
marine/snow/air patrol, by police, 213
mark system, 421
marshals: 158–159
fire marshals, 159
U.S. Marshals Service: 9, 161, 162, 165, 323
Martin, Trayvon, 94
Martinson, Robert, 426
Marx, Karl, 75
Marxist theory, 75
mass shootings, 16f
Matthew Shepard and James Byrd, Jr. Hate Crimes Prevention Act (2009), 37d
maximum security prisons: 442, 482, 533
McGregor, Conor, 15f
McKay, Henry, 72
McQuade, Samuel, 34
Mead, George, 74
measuring crime: 44–60
media: 21–24
benefits of media coverage t and: 22–23
crime reporting and: 23–24
effects on perception of justice, 22
First Amendment and: 23–242, 23if
misrepresentations of crime, 22
mediators: 7, 98, 141, 412, 413d
medical experts, 7
medium security prisons: 133, 441–442
mens rea (intent): 17d, 19d
mental illness
bipolar disorder: 448, 507d, 509t
criminological thinking and: 63f, 71
depression: 72, 86, 115, 199, 200, 507
depression and, 199
illegal substances and, 76
in law enforcement officers, 200

in military veterans, 308
parole decisions and, 471
post-traumatic stress disorder: 115, 196
in prison inmates: 455, 507–509
schizophrenia: 507, 509t
testing for, 114
merchants (in prison), 488d
Merton, Robert, 72
Mexican Mafia (or Le Eme) (prison gang), 493f
militarized policing, 149f
Miller, James, 105
Mills, C. Wright, 22
minimum security prisons: 441, 522
Minnesota Multiphasic Inventory-2, 183
Miranda v. Arizona (1966): 143, 250–251
misdemeanors: 40d, 334d
Missouri Bar Plan (merit selection), 315d
mistakes: 112–113
M'Naghten test, 114d
mobile digital terminals: 267d–268
Model Code of Judicial Conduct, 315d
Model Penal Code and Commentaries, 111d
Mohen Commission, 236d
Mollen Commission: 236–237d
monarchies, 106d
monetary bail: 336–337
deposit bail, 336d
fully secured, 336d
unsecured bond, 337d
money laundering: 12, 33d, 34
Monitoring the Future survey, 55d
Moral Code of Judicial Conduct, 315d
motor vehicle theft, 32d
mounted patrol, by police, 212
Muir, W., 205
municipal ordinances, 108
The Myth of Prison Rape (Fleisher and Krienert), 490

National Advisory Commission on Civil Disorders (Kerner Commission): 143, 236–237d
National Commission on Law Observance and Enforcement, 142
National Crime Victimization Survey (NCVS): 44, 51–54
history of, 52d
how it works, 52
limitations of, 54
Uniform Crime Report comparison, 53t
victimization rates, 57t
National Incident-Based Reporting System (NIBRS): 44, 49d–51
"dark figure of crime," 52d
Group A, Group B offenses: 50–51t
limitations of, 51
participation in, 51
representative sample: 51–52d
National Institute of Corrections, 438
National Prison Association, 422
National Registry of Exonerations, 96
National Survey on Drug Use and Health, 55d
Nazi Low Riders (prison gang), 493f
necessity: 111, 112d
negative reinforcements, 455d
negligence, 19d
negligent homicide, 105
Neta (prison gang), 493f

neurophysiological theories, 67
neurophysiology, defined, 67d
The New Jim Crow: Mass Incarceration in the Age of Colorblindness (Alexander), 497f
New York City Police Department, 173
New York City Police Department (NYPD), 173
9/11. *See* September 11, 2001, terrorist attacks
nitrogen hypoxia (capital punishment), 373
Nixon, Richard: 10, 147
no-knock searches, 245d
noble cause of corruption, 234d
noise flash diversionary devices, 491d
nolle prosequi, 335d
nolo contendere: 341, 342d, 370f
nominal dispositions, 393
nongovernmental organizations (NGOs), 168
North Carolina Department of Public Safety, 497f
not guilty by "reason of insanity,"342d

oath-helper, 282d
Obama, Barack, 150
objective standard of reasonableness, 320d
occupational crime, 33d
offender treatment specialists: 453–455
Office of the Solicitor General, 317d
Ohlin, Lloyd, 73
Oklahoma City federal building bombing, 148
Okobi, Chinedu, 220f
oleoresin capsicum spray (pepper spray), 491d
oligarchies, 106d
online courts, 404
online harassment: 31, 34, 35d
order maintenance, by police: 207–209
Ordinance of 1787, 288d
ordinance violations, 40d
Origin of the Species (Darwin), 66

Packer, Herbert: 99–100, 102
Pangea XI operation, 154f
paralegals: 327–328, 327d–328
parens patriae: 386, 387d
parole, 132d
amnesty, commutations, reprieves: 472d–473
Anti-Drug Abuse Act and, 26
autonomous model, 444
capital punishment cases, 376
community corrections and, 130
complete/partial sealing, expungement, 474
consolidated model, 444
discretionary parole: 133d, 471
federal administration, 161
felonies and, 38
institutional model, 444
mandatory parole: 133d, 471
medical parole, 463
origins: 421–422
pardons, 474
parole boards: 133, 134d, 443–444
pre-parole investigation reports, 450
reentry barriers: 473–474
reintegration programs: 474–475
release and parole: 132–133
revocation hearings: 471–472d
sentencing: 368, 369
Sixth Amendment Rights and, 290
U.S. adult corrections data, 429t
U.S. Parole Commission, 443

About the Author

Ronald G. Burns is a professor of criminal justice at Texas Christian University (TCU). He has published over 75 articles in the areas of the criminal justice system, policing, white-collar crime, and multiculturalism in the criminal justice system. He is the author, coauthor, or editor of eight books, including *Environmental Law, Crime and Justice*; *Federal Law Enforcement*; *Policing: A Modular Approach*; *Critical Issues in Criminal Justice*; *Multiculturalism, Crime, and Criminal Justice*; *The Criminal Justice System*; *Environmental Crime: A Sourcebook*; and *Policing and Violence*. Dr. Burns graduated from Florida State University in 1997 and has been at TCU ever since.

List of Reviewers

Aaron Fichtelberg, *University of Delaware*

Adam J. McKee, *University of Arkansas-Monticello*

Alicia Wilcox, *Thomas College*

Amin Asfari, *Wake Technical Community College*

Beverly Crank, *Kennesaw State University*

Bobby L. Brown, *Central Georgia Technical College*

Carlos E. Posadas, *New Mexico State University*

Dana N. Baxter, *Davis & Elkins College*

Donna Massey, *University of Tennessee at Martin*

Dr. James C. Brown, *Utica College*

Dr. Eric Metchik, *Salem State University*

Erin Wolbeck, *California State University San Bernardino*

Ginger Silvera, *Cal State Dominquez Hills*

Hamid R. Kusha, Ph. D., *Anna Maria College*

James Wright, *Dalton State College*

Jay Zumbrun, *Community College of Baltimore County*

Jeff O'Donnell, *Community College of Allegheny County*

John J. Shook, *University of Dubuque*

John Polzer, *Texas Christian University*

Jonathon Kremser Ph. D., *Kutztown University*

Kelly Fisher, *Indiana University Kokomo*

Kristen Stives, *Auburn University Montgomery*

Lecinda M. Yevchak, *Penn State University-University Park*

Lee Ann Morrison, *Eastern Kentucky University*

Lorna L. Alvarez-Rivera, *Valdosta State University*

Mark Tate, *Las Positas College*

Marlene Ramsey, *Albany State University*

Megan Maiello, *Bronx Community College*

Mengie Michaux Parker Ph.D., *Indiana University East*

Michele L. Foster, *Kent State University*

Nicole Doctor, *Ivy Tech Community College*

Patrick Ibe, *Albany State University*

Paul Nunis, *Arkansas State*

Rachel Schmidt, *Suffolk County Community College*

Rey Flores, *Richland College*

Robert Meadows, *California Lutheran University*

Szde Yu, *Wichita State University*

Tauya Johnson-Forst, *College DuPage*

Timothy Hayes, *University of North Georgia*

William J. Ferrell Ph.D., *Indiana University Southeast*